College English and Communication

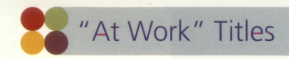

College English and Communication, 9/e
Sue C. Camp, Gardner-Webb University
Marilyn Satterwhite, Danville Area Community College
ISBN: 007310650X
© 2007

This text is designed to help students achieve success as a professional. It is an educational program designed for college-level business English and business communication courses. The comprehensive products include a student book, a student activity workbook, and a comprehensive Web site. The book offers coverage of reading, listening, speaking, writing, reports, employment communications, ethical communication, and technology, thus providing students with cultural material necessary to keep up with the speed of business today.

Business Communication at Work, 3/e
Marilyn Satterwhite, Danville Area Community College
Judith Olson-Sutton, Madison Area Technical College
ISBN: 0073138312
© 2007

A complete learning package, this text provides the opportunities to learn how to communicate orally, through speaking and listening as well as by letter, report, and e-mail. The text presents the foundations needed to develop sentences and paragraphs while also explaining how to use the appropriate approach to capture the messages necessary for effective communication.

Business English at Work, 3/e
Susan Jaderstrom, Santa Rosa Junior College
Joanne Miller
ISBN: 0073137871
© 2007

Written in a conversational tone, this text takes a totally new learning approach to relating business English to the workplace. Up-to-date topics of telecommunications, customer service, online references, electronic mail, and a host of other real-world subjects connect directly to an assortment of activities and exercises in grammar, punctuation, and writing. The activities in the text and online accommodate different student learning styles. All students regardless of their previous English background have the opportunity to be successful learning grammar in a business context.

College English and Communication

Ninth Edition

Sue C. Camp, Ed.D.
School of Business
Gardner-Webb University
Boiling Springs, North Carolina

Marilyn L. Satterwhite
Business and Technology Division
Danville Area Community College
Danville, Illinois

 **McGraw-Hill**
Irwin

Boston   Burr Ridge, IL   Dubuque, IA   Madison, WI   New York   San Francisco   St. Louis
Bangkok   Bogotá   Caracas   Kuala Lumpur   Lisbon   London   Madrid   Mexico City
Milan   Montreal   New Delhi   Santiago   Seoul   Singapore   Sydney   Taipei   Toronto

The McGraw·Hill Companies

 **McGraw-Hill**
Irwin

COLLEGE ENGLISH AND COMMUNICATION
Published by McGraw-Hill/Irwin, a business unit of The McGraw-Hill Companies, Inc., 1221
Avenue of the Americas, New York, NY, 10020. Copyright © 2007 by The McGraw-Hill
Companies, Inc. All rights reserved. No part of this publication may be reproduced or distributed
in any form or by any means, or stored in a database or retrieval system, without the prior written
consent of The McGraw-Hill Companies, Inc., including, but not limited to, in any network or other
electronic storage or transmission, or broadcast for distance learning.

Some ancillaries, including electronic and print components, may not be available to customers
outside the United States.

This book is printed on acid-free paper.

Printed in China

10 11 12 13 CTP/CTP 12

ISBN-13:   978-0-07-310650-2 (student edition)
ISBN-10:   0-07-310650-X (student edition)
ISBN-13:   978-0-07-310651-9 (instructor annotated edition)
ISBN-10:   0-07-310651-8 (instructor annotated edition)

Editorial director: *John E. Biernat*
Publisher: *Linda Schreiber*
Developmental editor: *Tommy Higham*
Marketing manager: *Keari Bedford*
Senior media producer: *Damian Moshak*
Lead project manager: *Pat Frederickson*
Senior production supervisor: *Sesha Bolisetty*
Lead designer: *Matthew Baldwin*
Photo research coordinator: *Kathy Shive*
Media project manager: *Joyce J. Chappetto*
Cover design: *Matthew Baldwin*
Interior design: *Matthew Baldwin*
Cover image: *© Getty Images*
Typeface: *10.5/12 Times Roman*
Compositor: *Interactive Composition Corporation*
Printer: *CTPS*

Library of Congress Control Number: 2005938404

www.mhhe.com

Brief Contents

Contents

Welcome to the ninth edition of *College English and Communication*. The world of business communication has changed since the first edition of *College English and Communication* was published in 1964. We now use computers instead of typewriters, e-mail is fast replacing "hard copy" memos as the preferred mode of internal business communication, and employers, more than ever before, require employees to have real-world communication skills. As we progress into the 21st century, the need for competent communicators will only increase. The Internet, the cellular technology boom, even the increase in digital television and digital video disks (DVDs) all reflect an innate human need to engage information in an authentic and immediate manner. Training tomorrow's business leaders to become competent communicators begins by providing instructors and students the tools they need to be successful in the "real-world."

These real-world skills do not exist in a theoretical vacuum. To achieve success in any career, you will need a solid foundation in grammar and mechanics and in reading, listening, speaking, and writing. In addition, you will need to understand how factors such as cultural diversity, ethics, nonverbal communication, and technology impact business communication. Today's businessperson also requires a complete understanding of how the Internet functions as a communication tool. This practical basis, combined with a solid pedagogical background, will help you become successful in your chosen profession.

College English and Communication, Ninth Edition, is designed to help you achieve success as both a professional and as what the ancient Roman rhetorician Quintilian referred to as a "good person speaking well." Responding to feedback from instructors and students of previous editions, the ninth edition retains the comprehensive, detailed presentation of previous editions and offers expanded coverage of reading, listening, speaking, writing, reports, employment communication, and technology. Cutting-edge coverage of vital topics such as global communication, digital communication, ethical communication, and the Internet round out the program, providing students with cultural material necessary to keep up with the speed of business today.

College English and Communication, Ninth Edition, presents an engaging combination of new and expanded coverage.

Coverage

Content

Unit openers. **Stories from the Real World** highlight professional communicators in their working environments and increase critical thinking skills.

Revised chapter openers. **Workplace Connection** answers the famous student question, "How can I use this information in the real world?" and provides a link between the theoretical and the practical.

Updated end-of-section materials. Section assessment materials include **Review of Key Terms, Discussion Point, Editing Practice,** and **Practical Application.**

Collaborative learning. Team activities are included for each chapter.

Career focus. **Communicating in Your Career** appears in every chapter and provides the opportunity to further enhance occupational communication.

Internet activities. **CEC Online** is a virtual treasure hunt of sorts, providing links to Web sites important to communicators. **Internet Quest** expands CEC Online and asks higher-level questions to challenge students' critical thinking ability.

Features

 **Going Global** is an introduction to multicultural aspects of business communication.

 **Digital Data** is designed to highlight the use of new technology for communication purposes.

Ethics in Action alerts students to ethical or legal issues in business communication.

Thinking Critically asks questions that require more advanced thinking skills such as interpretation, analysis, comparison, making judgments, or applying concepts.

 Employability Skills are based on the Secretary's Commission on Achieving Necessary Skills (SCANS) 2000. Employability Skills links information learned in class and in text to help students in their careers.

Enhanced Coverage

- Updated *Memory Hooks*
- Updated *Self-Assessment*
- Updated *Oops!*

Web Site Features

Unit closers. **Your Turn: Real Skills for the Real World** reviews all skills developed in the previous unit, then offers real-world practical applications.

End of chapter materials. Newly designed activities create cognitive links. Revised cases include one hypothetical and one "real world" activity designed to highlight the importance of communication on the job.

Concept Review and Application

Summary of Key Points sums up the chapter's major themes. The summary is organized by chapter objectives.

Case Studies on the Web site encourage you to apply the concepts you have learned. Each scenario provides you the opportunity to analyze a situation, using the knowledge you have gained from the chapter, and to then propose a solution, evaluate a proposal, or make a decision.

Communicating in Your Career and *Ethics in Action* offer opportunities for you to broaden your understanding of the material presented, prepare yourself to participate in classroom discussions, and enhance your performance on exams.

 CEC Online encourages you to use the Internet to discover how technology helps business communication.

Program Components

The ninth edition of *College English and Communication* is a complete, well-rounded program that includes the following components:

- *Student Activity Workbook* has been revised to include 50 percent new assessment material. Activities for each chapter are organized by section and often integrated, calling on you to apply more than one skill to complete an activity.

- *Instructor's Annotated Edition of the Student Activity Workbook* contains a page-for-page answer key for all activities, with the answer keys shown full size.

- *Instructor CD-ROM,* included with every Instructor's Annotated Edition, includes PowerPoint slides for every chapter, additional teaching materials, and EZ Test.

- *EZTest* provides comprehensive chapter tests for all 16 chapters of *College English and Communication, Ninth Edition,* with questions organized by section. Instructors have the option of using the prepared questions or adding their own. Question types include true/false, multiple choice, matching, completion, short answer, and essay.

- *College English and Communication Web Site* is a storehouse of additional materials, including study tips, games, password-protected instructor's materials, and more. The *Student Web Site* includes a plethora of materials for students, including Glencoe Interactive Grammar Student Software, additional assessment materials, and résumé examples.

Acknowledgments

We would like to thank the following educators for their invaluable comments and feedback on this revision.

Dr. Andy O. Alali
California State University, Bakersfield

Holly Bales
International Business College

Lisa Barley
Eastern Michigan University

Lia Geloso Barone, J. D.
Norwalk Community College

Bryan H. Barrows III, M. A.
North Harris College

Mary D. Been
Oregon Institute of Technology

Thomas Beery
Rhodes State College

Lyda Black
Shelton State Community College

Sheri L. Blok, PhD
Southeast Community College

Dom Bongiorni, PhD
Kingwood College

Timothy A. Borchers
Minnesota State University, Moorhead

Natalie Bryant
South Plains College

Judy Burnett
Florida Community College

Angela Butler
Mississippi Gulf Coast Community College

Danny R. Cantrell
West Virginia State University

Eric Carlson
Collin County College

Karen G. Carlson
Jamestown Business College

Elaine Cichon
Florida International University

Kathryn Cid
Lincoln Technical Institute

Carolyn Clark
Salt Lake Community College

Deborah L. Cook
Blinn College

James C. Cox
University of North Carolina

Terry M. Cunconan
Central Missouri State University

Bebe Cunningham
Lanier Technical Institute

Hetty Davies
Ferndale Adult Education

Evelyn Delaney
Daytona Beach Community College

Margaret M. Francis Dombeck
Centennial College of Applied Arts and Technology

Dr. James A. Doran
Stetson University

Matthew Gainous
Ogeechee Technical College

Arlette Giuliano
Bradford School of Business

Dr. Judith A. Grenkowicz
Kirtland Community College

James P. Hess
Ivy Tech State College—Fort Wayne

Jack Hoggatt
University of Wisconsin—Eau Claire

Deborah Holder
Piedmont Technical College

Mark E. Huglen, PhD
University of Minnesota, Crookston

Donald Kesler
Cochise College

Dr. Linda A. Kurth
Phoenix College

Ruth Lindemann
Danville Area Community College

Susan D. McClaren
Mt. Hood Community College

Dennis D. McDaniel, PhD
Saint Vincent College

Audra McMullen
Towson University

Ron Mcneel
New Mexico State University at Alamogordo

Paul Miller
Davidson College

Barbara Oliver
CHI Institute

Cynthia G. Randolph
Bethel College

Mageya R. Sharp
Cerritos College

Marilyn M. Shaw
University of Northern Iowa

Deborah Sheray
International Business College

Sue L. Stewart
Texas State University at San Marcos

Jay Stubblefield
North Carolina Wesleyan College

Billie Tomlin
Miami Dade Community College, Kendall

Harriet Tufte
NWTC Moorhead Campus

Charlotte Weybright
Michiana College

Sherry Wise
South Georgia

Dedication

With thanks for their encouragement and support, we would like to dedicate the ninth edition of *College English and Communication* to our families: Gladys, Charles Sr., Charles Jr. and Amber, Charles III, and John Mattison Camp II for Sue Camp; Bill, Marcy, and David for Marilyn Satterwhite.

College English and Communication, 9e Learning System

This book is designed to help students learn. It contains 16 chapters, divided into six units. You will learn more if you use the learning system. *College English and Communication, 9e,* uses the following integrated learning system:

1. **Concept Preview**—The chapter opener introduces the key concepts to be learned.

2. **Concept Development**—The chapter text explains concepts in a structured, visual format.

3. **Concept Reinforcement**—In-text examples, graphics, and special features enhance and strengthen your learning.

4. **Concept Review and Application**—End-of-chapter exercises and activities encourage you to apply what you learned.

1. Concept Preview

Chapter Sections introduce the topics that will be discussed. Scan the sections to familiarize yourself with the subject matter.

Chapter Objectives alert you to the major concepts to learn. Turn the objectives into questions, and, as you read the chapters, look for the answer to the questions.

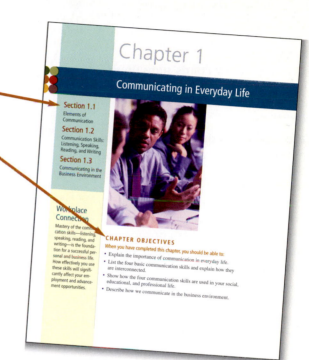

2. Concept Development

The **heading structure** shows the relationship among the topics in a section and breaks the material into easily digestible segments of information. Scan the headings to locate the information that will help you answer the questions you formed from the chapter objectives.

Key points are noted in the margin, reminding you of important elements.

Key terms are printed in boldface and defined when introduced.

3. Concept Reinforcement

Memory Hooks provide mnemonic devices and other easy-to-remember hints to help you retain important information.

Special features reinforce and enhance your understanding of concepts presented.

Self-assessment activities allow you to check your understanding of the material before you continue on to the next section.

4. Concept Review and Application

On the Web site

Summary of Key Points sums up the chapter's major themes. The summary is organized by chapter objectives.

Case Studies on the Web site encourage you to apply the concepts you have learned. Each scenario provides you the opportunity to analyze a situation, using the knowledge you have gained from the chapter, and to then propose a solution, evaluate a proposal, or make a decision.

Communicating in Your Career and **Ethics in Action** on the Web site offer opportunity for you to broaden your understanding of the

material presented, prepare yourself to participate in classroom discussions, and enhance your performance on exams.

CEC Online encourages you to use the Internet to discover how technology helps business communication.

Memory Hook

Use these five strategies to enhance, reinforce, and develop your listening skills:

- *Read* to gain background information.
- *Repeat* a person's name when you are introduced to someone.
- *Ask* questions to clarify information.
- *Take* good notes.
- *Use* a tape recorder, when permitted, to record a lecture or meeting.

5.1 Self-Assessment A

Check the following sentences for any errors in the use of plurals. Write *OK* if the sentence is correct. Circle any error(s) and write the correction(s) on the line provided.

1. The last three editor in chiefs were excellent grammarians. _____
2. David and Heather are the owners of two companies. _____
3. Krispy Kreme stores, which started in North Carolina in 1937, are now in seven countrys. _____
4. Three new district attornies were hired last week. _____
5. Two countys order computer supplies from these three companys. _____
6. Otto's Camera Shop has two wide-angle lenss on sale this week. _____
7. Two Marcies—Marcy Satterwhite and Marcy Pasierb—are in this class. _____
8. Miss Aguirre has two daughters-in-law who live in Texas. _____
9. *USA Today* has advertised for two editor in chiefs positions. _____

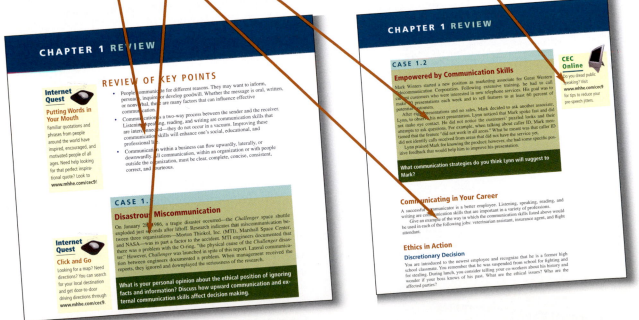

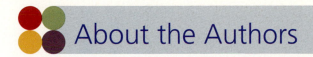

About the Authors

Dr. Sue C. Camp received her doctorate from the University of Tennessee at Knoxville, her master's degree from Winthrop University, and her bachelor's degree from Gardner-Webb University.

She has taught business education courses for over thirty years and has spoken to civic organizations, teacher associations, and other professional groups who are interested in learning about business communications. She is past president of her Rotary Club and is active in local charitable organizations.

Her awards include being named to Women of Achievement and Who's Who Among American Teachers. She received the Academic Excellence Award at Gardner-Webb University and has been listed in the University's Gallery of Distinguished Graduates.

Marilyn L. Satterwhite has been a community college professor and trainer for over 30 years. In addition to her first love—teaching—she has authored seven textbooks, all dealing with communication skills. She is a frequent speaker at workshops, conventions, and seminars for business educators, office assistants, executives, and other businesspeople who want to improve their communication skills.

Professional organizations in which she is active are the International Society for Business Educators, North Central and National Business Education Association, Illinois Business Education Association (including serving as its president in 2005), and many others. Her accomplishments and contributions to the field of business education and community service have been recognized in the following ways:

- NBEA Post Secondary Teacher of the Year.
- Eastern Illinois University Lumpkin School of Business Distinguished Alumnus.
- Association of Community College Trustees Central Region Faculty Member of the Year.
- National Institute for Staff and Organizational Development (NISOD) Teaching Excellence Award.
- National ATHENA recipient.
- Danville Woman of the Year.
- DACC Faculty of the Year.
- IBEA and NCBEA Distinguished Service Award.

College English and Communication

Unit 1

Introduction to Communication

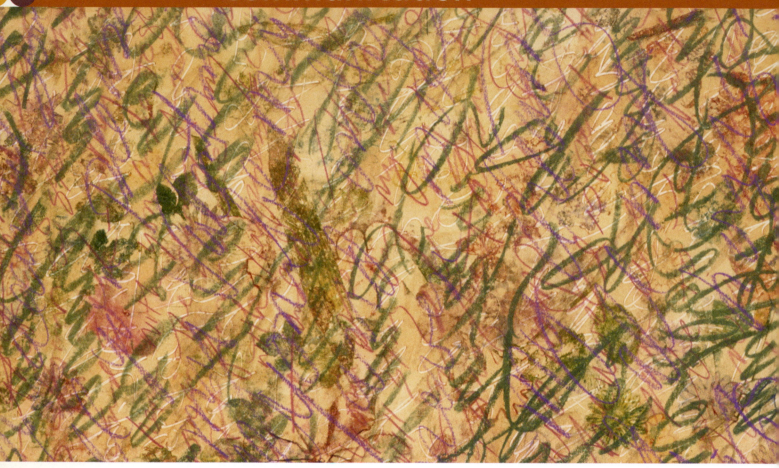

Unit Overview
In this unit, you will learn introductory communication principles.

A Japanese automotive company was building a manufacturing plant in the Midwest. A major Japanese supplier of this company also decided to build a small manufacturing facility in a neighboring town. The supplier's company was run using a team approach, common in Japanese companies.

Ann Adams, a recently hired management trainee, was one of the few American employees in management at the supplier's company. Ann was unaware of the differences between Japanese and American culture, particularly concerning the concept of teamwork in Japanese businesses. She used business and social practices commonly used by American companies in the area.

One of Ann's assignments was to research different communication systems to be used at the plant. She contacted local telephone providers for information on costs and services available. Ann also did some research on her own using the Internet. After analyzing the different systems, Ann wrote a report comparing the systems and recommending the one to adopt.

Ann's managers were upset with her for making recommendations without first consulting them. In Japanese businesses, almost all decisions are made by a team. The managers were used to being part of the decision-making process.

Ann was unfamiliar with the management style for a Japanese company, and her Japanese managers did not understand that her American management style was quite different from theirs.

As you read Unit 1, identify some of the problems Ann had in communicating with her managers from another culture, and describe how the problems could be eliminated or minimized.

Thinking Critically

What might Ann have done differently to handle the differences she had with the other members of management?

What action or actions might Ann take in order to work with management and to implement her ideas?

Chapter 1

Communicating in Everyday Life

Section 1.1
Elements of Communication

Section 1.2
Communication Skills: Listening, Speaking, Reading, and Writing

Section 1.3
Communicating in the Business Environment

Workplace Connection

Mastery of the communication skills—listening, speaking, reading, and writing—is the foundation for a successful personal and business life. How effectively you use these skills will significantly affect your employment and advancement opportunities.

CHAPTER OBJECTIVES

When you have completed this chapter, you should be able to:

- Explain the importance of communication in everyday life.
- List the four basic communication skills and explain how they are interconnected.
- Show how the four communication skills are used in your social, educational, and professional life.
- Describe how we communicate in the business environment.

Elements of Communication

Essential Principles

Communication, very simply defined, is the exchange of information. Communication is a vital part of our everyday lives, beginning at birth. Speaking, listening, reading, writing, and even observing are part of the communication process.

Today, in addition to traditional methods of communication such as letters and telephone conversations, communicating by electronic media is becoming increasingly common. Electronic media include e-mail, voice mail, cell phones, PDAs (personal digital assistants), wireless tablet PCs (personal computers), and videoconferencing.

Each of these media allows people in different locations to exchange messages quickly and conveniently. This increased use of electronic media is changing communication practices, especially with regard to ethics and confidentiality.

Types of Communication

Communication can be divided into three main categories: *oral,* *written,* and *nonverbal.*

Oral Communication

Oral communication uses spoken words to exchange ideas and information. Examples of oral communication include one-on-one conversations, meetings, voice mail messages, and teleconferencing. Spoken messages can be sent instantaneously, and they usually result in some immediate feedback. The disadvantage to oral communication is that there is often little opportunity to reflect on what is said. There is also no written record.

Written Communication

Written communication is the exchange of information through letters, words, and sentences. It can include letters, faxes, memos, e-mail, reports, news releases, tables, diagrams, charts, and graphs. Written communication provides proof that the information was exchanged. The disadvantage to written communication is that immediate feedback may not always be possible.

Nonverbal Communication

Nonverbal communication is communication without words. Nonverbal communication is an important form of communication. Think about it. Without saying a single word, you can express your feelings with body language—gestures, facial expressions, and body movements or positions.

SECTION OBJECTIVES

When you have finished Section 1.1, you will be able to:

- Identify the three types of communication and the four purposes of communication.
- List and define the six components of communication.
- Describe the four factors that influence communication.
- Discuss ways interpersonal skills affect communication.

WHY IT'S IMPORTANT

Good communcation is paramount to success in any profession.

KEY TERMS

- oral communication
- written communication
- nonverbal communication
- barriers
- intrapersonal communication
- interpersonal communication
- feedback
- human relations skills
- you-attitude
- I-attitude

KEY POINT

The three main categories of communication are:

1. **Oral**
2. **Written**
3. **Nonverbal**

5

Many times the nonverbal message is stronger and, therefore, more believable than the verbal message. The nonverbal message also may reinforce or contradict the verbal message. An example would be talking to someone who said she wasn't in a hurry but kept glancing at her watch.

Good communicators combine oral and nonverbal communication techniques to make their communication more effective. When this combination is faulty, the effect is easy to spot. Have you ever listened to a speaker who was an authority on a subject, but whom you considered boring because the speaker lacked any kind of nonverbal expression? Even if the subject interested you, you probably found it hard to keep your mind on the speech. Nonverbal communication can add emphasis and depth to spoken words and can even tell you whether or not to believe a speaker. Nonverbal communication plays an important role in the clear, effective exchange of messages.

Purposes of Communication

The first step in planning any message is to determine the purpose of your communication.

Recall for a moment what you said to various family members, friends, and school or business associates today. Each question you asked, each statement you made—from "How do you feel today?" to "I just found a ten-dollar bill!"—falls into at least one of the following four main purposes of communication:

- *To inquire.* "When did you get your HDTV [high definition television]?"
- *To inform.* "This HDTV was a birthday gift."
- *To persuade.* "You really will have a better quality picture on an HDTV."
- *To develop goodwill.* "Thank you for helping me select an HDTV."

You will learn how to plan business messages and to determine the purposes of such messages in Chapters 9, 10, and 11.

Components of Communication

Communication can take place only if you have *both* a sender and a receiver. Each time you have a conversation with someone or exchange written messages, be aware of each component of the communication model, as illustrated in **Exhibit 1.1** below.

Exhibit 1.1
Communication Components
Communicating in teams is an important aspect of internal communication. What qualities should team members demonstrate in order to communicate effectively as part of a team?

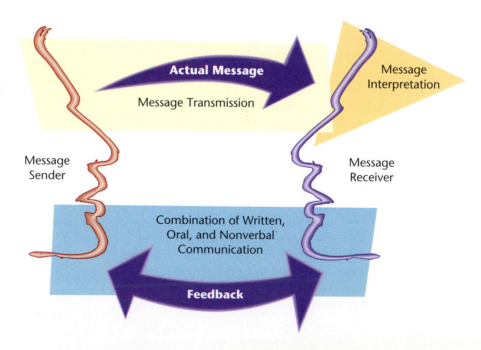

Components of Communication

The six basic components of communication are:

1. *Message sender.* The sender composes the intended message. The sender could be a writer, a speaker, or a person who sends a nonverbal message through gestures and body language.

2. *Actual message.* The actual message may be written, oral, or nonverbal; or it may combine two or more types of communication. It may or may not be the message the sender intended.

3. *Message transmission.* The message can be sent or delivered in a variety of ways. Written messages can be sent in the form of letters, memos, and reports. Written messages could also be sent electronically using fax machines or e-mail. Oral messages can be delivered through face-to-face conversations, by phone, and by voice mail. Nonverbal messages include gestures, body language, and facial expressions.

4. *Message receiver.* The receiver takes in, or receives, the message. The receiver's knowledge, interest, and emotional state will affect how the message is received.

5. *Message interpretation.* The receiver interprets the message. The interpretation may be different from the intended message or the actual message.

6. *Feedback.* The sender and the receiver respond to each other in writing, orally, nonverbally, or through a combination of these components. Feedback may include a written response, verbal questions, and nonverbal gestures such as body language and facial expressions.

The Communication Process in Action. As illustrated in **Exhibit 1.2,** the communication process worked like this: On a *60 Minutes II* segment on September 8, 2004, Dan Rather (*message sender*) of CBS News reported that a memo had surfaced indicating that President George W. Bush did not properly complete his National Guard service. Subsequently, the memo was proved to be false. Therefore, the initial report (*message transmission*) to everyone watching *60 Minutes II* (*message receiver*) was that Bush did not complete his National Guard service (*actual message*). This message caused Bush's popularity to drop in the polls (*message interpretation*). Subsequently, the memo was proved to be false and CBS News had to retract the memo and apologize (*feedback*). Several CBS News staffers lost their jobs due to failure to properly verify this memo. The retraction caused Bush's popularity to rise.

Factors That Influence Communication

Although the sender of a message knows the goals to achieve, the sender must keep in mind four key factors that will influence the communication either favorably or unfavorably. To be an effective communicator, the sender should account for how the following four factors affect the communication process:

1. The background of the receiver.

2. The appearance of the sender or of the sender's communication.

3. Barriers that might negatively affect the intended message.

4. The language and communication skills of the sender and the receiver.

Mastering Importance

Its important to master verbal communications.

(It's—*its* is the possessive form. *It's* is a contraction meaning *it is.*)

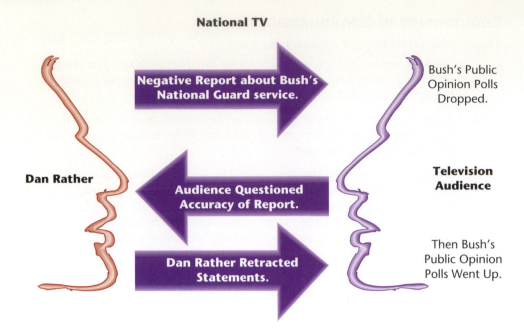

National TV

Negative Report about Bush's National Guard service. →

Bush's Public Opinion Polls Dropped.

Dan Rather

← Audience Questioned Accuracy of Report.

Television Audience

Dan Rather Retracted Statements. →

Then Bush's Public Opinion Polls Went Up.

Exhibit 1.2
Communication Components Applied
How could CBS News have improved the *60 Minutes II* report on George W. Bush's National Guard service?

Memory Hook

Recalling the four factors that influence communication is easy if you use the acronym *BABL* (pronounced "babble").

B —**B**ackground of the receiver.

A —**A**ppearance of the sender or of the sender's communication.

B —**B**arriers to effective communication.

L —**L**anguage skills of the sender and the receiver.

KEY POINT

A receiver's interest and motivation are often influenced by experience.

Background of the Receiver

The following four background elements can play an important role in determining the receiver's possible reaction and response to the message.

1. The *knowledge* both the sender and the receiver already have about the facts, ideas, and language used in the message.

2. The *personality* of the receiver—particularly the emotions, attitudes, and prejudices that are likely to influence the way the message is interpreted.

3. The receiver's *experiences* relevant to the message content.

4. The receiver's *interest* and *motivation* regarding the subject of the message.

To understand how these four factors can influence a receiver, imagine that you have just received a flyer from a computer store explaining its latest sale. If you have not previously purchased from this store, your *knowledge* of its quality and service is probably limited. Naturally, your reaction would be different from that of a person who is knowledgeable about the computer store. If your *personality* is quite conservative, you have probably decided to make only a small purchase. However, if your *experience* with this store has been good, your *interest* and *motivation* probably grew the minute you saw the cost savings available from this type of sale.

The communicator who weighs all these factors and anticipates the receiver's needs before preparing the message stands a greater chance of having the message accepted by the receiver than does the person who ignores these factors.

Appearance of the Sender or of the Sender's Communication

What do the following three situations have in common?

- A sloppy-looking speaker or salesperson.
- A receptionist or telemarketer who does not speak distinctly.
- A letter filled with errors.

The three situations above all transmit their messages in an unfavorable way. Every communication you transmit can be your goodwill ambassador and can help achieve a positive reaction if you remember that appearances do make a difference as shown in **Exhibit 1.3.** Written communication that appears neat and professional makes a positive first impression.

Barriers to Effective Communication

Barriers are factors that interfere with communication and might negatively affect the intended message. Barriers include physical distractions, emotional distractions, and cultural and language differences.

Under what circumstances is the message received? For example, is the room noisy? too warm or too cold? poorly lighted? Is the receiver more concerned with an

Exhibit 1.3
Making an Impression
Physical appearance contributes positively or negatively to the impression a person makes. ***Thinking Critically.*** *Which person's appearance makes the better impression? Why?*

Employability Skills

Working with Diversity

With many businesses becoming culturally diverse, the ability to work with people from diverse backgrounds is a key employability skill.

oops!

A Valuable Misunderstanding

Misunderstandings can arise when someone uses the wrong word. Consider this request made by an employee in a European hotel:

"Please leave your values at the front desk."

(the concrete noun, *valuables,* not the abstract noun, *values*)

KEY POINT

Three types of barriers to communication are:

1. **Physical distractions**
2. **Emotional distractions**
3. **Language differences**

upcoming exam or the argument he or she had this morning? Such distractions interfere with, and draw the receiver's attention away from, the message and create barriers to effective communication. Sometimes, the resulting lack of concentration can lead to incomplete communication by message senders and erroneous conclusions by message receivers.

Physical Distractions. *Physical distractions* are usually easier to prevent in a speaking or listening situation because the surroundings can often be controlled or changed. In a writing or reading situation, however, the writer has little influence over the reader's surroundings. Writers should take special care in developing error-free messages. Remember, people do judge you based on the appearance of your communication.

Emotional Distractions. *Emotional distractions* on the part of the receiver can prevent him or her from concentrating on, and giving full attention to, the communication. Emotional distractions may include thinking about a personal matter or allowing an emotion such as anger to influence how you interpret a message.

Nonverbal Barriers. *Nonverbal barriers* such as language differences, inattention, and misunderstanding caused by different interpretations of a word or an expression can have a negative influence on the communication process. Cultural diversity can also be a barrier to effective communication. For example, executives in the United States and Japan might have different ideas about what constitutes politeness in a letter. Chapter 3 discusses cultural diversity in more detail.

Language and Communication Skills

Every businessperson is involved in some form of communication with others and must be able to use language effectively to send and receive messages. Words are the major tools of language, and they must be chosen carefully to express the intended meaning. How well the sender of the message uses these tools and how well the receiver interprets their use are major factors in the effectiveness of the message.

In today's multicultural society, it is important to be sensitive to cultural diversity when using any form of communication. An awareness of, and respect for, cultural differences will help you to avoid any miscommunications.

Selecting the correct words is particularly important if the receiver's first language is not English. Use of slang and jargon in communicating with people who do not understand the terminology can also cause a barrier to communication. If the receptionist tells the international caller, Mr. Wong, that Mrs. Wyatt can't take his call because she's *tied up* in a meeting, Mr. Wong could interpret the message literally (Mrs. Wyatt is *tied with ropes to a chair* in the meeting).

As a message sender, you must communicate facts, ideas, opinions, and instructions in a coherent manner with clarity, confidence, and knowledge. To do this, you must have a broad vocabulary and the ability to spell, pronounce, and select the correct words. You must be able to speak and write clearly, concisely, and without error. As a message receiver, you must also be able to read and listen with understanding. *Both* the sender and the receiver share the responsibility for effective communication.

In spoken communication, word choice, grammar, pronunciation, and listening are also factors in effective communication. A receiver may be distracted by incorrect grammar, incorrect pronunciation, or misused words, and, consequently, he or she may not receive the intended message. For example, a diner in a restaurant may focus on the errors, rather than the message when a server says, "We *done* the meal as *good* as we could so a 15-percent *gratuity* would be appreciated."

In written communication, something as simple as using the wrong word, making a spelling or grammatical error, using an incorrect format, or misusing a punctuation mark may change the intended meaning of the message. Even if the receiver understands the message, his or her opinion of the sender's intelligence and credibility may be negatively influenced by the error. For example, a receiver may not do business with a company because of a poorly written sales letter. The receiver may feel that a company careless about its letters may also be careless about filling orders promptly and accurately.

Each of these language tools is discussed more fully in later sections of this book. Keep in mind, however, that these tools apply not only to writing but also to reading, listening, and speaking. If the communication process is to be successful, the message sender must be an effective writer or speaker, and the receiver must be an effective reader or listener.

Responsibilities of the Sender and the Receiver

As illustrated in **Exhibit 1.1,** both the sender and the receiver bear a responsibility for ensuring that effective communication occurs. Let's take a look at the particular responsibilities of the sender and the receiver.

Evaluate Each Communication Situation

Effective communication requires the sender to understand his or her own intrapersonal communication. **Intrapersonal communication** refers to the way each person views and interprets information based on previous life experiences. Intrapersonal communication, or communication with yourself, must take place before you can communicate with another person. **Interpersonal communication** is communication that occurs between two people, such as a doctor and a patient, an attorney and a client, and a financial adviser and a client.

Avoid Miscommunication.　Ideally, the intended message, the actual message, and the interpreted message will be the same. Miscommunication occurs when components of one or more of these three messages are different for either the sender or the receiver. For example, consider the following situation:

College freshman Robin Wilkerson was upset with her semester grades, but she had to tell her parents. Robin (*message sender*) sent them a letter (*message transmission*) in which she stated her grades (*intended message*): "I got only one D this semester" (*actual message*). When her parents (*message receivers*) read her letter, they viewed it this way: "Robin got only one D this semester. That is much better than the three Ds she got last semester!" (*interpreted message*).

Miscommunication occurred because Robin's *actual message* did not convey that she also received two Fs. Her parents interpreted her partial message in a positive way. This is not an example of miscommunication, however, if Robin deliberately set out to deceive her parents. Was it ethical if she did intend to deceive them?

Maintain Goodwill.　Effective communication takes place (1) when the message is received and understood and (2) when the communication maintains *goodwill* between the sender and the receiver. You can tell a person no and make an enemy for life; but if you use a customer service approach and incorporate human relations skills into your communication, you are more likely to have an effective communication. Chapter 13 discusses customer service communication in more detail.

Remember that communication is effective when it:

- Enables the receiver to interpret the message exactly as the sender intended.
- Results in the desired response from the receiver.
- Develops goodwill between the sender and the receiver.

Give and Receive Feedback.　Miscommunication and communication breakdowns can often be avoided by using the feedback technique. **Feedback** involves getting an

KEY POINT

Communication takes place when the intended message, the actual message, and the interpreted message are the same.

Digital Data

Information Tools

Personal digital assistants (PDAs) are handheld tools that help you organize and manage large amounts of information. PDAs are useful as a calendar; valuable for storing contact names and phone numbers, and home and e-mail addresses; keeping personal and business records.

Exhibit 1.4
Listening
Feedback from a listener may include facial expressions, posture, and eye contact. ***Thinking Critically.*** *What might the listener's feedback indicate to the speaker? What could the speaker do to get oral feedback from the listener?*

oral, written, or nonverbal response from the receiver. In the process of transmitting a face-to-face message, the sender can use clues from the receiver to determine if the receiver is interpreting the message correctly. For example, a puzzled look on the receiver's face can signal that the message is confusing as illustrated in **Exhibit 1.4.**

Asking questions is one way to get feedback. The sender can ask the receiver questions to determine whether the message is being received accurately. In turn, the receiver can ask the sender questions to clarify any content that is unclear.

Feedback cannot be achieved as easily with written communication because the sender and receiver are separated, and the receiver's response is usually not immediate. The wrong response, questions from the receiver, or no response at all may indicate a temporary breakdown in communication.

Understand Personal Needs

One significant factor in successful interpersonal skills is understanding the needs of the receiver of a message. Abraham Maslow, a famous psychologist, divided human needs into five levels as shown in **Exhibit 1.5.**

- *Physical needs.* Physical needs are essential to life and include food, clothing, and shelter. Until these basic needs are satisfied, receivers have difficulty thinking of anything else.
- *Security needs.* Security needs include the desire to be safe from physical harm and mental abuse.
- *Social needs.* Social needs, which are evident in a desire to be part of a group, can be met through family, social contacts, work relationships, or other group situations.
- *Esteem needs.* Esteem needs are satisfied through a feeling of self-importance, self-respect, prestige, power, or recognition. Winning a contest, being selected as chairperson of an event or organization, and receiving a scholarship are some situations that satisfy esteem needs.
- *Self-actualizing needs.* These needs are met through a sense of achievement, competence, and creativity, and by helping others meet their own needs. People who reach the top in their fields often want to use their abilities and resources to benefit others. They may also want to help others attain similar success by becoming a mentor, a role model, or a volunteer for organizations such as Big Brothers/Big Sisters, Boy Scouts, and Girl Scouts.

KEY POINT

Maslow organizes human needs into five levels:

1. **Physical**
2. **Security**
3. **Social**
4. **Esteem**
5. **Self-actualizing**

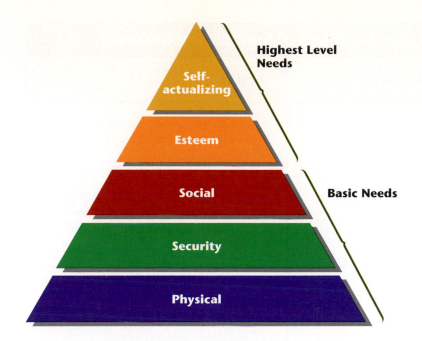

Highest Level Needs

Self-actualizing

Esteem

Social — Basic Needs

Security

Physical

Exhibit 1.5
Maslow's Hierarchy of Needs
Exhibit 1.5 illustrates Maslow's hierarchy of needs, with the lowest-level needs at the bottom and the highest-level needs at the top. ***Thinking Critically.*** *How does the lack of these basic needs interfere with effective communication?*

Assess the Needs of the Receiver

In order to communicate effectively, the sender must carefully examine each situation and assess the needs of the receiver. Needs motivate people to act or react in certain ways. By helping the receiver satisfy the higher two levels of needs—*esteem* and *self-actualizing*—the sender can improve communication. Furthermore, by *empathizing* with the receiver, that is, imagining yourself in that other person's situation, you will be better able to determine the best way to motivate the receiver to do what you want.

Keep in mind that the receiver may be motivated by more than one need at any given time. For example, a person may accept a position as officer of an organization to satisfy both social and esteem needs.

To communicate effectively, you need to demonstrate human relations skills when interacting with others. Use the human relations techniques described in the following paragraphs as a guide.

Apply Interpersonal Skills

The average person speaks about 18,000 words each day. Most of those words are spent communicating on a one-to-one basis or in situations involving only a few people. **Human relations skills,** also known as *interpersonal skills,* involve the ability to understand and deal with people in such a way that a favorable relationship and goodwill are maintained. It makes sense, therefore, that everyone should develop effective interpersonal skills.

Use the You-Attitude. Using the you-attitude when writing and speaking helps to build goodwill and to maintain an environment of friendliness. The **you-attitude** means putting your reader or listener first and being considerate of the other person. An example of the you-attitude is, "For your convenience, we are extending our hours to 7 p.m."

The **I-attitude** is the opposite of the you-attitude; it is putting your own interests, well-being, and comfort ahead of anyone else's. An example of the I-attitude is, "Because it fits my schedule better, I have decided to extend the store's hours until 7 p.m."

Demonstrate a Positive Attitude. A good communicator demonstrates a positive attitude by building good working relationships with peers, superiors, subordinates, customers, and clients. Showing enthusiasm about your job and your organization and cooperating with others are ways to demonstrate a positive attitude.

KEY POINT

Using the you-attitude in speaking and writing helps to build and maintain goodwill.

Exhibit 1.6
Responsibilities of the
Sender and Receiver
Applying a combina-
tion of these commu-
nication responsibili-
ties fosters productive
communication.
Thinking Critically.
Which of these re-
sponsibilities is most
important to the
sender and to the
receiver?

Responsibilities of Sender and Receiver	
Responsibilities	**Actions**
Evaluate the situation	• Avoid miscommunications • Give and receive feedback • Maintain goodwill
Understand your needs and the receiver's needs	• Fulfill each of your own and your receiver's needs according to Maslow, especially esteem and self-actualizing
Apply interpersonal skills	• Use the you-attitude appropriately • Demonstrate a positive attitude • Be a good listener • Maintain confidentiality • Be considerate

Be a Good Listener.   A good communicator is also a good listener. It is important to listen carefully and to let the speaker know you are interested. Ask questions when you are unsure of the content of the message, and take notes when appropriate.

Maintain Confidentiality.   A good communicator understands the importance of confidentiality. This means releasing information to authorized personnel only and releasing information at the appropriate time, not early and not late.

Be Considerate.   Treat others as you would like to be treated. A good communicator is courteous, honest, and patient in dealing with other people and respects the opinions of others. This means using tact and diplomacy in some instances. It also means using words and terms that your receiver understands. Another way to show courtesy is to be prompt in answering correspondence and in returning telephone calls.

Recent studies indicate that workers need to possess good communication skills in order to be competitive in the changing workplace and in the global economy. Practicing the human relations techniques described in this section will help you improve your communication skills. Review the responsibilities of sender and receiver in **Exhibit 1.6** above.

Assessment   Section 1.1

Review of Key Terms

1. How does *nonverbal communication* affect the verbal message? Provide an example. _____

   _____

2. What types of *barriers* interfere with communication? _____

   _____

   _____

3. What is the difference between *intrapersonal* and *interpersonal* communication? _____

_____

_____

Editing Practice

Spelling Alert!   Correct the following spelling errors. A sentence may have more than one misspelled word.

4. The rest of you order is back-ordered and shoud be hear in 7 to 10 days.

_____

5. Although Joaquin maled the package last week, Alicia hasnt recieved it yet. _____

6. You're plane is quit late. _____

7. Ms. Lamay finaly wraped up her project. _____

8. With the car radio blaring, Bryan past the hospital quite zone. _____

Practical Application

Analyzing Information

9. Give an example of a *you-attitude* statement and an *I-attitude* statement. Then, list several basic human relations techniques that, if applied, could improve communication. _____

_____

_____

10. Today, immediately after a conversation with a fellow student, analyze what was said by jotting down answers to the following questions:

   - What was the sender's intended message?
   - What was the sender's actual message?
   - What was the receiver's interpretation of the message?

   Compare notes with your team to determine if all messages are the same. If not, discuss what factors may have influenced the message.

_____

Discussion Point

Making Comparisons

11. Discuss the differences among oral, written, and nonverbal communication. Why is each type of communication essential to effective communication? _____

_____

_____

_____

12. Name the four key factors that influence communication and describe each one briefly. _____

_____

SECTION OBJECTIVES

When you have finished Section 1.2, you will be able to:

- Explain how the four communication skills are interconnected and how they reinforce one another.

- Show how the four communication skills relate to your social, educational, and professional lives.

- Give examples to illustrate the importance of listening, speaking, reading, and writing skills in your life.

WHY IT'S IMPORTANT

Good communicators are effective, energetic, and personable.

KEY TERMS

- oral communication
- written communication
- educational distraction
- environmental distraction
- emotional-physical distraction
- reflective listening

The Communication Skills: Listening, Speaking, Reading, and Writing

Essential Principles

In Section 1.1 you learned that communication is a two-way process that requires a sender and a receiver. You cannot communicate in a vacuum. You cannot communicate by speaking if there is no one to listen. You cannot communicate by writing if no one will read your words. Each side—sender and receiver—must do its part.

As you have probably noticed, communicators are paired: speaker-listener and writer-reader. **Oral communication** requires a speaker and a listener. Oral communication is most effective when the sender has good speaking skills and the receiver has good listening skills. Similarly, **written communication** requires a writer and a reader. Written communication is most effective when the sender has good writing skills and the receiver has good reading skills.

If only half of the pair operates effectively, something is lost in the communication process. Suppose, for example, that someone writes a clear, step-by-step description of how to install a modem. No matter how clear that message, some information will be lost if the reader does not focus full attention on the message or does not understand some of the words or references. The reader will not understand what the writer is trying to say. Communication, then, is a partnership in which each side is responsible.

Combining the Communication Skills in Your Social, Educational, and Professional Lives

An essential ingredient of successful family, social, and business relationships is effective communication. A communication breakdown can lead to misunderstandings and serious problems in our personal and business lives. Good communication skills can positively affect most aspects of our relationships with others.

Learning to be a successful, effective communicator is somewhat like learning to be a good basketball player or a good chess player. Once you have learned the basic skills, you become better as you practice the skills and gain confidence.

Listening, speaking, reading, and writing are important and useful skills in and of themselves. When used together, they reinforce one another, producing a higher, efficient level of communication. Being combined with the others can strengthen each of the four skills. Take listening, for example.

Listening Skills

Listening is concentrating on what you hear and is one of the primary means of receiving information. The problem with listening, though, is that if you miss something or forget part of what you heard, you cannot replay the message, unless you have recorded it. When you know something about the subject, however, when you have "read up on it" or "done your homework," you will find it easier to grasp the information presented orally. Reading, then, can reinforce listening; it helps you gain more from what you hear.

Common barriers or distractions to good listening fall into three categories—educational, environmental, and emotional-physical. **Educational distractions** include a lack of knowledge of the subject matter and vocabulary. **Environmental distractions** include external factors such as the temperature in the room, the noise level, and so on. **Emotional-physical distractions** include internal factors such as your state of mind or your health. For example, having a headache or being extremely worried about tomorrow's big exam can adversely affect your ability to listen.

Speaking, too, can reinforce your listening skills. As mentioned before, good listeners ask questions to clarify points and obtain additional information. Speaking can also be used as a memory aid. Repeating a person's name right after you hear it, for instance, will help you to remember the name later.

Writing reinforces listening skills on an ongoing basis. You jot down the name and address of a restaurant someone recommends, or you take a telephone message for a co-worker. You take notes when your supervisor explains how a job should be done. You can then refer to your notes when you need them. Listening skills are important in all aspects of your life.

Memory Hook

Use these five strategies to enhance, reinforce, and develop your listening skills:

- *Read* to gain background information.
- *Repeat* a person's name when you are introduced to someone.
- *Ask* questions to clarify information.
- *Take* good notes.
- *Use* a tape recorder, when permitted, to record a lecture or meeting.

Your Social Life.   In a social setting, good listeners—those who understand what the speaker is saying and why—are much in demand. We often choose a good listener to be a good friend: someone to turn to when we want to talk about our problems or fears or to share our triumphs or joys. Good listeners often reap the benefit of the experience of others and enjoy the satisfaction of close personal relationships.

Your Educational Life. Good listening skills help you absorb an instructor's lectures, explanations, and directions for assignments. The process of taking notes on the oral information enhances listening. Your notes provide a record of the information you received and enable you to review the information at a later time.

Your Professional Life. Listening is assisted by the other communication skills in every profession. Consider Barbara Wright, for example, who is an administrative assistant in a medical center. She listens in weekly staff meetings to caseworkers and medical staff as they discuss current problems and cases. To help her remember those discussions and what she's been assigned to do, Barbara takes notes. Then she types her notes on her computer to create a permanent record and handy reference. Barbara also reads as many medical articles as she can. This background reading helps her better understand what her co-workers are talking about.

Barbara also uses speaking skills in her job. She participates in the staff meetings, and she spends time each day on the telephone, answering questions and providing information to co-workers and clients. Barbara has discovered that reading, writing, and speaking have helped her become a more effective listener.

Speaking Skills

The communication skill you will probably use the most is speaking. Speaking can be an excellent way to transmit information. Speaking also plays a part of being a good listener. You provide feedback by letting the speaker know you understand, by offering advice, and by asking for more details.

Reflective listening is an important tool in many listening situations, particularly in one-on-one situations. **Reflective listening** (see **Exhibit 1.7**) is attentively listening to the speaker's actual words, as well as tone of voice, and observing the body language and emotions displayed. Then, periodically stop the speaker and "play back" in your own words what you heard and observed. "You said . . ."; "You felt . . ."; "Is that correct?" Reflective listening is usually not practical in a speaker-audience situation. It is not appropriate when the speaker needs specific help or information from you.

Oops!

Homonym Horror

Browsing and searching through the Internet was a waist of time when I had the information in this book.

(waste—not *waist*)

Exhibit 1.7
Reflective Listening
How can a listener display reflective listening? *Thinking Critically.* Name *two ways you could show reflective listening.*

Your Social Life.   You use your speaking skills to share your thoughts, wants, accomplishments, and feelings with others. You also ask questions to gain information and show interest. Speaking can be face-to-face or over the telephone or computer.

Your Educational Life.   Asking questions, summarizing information, and expressing ideas are an important part of the learning process. Your spoken feedback tells your instructor what information you understand and what information needs clarification. Your speaking skills will help you master the course material.

Your Professional Life.   Communicating by speaking is an important skill in the work world. Let's look at how Andrea Rosado uses speaking on her job as a paralegal. Andrea spends a good portion of her day speaking with attorneys, other paralegals, and clients. She makes telephone inquiries regarding legal cases she's working on, and she engages in discussions with attorneys and colleagues.

Reading, writing, and listening skills support Andrea's speaking skills. Andrea knows that reading is an essential part of her job. She must analyze the facts of a case and conduct research to identify laws, judicial decisions, and legal articles that may have a bearing on the case. Andrea uses her writing skills to prepare legal briefs and legal correspondence. Listening is also an important skill for Andrea. As a paralegal, she must listen to clients to obtain information, and she must listen to instructions from her supervising attorney.

Reading Skills

Reading is one of the principal means of obtaining information. The information may be in printed form, such as a book or magazine, or in electronic form on a computer screen. Reading is an efficient way to learn because it allows you to control the flow of information. You can reread a passage you have not fully understood, and you can take notes, which will help you when reviewing the material. Reading allows you to skip over material you don't need.

Your Social Life.   Reading newspapers, magazines, and books helps you to broaden your knowledge and understanding of the world and to become a more interesting person. Reading gives you more information and ideas to share with others.

Your Educational Life.   In any kind of educational setting, reading is one of the principal means of acquiring course-related information.

Reading skills are important for students at every level. Take Julius Mitchell, for example. Julius works for an electrical supply company during the day and attends a community college at night. He found the reading assignments for some of his courses difficult at first. However, things improved when he started taking notes on his reading. Taking notes helped Julius organize and remember the information. These notes made studying for exams easier, since Julius could review his notes rather than rereading the entire text.

Julius discovered that he gets more out of a class when he has read the assignment ahead of time. The lectures help him to review basic material and to clarify difficult points. Julius has also found that he likes participating in discussions when he is prepared for class. Talking about the material in class reinforces Julius's reading and aids him in mastering the material.

Your Professional Life.   Reading will be part of any job, starting with the employment forms you must read when you are hired. Memos, letters, reports, computer manuals, schedules, procedures manuals, and policy manuals are just a few of the documents that will require reading skills.

Writing Skills

Writing skills are important for creating and communicating information. Although writing has many advantages, the major one is that it provides a physical record that can be used as proof, if necessary.

Your Social Life. Writing is probably the communication skill that is least used in our personal lives today. Many of us tend to make a telephone call rather than write a letter to a friend who lives some distance away. But we need to know how to write a note of appreciation or to express condolences.

Similarly, we all need to know how to write business correspondence, such as letters of request, letters of complaint, or notification of a change of address. Committing your personal business to writing gives you a record of the exchange should it ever be required.

Your Educational Life. Excellent writing skills can help you to earn higher grades on research papers and tests. You learn more through writing about a subject because you must think about the material and organize the information you have before you can start to write about it.

Your Professional Life. On the job, you use your writing skills to compose e-mail messages, memos, letters, and reports. In many jobs, writing is a supporting skill, but in some jobs—a newspaper reporter or author, for example—writing is the primary skill. Writing via some form of electronic communication will become an increasingly important part of our lives in the future.

The Value of Good Communication Skills

As you can see, the four communication skills apply to your social, educational, and professional lives in much the same way. With the rapid rate of technological advancements, you can expect to have several different jobs during your working life. You'll need to learn new software programs or managerial skills, for example. Your communication skills are tools that will help you to adapt to a variety of work situations.

The four communication skills are interconnected, and using all of them will strengthen your ability to communicate. Let's see how Tisha Tillotson uses all four communication skills in her job. Tisha works as an investigative reporter for the *News Gazette*. She has always liked to write and now works as a full-time journalist. Tisha knows that listening, speaking, and reading skills are crucial in writing newspaper articles.

For example, Tisha had to read the minutes of last year's town meetings to get the history of the new recycling program. She found that she needed more information about recycling plans in other communities and the technology involved. Tisha spent the morning in the public library, reading and taking notes. Next, she wanted to find out what various town officials and citizens thought about the new program. Was the proposed program worth the expense? Would it really help to cut down on the amount of garbage? Would the plastic bottles be processed and reused as promised? Tisha drew up a list of questions, she listened carefully to the answers of her interviewees, and she took notes.

Tisha then assembled the material for her story. She was able to plan what she was going to say before she actually sat down at her computer to write.

When analyzing Tisha's job, you see how the four communication skills are interconnected. Each of the communication skills—listening, speaking, reading, and writing—is strengthened and reinforced by the other skills.

The following chart illustrates that the largest job growth occurs with jobs in which the four communication skills are essential.

Occupations with the Largest Job Growth, 2002–2012 (Numbers in Thousands of Jobs)				
Industry Description	**Employment**		**Change**	
	2002	**2012**	**Number**	**Percent**
Registered nurses	2,284	2,908	623	27
Postsecondary teachers	1,581	2,184	603	38
Retail salespersons	4,076	4,672	596	15
Customer service representatives	1,894	2,354	460	24
Combined food preparation and serving workers, including fast food	1,990	2,444	454	23
Cashiers, except gaming	3,432	3,886	454	13
Janitors and cleaners, except maids and housekeeping cleaners	2,267	2,681	414	18
General and operations managers	2,049	2,425	376	18
Waiters and waitresses	2,097	2,464	367	18
Nursing aides, orderlies, and attendants	1,375	1,718	343	25

SOURCE: U.S. Department of Labor, Bureau of Labor Statistics

 Assessment   Section 1.2

Review of Key Terms

1. What are the three categories of common barriers or distractions to good listening? Give a definition of each category. _____
    _____
    _____
    _____

2. What effect does *written communication* have on one's professional life?
    _____
    _____

Editing Practice

Proofreading Alert! Proper proofreading involves checking the spelling, grammar, and punctuation within a sentence. Proofread the following paragraph and mark all the errors. Then, rewrite or type the corrected paragraph.

3. As per our telephone conservation, we are senting you corected speci-facations. Note that instalation of a two-way comunication systems is now required. In addition, the thermastat is to be re-located to the upstair hall. Please send us your revise bid, propperly typed on your company stationary, no latter then Oct. 1.

_____

_____

Practical Application

Thinking Critically

4. Write a brief paper on the value of letter writing in either your social life or your business life:

    a. How has e-mail changed letter writing?
    b. Letter writing is a lost art.
    c. Writing letters is a wonderful way to communicate.

    _____

5. One communication skill is featured in each of the following examples. Explain how another communication skill might be used in each situation to reinforce the main skill.

    - Listening to a neighbor's complaints about a barking dog.

      _____

    - Speaking to a group about the pros and cons of four popular word processing programs. _____

      _____

      _____

    - Writing a report about public opinion on local property tax rates. _____

      _____

    - Reading several consumer and photography magazines in the library that evaluate digital cameras. (You want to buy a digital camera.) _____

Discussion Point

Identifying the Main Idea

6. Describe how communication is a two-way process and explain why communication skills are paired. _____

    _____

    _____

Communicating in the Business Environment

The Importance of Good Communication in Business

Imagine that you are an employee who has made suggestions on how to improve your department or company. How would you feel if your supervisor listened to your ideas and actually put some of them into effect? You would probably feel great. You might respond by working even harder than you were working before. You would have experienced *effective communication.*

Flow of Communication

Communication not only links members of a certain department but also serves as a vital link between people in different departments. In a company, each department functions as a spoke in a wheel; all the spokes are needed for the wheel to function properly. If several spokes are missing, broken, or not aligned properly, the wheel becomes wobbly and eventually will break.

Upward communication is communicating with people who rank above you, such as your boss or instructor. **Lateral** or **horizontal** communication is communicating with people who are at the same rank or level as you—your co-workers or classmates, for instance. **Downward communication** is communicating with people who rank below you, such as the people you might manage at work. The direction your communication flows at any given time will influence how you communicate—the words you use and the method you choose.

Not only does good communication make a company operate efficiently, it also creates a sense of unity—a team spirit—and a striving for common goals among employees.

Exhibit 1.8 illustrates the flow of communication within an organization and shows the directions in which communication can travel. The arrows at both ends of a line show that communication flows both ways.

Types of Business Communication

Communication that takes place in a company or an organization falls into two categories: internal communication and external communication. The tone used in internal communication usually differs from that used in external communication. *Tone,* as it applies to business communication, usually refers to the general manner of expression or effect of a written document, conversation, discussion, or speech.

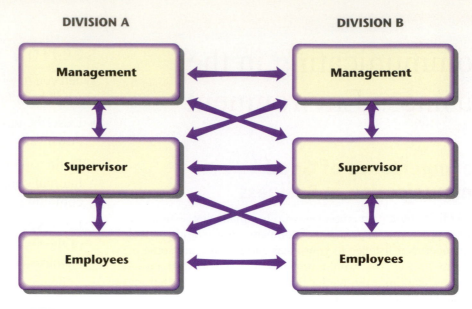

DIVISION A **DIVISION B**

Management ↔ Management

Supervisor ↔ Supervisor

Employees ↔ Employees

Exhibit 1.8
Communication Flow
Communication within an organization flows in three directions—upwardly, laterally, and downwardly—to accomplish company objectives. How could management effectively communicate with company employees? List three methods of internal communication.

Internal Communication

Internal communication is the transmittal of information between and among persons within a business or organization. Within a company, internal communication is used to accomplish company goals and objectives. Managers must, for example, let employees know when and why a specific job must be done. On the other hand, nonmanagement personnel use communication for understanding and clarifying how a specific job must be done. Nonmanagement personnel communicate to convince management that their knowledge and personal attributes qualify them for pay increases or promotions. Other examples of internal communication include suggestions for improving products and services and guidelines for completing a process.

Internal communication may be carried out with people in the same department, in other departments, and at other company locations.

Also, employees may communicate individually or as members of a team. Internal communication may include face-to-face conversations, telephone calls, e-mail messages, and brainstorming ideas at a meeting as illustrated in **Exhibit 1.9** on page 25.

In internal communication, a person's tone may be friendly and informal. As an employee, you must assess a situation and use the most appropriate tone. For instance, when telling a colleague about an idea you have to make your department more productive, you would use different words, different phrasing, and a different tone from the words, phrasing, and tone you would use if you were making the same suggestion to the manager of your department.

External Communication

External communication is the transfer of information to and from people outside the company. The goal of a company's external communication is to persuade the recipients to respond favorably to company needs. A sales letter, for example, tries to get a potential customer to buy a product or a service. A job listing tries to attract qualified personnel to fill a certain position.

Exhibit 1.9
Team Communication
Communicating in teams is an important aspect of internal communication. What qualities should team members demonstrate in order to communicate effectively as part of a team?

In external communication, a person's tone is often more polite and formal. Using the right tone in external communication is more challenging than using the right tone in internal communication because you are representing your company as well as yourself. Often, customers and clients will transfer their opinions of you and your communication skills to the company itself. They will base opinions not only on what you say or write but also on your appearance and manner. In other words, the whole package counts.

Although your physical appearance may not be as important as the content of what you say or write, your appearance creates a first impression. Keep in mind that the first impression you create will often influence how closely your customer or client will pay attention to what you have to say. As a result, your appearance, or the appearance of your communication, can work either for you or against you.

The Six Cs of Business Communication

Effective business communication meets the test of the six Cs—*clear, complete, concise, consistent, correct,* and *courteous.* The six Cs apply to any communication situation, whether you are speaking or writing, and whether you are communicating with someone inside or someone outside your organization. Using the six Cs will make your communication coherent and easy to follow.

Clear

It isn't enough to communicate so you can be understood; you must communicate so clearly that you cannot be misunderstood. Being specific rather than vague is a way to meet this test. If you leave your car for "routine service," will you be upset when you receive a bill for $368? Asking the Service Department to call you if the car will require more than $70 worth of service work would eliminate this miscommunication.

Complete

Complete communication includes enough details so that the recipient will not need to ask for more information. Imagine receiving a notice from your dentist for a return visit on Wednesday at 3 p.m. Which Wednesday would you go? To be complete, a communication should answer the following questions: Who? What? Where? When? Why? and How? or How much?

KEY POINT

Effective business communication is:

1. **Clear**
2. **Complete**
3. **Concise**
4. **Consistent**
5. **Correct**
6. **Courteous**

Concise

Unnecessary words hamper communication because the extra words used to express the idea or thought clutter the message. The following sentence is wordy: "I am writing this letter to inform you that your airline tickets will be mailed ten days before your scheduled departure." Look how much more effective a more concise version is: "We will mail your airline tickets to you ten days before your scheduled departure." You've eliminated seven words, and none of the meaning is lost from the original message.

Consistent

All communication should be consistent in *fact, treatment,* and *sequence.* Consistency in *fact* refers to agreement with a source document or an established fact. For example, an open house scheduled for April 31 should be questioned since April has only 30 days. Consistency in *treatment* means treating similar items the same way. An example of consistent treatment would be using a courtesy title (Mr., Mrs., Miss, or Ms.) with the names of all recipients of a letter or indenting all paragraphs in a letter. Consistency in *sequence* refers to the arrangement of listings such as alphabetical, chronological, or numerical. Imagine a telephone book that is not arranged in alphabetical order. If a workshop is scheduled for three days, the dates should be given in chronological order: for example, May 3, May 6, and May 10.

Correct

All the information in a message should be accurate—the content, the spelling, the capitalization, and the punctuation.

Courteous

Your communication should use the you-attitude instead of the I-attitude. This means keeping the reader or listener in mind when you write or say something. Use positive words instead of negative words and use tactful language. Use formats, such as lists, short paragraphs, and tables, that are easy to read and comprehend.

 ## Memory Hook

The six Cs of effective communication are easy to remember because each one starts with the letter C.

Clear **C**onsistent

Complete **C**orrect

Concise **C**ourteous

To recall the six Cs, remember this sentence: Clara gave clear, complete, and concise directions on how to greet customers in a consistent, correct, and courteous way.

 ## Assessment Section 1.3

Review of Key Terms

1. How is *upward communication* different from *lateral* or *horizontal communication*? _____

_____

2. What is the difference between *external* and *internal communication*?

_____

_____

_____

Editing Practice

Call an Editor! Which of the six Cs of communication is violated in each of the following sentences?

3. We would like to take this opportunity to welcome all retirees. _____

_____

4. We demand that you make a payment now. _____

5. The pictures will be sent seperately. _____

6. The sales manager told the associate that he would not attend the meeting. _____

7. The new Wal-Mart store will have the ribbon-cutting ceremony on Wednesday, August 28. _____

8. The prices will be $2, $6, and $4. _____

Practical Application

Analyzing Information

9. Explain and give examples of the six Cs of business communication.

_____

10. In your teams, write a paragraph about what combination of communication skills you would use and why.

a. Applying for a job advertised in the want ad column in the newspaper that gives a box number for reply.

b. Receiving a message on your telephone answering machine to call an employer to set up an appointment for a job interview.

c. Preparing a research paper on a topic about which you have limited knowledge.

d. Conducting a workshop on refinishing furniture (assume you are not an expert).

_____

_____

Discussion Point

Identifying the Main Idea

11. How is communication in an organization like the spokes of a wheel? _____

_____

_____

12. Discuss how speech and appearance can provide the tone for a company you represent. Brainstorm examples of both positive and negative tones. _____

_____

Chapter 2

Interpreting Communication

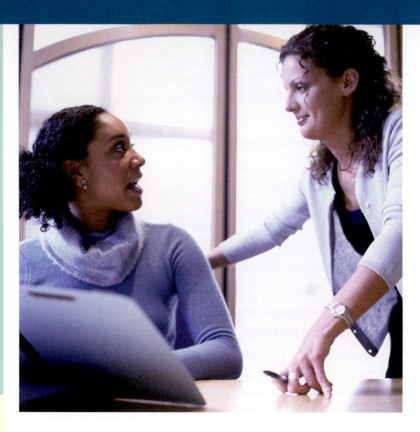

Workplace Connection

Listening and reading, two of the four communication skills, are utilized to receive information. Being successful as a student or an employee depends on your ability to listen and to read effectively.

CHAPTER OBJECTIVES

When you have completed this chapter, you should be able to:

- Discuss the basics of nonverbal communication and their importance in all interactions.
- Explain the mental and physical processes in listening.
- Discuss and contrast listening in casual and business settings.
- List suggestions for improving your reading skills.

The Basics of Nonverbal Communication

Essential Principles

Without realizing it, communicators send numerous nonverbal messages every day. Nonverbal communication is communication without words. Note the occurrences of nonverbal and verbal communication in the following scenario:

> The impeccably dressed president of the company entered the high-tech meeting room with a stranger at his side—a woman in crisp, smart business attire. As the president warmly and respectfully introduced her to the company's middle management, the woman's easygoing smile acknowledged the participants.
>
> With a sense of professional excitement, the president explained that the woman was a seasoned management consultant who was going to help implement a number of organizational changes within the company. As a number of the managers glanced at each other with questioning looks, the president quickly assured the managers that no jobs or salaries were in danger. He then added that he was very enthusiastic about the company's enhanced prospects once the changes were completed.
>
> After her introduction, the management consultant told a well-delivered, business-related joke, which put the group at ease. She then told the group she was looking forward to working with the entire management team, and she noted that she would actively seek their input. She explained she expected to learn a great deal from them as she recommended and helped implement the upcoming changes for the company. The managers listened closely to everything she had to say.

The scenario demonstrates both verbal and nonverbal communication. The verbal communication was the president's calling a meeting of managers to introduce the management consultant's role in reorganizing the company. The importance of the meeting was expressed nonverbally by the inclusion of all the company's management. Both the president and the consultant's relaxed and warm manner conveyed the good news nonverbally. The nonverbal communication included the president's actions, his attire, his facial expressions, his voice, as well as his interaction with the consultant. The management members also exhibited nonverbal communication, first with questioning looks, later with laughter, and finally with their undivided attention to what the consultant had to tell them.

SECTION OBJECTIVES

When you have finished Section 2.1, you will be able to:

- Define nonverbal communication and how it applies to life situations and the workplace.
- Discuss the personal and professional importance of nonverbal communication.
- List the five categories of nonverbal communication.

WHY IT'S IMPORTANT

Nonverbal communication, simply defined, is communicating without words; it is the conscious and subconscious use of actions, behaviors, and interactions with one's surroundings, which convey a message.

KEY TERMS

- nonverbal communication
- paralanguage
- body language
- touch
- space

The Importance of Nonverbal Communication

Two well-known adages express the importance of nonverbal communication:

- Actions speak louder than words.
- A picture is worth a thousand words.

Most people agree that actions speak louder than words. Our friends, co-workers, and others often attach more meaning to our nonverbal messages than they do to our verbal messages, because they feel nonverbal messages more accurately reflect attitudes and feelings. For example, suppose two employees are vying for the same promotion to branch manager. When the promotion decision is announced, the employee not getting the promotion congratulates the new branch manager and says, "I'm happy for you." However, his nonverbal facial expression might communicate disappointment about the promotion and that he is actually not happy for the new branch manager. Professional courtesy and protocol have compelled the person who did not get the promotion to congratulate the new branch manager. Reading the true feelings of disappointment in his face, the new branch manager takes the opportunity to respond warmly and sincerely, by crossing the room to shake hands. The nonverbal communication these two shared speaks volumes more than the words they exchanged.

Is a picture indeed worth a thousand words, as the second adage says? Nonverbal communication is like a mental snapshot the mind records during the communication process. Remember you're not only reading cues from nonverbal communication, you're also sending them. The mental snapshot, or image, affects our perception of a particular situation. People you interact with will examine their own snapshots for communication clues that indicate to them how you feel about what you are saying. Strangers will have immediate positive or negative first impressions about you.

Nonverbal communication is extremely important—so important that its absence is noticed and can be detrimental. The absence of nonverbal communication can deliver a negative message and affect relationships. Suppose, for example, two business associates have had a strained relationship. The failure of one associate to shake hands, when the other associate offers his hand in greeting, clearly communicates that the relationship is still strained.

A fundamental reality exists in human nature regarding verbal and nonverbal communication. When nonverbal cues contradict verbal cues, people tend to trust their perception of the nonverbal cue. Therefore, even from the first impressions people make of you, through personal and professional relationships as they grow, the nonverbal information you broadcast will weigh heavily on your influence and impact on people.

Nonverbal perceptual checks are helpful in both personal and professional growth. On a personal level, you would strive to view yourself as others see you and attempt a level assessment. More organized settings, such as the workplace, may have performance reviews. These reviews may also include feedback on the message your nonverbal personality conveys. Here, an employee has the opportunity to ask: "Is there anything negative you see in my body language? Is there anything I could work on in my nonverbal presentation?" This type of feedback is valuable information that targets the likely areas of habitual behavior that need attention or possibly signal a need for personal growth.

Categories of Nonverbal Communication

Nonverbal communication can be divided into five categories. As you study each one, refer to the example of the management meeting at the beginning of this section. Can you identify each of the following categories in the example?

Paralanguage

Paralanguage includes nonverbal communications such as tone, pitch, quality, rate of speech, laughing, crying, belching, and even hesitating or sighing. Paralanguage can help reinforce a verbal message. For example:

- A father says, "awww" to his daughter who has just fallen.
- An ill student with a scratchy voice calls her professor to let him know she will not be able to give her presentation.
- A customer clears his throat to let a busy cashier know he is ready to check out.

Kinesics

Body language, or kinesics, is the gestures, movements, and mannerisms by which a person communicates with others. Physical attributes such as appearance, facial expressions, eye contact, and posture all contribute to kinesics or body language. Facial expressions communicate our thoughts and emotions. See **Exhibit 2.1** for examples. Here are examples of body language.

- Physical appearance includes clothes, jewelry, and grooming. Wearing the appropriate clothing to specific events demonstrates taste and style. Wearing jeans to a formal dinner would convey that the person has poor judgment.
- Facial expressions indicate our emotions: happy, sad, confused, angry, etc. Eye contact, in the American culture, conveys confidence, honesty, and interest in the conversation.
- Gestures can express many things: a friendly wave to say hello, a frantic wave from a trader on the New York Stock exchange, a supervisor holding up his hand to defer questions in a meeting, and the American okay gesture to convey agreement.
- Posture sends a message. Standing or sitting erect denotes that you are paying attention to the matter at hand. Leaning forward conveys increased interest, while leaning back conveys disinterest or a feeling of discomfort or defensiveness.

Memory Hook

Eye contact is a useful nonverbal tool. Good eye contact lets your speaker know that you are paying close attention. Poor eye contact conveys that you are not interested in what the speaker is saying.

Exhibit 2.1
Facial Expressions
Expressions often reveal what is going on in the mind. *Thinking Critically. What emotion or idea does each snapshot demonstrate?*

Employability Skills

Self-Esteem

Maintaining a positive view of self is important when working in a team environment. It's important for all individuals to have positive self-esteem for a team to work effectively and efficiently.

Going Global

Worldly Etiquette

Consider differences in etiquette when doing business abroad. While Americans shake hands before and after a business meeting, Asian cultures, such as Korean or Japanese, usually bow instead of shaking hands.

Going Global

Personal Space, Worlds Apart

Consider how different cultures interpret personal space. In Mexico, people communicate by standing very close together and might even touch arms. In Japan, people are not inclined toward physical display and stand farther away from each other than we do in the United States.

Memory Hook

The human smile is one of the most effective nonverbal ways in which we express our happiness or approval. Smiles are contagious. An old adage says, "Smile and the whole world smiles with you." (Author unknown)

Environment

Our environment communicates many different messages. Environmental factors of nonverbal communication include objects in our surroundings or the surroundings themselves. For example:

- A large desk in a corner office with windows communicates high status within an organization.
- Fast-food restaurants are usually designed to move customers through quickly, using bright colors and plastic seating that is comfortable for only about 10 minutes.
- Some organizations arrange product catalogs or sales awards in the reception area. This is done to give visitors a positive first impression.
- Color communicates a variety of messages. Many hospital delivery rooms are painted in soothing colors to relax expectant parents.

Touch

Touch, or haptic communication, is a primary method for achieving connection with people, indicating intention, or expressing emotion. Like other factors of nonverbal communication, the use of touch is culturally bound. Consider the following:

- In a business setting, the most appropriate form of communication is the handshake.
- A limp handshake can communicate nervousness or a feeling of inferiority; a firm handshake communicates confidence.
- Haptic communication is status-driven. That is, a manager may give an employee an encouraging pat on the back, but not vice versa.
- People in business must avoid touch that could be considered condescending or sexual harassment. Sexual harassment is any unwanted verbal or physical action related to sex.

Space

Space, as it relates to nonverbal communication, is the physical distance maintained with others. How you use space to communicate depends upon cultural norms, your relationship with the receivers of your communication, and the activities involved.

For North Americans, space generally falls into four categories:

- Intimate distance: From physical contact to 18 inches. This distance is reserved for personal expression with those we know well.
- Personal distance: From 18 inches to 3 feet. This distance is used for casual and friendly conversations.
- Social distance: From 3 feet to 7 feet. This distance is used in the workplace for business-related conversations, small meetings, and social functions. It is also used for other conversations that are not personal in nature.

- Public distance: From 7 feet and beyond. This distance is usually for public speaking. Obviously, this distance in a personal conversation would constitute a huge communication barrier.

Conflicting Signals

Messages are made stronger when both the verbal and the nonverbal communications convey the same thing. Sometimes, subconsciously, we send two distinctly different messages. For example, when discussions become emotionally driven, one participant may say to the other, "You're angry." Immediately, the other emotionally charged participant shouts, "I'm not angry!" Here there is a conflict between what is actually said and the volume and tone of the voices. Another common example is that of a quiet, preoccupied, and withdrawn person. When asked if anything is wrong, the person insists he or she is fine. Depending on the circumstances, most questioners would either leave the person alone or ask more questions. The person who answers the question by saying, "I am fine," however, does nothing to alter the questioner's view that something is wrong.

Using Nonverbal Communication

As effective communicators, we strive to combine verbal and nonverbal communications to increase the efficiency and impact of our messages. In doing so, we make sure that what we express verbally and nonverbally is not in conflict. In addition, care should be taken not to intimidate people by encroaching on their personal space.

Interpretation of the nonverbal cues and messages we receive is an essential responsibility of any communicator. Nonverbal feedback can be extremely helpful in understanding countless settings, for example, when a subordinate listens to instructions for performing a specific task. A puzzled expression from the subordinate lets the supervisor know more explanation is needed.

A word of caution about nonverbal communication—perception is the cornerstone for interpreting nonverbal signals. Misperceptions can result in misinterpretation of nonverbal signals. And if any action is based on possible misperception or misinterpretation, the consequences of that action must be seriously considered.

2.1 Self-Assessment

Answer *T* for *True* and *F* for *False* for the following questions.

1. Most people agree that words speak louder than actions. _____

2. The definition of kinesics does not include gestures as a way to communicate. _____

3. The environmental category of nonverbal communications includes facial expressions. _____

4. Haptic communication is another term for touch communication. _____

5. A firm handshake and a limp handshake communicate the same message when greeting a business associate. _____

6. The handshake is used in all countries as the standard way to greet others. _____

7. Nonverbal communication is the exchange of information without words. _____

oops!

Accessible

Employees can excess the company directory by using the new telephone system.

(access is the correct word, not excess)

8. Nonverbal communication does not convey a message. _____

9. When nonverbal cues contradict verbal cues, people tend to trust their reading of the nonverbal cues. _____

10. Paralanguage can help reinforce a verbal message. _____

11. Verbal communication more accurately reflects attitudes and feelings. _____

12. The absence of nonverbal communication can deliver a negative message. _____

Bonus Question

13. How do body language and environment affect communication?

   _____
   _____
   _____

Assessment   Section 2.1

Review of Key Terms

1. How can *nonverbal communication* affect a speaker's message? _____

   _____
   _____
   _____

2. How does a speaker's *paralanguage* affect an audience? _____

   _____

3. What kind of *body language* would a speaker use to portray unfortunate news? _____

   _____

Editing Practice

Proofreading Alert!   Make corrections to the following sentences; rewrite poorly worded sentences.

4. Will you and him attend the CEO's annual address? _____

   _____

5. Please continue on as though nobody said anything. _____

   _____

6. You should follow-up on your *Car and Driver* article with a visit to the manufacturers office. _____

   _____

7. This company has always in the past—and always will—be noted for its fair treatment of all employees. _____

_____

8. The new assignment schedule was only given to Morgan and I last week.

_____

_____

Practical Application

Analyzing Details

9. Politicians, business leaders, and television journalists are aware of how their nonverbal communication may affect their audience and use it to their advantage. Prepare a video of one of these professionals giving a speech or delivering news. Note factors—both pro and con—that affect their speaking effectiveness. Then, as a team write a paragraph analyzing how nonverbal communication made the message more effective. _____

_____

_____

Discussion Point

Evaluating Concepts

10. Discuss how nonverbal cues can be misinterpreted. In your discussion, include how cultural differences play a role. _____

_____

_____

_____

11. Discuss how being successful as a student or an employee depends on your ability to listen and to read effectively. _____

SECTION OBJECTIVES

When you have finished Section 2.2, you will be able to:

- Identify the five components of the listening model.
- Explain how hearing differs from listening.
- Describe the difference between active and passive listening.
- Describe how to overcome listening barriers.

WHY IT'S IMPORTANT

Listening is an integral part of the communication process, and much of the routine workday is spent using this skill.

KEY TERMS

- listening
- hearing
- interpreting
- retaining
- recalling
- passive listening
- active listening
- listening barriers
- external noise
- internal noise
- listening priorities

Learning the Basics of Listening

Essential Principles

Often, we think just because we have ears, we can listen. **Listening,** however, is to hear something with thoughtful attention. **Hearing,** on the other hand, is the physical function of detecting sound. Those who are hearing-impaired "listen" to sign language. That is, they receive the sign language and use their perception to analyze and give meaning to the communication just received.

The Listening Model

As you can see from **Exhibit 2.2,** listening has five components. You do not choose which sounds you will hear. You do, however, decide on which sounds to focus your attention. Then, you assign meaning and importance to those sounds.

Listening—A Neglected Skill

From your first years of development, you began listening without studying how to listen or even being aware of the way you were listening. Listening is different from the other communication skills in that you were probably not taught to listen. When you learned to speak, someone corrected you if you made mistakes or mispronounced words. Learning to read and write involved even more formal instruction and practice. Many people assume listening is automatic, but it is really an acquired skill. Hearing happens unconsciously; listening effectively requires active concentration.

To become a better listener, you must be aware of the type of listening required in each situation and learn how to make your listening more productive.

Types of Listening

There are two types of listening: passive and active. The difference between these is the level of the listener's involvement.

Passive Listening

Passive listening means concentrating at a low level and absorbing just enough of the speaker's words to stay involved in a conversation or speech. Passive listeners actually understand or remember little of what is said. Often, passive listeners let the speaker's inflection or tone of voice signal when they should react by nodding, smiling, or saying, "I see." Such reactions can suggest that the speaker has a listener's attention even though that may not be the case.

The Listening Model

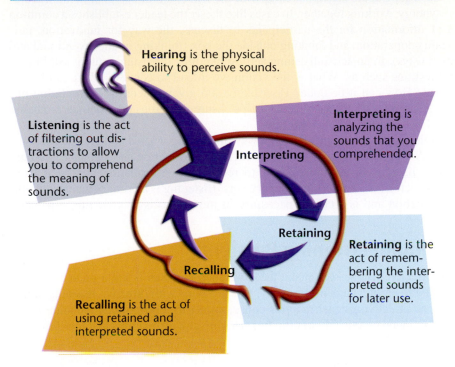

Hearing is the physical ability to perceive sounds.

Interpreting is analyzing the sounds that you comprehended.

Listening is the act of filtering out distractions to allow you to comprehend the meaning of sounds.

Interpreting

Retaining

Retaining is the act of remembering the interpreted sounds for later use.

Recalling

Recalling is the act of using retained and interpreted sounds.

Exhibit 2.2
Listening Model
The listening model involves five elements. ***Thinking Critically.*** *Which are most challenging for you?*

Passive listening is appropriate only when you listen for pleasure and when it doesn't matter whether or not you retain what you hear. Imagine yourself in a comfortable chair reading a magazine, listening to music.

In these situations, you listen passively because you don't need to register every piece of sound information you hear. Often, you use the music as background noise and listen attentively only when you hear something—for example, your favorite song—that suddenly captures your attention.

Active Listening

Active listening uses a high level of concentration because you are listening for information. In school or in the workplace, active—not passive—listening is appropriate. Listening carefully to an instructor's explanation of an assignment or to your supervisor's directions about the procedure to follow for performing a particular task are examples of active listening. Workplace conversations are filled with names, dates, places, prices, requests, and suggestions. Each conversation has its own level of importance and priority.

Participating mentally, active listeners concentrate at a high level on what is being said. The computer programmer, for example, must listen to the company accountant to understand what is needed in the new accounting program. The administrative assistant must listen to which specific data are needed prior to setting up a new database. The travel agent must accurately hear the correct times, dates, and destinations for booking a trip. The medical assistant must hear the doctor's exact instructions for patient care. Knowing how to listen actively is essential to being successful in any workplace environment.

KEY POINT

Passive listening is appropriate when it is not important to remember what you hear.

In the ever-changing environment of today's workplace, professional meetings sometimes require acute active listening with the leader's ultimate goal being the creation of synergy, working together. In cases like these, the leader establishes a common ground of information for the participants to discuss, the way for innovation, new ideas, team cooperation, and thinking outside the box (thinking in unconventional and innovative ways). In an active listening setting like this, the listener might ask him or herself questions such as: What is the vision we intend to convey? What can be accomplished? How can it be done? How likely is a given outcome? Formulating numerous questions for a scenario like this helps ensure numerous perspectives are being considered in this dynamic team process.

Excluding sight, listening is the main way of learning what is going on in your surroundings. Active listening provides you with vital information and signals. If you are prepared to listen, you are more likely to receive the information you need from friends, instructors, co-workers, and supervisors. Listening is a primary means of gathering information and is crucially necessary in most aspects of your life, especially your work.

Overcoming Listening Barriers

Being an effective listener can make the difference between being a great employee and a mediocre employee. Unfortunately, few are born with effective listening skills. Becoming an effective listener requires conscious effort. Overcoming listening barriers takes continued practice. **Listening barriers** are any distractions that interfere with listening. Some examples are:

- Not concentrating on what is being said.
- Becoming distracted by noise.
- Talking instead of listening.
- Having preconceived thoughts and opinions.
- Not being interested in what is being said.

Concentrate on the Speaker's Message

One key to effective listening is realizing that it is your responsibility to stay focused. Often the listener blames his or her lack of concentration on the fact that the speaker is boring or that the listener has something else on his or her mind. Sometimes, instead of listening, a person might decide to "tune out" and later ask a friend or co-worker to explain the gist of a speaker's message.

Most people—even good listeners—occasionally find they have lost their focus when they should be listening. When this happens to you, simply create a default refocus in your attention by saying to yourself something like: "Mind, come back to where body is." Then, immediately refocus on the priorities of listening.

Use Filters to Manage and Control Noise

Noise can affect your ability to listen. The two basic kinds of noise are external noise and internal noise. **External noise** includes sounds from conversations, radios, television, CD players, machinery, etc. **Internal noise** includes distractions such as pain, fatigue, preoccupation with other thoughts, hunger, worry, or a personality conflict with the speaker.

KEY POINT

To manage noise, a listener should identify what noise can be controlled and what noise cannot be controlled.

An effective listener filters out unwanted external and internal noise. Proactive techniques in effective listening can include avoiding distracting noise when possible and managing the noise you cannot control. For example, you can turn down the volume on a radio, but you can't turn down the noise of the machinery you may be operating. However, you can manage the machinery noise by wearing ear protection. Seeking medical attention and getting enough sleep are ways of controlling the internal noise resulting from headaches and fatigue.

Resist Talking Instead of Listening

As a listener, keep this suggestion in mind: When you are talking, you cannot listen effectively. It is impossible to be both sender and receiver at the same time. You can even become your own distraction.

As a listener, you may be tempted to interrupt the speaker in order to make a point or to share information you feel is important. However, a listener should resist the urge to interrupt. Wait until the speaker has finished making a point and then respond with an appropriate comment.

Focus on the Message

As a good listener, you will want to be sure your own ideas do not interfere with listening to the ideas of others. First, although you may be aware that a speaker's ideas or opinions conflict with your own, you cannot be certain what someone will say until you actually hear it. Second, you may know the speaker's views but not the reasons for those views; passing judgment without hearing the speaker's arguments would be premature. Third, even if the speaker advocates ideas or actions you oppose, you should still listen carefully. By listening, you will learn about the opposing view and be able to argue against it more effectively. Listening could even change your mind.

Listen with a Positive Attitude

To be a good listener, you don't have to agree with the speaker. However, to be an effective listener, you do have to keep an open mind and believe the speaker might have something useful to offer.

It is easy to see how taking a positive attitude toward listening is in your best interest. For example, the main purpose of attending a lecture or a class discussion is to learn. Therefore, if students want to learn, they will also need to listen. In the business world, the employee who wants to do a good job will listen carefully to the supervisor's explanations and directions. To be productive, supervisors also need to listen carefully to workers' problems and needs. Good listeners learn to listen even when they don't want to listen.

Turning Good Listening Skills into Effective Communication

Think back to a recent occasion when someone told you how to do something new. Did you listen carefully and understand fully what you were supposed to do, or did you realize a few minutes later that you had actually missed or misunderstood certain steps in the directions? Suppose you had to ask for the directions to be repeated. Refer to the list of listening barriers (see page 38) to determine what may have prevented you from hearing all the directions the first time.

Improving Your Listening Skills

When you read, your attention may sometimes wander from the writer's message, yet you know you can return later to reread the content you missed. Spoken words, however, disappear once spoken and cannot be recaptured.

Imagine yourself in this situation: As your flight taxis down the runway, the flight attendant gives the routine speech about safety and emergency procedures. The flight attendant and the topic are boring, the plane's air-conditioning has not yet reached a comfortable temperature, you're leafing through a magazine, and the person seated next to you is listening, unfortunately, at the same level that you are. After a smooth take-off, the pilot levels off at 35,000 feet. Suddenly, the plane loses cabin pressure and the oxygen masks drop before you and your seatmate. You immediately realize you should have focused on the flight attendant's speech. An instant replay of the speech is impossible. Your only option is to improvise. After a few minutes, cabin pressure is

KEY POINT

Usually a listener has only one chance to absorb and comprehend a speaker's words.

reestablished, and the flight continues without incident. During the safety instruction speech, you and the other passengers would have benefited from active—not passive—listening.

In most listening situations, you have only one chance to absorb and comprehend a speaker's words, so you cannot afford to let your attention wander.

One reason we as listeners stop paying attention is that we hear faster than most speakers can speak. The average person can speak 125 to 150 words a minute, but a good listener processes 300 or more words a minute. Because of this ability to understand faster than people speak, listeners tend to relax and listen to only part of what is being said. However, missing a sentence or even a single word can change the speaker's message.

To avoid the risk of misunderstanding the message or missing an important part of it, listen actively to everything that is said. Still, it is humanly impossible to listen attentively all the time. At some point, you need to take a break, mentally and physically, from listening. If possible, schedule breaks during long periods of listening. Also, try to vary your activities, appointments, and tasks so that you do not have long blocks of time when you must listen intensely.

Paraphrasing

One powerful and effective way of "owning" the content presented to you by a speaker is to paraphrase the message. In doing so, the listener crystallizes her or his understanding of the content, and the speaker has the opportunity to correct any discrepancies from the core of her or his intended message.

Evaluate Your Skills

Everyone has listening weaknesses. Before you can improve your listening skills, you must identify your weaknesses. Begin by answering the questions in the listening checklist in **Exhibit 2.3** on page 41.

Prepare Yourself Physically and Mentally

Listening is a combination of physical and mental activities. Although the mental part of listening is more complex, you must also remember to take responsibility for the physical part of listening.

If you are experiencing any hearing difficulties, schedule a hearing examination with a medical professional. This person will examine any abnormalities and present options for necessary treatment. The causes of hearing impairment are numerous. Some people are born with hearing deficiencies; others encounter them as a result of accidents, illness, or exposure to loud noises such as machinery or other habitual and work-related sources of extreme noise. Most companies with excessive noise in the workplace require their employees to wear hearing protection to prevent damage to this vital sense. Unprotected exposure to loud sounds, whether work-related or leisure-related, can permanently damage your hearing. The public health service in your community might have information about local agencies that offer free hearing tests.

The most important factor in effective listening is being mentally prepared. Mental preparation involves a receptive frame of mind and certain communication tools, such as an extensive vocabulary. Good listeners clear their minds of extraneous thoughts—meeting deadlines, making car payments, scheduling a dental appointment, deciding where to eat lunch, making plans for the weekend—so their minds are open to receive the speaker's message.

If your professional goals include progressing through positions of added responsibility and reward, then the general vocabulary you acquired in high school and college may not be adequate for effective listening in the workplace. Almost every field has its own lexicon or specialized vocabulary, and the listener must master this vocabulary to understand the material under discussion. If you work in a computerized office, for example, you will probably need to be familiar with such terms as default drive, local area network, and file server. To master the special vocabulary in your field,

Listening Checklist

- Have you had your hearing tested recently?
- Do you try to filter out distracting sights and sounds when you are listening to someone?
- Do you avoid interrupting speakers before they finish expressing their thoughts?
- Do you avoid doing something else—such as reading—while trying to listen?
- Do you always look at the person who is talking to you?
- When people talk to you, do you try to concentrate on what they are saying?
- Do you listen for people's ideas and feelings as well as for factual information?
- Do you believe that you can learn something from others?
- If something is unclear, do you always ask the speaker to repeat or explain information?
- Do you ever refuse to listen because you do not agree with the speaker's ideas?
- Do you ever stop listening because you do not like a speaker's appearance or mannerisms?
- Do you ever think about what you will say next while another person is talking?
- Do you ever have to ask the speaker to repeat some important information because you cannot remember what was said?
- Do you ever let your mind wander because you believe that what the speaker is saying will not interest you?
- Do you sometimes stop listening because you feel that you need to spend too much time and effort to understand what the speaker is saying?

Exhibit 2.3

Listening Checklist

The listening checklist allows you to evaluate your listening abilities.
Thinking Critically. *Which question did you find most difficult to answer?*
Explain.

ask people in your company to recommend appropriate textbooks. Then, as you read, write down any unfamiliar words and look them up in the dictionary or consult the glossary often found in textbooks written about specialized fields. When you communicate with co-workers and supervisors, follow the same procedure of collecting and learning new and useful words so they become part of your own vocabulary.

Set Listening Priorities

Because you are often bombarded with several messages at once, you must set **listening priorities.** When more than one listening opportunity is available to you, determine which one deserves your focus. For example, while your instructor is discussing procedures in specialized e-mails, the person behind you might be talking about weekend plans, and in the background, you may be aware of an ambulance siren and a honking horn. If your priority is to listen for information on e-mails, you must concentrate on the primary message (the lecture) and try to block out the conversation and noises, which are barriers. Continued practice at blocking out distracting sounds improves mental focusing capabilities and efficiency in work practices.

Make Efficient Use of Available Time

As you read earlier, a listener comprehends words at least twice as fast as most people speak. To some listeners, this seemingly extra time is a problem because they allow their thoughts to wander from the subject. Active listeners, however, use this time to concentrate on the speaker's words so they can better understand what is being said. Specifically, good listeners use their available time to employ the strategies outlined in the Memory Hook below.

Identify Ideas and Relationships. As you begin to grasp the speaker's ideas, look for relationships among them. For example, which idea is most important? Do the other ideas support the main one? What is the speaker leading up to? Can you anticipate what the speaker is going to say next? What cues does the speaker give to show relationships among the ideas?

Imagine listening to the following excerpt from a speech:

> *Two major costs in a vacation to Alaska are airfare and hotel accommodations.* For instance, if your plane ticket is $1,500 per person and your hotel room is $300 per night for two people, an eight-day trip for two will start at $5,400. Of course, there are other costs such as meals, tours, and souvenirs.

Note the first sentence, in *italics*, contains the main idea. The word *major* is a cue to the importance of that first sentence. In the next sentence, the speaker also uses the phrase *for instance* as a cue to indicate that what follows will support the main idea. Experienced speakers use verbal cues such as these to emphasize important ideas.

Speakers also use numerous nonverbal cues, such as pauses and changes in volume or tone of voice. Speakers reinforce certain points by using body language such as gestures, nodding or shaking the head, or counting on their fingers. They also reinforce points by writing them on flip charts or using visual aids such as handouts, transparencies, or computer-generated slide shows. All of these cues help you identify the speaker's ideas and see the interrelationships among them.

Verbal Cues for General Listening
- First
- Second
- Third
- Another consideration
- On the other hand
- The most important thing
- Finally
- In summary

Verbal Cues for Class Lectures
- You'll see this information again.
- This concept is important.
- Remember how to apply this information.

Summarize Main Points. As you listen, summarize the speaker's words by paraphrasing them in your own words. By reducing the speaker's message to its most basic terms, you will be able to understand and remember the message better. The following example shows how you might paraphrase the speaker's points in your own words.

What the Speaker Says
Empathy is the essence of customer-oriented selling. Empathetic salespeople are able to see things from a customer's point of view and to be sensitive to a customer's problems. For example, such a salesperson might say, "I can understand why you feel that way. If I were in your situation, I would feel the same." But the salesperson must be sincere in this. Customers are astute and can tell when salespeople don't mean what they say. When customers sense that you have their best interests at heart, they let down their defenses and begin really listening to you.

Your Summary of the Speaker's Points
Salespeople should see the situation from the customer's point of view and be sympathetic but sincere in their comments.

KEY POINT

Paraphrasing involves putting the speaker's ideas into the simplest, clearest, and most direct words possible without changing the intended meaning.

Assess the Message. As you summarize the speaker's message and see the organization and the relationship structure of the speaker's ideas, you will probably find yourself beginning to agree or disagree with the speaker. When this happens, try to trace your response to the speaker's reasons or arguments. Ask yourself if the arguments and ideas of the speaker really lead to his or her conclusions. Also, determine if the speaker is trying to convince you with reason or to persuade you by pleading, coaxing, or insisting. Make sure you are in favor of the speaker's views for substantive and tangible reasons, not just because they are presented with humor, enthusiasm, or charm.

Formulate Questions. Formulating questions helps you stay focused on what the speaker is saying. You might ask questions of the speaker to clarify a point that is unclear or to determine if you have interpreted the material correctly.

Associate Ideas with Familiar Concepts. As you listen to the speaker's ideas, relate this information to what you already know about the topic or related topics. Doing so allows you to quickly grasp the information presented by the speaker. For example, suppose you are listening to a sales presentation on the functions of several fax machines. As you listen to the speaker, you would want to think about and compare the presented functions with the functions of your present fax machine.

Consider Ways to Use the Information. One of the best ways to personally integrate a speaker's message is to determine how you can best use the information in the message. For example, if you are responsible for handling customer inquiries, you can directly benefit from listening to your supervisor's explanation of a new procedure for dealing with customers.

Take Notes. You are most likely to take notes in meetings or in a lecture or conference setting. As you will learn in Section 2.3, taking notes is an excellent way of recording spoken information for future reference. Notes, however, should be more than just aids to memory. They should also be tools that help the listener concentrate on the speaker's message.

2.2 Self-Assessment

Answer *T* for *True* and *F* or *False* for the following questions.

1. The general vocabulary you developed in high school is adequate for effective listening on the job. _____

2. Listening is the physical function of detecting sound. _____

3. People choose which sounds they will hear. _____

4. Listening is an acquired skill. _____

5. The difference between active and passive listening is the level of the listener's involvement. _____

6. Even good listeners occasionally lose their focus when they should be listening. _____

7. When you paraphrase a speaker's thoughts, you put them in your own words. _____

8. Speakers may use body language to reinforce certain points. _____

9. A speaker can talk twice as fast as a listener can comprehend spoken words. _____

10. Having your hearing checked is one way to physically prepare yourself to listen. _____

Bonus Question

11. How does hearing differ from listening? _____

_____

_____

Assessment   Section 2.2

Review of Key Terms

1. What is the difference between *hearing* and *listening*? What is the difference between *active* listening and *passive* listening? _____

_____

_____

_____

_____

2. How can a good listener avoid *internal noise*? _____

_____

Editing Practice

Using Language! Check the following sentences for any errors in the correct use of words. Write *OK* if the sentence is correct. Rewrite the sentence correctly if it contains errors.

3. The speaker's presentation had an amazing affect on the audience. ____

_____

4. The insurance investigators asked for the corporation of everyone in re-creating the series of events. _____

_____

5. Our personnel handbook contains a section on the discrimination of confidential information. _____

_____

6. The defendant is to be arranged in court next week. _____

_____

Practical Application

Thinking Critically

7. A good listener is able to distinguish between facts and opinions. Identify each of the following statements as a fact or as an opinion.

   - Making sure our water supply remains clean is our state's most important task. _____
   - Six hours of math is a requirement for graduation. _____
   - Wearing a suit to a job interview will give the interviewee more self-confidence. _____

8. As a team, select at least three possible areas of employment. Then, list five specialized vocabulary words from each area that you might hear used on the job. Define all terms and present the specialized vocabulary to the class.

   _____

Discussion Point

Analyzing Details

9. Name one kind of barrier that can affect a listener. How can one overcome this barrier? _____

   _____

   _____

10. How can a person improve his or her listening skills? _____

   _____

   _____

   _____

   _____

Listening in Casual and Business Settings

Listening in Casual Conversations

When you list your best friends, the names at the top of the list are likely those in whom you confide. The primary reason these people are at the top of your list is that they are good listeners. Good listening helps build friendships and also helps forge important professional relationships. The following techniques can help you establish rapport in casual, small-group conversations.

Listen Attentively

The ability to listen attentively is one of the most important skills connected with effective communication. Being attentive and showing interest in what the other person has to say are two attributes of the good listener that lead to more effective communication. For example, if a customer complains to you about something over which you have no control, help soothe the customer by listening attentively. Often, you need to say little because what the customer most wants is for someone to listen.

Listen for Ideas and Feelings

A good listener listens for ideas and feelings as well as for factual information. A good listener also listens to the tone of the speaker's voice to pick up subtleties in meaning. Read the following statement out loud:

"Thanks, Manuel, for your help on the project."

If the sentence were expressed sincerely, it would indicate Manuel helped with the project. However, if the sentence were spoken sarcastically, it would indicate that Manuel had not helped with the project, but was expected to. Try reading the sentence aloud and attempt conveying first sincere appreciation and then sarcasm. Observe the striking contrast in meaning the same words can have when expressed with a different tone or attitude.

Establish Eye Contact

A speaker likes to have the listener's complete attention. One way to communicate your interest in what the speaker is saying is by establishing eye contact. Do not stare at the speaker. Instead, glance away periodically to reflect on the topic or observe your surroundings.

Use Body Language to Show You Are Listening

As a listener, you can employ body language to convey to a speaker or speakers your interest in what they are saying. In **Exhibit 2.4,** the eye contact, facial expression, and other body

SECTION OBJECTIVES

When you have finished Section 2.3, you will be able to:

- Identify techniques for listening in casual and small-group conversations.
- Identify effective listening techniques for conference situations.
- Define videoconferencing and distance learning.
- List tips for efficient note taking.

WHY IT'S IMPORTANT

Most employers will tell you that effective listening is an important skill in their specific work environments. Employees with poor listening skills can be costly. Poor listening can cause mistakes, misunderstandings, lost sales, lost customers, and ultimately lost jobs on the part of employees who simply did not listen!

KEY TERM

- teleconference

KEY POINT

Use body language to convey your interest in what a speaker is saying.

Exhibit 2.4
Listening to Casual Conversation
Thinking Critically. *Do these people appear to be listening to each other?* Explain.

language communicate that both people are eagerly listening and participating in the conversation.

Here are a few nonverbal cues that let people know you are listening to them:

- Stand or sit facing the speaker.

- Give the speaker your undivided attention. In other words, don't continue reading a report or working on your computer during the conversation. Also, don't look at your watch frequently. Doing so signals a preoccupation with other matters and possible conflicting time commitments.

- Use facial expressions to convey you are listening intently to the conversation. Nodding affirmatively encourages a person to continue the conversation.

- Take notes about the conversation if it is appropriate. For example, taking notes when a supervisor gives instructions on a new procedure demonstrates that you realize the importance of the conversation. The notes will later help you perform the procedure correctly.

- Follow the listening customs of different countries. For example, standing too close to someone is considered rude in the United States. Some cultures have strict rules regarding interactions between men and women.

Listening in Traditional and Teleconference Situations

Many people think the last lecture they will hear is in a college classroom. To keep up with the changes occurring in their professions, however, employees at all levels are involved in frequent training or retraining. This updating of professional skills can take place within an organization's walls, at conference centers, over the Internet, or by teleconference.

A **teleconference** is a meeting that uses advanced telephone and sometimes computer technology to bring people from several locations together to participate simultaneously in a conference. For example, the speaker may be in Florida, and the

Digital Data

Videoconferences are beneficial for several reasons. They allow employees to communicate with colleagues, partners, and clients who are at inconvenient distances. Videoconferences save companies time and travel expenses.

listeners can be scattered throughout the United States or other parts of the world. Depending on the parameters of the conference and the technology available at various locations, the conference may be one-way, without interaction between the speaker and the listeners, or two-way, which allows interaction between the speaker and the listeners.

In addition to conferences, employees must attend meetings held by their supervisors. In most cases, the employees are responsible for retaining the information disseminated. The following techniques for effective listening in a conference situation are also helpful in improving listening skills in classroom lecture situations.

Determine Your Listening Objectives and Prepare Accordingly

Know why you are attending the session and what the expected outcomes are. Are you attending the session to learn how to design Web pages for your company? Are you expected to learn enough about Web page construction to teach the process to your co-workers?

Find out the subject matter to be covered and learn something about it before you attend the session. If you know, for example, that you are going to attend a training session on a specific software application, you should read a manual or textbook about the subject before you attend the session. This preparation will give you a frame of reference that prepares you to absorb the information you will hear. Keep in mind that homework does not end with college.

Overlook Personal Characteristics of the Speaker

Don't prejudge a speaker on the basis of distracting personal characteristics such as mannerisms, voice, speech patterns, or appearance. Good listeners do not confuse the speaker's message with the manner of speaking or the speaker's appearance. Also, you will sometimes encounter speakers with unusual voices or accents. In these instances, very active and focused listening is required to adapt to the challenging characteristics of the speaker's voice. In situations like these, maintaining your mental focus on the speaker's message is your main priority.

As a listener, you can manage any adverse feelings you may have for the speaker by putting yourself in the speaker's place. Consider how you might react if you were speaking.

Choose Strategic Seating

Arrive early and, if possible, choose a seat at the front and center of the room. Select a location that limits distracting sights and sounds. Choose a seat away from the windows if you think that the sun glare might be a distraction. If you feel the hallway will be noisy, choose a seat as far away from the door as possible. If you have either visual or hearing impairments, choose a seat that offers the best opportunity to see and hear the speaker. Also, some meeting rooms have inconsistent lighting, and choosing a seat in a well-lit area has clear advantages.

Prepare for Comfort

Physical discomforts are big distractions. If you have a tendency to get chilled while sitting still in an air-conditioned room, take a sweater or suit jacket with you. A room that is too warm makes listening difficult. Considering your wardrobe for settings like these is wise.

Comfort also includes having any equipment you are using in a meeting—PDAs, laptops, or other devices—fully charged and ready to use so they don't become a distraction rather than an aid to your work.

Nothing Personal

Philip's supervisor told him to limit personnel e-mail messages at the office.

(personal is the correct word, not *personnel*)

KEY POINT

One way to determine your listening objectives is to find out what the expected outcomes are.

Exhibit 2.5
Ready to Take Notes
Thinking Critically.
What information
does the listener
portray by sitting
at the front of a
conference room?

oops!

Lapse in Attention

Preoccupied with her mother's illness, Pamela was not paying close attention when her boss gave her instructions to make hotel reservations for a visiting consultant. Pamela wrote down the wrong date, and when the consultant arrived, there were no hotel rooms available.

KEY POINT

To improve retention:

1. **Read your notes within 24 hours.**
2. **Highlight only major points in your notes.**

Ask Questions if Permitted

Most speakers indicate a specific time for questions. Some allow questions during the session. Other speakers prefer to answer questions at the end of the session. Asking questions at very large or formal conferences is often inappropriate or impossible. Jotting your questions with your notes, while waiting for the opportunity to question the speaker, is a valuable use of your time.

Take Notes

As you listen, concentrate on taking notes on key ideas or concepts. You will often discover later that these notes are invaluable, since information that was completely clear in the meeting or conference can become vague or unclear before you actually apply it. Some tips for taking notes appear in this section (see page 51). You may want to add your own tips to the list.

Avoid Substituting Note Taking for Active Listening. Occasionally, listeners will just "try to get it all down on paper," promising themselves they will review their notes later. When this happens, the listener transfers the information directly to paper without thinking about what was said. In other words, the information goes in the ears and out the pencil while nothing is retained in the brain. As a result, little learning takes place since focused thinking is at the core of attentive listening and note taking.

If possible, compare your notes with those of another attendee. The comparison should help fill in gaps for both of you.

Read Your Notes within 24 Hours. Read your notes as soon as possible after taking them. Reading your notes soon after they are taken will enable you to include any necessary explanations or additions while the information is still fresh in your mind. Studies show that a significant amount of memory loss takes place after 24 hours. Read your notes again within the next 48 hours, and again as time permits, until you have mastered the information.

Highlight Major Points. Use a highlighter pen or underscoring to emphasize major points in your notes. Some people have a tendency to color virtually the entire page

Tips on Taking Lecture or Meeting Notes

- Have two pens and a notebook or legal pad for taking notes.
- Write the date and the topic at the top of every page.
- Begin a new page for each meeting or session.
- Write additional notes directly on handouts. Be sure to note the date and topic on the handouts.
- Leave a wide left-hand margin in your notes where you can write additional information later.
- Don't try to take down everything the speaker says. If you do, you will miss some of the main points.
- Listen for cues that something is important. Some examples are: "Here are three tasks you should complete before the interview . . ."; "This concept will be on your exam . . ."; "Let me summarize the points I have made today. . . ."
- Note the content of visual aids such as posters, transparencies, and slide shows.
- Record only the main points and important details. As time permits, go back and fill in details in the left-hand margin.
- Ask questions if permitted.
- Use your own set of symbols to target information that needs special treatment. For example:
  - * Something that needs follow-up.
  - ! Important fact or critical information.
  - ? A point that is unclear.
  - \> Something you want to ask the speaker about when questions are appropriate.
  - ❑ Topic that needs further study or research.

with a highlighter. This practice defeats the purpose of highlighting. Highlight only the major points. Some listeners may use highlighter pens as they take notes; others will highlight after they take notes.

Keying and Printing Notes as a Learning Strategy.   If the material is unusually hard to master, you may choose to key your notes and possibly expand on them while the information is still fresh in your mind. Keying the information helps you learn it, and having a neat printout makes your notes easier to read, study, and share with others.

Your listening skills can be improved. The challenge is yours. To meet that challenge, practice the listening and note-taking tips presented.

2.3 Self-Assessment

Answer *T* for *True* and *F* for *False* for the following questions.

1. Focusing on speakers' individual and idiosyncratic characteristics of speech delivery is essential to understanding their core message. _____

2. Reviewing your notes within 24 hours of taking them is a valuable practice. _____

3. Asking questions of the speaker is a good way to clarify uncertain information. _____

4. In choosing your seat at a lecture or meeting, one is most often as good as another. _____

5. Trying to get it all down on paper is the best method of note taking.

   _____

Assessment   Section 2.3

Review of Key Terms

1. What nonverbal clues from a speaker should listeners notice? Do listeners give speakers nonverbal feedback? Explain your answer. _____

   _____

   _____

   _____

2. How can you be an effective listener during a *teleconference*? _____

   _____

   _____

   _____

Editing Practice

Grammar Alert! Check the following sentences for any errors in the use of superlatives. Write *OK* if the sentence is correct. Underline the error and write the correction in the space provided.

3. This quarter our expenses are high compared to last quarter's. _____

   _____

4. Of the three ideas, Vanna's is the more practical. _____

   _____

5. My essay is more clear than Anna's. _____

   _____

6. Maria's Italian Garden is the better restaurant in New York City. _____

    _____

7. Kris's office is more larger than yours. _____

    _____

Practical Application

Taking Notes

8. Listen to a short speech presented by your instructor and take notes.
    Then, compare your notes with the notes of several other classmates.
    Determine if there are any discrepancies between your notes and those
    taken by your classmates. What are some factors that may account for
    the discrepancies? _____

    _____

9. As a team write a description of a job situation that demonstrates some
    of the listening techniques presented in this chapter.
    Include examples of poor listening skills. Role-play or video-
    tape the case for the class. Classmates should identify good
    and poor listening techniques. _____

    _____

Discussion Point

Making Generalizations

10. Brainstorm a list of various business situations that require good listen-
    ing skills. _____

    _____

    _____

11. Note taking during meetings is important. What techniques can you
    use so that you are not writing down everything the speaker is saying?

    _____

    _____

    _____

SECTION OBJECTIVES

When you have finished Section 2.4, you will be able to:

- Discuss the difference between reading and comprehending a text.
- Explain the purpose of scanning or previewing material before reading it.
- Describe strategies to improve retention.
- Define distance learning.

WHY IT'S IMPORTANT

Skillful reading is essential for success in college and business. Students are tested on what they have read, and employees are often held accountable for actions based on their reading.

KEY TERMS

- comprehension
- retention
- distance learning

Reading Business Documents

Strategies for Comprehending and Retaining Content

We live in the Information Age. The amount of information on any subject in every field is growing at an astounding rate. Thus, the ability to read well will be even more important in the future than it is today. Employees at all levels will have to read to keep up with the changes in their jobs.

Understanding What You Read

Reading is more than the physical act of looking at words on a page or on a computer screen. Have you ever read something only to find when you're finished that you have no idea what you read? The words might as well have been in a foreign language you do not understand. Just as you can hear something but not listen, you can read words but not understand or remember what you read.

Improving Reading Comprehension

The ability to read quickly is important in our productivity-oriented business world. But even more important than reading speed are **comprehension** (understanding) and **retention** (remembering). Many of the suggestions made for increasing reading speed also contribute to greater comprehension. Additional hints are presented in the Memory Hook (see page 55) and explained in the text that follows.

Scan or Preview Material. Before you commit to reading a body of content, scan the material. If you are reading a textbook or a report, look over the table of contents. Also check to see if a glossary is included or if there are any other features that help you understand the textbook. If you are reading a chapter in a textbook or a section in a report, read the main headings and subheadings for an overview of the subject flow. Also look at illustrations and read captions and numbered passages that offer depth to the content. This preliminary overview will help you assess your objectives for reading and will also help you identify important points.

If you are reading a textbook for a course, always read the exercise or assigned work before reading the chapter. Reading this material first helps you to focus on what you need to learn or to identify information on which you need to take notes.

To preview material, follow these steps:

1. Read headings.
2. Read the first paragraph of the chapter, section, or article.
3. Read the first sentence of each of the remaining paragraphs.

Memory Hook

To help you remember the five strategies for improving reading comprehension and retention, use this sentence: Smart readers take on maximizing retention.

S –Scan or preview material.

R –Read.

T –Take notes.

M –Make an outline.

R –Reread and review.

4. Read the last paragraph of the chapter, section, or article.

5. Review any illustrations.

By previewing material, you can anticipate what information will be presented.

After reading the whole piece, read the most important points twice to reinforce your comprehension and retention of the information. With particularly important blocks of information, setting aside time to memorize the material is recommended for efficient retrieval and confident personal use.

Read the Material. As you read, focus your full attention and concentrate on reading. Reading is the receiving of the raw input of written communication. However, reading is not synonymous with absorbing and mentally processing the information contained in the written communication. Comprehending what you read is an active process. Your mind must work to understand the information you are reading. The more complex the written information is, the harder the reader must work.

As an efficient reader, you will target the information you need, then relate it to knowledge you have already acquired. Look for the main ideas, and constantly relate what you already know to the new material being presented.

Your environment and state of mind will enhance or detract from your comprehension. It is extremely difficult to watch an action-packed television show and read technical material at the same time. Constant interruptions can cause you to lose your concentration. After an interruption, it often takes a few minutes to refocus. If you are worried about something or thinking of another project, your concentration, and consequently your comprehension, will suffer. It is important to learn to focus your full attention on material you are reading in order to comprehend and retain the information.

Take Notes. To help you remember what you have read, take notes that include the main ideas. How do you find these main ideas? Usually, writers deal with only one main idea per paragraph, and they often place the main idea in a topic sentence, often the first sentence in the paragraph. In addition to the main idea, you should also note the facts, examples, and supporting points that explain, support, or develop each main idea. Noting page numbers in your notes is helpful for future references back to the book.

When you read for specific information such as a flight number, an automobile part number, or an account number, it is important to make a written note of the information. The written notation becomes an efficient and reliable way to accurately refer to data.

Make a note of unfamiliar words you encounter while reading. Look up the meanings of these words and add useful words to your personal vocabulary. The more words you know, the easier it is to read and comprehend information.

KEY POINT

Scan the table of contents, headings, and other features to get an overview of the material.

oops!

Check and Double-check

The new assistant's first task was to proofread a letter to our client and fix all the errors. She did a great job and finalized the letter by printing it on the company stationery. The assistant was so excited that she did a good job that she sent out the letter without her supervisor's signature.

KEY POINT

Reading involves recognizing written words. Comprehending involves understanding what you have read.

Make an Outline. One way to organize your reading notes is to make an outline. In an outline, list the main ideas on separate lines, with supporting points listed underneath. Number the main ideas, beginning at the left-hand margin, and indent supporting points, as in the following example:

Buying Your First Sports Utility Vehicle

I. Buying a Sports Utility Vehicle

    A. Reasons

    B. Price Range

    C. Models

II. Paying for a Sports Utility Vehicle

    A. Savings

    B. Payments

    C. Loan

When you make an outline, use phrases or short sentences. Your outline should include just enough information to remind you of a concept, without including all the details.

Reread and Review. How often you reread or review material will depend on its difficulty and how you plan to use the information. Often, quick scanning or rereading of your notes will be adequate for review if the first reading was done carefully. However, if the material is technical and filled with new concepts and specific subject matter jargon, including new vocabulary, it may be necessary to read the text a second or third time to fully comprehend the material.

If you follow the suggestions made in this section and apply yourself seriously to a reading improvement program, you will see results. Not only will you be able to understand more of what you read, but you will also retain more information from what you read.

Effective Note Taking While Reading

The process of writing information increases your ability to comprehend and remember it. The purpose of taking notes while you read is to highlight the most important points in the material. The reading can be from articles, textbooks, the computer screen, or a host of other sources.

Take Useful Notes

The following suggestions and tips will help you take better notes.

Find the Important Points

How do you find the most important points? In written material, important points are often indicated through formatting techniques. Text material is usually broken down into sections by headings, and important words or phrases are in **bold** or *italic* type. Sometimes key points are formatted in a special way, such as in a box or with shading around or behind the text or by placing key points in the margins as this book does. Another method of emphasizing important points is to number them or put them in a bulleted list.

Marginal Notes and Underlining Techniques on Other Documents. Sometimes you need to add notes to the source such as a handout, textbook, a periodical, or computer documentation. If you have your own copy or a photocopy of the material, you could:

- Underline or highlight the important points.
- Make notes in the margins.

Important Date

The memo stated: "The files will be destroyed on July 25." July 15 is the date that should have been indicated. The person who requests the files on July 20 may find they have already been destroyed.

KEY POINT

Important points in written material are often indicated by formatting techniques such as headings and **bold** or *italic* type.

Tips for Taking Reading Notes

Notes are a condensed version of the important points in an article or chapter. Follow these tips when taking notes:

- Use lined paper or note cards and list each new idea on a new line.
- Use phrases, not complete sentences, to save time.
- Use abbreviations when possible.
- Never take verbatim notes, unless you need a direct quote, even if you know shorthand.
- Use pen rather than pencil. A pencil point gets dull and pencil lead can smear.
- Use underlining and asterisks to indicate important points.
- Number items, put information in bulleted lists, or use an outline to make it easier to review notes.
- Leave space in the margins for additional notes.
- Write on only one side of the paper or note card.
- Watch for clues: repetition of words or topics, anything written on the board, handouts with key phrases or terms.
- Try to get to know someone in your class, just in case you need notes, or want to study with someone.
- Use a second note page for listing questions and their answers. Write potential test questions at the bottom of the page.
- Begin each day's notes with a heading that includes the name or number of the course, the instructor's name, and the date and topic of the day.

Digital Data

Convenience of Distance Learning

Technology is making learning more convenient. **Distance learning** is an increasingly popular vehicle for delivering education or work-related training. Distance learning involves students at varying locations, such as at home or at work, taking courses offered by a college or other educational or training institution. In a distance learning course, you may be taking notes from a live lecture originating from another part of the state, country, or world, via your computer screen.

2.4 Self-Assessment

Answer *T* for *True* and *F* for *False* for the following questions.

1. Since the information is already in print, taking notes for reading is generally considered unnecessary. _____

2. The best reading strategy involves starting with the material from page 1 and reading until the task is complete. _____

3. While writing notes on your own textbooks, handouts, and other personal documents is recommended to enable enhanced retention and comprehension, it is wrong to write on printed source material that you do not own. _____

Employability Skills

Reading

When working with important business documents, reading skills are essential in understanding, processing, and interpreting written information.

4. Important points are often highlighted in numerous ways in printed information. _____

5. Abbreviations, symbols, and phrases save time in note taking. _____

Bonus Questions

1. Why should you read your class notes within 24 hours? _____
    _____
    _____

2. How can note taking be substituted for active learning? _____
    _____
    _____

3. What is the difference between reading and comprehending a text?
    _____
    _____
    _____

4. What are the most effective listening techniques for conference situations? _____
    _____
    _____
    _____

Assessment   Section 2.4

Review of Key Terms

1. What five strategies can readers use to improve their *comprehension* and *retention*? _____
    _____

2. How can improved reading skills assist in *distance learning*? _____
    _____
    _____

Editing Practice

Proofreading Alert! Copying amounts of money, numbers, dates, and other figures often results in errors because of reading mistakes. Proofread the copied list (B) to determine if any items have been copied incorrectly.

	List A	List B
3.	789836B	789863B
4.	43287v698	43287V698
5.	$2786.54	2786.54
6.	S768R3456J789	S768R3546J789

Practical Application

Analyzing Material

7. Read the following paragraph. Identify the main idea and two supporting points you would write if you were taking notes.

   There are three important traits every employee should possess in order to be valuable to an employer. Customers and clients expect prompt service, so being dependable is extremely important. Because technology changes things so rapidly today, employees must have the ability to learn quickly and adjust to changes. Finally, an employee must be able to be a team player and cooperate with fellow employees.

   _____

   _____

   _____

8. Have everyone on your team read the same magazine article. Write a brief summary of what your team has read and create questions about the text that could be asked if you were tested about the material. Write a brief answer to each question, remembering to explain new concepts. _____

   _____

   _____

Discussion Point

Thinking Critically

9. What are the benefits of scanning or previewing material before reading it? _____

   _____

10. If you were going to take notes while reading an unfamiliar topic, how would you approach the task? _____

    _____

    _____

    _____

    _____

    _____

Chapter 3

Communicating Globally

Workplace Connection

Because we live in a multicultural society, each of us must understand all aspects of communicating globally. To be successful communicators, we must respect all ethnic groups and cultures.

CHAPTER OBJECTIVES

When you have completed this chapter, you should be able to:

- Describe differences and similarities between domestic and international communication.
- Explain the importance of ethics and professional courtesy in business communication.
- Give examples of nondiscriminatory language.

Domestic and International Communication

Essential Principles

Through advances in technology and telecommunications, our world expands each day. People can travel to almost any part of the world in a matter of hours. Soon, instant, realistic virtual travel will be possible without leaving our desk chairs. Our messages can travel to most parts of the world in a matter of minutes, seconds—even nanoseconds! As we communicate on an increasingly global basis, it is crucial that we understand the people we communicate with and their culture. **Culture** refers to the customs, beliefs, lifestyles, and practices of a group of people.

Cross-cultural communication means communicating—either in writing, verbally, or nonverbally—with people who are from a culture different from your own. To communicate effectively, you must understand and respect cultural differences and be adaptable. Many of the same principles of cross-cultural communication need to be observed in both domestic and international communication. **Domestic** refers to one's own country, or originating within and pertaining to one particular country. **International** goes beyond one's national boundaries or viewpoints, involving two or more countries. An example of an international company would be a delivery company such as DHL or a food franchise such as McDonald's that has branches, business dealings, or employees in more than one country.

Domestic Communication

Different cultural and religious groups in the United States sometimes speak their own languages and observe traditional customs and religious practices. Examples of such groups include:

- Amish settlements in the Midwest and Pennsylvania.
- Chinese quarters, or Chinatowns, in New York City, San Francisco, and other large cities.
- Hasidic Jewish neighborhoods in New York City and other large cities.
- Hispanic neighborhoods in Miami and in cities in southern California and southern Texas.
- Native American communities in the Southwest and the Northwest.
- Polish neighborhoods in Chicago.
- Vietnamese communities in Minnesota, Wisconsin, and Texas.
- West Indian communities in New York City.

SECTION OBJECTIVES
When you have finished Section 3.1, you will be able to:

- Define the word *culture*.
- Give examples of some ethnic groups in the United States.
- Explain what a multinational company is.
- Provide several examples of cultural differences between the United States and other countries.
- Describe the differences and similarities between domestic and international communication.

WHY IT'S IMPORTANT
Communicating with someone from another culture in your career is becoming more common. In order to be effective, you should understand the essentials of cross-cultural communication.

KEY TERMS
- culture
- cross-cultural communication
- domestic
- international
- multinational company
- abbreviation
- acronym
- exchange rate

When working with people from different cultural, religious, and ethnic groups, keep in mind these guidelines:

- Research the customs of the communities in which you do business.
- Keep track of significant religious holidays that affect a company's employees and clients.
- Do not make comments or jokes based on cultural or religious practices.
- Do not imitate cultural language expressions or accents in an attempt to be friendly.

We need to be aware of, and respect, cultural preferences and beliefs that are different from our own. In a contemporary example, a Japanese company built a small facility in the United States and hired an American management trainee. The trainee was to research different communication systems that could be used at the facility. After analyzing several different systems, the trainee wrote a comparison report in which he recommended the system to adopt, and then he ordered the system. The Japanese managers were upset with the trainee for ordering the system without first consulting them. In the Japanese business culture, a team of participants makes almost all decisions.

Being unaware of significant religious holidays can also create problems. To illustrate, if a business conference were scheduled at the same time as the Jewish High Holy Days of Rosh Hashanah or Yom Kippur, Jewish members would be forced to choose between sacrificing either a solemn religious observance or an opportunity for professional development.

It is also critical that you know the business protocol in a country where you and your company do business. A lack of such knowledge could easily result in behaving in an impolite or disrespectful fashion. The Japanese, for example, place a high value on another's business card, which is treated with care. Cards are to be presented face up and accepted with both hands. Ideally, the information will be in English on one side of the card and in Japanese on the other. It is considered very disrespectful to write on a person's business card.

Regional Differences

People in different geographic regions of the country use different words to express the same ideas. A carbonated drink, for instance, may be called pop, soda, soda pop, or a soft drink, depending on the region of the country and who the speaker is. The same is true of coffee, which may be called java, a caffeine fix, a cup of joe, latte, or mud.

Holidays

Most Americans celebrate the same federal holidays, but people in many groups and religions celebrate additional holidays. The federal holiday celebrations may even be observed on different days, depending on the state you live in. For example, most states observe President's Day on the third Monday in February, but some places observe Lincoln's birthday on February 12 or Washington's birthday on February 22 instead.

U.S. Time Zones

KEY POINT

Differences in time zones across the United States affect working hours for businesses.

From Honolulu, Hawaii, in the west to Bangor, Maine, in the east, the United States spans seven time zones. This time difference must be taken into consideration with some forms of domestic communication. When it is 9 a.m. in Maine, it is 6 a.m. in California, and 4 a.m. in Hawaii. Most of the states move forward 1 hour from standard time to daylight savings time in the spring and back 1 hour in the fall. Arizona, Hawaii, Puerto Rico, the Virgin Islands, and American Samoa do not observe daylight savings time.

Being aware of these cultural, regional, holiday, and time zone differences when conducting business will enable you to do a better job of communicating. Some of these same considerations regarding domestic communication also apply to international communication.

International Communication

Many U.S. companies have operations and offices throughout the world. Likewise, many foreign companies have branch offices and/or manufacturing plants in the United States. Multinational companies are commonplace. A **multinational company** is a company that does business in or has operations in more than one country. To illustrate, Coca-Cola, although based in the United States, derives less than 30 percent of its income from its home country. Nestlé, on the other hand, is based in Switzerland, but it has factories in 80 countries, including the United States.

Other examples of multinational companies include Disney, FedEx, IBM, McDonald's, and Nike. If you are an employee of a multinational company and you are based in the United States, you need to be aware of cultural and other differences when communicating with your company's offices in other countries.

Language

Although English is recognized worldwide as the language of business, it is a *second* language for people in most other countries. Slang, clichés, and jargon make English one of the most complex languages in the world. When communicating with people in other countries, follow these guidelines:

- Limit figures of speech and clichés. Instead of writing *bare minimum,* use *minimum.* Instead of *quick as a wink,* use *quick.*

- Avoid using cute, fancy, or trendy terms for standard English words. Instead of writing *legal eagle,* use *lawyer.* Instead of *policy wonk,* use *policy expert.*

- Use specific terms. Instead of writing *just a little way down the road,* use *15 miles* or *24 kilometers.* Instead of *unsanitary conditions,* use *unsafe drinking water.*

- Be aware of the multiple definitions of words. Some words carry more than one meaning and may be confusing to someone whose first language isn't English. For example, the word *bug* may refer to an insect, the flu, or a computer software virus. The word *break* in the sentence *There was a break in the negotiations* can refer to an opening or opportunity for agreement or a halt in the talks. Make sure the context makes the meaning clear. This problem is especially troublesome in speech because words that are spelled differently may be pronounced similarly: think of *sum* and *some* or *bough* and *bow.*

- Avoid any form of slang or jargon. American slang, such as *bad* meaning *good, cool* meaning *in style,* and *wicked* meaning *good, great,* or *in style,* would be confusing to a person whose first language isn't English.

- Avoid using abbreviations or acronyms. An **abbreviation** is a shortened form of a word or phrase. *Atty.* is an abbreviation for the word attorney; *St.* is an abbreviation for either saint or street. An **acronym** is a word usually formed from the first letter or letters of each word in the phrase. Examples include, among many others, *PIN* for *personal identification number* or *CPU* for *central processing unit.* Because acronyms can stand for more than a single term—does *IRA* mean *Irish Republican Army* or *individual retirement account?*—it is best to avoid them.

- Use visual aids. Wherever possible use visual aids to clarify your message. A map, a sketch, or a picture usually enhances verbal or written communication.

If your message must be translated, be aware that many English words do not have exact translations. Many companies have learned the hard way that some translations cause problems. In his book *The Tongue-Tied American* (New York: Continuum Publishing Corporation, 1980, pp. 6, 7, 32), Paul Simon gives these examples of problem translations.

- Chevrolet would have a hard time selling its Nova model in Latin American countries. In Spanish, the phrase *nova* literally means, "It does not go."
- General Motors' slogan "Body by Fisher" translates to "Corpse by Fisher" in Flemish.
- The slogan "Come alive with Pepsi" translates to "Pepsi brings your ancestors back from the grave" in Chinese and translates to "Come alive out of the grave" in German.
- Parker pen put on a sales campaign in South America. A less-than-accurate Spanish translation promised buyers that the new ink in the pen would prevent unwanted pregnancies.
- Schweppes Tonic Water advertisements in Italy translated as "bathroom water."
- Cue toothpaste, a Colgate-Palmolive product, was advertised in France with no translation errors, but *Cue* happens to be the name of a widely circulated pornographic book.

Yet another example, which was referenced in a *Washington Post* article in August 1999, notes that Nike, Inc., had to stop selling a new line of basketball shoes in Arabic countries because they unknowingly used a logo on the shoe that closely resembled the Arabic word for *Allah*, or *God*. Obviously, Muslims could and did find this offensive.

Because of these kinds of translation problems, companies sometimes change product names or slogans before marketing products in other countries. For example, Diet Coke is known as "Coke Light" in many parts of the world.

Cultures

Many international cultures have a high regard for formality and social rules. In the United States, most people are very time conscious and view being punctual as important. In many other cultures, however, it is *not* considered rude to be quite late for an appointment or to keep a person waiting for a long time. In fact, in some cultures arriving either early or on time is considered rude.

Customs in various countries regarding clothing styles, greetings, and eye contact are also different. Some examples include the following:

- *Clothing styles.* Women in some cultures do not appear in public with their faces uncovered, while other cultures accept skimpy or topless swimwear in public.
- *Greeting others.* In some cultures, men kiss each other on the cheek or bow from the waist when they meet rather than shake hands as men and women do in the United States.
- *Eye contact.* In some cultures, it is considered extremely rude to have direct eye contact with people with whom you are talking. By contrast, in the United States, direct eye contact is expected. Lack of eye contact is interpreted as disinterestedness, unfriendliness, or perhaps even dishonesty.

It is important to learn about other cultures and countries so you are aware of cultural differences and can be patient and flexible in communicating with others. Just as

Exhibit 3.1
Greeting Customs
Although the American custom of hand-shaking has been adopted by many cultures, it is polite to follow the greeting customs of a particular culture. Why is showing respect for other cultures important?

many different cultures exist in the United States, other countries are also multicultural and include different ethnic groups. For example, in Belgium the population is divided into two major cultural groups—the Flemings and the Walloons. The Flemings live in northern Belgium and speak dialects of Dutch, while the Walloons live in southern Belgium and speak dialects of French. The differences in language and other aspects of their culture have caused some friction between the two groups, even though the country is small and operates under one government. Good business communication can be hindered unintentionally by lack of knowledge about other countries and cultures.

There is an old saying "When in Rome, do as the Romans do," which is very appropriate to international communication. When you travel to another country, you have a responsibility to learn about the local customs and business practices to avoid offending anyone and to promote positive communication and business practices. Consult books on customs and business practices in other cultures to increase your cultural awareness. When a person from another country or another culture communicates with you, you should recognize the cultural differences and not let those differences interfere with your communication.

Gestures

We need to be aware that gestures also mean different things in different countries. Gestures that are common in the United States can cause international incidents when used in other countries. Take the example mentioned in Roger Axtell's *Gestures—the Do's and Taboos of Body Language Around the World* (New York: Wiley, 1999) of President George H. Bush's state visit to Australia in 1993. The President flashed the "V" for victory sign to crowds of Australians from his limousine. Unfortunately, he turned the back of his hand toward the people when he made the sign. The next day, newspaper headlines read, "President Insults Australians." President Bush was unaware that in Australia, as in England, the reverse "V" is an obscene gesture.

Going Global

Effective Global Communication

Many factors make communication challenging in a global environment. For example, language differences, customs, religious beliefs, and cultural beliefs make it difficult to communicate effectively.

KEY POINT

Regard for formality and social rules varies from culture to culture. Be sure to have an understanding of social customs before traveling abroad.

Some other common examples that Axtell mentioned include:

- Our circular-shaped OK symbol is formed by the index finger and thumb. In Japan, this is a signal for money, whereas in some other countries it is considered an obscene gesture.
- The American thumbs-up gesture in Japan signifies the number 5.
- Crossing your legs with one ankle over the other knee so that the sole of your shoe faces other people in the room is considered an insult in Egypt.

There is, however, a universal gesture that is understood everywhere in the world and is seldom, if ever, misunderstood—the smile.

Holidays

Other countries celebrate different holidays from those celebrated in the United States, and businesses are closed on different days. For example, Independence Day (the Fourth of July) and Thanksgiving are observed only in America; these two holidays are normal working days in other countries. Likewise, other countries have their own national holidays. Even though the United States celebrates St. Patrick's Day informally, in Ireland it is a legal holiday. May Day on May 1 is a legal holiday in Great Britain and Russia. A holiday similar to our Independence Day is celebrated on different dates in these other countries:

- Greece (Independence Day)   March 25
- Italy (Liberation Day)   April 25
- Japan (Constitution Day)   May 3
- India (Independence Day)   August 15
- France (Bastille Day)   July 14
- Mexico (Independence Day)   September 16

The Christmas holiday is also celebrated in different ways and on different dates elsewhere. In the Netherlands, Belgium, and Luxembourg, St. Nicholas gives children presents on the eve of December 6. Children leave a snack, such as carrots, in their wooden shoes for St. Nicholas's white horse. December 25 in these nations is strictly a religious holiday.

In recent years, many African Americans have begun celebrating the cultural holiday Kwanzaa. It begins on December 26 and lasts for seven days. Each day is dedicated to celebrating a different principle of African culture.

The Islamic holy month of fasting, called Ramadan, is celebrated during the ninth month of the Islamic year—which corresponds to the ninth month of their calendar—by Muslims the world over. During each day of this month, Muslims may not eat or drink from dawn to sunset. (The Islamic calendar is a lunar calendar which contains 354⅓ days a year. The Christian calendar contains 365¼ days a year.)

International Time Zones

The difference in time zones, as illustrated in **Exhibit 3.2,** must likewise be considered in some forms of international business communication. When it is 9 a.m. in Chicago, it is 5 p.m. in Finland. If you are working in Chicago and wish to call a business in Finland, you will need to call before 9 a.m. in Chicago.

Measurements and Currency

Most of the world uses the metric system (a decimal system based on meters, kilograms, liters, kilometers, and so on) for measurement. Only the United States,

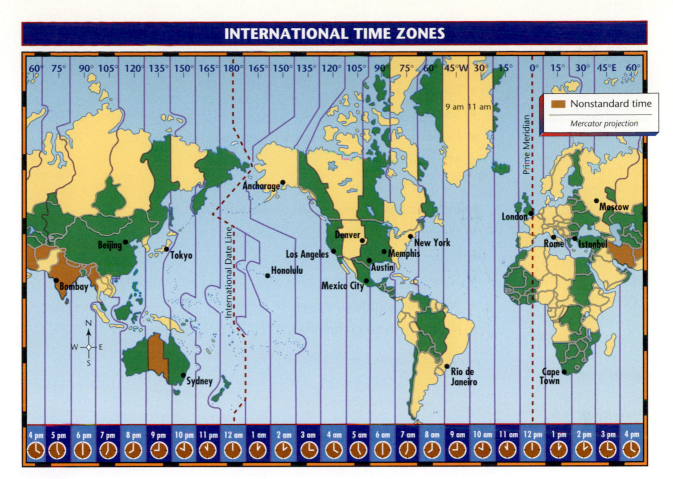

Exhibit 3.2
World Time Zones
Map of International Time Zones. The earth's surface is divided into 34 time zones. *Thinking Critically. How might a lack of knowledge about time zones hinder international communications?*

Liberia, and Burma use the Imperial System, sometimes called the English or British System, whose customary units of measurement include feet, pounds, gallons, and miles, among others. When communicating with a person who uses the metric system, don't assume that person is familiar with the English system of measurement and can thus convert your figures correctly into the metric system.

In addition, practically all nations have their own unique currencies. Japan has the yen, Israel the shekel, Mexico the peso, and South Africa the rand. Twelve European countries now use a common currency called the Euro. Australia, Canada, Hong Kong, Singapore, Taiwan, and the United States all use currencies called the dollar, but each one has a different value. The **exchange rate** is the ratio at which the principal unit of two currencies can be traded, and it fluctuates daily. For example, on any given day, a U.S. dollar may be the equivalent of $1.80 in Australian dollars, $1.50 in Canadian dollars, $7.80 in Hong Kong dollars, or $33.20 in Taiwanese dollars.

OOPS!

Tips for Effective International Communication

- Recognize your own biases.
- Show respect for differences.
- Look for common ground between cultures.
- Maintain formality.
- Tolerate the cultural mistakes of others.
- Be patient with nonnative speakers of English.
- Listen with a nonjudgmental attitude.
- Listen for what is NOT said.
- Have an understanding of cross-cultural body language.
- Avoid interrupting.
- Remember that communication is a collaborative effort.

Memory Hook

In order to be an effective communicator in the business world, it is crucial that you understand the people you communicate with and the culture in which they live.

Assessment   Section 3.1

Review of Key Terms

1. Why is cultural knowledge important in the business world? _____ _____ _____

2. Define the term *multinational company.* _____ _____

Editing Practice

Spelling Alert! Proper proofreading involves checking the spelling, grammar, and punctuation within the sentence. Proofread the following paragraph. Make a list of all the errors. Then, rewrite or type the paragraph.

3. Inter-culturel expereinces are important to help us understand people form all parts of the world. We tend to assume that every one has the same beleifs, customs, and practises we do. It is important to be aware of these diferences so that we can become more tolerant and understanding of people from other contries. _____

_____

_____

_____

_____

_____

Practical Application

Analyzing Information

4. On July 14, Maria Hong discovers she needs to telephone the Paris office to explain that the merchandise her company ordered will be two weeks late. She knows that the receptionist speaks English. Maria has never made an overseas phone call. What does she need to know before she places the call? _____

_____

_____

_____

5. As a team choose a country that you would like to research. Assume you are writing a memo for employees who will be traveling there for business. Write a brief summary of the country that describes its customs in business clothing and social etiquette, its national holidays, its time zone, its currency, and any other important information employees should know.

_____

_____

Discussion Point

Thinking Critically

6. How does jargon or slang interfere with cross-cultural communication?

_____

_____

7. If a businessperson were traveling to a foreign country to do business, how would he or she promote a positive business relationship? _____

_____

_____

_____

Ethics and Professional Courtesy in Business Communication

Essential Principles

The issue of ethics doesn't surface unless there are choices to be made. For example, if you find a billfold without identification on the floor in a store, you have several choices. You could: (1) walk away and leave the billfold on the floor; (2) turn in the billfold to the customer service desk; (3) stick the billfold in your pocket and leave the store with it; (4) remove any money that was in the billfold and leave it on the floor; or (5) remove any money that was in the billfold, then turn it in to the customer service desk. The *ethical* person will choose option 1 or 2; the *unethical* person will choose from among the last three options.

Ethics

We often hear about business practices being legal and being ethical. What is the difference? Laws determine whether or not something is legal. **Ethics** are the moral principles of right and wrong by which a person is guided. The goal of every business communicator should be to conduct all business in a legal and an ethical manner. It is possible for an activity to be legal but unethical. For instance, suppose you purchase a computer from a store with a 30-day return policy with the intention of using it solely to key in your term paper and then you return the computer for a full refund. Your behavior would be legal but unethical.

Treating Others with Honesty and Fairness

One way of incorporating ethics into business communication is to be honest and fair and to treat others as you would like to be treated. A new sales associate, with no previous retail experience, was advised by her hardware manager that a certain brand of mediocre-quality tools paid a higher commission rate than the top-quality tools. A **commission** is a fee paid to the sales associate as a result of the sale. The manager suggested making the following response to prospective customers who asked about the quality of the mediocre brand: "It's a very popular item." This statement implies that the tools are of a good quality. While it is not a lie, the statement is misleading—and unethical.

Stating Facts Instead of Opinions

Business communication should be ethical and should communicate information that is true. Another way of incorporating ethics into business communication is to use objective language and verifiable information. For example, suppose you are asked for a recommendation about a former employee's dependability. Instead of saying "Felicia will not be dependable," say "Our attendance records show that Felicia missed work 11 times in the last three months." Stating a verifiable fact instead of your opinion lets the receiver form his or her own opinion of Felicia. Many human resource departments have strict guidelines in place that specify how to respond to these queries.

Another example of providing honest, verifiable information occurs when a company requests a background check on a prospective employee from an employment background checking agency. If the reporting agency faxes the company a copy of an official court record, the court record gives verifiable fact rather than opinion.

KEY POINT

Ethics are the moral principles of right and wrong by which a person is guided.

Ethical Communication

Ethical business communication should not withhold information that could cause the communication to be misinterpreted. For example, the U.S. tobacco industry allegedly withheld or misrepresented facts about the dangers of tobacco in reports to the public. Withholding information about the dangers of tobacco and thus misleading the public is an example of unethical communication.

Another example of unethical communication is the recent case of a tire manufacturer's failure to inform consumers about defects in certain sizes of tires that caused tread separation. These defects resulted in life-threatening, and sometimes fatal, accidents. Testing agencies that distort or skew the results of their vehicle safety tests are also unethical when they represent their skewed findings as fact.

A subtler example of unethical communication occurred in the following situation. An environmental group released data indicating the city water was unsafe to drink at the same time that the water company released data indicating the city water was safe to drink. The water company tested samples of water leaving its plant. The environmental group tested water at points along feeder waterways, just downstream from a golf course that uses fertilizer and other chemicals to enhance the appearance of the grass on the fairways and greens. Both groups were accurately reporting the results of their tests. However, drinking water should be tested *after* it has been processed, treated, and released by the water company to homes and businesses. Clearly, since the two groups were using different sources for their data, the test results were different. Which group released ethical communication?

Exhibit 3.3
Ethics
When you are faced with an ethical dilemma, it may help to discuss the matter with a person who you believe is ethical. *Thinking Critically. How might you ask someone for such advice?*

Here are some other examples of the types of unethical situations you might encounter on the job:

- Your supervisor asks you to "adjust" some figures in a report to make the results look better.
- You work in the lab of a company that makes no-fat cookies, but you know they contain some fat.
- Your city promotes recycling to appeal to environmentalists, but you know that the "recycled" materials really go to the landfill with the rest of the garbage.

International Ethics—Bribery

Bribery is the act or practice of giving or receiving money or other valuable items to influence a person's behavior or action.

Bribery is a practice that many U.S. companies encounter in international business dealings. Although bribery is against U.S. law—for transactions both inside and outside the United States—it is, nevertheless, accepted and even common in many other countries, which puts U.S. companies at a disadvantage when doing business in those countries. Bribery is less common in Scandinavian and European countries and more common in some South American and Far Eastern countries.

The problem of overt bribery is decreasing as more and more countries adopt the U.S. attitude about it. Subtle and indirect forms still exist, however, such as exchanging gifts, paying for elaborate parties, and agreeing to humanitarian efforts that are not connected with the actual business being done. One example of a subtle bribe was a computer company's agreeing to provide food and housing for poor people in a particular country in order to do business there.

Maintaining Confidentiality

Confidential information is spoken or written information that is private or secret and should be released only to people with a proven need to know. Confidentiality is another important aspect of ethics. Right-to-privacy laws have been passed to legislate confidentiality in certain instances. For example, medical records, attorneys' client files, certain education and court records, and banking and financial records are considered confidential information. Businesses and industries that develop new products and technologies, such as the electronics and pharmaceutical industries, have confidential information that should not fall into the hands of competitors. You may be asked to sign a **nondisclosure agreement** when beginning a new job with such a firm. By signing this statement, you are agreeing, as an employee, not to tell any of the company's trade secrets or procedures, for example, nor will you use customer lists to promote your own business outside the office.

Confidentiality is becoming an increasing problem with the rapidly increased use of the Internet. It's possible for companies to determine from your visits to various Web sites what your interests are, as well as personal information about you. They then compile this information into lists that they sell to other organizations. This practice isn't illegal as of the writing of this book, but is it ethical? At the present time there is considerable controversy among political and legal experts about how much, if any, control should be placed on the obtaining of information about a person from the Internet without her or his permission.

Government and legal authorities are in a quandary over how to deal with this problem. On one hand, we need to consider the violation of individual confidentiality. On the other hand, we must follow the Freedom of Information Act. The bottom line, however, remains consistent: It is unethical to release confidential information to anyone who is not authorized to have access to it.

society for technical communication

901 N. Stuart Street, Suite 904 • Arlington, VA 22203-1822
703-522-4114 • FAX 703-522-2075 • stc@stc-va.org • www.stc-va.org

William C. Stolgitis
Executive Director and Counsel

Exhibit 3.4
A Code of Ethics
This illustration shows one organization's code of ethics. ***Thinking Critically.*** *What are the advantages to a group or company of publishing a code of ethics?*

Code of Ethics

Being ethical means being honest, fair, and objective in all forms of communication. The true test of being ethical is to work toward the good of all rather than toward the good of a specialized group at the expense of some other group.

Some organizations and companies develop a written code of ethics so employees and customers or clients have a written record of the philosophy of the group. **Exhibit 3.4** illustrates one such example of a code of ethics. A **code of ethics** states the goals of the organization in terms of how it operates and how it treats customers and competitors. Some companies have all their employees sign a statement of business ethics.

Professional Courtesy

Professional courtesy, also known as business etiquette, is simply using good manners and appropriate behavior in business transactions and written and verbal communication.

Going Global

Communication Today

The advance of technology has helped business-people around the world communicate information more quickly than ever before. Cellular phones, facsimiles, and e-mails have taken over the traditional ways of sending mail and handling business.

KEY POINT

Common courtesy calls for promptly introducing people who don't seem to know each other.

Making Introductions

One example of professional courtesy is *making introductions* when people do not know each other. In introducing people, the person you show greatest respect to is mentioned first. For example, "Bridget Allen (your supervisor), I'd like you to meet Richard Trower (new employee). Richard is the new designer in the Web Development and Administration Department."

Promptly introduce people to each other who have not met rather than leave them to introduce themselves to one another. In the United States, after you have been introduced to someone, you should make eye contact, smile, and acknowledge the introduction with such statements as "I'm happy to meet you, Richard" or "I'm pleased to meet you, Richard." As we noted earlier, in Japan this direct eye contact would be considered rude. In the United States, a firm handshake initiated by either person, regardless of gender, is also appropriate. In other cultures, there are different methods of responding to an introduction. Once again, in Japan a bow from the waist is the accepted method for responding to an introduction. The lower the bow, the more respect you show for the individual.

Acknowledging Invitations and Thoughtful Actions

Another form of business etiquette involves acknowledging invitations for various events. If the invitation includes an **RSVP** notation, which is an abbreviation of a French phrase meaning "Please reply," a reply by phone or in writing is required. A written invitation usually requires a written response unless a phone number is given. The host needs your reply in order to plan enough food; seats; handouts; and individualized materials, such as name tags, table tents, and so on, for the event. It is simply professional courtesy to let the sender know whether or not you will be attending. Occasionally, the notation *RSVP Regrets Only* appears on an invitation. That means the host is expecting you to attend unless you indicate otherwise.

Special favors, such as recommending you for a job, and thoughtful actions, such as sending flowers or a gift, should be acknowledged in writing with a thank-you note. E-mail could be used in many cases; however, a short typed or handwritten note sent by traditional mail is more personal than e-mail. Letitia Baldrige, business protocol expert and former social secretary to First Lady Jacqueline Kennedy, says, "It's perfectly acceptable to send thank-you notes by e-mail, especially for lunch or a meeting." For more formal occasions, such as a museum dinner or a client wedding, Baldrige recommends the old-fashioned handwritten thank-you note.

Assessment   Section 3.2

Review of Key Terms

1. How are *ethics* incorporated into business communication? _____
   _____
   _____
   _____

2. How does one communicate *professional courtesy*? _____
   _____
   _____

Editing Practice

Grammar Alert! Write or type each of the following sentences, correcting the grammar errors. A sentence may have more than one grammar error.

3. Mr. Weber feel that punctuality and good manners is the most valuable skills an employee can possess. _____

_____

4. The accounting procedure, as well as other aspects of daily operations, are under administrative review. _____

_____

5. Mrs. Soong often teaching in addition to making real estate appraisals.

_____

6. Although the president provide positive criticism, most of his comments sounds reasonable. _____

_____

7. The hotel manager and me made a extra effort to accommodate the hurricane victims. _____

_____

Practical Application

Evaluating Concepts

8. Steve Sandusky works as a graphic designer for a company that has a "no moonlighting" policy. *Moonlighting* means "holding a second job in addition to a regular job."

    Steve needs $2,000 to pay for car repairs. Steve's brother knows of a design firm that needs a temporary graphic designer to work three hours a night for six weeks. This job would more than pay for Steve's car repair.

 Make a list of the pros and cons of Steve's taking the freelance work. What are the pros and cons of his turning down the work? Which decision should Steve make and why? _____

_____

Discussion Point

Identifying the Main Idea

9. Explain why many businesses incorporate a written code of ethics.

_____

_____

10. How has the Internet created problems in regard to confidentiality?

_____

_____

_____

_____

SECTION OBJECTIVES

When you have finished Section 3.3, you will be able to:

- Define the terms *discrimination* and *discriminatory language*.
- Describe gender-specific words and give some examples.
- Change gender-specific words to generic, neutral words.
- Change discriminatory language to neutral language.

WHY IT'S IMPORTANT

Discrimination is the act of treating or judging someone on the basis of things like age, category, class, ethnic group, religion, sex, or skin color rather than on individual merit.

KEY TERMS

- gender-specific words
- gender-bias words
- discriminatory language
- stereotyping
- ethnocentrism
- prejudice

Nondiscriminatory Language

Avoiding Discrimination in Communication

Use gender-neutral words and nondiscriminatory words to avoid offending any person or group.

Use Gender-Neutral Words

Gender-specific words indicate whether a subject is male or female. Such **gender-bias words** show favoritism toward or imply a greater importance of one gender over another. Gender-specific words do not accurately reflect today's world and are not appropriate in today's business communication. Instead, use gender-neutral words that do not indicate maleness or femaleness.

Avoid expressions such as "He's the best man for the job," which implies that men are more capable than women. Instead, say, "He's the best person for the job." Similarly, avoid a phrase such as "officers and their wives," which implies that all officers are male. A more neutral statement would be "officers and their spouses" or "officers and their guests."

Gender-Neutral Pronouns

Using gender-neutral pronouns such as *his/her* are acceptable but often awkward when repeated in a document. Another solution is to change the noun that the pronoun refers to into the plural form, or simply to rewrite the text. Be careful not to change the meaning of the original text, however.

Correct: Each employee must wear *his/her* name tag when *he/she* enters a restricted area of the plant.

Better: All employees must wear *their* name tags when *they* enter a restricted area of the plant.

Better: Name tags must be worn by all employees when entering a restricted area of the plant.

Gender-Specific	Gender-Neutral
businesswoman	businessperson, business worker
chairman	chairperson
fireman	firefighter
foreman	supervisor
housewife	homemaker
mailman	mail carrier

Gender-Specific	Gender-Neutral
woman doctor	doctor
newsman	newscaster, reporter
old man/woman	senior citizen
saleswoman	sales associate, salesperson, sales representative
spokesman	spokesperson
stewardess	flight attendant
weatherman	weather analyst, weather reporter
waitress	server

Use Nondiscriminatory Words

In today's world, you must avoid using offending or discriminating language against anyone who may have characteristics, beliefs, values, and attitudes different from your own. This language is called **discriminatory language.**

Use unbiased and nondiscriminatory language when communicating—especially when referring to a person's physical or mental condition, race, religion, age, and so on. Ours is a sensitive world, and you do not want to offend anyone—even unintentionally. Always use bias-free language. Some words have negative connotations or meanings. For example, *handicapped* is more negative than *physically challenged.*

Here are some guidelines for using nondiscriminatory language:

1. Describe people in terms of their skills and abilities, not in terms of their gender, race, cultural background, appearance, religion, age, or physical challenges.

   Not
   - My deaf assistant has great computer skills.
   - A well-informed Asian dentist conducted the 10 a.m. tour.

   Better
   - My assistant has great computer skills.
   - A well-informed dentist conducted the 10 a.m. tour.

2. Don't make assumptions about people based on their gender, race, cultural background, looks, religion, age, or physical challenges.

   Not
   - Eliot was a top salesman at the Harlem branch office because he is black.
   - Elderly clients are grumpy and hard to deal with.

   Better
   - Eliot was a top salesperson in the Harlem branch office.
   - Some clients are grumpy and hard to deal with.

3. Use preferred terms for different groups:
   - *African American, blacks:* Both terms are widely accepted, but *African American* is currently preferred. Be aware of specific groups such as West Indians and Black Muslims.
   - *Asian:* Do not use *oriental* and be as specific as possible: *Japanese, Chinese, Indian.*
   - *English:* Not all the British are English. Some are Welsh, Scottish, or Irish.

oops!

What's in a Name?

Mr. Thompson asked his new assistant to type and send a letter to Terry Israel, director of marketing. The assistant included a courtesy title on the letter and sent it to Mr. Terry Israel. Terry was upset because she did not appreciate being addressed as a man.

oops!

Inflammatory Language

Vicky Stewart, an American executive, was walking down Michigan Avenue in Chicago with a Japanese trade representative on a cold, windy day. She said, "There sure is a nip in the air today." Vicky wasn't aware that Nip is a derogatory slang term for Japanese.

- *Hispanic:* This term is generally acceptable, but because so many individual groups are of Latin American descent, it is best to be specific whenever possible: *Mexican, Puerto Rican, Cuban.*

- *Jewish:* Do not use *Hebrew,* which refers to a language, or *Israelite,* which is a biblical term. Also, not all Israelis are Jews and not all Jews are Israelis.

- *Muslim:* Avoid using *Muhammadan. Moslem,* however, is acceptable. Remember that not all Muslims are Arabs and not all Arabs are Muslim.

- *Native American:* This term is generally acceptable. *American Indian,* but not *Indian,* which is used for natives of India, may also be acceptable. It is best to be as specific as possible: the *Sioux,* the *Iroquois.*

4. Use preferred terms to describe specific conditions: However, use such descriptions only when it is necessary to the meaning of the sentence:

Not	Preferred
• blind	• person with visual impairment
• weird, crazy	• eccentric, offbeat
• stutterer	• person with speech impairment
• handicapped, disabled, crippled	• person with a physical challenge
• retarded	• person with developmental delay
• AIDS victim	• person living with AIDS
• hyper	• person with ADHD disorder
• manic depressive	• person with bipolar disorder
• anorexic, bulimic, compulsive eater	• person with eating disorder
• paraplegic, quadriplegic	• person living with spinal cord injury

Avoiding Stereotyping, Ethnocentrism, and Prejudice

Stereotyping is a simplified and standardized conception or image of a person, group, etc., held in common by members of a group. Stereotypes are often negative and based on false or incomplete information. Stereotyping is often a result of ethnocentrism. **Ethnocentrism** is the belief that one's own ethnic group or culture is superior to all other ethnic groups or cultures. A **prejudice** is a negative attitude about an individual, a group, or a race, or about its supposed characteristics. Prejudices are conclusions that are drawn without sufficient facts.

Your view or interpretation of events and people is based on your personal experiences and on information you have heard or read. If you have had a negative experience during your first contact with someone from a group, you tend to assume all people in this group are the same. For example, if your first experience with a motorcycle rider was a bad one where the person was a gang member, had numerous tattoos, wore black leather, and used excessive profanity, you would probably have a negative opinion of motorcycle riders from that point on. Whereas, if your first experience with motorcyclists was at a fundraiser they sponsored for a child with terminal cancer, and you observed how concerned the bikers were for the child and how hard they worked to raise money, you would probably have a positive opinion of bikers in general.

Discriminatory Actions

You can offend another person through your actions as well as your words. People who are blind are frequently spoken to in a loud voice. Remember, they are visually impaired, not hearing-impaired. Likewise, people who wear a hearing aid frequently find that others still speak to them as though they were hearing-impaired. Remember, the hearing aid usually corrects the hearing impairment. Moreover, if the volume of speaking is much above normal, the voice of the speaker is distorted, and the volume on the hearing aid will need to be adjusted.

People who don't speak English aren't deaf; they just don't understand. Don't shout; speaking louder won't help them understand, but speaking a little more clearly and slowly may help. Helping someone who uses a wheelchair, or helping a blind person navigate stairs by taking that person's arm, may offend that person if he or she feels proud and self-sufficient.

As you communicate in school and at work, strive to use language that is inclusive and not biased. Doing so will help you avoid misunderstandings and treat others equally and fairly. For example, if a female teacher has a class that is predominantly female and she directs all her comments to the female students, she is being biased and excluding the male students. If a male manager constantly tells "blonde" jokes, female employees who are blonde may feel they are not being treated fairly or respectfully. Referring to female employees as "the girls" is another example where choice of words may offend those employees.

Going Global

Avoiding Sexist Language

When writing or speaking, be sensitive in your choice of words and try to use gender-neutral words. Some people might be offended by sexist language—for example, referring to a female police officer as a policeman.

Exhibit 3.5
Friendly Conversation
Nondiscriminatory behavior involves focusing on what you have in common with someone, rather than the differences between you.
Thinking Critically. How might this be accomplished?

Employability Skills

Speaking

Speak clearly and slowly when doing a presentation for international clients. You can avoid creating confusion when you enunciate carefully and choose the appropriate words to communicate your ideas.

Review of Key Terms

1. How can one avoid *discrimination* in writing? _____
   _____

2. How can *discriminatory language* create a hostile work environment?
   _____
   _____

Editing Practice

Using Language! Mark and correct any biased and discriminatory language in the following sentences.

3. The old postman was very dependable. _____

4. The cute stewardess showed us how to operate the oxygen mask. _____
   _____

5. Danny Jones, the black quadriplegic, sang the national anthem at the ceremony. _____

6. Her Mormon parents always stressed the importance of honesty. _____
   _____

7. Lisa works with crazy people at Garden State Hospital. _____
   _____

8. The white basketball players lost the game yesterday. _____
   _____

9. I was surprised when that lady attorney won the big lawsuit. _____
   _____

Practical Application

Analyzing Information

10. Make a list of gender-specific words and change them to neutral ones.
    _____

11. Mary, whose ancestry is Polish, works at an accounting firm. She likes her job, but often she overhears jokes about people of Polish ancestry. Although the jokes are not directed at Mary, they offend her. What should Mary do? As a group, develop strategies for avoiding offensive language. _____
    _____
    _____

Discussion Point

Thinking Critically

12. How has gender equality in the workplace affected language? _____
_____
_____

13. How do people develop stereotypes? Do you think people can change
their prejudices? Explain. _____
_____
_____

Unit 2

Developing Language Skills

Unit Overview
In this unit, you will learn to expand and apply your language skills.

Chapter 4
Exploring Language Elements

Chapter 5
Mastering Nouns and Pronouns

Chapter 6
Expanding Language Skills

Ashley had been working as administrative assistant to Mr. Moxley, the head of the shipping department, for about two years. When the administrative assistant to the company president retired, Ashley applied for the position. Ashley was disappointed when she did not get the promotion and asked Mr. Moxley if he knew the reason.

Mr. Moxley was quite candid. He reminded Ashley that all her performance evaluations had indicated that she was weak in grammatical skills and that the reports and letters she produced always had to be corrected for grammatical errors. Mr. Moxley explained, "The company president has to have someone that he can depend on to make sure that his communications are correct."

When Ashley reminded Mr. Moxley that she had taken courses in grammar, Mr. Moxley replied, "Yes, I'm sure you have, but sometimes we need to refresh skills that are important in our job. The most convenient way is to review grammar concepts in a reference manual or a communications textbook. Another way to refresh grammar skills is to enroll in a course at a community college or private business school."

Ashley decided that she would not be passed over for the next available promotion. She searched her closets and found her communications text. She began to review the text immediately and placed the text beside her dictionary in the office as a ready reference—where the book should have been all along. After confirming that her company had a tuition reimbursement policy, Ashley enrolled in a grammar course at the local community college.

With the help of her grammar course, Ashley's grammar skills improved. As a result, her next performance evaluation was positive. Moreover, in the evaluation report Mr. Moxley wrote about Ashley's efforts to refresh grammar skills to improve her job performance.

Ashley's efforts paid off. She got the next available promotion, which included a salary increase.

As you read Unit 2, identify areas of grammar usage in which you could make improvements. Like Ashley, plan what you will do to strengthen your language skills.

Thinking Critically

Give an example of a work, home, or school situation in which you were asked to improve in some area.

How did you react to being asked to improve?

If you were in Ashley's situation, how would you have reacted to Mr. Moxley's explanation?

Which actions would you have taken?

Chapter 4

Exploring Language Elements

Workplace Connection

As you study this chapter, view your instructor as the coach and yourself as a team player—not a spectator. Just as competitive athletes do, you will review the rules and practice applying them so that you can successfully compete when communicating in your chosen occupation.

CHAPTER OBJECTIVES

When you have completed this chapter, you should be able to:

- Identify the eight parts of speech.
- Distinguish between sentences and fragments.
- Use regular and irregular verbs correctly.
- Apply the principles of subject-verb agreement.

The Parts of Speech

Essential Principles

All the many thousands of words in our language can be grouped into eight categories: nouns, pronouns, verbs, adjectives, adverbs, prepositions, conjunctions, and interjections. These categories are called the parts of speech. As you will see, each category, or part of speech, has certain characteristics, one of which is how the words from the category function in a sentence.

Nouns

The word *noun* is derived from a word meaning "name." A **noun** is the name of a person, place, thing, idea, concept, or quality. Nouns may be proper or common. A *proper noun* "names a specific person, place, or thing." A *common noun* "names a general person, place, or thing." The list in **Exhibit 4.1** gives examples of proper and common nouns.

In a sentence, nouns function as subjects, direct objects, indirect objects, objects of a preposition, appositives, and complements. These functions will be discussed in Chapter 5.

Common and Proper Nouns	
Proper	**Common**
Persons: Mr. Arnold Werner, Sarah	managers applicants
Places: Rocky Mountains West Coast	beaches mountains
Things: London Bridge Xerox Corporation	compact disks laptops
Ideas, concepts, or qualities: Buddhism Christianity	democracy honesty

Exhibit 4.1
Common and Proper Nouns
This table shows common and proper nouns. *Thinking Critically. How does knowing the difference between common and proper nouns affect your communications with others?*

Pronouns

Pronouns are words that replace nouns. Examples include: *I, you, she, he, it, we, they, me, her, us, them, my, mine, your, his, its, our, ours, their,* and *theirs.* Pronouns add variety to our speech and our writing and provide us with shortcuts.

- She asked William to order the new microwave. (Another way of saying "Jenny asked William to order the new microwave.")
- She gave them the keys to their offices. (Another way of saying "Sarah gave Samuel and Vanessa the keys to Samuel's and Vanessa's offices.")

Since pronouns replace nouns, they also function as subjects, direct objects, indirect objects, objects of prepositions, appositives, and complements.

KEY POINT

Nouns name:

1. Persons
2. Places
3. Things
4. Ideas
5. Concepts
6. Qualities

4.1 Self-Assessment A

Identify the nouns and pronouns in the following sentences. Label each noun *N* and each pronoun *P*.

1. Can we order a ticket for a play on Broadway? _____
   _____

2. I believe that Oscar will plan our tour if we ask him. _____
   _____

3. They drove the Lamborghini to Chicago last week. _____
   _____

4. You and I will meet next Saturday to plan the wedding. _____
   _____

5. She plans to visit Orlando and Miami to tour the sights. _____
   _____

6. Mark and Anna tell me the Northeast is their favorite part of the country. _____

Verbs

Verbs are words that express action, a state of being, or a condition. Verbs that express an obvious action are called *action verbs* because they give sentences life. Some examples are:

- Our company imports Swiss chocolate and uses it in various desserts. (*Imports* and *uses* are action verbs.)
- Ms. Baxter bought one Swiss chocolatier's inventory and shipped it to our Pennsylvania plant. (*Bought* and *shipped* are action verbs.)

Some verbs do not indicate an obvious action but express a condition or a state of being. These verbs are called *linking verbs.* Linking verbs include forms of the verb "to be," such as *am, is, are, was, were, be,* and *been.* The *sense verbs—look, feel, sound, taste,* and *smell*—as well as the verbs *appear* and *become,* are also linking verbs. Some examples are:

- Of course, I am delighted about Arik's graduation, but his parents are thrilled. (*Am* and *are* are verbs that show state of being.)
- Chelsea will be an assistant manager in March. By that time, Robert will have been a manager for 12 years. (*Will be* and *will have been* are verbs. Note that each consists of more than one word.)

In a sentence, verbs function as predicates. You will learn about predicates later in this section.

4.1 Self-Assessment B

Write the verbs in the following sentences.

1. Betty seems happy about her new promotion. _____

2. The receptionist was planning to call each new patient. _____

3. Mr. Walters has been in Charlotte since 2004. _____

4. Rhonda hired two new associates after she promoted Tyler. _____

_____

Supply a verb for each blank in the following sentences, and indicate whether the verb is an action verb or a linking verb.

5. He _____ to begin work on his bachelor's degree in nursing within two years.

6. Jeremy _____ his associate degree in nursing in May and _____ his new job two months later.

7. He _____ proud of his degree and his new job.

8. Karl _____ his CPA exam last month.

Adjectives

Adjectives describe nouns and pronouns by limiting, or making more specific, the noun or pronoun. Another word for limiting is *modifying.* Adjectives may show what kind of, which one, or how many. Some examples are:

- What kind of: *hectic* week, *interesting* article, *expensive* vacation
- Which one: her *former* supervisor, *that* book, *those* folders
- How many: *one* doctor, *several* patients, *several* tickets

The words *a, an,* and *the* are special types of adjectives called *articles. A* and *an* are *indefinite articles* because they do not identify a specific item. *The* is *a definite article* because it identifies a specific item. When an adjective describes a noun, the adjective usually precedes the noun. When an adjective describes a pronoun, the adjective generally follows a linking verb or a sense verb. Some examples are:

- She was impatient with the slow growth of her investment.
  (The adjective *impatient* describes the pronoun *she.*)
- She feels ill. (*Ill* describes the pronoun *she.*)

Adjectives that follow linking verbs and sense verbs can also describe nouns. Some examples are:

- Nancy feels *ill.*
- The group was *nervous* before its presentation.

Adverbs

Adverbs are also modifiers; like adjectives, adverbs describe or limit adjectives, verbs, or other adverbs. They specify how, when, where, why, in what manner, and to what extent. Some examples are:

- Lou Ann was unusually quiet during the meeting yesterday.
  (The adverb *unusually* modifies the adjective *quiet.*)
- Alex nearly fell when he tripped over the telephone cord.
  (The adverb *nearly* modifies the verb *fell.*)

Note that many adverbs end in *ly* and are therefore very easy to identify. Some examples are:

badly	successfully
completely	suddenly
immediately	surely

We form these adverbs simply by adding "*ly*" to the adjectives *bad, complete, immediate, successful, sudden,* and *sure.*

Although most words that end in *ly* are adverbs, not all adverbs end in *ly*. Here are some adverbs that do not end in *ly*:

almost	quite
always	soon
here	then
much	there
never	very
not	well

 4.1 Self-Assessment C

Identify the words in parentheses as either adjectives or adverbs.

1. The (beautiful) weather (here) attracts (many) tourists each summer. ___
   _____

2. Fred will forward the e-mail (immediately) to your (new) address. _____
   _____

3. Several (experienced) electricians are (eagerly) waiting to begin work.
   _____

4. A (professional) presentation (always) has (attractive) visual aids. _____
   _____

5. The (last) applicant whom we interviewed was (more) qualified than we had expected. _____

6. Staff members were (excited) about the equipment. _____

Prepositions

Prepositions are connecting words that show the relationship between a noun or pronoun and other words in a sentence. Prepositions are always used in phrases. Some examples are:

Preposition	Prepositional Phrase
by	*by* the bus terminal, *by* tomorrow noon
for	*for* us, *for* Katelyn
from	*from* Robert, *from* Mr. Chen
in	*in* the evening, *in* September
of	*of* the organization, *of* my friend
to	*to* the park, *to* my brother

In addition to the prepositions listed above, many other commonly used prepositions include:

at	on
after	onto
before	over
between	out
into	through
off	with

Prepositional Phrases

Prepositional phrases are frequently used in sentences. A prepositional phrase contains an *object,* which is the noun or pronoun following the preposition. Some examples are:

- The pilot left here *after the meeting* and went directly *to the airport.*
- *At the airport,* she boarded the plane *with her crew.*
- The horse leaped *over the fence, across the ditch,* and *over the hedges.*

Conjunctions

Conjunctions are words that join words, phrases, or clauses. Note how the conjunctions *and, but, or,* and *nor* are used in these sentences.

- Dayle and Joe attended the convention in Las Vegas. (*And* joins two words—the nouns *Dayle* and *Joe.*)
- The team members did not go to the meeting but to the gym. (*But* joins two prepositional phrases.)
- Elizabeth will visit the construction site, or she will go to the main office. (*Or* joins two independent clauses.)
- The defendant would not respond to their accusations, nor did she offer to answer any of their questions. (*Nor* joins two independent clauses.)

> ### KEY POINT
> Prepositions connect and relate nouns or pronouns to other words in a sentence.

Identify each word in parentheses and label it as either a preposition *P* or a conjunction *C.*

1.   Grace likes the bagel shop (on) the corner, (but) Kevin prefers the one (on) Warren Street. _____

2.   (With) Ms. Hannah's approval, the new policy will begin (on) Monday (or) Tuesday. _____

3.   The letter (to) Mr. Turner gave the reason (for) the investigation. _____

4.   Ben did not order two (of) these vans, (nor) has he ordered any other vehicles (through) our dealership (during) April. _____

5.   Dickson (and) Polly went (to) the tax workshop (in) Washington (with) their manager, Ms. Bridges. _____

Interjections

Interjections are words used alone that express an extremely strong feeling. Interjections are often followed by exclamation marks. Some examples are:

- *Congratulations!* All your hard work has finally paid off handsomely. (Note that the interjection *Congratulations!* is treated as an independent sentence.)

- *Wow!* I never dreamed I would get a sales award.

- *Wait!* Don't send that e-mail to everyone!

- *Oops!* I missed my dental appointment.

Assessment   Section 4.1

Review of Key Terms

1.   How does a *pronoun* take the role of a *noun*? _____
     _____
     _____

2.   What are *prepositions* and why are they important? _____
     _____
     _____

Editing Practice

3.   **Spelling Alert!**   Find and correct any spelling errors in the following excerpt from an informal note.

     Heres the sales figures from January, Feburary, and March. If their is any posible explanation for the sales delcine in March, I would appreciate that information before noon tomorow. We frequently have declines in sales in Feburary, but not in March. _____

_____

_____

_____

Practical Application

Identifying Parts of Speech

4. Identify the part of speech for each of the italicized words.

   a. *Stefan* submitted his report *on* time, *but* his *formatting* was done very *poorly.*

   b. I personally *agree* that *Miami* would be the *best* location for our January *national* meeting.

   c. A *special* award *will be given* to associates if *they* achieve perfect *attendance.*

   d. *Excellent!* We have *just* won the *department* sales award *for* our entire region.

   _____

   _____

   _____

   _____

5. Choose a painting from a book that everyone on your team likes. Brainstorm a list of words or phrases that describes the painting its mood, and the team's feeling toward the painting. Then use those words to write a descriptive paragraph about the painting and your own reaction to it. Include active verbs, adjectives, adverbs, and interjections in your description. _____

   _____

   _____

Discussion Point

Making Comparisons

6. How are *action verbs* different from *linking verbs*? _____

   _____

   _____

7. Compare the role and characteristics of *adjectives* with the role and characteristics of *adverbs.* _____

   _____

   _____

SECTION OBJECTIVES

When you have finished Section 4.2, you will be able to:

- Define the word *sentence.*
- Distinguish between a subject and a predicate.
- Distinguish between normal and inverted sentence order.
- Identify the types of sentences.
- Identify clauses, phrases, and sentence fragments.

WHY IT'S IMPORTANT

To communicate effectively, it is essential to understand the structure of a sentence. We build sentences by combining parts of speech.

KEY TERMS

- sentence
- subject
- simple subject
- compound subject
- predicate
- simple predicate
- complete predicate
- declarative sentence
- interrogative sentence
- imperative sentence
- exclamatory sentence
- clause
- phrase
- prepositional phrase
- infinitive phrase
- verb phrase
- sentence fragment

The Sentence

Essential Principles

The parts of speech are used to form sentences, the basic units we use in reading, writing, and speaking. Therefore, the ability to use and to understand sentences effectively determines your ability to communicate.

A **sentence** is a group of words that expresses a complete thought and contains a subject and a predicate. An interjection such as *Yes! No!* or *Congratulations!* may be used as an elliptical expression that stands for a sentence. An *elliptical expression* can represent a complete statement or command and may be an answer to a question. The subject and the predicate are the key elements needed to build a sentence.

Subjects

The **subject** of a sentence names (1) the person or persons speaking, (2) the person or persons spoken to, or (3) the person(s) or thing(s) spoken about. A subject is usually a noun or pronoun. Some examples are:

1. **Who is speaking:**
   - I voted for Tyler in the last election. (*I* is the complete subject of the sentence, the person who is speaking.)

2. **Who is spoken to:**
   - You have been invited to speak at the banquet, Linda. (The subject *You* identifies the person spoken to, Linda.)
   - Open a checking account. (Here the subject is still *you,* but this sentence is an *imperative sentence*—an order. In such sentences, the speaker usually directly addresses the person spoken to; therefore, it is clearly understood that the subject is you.)

3. **Who is spoken about:**
   - Tony purchased the condominium in July. (Who is spoken about? Answer: *Tony,* the subject of the sentence.)
   - She is the owner of the coffee shop. (Who is spoken about? Answer: *She,* the subject of the sentence. The person spoken about is referred to by the pronoun *She.*)

4. **What is spoken about:**
   - This insurance policy covers loss by fire and theft. (What is spoken about? Answer: *This insurance policy.*)
   - It covers loss by fire and theft. (What is spoken about? Answer: *It,* a pronoun that substitutes

for the complete subject *This insurance policy. It* is the subject of the sentence.)

- That disk belongs to Donna. Those disks belong to Jay. (*That disk* and *Those disks* are the complete subjects. *That disk* is the thing spoken about; *Those disks* are the things spoken about.)

4.2 Self-Assessment A

Write the subjects of the following sentences. Determine whether each subject is (1) the person or persons speaking, (2) the person or persons spoken to, or (3) the person(s) or thing(s) spoken about.

1. Repairs should be finished by Friday. _____

2. I feel that the cost for installing the garage door is too high. _____

3. Caroline Madison will be the top listing agent for most of the year. ____
_____

4. You will join the tour in New York City. _____

5. Donna Simpson will be assigned a company car. _____

Simple Subjects

The **simple subject** is the main word or words in the complete subject—the core of the subject. Some examples are:

- The owner of the restaurants is Cory Brookes. (The complete subject is *The owner of* the restaurants. The main word, or simple subject, in this complete subject is *owner.*)
- Five former lawyers in the Myers, Myers & Brantley law firm have filed a complaint. (The complete subject of this sentence is *Five former lawyers in the Myers, Myers & Brantley law firm.* Within this complete subject, the simple subject is *lawyers.*)

Because the subject of the first example is *owner,* not restaurants, the correct verb must be *is.* In the second example, the subject is *lawyers,* not *firm,* therefore, the correct verb must be *are.* You will learn more about subject-verb agreement in Section 4.4.

Compound Subjects

A **compound subject** is two or more subjects joined by a conjunction, such as *and, but, or,* or *nor.* Some examples are:

- The mechanics and technicians at our local plant have requested additional safety procedures. (The complete subject is *The mechanics and technicians at our local plant.* There are two main words in this complete subject—*mechanics* and *technicians*—which are joined by the conjunction *and.* The compound subject is *mechanics and technicians.*)
- A cruise to Alaska or a one-week vacation on Maui is going to be the first prize. (The complete subject is *A cruise to Alaska or a one-week vacation on Maui.* The two main words in this complete subject are *cruise* and *vacation,* which are joined by the conjunction *or.* The compound subject is *cruise or vacation.*)

Every time you identify the subject correctly, you simplify your work in identifying the predicate.

4.2 Self-Assessment B

Write the simple subject or the compound subject for each sentence.

1. One seminar participant asked about more software training for associates. _____

2. All employees were offered flu shots in November. _____

3. Two hair salons and a bookstore are relocating to the strip mall. _____

4. Four comprehensive depositions on the Terrell case are filed in the cabinet beside my desk. _____

5. Has Susan or Jeff filed to run for mayor? _____

Predicates

The **predicate** is the part of the sentence that tells what the subject is or does, or what is done to the subject. The **simple predicate** is the main verb of the sentence plus any helping verbs, usually the various forms of the verb to be. The **complete predicate** is the simple predicate and all the words that modify it. Some examples are:

- Mr. Carswell will organize the teams for the competition. (The simple predicate is *will organize*, which is what Mr. Carswell will do. The complete predicate is *will organize the teams for the competition.*)

- Steven and Michael are the managers of these departments. (The simple predicate is *are*, which tells what Steven and Michael are. The complete predicate is *are the managers of these departments.*)

oops!

House Hunting or Haunting?

Mr. Robertson and his family are moving into our neighborhood next month. They will be haunting for a new house real soon.

(hunting is the correct word, not *haunting*)

4.2 Self-Assessment C

Write the complete predicate for each of the following sentences.

1. My performance appraisal is scheduled for June 10. _____

2. Our depositors have responded favorably to our new bank statements. _____

3. Martha and Todd are our best home decorators. _____

4. Betty has enrolled in a business communications course. _____

5. All applicants should have at least three years' experience. _____

Normal Order: Subject, Then Predicate

The normal order of a sentence is subject first, then predicate. Some examples are:

- Three members of management were at last night's meeting concerning health benefits. (The complete subject is *Three members of management.* The complete subject precedes the complete predicate, which is *were at last night's meeting concerning health benefits.* Therefore, this sentence is in normal order.)

- At last night's meeting concerning health benefits were three members of management. (The words are the same, but the order is different. The sentence is in *inverted order:* the predicate precedes the subject. This sentence, therefore, is not in normal order.)

Most questions are phrased in inverted order rather than normal order. An example is:

- Has Phillip estimated the cost of constructing the kennel? (Why is this question in inverted order? The subject is *Phillip,* and part of the verb—the word *Has*—precedes the subject. Normal order would be, Phillip has estimated the cost of constructing the kennel.)

It is important to be able to distinguish between normal order and inverted order. What, if anything, is wrong with this sentence?

- Where's the photographs that Michelle left for us?

Many people almost automatically start sentences with *Where's, There's,* and *Here's,* even when these words are incorrect. Normal order quickly points out the error. An example is:

- The photographs that Michelle left for us is where? (Simply put, "The photographs . . . is where?" *Photographs is,* is incorrect; we must say *Photographs are.* Thus, the correct form for the question is, "Where are the photographs that Michelle left for us?")

It is important to spot inverted order not only in questions but also in statements. Look at this sentence:

- On the desk in my office is the photographs that Michelle left for us. (In normal order, this sentence reads "The photographs that Michelle left for us is on the desk in my office." The subject *photographs* is plural and does not agree in number with the verb *is,* which is singular. This error is masked by the inverted order. The original sentence should read, "On the desk in my office are the photographs that Michelle left for us.")

Types of Sentences

You use sentences to make statements, ask questions, state a command or request, and express strong feeling. There are four types of sentences to serve these purposes:

Type of Sentence	Definition	Example
Declarative	makes a statement	You are tall.
Interrogative	asks a question	How old are you?
Imperative	states a command or request	Proofread the letter.
Exclamatory	expresses strong feeling	I can't believe it!

Employability Skills

Serving Customers

To establish a good relationship with all your customers, try not to use figures of speech to convey a message. Serving customers well means making sure that they understand and are satisfied with the service. Use words or phrases that are clear to avoid any miscommunication or confusion.

KEY POINT

An independent clause expresses a complete thought and can stand alone as a sentence. A dependent clause does not express a complete thought and cannot stand alone.

4.2 Self-Assessment D

Identify each of the following sentences and label it as declarative *D*, interrogative *INT*, imperative *IMP*, or exclamatory *E*.

1. Who attended the program on cosmetic surgery? _____

2. Please give me the latest sales figures by noon. _____

3. Both Elaine and Shauna are applying for the position. _____

4. Congratulations on winning the award for helping senior citizens! _____
   _____

5. Fred answered my e-mail today. _____

Clauses and Phrases

Words that are grouped together are classified as a clause if the group of words includes both a subject and a predicate. A group of related words that does not have both a subject and a predicate is called a phrase.

Clauses

A **clause** is a group of words containing both a subject and a predicate. If the clause expresses a complete thought and can stand alone as a complete sentence, it is an *independent clause.* If the clause cannot stand alone, then it is called a *dependent clause.*

Note that the following sentence has a subject and a predicate and can stand alone. The sentence is an independent clause.

- Janetta Draymore is a well-known expert in computer science. (The subject is *Janetta Draymore*, and the complete predicate is the rest of the sentence. Because this group of words can stand alone, it is an independent clause.)

The clause that follows has a subject and predicate but cannot stand alone. Therefore, it is a dependent clause.

- If Mary Courtney accepts the nomination. (The subject of this clause is *Mary Courtney,* and the complete predicate is *accepts the nomination.* But does this group of words make sense by itself? No. This is a dependent clause. More information is required if this group of words is to make sense.)

Dependent clauses cannot stand alone as sentences; therefore, they must be joined to independent clauses for their meaning to be complete.

- If Mary Courtney accepts the nomination, she must resign her present position. (*She must resign her present position* is an independent clause. Thus, the dependent clause *If Mary Courtney accepts the nomination* is joined correctly to an independent clause.)

4.2 Self-Assessment E

Determine which of the following groups of words are complete sentences and which are dependent clauses that are incorrectly treated as sentences. For each dependent clause, suggest an independent clause that would complete it.

1. Before the nurses meet to evaluate their patients. _____
   _____

2. When Dr. Rosa Peréz meets with the hospital nursing staff. _____
   _____

3. If Omar is unable to employ another administrative assistant by April 1.
   _____

4. Anna and Lee will arrange a work schedule for each police officer. _____
   _____

5. Because Don, the new manager, will not return until Friday, our weekly
   staff meeting will be rescheduled. _____

Phrases

A **phrase** is a group of words that has neither a subject nor a predicate. As you study the following three kinds of phrases, note that none has a subject or a predicate.

Prepositional Phrases.   A **prepositional phrase** consists of a preposition, an object, and any modifier of the object. Phrases such as *for the associates, among the interns, with Adam Murphy, in the office, at the meeting, between you and me,* and *from Dr. Sanders* are prepositional phrases. The nouns and pronouns at the ends of prepositional phrases are not subjects; they are *objects of the prepositions.*

As you read the following examples, note how prepositional phrases can be used (1) as adjectives, (2) as adverbs, and occasionally (3) as nouns.

1. **As adjectives:**
   - The woman with the laptop computer is Brenda Taylor. (Which woman? The prepositional phrase *with the laptop computer* describes the noun *woman.* Therefore, this prepositional phrase serves as an adjective.)

2. **As adverbs:**
   - Oscar sent the report to the research department. (Sent it where? The prepositional phrase *to the research department* answers the question Where? This prepositional phrase serves as an adverb.)

3. **As nouns:**
   - After 5 o'clock is the best time to meet. (The prepositional phrase *After 5 o'clock* serves as the noun or subject of the sentence.)

Infinitive Phrases.   An infinitive is the "to be" form of a verb. Some examples are: *to read, to study, to analyze, to review, to compute, to question, to be, to have, to do,* and so on. An **infinitive phrase** includes the infinitive and any other words that are related to it. Infinitive phrases may be used (1) as nouns, (2) as adjectives, and, less frequently, (3) as adverbs.

Some examples of infinitive phrases are:

1. **As nouns:**
   - To create new slogans is the objective of this meeting. (The complete infinitive phrase is *To create new slogans;* the phrase is the subject of the verb *is.*)

2. **As adjectives:**
   - Sandra Smith is the person to ask about employment opportunities. (Here the infinitive phrase *to ask about employment opportunities* modifies the noun *person* and serves as an adjective.)

3. **As adverbs:**
   - Raymond bent down to tie his shoe. (Bent down for what reason? Here the infinitive phrase answers the question *why?* The infinitive phrase *to tie his shoe* serves as an adverb.)

Verb Phrases.   In a **verb phrase,** two or more verbs work together as one verb. In such cases, the main verb is always the last verb in the phrase; the other verbs are helping verbs. Some common helping verbs include: *is, are, was, were, can, could, has, had, have, should, will,* and *would.* Some examples are:

- The architect will complete our house plans by July 5. (*Will complete* is a verb phrase. The main verb is *complete; will* is a helping verb.)
- By July 5 our house plans will have been completed. (The main verb is *completed,* the last word in the verb phrase. *Will have been* is a helping verb.)

Verb phrases are often interrupted by adverbs, as shown in the following examples:

- The architect will soon be showing our house plans to the builder. (The verb phrase *will be showing* is interrupted by the adverb *soon.*)
- Our staff members have already been told about possible computer network problems tomorrow. (The verb phrase *have been told* is interrupted by the adverb *already.*)

4.2 Self-Assessment F

Identify the following words in parentheses and label them as prepositional phrases *PP,* infinitive phrases *IP,* or verb phrases *VP.*

1. Mr. King wants (to drive your van) when he goes (to the electronics show) (with the manager). _____

2. (To attend the computer classes), customers (have been asked) (to register) (in advance). _____

3. Rubin's essay (will be submitted) (to the contest committee) (by next Friday). _____

4. Several self-defense classes (have been scheduled) (for college students). _____

5. (To become a chef) (at Antonio's), you (must have had) at least five years' experience (at a three-star restaurant). _____

Sentence Fragments

A sentence is a group of words that expresses a complete thought and contains a subject and a predicate. When the writing is "an incomplete thought," it is called a **sentence fragment.** You can distinguish between a complete sentence and a fragment by applying the "no sense, no sentence" rule. An example is:

- Randy wants to attend the seminar because the topic is how to create Web pages. (This is a complete thought. This group of words makes sense and is a sentence.)

If, however, you try to split off part of the sentence, you create a fragment.

- Randy wants to attend the seminar. Because the topic is how to create Web pages. (The first group of words is a sentence. The words *Because the topic is how to create Web pages* do not make sense by themselves. The word *because* leads us to expect more.)

In the preceding example, the word *because* begins a clause that cannot stand alone. Note that the following words often introduce dependent clauses. Some examples are:

after	before	provided that	when
although	even if	since	whenever
as	for	so that	where
as if	how	than	wherever
as soon as	if	that	whether
as though	in case that	unless	while
because	in order that	until	why

KEY POINT

A sentence is a group of words that expresses a complete thought. A fragment is a phrase or clause incorrectly treated as a sentence.

4.2 Self-Assessment G

Identify each group of words as either a sentence or a fragment. Then, rewrite each fragment to make it a complete sentence.

1. If Mr. Lee decides to accept our terms. _____
   _____

2. Juan or Rafael will be chosen as our representative. _____
   _____

3. Our policy manual mandated these safety procedures about five years ago. _____

4. Although David's passport was valid at that time. _____
   _____

5. Because two signatures are required for checks over $250. _____
   _____

Review of Key Terms

1. What is the role of a *subject* in a sentence? What is the role of a *predicate* in a sentence? _____

   _____

   _____

   _____

2. Distinguish between a *sentence* and a *fragment.* _____

   _____

   _____

Editing Practice

Grammar Alert!   Correct any agreement errors in the following.

3. Under the stack of papers on my desk is the disks that I made for the presentation. _____

   _____

4. The veterinarian with the talking parrots have a new office downtown.

   _____

5. Linda and Rick sings in a choir that performs during the holidays. _____

   _____

6. A casual dinner at the lake or a formal gala at the country club are going to be the location of our regional sales meeting. _____

   _____

   _____

Practical Application

Clauses

7. Identify each of the following clauses as dependent or independent. If a clause is dependent, complete the sentence to make a complete thought.

   a. When the tree came crashing through the window.
   b. Mario is the intern who wrote the procedures.
   c. Since she told us not to work overtime.
   d. After the taxi took us to the conference hall.
   e. Until I took a computer course, I could not get a promotion.

   _____

   _____

   _____

   _____

   _____

8. Choose a profession and write a paragraph about the educational requirements or special training the job requires. Include at least three sentences that use dependent clauses. Once you have developed your sentences, share them with your team. Determine how dependent clauses are used most effectively in sentences and report back to your instructor.

_____

_____

Discussion Point

Thinking Critically

9. How can inverted sentence order create problems in agreement? _____

_____

_____

10. What is the difference between a *phrase* and a *clause*? _____

_____

_____

_____

SECTION OBJECTIVES

When you have finished Section 4.3, you will be able to:

- List the four principal parts of a verb.
- Explain what makes most verbs regular rather than irregular.
- Define the term *verb tense*.
- Discuss the differences between being, transitive, and intransitive verbs.

WHY IT'S IMPORTANT

Many of us regularly make serious verb tense errors. This section will assist you in using verbs correctly.

KEY TERMS

- verb
- being verb
- regular verb
- principal parts of verbs
- verb phrases
- verb tenses
- present tense
- past tense
- future tense
- present perfect tense
- past perfect tense
- future perfect tense
- present progressive tense
- past progressive tense
- future progressive tense
- irregular verb
- transitive verb
- intransitive verb

Verbs

Essential Principles

Among the most serious and the most common errors we make as we speak and write are verb-tense errors. Yet forming most verbs correctly is easy, because most verbs follow one simple pattern, as you will see in the first half of this section. The verbs that do not follow this regular pattern are the ones that cause problems; these irregular verbs are discussed in depth in the second half of this section.

Identifying Verbs

As you read in Section 4.1, a **verb** is a word that describes an action, a condition, or a state of being. The verb in a sentence is referred to as a *predicate*. The following examples illustrate action verbs and two types of linking verbs.

Action

In the following sentences, the verbs *supported, arrived, will write, is preparing,* and *will be competing* all describe actions.

- Scott *supported* our candidate.
- The special delivery package *arrived* promptly at 9:30 a.m.
- The executives of the power company *will write* to all the people who complained about the service interruption.
- The paralegal *is preparing* the contract now.
- John Kimble *will be competing* in the upcoming marathon.

Condition

The verbs *seems, felt, became, appears,* and *grew* in the following examples all describe conditions.

- Lisa *seems* excited about her new job.
- Jack and Melvin *felt* better after the carbon monoxide fumes had dissipated.
- Most of the trainees *became* fidgety during the explanation of safety procedures.
- Ms. Bankhead *appears* to be an excellent teacher.
- Mr. Wray *grew* hungry before his medical tests were completed.

Being

The **being** verbs *is, are, am, will be,* and *was* do not describe actions or conditions in the following sentences, yet each is a verb.

- Lynne Morris *is* happy with the new wireless system.
- Jan and Hilton *are* home from their trip to South Africa.
- I *am* eager to begin working in my new position.
- Ms. Ramsey *will be* a likely nominee for employee of the month.
- Mr. Yelton *was exhausted* after his business trip to Puerto Rico.

Practice identifying verbs correctly—that's the first step to using them correctly.

4.3 Self-Assessment A

Identify the verbs in the following sentences.

1. The chief executive officer has accepted Larry's proposal. _____

2. Madison invited her manager to speak at the meeting. _____

3. Angela seemed convinced that she had good intentions. _____

4. Ray was in Raleigh when his promotion was announced. _____

   _____

5. Both real estate agents want the highway business property for their clients. _____

6. Dana and Jaya are at the airport to meet his flight. _____

Regular Verbs

As we speak and write, the verbs we use indicate the time of the action, the condition, or the state of being. We select a verb form to indicate the time when the action occurred: *a present time:* "I *laugh*," "I *am laughing*"; *a past time:* "I *laughed*," "I *have laughed*," "I *had laughed*," "I *was laughing*"; or *a future time:* "I *will laugh*," "I *will be laughing*." This time element for a verb is called its *tense.* Fortunately, most verbs in English follow the same simple pattern to indicate time. These verbs are **regular verbs.**

Principal Parts of Regular Verbs

Knowing how to form the **principal parts of verbs** is necessary if you are to use verbs correctly in all forms of communication. All verb tenses are formed from the principal parts of a verb. These parts are (1) the present tense form, (2) the past tense form, (3) the past participle, and (4) the present participle.

How can you distinguish between the *past tense* form and the *past participle*? Look at the word in context and see how it is used in a sentence. A past tense form never has a helping verb; a past participle always has a helping verb.

- Alan faxed us at 10 p.m. (Here, *faxed* is a past tense form; it has no helping verb.)
- Carol called at 11 p.m. to tell us about the meeting, but Alan had faxed us at 10 p.m. (Here, *faxed* is a past participle. When *faxed* is used with the helping verb *had*, the combination forms a tense called the *past perfect*. Together, *had faxed* is a verb phrase or simple predicate and *faxed* is its main verb.)

KEY POINT

The principal verb forms are:

1. **The present tense.**
2. **The past tense.**
3. **The past participle.**
4. **The present participle.**

Look at **Exhibit 4.2** below. As you read this table, say to yourself "I move," "I prepare," and so on. Then, notice that simply adding "d" to verbs that end in *e* forms the past tense. For verbs that do not end in *e*, add "ed": *called, entered, listened*. For some verbs ending in *y*, change the *y* to *i* before adding "ed."

Further simplifying this pattern for regular verbs is the fact that the past participle is the same form as the past tense. The present participle is formed by adding *ing* to the present tense form. Note that, for verbs ending in *e*, you must drop the *e* before adding *ing: moving, preparing, hiring*. Except for a limited list, all the verbs in English follow this pattern.

Verbs			
Present Tense	**Past Tense**	**Past Participle**	**Present Participle**
move	moved	moved	moving
prepare	prepared	prepared	preparing
hire	hired	hired	hiring
call	called	called	calling
enter	entered	entered	entering
listen	listened	listened	listening
study	studied	studied	studying

Exhibit 4.2
Verbs
This table lists verbs in their present, past, past participle, and present participle forms. ***Thinking Critically.*** *How does understanding a verb in context allow you to check your usage?*

4.3 Self-Assessment B

Fill in the missing parts for each entry.

	Present Tense	Past Tense	Past Participle	Present Participle
1.	paint	painted	_____	painting
2.	carry	carried	carried	_____
3.	type	_____	typed	typing
4.	answer	answered	_____	answering
5.	bake	baked	_____	baking
6.	mark	_____	marked	marking
7.	marry	married	married	_____
8.	trust	_____	trusted	trusting
9.	use	used	_____	using
10.	walk	walked	walked	_____

oops!

Past Tense Makes Sense

I lay the computer manual on the kitchen counter.

(laid—the verb *lay* needs to be past tense)

Verb Phrases

As you read in Section 4.2, a **verb phrase** consists of the main verb and any helping verbs used together to function as one verb. A verb phrase may also contain an interrupting adverb. The main verb in the phrase is always the last verb. The other verbs are the helping, or auxiliary, verbs. Some examples are:

> can *move*
> did *prepare*
> will *hire*

The main verbs in the preceding three examples are *move, prepare,* and *hire.* The verbs *can, did,* and *will* are helping verbs. Note that *move, prepare,* and *hire* are the present tense forms listed in **Exhibit 4.2** on page 104. Some examples are:

> has been *moved*
> have *prepared*
> will soon be *hired*

The main verbs are *moved, prepared,* and *hired,* which are the past participles listed in the third column in **Exhibit 4.2** on page 104. The verbs *has been, have,* and *will be* are helping verbs. The word *soon* is an interrupting adverb. Some examples are:

> are *moving*
> is *preparing*
> will be *hiring*

KEY POINT

The last verb in the verb phrase is *always* the main verb.

Again, the last word in each phrase is the main verb: *moving, preparing,* and *hiring.* These are the present participles listed in **Exhibit 4.2** on page 104. The words *are, is,* and *will be* are helping verbs.

Now note how verb phrases are used in sentences. Remember that a verb phrase can be interrupted by another word, most often an adverb. Some examples are:

- Barbara will be moving into her new office in May. (The verb phrase is *will be moving*; the main verb is the last verb, *moving.*)
- Anne-Marie has also been preparing for the debate. (The verb phrase *has been preparing* is interrupted by the adverb *also.* The main verb is *preparing.*)
- Our new president has already been hired. (*Hired* is the main verb in the phrase *has been hired; already* is an adverb.)

In questions, the verb phrase is often more difficult to identify because the sentence order is inverted. Finding the verb phrase in inverted sentences is easier if you change the sentence to the normal order first.

- When did your client purchase additional stock? (The verb phrase is *did purchase.*)
- Have Rob and Lori already been transacting business over the Internet? (The verb phrase *have been transacting* is tricky to identify because of the inverted order and the interrupting adverb *already.*)

4.3 Self-Assessment C

Identify the verb phrases in each of the following sentences. Underscore the main verb.

1. Kathy and Ryan have been waiting two years to buy their first house.
   _____

2. Should they have attended every class? _____

3. Mr. Zanora will be inspecting all the equipment tomorrow morning. ___
   _____

4. Glenn can complete this project by Monday. _____

5. Does Jenny want to speak to her attorney? _____

6. Denise and Paul have already received their passports. _____

7. Ms. Donovan has been drafting her graduation speech. _____

8. Daniel has been promoted to vice president of sales. _____

9. The actors will enter the theater through the stage door. _____

10. Barbara will introduce the speaker. _____

Chapter Four   *Exploring Language Elements*

Verb Tenses

As we saw earlier in this section, the **tense** of a **verb** is the form that tells when the action did or will occur.

Present Tense. Remember that terms such as *to spend, to run, to sell, to listen,* and *to call* are infinitives. Omit the word *to* from these forms to create the present tense forms. Some examples are:

I call	we call
you call	you call
he	
she } calls	they call
it	

As you see, there are only two present tense forms, *call* and *calls*. Use *call* with *I, you, we,* and *they.* Add "s"—*calls*—to create the present tense of the verb form used with *he, she,* and *it* and with singular nouns. Some examples are:

- We call every morning. (*Call* with the pronoun *we.*)
- He calls every morning. Steve calls every morning. (*Calls* with the pronoun *he* and the singular noun *Steve.*)
- They enjoy traveling. (*Enjoy* with the pronoun *they.*)
- She enjoys traveling. Sally enjoys traveling. (*Enjoys* with the pronoun *she* and the singular noun *Sally.*)

The **present tense** is used to show action that is happening now. It is also used to indicate that something is always true, as in, "the sun rises in the east."

KEY POINT

Regular third person singular verbs always end in *s*.

Past Tense. The **past tense** is formed by adding "ed" to the present tense form, or *d* if the present tense form already ends in *e*. Some examples are:

I called	we called
you called	you called
he	
she } called	they called
it	

As you see, there is only one past tense form for a verb. The only exception is the verb *to be,* which will be discussed later. The **past tense** is used to indicate action that has already been completed.

Future Tense. The **future tense** indicates action that is to take place in the future. To form the *future tense* of a verb, use *will* or *shall* plus the infinitive form without the word *to.* In ordinary situations, use *will* to form the future tense. In formal situations, use *shall* to form the future tense for the first person (*I, we*). Some examples are:

I shall call	we shall call
you will call	you will call
he	
she } will call	they will call
it	

Each of the three tenses, *present, past,* and *future,* has a correlated *perfect tense.* Perfect tenses are commonly used in everyday conversation and writing.

Present Perfect Tense. The **present perfect tense** is used to show that an action began in the past and may still be occurring. This tense is formed by using the helping verbs *has* or *have* with a past participle. Some examples are:

- Lana has redecorated the reception area. (Present perfect tense for an action that was begun in the past.)
- Terry and Wade have debated the issue for at least five years. (Present perfect tense for an action that began in the past and may be still continuing in the present.)

Past Perfect Tense. The **past perfect tense** is used to show which of two past actions occurred first. To form the past perfect tense, use *had* plus the past participle of a verb. An example is:

- Nancy had signed the agreement before she received the advice from her attorney. (The verbs *had signed* and *received* show two past actions. The past perfect tense *had signed* is the first action. After that action was completed, a second action occurred—Nancy received something. *Received* is in the past tense to show that this action occurred second.)

Future Perfect Tense. The **future perfect tense** shows that an action will be completed by some specific time in the future. The action may have already begun, or it may begin in the future. The important point is that it will end by a specific future time. To form the future perfect tense, use the verb *will have* or *shall have* plus the past participle of a verb. An example is:

- The landscape artist will have completed her sketches long before the architect finishes his. (*Will have completed* is a future perfect tense verb describing an action that will end by some specific time— *long before the architect finishes his*—in the future.)

The Progressive Tenses. Closely related to the six tenses just discussed, *present, past, future, present perfect, past perfect, and future perfect,* are the *progressive tenses,* which depict actions that are still in progress. The **present progressive tense** describes an action that is in progress in the present. To form this tense, use *am, is,* or *are* with a present participle. Some examples are:

- I am using my computer to do research. (*Am using* shows action in progress now.)
- You are reading Tom's autobiographical sketch. (*Are reading* shows action in progress now.)
- He is driving his new truck. (*Is driving* shows action in progress now.)

The **past progressive tense** describes an action that was in progress at a certain time in the past. It is formed by using *was* or *were* with a present participle. An example is:

- They were assessing the losses when the insurance agent arrived. (*Were assessing* shows action that was in progress in the past.)

The **future progressive tense** describes an action that will be in progress at a certain time in the future. It is formed by using *will be* or *shall be* with a present participle. An example is:

- Max will be interviewing for a scholarship next Monday. (Is this action in progress now? No. In the past? Again, no. *Will be interviewing* shows an action that will be in progress in the future—specifically, next Monday.)

Conjugating Regular Verbs

Exhibit 4.3 on page 110 illustrates the three elements that determine verb forms: *person* (*I, you,* and so on), *number* (singular or plural), and *tense.* Every regular verb follows the same basic conjugation pattern shown there. When you are unsure about the correct form of a particular regular verb, check that verb against the table.

4.3 Self-Assessment D

Use each of the following regular verbs in a sentence.

1. have studied _____

2. wished _____

3. has stopped _____

4. evaluates _____

5. had remembered _____

6. are listening _____

7. will have adjusted _____

   _____

8. will be _____

Irregular Verbs

Most verbs follow the regular pattern shown in **Exhibit 4.2** on page 104 for forming the present tense, the past tense, the past participle, and the present participle. However, more than 50 commonly used **irregular verbs** do not follow this pattern. The rest of this section discusses these irregular verbs.

Principal Parts of Irregular Verbs

Review **Exhibit 4.4** on page 111. During your review, try fitting some of the irregular verbs into the regular pattern. For example, say "speak, speaked" instead of "speak, spoke" or say "leave, leaved" instead of "leave, left." Can you hear the errors? For many of us, the only alternative is to memorize these forms, especially those that are used frequently.

Exhibit 4.3

Verb Conjugation
This table shows the conjugation of the infinitive verb *to hope*. **Thinking Critically.** *How does reviewing such a chart enable you to improve upon your written and spoken communications?*

KEY POINT

To use the conjugation table, substitute singular nouns in place of the pronouns *he* or *she* and plural nouns in place of the pronoun *they*.

Verb Conjugation

Singular	Plural
Present Tense I hope you hope he, she, or it hopes	we hope you hope they hope
Past Tense I hoped you hoped he, she, or it hoped	we hoped you hoped they hoped
Future Tense I shall hope you will hope he, she, or it will hope	we shall hope you will hope they will hope
Present Perfect Tense I have hoped you have hoped he, she, or it has hoped	we have hoped you have hoped they have hoped
Past Perfect Tense I had hoped you had hoped he, she, or it had hoped	we had hoped you had hoped they had hoped
Future Perfect Tense I shall have hoped you will have hoped he, she, or it will have hoped	we shall have hoped you will have hoped they will have hoped
Present Progressive Tense I am hoping you are hoping he, she, or it is hoping	we are hoping you are hoping they are hoping
Past Progressive Tense I was hoping you were hoping he, she, or it was hoping	we were hoping you were hoping they were hoping
Future Progressive Tense I shall be hoping you will be hoping he, she, or it will be hoping	we shall be hoping you will be hoping they will be hoping

Principal Parts of Irregular Verbs

Present Tense	Past Tense	Past Participle	Present Participle
am	was	been	being
begin	began	began	beginning
bid (to command)	bade	bidden	bidding
bid (to offer to pay)	bid	bid	bidding
bite	bit	bitten	biting
blow	blew	blown	blowing
bring	brought	brought	bringing
burst	burst	burst	bursting
choose	chose	chosen	choosing
come	came	come	coming
do	did	done	doing
draw	drew	drawn	drawing
drive	drove	driven	driving
eat	ate	eaten	eating
fall	fell	fallen	falling
fight	fought	fought	fighting
flee	fled	fled	fleeing
fly	flew	flown	flying
forget	forgot	forgotten	forgetting
get	got	got or gotten	getting
go	went	gone	going
grow	grew	grown	growing
hang (to put to death)	hanged	hanged	hanging
hang (to suspend)	hung	hung	hanging
hide	hid	hidden	hiding
know	knew	known	knowing
leave	left	left	leaving
lie	lay	lain	lying
pay	paid	paid	paying
read	read	read	reading
ride	rode	ridden	riding
run	ran	run	running
send	sent	sent	sending
set	set	set	setting
shake	shook	shaken	shaking
sing	sang	sung	singing
speak	spoke	spoken	speaking
strike	struck	struck	striking
take	took	taken	taking
tear	tore	torn	tearing
throw	threw	thrown	throwing
wear	wore	worn	wearing
write	wrote	written	writing

Exhibit 4.4
Principal Parts of Irregular Verbs
This table shows the principal parts of some irregular verbs.
Thinking Critically. *How does knowing these irregular verbs improve your communications with others?*

4.3 Self-Assessment E

Check the following sentences for any errors in the use of verb tenses. Write *OK* if the sentence is correct. Rewrite the sentence correctly if it contains errors. *Hint:* Remember that a past tense form never has a helper and that a past participle or a present participle always has a helper!

1. Sue, of course, spoken about her trip to Africa many times. _____

    _____

2. Monica had began her research paper weeks before her instructor assigned it to her. _____

3. Jason has went to the post office to get his package. _____

4. Ask Liz if she seen Mary's personnel folder. _____

5. The prosecutor knowed the facts before the trial. _____

6. He stood at the door and knocked. _____

7. Travel expenses have decreased during the last three months. _____

KEY POINT

Only the verb *to be* has three present tense forms (*am,* is, and *are*) and two past tense forms (*was* and *were*). All other verbs, regular and irregular, have only two present tense forms and one past tense form.

Being Verbs

The being verbs are the forms of the verb *to be*. They show no action. Study the present tense and the past tense forms that follow:

Present Tense	Past Tense
I am	I was
you are	you were
he ⎫	he ⎫
she ⎬ is	she ⎬ was
it ⎭	it ⎭
we are	we were
you are	you were
they are	they were

As you see, there are three present tense forms: *am, is,* and *are*. The two past tense forms are *was* and *were*.

Verb Phrases with Forms of *To Be*. As you saw earlier in this section, verb phrases are formed by using helping verbs with (1) the infinitive form *be*, (2) the past participle form *been*, or (3) the present participle form *being*. Some examples are:

*   The infinitive form *be* with a helping verb: *will be, shall be, may be, can be, would be, might be,* and so on.
*   The past participle *been* with a helping verb: *has been, have been, had been, will have been, shall have been, could have been, might have been,* and so on.
*   The present participle *being* with a helping verb: *am being, is being, are being, was being,* and *were being*.

Try to memorize the eight forms of the verb *to be*: *am, is, are, was, were,* a helper plus *be,* a helper plus *been,* and a helper plus *being.* Because being verbs are so often used as helping verbs, be careful to distinguish between being verbs that are helpers and being verbs that are main verbs in the phrase. Some examples are:

- Brendan should have been here by now. (The verb phrase is *should have been,* and the main verb is *been.* This verb phrase is a being verb.)
- That contract should have been signed. (Now, the verb phrase is *should have been signed. Should have been* is only a helping verb. The main verb is *signed.* Only the helping verb is a being verb.)
- Brian Patrick is the vice president of technology. He was formerly the director of technical services. (Both *is* and *was* are being verbs. There are no helping verbs.)

4.3 Self-Assessment F

Write the verbs and verb phrases in the following sentences. Identify each being verb that is a main verb by writing *B* next to the verb.

1. Our company is proud of its community volunteer participation. _____

2. Incidentally, the jury has been deliberating for over a month. _____

    _____

3. Mario Gomez was employed as a physician's assistant. _____

4. Both Ms. Burten and Mrs. Webb have been members of the advisory board for five years. _____

5. Most citizens, however, have been sympathizing with the defendant.

    _____

6. Joseph, the industrial engineer for our company, is in a meeting. _____

Were **Instead of** *Was.*   Good writing requires that we sometimes use *were* instead of *was* after *if, as if, as though,* and *wish.* Whenever such statements describe (1) something that is highly doubtful or impossible or (2) something contrary to fact or simply not true, use *were* instead of *was.* If, on the other hand, the statement is true or could be true, as often happens after the word *if,* then do not substitute *were* for *was.* Some examples are:

- We wish it were possible for us to predict future stock prices, but SEC regulations prohibit us from making such claims. (It is not possible. Therefore, *were* is correct.)
- If I were you, I would purchase this stock while it is still selling at 32. (Of course, I am not you—thus *were* is correct.)
- Mr. Webber acts as if he were the only candidate for the position. (Mr. Webber is not the only candidate for the position, so this statement is contrary to fact and takes the verb *were.*)
- If Hannah was here earlier, she probably left a message with her assistant. (Hannah could indeed have already been here; thus, this statement could be true. Do not substitute *were* for *was.*)

4.3 Self-Assessment G

Check the following sentences for any errors in the use of verb tenses. Write *OK* if the sentence is correct. If it contains errors, circle any error(s) and write the correction(s) on the line provided.

1. At times Zach acts as if he is the only athlete in the state! _____

2. If I were president of the United States, I would make some drastic changes. _____

3. If Kristen were at work this morning, I certainly did not see her. _____

4. Andrew sometimes acts as if he was at a party instead of at work. _____

5. She has said that if she was younger, she would study forensic medicine.

    _____

Lie, Lay; Sit, Set; Rise, Raise

Just as we saw with the being verbs, the verbs *lie* and *lay, sit* and *set,* and *rise* and *raise* deserve extra attention. To be able to use these verbs correctly, you must first understand the distinction between transitive and intransitive verbs.

Transitive Verbs.   A **transitive verb** is a verb that has an object or a receiver of the verb's action. To find that object, say the verb and ask "What?" or "Whom?" The answer to that question is the direct object. If a direct object follows a verb, that verb is transitive. Some examples are:

KEY POINT

Transitive verbs have direct objects that answer the question "What?" and indirect objects that answer the question "To whom?" or "For whom?"

- Laura accepted Ken's gift. (Say the verb: *accepted.* Ask "What?" or "Whom?" Accepted what? Answer: Accepted *Ken's gift.* The object of the verb *accepted* is *gift.* Use the answer to determine whether the verb is transitive. Yes, *accepted* is transitive because it has an object, *gift.*)

- Ms. Drake invited Delores to the business luncheon. (Say the verb: *invited.* Ask "What?" or "Whom?" Invited whom? Answer: Invited *Delores.* The object of the verb *invited* is *Delores.* Transitive? Yes, *invited* is a transitive verb because it has an object, *Delores.*)

A **direct object** is a person or thing that directly receives the action of the verb. An **indirect object** is a person or thing that indirectly receives the action of the verb. The indirect object tells "to whom" or "for whom" something is done. Note that an indirect object does not appear without a direct object. Also, the indirect object will always appear before the direct object and is usually a person or persons rather than a thing. Some examples are:

- The flight attendant served the passengers a snack. (Say the verb: *served.* Ask "What?" or "Whom?" Served what? Answer: Served *a snack.* The object of the verb served is *snack.* Transitive? Yes, *served* is a transitive verb because it has an object, *snack.* If *snack* is the direct object, what is *passengers*? *Passengers* appears before the direct object, it refers to persons, and it answers the question "to whom?" *Passengers* is the indirect object.)

- Kelly gave the trainee the laboratory key. (Say the verb: *gave*. Ask "What?" or "Whom?" Gave what? Answer: Gave *the laboratory key.* The object of the verb *gave* is *laboratory key.* Transitive? Yes, *gave* is a transitive verb because it has an object, *laboratory key.* If *laboratory key* is the direct object, what is *trainee? Trainee* appears before the direct object, qualifies as a person, and answers the question "to whom?" *Trainee* is the indirect object.)

Sometimes the subject rather than the object of the sentence serves as the receiver of the verb's action. You can identify transitive verbs that are used this way because they include a being verb helper and a past participle. Some examples are:

- The award should have been given to Grace. (Do you have a being verb helper? Do you have a past participle? The answer to both questions is yes. Therefore, this verb is transitive. What receives the action? *the award.*)
- The concert was canceled, according to Gail. (Again, we have a being verb helper, *was,* and a past participle, *canceled.* Thus, we know that the subject, *concert,* receives the action of the verb. What was canceled? *the concert. Was canceled* is a transitive verb.)
- Marilyn has been nominated to the Executive Committee. (What is the verb in this sentence? Is it transitive? If so, explain why.)

Intransitive Verbs. Verbs that do not have objects are **intransitive verbs.** Being verbs never have objects. Therefore, being verbs are never transitive; they are always intransitive. Some examples are:

KEY POINT
Intransitive verbs do not have objects.

- Elizabeth Bordieu visits very often. (Visits what? Visits whom? No answer. *Visits* is an intransitive verb.)
- Wilma Vanderford will leave at 8 p.m., according to her itinerary. (The verb *will leave* has no object; it is an intransitive verb.)

4.3 Self-Assessment H

Identify the verbs and verb phrases in the following sentences. Label each verb or verb phrase as *B* for being, *T* for transitive, or *I* for intransitive.

1. Has Marie-Clair told Gracie about the storm damage? _____

2. Both of them have apparently left for the day. _____

3. As always, Tom Jones has been very helpful in getting employees to donate blood. _____

4. A new principal had been appointed as of May 1. _____

5. Celeste and Maria will be at the clinic by 7 a.m. each morning. _____

6. The documentary will be televised on May 5. _____

Identify the objects and label them as either indirect objects *IO* or direct objects *DO*. Write your answers in the space provided.

7. Lauren Henderson sent him a confirmation by e-mail. _____

_____

8. Blake sold books and magazines to help finance his education. _____

_____

9. The control tower gave the pilot the latest weather report. _____

_____

10. The manager presented Jillian and Justin awards for volunteerism.

_____

Now, review carefully the principal parts of the irregular verbs *dive, eat, lie, lay, sit, set, rise, raise,* and *wear.*

Present Tense	Past Tense	Past Participle	Present Participle	Infinitive
dive	dove	dove	diving	to dive
eat	ate	eaten	eating	to eat
lie	lay	lain	lying	to lie
lay	laid	laid	laying	to lay
sit	sat	sat	sitting	to sit
set	set	set	setting	to set
rise	rose	risen	rising	to rise
raise	raised	raised	raising	to raise
wear	wore	worn	wearing	to wear

 Memory Hook

Now that you have learned to distinguish between transitive and intransitive verbs, you will have an easier time using *lie* and *lay, sit* and *set,* and *rise* and *raise.* The letter *i* is the key. Use the *i* in intransitive to remember that the *i* verbs—*lie, sit,* and *rise*—are intransitive and, therefore, do not have objects. The other three verbs—*lay, set,* and *raise*—are all transitive.

One common trap is to confuse *lay* in its present tense form with *lay* as the past tense form of *lie.* How can you tell which is which? You can tell by remembering what you have learned about transitive verbs. Look at the following examples:

- Last Monday, Joy (lay/laid) her card on the receptionist's desk.
- After jogging, I usually (lie/lay) down for about 20 minutes.
- Yesterday I (lie/lay) down for only five minutes or so.

Analyze the above sentences. Does the verb in the first sentence above have an object? Yes, *card.* Therefore, a transitive verb is needed. As you just learned, *laid* is the past tense form of the transitive verb *to lay,* so *laid* is correct. In the second sentence, is there an object? No. *Down* is not an object; it is an adverb. Here you need a form of the verb *to lie,* so the answer is *lie—I lie down.* In the third sentence, the word *yesterday* shows that the past tense is needed. Does the verb have a direct object? Answer: no. Thus, the correct answer is *lay,* the past tense form of *lie,* an intransitive verb.

As you see, some thinking and analysis are needed when choosing among the forms of *lie* and *lay.* Do not choose hastily.

Exhibit 4.5
Coming Together
Read the following sentence: "Please raise and sing the national anthem." ***Thinking Critically.*** *What is wrong with the use of the verb raise?*

Note the example using *raise* in **Exhibit 4.5.** Now, let's apply the same principles to the transitive verbs *set* and *raise* and to the intransitive verbs *sit* and rise.

- Rhoda and Willette (sit/set) the flowers on the windowsill before they left for lunch. (Is an object needed here? Yes. Which is the transitive verb? *set.* Set what? Set *the flowers.*)

- As soon as the temperature (rises/raises), the air conditioner will automatically go on. (What is needed, a transitive verb or an intransitive verb? Intransitive, because the verb has no object in this sentence. Which, then, is the intransitive verb? *rises.*)

4.3 Self-Assessment I

Practice your ability to use the verbs *lie, lay, sit, set, rise,* and *raise.* Write the correct verb for each sentence.

1. The disks that you were looking for had been (lain/laid) carelessly on a table in the break room. _____

2. Please (rise/raise) when the national anthem is played. _____

3. Mr. Nelson will (rise/raise) the roof when he hears about this quality control problem. _____

4. Ask the movers to (sit/set) the lamp on the table. _____

5. When she works on special design proposals, Bethany usually (sits/sets) at the computer in my office. _____

6. According to my new contract, my salary has been (risen/raised) by about 10 percent. _____

7. When you print this special report, you should (sit/set) both margins for 2 inches. _____

8. Because Jeremy felt ill, he (lay/laid) down after dinner. _____

Review of Key Terms

1. What is a *verb tense*? What are the four principal parts of a verb? _____
   _____
   _____
   _____

2. What is the difference between a *transitive verb* and an *intransitive verb*? _____
   _____
   _____

Editing Practice

Spelling Alert!   Select the correct word for each sentence.

3. Ernesto stated that he had the (capital/capitol) to start a restaurant.
   _____

4. The lifetime warranty is the (principal/principle) reason that we are buying our tools from your company. _____

5. The campaign cost cannot (exceed/accede) $20,000. _____

6. We have (all ready/already) printed 500 copies of the brochure. _____

Practical Application

Verb Tenses

7. Identify the verb phrases in the following sentences. Then, underline the main verb and identify it as past participle, *PP*; or present participle, *PT*.

   a. The merger agreement should be signed by today.
   b. Sarah is requesting a raise.
   c. Heather is preparing a revised itinerary.
   d. Joyce will be recognized for 35 years of service.

   _____
   _____
   _____
   _____

8. Identify the verb tenses in each pair of sentences. Then, in a group, explain the differences.

   a. Kathleen flew to Mexico./Kathleen has flown to Mexico.
   b. I will hire a replacement for Sherry./I will have hired a replacement for Sherry.

   _____
   _____

Discussion Point

Interpreting Details

9. How are the six verb tenses for regular verbs formed? _____

_____

_____

_____

_____

_____

10. How does a writer know if he or she should use *were* or *was* after *if, as if, as though,* and *wish*? _____

_____

SECTION OBJECTIVES

When you have finished Section 4.4, you will be able to:

- State the basic rule of predicate agreement.

- Explain how to determine whether a collective noun is singular or plural.

- Describe subjects other than collective nouns that may be either singular or plural.

- Identify relative-pronoun clauses and their antecedents.

WHY IT'S IMPORTANT

Subject-verb agreement is something you probably don't think about on a daily basis. However, if you hear someone say, "he don't," it sticks out as incorrect. This section will help you use predicate agreement correctly.

KEY TERMS

- predicate agreement
- collective noun
- relative pronoun

Predicate Agreement

Essential Principles

Popular songs, television shows, and movies do little to avoid subject-verb agreement errors such as *he don't* and *I been*. As a result, listeners and viewers hear such errors over and over so often that they may start to believe that *he don't* and *I been* are grammatically correct.

They are not. Pay special attention to the subject-verb agreement rules to make sure you avoid such errors in your speaking and writing. In Section 4.1 of this chapter, you learned about predicates and simple subjects. Now let's review how these elements are related.

Basic Agreement Rule

Predicate agreement means that a **predicate** must **agree** with its simple subject in number and in person. This statement is the basic rule of agreement for all sentences. Remember, a complete predicate includes a complete verb, its complement, and any modifiers. Generally speaking, the complete predicate contains the complete verb and all the words that come after it. The verb within this complete predicate must agree with the subject of the sentence in both number and person. In addition, if the predicate includes any pronouns that refer back to the subject, those pronouns must also agree with the subject in both number and person.

Agreement of Subject and Verb. Note how the following verbs agree in number with their subjects in the following sentences:

- Jim Wisenberg wants to approve the proposal Monday. (The verb *wants* agrees with the subject, *Jim Wisenberg*—both are singular.)

- Jim Wisenberg, our manager, wants to approve the proposal Monday. (Neither the subject nor the verb has changed. *Wants* agrees with *Jim Wisenberg*.)

- Two managers want to approve the proposal Monday. (Now the subject is the plural, *managers*. The plural form of the verb, *want*—not *wants*—is correct.)

Agreement of Pronoun with Subject. If the *complete predicate* includes a pronoun that refers to the subject, that pronoun also must agree with the subject in number. Some examples are:

- Mr. Gaines wants to change his office carpet. (The singular pronoun *his* agrees with the singular subject, *Mr. Gaines.*)

- Mrs. Redmond is eager to receive her cash bonus. Mr. and Mrs. Redmond are eager to receive their cash bonuses. (*Her* agrees with the singular subject, *Mrs. Redmond.* In the second sentence, *their* agrees with the plural subject, *Mr. and Mrs. Redmond.*)

4.4 Self-Assessment A

Choose the correct verbs and pronouns in the following sentences.

1. The tour group (has/have) changed (his/her/its/their) destination since our Thursday meeting with (his/her/its/their) directors. _____

2. The Neal Eye Center (is/are) regarded as a leader in (his/her/its/their) specialty. _____

3. John Rudasill (wants/want) to close (his/her/its/their) savings account. ___
   _____

4. Mary O'Leary, one of our senior associates, (is/are) planning to liquidate (his/her/its/their) company stock before (he/she/it/they) purchases a home at the beach. _____

5. The Werner Corporation (does/do) not usually disclose (his/her/its/their) financial statements. _____

6. Both accountants (is/are) going to bring (his/her/its/their) laptops with (him/her/it/them). _____

Memory Hook

Although plural nouns usually end in _s_ or _es_, an _s_ ending on a verb indicates that it is a singular verb. To help you recall this fact, remember that the word singular has an _s_; the word _plural_ does not.

Singular Noun and Verb	Plural Noun and Verb
The student wants	The students want
One associate has	All associates have
Mrs. McMurry is	Mr. and Mrs. McMurry are

Simple-Subject Agreement Problems

The most common problems concerning agreement of subjects and verbs are reviewed in the following discussion. Study them carefully.

Inverted Sentences. Agreement problems most often arise when the subject is difficult to identify, as in sentences with inverted word order—where the verb precedes the subject. An example is:

Inverted Word Order
- On your desk (is/are) the necklaces. (At first glance, the subject and verb may appear to be "desk is," but a closer look shows that the subject of this inverted sentence is _necklaces_. The correct verb is _are_.)

oops!

Set, not *Sit*

When the courier arrives this afternoon, please ask him to sit the package at the front desk. (set—incorrect usage of a transitive verb)

KEY POINT

In sentences starting with *there*, the true subject follows the being verb and determines the number of the verb.

Other situations in which sentences are in inverted order include questions and sentences beginning with *there*.

Questions
- Are the necklaces on the desk? (Here the subject, *necklaces*, comes after the verb, *are*, because the sentence asks a question.)

Sentences Beginning with *There*
- There (is/are) still several vacancies. (Until you identify the subject, *vacancies*, you cannot choose the correct verb, *are*.)
- Do you know whether there (is/are) additional elevators in the hotel? (The simple subject of the dependent clause "whether there (is/are) additional elevators in the hotel?" is *elevators*. Therefore, *are* is the correct verb.)

Other examples include sentences beginning with *there has been* and *there have been*.

Intervening Phrases and Clauses. Another construction that may confuse the writer or speaker is one in which words separate the subject from its verb. Again, the trick is to identify the simple subject. Some examples are:

- The reason for the delays (is/are) that wind damaged the amphitheater. (The subject is the singular noun *reason*. Therefore, the correct verb is *is*. Although the plural word *delays* immediately precedes the verb, *delays* is not the subject of the verb. *Delays* is part of the prepositional phrase *for the delays*.)
- The business manager, who must sign all expense forms submitted by our executives, (has, have) restricted the travel budgets for everyone. (The subject is *business manager*, not *executives*. Therefore, the correct verb is *has*.)

4.4 Self-Assessment B

Check the following sentences for any errors in simple-subject agreement. Write *OK* if a sentence is correct. Be sure to identify the subject for each sentence. If it contains errors, circle any error(s) and write the correction(s) on the line provided.

1. When we checked the telephone directory, we found that there is only five area codes for that state. _____

2. The lawn, except for the wooded areas, are to be seeded next month.

   _____

3. Are you sure that there's no more than three stoplights within two miles of the proposed mall? _____

4. Our entire company, which consists of more than two thousand employees, are eager to participate in the contest to conserve resources. _____

5. There are, as you told me earlier, several explanations for increased absenteeism during January. _____

6. Did you know that there's a few stubborn individuals who wash their cars when conservation is mandated? _____

Pronoun Agreement with Common-Gender Nouns. When the gender of a noun is clearly masculine (man, father, brother, son) or clearly feminine (woman, mother, sister, daughter), choosing between the pronouns *he* or *she, him* or *her* is no problem. Common-gender nouns are those that can be either masculine or feminine, such as *employee, student, teacher, officer, owner, secretary,* and so on. The traditional rule has been to use masculine pronouns to represent common-gender nouns. However, good communicators today avoid using masculine pronouns to refer to common-gender nouns. Instead, they use pronoun combinations such as *he* or *she, him* or *her,* and *his* or *her* to avoid suggesting either masculine or feminine gender. Some examples are:

- Every student knows his or her role in the upcoming tornado drill. (*His or her* agrees with the common-gender noun *student.*)
- An instructor must be sure that he or she is familiar with the safety regulations. (*He or she* agrees with the common-gender noun *instructor.*)

When such combinations are used too often, they make the message difficult to read. In such instances, consider using plurals to avoid the need for pronoun combinations.

- Instructors must be sure that they are familiar with the safety regulations. (*They* agrees with the plural *instructors.*)

Indefinite-Pronoun Subject. The indefinite pronouns *any one, anybody, anyone, anything, each, either, every, everybody, everyone, every one, everything, neither, no one, nobody, nothing, somebody, someone,* and *something* are always singular. When they are used as subjects and when they modify other subjects, their predicates must be singular. Some examples are:

- Each of the printers has a 10-foot cable that connects it to the computer. (The singular verb has and the pronoun *it* agree with the subject *each.*)
- Each printer has a 10-foot cable that connects it to the computer. (Here *each* modifies the subject, *printer.* In this case too, *each* is singular.)
- Anyone in your precinct who wants to volunteer his or her time should be sure he or she registers. (*Wants, his* or *her, he* or *she,* and *registers* are all singular and agree with the singular indefinite pronoun *anyone.*)

Memory Hook

To remember the indefinite pronouns, memorize the phrase "All employees need salaries." The indefinite pronouns are listed beneath the word in the phrase that shares the same first letter.

All	Employees	Need	Salaries
anybody	everybody	nobody	somebody
anyone	everyone	—	someone
anything	everything	nothing	something
any one	every one	no one	—
—	either	neither	—
—	every	—	—
—	each	—	—

4.4 Self-Assessment C

Check the following sentences for any agreement errors in the use of indefinite pronouns. Write *OK* if the sentence is correct. For each sentence, identify the simple subject. If a sentence contains errors, circle any error(s) and write the correction(s) on the line provided.

1. Nobody in these two divisions have submitted his or her objectives for next year. _____

2. Every student is permitted to use the indoor pool, but he must present his identification at the desk when entering. _____

    _____

3. Anyone who wants to volunteer for community service next weekend should complete and return this form to his or her supervisor. _____

    _____

4. Neither of the medical clinics we visited have enough parking for its patients. _____

5. Every manager in this company is sure to want his staff members to participate in the team-building exercise. _____

6. Each of the sales representatives want to get their own company car. ___

    _____

Predicate Agreement with Special Subjects

Remember the basic agreement rule: A predicate must agree with its simple subject in number and in person. As you review some especially troublesome agreement problems, keep this rule in mind.

Collective-Noun Simple Subjects

A **collective noun** is one that refers to a group, or collection, of persons or things. Examples of collective nouns include: *class, jury, audience, department, company, committee,* and *association.* Because a collective noun may be either singular or plural, its correct number may not be easily recognized. Use the following Memory Hook to help you.

Memory Hook

When the *class,* the *jury,* and so on acts as one group, treat the collective noun as singular. When the members of the collective noun act as individuals, treat the noun as plural. In other words, remember: One group is singular. Individuals are plural.

- In a major case, the jury (does/do) not give (its/their) verdict quickly. (Is the jury acting as one group, or are the jury acting as individuals? Answer: as one group. Therefore, treat *jury* as a singular noun: ". . . the jury does not give its verdict quickly.")
- The jury (is/are) arguing about the charges. (Is the jury acting as one group, or are the jury acting as individuals? In arguing, they would be acting as individuals. Treat *jury* as a plural noun: "The jury are arguing about the charges."

4.4 Self-Assessment D

Check the following sentences for any subject-verb agreement errors. Write *OK* if the sentence is correct. If it contains errors, circle any error(s) and write the correction(s) on the line provided.

1. The college faculty was questioned individually concerning their views on the matter. _____

2. The college faculty was debating the issue among themselves. _____
   _____

3. The college faculty do not change its constitution without a two-thirds majority vote. _____

4. The committee are meeting this afternoon. _____

5. The biology class are leaving for a field trip on Friday afternoon.
   _____

6. The passengers were told that there would be a weather delay. _____
   _____

7. The jury was discussing the evidence among themselves. _____
   _____

Part, Portion, or Amount Subjects

Other subjects that may be either singular or plural are those that refer to a part, a portion, or an amount of something. Thus, *all, some, half, two-thirds* (or any fraction), and *none* may be either singular or plural depending on the nouns they refer to. The noun may belong to an "of" phrase. To decide, find the answer to "Part of what?" "Portion of what?" "Amount of what?" Use the complete subject, not the simple subject, for your answer. Some examples are:

- Some of the condominium (has/have) been remodeled. (Use *condominium has.* Some refers to the singular condominium in the prepositional phrase *of the condominium.*)
- Some of the condominiums (has/have) been remodeled. (Use *condominiums have.*) Here, some refers to more than one condominium and takes the plural verb *have.*

Memory Hook

Use the following sentence to help you remember words that are used as indefinite-amount subjects:

People at NASA eat M&Ms a Fraction of the time.

N –None

A –Any

S –Some

A –All

M –More

M –Most

F –Fractions

A Number, *the* Number

A number is always plural. *The number* is always singular. Note that an adjective before *number* has no effect on the choice. Note also that articles, which are adjectives, affect the choice. However, the adjective *large* has no effect. Some examples are:

- A large number of associates have requested vision insurance. (Use *have,* because *a number* is always plural.)
- The number of associates is increasing. (*The number* is always singular, so *is* is correct.)

4.4 Self-Assessment E

Check the following sentences for any agreement errors in the use of *a* number and *the* number. Write *OK* if the sentence is correct. If it contains errors, circle any error(s) and write the correction(s) on the line provided.

1. Some of the tools, as Sheila noted, has already begun to rust. _____
   _____

2. The number of volunteers have risen to ten. _____

3. None of our tents was damaged by the heavy rain and wind. _____
   _____

4. Nearly two-thirds of the offices was affected by power outages during the ice storm. _____

5. A number of workers is concerned about personal safety issues in our parking lot. _____

6. Some of the camping equipment, Don told me, was not adequately inspected before the expedition. _____

Predicate Agreement with Compound Subjects

To complete your study of predicate agreement, you will now work on predicate agreement with compound subjects—that is, two or more subjects joined by *and, or,* or *nor*—and one other predicate agreement problem: agreement with the **relative pronouns** *who, that,* and *which.*

Subjects Joined by *And*

A compound subject joined by *and* is plural and must take a plural verb. Some examples are:

- Anne and Robert have filed their tax returns. (The compound subject *Anne and Robert* is plural; the plural verb *have filed* is correct.)
- A video company and a software distributor *have asked* for more information on the property. (The plural form *have asked* is correct because the compound subject is joined by *and.*)

Two exceptions to this rule are possible:

1. If the two nouns joined by *and* refer to one person, then that subject is really singular and takes a singular verb. Some examples are:
   - My business partner and investment adviser is my brother, Mike. (Although the compound subject is joined by *and,* only one person is serving as both business partner and investment adviser. The singular verb *is* is therefore correct.)
   - Strawberries and cream is going to be served for dessert. (One dessert, *strawberries and cream,* is the intended meaning.)

Note that if two different people or two different desserts were intended, the verbs would then be plural. Some examples are:

- My business partner and my investment adviser are not in agreement on this issue. (Two different people are intended.)
- Strawberries and ice cream are among the desserts included in the fixed-price lunch. (Here, two different items on the menu are referred to.)

2. If two or more subjects joined by *and* are modified by *each*, *every*, or *many a*, then the predicate is singular. An example is:

- Each secretary and assistant has been asked to return the completed questionnaire to the personnel department by May 15. Every supervisor and manager is supposed to check the questionnaires. Many a factory, office, and store throughout the country is now following this procedure. (In each sentence, the predicate is singular because the subjects are modified by *each*, *every*, or *many a*. Members of the plural groups are being considered singly.)

4.4 Self-Assessment F

Check the following sentences for any agreement errors in the use of subjects joined by *and*. Write *OK* if the sentence is correct. If it contains errors, circle any error(s) and write the correction(s) on the line provided.

1. Many a lawyer and taxpayer have complained about the complexity of income tax regulations. _____

2. Pancakes and syrup is usually what I want for Saturday breakfast. _____

3. The letter and the envelope is from two different grades of stationery.

   _____

4. Pizza and ice cream is at the top of most children's favorite-foods list.

   _____

5. Every partner and associate in the law firms we contacted are writing to their representatives to show support for the legislation. _____

   _____

6. Each returning patient and new patient are required to complete the medical history form. _____

Subjects Joined by *Or* or *Nor*

For subjects joined by *or* or *nor*, simply match the predicate to the subject that follows *or* or *nor*. Some examples are:

- The owner or her assistants (is/are) going to discuss (her/their) new spring clothing line at the sales meeting tomorrow. (Matching the predicate to the subject that follows *or*, the correct choices are *are* and *their*.)
- The assistants or the owner (is/are) going to discuss (her/their) new winter clothing line at the sales meeting tomorrow. (Now the subject that follows *or* is the singular word *owner*. Therefore, the choices are *is* and *her*.)

- Neither the owner nor her associates (knows/know) where the Italian designer went. (Which subject follows *nor*? The plural *associates*. The choice is therefore *know.*)
- Either the three Japanese couturiers or SmartShirt (is/are) going to present (its/their) collection this afternoon. (The subject that follows *or* is *SmartShirt,* singular; thus, the choices are *is* and *its.*)
- Neither the actors nor the director (is/are) ready for the play. (Matching the predicate to the subject that follows *nor,* the correct choice is *is.*
- Either Sherry or her students (is/are) leaving early. (The subject that follows *or* is *students,* plural; thus, the answer is *are.*

4.4 Self-Assessment G

In the following sentences, select the words in parentheses that match the compound subject.

1. Either the salesclerks or Mrs. Paschal (like/likes) to present (their/her) customers' jewelry in expensive gift wrap. _____

2. Either her associates or Katlin herself (is/are) going to lead the tour to Egypt. _____

3. My sister-in-law or her friends (is/are) interested in purchasing craft items for (her/their) stores. _____

4. Rosa Delgado or her buyers (has/have) completed (her/their) garment selection for the fall season. _____

5. Neither Mrs. Anderson nor the accountants (has/have) volunteered to work Saturday evening to complete the audit. _____

Predicate Agreement in Clauses Introduced by Relative Pronouns

The pronouns *who, that,* and *which* are called *relative pronouns* because they relate to other words, called *antecedents.* The antecedent of the relative pronoun is a noun or a pronoun that is usually immediately before the relative pronoun. Some examples are:

- Maria Lopez is one who strives for perfection. (The relative pronoun is *who,* and its antecedent is *one.*)
- Maria Lopez is one of those who strive for perfection. (The relative pronoun is *who,* and its antecedent is *those.*)
- Maria Lopez is one of those people who strive for perfection all the time. (The relative pronoun is *who,* and its antecedent is the noun immediately before it, *people.*)
- The calculator that is on the shelf works accurately. (If *that* is a relative pronoun, what is its antecedent? *calculator.*)
- This special offer is good until Saturday, which is the last day of our sale. (The relative pronoun *which* refers to *Saturday,* its antecedent.)

Note that in each sentence, the verb in the clause introduced by a relative pronoun agrees with the antecedent.

> **KEY POINT**
>
> Omit the relative pronouns *who, that,* and *which* to make finding the correct verb easy.

relative pronoun

Kirk Watson is one manager who strives for perfect sales figures.

noun and antecedent of *who*

Exhibit 4.6
Subject Verb Agreement
Analyzing which word is the relative pronoun, which word is the verb, and which word is the antecedent can assist you in checking agreement. ***Thinking Critically.*** *What is wrong with the use of the verb in the following sentence?* Tony submitted the reports that was due yesterday.

 ## Memory Hook

To help you choose the correct verb in clauses introduced by a relative pronoun, omit the relative pronoun and use the antecedent as the subject of the clause. For example, omitting the relative pronouns from the preceding (see page 129) bulleted sentences would give:

one . . . strives
those . . . strive
people . . . strive
calculator . . . is
Saturday . . . is

Let's look at some other examples:

- Lisa prefers one of those microwaves that (has/have) rotating shelves inside (its/their) ovens. (By omitting the relative pronoun *that,* you can determine the agreement:
  microwaves . . . have . . . their.)

- Cheryl Asuras is one of those sales representatives who (does/do) (her/their) best selling under pressure. (Omit *who,* and you have sales representatives . . . do . . . their.)

Note: **An exception is a clause preceded by *the only one.* Such clauses must take singular predicates.**

- Nicole is the only one of the members who has cast her vote for the expansion. (*Has* and *her* are correct.)

4.4 Self-Assessment H

Check the following sentences for any agreement errors in the use of clauses introduced by a relative pronoun. Write *OK* if the sentence is correct. If it contains errors, circle any error(s) and write the correction(s) on the line provided.

1. Jane prefers one of those curling irons that has three temperatures. ____
   _____

2. We are ready to admit everyone who has his or her presentation prepared. _____

3. Anybody who qualifies may purchase their uniforms at the sale price. __
   _____

4. Everyone realized that it was too soon to expect preliminary results from the investigation. _____

5. Tomi is one of those insurance sales representatives who personally collect from their clients on a monthly basis. _____

6. Taylor, Inc., is one of those dealerships which has shown an interest in leasing cars and vans. _____

7. Management will soon close one of the several restaurants that is now operating at a loss. _____

8. Zach is one of those accountants who always double-check their figures. _____

9. Mr. Dexter prefers one of those offices that has two windows in it.
   _____

10. Rachel is the only one of the council members who want to change the zoning. _____

Bonus Question

11. What is the rule for predicate agreement with compound subjects? ____
    _____
    _____
    _____
    _____

Review of Key Terms

1. What is the basic rule of *predicate agreement*? _____
   _____

2. How can a writer determine if a *collective noun* is singular or plural?
   _____
   _____

Editing Practice

Proofreading Alert!　You typed the following copy quickly but didn't have time to proofread it. Do so now.

3. We appreciate your request for information about the Mountain Top Inn. To answer you questions about convention facilitys, we have enclosed our latest brochure.

   As you will see in the broshure, the Mountain Top Inn can accomodate large groups of people as well as intimate getaways with the same quality service that have made us famous for more than 40 years. _____
   _____
   _____
   _____
   _____
   _____

Practical Application

Subject-Verb Agreement

4. As a team, identify any errors in the use of subject-verb agreement in the following sentences.

   a. Each editor, proofreader, and designer were invited to an open house at the new publishing company.
   b. Don't José know how to use his voice mail?
   c. Some of the shipments from Florida has been delayed by the hurricane season.
   d. Neither the mouse nor the printer cable are with the computer.
   e. A number of people has complained about the defective products.
   _____
   _____
   _____
   _____
   _____

5. As a team, write a paragraph in which you recommend a colleague for a job. Use at least five of the following terms as subjects: *everybody, most, nobody, some, a number, anybody, either, none, all, neither.* _____

_____ _____

Discussion Point

Thinking Critically

6. What are some common problems concerning subject and verb agreement? How can they be avoided? _____

_____

_____

_____

_____

_____

7. Compare the agreement rule for subjects joined by *and* with subjects joined by *or* or *nor.* _____

_____

_____

Chapter 5

Mastering Nouns and Pronouns

Section 5.1
Nouns: Plural Forms

Section 5.2
Nouns and Pronouns:
Possessive Forms

Section 5.3
Pronouns: Nominative
and Objective Forms

Workplace Connection

Learning the basic grammar rules for forming possessives and plurals of nouns will help you communicate more effectively with prospective employers. Employers judge applicants based on their ability to speak and write correctly.

CHAPTER OBJECTIVES

When you have completed this chapter, you should be able to:

- Use nouns and pronouns appropriately.
- State the rules for using apostrophes.
- Give examples of nominative and objective pronoun forms.

Nouns: Plural Forms

Essential Principles

Written communication needs to be precise to communicate effectively. This is especially true when forming plurals. For example, when we say "several of our *customers*," or "this *customer's* opinion," or "all *customers'* orders," we do not ordinarily think of the differences in the written forms of *customers, customer's,* and *customers'*. We pronounce all three words in the same way. In writing, however, these three words are not interchangeable. Each has its own distinct meaning and use.

> *Customers* is a plural.
>
> *Customer's* is a singular possessive.
>
> *Customers'* is a plural possessive.

In this section and the next, you will master the use of plurals and possessives.

Plurals of Common Nouns

Add "s" to most common nouns to form their plurals. Some examples are:

Singular	Plural
service	services
computer	computers
employee	employees
valley	valleys

Add "es" to nouns that end in *s, sh, ch, x,* and *z* to form their plurals. Some examples are:

Singular	Plural
class	classes
dash	dashes
porch	porches
tax	taxes

Plurals of Proper Nouns

Add "s" to most proper nouns to form their plurals. Some examples are:

Singular	Plural
Mr. Rivero	the Riveros
Mrs. Amalfi	the Amalfis
Ms. Weinberg	the Weinbergs

Add "es" to proper nouns that end in *s, sh, ch, x,* and *z*. Some examples are:

Singular	Plural
Mrs. Valdez	the Valdezes
Michael Douglas	the Douglases
Mr. Lynch	the Lynches
Ms. Fox	the Foxes
Jane Herz	the Herzes

Plurals of Compound Nouns

KEY POINT

Form the plural of a compound noun by making the main word in the compound plural.

A **compound noun** is a noun that consists of two or more words. Compound nouns may be written with a hyphen, with a space between them, or as one word. Make the main word, the most important word in the compound, plural. For example, a *bulletin board* is a board on which we post bulletins. The main word is *board*; therefore, the plural is *bulletin boards,* not *bulletins board.* Some other examples are:

Singular	Plural
mother-in-law	mothers-in-law
general manager	general managers
major general	major generals
editor in chief	editors in chief
chief of staff	chiefs of staff
timetable	timetables

Plurals of Common Nouns Ending in "y"

oops!

Trouble with the In-law's

Jane did not have a good relationship with her sister-in-laws so she did not attend the recent family gathering.

(sisters-in-law—The most important noun, *sisters,* is plural.)

Add "s" to form the plural if there is a *vowel* immediately before the *y*. Some examples are:

Singular	Plural
attorney	attorneys
key	keys
valley	valleys
convoy	convoys

Change the *y* to *i* and add "es" if there is a *consonant* immediately before the *y*. Some examples are:

Singular	Plural
company	companies
secretary	secretaries
territory	territories
salary	salaries

Note that *proper nouns* ending in *y* do not follow these rules. For proper nouns, simply add "s" to form the plural. Some examples are:

Singular	Plural
Ms. Langley	the Langleys
Mrs. McCarthy	the McCarthys
one Amy	two Amys

Exhibit 5.1 explains the rules for plural nouns.

Plural Nouns		
Endings	**Noun Types**	**Plural Forms**
Ends in letters other than *s, sh, ch, x, z*	Common, proper	Add "s"
Ends in *s, sh, ch, x, z*	Common, proper	Add "es"
All endings	Compound	Make *main* word plural (see two rules above)
Vowel immediately before *y*	Common noun ending in "y"	Add "s"
Consonant immediately before *y*	Common noun ending in "y"	Change *y* to *i* and add "es"
Proper noun ending in *y*	Proper noun ending in "y"	Add "s"

Exhibit 5.1
Plural Nouns
Compound nouns made up of two or more words can have all types of endings. ***Thinking Critically.*** *How can you decide which word is the main word in a compound noun?*

5.1 Self-Assessment A

Check the following sentences for any errors in the use of plurals. Write *OK* if the sentence is correct. Circle any error(s) and write the correction(s) on the line provided.

1. The last three editor in chiefs were excellent grammarians. _____

2. David and Heather are the owners of two companys. _____

3. Krispy Kreme stores, which started in North Carolina in 1937, are now in seven countrys. _____

4. Three new district attornies were hired last week. _____

5. Two countys order computer supplies from these three companys. _____
_____

6. Otto's Camera Shop has two wide-angle lenss on sale this week. _____

7. Two Marcies—Marcy Satterwhite and Marcy Pasierb—are in this class.
_____

8. Miss Aguirre has two daughters-in-law who live in Texas. _____

9. *USA Today* has advertised for two editor in chiefs positions. _____
_____

Special Plurals

Forming certain plurals is a problem for writers because these plurals do not follow the rules. For example, how would you form the plural of the courtesy titles, Mr. and Mrs.?

Going Global

Always Be Courteous

The use of titles (for example, *Mr., Dr., Professor*) is a way of showing respect. Courtesy titles are considered very important in many countries. In Germany, for example, advanced degrees are always acknowledged (for example, *Frau Doktor Miller, Herr Doktor Miller*).

Plurals of Titles with Names

The commonly used courtesy titles and their plurals are:

Singular	Plural
Mr.	Messrs.
Mrs.	Mmes.
Ms.	Mses.
Miss	Misses
Dr.	Drs.

- *Messrs.* is derived from *Messieurs,* the French word for "Misters."
- *Mmes.* is derived from *Mesdames,* the French word for "My ladies."

When forming the title of a name, make *either* the title *or* the name plural, *not both.* Some examples follow. Both plural forms are correct. The trend is to make the last name plural rather than the title. Pluralizing the title is usually reserved for formal usage.

Singular	Plural Title	Plural Name
Ms. Toto	the Mses. Toto	the Ms. Totos
Mr. Werner	the Messrs. Werner	the Mr. Werners
Mrs. Ford	the Mmes. Ford	the Mrs. Fords
Miss Khan	the Misses Khan	the Miss Khans

KEY POINT

To form the plural of a title used with a name, make either the title or the name plural.

Plurals with Apostrophes

In some situations, an **apostrophe** is used to form the plural. Use an apostrophe plus "s," to form plurals of lowercase letters and lowercase abbreviations. Some examples are:

- The *t's* and *f's* on this page are unclear.
- The receptionist handles all c.o.d.'s for our office.

To form plurals of capital letters and abbreviations ending with capital letters add only the lowercase "s." For example, the plural of URL (uniform resource locator), is URLs. An example of a URL is CNN.com. Other examples of such abbreviations are VIPs (very important persons), CEOs (chief executive officers), CDs (compact disks), PCs (personal computers), DVDs (digital video discs), and SUVs (sport utility vehicles). These abbreviations have become commonly accepted words in our culture. They are written in all capitals to show they are abbreviations.

If adding an "s" to form a plural abbreviation would cause confusion, add an apostrophe before the "s." Some examples are:

- He got *A's, I's,* and *U's* on his report—not *As, Is,* and *Us.*

An apostrophe is not required to form plurals in phrases such as *ups and downs, temperatures in the 30s,* and *in the 1990s.*

Plurals with Special Changes

Some nouns form their plurals in an irregular manner. Some examples are:

Singular	Plural
man	men
woman	women
child	children
mouse	mice
goose	geese
shelf	shelves
oasis	oases
ox	oxen

Exhibit 5.2 shows how to make special plurals.

Exhibit 5.2
Special Plurals

Special Plurals	
Title with names	Make either title or name plural—not both.
Plurals of lowercase letters and abbreviations	Add an apostrophe.
Capital letters and abbreviations ending with capital letters	Add an "s."
Confusion if adding only "s"	Add an apostrophe plus "s," e.g., *Ms* vs. *M's*.
Irregular plurals	Use a different word, e.g., *leaf, leaves*.

5.1 Self-Assessment B

Check the following sentences for the correct use of plurals. Write
***OK* if the sentence is correct. Circle any error(s) and write the**
correction(s) on the line provided.

1. Hugo asked us to send these letters to the Misses Smiths. _____
   _____

2. The temperature in Fort Lauderdale during March break is usually in the high 70s. _____

3. Because of her illness, she received two Is for her incomplete courses.
   _____

4. Yes, the Messrs. Gieseler are buying the property on Macey Avenue.

    _____

5. Many woman are senior managers in American companys. _____

    _____

6. Students with current ID's can park at the Getty Center in Los Angeles without making a reservation. _____

7. Please take yesterday's bread and pastries off all the shelfs. _____

8. Two men and two woman partners have joined the firm: Mr. Krantz and Ryan and Ms. Kramer and Sung. _____

9. This year, we will be serving gooses at our Thanksgiving dinner. _____

    _____

10. All the CEO's are giving up their bonuses this fiscal quarter. _____

    _____

Plurals of Nouns Ending in "o"

Add "s" to form the plural of nouns ending in *o* preceded by a vowel. Some examples are:

Singular	Plural
studio	studios
video	videos
ratio	ratios
Oreo	Oreos

Add "es" to form the plural of nouns ending in *o* preceded by a consonant. Some examples are:

Singular	Plural
potato	potatoes
tomato	tomatoes
echo	echoes
hero	heroes
veto	vetoes
cargo	cargoes

Note, there are exceptions to the rule. For example, *casino* becomes *casinos* and *disco,* short for *discotheque,* becomes *discos.* Consult your dictionary when you are unsure of a plural form.

Nouns ending in *o* that relate to music and art form their plurals by adding "s." Some examples are:

Singular	Plural
piano	pianos
alto	altos
solo	solos
oratorio	oratorios

Plurals of Nouns Ending in "f" or "fe"

To form plurals of some nouns ending in *f* or *fe*, simply add "s." Some examples are:

Singular	Plural
plaintiff	plaintiffs
proof	proofs
roof	roofs
safe	safes
belief	beliefs
chief	chiefs

In other cases, change the *f* or *fe* to *v* and add "es." Some examples are:

Singular	Plural
shelf	shelves
half	halves
life	lives
wife	wives
knife	knives
self	selves

5.1 Self-Assessment C

Write the plural forms of the following nouns. If necessary, consult a dictionary.

1. tomato _____

2. logo _____

3. thief _____

4. loaf _____

5. concerto _____

6. gulf _____

7. sheriff _____

8. handkerchief _____

9. volcano _____

10. solo _____

Plurals of Foreign Nouns

There are many nouns in the English language that are of foreign origin, usually borrowed from Latin or ancient Greek. These foreign nouns have become part of our everyday communications. Plurals of these nouns are *not* formed according to the English rules. When unsure, consult your dictionary. Some examples are shown in **Exhibit 5.3.**

Borrowed Plurals

Singular	Plural
addendum	addenda
alumna (female)	alumnae
alumnus (male)	alumni (now being used for both male and female)
analysis	analyses
axis	axes
bacterium	bacteria
crisis	crises
criterion	criteria
datum	data
hypothesis	hypotheses
synthesis	syntheses
syllabus	syllabi

However, some words of foreign origin have two plural forms—the "original" plural form and an English plural form, a plural formed by treating the singular noun as if it were an English word. Some examples are included in **Exhibit 5.4.**

Exhibit 5.4
English and Foreign Plurals
Some words borrowed from Latin and ancient Greek have two plural forms. **_Thinking Critically._** _Which would you probably use in informal writing?_

English and Foreign Plurals

Singular	Foreign Plural	English Plural
appendix	appendices	appendixes*
curriculum	curricula	curriculums*
formula	formulae	formulas*
index	indices	indexes*
medium	media	mediums
memorandum	memoranda	memorandums*
nucleus	nuclei*	nucleuses
stadium	stadia	stadiums*
vertebra	vertebrae*	vertebras
syllabus	syllabi	syllabuses

*Indicates the plural form generally preferred in English usage.

Employability Skills

Writing

The ability to communicate effectively in writing is a core employability skill identified by a national study (SCANS).

Nouns That Are Always Singular or Always Plural

The following nouns are *always singular,* even though they end in *s.* Use a singular verb to agree with a singular noun. Some examples are:

aerobics	aeronautics	civics
economics	genetics	mathematics
molasses	news	physics
statistics		

The following nouns are *always plural*. Use a plural verb to agree with a plural noun. Some examples are:

auspices	antics	belongings
jeans	pants	proceeds
riches	series	scissors
slacks	statistics	thanks
tidings	tongs	

Nouns with One Form

The following nouns have only one form. The noun may be used as either a singular or a plural, depending on the intended meaning. Some examples are:

aircraft	Chinese	corps
deer	French	moose
odds	politics	salmon
sheep	wheat	series

When a number modifies a noun, the subsequent nouns usually have the same form to denote either a singular or a plural number. Some examples are:

four-*score* years	three *thousand* forms
two-*dozen* seniors	five *hundred* applicants

5.1 Self-Assessment D

Check the following sentences for any errors in the use of plurals. Write *OK* if the sentence is correct. Circle any error(s) and write the correction(s) on the line provided.

1. Three editor in chiefs from our organization will attend the national conference next month. _____

2. Professor Bello handed out syllabus to the entire class yesterday. _____ _____

3. The auditor's analyses of the treasurer's records will be completed by Friday. _____

4. Germany's discoes are always busy on Friday and Saturday nights. _____ _____

5. Bacterias are the primary source of spoiled food. _____

6. Our Internet site had over 9,000 hits last month. _____

7. Lake Land College has over 10,000 alumni. _____

8. The local woman' shelter is always in need of blankets and personal use items. _____

9. A civic class is required for graduation. _____

10. These exercises will provide stimuluses to the leg muscles to make them stronger. _____

Review of Key Terms

1. What do the terms *compound noun* and *foreign noun* mean? Give two examples of each. _____

_____

_____

2. Give an example of a *courtesy title.* When would you use this title? ____

_____

_____

Editing Practice

Call an Editor! Supply the correct plurals to complete the following paragraph. Hint: A maid of honor is an unmarried attendant, and a matron of honor is a married attendant.

3. Katja and Jasna Bolinski, twin daughters of Al and Rita Bolinski, were married to John Whitmire and Wade Randolph, respectively, in a double ceremony. The brides chose one ceremony instead of two c_____.

   Because they have always had a close relationship, M_____ Natali and Deirdre Bolinski, the brides' sisters, served as m_____ of h_____. After the wedding, the B_____, parents of the brides, entertained at a reception. The couples will live in adjoining duplex a_____. These adjoining a_____ are on the corner of Washington and Lafayette A_____.

Discussion Point

Thinking Critically

4. When Dan Quayle ran for vice president of the United States, he was embarrassed in a nationally televised program because he could not spell the word *potato.* His confusion arose because of the spelling of the plural form, *potatoes.* Forming plurals of nouns that end in *o* can be difficult. Explain the rule that Mr. Quayle needed to know and give some examples to illustrate your answer. _____

_____

_____

_____

_____

_____

_____

Bonus Question

5. Write the plural forms of the following words: *casino, cargo, oratorio, solo.* _____

Nouns and Pronouns: Possessive Forms

Essential Principles

The **possessive form of nouns and pronouns** is used to show ownership. Errors in the use of the possessive form of nouns and pronouns are common and very noticeable in writing. This section will help you master the correct usage of possessive nouns and pronouns.

An apostrophe is *always* used with a noun to show possession. The following rules will help you place the apostrophe in the correct position to show possession.

Adding an Apostrophe Plus "s"

Add an *apostrophe* plus "s" for:

A Noun That Does Not End in *s*. An example is:

- The man's portfolio and the woman's report are on my desk. (The portfolio *of the man,* or *belonging to the man,* and the report *of the woman,* or *belonging to the woman.* . .)

A Singular Noun Ending in *s*, if the Possessive Form Is Pronounced with an Added Syllable. Some examples are:

- One *witness's* comment was especially effective. My *boss's* recommendation was helpful.

Memory Hook

The possessive word comes *before* the object of possession:

- the *manager's* reports (the reports *of the manager,* or the reports *belonging to the manager*)
- the *students'* assignments (the assignments *of the students,* or the assignments *belonging to the students*)

By separating the ownership words from the objects of ownership, you will be able to apply the rules of possession easily.

SECTION OBJECTIVES

When you have finished Section 5.2, you will be able to:

- Apply the essential principles for forming the possessives of nouns.

- Identify correct possessive forms of compound nouns, of nouns showing joint or separate ownership, and of nouns used before gerunds.

- Use the correct possessive forms of personal pronouns.

WHY IT'S IMPORTANT

We frequently need to indicate separate or joint possession of both tangible and intangible items. This task often presents a challenge, especially in written communications.

KEY TERMS

- possessive form of nouns and pronouns
- gerund

Adding Only an Apostrophe

Add only an apostrophe for:

A Plural Noun That Ends in *s*. Some examples are:

- The *executives'* meeting has been rescheduled. (The meeting *of the executives* . . .)
- Approximately *two months'* time has been allotted for the project. (A time *of* approximately *two months* . . .)
- The *Browns'* new tractor arrived today. (The new tractor *of the Browns* or *belonging to the Browns* . . .)

A Singular Noun Ending in *s*. If the possessive form *is not* pronounced with an added syllable, then add only an apostrophe. Note, this rule applies to proper names that would sound awkward with an extra syllable. An example is:

- Bruce Struthers' promotion will be announced tomorrow.

Exhibit 5.5 reviews the rules for forming possessive nouns.

Forming Possessive Nouns	
Noun Type	**Rule**
Noun (singular or plural) that does not end in *s*	Add an apostrophe plus *s*.
Singular noun that ends in *s* (if possessive form is pronounced with an added syllable e.g., boss's)	Add an apostrophe plus *s*.
Singular noun that ends in *s* (if possessive form is *not* pronounced with an added syllable, e.g., *Jones'*)	Add only an apostrophe.
Plural noun that ends in *s*	Add only an apostrophe.

Exhibit 5.5
Singular and Plural Possessives
In deciding which word names the possessor and which word is the object of possession, ask yourself the following question: ***Thinking Critically.*** *Who or what owns X?* This will help you decide which word is the possessive.

5.2 Self-Assessment A

Check the following sentences for any errors in the use of possessives. Write *OK* if the sentence is correct. Circle any error(s) and write the correction(s) on the line provided.

1. John Rileys' investments have been successful in the last six months. ____

    _____

2. The actress' own account of Hollywood's history will appear in Sunday's newspaper. _____

3. Sam Brown and his friend John Canfield want to rebuild their fathers businesses. _____

4. Womens nutritional needs are discussed in Elinor's article. _____

5. The applicant's résumés are in the folders on your desk. _____

6. All our sales representatives vehicles are leased. _____

7. One accountants report criticized our companys' change in financial procedures. _____

8. Intel Corporations largest division is in an area known as Silicon Forest in Portland, Oregon. _____

Possessive Form of Nouns—Special Cases

As well as knowing the basic rules for forming the possessives of nouns, you need to know how to form the possessives of nouns in the following situations.

Compound Nouns

To form the possessive of a compound noun, make the *last word* possessive. If the last word ends in *s*, add an apostrophe. Otherwise, add an apostrophe plus "s." Some examples are:

- Two *major generals'* recommendations are outlined in this report. (*Major generals,* the compound noun, ends in *s.* To form the possessive, add an apostrophe.)
- My *brother-in-law's* bid was accepted by the City Planning Department. (The compound noun is *brother-in-law.* The last word, *law,* does not end in *s,* so add an apostrophe plus "s.")

KEY POINT

The last word in a compound noun is used to form the possessive of a compound noun (for example, the major generals' reports; the editors in chief's articles).

Joint Ownership and Separate Ownership

Joint Ownership. To show *joint ownership,* when two or more people own the same thing, add an apostrophe, or add an apostrophe plus "s," to the *last part* of the compound. Some examples are:

- *Susan and Randy's father* started this restaurant in 1995. (The father of Susan and Randy is *one person.*)
- *Nancy and Larry's house* is the newest on East Road. (The house belonging to Nancy and Larry is *one thing.*)

Separate Ownership. To show *separate ownership,* add an apostrophe, or add an apostrophe plus "s," to each part of the compound noun. Some examples are:

- *Erin's and George's fathers* started this restaurant in 1995. (Erin's father and George's father are *two different people.*)
- *Irwin's and Vicki's design studios* are in Miami. (The *two design studios* that are separately owned.)

Nouns Used Before a Gerund

A **gerund** is a verb form that ends in *ing* and is used as a noun. A noun or pronoun used immediately before a gerund must be in the possessive. Some examples are:

- *Hal's proofreading* was very helpful to us in meeting the deadline. *His proofreading* was very helpful to us. (The possessive form *Hal's* or *His* is used before the gerund *proofreading.*)
- We were unaware of *Nancy's leaving early.* We were unaware of *her leaving early.* (The possessives *Nancy's* and *her* are needed before the gerund *leaving.*)

The next section provides examples of the possessive forms of personal pronouns such as *my, your, his, her.*

5.2 Self-Assessment B

Check the following sentences for any errors in the use of possessives. Write *OK* if the sentence is correct. Circle any error(s) and write the correction(s) on the line provided.

1. Don and Sylvia's oldest daughter begins college next September. _____

2. Revising the e-mail policy was someone else idea, not Adrians'. _____
   _____

3. As you know, the two vice president's reports contain confidential information. _____

4. Juan and Maria were engaged last week. Juan's and Maria's wedding is planned for next June. _____

5. My two sisters-in-law's parents live in Atlanta. _____

6. John's running is his favorite pastime. _____

7. My mother-in-laws' store is being renovated. _____

8. I find Anitas shouting very upsetting. _____

KEY POINT

Do not use apostrophes with possessive forms of personal pronouns.

Possessive Forms of Personal Pronouns

Possessive forms of nouns always have apostrophes. However, personal pronouns, such as *I, you, he, she, it, we, you, they,* become possessive by:

- Adding an *s* (as in *its*); or
- Changing their spelling (as in *my, mine*).

The possessive forms of personal pronouns are listed in **Exhibit 5.5.** Note, possessive forms of personal pronouns *never* have apostrophes.

Study the following examples that show the correct uses of these forms.

- Valerie asked *her* assistant to revise the report.
- The red Honda Civic is *ours*; the white one is *theirs*.
- Would you please lend me *your* calculator; *mine* is at home.
- The college is holding *its* graduation ceremony next week.
- Is this book *yours*?

Possessive Forms of Pronouns—Special Cases

The possessive pronouns *its, their, theirs, your,* and *whose* are sometimes confused with words that sound similar, called *homophones.*

It, It's. The possessive pronoun *its* means *belonging to it* or *of it.* The contraction *it's* means *it is.* Some examples are:

- This computer monitor is expensive but *its* screen has high resolution. (The possessive pronoun *its* is correct—the screen *belonging to,* or *of,* the computer.)
- I like this monitor because *it's* easier to read. (The contraction *it's* is correct; it stands in place of *it is.*)

Their, There, They're. Confusion arises with this possessive pronoun and its homophones because we pronounce the three words in the same way. However, they have different meanings. *Their* is a possessive pronoun meaning *belonging to them, there* identifies a place, and *they're* is a contraction of *they are.* Some examples are:

- Sally and Mac have moved to *their* new house. (*Their* is a possessive pronoun. Whose new house? Sally and Mac's new house, or *their* new house.)
- *They're* very happy *there.* (*They are* very happy *there*—in that place.)

Personal Pronoun Forms		
Nominative Forms*	**Possessive Forms**	
I	my	mine
you	your	yours
he	his	his
she	her	hers
it	its	its
we	our	ours
you	your	yours
they	their	theirs
who	whose	whose

*For more information on nominative forms, see pages 153 and 154.

Exhibit 5.6
Personal Pronoun Forms
Personal pronouns take the place of people, places, or things. Their possessive forms have no apostrophe. ***Thinking Critically.*** *What is the difference in meaning of your and you're?*

KEY POINT

- *They're* is a contraction of *they are.*
- *There's* is a contraction of *there is.*
- *It's* is a contraction of *it is.*

Who's Who?

Whose in charge of the security at this building?

(*Who's*—the contraction for *who is,* not the possessive pronoun *whose.*)

Theirs, There's. The pronoun *theirs* and the contraction *there's* are pronounced the same way. However, the contraction *there's* means *there is.* Some examples are:

- Is this book *theirs*? (Does this book *belong to them*?)
- *There's* the book we want. (*There is* the book we want.)

Your, You're. The possessive pronoun *your* means *belonging to you.* The contraction *you're* means *you are.* Some examples are:

- Where are you going on *your* vacation? (The vacation *belonging to you.*)
- Jack said *you're* very excited about *your* trip to Mexico. (Jack said *you are* very excited about *your* trip to Mexico.)

Exhibit 5.8 shows possessive pronouns that are easily confused with contractions.

Possessive Pronouns and Homophones	
Possessive Pronouns	**Homophones**
its their theirs your	it's there, they're there's you're
*For more information on nominative forms, see Section 5.3.	

Exhibit 5.8
Possessive Pronouns and Homophones
Some possessive pronouns are easily confused with like-sounding words. ***Thinking Critically.*** *How are the homophones in the table alike and different from their possessive pronouns?*

Whose, Who's.   The possessive form of the relative pronoun *who* is *whose*. *Who's* is a contraction that means *who is* or *who has*. Some examples are:

- Do you know *whose* briefcase this is? (Do you know *to whom this briefcase belongs*?)
- Do you know *who's* going to the meeting? (Do you know *who is* going to the meeting?)
- Do you know *who's* applied for the position? (Do you know *who has* applied for the position?)

5.2 Self-Assessment C

Check the following sentences for any errors in the use of possessive personal pronouns. Write *OK* if the sentence is correct. Circle any error(s) and write the correction(s) on the line provided.

1. Do you think theres enough evidence to fire him? _____
   _____

2. Whose going with you to the United Way meeting? _____
   _____

3. They're going to move while her sister is in Europe. _____

4. Where does the symphony hold it's Gala? _____

5. Please let me know when your ready to start a walking program. _____
   _____

6. Many of our members prefer to communicate by e-mail because its easier. _____

7. As Mr. Hicks explained, theirs only one section of Financial Accounting offered this summer. _____

8. Whose at the Tech Prep Steering Committee meeting this morning from our department? _____

Assessment   Section 5.2

Review of Key Terms

1. What is the function of the possessive form of nouns and pronouns? Use an example to illustrate your answer. _____
   _____
   _____

2. "A noun or pronoun used before a gerund must be in the possessive form." Please explain this statement. _____
   _____

Editing Practice

Proofreading Alert! Check the following sentences for any errors in the use of possessives. Write *OK* if a sentence is correct. Rewrite the sentence if it contains errors.

3. Each managers' suggestion was discussed in detail. _____

   _____

4. Louise Havel, whose an excellent copywriter, has developed many award-winning slogans for our products. _____

   _____

5. I think that the womens' locker room should be renovated. _____

   _____

6. Carole's and Diane's interior design business is very successful. _____

   _____

7. Please let me know by Friday if your interested in joining the project team. _____

8. Denise and Chong's bosses are both at the weekly meeting. _____

   _____

9. We're not sure if its possible to fix this network problem today. _____

   _____

10. Everyone agreed that Jill Carters credentials are impressive. _____

    _____

11. Mickey's decision to check the e-mail saved us from an embarrassing situation. _____

12. I was surprised to find this message from the presidents assistant when I returned from vacation. _____

    _____

Discussion Point

Thinking Critically

13. Look up the meaning of *ownership* and *possess* in your dictionary. Using this information, explain the concept of ownership. How does this concept relate to the possessive forms studied in this section?

    _____

14. If possessive forms of nouns did not exist, how would your writing be affected? Is there any other way to indicate possession? Explain.

    _____

Pronouns: Nominative and Objective Forms

Essential Principles

To communicate well in writing, you must use the correct forms of *nominative and objective pronouns* and the *pronouns ending in self* in a number of different contexts.

The term **case** refers to the form of a pronoun. The case of a pronoun shows how the pronoun relates to other words in a sentence. There are three cases, or forms, of pronouns—possessive, nominative, and objective. In the previous section, you studied the possessive forms of pronouns. This section covers the other two forms—the nominative and the objective cases, and pronouns ending with *self*.

Exhibit 5.9 shows the nominative and objective case pronouns.

Nominative and Objective Pronoun Cases			
Nominative Case		**Objective Case**	
Singular	**Plural**	**Singular**	**Plural**
I	we	me	us
you	you	you	you
he	they	him	them
she	they	her	them
it	they	it	them
who	who	whom	whom
whoever	whoever	whomever	whomever

Exhibit 5.9
Nominative and Objective Pronoun Cases
This table details singular and plural pronouns. ***Thinking Critically.*** *How does a pronoun's position in a sentence affect its case?*

Nominative Case Pronouns

Follow these three rules for using nominative case pronouns correctly in writing.

Rule 1: Subject of a Verb.   If a pronoun is the subject of a verb, that pronoun must be nominative. Some examples are:

- *I* have reviewed the income statement. (*Who* has reviewed it? *I* [nominative case, singular] have reviewed, not *Me* [objective case, singular].)
- *She* and Ricardo will speak at the graduation ceremony. (*Who* will speak? *She* [nominative case, singular] will speak, not *Her* [objective case, singular]. *She* is the subject of the verb phrase *will speak*.)
- *Who* is the director of customer service? (*Who* [relative pronoun, nominative case] is the subject of the verb *is*.)

Rule 2: Complement of a "Being" Verb.   The "being" verbs are *am, is, are, was,* and *were*; and *be, being,* and *been* with helping verbs. If a pronoun follows and completes the meaning of a "being" verb, that pronoun must be nominative. (See Rule 3 for an exception.) Some examples are:

- Perhaps it was (they/them) who sent us these samples. (The "being" verb is *was.* The pronoun that follows *was* must complement the "being" verb. Therefore, the pronoun must be the nominative *they.*)
- It must have been (he/him) in the boss's office. (The "being" verb phrase is *must have been.* Therefore, the nominative form *he* correctly complements the "being" verb.)

Rule 3: Pronoun Completes the Infinitive.   If a pronoun follows and completes the meaning of the infinitive verb *to be* when *to be* has no subject, then that pronoun must be nominative. An example is:

- The patients appear to be (they/them). (There is no noun or pronoun immediately before the infinitive verb *to be.* Therefore, use the nominative form *they.*)

Memory Hook

To help you remember Rule 3 about the infinitive verb *to be,* make this connection:

- *No* subject—**N**ominative case

Let the *no* in the word *nominative* remind you to choose the nominative pronoun when there is *no* subject before the infinitive verb *to be.*

5.3 Self-Assessment A

Check the following sentences for any errors in the use of pronouns. Write *OK* if the sentence is correct. Circle any error(s) and write the correction(s) on the line provided.

1. Some members felt the Citizen of the Year should be him. _____

2. All the board members agree that the winner should be he. _____

3. Amy, if you were me, would you have gotten a dog? _____

4. When a telephone customer service rep asks for you by name, you should reply, "This is she." _____

5. When Mrs. O'Bryan saw Larry's silhouette, she thought him to be I. _____

Objective Case Pronouns

The **object** is a person or thing that receives the action of the verb.

Rule 1: Pronouns as Objects of Verbs, Prepositions, or Infinitives. Use the objective case pronoun forms *me, us, him, her, them, whom, whomever,* when the pronouns are objects of verbs, prepositions, or infinitives. Some examples are:

- Mr. Pappas promoted *me* to executive assistant. (The verb is *promoted.* The object of the verb is *me* [objective form], not *I.*)

- Mei-Yu had already given a copy to *us,* so we bought an extra copy for *him.* (*Us* is the object of the preposition *to,* and *him* is the object of the preposition *for.*)

- To *whom* did Elmer send a package on Monday? (*Whom* is the object of the preposition *to.*)

- Ms. Rosenberg plans to visit *them* next week. (*Them* is the object of the infinitive verb *to visit.*)

Rule 2: Subjects of Infinitives. Use the objective case pronoun forms for subjects of infinitives. An example is:

- Ken wants *us* to travel to England in June or July. (*Us* is the subject of the infinitive verb *to travel.*)

Rule 3: A Noun or Pronoun Precedes *To Be*. Use the objective case pronoun following the infinitive verb *to be* when a noun or pronoun immediately precedes *to be.* An example is:

- When she first answered the telephone, Eva thought Robert to be *me.* (The noun *Robert* immediately precedes the infinitive verb *to be;* therefore, the objective form *me* is correct.)

Special Problems of Pronoun Usage

In certain situations, selecting the correct case form of pronouns may be confusing. The following discussion will help you in such situations.

Digital Data

Be Skeptical about Grammar Checking

The grammar checking function of your word processing software will point out words that are misused or overused. However, this software doesn't know what you are trying to say and, therefore, cannot guarantee that you have communicated clearly in writing.

Who, Whom; Whoever, Whomever. You have already learned that the pronouns *who* and *whoever* are in the nominative case, and the pronouns *whom* and *whomever* are in the objective case. You also know that we use the nominative case (*who* and *whoever*) for subjects of verbs and for complements of being verbs. Use the objective case (*whom* and *whomever*) as you would use other objective forms—that is, for objects of verbs (direct objects and indirect objects) and for objects of prepositions. Still, many people have trouble with these pronouns—usually because of complications in context. Use the Memory Hook on page 157 to help you decide which pronoun case to use.

In Interrogative Sentences. Questions are generally worded in inverted order; that is, the subject comes after the verb. Therefore, in applying the Memory Hook test on page 157 to questions, change the sentence to normal order before substituting *he* or *him*.

(*Who? Whom?*) is the doctor Ed Billingsly recommended? (Normal order: "The doctor Ed Billingsly recommended is *he*." A pronoun in the nominative case is correct because the pronoun follows a being verb. *Who,* then, is correct because it is in the nominative case and complements the being verb *is*.)

(*Who? Whom?*) has the manager chosen? (Normal order: "The manager has chosen *him*." *Whom,* the objective case, is correct because *him* can be substituted and *him* is in the objective case.)

Of course, if the question is in normal order, simply substitute *he* or *him*.

In Clauses. When *who* or *whom* (or *whoever* or *whomever*) is used in a dependent clause within a sentence, you must (1) separate that clause from the rest of the sentence, (2) determine if the clause is in normal word order, and (3) proceed to substitute *he* or *him*.

1. Separate the clause, which *always* begins with the word *who, whom, whoever,* or *whomever*.

   We do not know (*who? whom?*) the caller could have been. (Separate the dependent clause from the rest of the sentence: "*who? whom?* the caller could have been.")

   Share this piece of information with (*whoever? whomever?*) you worked with on the Haggerty account. (Separate the clause: "*whoever? whomever?* you worked with on the Haggerty account.")

2. Change the inverted clause to normal order.

   . . . (*who? whom?*) the caller could have been (Normal order: "the caller could have been *who? whom?*")

   . . . (*whoever? whomever?*) you worked with on the Haggerty account (Normal order: "you worked with *whoever? whomever?* on the Haggerty account.")

3. Substitute *he* or *she* or *him* or *her* in each clause.

   . . . the caller could have been *he* (Remember that a nominative form must be used to complete a being verb; thus *he* and *who* are correct.)

   . . . you worked with *him* on the Haggerty account (*Him,* objective case, is correct, because *him* is the object of the preposition *with*. Therefore, *whomever* is correct.)

Note: Interrupters such as *I think, she says, you know,* and *we believe* should be omitted when selecting *who* or *whom* in clauses.

The supervisor (*who? whom?*) I believe we should hire is Celeste Harrill. (Separate the clause: "*who? whom?* I believe we should hire." Omit the interrupting words *I believe* and put the clause in normal order: "We should hire *her*." *Whom,* objective case, is correct because *her,* objective case, can be substituted.)

Memory Hook

You know that *him* is in the objective case. Let the *m* in *him* remind you of the *m* in *whom* and in *whomever,* which are also in the objective case. You may even substitute *him* to test whether the objective case is correct.

The doctor (*who? whom?*) Ed Billingsly recommended is Dr. Richard Bromberg. (Make this substitution: "Ed Billingsly recommended him." Because the objective case *him* is correct, the choice must be *whom.*)

Patricia doesn't know (*who? whom?*) the director has selected. (Make this substitution: "The director has selected *him*." The correct choice, therefore, is *whom.*)

We do not know (*who? whom?*) Dale Byrd is. (Make this substitution: "Dale Byrd is [*he*]." Because the nominative *he* can be substituted, the correct answer is *who.*)

5.3 Self-Assessment B

From the choices in parentheses, select the correct pronoun for each of the following sentences.

1. Perhaps the person (who/whom) you saw during the press conference was Jean MacDonald. _____

2. Eleanor is the salesperson (who/whom) should be assigned to this campaign. _____

3. The election committee can fine (whoever/whomever) does not observe the rules. _____

4. Mitch Chaffee, (who/whom) we consider the best network specialist in our company, will represent us at the seminar. _____

5. (Whoever/Whomever) wrote this manual did an excellent job. _____

    _____

6. We asked Peter, (who/whom) has experience in tax matters, for his advice. _____

Case Forms: Special Situations

There are situations in writing in which it is rather difficult to correctly select the nominative or objective form. These situations are discussed below.

Pronouns in Compound Subjects or Compound Objects

Compound subjects or **compound objects** are nouns and pronouns joined by the coordinating conjunctions *or, and,* and *nor.* When the pronoun is part of a subject, use the nominative case. When the pronoun is part of an object, use the objective case. Some examples are:

Nominative in Subjects	Objective in Objects
Kevin and I want . . .	. . . for *Kevin and me*
Ms. Royce and he asked . . .	. . . asked *Ms. Royce and him*
She and I will write . . .	. . . written by *her and me*
They and we agree . . .	. . . agree with *them and us*

To choose the correct pronoun in compounds, remove the other parts of the compound and test the pronoun choices with the rest of the sentence. Some examples are:

- Judy Sinclair and (I/me) leave for Mexico City on Monday. (When you omit the words *Judy Sinclair and,* the answer becomes "*I* leave . . . ," not "*me* leave . . .")
- Sylvia sent copies to Mr. Chernof and (I/me). (Omit the words *Mr. Chernof and,* and the answer becomes "Sylvia sent copies to *me.*")

Pronoun Phrases

When faced with a pronoun choice in phrases such as *we supervisors* or *us supervisors,* remove the noun that follows the pronoun and test the pronoun choices. An example is:

- (We/Us) supervisors met with the union delegates. (Remove the noun *supervisors* and test the pronoun choices. "*We* . . . met with . . ." or "*Us* . . . met with?" It becomes clear that the nominative pronoun *we* is correct.)

<aside>
KEY POINT

To choose the right pronoun in compounds, test pronoun choices by themselves with the rest of the sentence.

- **Tom and me/I went to the movies.**

Remove the word *Tom* and "I went to the movies," not "Me went to the movies," becomes the obvious choice.
</aside>

Pronouns with *Than* or *As*

Another pronoun problem may arise in sentences that contain *than* or *as.* Some examples are:

- "Roxanne has more vacation time *than* (I/me)."
- "This problem affects Aaron as much *as* (I/me)."

When the word *than* or *as* is used in such comparisons, it usually represents an incomplete clause. To improve your writing, complete the clause, and then the correct pronoun becomes clear. Some examples with explanations are:

- Roxanne has more vacation time than I (have vacation time). (By completing the clause, it is clear that the clause is "*I* have vacation time," not "*me* have vacation time.")
- This problem affects Aaron as much as (this problem affects) me. (The words "this problem affects" are understood and therefore not repeated. However, by using them to complete the clause, your pronoun choice becomes clear.)

Check the following sentences for any errors in the use of pronouns. Write *OK* if the sentence is correct. Circle any error(s) and write the correction(s) on the line provided.

1.   The voting information was sent only to we three union stewards. _____

    _____

2.   The procedure is to ask Dr. Cordez or I for an advance. _____

    _____

3.   The majority of the committee members voted for Tanya and he. _____

    _____

4.   The college president asked we students for our comments on the new registration system. _____

5.   Peter is certainly a more effective speaker than me. _____

6.   As you can see, Paul keyboards more quickly and accurately than she.

    _____

7.   Only Radmilla or him has the authority to approve changes in the shift schedule. _____

8.   Alice assumed that none of we nurses wants to change the schedule.

    _____

9.   Between you and me, I think that Elizabeth Garcia will become regional manager when Mr. Lowe retires. _____

Pronouns Ending in "Self"

Pronouns ending in *self*, such as *myself, yourself, himself, herself, itself, ourselves, yourselves*, and *themselves*, perform two functions. (1) They emphasize or intensify the use of a noun or another pronoun (intensive use). (2) They refer to a noun or pronoun that has already been used in a sentence (reflexive use).

Intensive Use

Pronouns ending in *self* provide emphasis. An example is:

- Suzanne *herself* announced the competition results. (This is more emphatic, than, "Suzanne announced the competition results.")

Reflexive Use

Pronouns that end in *self* refer to a noun or another pronoun that has already been used in the sentence. An example is:

- Angela distributed the copies and kept one for *herself*. (*Herself* clearly refers to Angela and saves us from saying, "Angela distributed the copies and kept one for Angela.")

KEY POINT

Pronouns ending in *self* put the emphasis on, or refer to, a noun or another pronoun in the same sentence.

Employability Skills

Organizing Ideas

Organizing ideas is a key component of communicating with co-workers and customers. Business documents that present information in an organized manner help prevent miscommunication.

Common Errors

Lack of Clear Antecedent. A pronoun that ends in *self* must have a clear antecedent within the sentence. An **antecedent** is a noun or noun phrase that is referred to by the pronoun. An example is:

- Gordon Taada and *myself* developed the strategy. To whom does *myself* refer? The sentence should read, "Gordon Taada and *I* developed . . ."

Misplacing the Pronoun. A pronoun must be placed correctly in the sentence. An example is:

- When we asked the painter for his advice, he said that he prefers spray painting *himself*. (Obviously the person does not want to spray paint *himself*. Change the position of the pronoun in the sentence to correct this error. ". . . he said that he *himself* prefers spray painting.")

Going Global

Name That Order

Writing an individual's name varies depending on the language. In English, your first name comes before your last name (for example, Sally Smith). In Korean, the family name, or last name, is always written first (for example, Kim Hyun Ju).

5.3 Self-Assessment D

Check the following sentences for any errors in the use of pronouns. Write *OK* if the sentence is correct. Circle any error(s) and write the correction(s) on the line provided.

1. As Chelsea and himself said, "It's history now." _____

2. The dean herself will talk to the board about the child care center. _____

3. After seeing the new dorm, Andrea specifically said that she wants to live there herself. _____

4. When Suzzana and myself suggested 10 a.m., we did not realize you lived four hours away. _____

5. The blacksmith himself made the horseshoes. _____

Assessment   Section 5.3

Review of Key Terms

1. What does the term *case* mean in reference to pronouns, and what are these cases? Use examples to illustrate your answer. _____

_____

_____

_____

2. What is the difference between an object and an objective case pronoun? Provide examples of each. _____

_____

_____

_____

3. How does a lack of a clear antecedent make a sentence confusing? Provide an example of a sentence with a clear antecedent and a sentence with an unclear antecedent. _____

_____

Editing Practice
Grammar Alert!

4. Rewrite the following paragraphs, correcting errors in plurals, possessives, and pronoun usage.

   As I am sure you know, our competitors are eager to compete with us for the ToysPlus account. John and myself have begun the proposal process by reviewing the video's of there most recent advertising campaign. Here's the three areas of emphasis for selling their playground equipment: safety, exercise, and cost.

   This six month's project should incorporate your most creative thoughts. The president has issued herself a special incentive. If we get the ToysPlus account, us, the advertising campaign staff, will get an extra weeks' vacation with pay.

   Kaitlyn and Scot Weston, the owners of ToysPlus, want to work with our company. However, the Westons' are looking for the best advertising campaign available. Obviously, you and me must give this campaign our best effort. _____

_____

_____

_____

_____

_____

_____

_____

_____

_____

_____

Practical Application
Thinking Critically

5. The word *noun* is derived from *nomen,* a Latin word. Use a dictionary to find the meaning of *nomen.* Then, find at least two related words. How does the meaning of *nomen* relate to the meaning of the word *noun* given in this section? _____

6. Write three sentences using incorrect pronoun case, and exchange your sentences with a partner. Ask your partner to explain why your pronoun case is incorrect and correct each other's sentences. _____

Chapter 6

Expanding Language Skills

Workplace Connection

Your ability to write and to speak correctly can make the difference in whether or not you get the job you want or the promotion you seek. Conjunctions and prepositions clarify relationships among ideas; adjectives and adverbs make language more expressive.

CHAPTER OBJECTIVES

When you have completed this chapter, you should be able to:

- Understand how and when to use conjunctions.
- State the function of prepositions.
- Explain the importance of adjectives.
- Discuss how adverbs work.

Conjunctions

Conjunctions

As you will recall from Section 4.1, a **conjunction** is a word that is used to join words, phrases, or clauses within a sentence. Some examples are:

- The delivery and the installation are included in the quoted price. (In this sentence, the conjunction *and* joins the words *delivery* and *installation*.)
- The patient may get a report from my office or from the laboratory. (The conjunction *or* joins two prepositional phrases, *from my office* and *from the laboratory*.)
- Rebecca wants to buy a wireless mouse for her laptop, but she is waiting for the price to go down. (The conjunction *but* joins the two independent clauses.)

Writing varied sentences and punctuating them correctly become much easier once you have mastered the uses of conjunctions. This section presents three different kinds of conjunctions, discusses the most common pitfalls in using conjunctions, and then considers parallel structure.

Types of Conjunctions

There are three types of conjunctions: *coordinating, correlative,* and *subordinating.* As you will see, coordinating and correlative conjunctions connect two or more items of equal grammatical rank. Subordinating conjunctions, however, connect a clause that is subordinate to a main clause.

Coordinating Conjunctions

The four **coordinating conjunctions**—*and, but, or,* and *nor*—are very commonly used. Note that they connect only like elements of grammar: two or more words, two or more phrases, or two or more clauses. Some examples are:

- Pepperoni and beef are on your pizza. (The conjunction *and* connects two words, *pepperoni* and *beef.*)
- Pepperoni, beef, and peppers are on your pizza. (Here the conjunction *and* joins three words.)
- Natalie has been with clients or with her staff since early morning. (The conjunction *or* joins two prepositional phrases, *with clients* and *with her staff.*)
- Dr. Austin planned to spend five days at the mountain resort, but he couldn't get a hotel room. (The conjunction *but* connects two independent, or main, clauses.)

SECTION OBJECTIVES

When you have finished Section 6.1, you will be able to:

- Describe the three types of conjunctions and give examples of the use of each type.
- Identify the pitfalls in the use of conjunctions and explain how to avoid those pitfalls.
- Discuss ways of ensuring parallel structure with coordinating and correlative conjunctions.

WHY IT'S IMPORTANT

Understanding how and when conjunctions are used can help make your writing more interesting.

KEY TERMS

- coordinating conjunctions
- correlative conjunctions
- subordinating conjunctions
- parallel structure

KEY POINT

Coordinating conjunctions and correlative conjunctions join like elements of grammar.

Correlative Conjunctions

Correlative conjunctions are pairs of conjunctions that are regularly used together to connect like elements. Note, again, that both *coordinating* and *correlative conjunctions* connect like elements *only*. The most commonly used correlative conjunctions are these:

both . . . and

either . . . or

neither . . . nor

not only . . . but also

whether . . . or

Just as with coordinating conjunctions, correlative conjunctions connect words, phrases, or clauses equal in grammatical rank. Some examples are:

- Not only Alan but also Dexter will fly to Chicago next Friday. (Here the correlatives *not only . . . but also* connect two words, Alan and Dexter.)

- Jack will work on our electrical system either during the week or during the weekend. (Two phrases, *during the week* and *during the weekend,* are joined.)

- Wesley intends both to play football and to graduate with honors. (Here two clauses are connected.)

Subordinating Conjunctions

Subordinating conjunctions join clauses of unequal rank. A *subordinating conjunction* introduces a subordinate, or dependent, clause and connects it to a main, or independent, clause. Some examples are:

- Although we completed the tax return, we were unable to duplicate it because the copier has been broken for several days. (*Although* is a subordinating conjunction that introduces the subordinate clause *although we completed the tax return*. Furthermore, *although* connects this subordinate clause to the main clause.)

- You should submit a $200 deposit if you plan to go to London with our group. (The subordinating conjunction *if* introduces the subordinate clause *if you plan to go to London with our group* and connects this clause to the main clause.)

Study the following list of commonly used subordinating conjunctions so that you will be able to identify subordinate clauses.

Exhibit 6.1
Subordinating Conjunctions
Subordinating conjunctions form subordinate clauses which indicate ideas of unequal rank. ***Thinking Critically.*** *How can identifying subordinate clauses improve your comprehension?*

Subordinating Conjunctions		
after	how	until
although	if	when
as	in case that	whenever
as if	in order that	where
as soon as	provided that	wherever
as though	since	whether
because	so that	while
before	than	why
even if	that	
for	unless	

6.1 Self-Assessment A

Underline the conjunctions used in the following sentences. Label each conjunction as coordinating *CO*, correlative *CR*, or subordinating *S*.

1. Have you submitted both the reimbursement form and your receipts?
   _____

2. Our consultant and the patient coordinator carefully reviewed the complaints received during the last year. _____

3. If you prefer getting your phone calls at work, please give me your number. _____

4. Unless you find your wallet immediately, you must cancel the credit cards that were in it. _____

5. Julie, do you know whether Bill or Mark was invited to speak at graduation? _____

6. Yes, I'm sure that Demitri called Bill this morning. _____

7. Please ask either Harry or Greg to examine the fruit trees at the end of the road. _____

8. You may subscribe to the journal, or you may read it at the library. _____

9. Tracey will discuss his expenses as soon as he returns from his mission trip to Mexico. _____

10. While Ms. Russell was on a business trip, her application was reviewed by the search committee. _____

Pitfalls of Using Conjunctions

There are two major conjunction pitfalls: (1) choosing a conjunction that does not accurately convey the meaning intended; and (2) choosing a preposition when a conjunction is needed.

Choosing the Correct Conjunction

But or And.   The conjunction *but* provides a contrast while *and* simply joins two elements. Use *but* when a contrast is intended. Some examples are:

- The difference between the motel accommodations is minimal, *but* only one motel is oceanfront. (*but* for contrast)
- The two motels are similar in price and both are oceanfront. (*and* to join two items)

Who, Which, or That.   Use *who* to refer to persons and *which* to refer to objects. Never say or write *and who* or *and which*. Some examples are:

- Send a copy of the report to Dave Austin, *who* is the vice president. (*Who* refers to a person.)

oops!

With Whom Did You Meet?

Jackson Poleta, who you met during last week's meeting, has resigned.

(*Whom*, the object, is correct, not *who*.)

- Rex asked us to present our petition to the board, *which* is responsible for all major decisions. (*Which* refers to an object.)

That is used to refer to persons, objects, or animals. Some examples are:

- The person *that* you met yesterday is Ron Taylor. (*That* refers to a person. Note that *whom* could also have been used.)
- One idea *that* you will deem exciting is restoring the antique carousel. (Here, *that* refers to an object.)
- The registered dog *that* Carrie bought was a chocolate lab. (*That* refers to an animal.)

Since or Because, Not Being That.   There is no such conjunction as *being that*. Use *since* or *because* instead. An example is:

- Because Mr. Rupert had a virus, he decided to work at home yesterday and today.

The Reason Is That; Pretend That.   Do not say or write *the reason is because* and *pretend like*. Instead, *the reason is that* and *pretend that* are correct. Some examples are:

- The reason for the delay in the flight arrival time is that violent storms prohibited the plane from taking off.
- The driver should not pretend that he didn't know that he was speeding.

Unless, Not Without or Except.   *Without* and *except* are prepositions. A preposition always introduces a prepositional phrase. A preposition is not a substitute for the subordinating conjunction *unless*. A prepositional phrase consists of a preposition plus its noun or pronoun object and any modifiers. Some examples are:

- You cannot return the merchandise without Ms. Cochran's approval. (*Without Ms. Cochran's approval* is a prepositional phrase: *approval* is the object of the preposition *without,* and *Ms. Cochran's* is a modifier.)
- You cannot return this merchandise *unless* Ms. Cochran approves it. (The subordinating conjunction *unless* introduces a clause. To say or write *without Ms. Cochran approves it* is incorrect. The preposition *without* cannot introduce a clause.)

As, As If, As Though, Not Like.   Remember that *like* is a preposition as in "a desk like mine," or a verb as in, "I like this desk." It is not a conjunction. Therefore, do not use *like* when *as, as if,* or *as though* is intended. An example is:

- Ralph acted *as if* he was disappointed.

6.1 Self-Assessment B

Check the following sentences for any errors in the use of conjunctions. Write *OK* if the sentence is correct. Rewrite the sentence part that contains errors.

1. One reason for the decrease in computer prices is because technology is continuing to advance. _____

2. The bride mentioned several singers which would be appropriate for the wedding. _____

3. Chad was instructed not to pay the invoice unless he receives both shipments from the vendor. _____

4. You should, of course, act like you are interested in the presentation.

   _____

5. Please do not use the expensive stationery except the mail is going outside the organization. _____

6. The manager told Dana not to sit around like he has no work to do.

   _____

7. Do not mail the payment without you check to see if we have enough funds to cover it. _____

8. Tony's car is not the latest model on the market, and he is really enjoying driving it. _____

9. Anna said, "It seems like almost every home has at least one computer."

   _____

10. Please make sure that Mr. Wesson doesn't leave before he approves the travel reimbursements. _____

Parallel Structure

Observing the rules of *parallel structure* will provide balance to your writing. **Parallel structure** expresses parallel ideas in parallel form. Some examples are:

- The new accountant works quietly and accurately. (The conjunction *and* joins two parallel elements—two adverbs, *quietly* and *accurately*.)

- The new accountant works quietly and with accuracy. (The same ideas are expressed here, but they are not expressed in parallel form. An adverb, *quietly*, joined to a prepositional phrase, *with accuracy* is incorrect. These two grammatical elements are not alike; they are not parallel.)

With Coordinating Conjunctions

Coordinating conjunctions connect like elements: an adjective with an adjective, a prepositional phrase with a prepositional phrase, and so on. Therefore, make sure

Speaking in Parallels

Helen speaks quietly and with confidence.

(*Confidently* is parallel with *quietly*.)

that the elements before and after a coordinating conjunction match. Some examples are:

- Our security system is checked carefully and (regularly/with regularity). (An adverb, *carefully*, appears before the coordinating conjunction *and*; therefore, the adverb *regularly* should follow *and*.)
- Running the first mile is relatively easy, but (finishing/to finish) the marathon is quite challenging. (*Finishing* matches *running*. Both *running* and *finishing* are gerunds.)

6.1 Self-Assessment C

Check the following sentences for any errors in the use of parallel structure with coordinating conjunctions. Write *OK* if the sentence is correct. Rewrite the sentence correctly if it contains errors.

1. You may send us your comments by Federal Express, by fax, or you can send them by e-mail. _____

2. Barbara enjoys reading, exercising, and to travel. _____

3. Nancy Lee, the nutritionist, said that the squash could be eaten steamed, fried, or is edible raw. _____

4. Our response should be courteous, quick, and with accuracy. _____

5. The doctor told the patient that avoiding certain foods is necessary, but to exercise is also essential to his overall health program. _____

6. "Both doctors," the patient commented, "seem to be competent and professional." _____

Digital Data

Cell Phones—A Modern Staple

Cell phones have become essential tools in everyday communication. Individuals from all walks of life and occupations use cell phones. They have not only increased accessibility but also have become a staple of communication.

With Correlative Conjunctions

To achieve parallelism with correlative conjunctions, simply make sure that the element that follows the first conjunction is the same part of speech as the element that follows the second conjunction. Some examples are:

- Katie wants either Adam or me to select the carpet for the reception area. (The elements that follow *either . . . or* are the noun *Adam* and a pronoun *me*. Nouns and pronouns are considered like elements because pronouns are substitutes for nouns. Thus the phrase *either Adam or me* is parallel.)
- The color green is predominant not only in the reception area's furnishings but also in its carpet. (Notice the parallelism of two prepositional phrases, one after each of the correlatives.)
- Not only did the volunteers do all the painting, but they also hung the wallpaper. (*Not only* is followed by an independent clause, and *but also* is followed by an independent clause and may be interrupted by *they*. The sentence is parallel. Do not be misled by the inverted order of the first clause.)

Misplaced Conjunctions

Be sure that the placement of the correlative conjunction is correct. A misplaced conjunction can change the meaning of a sentence. Some examples are:

- Matt likes either to eat pizza or to eat spaghetti. (correct)
- Matt likes to eat either pizza or spaghetti. (correct)
- Matt likes to eat either pizza or to eat spaghetti. (incorrect)

 ## 6.1 Self-Assessment D

Check the following sentences for any errors in the use of parallel structure with correlative conjunctions. Write *OK* if the sentence is correct. Rewrite the sentence correctly if it contains errors.

1. Among the activities I like best are reading mystery novels and to "surf" the Internet. _____

2. In an effort to save fuel, we are trying to either form car pools or to use public transportation. _____

3. Coupons are usually either mailed to our best customers or to our prospective customers. _____

4. Our college catalog is both well written and has colorful illustrations.

   _____

5. For 50 years, the antique shop has been owned either by Mr. Ormanni or his father. _____

6. Patrick neither went to the library nor to the bookstore. _____

Assessment   Section 6.1

Review of Key Terms

1. What are the three types of *conjunctions*? Describe the function of each one. _____

   _____

   _____

   _____

   _____

2. What is *parallel structure*? _____

   _____

Editing Practice

Proofreading Alert!   Correct any errors in the following sentences.

3. I was not aware of Margaret leaving early, but apparently she had permission to do so. _____

4. My calculations do not agree with your's. _____

5. Please check the ratioes that are listed in the first table in the report.

_____

6. Donald don't want to take our clients to play golf Friday afternoon.

_____

Practical Application

Using Conjunctions Correctly

7. Correct any conjunction errors in the following sentences.

    a. During the trip, Thad spent money like it were growing on trees.

    b. The reason Sherry is buying more clothes is because she just got her first professional job.

    c. Last month, they not only agreed to drop the lawsuit but also to accept a refund for the damaged merchandise.

_____

_____

_____

8. Revise the following paragraph so that (a) short, choppy sentences are combined, using conjunctions, and (b) each sentence has parallel structure. As a team, present the findings to your class.

Mr. Mendoza is going to tour our plant this month. Mr. Cassio is going to tour our plant this month. They are concerned about recent problems in understocking, shipping, and returned goods. The warehouse is not the only place they will check. They also will visit customer relations.

_____

_____

_____

_____

_____

Discussion Point

Thinking Critically

9. How can writers verify that their sentences are parallel when using coordinating and correlative conjunctions? _____

_____

_____

10. Explain how the conjunctions *but* and *or* can make writing "more thoughtful." _____

_____

_____

Prepositions

Prepositions

A **preposition** is a connecting word. It connects a noun or a pronoun to the rest of the sentence. The preposition combined with that noun or pronoun makes up a **prepositional phrase.** Examine the following commonly used prepositions and some sample prepositional phrases. Note: *But* is a preposition only when it means "except." In other cases, *but* is a conjunction. Some examples are:

Prepositions			Prepositional Phrases
about	but (except)	off	above the window
above	by	on	after our presentation
after	except	over	before his birthday
among	for	to	from Jon and Mike
at	from	under	into the soup
before	in	until	like that magazine
below	into	up	off the roof
beside	like	upon	to the park
between	of	with	with my brother

The noun or pronoun that follows the preposition in a phrase is the **object of the preposition.** The phrase may include modifiers, for example, *new* in *to the new instructor* modifies *instructor,* which is the object of the preposition *to.* Also, a phrase may have compound objects, as in *from Brian and Tammy.*

Because prepositional phrases often interrupt the subject and the verb in a sentence, your ability to make subjects and verbs agree will sometimes depend on your ability to identify prepositional phrases. Examine the following examples:

- The computer analysts in this company are reviewing the computer security rules carefully. (The prepositional phrase *in this company* separates the subject *computer analysts* from the verb *are.* A careless speaker, therefore, may incorrectly say "company is," which is wrong.)
- One employee from both departments has agreed to represent his or her department. (The prepositional phrase *from both departments* separates the subject *employee* from the verb *has agreed.*)

SECTION OBJECTIVES

When you have finished Section 6.2, you will be able to:

- State the function of prepositions.
- Explain why certain prepositions are used with certain words even though no rule is involved.
- Identify several pitfalls in the use of prepositions and cite the rules for avoiding those pitfalls.

WHY IT'S IMPORTANT

Such prepositions as *for, in, of, on,* and *to* are used so often that native speakers generally pay no attention to them.

KEY TERMS

- prepositions
- prepositional phrases
- object of the preposition
- idiomatic usage

6.2 Self-Assessment A

Write each prepositional phrase in the space provided. Underline the preposition in each phrase.

1. Only one of the customers indicated that she was unhappy with the billing procedures. _____

2. Anita went into the auditorium, I think, with her guest. _____
   _____

3. The final decision on the site of the midtown helicopter-landing pad will be made by the planning board. _____
   _____

4. Because Mr. Davis was in a hurry, Seth drove him to the airport. _____
   _____

5. You will need the statistical reports that were put in my file cabinet.
   _____

6. Between you and me, I do not believe that dropping out of college was a smart idea. _____

7. The main reason for the delay is that Zach is still on the computer. _____
   _____

8. The invoices that Betty placed on my desk have been approved and sent to the Accounts Payable Department. _____
   _____

Employability Skills

Self-Esteem

The ability to believe in one's self is important in a work environment. Self-esteem and a positive attitude are valuable attributes that employers look for in their employees.

KEY POINT

Using the incorrect preposition can change the meaning of what you are trying to say.

Words Requiring Specific Prepositions

Through years of use, certain expressions have come to be considered "correct" even though there may be no rule or logical reason to make them so. Such usage, called **idiomatic usage,** governs many expressions in our language. The use of certain prepositions with certain words is *idiomatic*. Long-accepted use has made it correct to use these prepositions. Examples are given in **Exhibit 6.2** on page 173.

Common Idiomatic Errors

The idiomatic expressions that are used and misused most often are given special attention below. Be sure to learn to use these expressions correctly.

Agree With, Agree To. Use *agree with* when the object of the preposition is a person or an idea; use *agree to* when the object is not a person or an idea. Some examples are:

- Does Sidney agree with Mr. Porter on the need to improve security in the parking deck? (Because the object of the preposition is a person, the preposition *with* is correct.)
- Yes, Sidney agrees to the recommendation to improve security in the parking deck. (Here, the object of the preposition is *recommendation*; because the object is not a person or an idea, *agrees to* is correct.)

Idiomatic Expressions with Prepositions

abhorrence of
abhorrent to
abide by a decision
abide with a person
abound in *or* with
accompanied by a person
accompanied with an item
acquit of
adapted for (made over for)
adapted from a work
adapted to (adjusted to)
affinity between
agree to a proposal
agree with someone
agreeable to (*with* is
   permissible)
angry at *or* about a thing *or*
   condition
angry with a person
attend to (listen)
attend upon (wait on)
beneficial to
bestow upon
buy from
compare to the mirror image
   (assert a likeness)
compare with the reverse side
   (analyze for similarities or
   differences)
compliance with
comply with
confer on *or* upon (give to)
confer with (talk to)
confide in (place confidence in)
confide to (entrust to)
conform to
in conformity to *or* with
consist in (exist in)
consist of (be made up of)
convenient for (suitable for,
   easy for)
convenient to (near)
conversant with

correspond to *or* with (match;
   agree with)
correspond with (exchange
   letters)
credit for
deal in goods *or* services
deal with someone
depend *or* dependent on (but
   independent of)
different from (not than or to)
disappointed in *or* with
discrepancy between two things
discrepancy in one thing
dispense with
employ for a purpose
employed at a stipulated salary
employed in, on, or upon a
   work or business
enter at a given point
enter in a record
enter into (become a party to)
enter into *or* upon (start)
exception to a statement
familiarize with
foreign to (preferred to from)
identical with
independent of (not from)
inferior *or* superior to
need of *or* for
part from (take leave of)
part with (relinquish)
plan *or* planning to (not on)
profit by
in regard to
with regard to
as regards
retroactive to (not from)
speak to (tell something to a
   person)
speak with (discuss with)
wait for a person, a train, an
   event
wait on a customer, a guest

Exhibit 6.2
Idiomatic Expressions
Speakers of English in countries such as Australia and Britain differ in their idiomatic usage compared with speakers of English in the United States. ***Thinking Critically.*** *How can misunderstandings in idiomatic usage hinder communication?*

Angry With, Angry At. Use *angry with* when the object of the preposition is a person; use *angry at* or *about* when the object is not a person. Some examples are:

- Lisa appeared to be angry with Mr. Parker because she was not recommended for the transfer. (*With* is correct because its object is a person, *Mr. Parker.*)
- Lisa appeared to be angry at the decision not to transfer her. (Now, the object of the preposition, *decision*, is not a person; thus *angry at* or *about* is correct.)

Part From, Part With. *Part from* means "to take leave of"; *part with* means "to relinquish" or "to give up." *Part from* is generally used when the object of the preposition is a person. *Part with* is generally used when the object is not a person. Some examples are:

- As soon as we part from Greg Teague at the airport, we will return to the office. ("We" *part from* a person.)
- Although we certainly appreciate the features of the new telephones, we hate to part with our old telephones that were reliable and durable. (*Part with* means "to relinquish" or "to give up.")

Discrepancy In, Discrepancy Between, Discrepancy Among. Use *discrepancy in* when the object of the preposition is singular. Use *discrepancy between* when the object specifically denotes two in number. Use *discrepancy among* when the object denotes three or more persons or things. Some examples are:

- I checked the client's account carefully and found no discrepancy in it. (Only one *account* is mentioned.)
- Compare these two spreadsheets; then let me know if you find any discrepancy between the two. (*Two spreadsheets* are mentioned.)
- There were many discrepancies among the statements from the eyewitnesses. (More than two statements are mentioned.)

In Regard To, With Regard To, As Regards. The three terms *in regard to*, *with regard to*, and *as regards* are equally correct, but be sure to remember that only the word *regard*, not *regards*, can be used in the phrases *in regard to* and *with regard to*. Some examples are:

- Jonathan has already consulted Mr. Abernathy (in/with) regard to the new software. (Either *in* or *with* is correct.)
- (In/With/As) regards the new software, please consult Mr. Abernathy. (Only *As* is correct—*As regards.*)

Note: In many cases, you can simplify and improve your sentence by substituting the word *about* for *in regard to*, *with regard to*, or *as regards*. An example is:

- Jonathan has already consulted Mr. Abernathy *about* the new software.

Different From, Identical With, Plan To, Retroactive To. Memorize the correct prepositions that go with these phrases, so that you will use them properly. Some examples are:

- different from (not *than*)
- identical with (not *to*)
- plan to (not *on*)
- retroactive to (not *from*)

Check the following sentences for any errors in the use of prepositions. Write *OK* if the sentence is correct. Correctly write the part of the sentence that contains errors.

1. The jury members were amazed to find several discrepancies in the testimony. _____

2. Beverly and I proofread both draft copies of the wedding invitation; fortunately, we found no discrepancy in the two of them. _____

   _____

3. It is my understanding that the new policy will be retroactive from May 1. _____

4. We found a bridal gown that is identical to the one that was damaged during the flood. _____

5. Both Pete and Sam agree with Amelia concerning the need to upgrade our graphics software. _____

6. The company wrote to him in regards to the item that was lost in the mail. _____

7. Benita and David said that the most difficult aspect of transferring to our Atlanta branch was parting from all their good friends. _____

8. Sue enthusiastically told us how the safari is different than her previous vacations. _____

9. Camille was angry at the telemarketer because the telephone call came during dinner. _____

10. The bride plans on opening the wedding gifts after dinner. _____

Pitfalls of Using Prepositions

Deciding when to use *between* and when to use *among* is one preposition choice that traps many writers and speakers. Other pitfalls concern adding unnecessary prepositions or, conversely, omitting prepositions that are necessary.

Commonly Confused Prepositions

Study the following examples to avoid the most common preposition pitfalls.

Between, Among. Use *between* when referring to two persons, places, or things, and use *among* when referring to three or more. Some examples are:

- The marathon was tied between Evelyn and Caley. (*Between* two people.)
- The reactions to the new product were divided among our three experts. (*Among* three experts.)

Adverbs Beside the Point

She sat besides the guest of honor at the inauguration.

(*Beside*, the adverb, is correct, not *besides*.)

Between may also be used to express a relationship of one thing to each of several other things on a one-to-one-basis. Some examples are:

- A separate agreement was signed between the university and each of the three students.
- Between each artist and each gallery exists an unspoken respect.

Beside, Besides. *Beside* means "by the side of"; *besides* means "in addition to." Some examples are:

- Yes, the man seated beside Mr. Wexler is Larry Newton, our guest speaker. (The man is seated *by the side of* Mr. Wexler.)
- Do you know who is scheduled to speak besides Mr. Wexler? (Someone is speaking *in addition to* Mr. Wexler.)

Inside, Outside. Do not use the preposition *of* after *inside* or *outside*. When referring to time, use *within*, not *inside of*. Some examples are:

- The ticket booth is on the left, just *inside* the main entrance. (*Inside of* is incorrect.)
- We expect to have both cars painted *within* the week. (*Inside of* is incorrect.)

All, Both. Use *of* after *all* or *both* only when *all* or *both* refers to a pronoun. Omit *of* if either word refers to a noun. Some examples are:

- All the truck drivers blocked the highway so the bank robbers' getaway car couldn't escape. (*Of* is not needed.)
- All *of* them received a personal note of gratitude from the governor. (*Of* is required here with the pronoun *them*.)

At, To; In, Into. *At* and *in* denote position; *to* and *into* signify motion. Some examples are:

- Kari arrived at the faculty meeting and immediately went to the podium. (*At* for position; *to* for motion.)
- They went into the restaurant and requested seats in the nonsmoking section. (*Into* for motion; *in* for position.)

Note: When either *at* or *in* refers to a place, use *in* for larger places and *at* for smaller places. An example is:

- Crystal lives in Gaston County and teaches at the local community college. (*In* Gaston County indicates the larger place; *at* the local community college indicates the smaller place.)

Behind, Not In Back Of. Use *behind*, not *in back of*. *In front of*, however, is correct. Some examples are:

- Until the presentation begins, place the promotional display behind, not in front of, the curtain.
- Please place the old documents behind the new ones.

From, Off. *From* is generally used with persons; *off* is used with things. *Off* is used with persons only when something on the person is physically being lifted away. Never use *of* or *from* after *off*. Some examples are:

- Get some ink cartridges from Sophia.
- After ten minutes, take the ice pack off your arm. (Something is physically being lifted away.)
- Let's take these watermelons off the truck.

Where, Not Where . . . At or Where . . . To.   Adding *at* or *to* to *where* is a glaring error in usage. Some examples are:

- We do not know *where* Dr. Madden *is*. (*Is at* is incorrect)
- Where did Charles *go?* (*Go to* is incorrect)

Help, Not Help From.   Do not use the word *from* after the verb *help*. Some examples are:

- The lecture was so stimulating that we could not help asking Dr. Thompson how we could contribute to the homeless shelter.
- I could not help depending on her computer knowledge.

Opposite, Not Opposite To.   Do not use the word *to* after *opposite*. Some examples are:

- The service station is directly opposite the cafe.
- I live opposite the factory.

Like, Not Like For.   Omit the word *for* after *like*. Some examples are:

- Mr. Adams told Ms. Varner that he would like her to sell his oceanfront home.
- I would like you to join us for dinner.

6.2 Self-Assessment C

Check the following sentences for any errors in the use of prepositions. Write *OK* if the sentence is correct. Write any needed corrections in the space provided.

1. The students cannot help from cheering when they win a contest. _____
   _____

2. Do you know where the manager and his assistant have gone to? _____
   _____

3. Let's leave all of these decorations packed in boxes. _____

4. Both of the squad members received awards for their roles in resuscitating heart attack victims. _____

5. Anne's mother would like for her to go to graduate school. _____

6. We are sure that the coffee shop is opposite the medical clinic. _____

7. Perhaps you should go in the new health club to inspect its facilities.
   _____

8. According to the e-mail this morning, we may get our flu shots tomorrow inside of working hours. _____

9. The new courthouse is opposite to the town hall. _____

10. The nurse will take the cast from your wrist. _____

11. Please meet me in back of the restaurant at 8 p.m. _____

12. The office duties were divided between Megaly, Miguel, and Suzanna.

    _____

13. When the tornado alarm sounded, Patrick quickly ran in a nearby
    school. _____

14. Is the man standing besides Dan the consultant that you know?

    _____

15. Does the fleet supervisor know where all of his cars and trucks are at?

    _____

Assessment   Section 6.2

Review of Key Terms

1. What is a *prepositional phrase*? What is its role in a sentence? _____

   _____

   _____

   _____

2. What is *idiomatic usage*? Provide examples of some idiomatic
   expressions with prepositions. _____

   _____

   _____

   _____

Editing Practice

Vocabulary Alert!   Select the word from the list below that best completes each
sentence.

comptroller	cumulative	enumerate	exorbitant	unscrupulous

3. Mr. Diaz, the _____ of our company, assists with all our financial
   affairs.

4. The _____ hardware store sold generators at _____ prices
   during the recent tornado.

5. To make the memo easier to read, _____ the items that are back-
   ordered.

6. The first column lists the monthly sales, and the second column lists the
   _____ sales for each year.

Practical Application

Using Prepositions Correctly

7. Using too many prepositional phrases in one sentence can lead to a confusing sentence. As a team, rewrite the following sentences by eliminating some prepositional phrases.

    a. There will be a negotiation of a settlement by the lawyers that is agreeable to both parties by tomorrow.
    b. There will be an evaluation of the training program by personnel to ensure quality training within our company.

    _____

    _____

    _____

Discussion Point

Thinking Critically

8. How does one know when to use *between* and when to use *among*?

    _____

    _____

9. How can writers avoid agreement errors when using prepositional phrases? _____

    _____

SECTION OBJECTIVES

When you have finished Section 6.3, you will be able to:

- Define adjectives.
- Identify and describe the various types of adjectives.
- Explain how to form the comparative and superlative forms of descriptive adjectives.
- Describe situations in which compound adjectives are and are not hyphenated.

WHY IT'S IMPORTANT

Used wisely, adjectives make nouns and pronouns interesting, vivid, and specific.

KEY TERMS

- adjectives
- articles
- descriptive adjectives
- possessive adjectives
- limiting adjectives
- proper adjectives
- compound adjectives
- demonstrative adjectives
- positive degree
- comparative degree
- superlative degree
- absolute adjectives
- predicate adjectives
- predicate nominatives

Adjectives

Adjectives

Any word that modifies or describes a noun or a pronoun is an **adjective.** An adjective usually precedes the noun it modifies. It tells "what kind," "how many," "which one," and "in what order." Some of the most commonly used kinds of adjectives are described below.

Articles

The words *a, an,* and *the* are called **articles.** Note how these special adjectives are commonly used.

- The sailboat captain pointed out a beautiful sunset.
- The gelatin salad recipe includes a banana and an apple.

Descriptive Adjectives

The most commonly used adjectives are descriptive adjectives. **Descriptive adjectives** describe or tell "what kind of." An example is:

- In a strong, clear voice, Belinda rejected the irresponsible policies that some real estate companies use to lure unsuspecting consumers into buying overpriced and sometimes worthless property. (*Strong, clear, irresponsible, real estate, unsuspecting, overpriced,* and *worthless* are all descriptive adjectives.)

Possessive Adjectives

Possessive personal pronouns, such as *my, your, his, her, its, our, their,* and *possessive nouns,* such as *Jason's, Linda's,* can be used as adjectives to modify nouns. They are called **possessive adjectives.** An example is:

- *Your* lawyer evaluated *our* request and referred it to *Don's* office.

Limiting Adjectives

Adjectives that tell "how many," "how much," or "in what order" are called **limiting adjectives.** Some examples are:

- The top five seniors will receive at least three full scholarships. (*Top* tells "in what order," *five* tells "how many seniors," *at least three* tells "how many scholarships.")
- Each senior had won many awards. (*Each* modifies *senior; many* modifies *awards.*)

Proper Adjectives

Proper nouns are very often used as proper adjectives. Some examples are:

Used as a Noun	Used as an Adjective
in Atlanta	an Atlanta restaurant
near Chicago	a Chicago citizen
in Texas	Texas ranch

Proper adjectives include words derived from proper nouns, such as *Mexican, British, Canadian,* and *Israeli.*

Compound Adjectives

Two or more words joined to modify one noun or pronoun form a **compound adjective.** Some examples are:

- Joe wanted a long-term agreement but signed a one-year contract instead. (*Long-term* modifies agreement, and *one-year* modifies contract.)
- Cathy is a well-known author of time-management books. (*Well-known* modifies author, and *time-management* modifies books.)
- Marcus works as a real estate agent. (*Real estate* modifies *agent.*)

Demonstrative Adjectives

The pronouns *this, that, these,* and *those* are *demonstrative pronouns* that can function as **demonstrative adjectives.** Some examples are:

As Pronoun	As Adjective
this is	this desk
these are	these newspapers
that has been	that software
those might be	those computers

> **KEY POINT**
>
> Demonstrative adjectives "point" to the noun or pronoun they modify.

Note that *these* is the plural of *this*; both *these* and *this* indicate nearness to the speaker. *Those* is the plural of *that*; both *those* and *that* indicate distance from the speaker. Never use the pronoun *them* as a substitute for *these* or *those.* Some examples are:

- Please return those books to the library. (*Those* books, not *them* books.)
- These kinds of problems occur early in the semester. (*These* kinds, not *them* kinds, or *these* kind.)

6.3 Self-Assessment A

Identify the adjectives in the following sentences and label them as possessive *P*, limiting *L*, proper *PR*, compound *C*, descriptive *D*, or demonstrative *DM*. Disregard the articles *a, an,* and *the. Note:* Some adjectives may fit in more than one category.

1.   A special seminar is being scheduled for new paramedics to learn these life-saving procedures. _____

2. The Reno attorney who represents that company asked our associates for their opinions on Will's character. _____

_____

_____

3. Dr. Cooper's assistant announced that three well-known speakers will be featured at the fall conference. _____

_____

4. In six months, his older brother will visit this country and intern in our Atlantic City plant. _____

_____

5. In Andy's opinion, we should request a two-year assignment in scenic Alaska. _____

_____

6. One of Lenny's crucial accounts is a new client who represents an East Coast retail store. _____

_____

7. These bonds are tax-free investments, according to their new prospectus. _____

_____

8. The first T-shirt outlet we opened has contributed a substantial profit to our struggling company. _____

_____

Comparison of Adjectives

Descriptive adjectives can be compared. For example, *strong* and *clear* can be compared to show degrees of strength and clarity: *strong, stronger,* and *strongest; clear, clearer,* and *clearest.* These three forms of comparison are called the *positive,* the *comparative,* and the *superlative* degrees.

1. The **positive degree** expresses the quality of one person or thing. Some examples are:

   a *strong* foundation   a *clear* day

2. The **comparative degree** allows us to compare that quality in two persons or things. Some examples are:

   a *stronger* foundation   a *clearer* day

3. The **superlative degree** enables us to compare that quality in three or more persons or things. Some examples are:

   the *strongest* foundation   the *clearest* day

Now that we know how the three degrees are used, we need to know how they are formed.

KEY POINT

The comparative degree compares two persons or things. The superlative degree compares three or more persons or things.

Forming the Comparative and Superlative Degrees

The *comparative degree* is formed by adding "er" to the positive form or by inserting the word *more* or *less* before it. The *superlative* is formed by adding "est" to the positive form or by inserting the word *most* or *least* before it. Some examples are:

Positive	Comparative	Superlative
quick	quicker	quickest
funny	funnier	funniest
poor	poorer	poorest
decisive	more decisive	most decisive
	less decisive	least decisive

In addition, some commonly used adjectives form their comparative and superlative degrees by changing the form to another word completely. Memorize these for quick reference.

Positive	Comparative	Superlative
bad	worse	worst
good	better	best
little	less	least
many	more	most
much	more	most

Selecting the Correct Forms

For adjectives of only one syllable, form the comparative and superlative by adding "er" or "est" to the end of the adjective. For adjectives of three or more syllables, add the word *more* or *less* or *most* or *least* before the adjective. Adjectives of two syllables vary: some fall into the first category, adding "er" or "est"; others follow the second rule, using *more* or *less* or *most* or *least*. Sometimes an error may be obvious to you: *more useful*, not *usefuler; most useful*, not *usefulest.* If you are unsure, consult a dictionary.

Avoiding Comparison Errors

The following discussion highlights two of the most common comparison errors in using adjectives: making double comparisons and comparing absolute adjectives.

Making Double Comparisons.   Do not mix the different ways in which adjectives can be compared—use only one comparative form at a time. Some examples are:

- *better,* not *more better*
- *greatest,* not *most greatest*

Comparing Absolute Adjectives.   Adjectives whose qualities cannot be compared are called **absolute adjectives.** For example, a glass of water cannot be *fuller* or *fullest. Full* is already tops!

Here are some other adjectives that cannot be compared:

accurate	perfect	supreme
complete	perpendicular	true
correct	round	ultimate
dead	square	unanimous
empty	straight	unique
immaculate		

OOPS!

Nothing's Funnier Than Funniest

Your joke was the most funniest I've ever heard.

(*Funniest* cannot be further modified by *most.*)

Although they cannot be compared, the qualities of these adjectives can be approached, as indicated by the following:

more/nearly accurate   most/nearly correct
less/nearly complete   least/nearly perfect

You may hear, especially in advertisements, of products that are the *most unique,* but *unique* really says it all. Remember that absolute adjectives cannot logically be compared.

6.3 Self-Assessment B

Check the following sentences for any errors in the use of adjectives. Write *OK* if the sentence is correct. In the space provided, correctly write the sentence parts that have errors.

1. Which of the two medical centers is largest, City General or University Medical Center? _____

2. The local arts council agrees that Todd's pottery exhibit is very unique.
   _____

3. The hot water dispenser is fuller than the cold water dispenser. _____

4. These condominiums are more better than the condominiums on Elm Street because they are more quiet and more big. _____
   _____

5. Ms. Bostic is definitely a better piano teacher than Ms. Mobley. Indeed, she is probably the best piano teacher in the city. _____

6. Barry thought that we had enough lemonade, but the cooler was very empty. _____

7. Which refrigerator uses the most energy, Model RG384 or Model RG386? _____

8. Malcolm is more happier now that he is working in the computer field.
   _____

Selecting Adjectives for Clarity

Following some simple guidelines will ensure that your prose is expressive and precise.

More Than Any Other, More Than Anyone Else.   In comparisons with *more than,* include the word *other* or *else* if the person or thing is being compared with *other* members of the group. Some examples are:

- Carol is more ambitious than anyone else in the Retail Division.
  (Carol is a member of the Retail Division. Without the word *else,* the sentence would indicate that Carol is not part of the Retail Division but is being compared with people who are in this division.)

- Josh is more creative than any other writer in the Public Relations Department. (Josh is a writer in the Public Relations Department. Without the word *other,* this sentence would indicate that Josh is not a writer in that department.)

Repeated Modifier.   In the following examples, repeating the modifier *a, an, the,* or *my* indicates that two different people are intended. Some examples are:

- The analyst and the programmer (was/were) formerly with Speed Temporary Services. (Repeating *the* shows that two people are referred to. *Were* is the correct verb.)
- The analyst and programmer (was/were) formerly with the local school system. (One person who is both an analyst and a programmer is referred to. *Was* is correct.)

Selecting Adjectives for Added Polish

The following short discussions will help you make correct choices when referring to two, or more than two, persons or things.

Each Other, One Another.   Use *each other* when referring to two in number; use *one another* when referring to three or more. Some examples are:

- Jill and Dale work very effectively with *each other.*
- Several sales representatives talked with *one another* about the proposed new fringe benefits.

Either, Neither; Any, Any One, No One, Not Any, None.   Use *either* or *neither* when referring to one of two persons or things. When referring to three or more, use *any, any one, no one, not any,* or *none.* Some examples are:

- *Either* of the car dealers can locate the car that you want by searching the Internet. (There are only two car dealers; therefore, *either* is correct.)
- *Any one* of the small airlines will arrange a charter flight to the Grand Canyon for you. (There are three or more small airlines; *any one* is correct.)

Compound Adjectives

Hyphenate most **compound adjectives** that appear before a noun. Some examples are:

- air-conditioned buses
- first-quality merchandise
- fund-raising projects
- no-fault insurance
- a one-year contract
- tax-free bonds
- three-mile hike
- up-to-date report

When they appear after the noun, compound adjectives such as *air-conditioned* and *tax-free* retain the hyphen. Most other compounds do not. Some compound adjectives that almost always take hyphens before or after nouns include the following:

- adjective + noun + ed
- adjective + participle
- noun + adjective
- noun + participle

open-ended; single-spaced
high-ranking; soft-spoken
toll-free; year-round
computer-aided; decision-making

> **KEY POINT**
>
> Use a dictionary or a writer's handbook to help you decide whether to hyphenate a compound adjective.

oops!

Longtime use has made some compounds so familiar that they are no longer written with hyphens. Some examples are:

- high school teachers
- a life insurance policy
- real estate services
- social security benefits

When the adverb *well* is used with a participle as a compound adjective, it is usually hyphenated before and after the noun. An example is:

- The well-known author gave us some advice that was well-timed. (*Well-known* and *well-timed* are compound adjectives.)

Confusion may result when *well* and a participle appear after the noun and the participle is part of the verb. An example is:

- The speaker is well known. (In this sentence, *well* is an adverb and *known* is part of the verb.)

6.3 Self-Assessment C

Check the following sentences for any errors in the use of hyphens in compound adjectives. Write *OK* if the sentence is correct. Rewrite the sentence correctly if it contains errors.

1. Alice planned a 15 minute break after each two hour rehearsal.

    _____

2. Analysis has indicated that word of mouth referrals from our satisfied customers are the most effective way to attract new business. _____

    _____

3. Patricia Abbott's court appointed attorney is one of the best attorneys in the country. _____

4. My doctor and my dentist are well known in this region. _____

5. Ask Nelson or Daniel—any one of them should be able to help you.

    _____

6. When Steve and Alex get to know each other better, they will work with one another extremely well. _____

7. Haley Brenner is a five time winner in the company bowling competition. _____

8. Rafael's essay is better than any essay that we have read so far. _____

Predicate Adjectives

In Section 4.3, we discussed being verbs—verbs that express a state of being rather than action. *Being verbs* include all forms of the verb "to be," such as *am, was, will be,* and *should have been,* and such verbs as *feel, seem,* and *appear.* A **predicate adjective** follows a being verb and modifies or describes the subject of the sentence. Some examples are:

- Victor's voice seems hoarse. (*Hoarse* follows a being verb and modifies the subject *voice*.)

- The police officer has been helpful. (*Helpful* follows a being verb and modifies the subject *police officer*.)

Predicate nominatives also follow a being verb, but they rename—*not* modify—the subject. Some examples are:

- Tony was the most outstanding gymnast. (*Gymnast* follows a being verb and renames the subject *Tony*.)
- Roberto Curtez will be my first choice for receiving the promotion. (*Choice* follows a being verb and renames the subject *Roberto Curtez*.)

Pronouns can also be predicate nominatives. An example is:

- The new president is he. (*He* follows a being verb and renames the subject *president*.)

6.3 Self-Assessment D

Identify the words in parentheses and label them as either predicate adjectives, *PA*, or predicate nominatives, *PN*.

1. Each weekend always seems (brief). _____
2. Amelia is the (weather reporter) on Sunday nights. _____
3. The Webb Building is (vacant) and is (well suited) for our business. _____
4. Don is (president) of the local Rotary Club. _____
5. My preference for the trip is (Greece). _____

Assessment   Section 6.3

Review of Key Terms

1. How do *adjectives* make writing and speaking more meaningful? Provide several examples. _____

   _____

2. What is a *compound adjective*? What is the rule about using a hyphen in compound adjectives? _____

   _____

   _____

   _____

Editing Practice

Proofreading Alert!   Correct any errors in the use of homonyms—words that look or sound alike but have different spellings and meanings. *Note:* Using your software program's spell-check feature will not identify homonyms as errors because they are spelled correctly, but misused.

3. Let's take a brake before we get to tired. When we get tired, we may lose hour patients and not make the rite decision. We no that we should consider the situation carefully. _____

_____

_____

Practical Application

Using Adjectives Correctly

4. Correct any errors involving adjectives. On a separate sheet of paper, write the corrected sentences.

   a. Because they cooperated with one another so well, Nikki and Anthony were able to file their report weeks before the June 10 deadline.

   b. Tourists may purchase last minute gifts at the duty free shops at the airport.

   c. Although the price is higher, this VCR is no more better than that one.

   d. Most of them desks are too high for computer use.

   _____

   _____

   _____

   _____

5. It is often easy to use adjectives to describe a person or place. It is more difficult to use descriptive language with mundane objects. As a team choose a product, such as ceiling fans, office chairs, or mufflers, and write a paragraph using at least seven adjectives. Underline each adjective. _____

   _____

   _____

Discussion Point

Thinking Critically

6. Explain how to form the comparative and superlative forms of adjectives. Provide several examples for single-, double-, and multisyllable adjectives. _____

   _____

   _____

   _____

7. Besides descriptive adjectives, what other types of adjectives are there? Provide an example of each. _____

   _____

   _____

   _____

Adverbs

Adverbs

An **adverb** is a word that modifies an adjective, a verb, or another adverb. Adverbs answer questions such as "Why?" "When?" "Where?" "How?" "How much?" and "To what extent?" Many adverbs are formed simply by adding "ly" to an adjective. Adverbs that end in *y* change their *y* to *i* before adding "ly." Some examples are:

Adjective	Adverb
adequate	adequately
clear	clearly
happy	happily
immediate	immediately
perfect	perfectly

Most words that end in *ly* are adverbs, but not all adverbs end in *ly*, as the following list of common adverbs demonstrates. Some examples are:

also	never	soon
always	now	then
hard	often	there
here	quite	too
much	right	very

Note how adverbs are used in the following sentences.

- The real estate agent will meet us here. (Meet where? Answer: *here*. The adverb here modifies the verb *meet*.)
- That software has a very good database program. (How good? *Very* good. The adverb *very* modifies the adjective *good*.)
- Thomas worked quite well under the pressure of the tight deadlines. (How well? *Quite* well. The adverb *quite* modifies another adverb, *well*.)

Some words can be used either as adjectives or as adverbs, depending on their position in the sentence. Some examples are:

- He kicked hard as he swam to defeat his own record time. (Here *hard* is an adverb that modifies the verb *kicked*.)
- Tony complained that washing the windows was hard work. (Here *hard* is an adjective that modifies the noun *work*.)

SECTION OBJECTIVES

When you have finished Section 6.4, you will be able to:

- Discuss the ways in which adverbs are like adjectives and how they differ.
- Explain how to identify the comparative and superlative forms of one-syllable adverbs and of adverbs ending in *ly*.
- Name at least six conjunctive adverbs and six subordinating conjunctions and tell how each is used.
- Discuss several pitfalls of adverb use and ways to avoid them.
- Explain how recognizing linking verbs can help eliminate adjective and adverb confusion.

WHY IT'S IMPORTANT

Your ability to write and to speak correctly can make the difference in whether or not you get the job you want or the promotion you seek.

KEY TERMS

- adverbs
- adverbial clause
- conjunctive adverbs
- double negative

KEY POINT

Like adjectives, *adverbs* modify or describe. You will see several similarities between adverbs and adjectives as you read this section, including some common problems with their use.

Comparison of Adverbs

Adverbs can be compared in much the same way as adjectives. To indicate the comparative and superlative forms of a one-syllable adverb, add *er* or *est* to the positive form. Some examples are:

fast	faster	fastest
late	later	latest
soon	sooner	soonest

For adverbs ending in *ly*, use *more* or *most,* or *less* or *least*:

quickly	more quickly	most quickly
quickly	less quickly	least quickly
confidently	more confidently	most confidently

Certain adverbs form their comparative and superlative degrees by completely changing their forms. Some examples are:

well	better	best
badly	worse	worst
much	more	most

Conjunctive Adverbs

Conjunctive adverbs are adverbs that serve as conjunctions—words that join. These adverbs are also known as transitional words. Some examples are:

accordingly	likewise	still
consequently	moreover	then
furthermore	nevertheless	therefore
however	otherwise	thus

These adverbs join two independent clauses, as shown in the following sentences:

- Insurance premiums are a big expense; moreover, the premiums will go up again at the end of the year.
- Our expenses through June 30 are about 15 percent over budget; however, we expect the expenses to decrease as our quality increases.

Note, again, that each sentence consists of two independent clauses joined by a conjunctive adverb.

Adverbial Clauses

Subordinating conjunctions introduce dependent clauses that serve as adverbs modifying an adjective, verb, or adverb in the main clause. These clauses are called **adverbial clauses.** Here are some commonly used subordinating conjunctions:

after	before	unless
although	for	until
as	if	when
because	since	while

Note the following examples of adverbial clauses introduced by subordinating conjunctions:

- Anita Sanchez will become our chief executive officer when Melvin Morris retires. (The adverbial clause *when Melvin Morris retires* modifies the verb *will become* in the main clause.)

Employability Skills

Organizing Information

Organizing information is a key component in presenting a professional business document. By organizing information in a clear manner, you avoid confusion for your clients and make it easy to communicate ideas.

- Our new line of cellular phones will be profitable if we market it properly. (The adverbial clause *if we market it properly* modifies the adjective *profitable*.)

6.4 Self-Assessment A

Identify the italicized words in the following sentences by labeling each as simple adverb *SA*, conjunctive adverb *CA*, or subordinating conjunction *SC*.

1. *Because* Austin was behind in his work, he stayed *here late* two nights this week. _____

2. John *specifically* stated that he wanted an exercise room; *accordingly,* his architect designed a *very* modern room that was later furnished with top-of-the line equipment. _____

3. *Since* Arik opened his computer repair service, he has been *extremely* busy. _____

4. Lana and Josh have requested assistance *when* Mr. Tobias returns from Detroit. _____

5. The deadline for completion of the telephone system update is next Monday; *therefore,* our vice president has approved our working overtime. _____

6. *If* you would like information regarding the cost and availability of our electric scooter, please e-mail me at toysonwheels@yahoo.com. _____

7. The new copier works *quickly* and *quietly*; however, it does have more paper jams than our last copier did. _____

8. Doug has been *unduly* busy *since* his assistant had to be out of work for knee surgery. _____

Pitfalls of Adverb Use

Adverbs contribute to thoughtful prose; however, in speaking and in writing, be sure to avoid the pitfalls of adverb use described in the following paragraphs.

Position of the Adverb

Place an adverb as close as possible to the word that it modifies. The meaning of a sentence changes depending on where the adverb is placed. Some examples are:

- Only Miss Spradley has an oak credenza in her office. (No one else has one.)
- Miss Spradley has only an oak credenza in her office. (She has nothing else in her office, only an oak credenza.)

Double Negative

Adverbs that have negative meanings, such as *scarcely, hardly, only, never,* and *but,* should not be used with other negatives. Some examples are:

- Ricardo has *scarcely* any money left for his holiday shopping. (Not: "Ricardo *hasn't scarcely*. . . .")

KEY POINT

A **double negative** is two negative expressions used together. A double negative gives a positive meaning.

- With five copiers working, Shonda could hardly hear Rafael. (Not: "Shonda *couldn't hardly.* . . .")

Never or Not

Never and *not* are both adverbs, and both have negative meanings. *Not* expresses simple negation, but *never* means "not ever." Note the word *ever*. Use *never* only when an appropriately long time is intended. Some examples are:

- Ms. McNeilly has *not* sent me an e-mail this week. (*Never* would be incorrect because the meaning "not ever . . . this week" would be wrong.)
- Murphy has *never* been married. (Even though *not* could be substituted for *never, never* is a better choice because it indicates a longer period of time.)

Where for That

The subordinating conjunction *that,* not the conjunctive adverb *where,* should be used in expressions such as the following:

- We heard on television that the governor has endorsed Ben Dixon for attorney general. (Not: "We heard on television *where.* . . ." But: "We toured the house *where* the famous musician once lived.")

Badly or in the Worst Way for Very Much

Too often, we hear people say *badly* or *in the worst way* when they really mean *very much.* An example is:

- Carla said that she wanted a new laptop very much. (Not: "*wanted* a new laptop *badly*" or "wanted a minivan *in the worst way.*")

Adjective and Adverb Confusions

Remember that adjectives, not adverbs, must follow linking verbs. The being verbs, such as *am, is, are, was, were, be, been,* and *being,* are all nonaction, or linking, verbs. In addition to these, the sense verbs, such as *feel, appear, seem, look, sound, taste,* and *smell,* can be used as nonaction verbs. Some examples are:

- Mr. Landers was (happy/happily) when he heard about my new job. (The being verb *was* links the subject Mr. Landers to the adjective *happy.* The verb *was* shows no action.)
- Mr. Landers appeared (happy/happily) when he heard about my new job. (Like *was,* the linking verb *appeared* shows no action; thus the adjective *happy* is correct.)

Keep in mind that some of these verbs can also be used as action verbs. An example is:

- Dr. Kirkpatrick felt carefully for a possible fracture. (Here, *felt* is an action verb; thus the adverb *carefully* modifies the verb felt.)

Frequently Confused Pairs

Several adjective-adverb pairs cause special problems for writers and speakers. Learning the difference will help you express your ideas clearly. In the following pairs, the adjective is listed first.

Bad, Badly.   *Bad* is an adjective; *badly* is an adverb. An example is:

- Vance performs *badly* under pressure. (Performs how? *Badly.* The adverb *badly* modifies the action verb *performs.*)

The problem in selecting between *bad* and *badly* arises following nonaction verbs:

- Jennifer felt (bad/badly) when she learned of the earthquake damage. (Here, *felt* is a linking verb, not an action verb. The answer here, *bad*, will modify not the verb *felt* but the noun *Jennifer*. Thus, an adjective is required because an adverb cannot modify a noun: "Jennifer felt bad . . .")

Real, Really; Sure, Surely. *Real* and *sure* are adjectives. Use the *ly* endings to remind you that *really* and *surely* are adverbs. In the following examples, note that you can substitute the adverb *very* or *certainly* whenever *really* or *surely* is correct. Some examples are:

- Cheryl and Mary Ruth were (real/really) dedicated to helping children who were visually impaired. (*Very dedicated* makes sense. The adverb *really* is correct.)
- Tobias (sure/surely) was smart to have the house checked for termites. (*Certainly was* makes sense. The adverb *surely* is correct.)

Good, Well. *Good* is an adjective, and *well* is an adverb. The adjective *good* can modify nouns and pronouns; the adverb *well* can modify adjectives and verbs. Some examples are:

- Dr. Newton always prepares good lectures. (The adjective *good* modifies the noun *lectures*.)
- Dr. Newton always prepares lectures well. (The adverb *well* modifies the verb *prepares*. *Prepares* lectures how? Prepares *well*.)

Exception: *Well* can also be an adjective, but only when referring to personal health.

- Because Allison did not feel well, she left the office early. (Here, *well* is an adjective referring to a person's health.)

Remember the noun *well-being*, and you'll be sure to recall that *well* is an adjective only when it refers to health.

Some, Somewhat. *Some* is an adjective; *somewhat* is an adverb. To use *somewhat* correctly, test to be sure that you can substitute the phrase *a little bit*. Some examples are:

- As we anticipated, Mr. Nicols was (some/somewhat) surprised when he received the award. (Does *a little bit surprised* make sense? Yes. Thus, *somewhat* is correct.)
- As you requested, we have listed (some/somewhat) suggestions for reducing expenses. (Does *a little bit* ideas make sense? No. Thus, the adjective *some* is correct.)

Most, Almost. *Most* is an adjective, the superlative of *much* or *many*, as in *much, more,* and *most*. *Almost* is an adverb meaning *not quite* or *very nearly*. Some examples are:

- (Most/Almost) assistant managers aspire to become managers. (Because *very nearly assistant managers* makes no sense, *almost* cannot be correct. *Most assistant managers* is correct.)
- Zach brought (most/almost) enough umbrellas for our tour group. (*Very nearly enough umbrellas* does make sense. Thus, *almost* is correct.)

An adjective defines a noun or pronoun, and an adverb defines a verb, an adjective, or another adverb.

6.4 Self-Assessment B

Check the following sentences for any errors in the use of adverbs. Write *OK* if the sentence is correct. Rewrite the sentence correctly if it contains errors.

1. Needless to say, Rex and I felt badly when we heard that Jorge Rodrique was being transferred to San Diego. _____

2. Because you don't feel good, Oscar, we suggest that you work on your computer at home this week. _____

3. Dillon appeared angrily at the idea of selling his land to the developer.

   _____

4. Because of potential legal action, we were somewhat hesitant to discuss this sensitive issue with the employees involved. _____

5. During the preseason sale, you can get a real good deal on a boat.

   _____

6. Mr. Wray was some upset when he heard what had happened to his car.

   _____

7. Most of us in the technology field found the sales projections real disappointing. _____

8. After almost six months, our landscaping business is doing very well.

   _____

9. Because she was rushed, the dental hygienist treated the patients badly.

   _____

10. He was, of course, sure justified in asking the dental hygienist to be more patient. _____

Assessment   Section 6.4

Review of Key Terms

1. How do *adverbs* differ from *adjectives*? _____
   _____

2. What is the role of a *conjunctive adverb*? Write a sentence using a conjunctive adverb and punctuate it correctly. _____
   _____

Editing Practice

Proofreading Alert!   Proofread the following paragraph and correct any errors.

3. Ms. Brasfield called the managers office yesterday to request additional funds for her research project. She reported that she hasn't scarcely any

money remaining in her budget. She had read in a newsletter where more funds would be available in May. Ms. Brasfield believes that she is working on a real good project, and she would like to complete it.

_____

_____

_____

_____

_____

Practical Application

Using Adverbs Correctly

4. Correct any adverb errors in the following sentences. Write the corrected sentences.

   a. We needed help in the worst way when we realized our proposal was $5,000 over budget.

   b. Of course, we felt very badly when we heard of your injury.

   c. "Robert," the football coach said, "you played good today."

   d. Which of the four movies do you like better?

   e. Dana sure does a superb job of staffing for seasonal sales increases.

   _____

   _____

   _____

   _____

   _____

5. People often read reviews of restaurants before deciding if they will eat there. Choose two restaurants and write a one-page review comparing the two. Review the quality of the food, the service, and the expense. Underline all comparative adverbs. Share your findings in a team. What similarities did you find? _____

Discussion Point

Thinking Critically

6. Explain how to form the *comparative* and *superlative* forms of adverbs. Provide several examples. _____

   _____

   _____

7. What are some common errors writers make with adverbs? How can these errors be avoided? _____

   _____

   _____

   _____

   _____

Unit 3

Developing Writing Skills

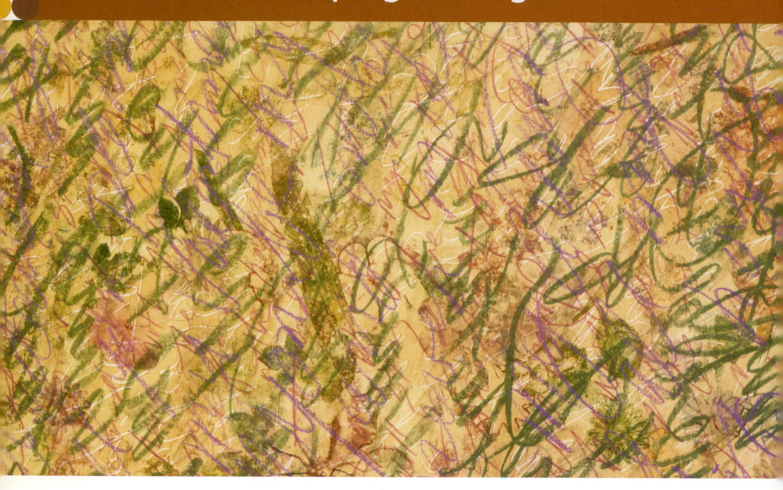

Unit Overview

In this unit, you will learn how to sharpen your writing skills to communicate effectively.

Chapter 7

Applying the Mechanics of Style

Chapter 8

Sharpening Writing Skills

Renata, born in Mexico, was the head teller of a large branch bank in a Texas city. Her native language was Spanish, but she spoke English quite well, even though she had lived in the United States less than two years. Renata had studied English at a community college and learned to write English correctly. Her problem areas were capitalization and punctuation. She knew that if she were promoted to assistant branch manager, she would have to write many more memos, letters, and reports and would need to be a polished writer.

Renata checked with several schools in the area, but none of them had a course that would help her specifically with punctuation and capitalization. Renata talked with Consuelo, an associate of hers, about her writing concerns. Consuelo understood completely, because she had had a similar problem after learning to speak and write English. She recommended that Renata speak with Allison in the human resources department about her desire to improve her writing skills.

Allison was impressed with Renata's current English skills but even more impressed that she had diagnosed her own difficulty and that she wanted to overcome it. Allison ordered several books that Renata could work through on her own and also arranged for a retired high school English teacher to work with her one night a week.

As a result of her efforts, Renata made rapid progress. She had diagnosed her own difficulty and had sought assistance in overcoming it. What role will improving her skills play in Renata's chances for promotion?

As you read Unit 3, follow Renata's example and identify areas of punctuation, capitalization, and numbers use in which you need to improve. What strategies will you use to help you improve your skills?

Thinking Critically

What are the benefits of recognizing areas for self-improvement?

How can taking initiative affect your job performance?

What strategies will you use to improve your punctuation skills?

Chapter 7

Applying the Mechanics of Style

Workplace Connection

Being able to properly punctuate your business writing adds to the evidence that you are indeed a professional.

CHAPTER OBJECTIVES

When you have completed this chapter, you should be able to:

- Use punctuation correctly.
- Apply capitalization rules to business writing.
- Use abbreviations appropriately.
- Apply number expression rules in business writing.

Sentence Enders

Essential Principles

Punctuation marks do for writing what pauses, changes in pitch, and gestures do for speaking: They provide the necessary road signs to help readers and listeners understand our messages correctly. The three punctuation marks—periods, question marks, and exclamation points—are used to end sentences. In addition, these marks have some other uses, which will be discussed in this chapter.

Periods

It's important to learn when to use periods and when not to use periods, as well as how to avoid some common pitfalls in using them. A **period** is a point used to mark the end of a sentence.

When to Use Periods

Use periods (1) to end declarative or imperative sentences, (2) to end requests that are phrased as questions simply for the sake of courtesy, and (3) to end indirect questions.

After Declarative and Imperative Sentences. Declarative sentences make statements, and **imperative sentences** order someone to act. Some examples are:

- All expense reimbursement requests must be submitted by Monday (declarative sentence).
- Please submit your expense reimbursement requests by Monday (imperative sentence).

After Requests Phrased as Questions. In an effort to soften commands and orders, speakers and writers often phrase such orders as questions. Because such statements are not really questions, use periods to end these sentences:

- Will you please put the appointment on my electronic calendar. (This is not a question—no answer is required.)
- May we have the live lobsters shipped by the fastest method. (This is a polite way of saying, "Send the live lobsters as fast as possible," not really a question.)
- Can you demonstrate the new software by next Thursday? (This question requires a yes-or-no answer and, therefore, requires a question mark rather than a period.)

After Indirect Questions. An **indirect question** is a question restated as a declarative sentence. Some examples are:

- Donald asked me if I had contacted Mr. Steinberg about our computer security. (The question is related as a declarative sentence, so it requires a period.)

- Alicia, have you contacted Ms. Steinberg about our computer security? (Stated as a question, the sentence requires a question mark.)

7.1 Self-Assessment A

Check the following sentences for errors in the use of end punctuation. For each item, insert a period or a question mark, and write _P_ if there should be a period and _Q_ for question mark.

1. May we schedule your physical for Monday morning at 10 a.m. _____

2. Will you please close the door _____

3. Jacob asked if he should work Monday _____

4. Emily, may I ride to the party with you tonight _____

5. Submit your evaluation to your supervisors by July 1 _____

6. May I please have your comments before you leave _____

7. Did John Catlett respond to the therapy _____

8. Mrs. Voorhees asked Sarah if she planned to wear a red hat to the luncheon _____

When Not to Use Periods

Do not use periods in the following instances.

After Sentences Ending in Abbreviations. Do _not_ use two periods for sentences that end with abbreviations that require periods. If a sentence-ending abbreviation requires a period, let that period serve both functions. An example is:

- As printed on your itinerary, the hot air balloon excursion will depart promptly at 5 a.m. (Not 5 a.m..)

After Headings or After Roman Numerals with Names or Titles. A heading that is set on a separate line (for examples, see some of the headings in this textbook) should not be followed by a period. Also, roman numerals used with names or titles should not be followed by periods.

- John Mattison Camp III has been appointed to our board of directors (Not "John Mattison Camp III. has been . . .").

After Numbers or Letters in Parentheses. Do not use periods after numbers or letters enclosed in parentheses that precede enumerated items in a sentence.

- Reduced Internet access fees have been negotiated for our associates with (1) America Online, (2) Internet of Austin, and (3) Speed Runner Cable Company.

Digital Data

Formatting Documents

It is important to apply the correct mechanics of style when formatting documents. Don't forget to use the italics feature in your word processor when you are listing the titles of books, newspapers, plays, operas, or movies.

KEY POINT

Do not use periods after the following:

1. **Sentence-ending abbreviations**
2. **Headings**
3. **Roman numerals with names or titles**
4. **Numbers or letters in parentheses**
5. **Even-dollar amounts**

When numbers or letters are not in parentheses and are displayed on separate lines, use a period after each.

- Our employees have access to:

  1. America Online.
  2. Internet of Austin.
  3. Speed Runner Cable Company.

Note: In the above example, each item in the list completes the introductory statement. Each item is the object of the preposition *to* in the introductory statement. Therefore, each item ends with a period. If the items did not complete the introductory statement, no periods would be needed.

If the introductory statement for a numbered list is grammatically complete, do not use periods after the items in the list. An example is:

- Our employees have access to all the following:

  1. America Online
  2. Internet of Austin
  3. Speed Runner Cable Company

In addition, if each item in a list is a complete sentence or a long phrase, use a period.

After Even Amounts of Dollars.   Except in tables (when it is important to align numbers), do not use periods or unnecessary zeros in even-dollar amounts. An example is:

- Thank you for sending your $100 contribution to support the homeless shelter (not $100. contribution and not $100.00 contribution).

As shown in the preceding example, omitting the period and use of unnecessary zeros improves the readability of the sentence.

7.1 Self-Assessment B

Check the following sentences for any errors in the use of periods. Write *OK* if the sentence is correct. If it contains errors, circle any error(s) and write the correction(s) on the line provided.

1. Our new health insurance does not cover the following employees: ＿＿＿

   a. Seasonal associates
   b. Part-time staff
   c. Temporary support personnel

2. Until April 1, you can join the new sports and health club for $600 a year. ＿＿＿＿＿＿＿＿＿＿＿＿＿＿＿＿＿＿＿＿＿＿

3. The best PowerPoint slide presentation was given by John R. Davis, Jr..

   ＿＿＿＿＿＿＿＿＿＿＿＿＿＿＿＿＿＿＿＿＿＿＿＿＿＿

4. The tour guide listed his complete name, Thurston P. Howell III., on the ship's passenger list. ＿＿＿＿＿＿＿＿＿＿＿＿＿＿＿

KEY POINT

Do not use periods after numbers or letters in parentheses or after even-dollar amounts.

oops!

Final Punctuation

My flight arrives at 9:55 p.m..

(9:55 p.m. is correct, not 9:55 p.m..)

5. The enclosed materials include (1) a hotel reservation form, (2) a flight request form, and (3) a brochure describing tourist attractions. _____

6. Your $570.00 refund for the unused portion of your airline ticket is enclosed. _____

Period Pitfalls

Using a period at the end of an *incomplete* thought, or fragment, is a **period fault.** Using a comma when a period is needed is a *comma splice.* Avoid these errors in your writing.

The Period Fault. An incomplete thought, or **fragment,** is not a sentence and therefore cannot stand alone. It should not end with a period. A period fault often occurs when a dependent clause is separated from the main clause. Generally, joining the incomplete thought to a main clause will solve the problem. Some examples are:

- Brent is taking a computer applications course. Because he believes it will help him get a promotion. (The second group of words cannot stand alone. This dependent clause should be joined to the preceding independent clause as shown in the following example.)
- Brent is taking a computer applications course because he believes it will help him get a promotion. (Now, the dependent clause does not stand alone but is joined correctly to an independent clause.)

The Comma Splice. A **comma splice** is a comma by itself used to join two independent clauses. Instead, a period is needed. Comma splices may also be remedied by using a semicolon or a conjunctive adverb. Some examples are:

- Your seeds and bulbs are enclosed, a planting guide for your location will be mailed within ten days. (Place a period after *enclosed* to separate these two independent clauses.)
- Jedd is recruiting students to tour Israel, he said that the reservation deadline is May 15. (A semicolon can be used to join these two independent clauses.)

A comma splice will sometimes create a *run-on sentence* in which two related ideas that can stand alone grammatically are joined together by a comma. A run-on sentence may be corrected by using a period, a semicolon, or a comma followed by a coordinating conjunction.

 ## 7.1 Self-Assessment C

Check the following sentences for any period faults or comma splices. Write *OK* if the sentence is correct. If it contains errors, circle any error(s) and write the correction(s) on the line provided.

1. Tomas was at a conference last week, but he called the office each day to check on his clients. _____

2. The flight was delayed for almost four hours. When a severe thunderstorm developed near the airport. _____

3. As we discussed at a recent committee meeting. We must continually update our technology. _____

4. Requests for specific software should be made by Tuesday noon, we get a discount on software ordered when we order our computers. _____

_____

5. Since he came to work here a year ago. Rafael has not missed a day of work. _____

6. Dr. Ramirez is being honored at a reception on Monday, he is retiring at the end of the year. _____

7. The cashier stamped the checks for deposit, he immediately placed them in the safe. _____

8. Even though Hagar exercises daily at the spa for about an hour. She jogs two miles each evening. _____

Question Marks

Use question marks after direct questions and in a series of questions. A **question mark** is a mark used in writing and printing at the conclusion of a sentence to indicate a question.

After Direct Questions

Direct questions always end with question marks. Some examples are:

- Have you finished the spreadsheet?
- Mrs. Alexander, have you mailed your tax return yet?
- Should we mark these packages "Fragile"?
- Reynaldo asked, "Will you complete the report by Thursday?"

Sentences that begin as statements but end as questions are considered questions. Use question marks at the end of such sentences:

- Caleb shipped the fruit by United Parcel Service, didn't he? (The question at the end of the statement—*didn't he?*—requires you to put a question mark at the end of the sentence.)
- Makayla is planning to go to the dentist today, isn't she? (Again, the question following the statement makes this an interrogative sentence. Use a question mark at the end of the sentence.)

In a Series of Questions

When a sentence contains a series of questions, the series may be joined by commas and a conjunction (like other series) and end with one question mark. Alternatively, each question may be separated from the main sentence and may have its own question mark. Some examples are:

- Have you distributed copies of the commendation to the employee, her supervisor, and the human resource department? (The items in the series are joined by commas and the conjunction *and*. The sentence ends with a question mark.)
- Have you distributed copies of the commendation to the employee? her supervisor? the human resource department? (Each item in the series is separated from the main sentence, and each ends with its own question mark. Note that a lowercase letter begins each item to show that it is grammatically connected to the main sentence.)

Are You Asking Me?

Did you schedule your dental appointment.

(*Appointment?* is correct, not *appointment.*)

Question Mark Pitfall

So many questions include the word *why, ask,* or *how* that some writers automatically use a question mark at the end of any sentence with one of these words. However, many sentences with *why, ask,* or *how* are simply indirect questions—that is, declarative sentences. Some examples are:

- Alice Vergeer asked why the copy machine had not been repaired. (This statement is an indirect question. Use a period.)
- Bob asked how we intended to decrease expenses. (This is a statement, not a question.)

7.1 Self-Assessment D

Check the following sentences for any errors in the use of periods and question marks. Write *OK* if the sentence is correct. If it contains errors, circle any error(s) and write the correction(s) on the line provided.

1. The new technician asked how to use the new lighting system? _____

2. Doesn't Courtney know that the Ethics Seminar has been canceled because of the tornado. _____

3. The paper towels for the lunch room are in the supply cabinet, aren't they. _____

4. Gary asked Kevin if he had completed rotating the tires on the pickup truck? _____

5. Brenda knows how to use the heart monitor, doesn't she. _____

6. When will Chris complete his training at the Naval Academy? _____

7. Ask the tour guide when we should meet for the tour of Navy Pier? _____

8. Has the Realtor already notified the buyer? The seller? And the title company? _____

Exclamation Points

During the typical day, we see many, many exclamation points as we read signs and advertisements: "Special Sale!" "Limited-Time Offer!" "Hurry! Place Your Order Today!" The **exclamation point** is used to show strong emotion or feeling. An exclamation point can be used after a single word or at the end of a sentence. In business writing, exclamation points are limited to special uses. Some examples are:

- Congratulations! You have been named Volunteer of the Year.
- We were awarded the construction contract. What great news!
- Mr. Cortez, your suggestions helped increase profits by 25 percent!

Sometimes the exclamation point may replace a question mark when a question is really just a strong statement. An example is:

- What happened to the fax machine! (This sentence is worded like a question but really is an exclamation.)

Do not overuse the exclamation point! Some inexperienced writers incorrectly use two or three exclamation points at the end of a sentence for extra emphasis. One exclamation point is enough.

Assessment   Section 7.1

Review of Key Terms

1. What kind of sentences should end with a period? _____
   _____
   _____

2. What is a *comma splice*? Provide an example. _____
   _____

Editing Practice

Grammar Alert!   Which of the following sentences should end with periods and which should end with question marks? Write *P* for *period* and *Q* for *question mark*.

3. Alfred, may I ride home with you this afternoon _____

4. Sun Lee asked if she should work overtime _____

5. Will you please submit your goals for next year to Athena by Monday
   _____

6. May we schedule your dental appointment for Monday morning at 8:30
   _____

7. Oksana asked Mr. Moreno if he plans to call his travel agent _____

Practical Application

Correcting Sentences

8. Correct any errors in the use of periods, question marks, or exclamation points in the following sentences.

   a. The professor asked the class if they would like an extra week to complete their research papers?
   b. Ms. Garcia's administrative assistant booked her a flight that leaves at 7 p.m.
   c. Although the sales meeting was postponed. We still celebrated Mr. Lee's retirement at the end of the week.

d. Our financial adviser suggested that we increase our (1.) life insurance, (2.) foreign investments, and (3.) professional liability coverage.

_____

_____

_____

_____

_____

_____

9. Find and read an article with information about the stock market. Then, write a group response that summarizes the article and includes the following end marks: period, question mark, and exclamation point. _____

Discussion Point

Making Comparisons

10. What is the difference between an _indirect question_ and a _direct question_? _____

_____

11. Why would some sentences end with an _exclamation point_ instead of a _question mark_? _____

_____

Commas

Essential Principles

Commas are like road signs. Road signs let the driver know when to slow down, when to stop, and in what direction the road is curving. Likewise, commas let the reader know when they should pause and slow down.

Effective speakers use pauses that enable their listeners to grasp and connect thoughts and to separate expressions that are not essential to the clarity of the message. Similarly, effective writers use **commas** to connect thoughts and to separate elements within sentences. You will find that using commas correctly will be an important asset to you in your business and personal writing.

Study the following applications so that you will be able to use commas correctly in all forms of business writing.

In Compound Sentences

To use commas correctly in compound sentences, you need to be able to distinguish a compound sentence from a *simple sentence* with a *compound predicate*. To accomplish this, review the distinction between simple and compound sentences.

A **simple sentence** contains a subject and a verb, and it expresses a complete thought. The subject or the verb may be compound. A simple sentence with a compound predicate has only one subject and a compound verb. Do *not* use a comma to separate a compound predicate. Some examples are:

- Alex moved to Bristol last week and started his new job with Cyber Technology today. (*Alex* is the only subject for the two verbs in the compound predicate—*moved* and *started.* No comma is needed.)
- The Solomon & Willis Company originally planned to develop a dude ranch on the acreage but later decided to sell the land instead. (*Company* is the subject for the compound predicate verbs *planned* and *decided.* No comma is needed.)

A **compound sentence** has two or more independent clauses, each with a subject and a predicate. Note in the following sentences how commas are used with the coordinating conjunctions *and, but, or,* and *nor* to join two independent clauses. Some examples are:

- Alex moved to Bristol last week, and he started his new job with Cyber Technology today. (The comma and the conjunction *and* join two independent clauses.)
- The Solomon & Willis Company originally planned to develop a dude ranch on the acreage, but it later decided to sell the land instead. (The comma and the conjunction *but* join two independent clauses.)

SECTION OBJECTIVES

When you have finished Section 7.2, you will be able to:

- Use commas correctly in compound sentences and in a series.
- Use commas correctly after introductory words, phrases, and clauses.
- Use commas correctly to set off interrupting elements.
- Use commas correctly with consecutive adjectives and repeated expressions.

WHY IT'S IMPORTANT

Commas help your readers make sense of information you present.

KEY TERMS

- commas
- simple sentences
- compound sentences
- series
- semicolons
- infinitive phrases
- participial phrases
- gerund phrases
- prepositional phrases
- interrupting elements
- parenthetic elements
- explanatory elements
- appositives
- consecutive adjectives
- direct address

KEY POINT

Each clause in a compound sentence can stand alone as a sentence.

- Hannah will take a refresher course in spreadsheets this semester, or she will take a course in database management. (The comma and the conjunction *or* join two independent clauses.)
- José does not plan to apply for the position, nor does he plan to transfer to another office. (The comma and the conjunction *nor* join two independent clauses.)

Memory Hook

To help distinguish between a simple sentence with a compound predicate and a compound sentence, use the following:

- **Simple sentence with compound predicate**
  subject + verb + verb
  <u>Tim</u> <u>finished</u> the analysis on time but <u>forgot</u> to report his results.
- **Compound sentence**
  subject + verb + conjunction + subject + verb
  <u>Tim</u> <u>finished</u> the analysis on time, *but* <u>he</u> <u>forgot</u> to report his results.

No Comma Between Very Short Clauses

When the independent clauses are very short, the comma is usually omitted. Read the following examples aloud; as you do so, note that each sentence sounds "natural" without a pause before the conjunction. Some examples are:

- Katrina washed the car and Omar waxed it. (The two independent clauses are short; the comma between car and *and* may be omitted.)
- Will went to lunch and Fred joined him later. (Again, two short independent clauses do not require a comma.)

Semicolon to Avoid Possible Misreading

If either clause of a compound sentence already contains one or more commas, a misreading may result. To avoid misreadings, use a semicolon, not a comma, to separate the clauses. An example is:

- This next benefits meeting will cover changing dental plans, submitting claims for reimbursement, and establishing flexible working hours; and a company-sponsored child care center will be the topic of next month's meeting. (The semicolon provides a stronger break and prevents misreading a company-sponsored child care center as part of the preceding series.)

When the two independent clauses in a compound sentence are very long, a semicolon is required. Better yet, rewrite very long clauses as separate sentences. An example is:

- The findings of our research staff clearly point to the possible effectiveness of polyvinyl chloride (PVC) as a replacement for the more expensive materials we are now using. We fully support the need to fund further research to explore the uses of PVC for our entire line of products.

7.2 Self-Assessment A

Check the following sentences for any errors in the use of commas. Write *OK* if the sentence is correct. If it contains errors, circle any error(s) and write the correction(s) on the line provided.

1. Grady does not plan to fly to Dallas nor does he plan to drive; he plans to take the train. _____

2. Wesley will officially retire in June, but will work part time next year.

   _____

3. Jennifer will be transferred to Boston in September but her replacement has not been appointed. _____

4. I telephoned the customer this morning but was disappointed with his attitude. _____

5. The surgery began at 10:30 a.m., but ended before noon. _____

6. Max should fix his air conditioner immediately, or he should get someone else to fix it. _____

7. Keith drove, and Nathan slept. _____

8. Hilton interviewed Beth, Dave, and Phil, and Leslie interviewed Sharon, Teresa, and Vince. _____

In a Series

A **series** consists of three or more items in a sequence. The items may be words, phrases, or clauses.

KEY POINT

Use a comma before the conjunction when listing three or more items in a series.

- The nurse checked the patient's blood pressure, temperature, and pulse (a series of words with the comma placed before the conjunction).

- Many of our employees do volunteer work in hospitals, at homeless shelters, and for various charitable organizations (a series of three phrases: *in hospitals, at shelters, for various charitable organizations*).

- Joan will head our New Orleans office, Danny will fill Joan's former position at headquarters, and Lisa will become Danny's assistant (a series of three independent clauses).

When *Etc.* Ends a Series

Etc. means "and so forth." Never write *and etc.* because that would mean "and and so forth"!

When *etc.* ends a series, use a comma before and after it unless *etc.* ends the sentence. Some examples are:

- Summer interns at the newspaper interview community leaders, research background information, write feature articles, etc. (Use a comma before *etc.* but no comma after *etc.*, because it ends the sentence.)

- Jeanne will meet the clients, take them to dinner, show them around the city, *etc.,* according to Kyle's instructions. (Use a comma before and after *etc.*)

Semicolons Instead of Commas in a Series

When the items in a series are long clauses or if the items already contain commas, use a **semicolon** to provide a stronger break between items. Some examples are:

- Ms. Russell has asked us to do the following: place the cartons on shipping pallets; move the pallets to the warehouse entrance for shipment; and obtain a signed receipt showing the time the pallets were picked up by the shipper. (A long pause in between the items is helpful to the reader.)
- During his first two months with the company, Ben met with clients in Miami, Florida; Trenton, New Jersey; and Kansas City, Kansas. (Using semicolons to separate the parts of the series enables the reader to grasp the meaning immediately.)

When Not to Use Commas

Do not use commas in the following situations.

At the End of a Series.   Do not use a comma after the last item in a series (the item following the conjunction) unless the sentence structure requires a comma. Only the items preceding the conjunction are separated by commas. Some examples are:

- Duane, Esther, and Tomas are responsible for the orientation sessions for new employees. (No comma is required after *Tomas,* the last item in the series.)
- Duane, Esther, and Tomas, who are training specialists in our home office, will conduct the orientation sessions for new employees. (The comma after *Tomas* is required because of the interrupting clause beginning with *who.*)

With Repeated Conjunctions.   When the conjunction is repeated between every two items in the series, no commas are needed:

- You may send us the contract by mail or courier or fax. (The conjunction *or* is repeated between series items; no commas are needed.)

In Certain Company Names.   Write a company's name exactly as it is printed on the company's letterhead. Some companies write their names *without* a comma before *and*; others use a comma. In all cases, no comma is used before an ampersand (&).

- Mallory, Paxton, and Stevens Company bought the property. (This example follows the official company name precisely.)
- Dewey, Cheatum & Howe is a reputable accounting firm. (Never use a comma before an *ampersand: &.*)

7.2 Self-Assessment B

Check the following sentences for any errors in the use of commas. Write *OK* if the sentence is correct. If it contains errors, circle any error(s) and write the correction(s) on the line provided.

1. At midnight, the security guard turns off the lights, locks the door, turns on the alarm, and etc. _____

2. The firm of Jonas, Jonas, & Smith represented our team. _____

3. Shorts, tees, tanks, etc. will be on sale after July 4. _____

4. Amy will request the van, Harriet will make the hotel reservations and Leslie will buy the theater tickets. _____

5. You can travel by van, train, or airplane, or if you prefer, you may drive your car. _____

6. Ben, John and Morris brought their gear and are going trout fishing tomorrow. _____

7. You can use your cellular phone in your car, on the train or on your sailboat. _____

8. Abigail, Max, and Molly, our summer interns, will temporarily replace our vacationing employees. _____

Following Introductory Words, Phrases, and Clauses

Commas follow introductory words, phrases, and clauses to provide a needed pause and thereby prevent possible misreading or confusion.

Introductory Words

Commas follow *introductory words* at the beginning of sentences or clauses. Some of the most commonly used introductory words are listed in **Exhibit 7.1.**

Common Introductory Words		
clearly	meanwhile	now
consequently	moreover	obviously
finally	namely	originally
first	naturally	therefore
however	no	yes

Exhibit 7.1
Common Introductory Words
Thinking Critically. What is another introductory word that you commonly use in business communications?

- Naturally, we were eager to hear the results of his medical tests. (The introductory word *naturally* is at the beginning of the sentence and is followed by a comma.)
- The medical tests showed that his surgery had been successful; naturally, we were thrilled that he would soon return to work. (Here, the word *naturally* introduces the second clause in the sentence. Again, it is followed by a comma.)
- We received the results from the medical tests today; we were, *naturally*, extremely happy that his surgery was a success. (Note that a comma is used before and after *naturally*.)

Introductory Phrases

Commas are often needed after infinitive phrases, participial phrases, and prepositional phrases.

After Infinitive Phrases. An infinitive phrase is introduced by *to*. An **infinitive phrase** that begins a sentence or a clause is followed by a comma unless the phrase is the subject of the sentence or clause. Some examples are:

- To finish the inventory report, Mary will have to work late every night this week. (The infinitive phrase *to finish the inventory report* introduces the sentence. It modifies the subject *Mary*.)
- To finish the inventory report is Linda's priority for the week. (Here, the infinitive phrase *to finish the inventory report* is the subject of the sentence.)

After Participial Phrases. A participal is a word having the characteristics of both a verb and an adjective. A **participial phrase** is always followed by a comma. Some examples are:

- *Waiting for the airplane to arrive,* Susan read the novel she had brought with her to the airport. (Use a comma after the participial phrase.)
- *Delayed by heavy snow,* Lisa needed an extra two hours to complete the trip. (Use a comma after a participial phrase.)

Do not confuse participial phrases with *gerund phrases*. A **gerund phrase** is a phrase that contains a gerund. A gerund is a verb form that ends in *ing* and is used as a noun. When a gerund phrase appears at the beginning of a sentence, it is always a subject. A participial phrase is always an adjective. Some examples are:

- Maintaining law and order is every police officer's responsibility. (*Maintaining* is a gerund. The gerund phrase *Maintaining law and order* is the subject of the sentence.)
- Maintaining law and order, the police officer improved the living conditions in our neighborhood. (Here, *Maintaining* is a participle—an adjective that modifies the subject *police officer.*)

After Prepositional Phrases. Use commas after long **prepositional phrases** and prepositional phrases that contain verb forms such as gerunds. Some examples are:

- For more detailed installation instructions, please call our toll-free number. (Long prepositional phrase.)
- After stopping the runaway car, Lynn received awards from the mayor and the governor. (Note the gerund *stopping* in the prepositional phrase.)

Do not use a comma if the prepositional phrase is short or if it flows directly into the main thought of the sentence. An example is:

- By noon the temperature should rise and the snow should begin to melt. (The prepositional phrase *By noon* is short and flows directly into the sentence.)

Introductory Clauses

A comma is needed after a dependent clause that precedes a main clause. An example is:

- When Lorenzo returned from the conference, he met with the engineers who had several recommendations for solving the problem. (A comma after a dependent clause that precedes the main clause.)

To apply this comma rule, you must be able to identify the words and phrases that commonly begin introductory clauses (see **Exhibit 7.2**).

Words That Introduce Clauses

after	how	though
although	if	till
as	inasmuch as	unless
as if	in case	when
as soon as	in order that	whenever
as though	otherwise	where
because	provided	whereas
before	since	wherever
even if	so that	whether
for	then	while

Exhibit 7.2
Words That Introduce Clauses
Thinking Critically.
Which word would best finish the follow-ing sentence? If at first you don't succeed, _____ try again.

7.2 Self-Assessment C

Check the following sentences for any errors in the use of commas. Write *OK* if the sentence is correct. If it contains errors, circle any error(s) and write the correction(s) on the line provided.

1. To succeed as a customer service rep, requires confidence, courtesy, and tact. _____

2. Unless you apply before August 1 you will not be considered for the Scholars program. _____

3. To enter the U.S. Capitol each person must present a current picture ID.

   _____

4. Unless the Zoning Commission approves our zoning request today we will not be able to start remodeling tomorrow. _____

5. Tia should be able to leave by 10 a.m.; therefore she should arrive in Dallas by 6 p.m. _____

6. Installing the new windows, took Fred and Anneliese most of the week. _____

7. Installing the new windows, Fred and Anneliese worked most of the week. _____

8. When you return from your trip to Boston we will start working on remodeling the Conference Room. _____

9. Before Marilyn was promoted to Dean she worked at least 50 hours a week. _____

10. Mr. Cronkhite finally gave his consent to the insurance plan; he approved moreover adding vision and dental benefits for everyone. _____

With a Dependent Clause Following a Main Clause

KEY POINT

When the dependent clause follows the main clause, use a comma only if the dependent clause offers nonessential information.

We have already seen that a dependent clause preceding a main clause is always followed by a comma. Some examples are:

- As we decided at our regular Monday morning meeting, we will evaluate the commission rates for all sales representatives. (Comma after a dependent clause preceding a main clause.)
- After Mr. Harrison has made his decision regarding recruitment, he will meet with each department head. (Comma after a dependent clause preceding a main clause.)

However, when the dependent clause *follows* the main clause, use a comma only if the dependent clause offers *nonessential* information—information not needed to complete the meaning. As you read the following examples, note how the dependent clauses differ. Some examples are:

- We will evaluate the commission rates for all sales representatives, as we decided at our regular Monday morning meeting. (The words *as we decided at our regular Monday morning meeting* are not critical to understanding the meaning of the sentence. They merely provide extra information. A comma separates nonessential words.)
- Mr. Harrison will meet with each department head after he has made his decision regarding recruitment. (No comma is needed here because the clause *after he has made his decision regarding recruitment* is important to the meaning of the sentence. It provides essential information, not additional information. It tells precisely when "Mr. Harrison will meet . . .")

When writing such sentences, you will, of course, know the meaning you intend and will have an easier job of deciding whether a comma is needed or not.

With Interrupting, Parenthetical, and Explanatory Elements

Use commas to set off nonessential information such as interrupting, parenthetical, and explanatory elements.

Interrupting Elements

Interrupting elements do not provide essential information. Use commas to set off interrupters. Some examples are:

- The increase in annual profits, naturally, has elated the stockholders. (Commas set off the interrupting word *naturally*.)
- Each division's proposed budget, consequently, can be increased because of the significant jump in profits during the last fiscal year. (Again, commas set off the interrupter *consequently*.)

Parenthetical Elements

Parenthetical elements are added words, phrases, and clauses within sentences to emphasize a contrast, express an opinion, soften a harsh statement, qualify or amend meaning, and so on. They should be set off by commas.

Some examples are:

- Any policy changes, in my opinion, must be approved by the personnel committee. (The parenthetical expression *in my opinion* is not essential to the meaning of the sentence and is set off by commas.)
- The text of the policy manual, but not the appendices, has been approved by the executive committee. (The parenthetical statement separated by commas emphasizes the contrast.)

Explanatory Elements

Additional information that is not essential to the meaning of the sentence is set off by commas and is called an **explanatory element.** To determine if information is nonessential, read the sentence without the information. If the sentence makes sense, use commas to set off the additional information. Some examples are:

- The systems analyst, suspecting a virus in the computer network, issued an advisory memo to all network users. (Read this sentence aloud. As you do so, note the pause at the beginning and at the end of the participial phrase *suspecting a virus in the computer network*. Use commas to set off such explanatory elements.)
- Leslie O'Malley, who developed this procedure, is a third-shift supervisor. (The clause *who developed this procedure* is set off by commas. Again, read this sentence aloud to note that you pause before and after the explanatory element.)

Note, however, that clauses that *are* essential are not set off by commas. An example is:

- Our company has five additional third-shift supervisors. The third-shift supervisor who developed this procedure is Leslie O'Malley. (In this sentence, the clause *who developed this procedure* does not provide extra information; it specifies one of the "five third-shift supervisors." Note that in reading this sentence aloud, you would not pause before and after the clause.)

> ### KEY POINT
>
> To determine if an element is interrupting, parenthetical, or explanatory, do this: Read the sentence without the element. If the meaning of the sentence isn't affected, use commas to set off the element. It is nonessential.

oops!

Punctuate Your Meaning

Omitting a punctuation mark can completely change the meaning of a sentence.

- The teacher said the student was very cooperative.
- The teacher, said the student, was very cooperative.

In each sentence, who was cooperative?)

Check the following sentences for any errors in the use of commas. Write *OK* if the sentence is correct. If it contains errors, circle any error(s) and write the correction(s) on the line provided.

1. An effective alternative Jon and I think will be to reschedule the meeting after the inventory has been completed. _____

2. The team members, not the manager, must determine the course of action. _____

3. The technician, who is installing the computer in the lab, is Andrea Mitchem. _____

4. Mrs. Jonas waiting for the fax from our San Diego office did not go out for lunch. _____

5. One possible solution as we discussed yesterday is to order immediately the supplies that we anticipate using next week. _____
   _____

6. Ms. Delgado, who designs our luggage, met with the international sales manager yesterday. _____

7. The income tax attorney, whom you should consult, is Melvin Campos.
   _____

8. The dividends received but not the stock owned are called earnings.
   _____

9. The only accountant on our staff, who is a CPA, is Robin Bradley. _____
   _____

10. Please order additional toner cartridges, if the special discount is still in effect. _____

KEY POINT

Use commas before and after an appositive that is nonessential to the meaning of the sentence.

With Appositives and Related Constructions

The use of commas with appositives, degrees and titles, calendar dates, and state names is explained in the following discussion.

Appositives

An **appositive** is a word or a group of words that gives more information about a preceding word or phrase but is not essential to the meaning of a sentence. The appositive is set off by commas. Some examples are:

- The new paralegal, Aaron Fielding, is working on the Raymond case. (The appositive, *Aaron Fielding,* offers additional information, which is not essential, and is set off by commas.)
- The controller of Peeler Accounting, an adjunct professor at the community college, is an expert in financial management. (The appositive, *an adjunct professor at the community college,* offers additional information and is set off by commas.)

When the appositive is very closely connected with the noun that precedes it, no commas are used to set off the appositive. This occurs most often with one- or two-word appositives such as names, which are read as a unit. Some examples are:

- My son Donald will graduate in June. (The appositive *Donald* is read as part of the unit *My son Donald,* so no commas are used. Strictly speaking, if the speaker has only one son, *Donald* could be set off by commas, since the name would not be needed to indicate *which* son, but in expressions like this, the name is considered part of the unit.)

- The motivational speaker Elizabeth Thomas will accompany Janice to the convention. (The appositive *Elizabeth Thomas* is closely connected to the noun preceding it; therefore, no commas are needed.)

- The year 2005 will mark the 100th anniversary of our firm. (Here, *2005* is essential to the meaning of the sentence. It is not set off by commas.)

Degrees, Titles, and Other Similar Terms

Several commonly used abbreviations offer additional information about the names that precede them. For example, *M.D.* following a person's name tells that he or she is a doctor of medicine, and *Inc.* following a company name tells that the firm has been incorporated.

Abbreviations such as *M.D., Ph.D.,* and *D.D.S.* are always set off by commas when they follow a person's name.

- Jane B. Davis, M.D., makes many medical mission trips a year.
- Leonard F. Casper, Ph.D., has a private counseling practice.

The abbreviations *Inc.* and *Ltd.* may or may not be set off with commas, depending on the preference of the company. Follow the style shown on a company's letterhead. Some examples are:

- The credit services division of Sanford & Son, Inc., has been moved. (*Sanford & Son, Inc.,* is the official company name.)

- Ms. Madison does freelance photography for Nature Inc. in New York City. (*Nature Inc.* is the official company name.)

Like *Inc.* and *Ltd.,* the abbreviations *Jr.* and *Sr.* may or may not be set off with commas. Follow the preference of each individual when writing *Jr.* or *Sr.* or roman numerals after a person's name.

- Dennis H. Carswell Jr. has been appointed assistant principal. (Mr. Carswell prefers no commas setting off *Jr.*)

- Jeremiah D. Wheeling, III, is the president of Wheeling Travels, Inc. (Mr. Wheeling prefers to use commas to set off *III.*)

Note that when commas are used to set off such abbreviations as *M.D., Inc.,* and *Jr.,* they are used in pairs. Do not use a single comma to set off such abbreviations unless the abbreviation appears at the end of a sentence. If the person's preference is not known, do not use commas to set off *Jr., Sr.,* or roman numerals after the name.

If a name is written in inverted order, a comma should be used regardless of the person's preference.

- Finney, Robert W., Jr.

Calendar Dates

In month-day-year dates, the year is set off with two commas. In month-year dates, the commas are omitted. Some examples are:

- We purchased the restaurant on October 15, 2005, and will open it in January.
- We purchased the restaurant in October 2005 and will open it in January.

When the month and day are preceded by the day of the week, use commas to set off the month and day.

- We will meet on Monday, March 18, to discuss the legal aspects of the case.

State Names

A comma is used to separate the city from the state and the state from the rest of the sentence. An example is:

- Our next national meeting will be held in Omaha, Nebraska, next April.

7.2 Self-Assessment E

Check the following sentences for any errors in the use of commas. Write *OK* if the sentence is correct. If it contains errors, circle any error(s) and write the correction(s) on the line provided. (*Note:* Abbreviations used with names reflect the preference of the person or company.)

1. His wife Amy enjoys flying and skydiving. _____

2. A secretary in the Accounting Department, Susan Reynolds will be our entrant in our community's outstanding citizen competition. _____

   _____

3. Joshua Bernard, one of our new employees, lived in Houston Texas for ten years. _____

4. On Friday Harry D. King, Jr. will be here as a consultant to the president. _____

5. During July 2000 two hurricanes damaged our restaurant on the New Jersey coast. _____

6. Two new staff writers, Jill Kirby and Anne Meyers were recently hired by the *Shelby Gazette*. _____

7. On April 1, 2005 our contract should be renegotiated. _____

   _____

8. One of our divisions Ace Pharmaceuticals has been a leader in disease prevention. _____

9. Michael Hilton flew to Little Rock, Arkansas to meet with the songwriter. _____

10. Send the damaged merchandise to Kline Discount and Salvage, Inc. this afternoon. _____

Which and That Clauses

Clauses that are not necessary to the meaning of a sentence should be introduced by *which* and set off by commas. Clauses that are necessary to the meaning of a sentence are introduced by *that*. They are not set off by commas. Some examples are:

- Only the part of the roof that was damaged by the storm will be replaced. (No commas separate a *that* clause.)
- The damaged roof, which includes the patio roof, will be replaced. (The *which* clause gives additional information and is correctly set off by commas.)

Comma Pitfalls

Two more comma pitfalls that trap many writers are: (1) using a comma to separate a subject from its predicate and (2) using a comma to separate a verb or an infinitive from its object or complement.

Comma Separating Subject from Predicate

Never separate a subject from its predicate by a comma. Some examples are:

- All written requests from our clients, must be initialed by the office manager before being given to the broker. (Incorrect. No comma should separate the subject, *requests,* from its verb, *must be initialed.*)
- All written requests from our clients, according to company policy, must be initialed by the office manager before being given to the broker. (Correct. Now, two commas separate a phrase that gives additional information.)

Comma Separating Verb from Object

Never separate a verb from its object or complement with a comma. Likewise, never separate an infinitive from its complement with a comma. Some examples are:

- Since 1995 Jacquelyn has been, one of the hospital's most dedicated volunteers. (Incorrect. A comma should never separate a verb, *has been,* from its complement, *one.*)
- Most of the staff were surprised to learn, that Ellen is retiring next month. (Incorrect. A comma should never separate an infinitive, *to learn,* from its complement, *Ellen.*)

Comma Separating Noun from Preposition

Never separate a noun from the qualifying preposition that follows it. An example is:

- The sales representatives, from Amex Corporation will be arriving shortly. (Incorrect. The prepositional phrase *from Amex Corporation* defines the noun *the sales representatives* and should not be separated by a comma.)

7.2 Self-Assessment F

Check the following sentences for any errors in the use of commas. Write *OK* if the sentence is correct. If it contains errors, circle any error(s) and write the correction(s) on the line provided.

1. Several clerks on the second shift, are being considered for first shift positions. _____

2. The enclosed brochure which also includes an order form for season tickets is also available through our Web site. _____

3. All computer software, that is listed in our catalog, may also be purchased in our retail store at the mall. _____

4. Nancy has urged members to recycle products, that can be recycled effectively. _____

5. Our San Diego outlet which is one of the largest seashell outlets in the United States is our company's most profitable outlet. _____

    _____

6. The college president is writing an article for the DACC Foundation's Annual Report, which has become a tradition at our school. _____

With Consecutive Adjectives

Consecutive adjectives are adjectives that come together but separately modify a noun. When consecutive adjectives *separately* modify a noun, use a comma to separate the adjectives. To test whether the two adjectives separately modify the noun, use the word *and* between the adjectives. Some examples are:

*   Malinda addressed the audience in a dynamic, entertaining way. (A comma is required between the adjectives *dynamic* and *entertaining*. Note that the word *and* can be used between the modifiers: *in a way that is dynamic and entertaining.*)

*   Philip and Courtney are creative, knowledgeable computer analysts. (Use a comma between the adjectives that separately modify the compound noun computer analysts: *creative and knowledgeable.*)

Note that no comma follows the last adjective in a series—that is, no comma separates the last adjective from the noun. An example is:

*   The new outpatient clinic is staffed by skilled, experienced personnel. (No comma is used to separate the last adjective, *experienced,* from the noun *personnel.*)

Commas are not needed in the following examples:

*   Olivia Baxter's unique negotiation style is her greatest attribute. (Using the word *and* between the modifiers *unique* and *negotiation* makes no sense. These adjectives do not separately modify the noun; therefore, a comma is not used here.)

- We discussed conservative financial investments with our adviser. (You would not say "investments that are conservative and financial." Here, the adjective *financial* modifies *investments*. But the adjective *conservative* modifies the unit *financial investments*. In other words, "financial investments that are conservative.")

7.2 Self-Assessment G

Check the following sentences for any errors in the use of commas. Write *OK* if a sentence is correct. If it contains errors, circle any error(s) and write the correction(s) on the line provided. Test by using the word *and* between adjectives.

1. William is considered a brilliant ambitious resourceful management intern. _____

2. Cherlyn and Kelvin showed the slides of their fascinating educational trip to Asia. _____

3. The earliest possible date that we can meet is December 9. _____
_____

4. Their portfolio contains solid high-yielding investments. _____
_____

5. Kester & Lennoz manufactures lightweight thermal blankets. _____

6. Mr. Wilder has developed a creative talented consulting team of highly experienced professionals. _____

For Omissions, with Repeated Expressions, and in Direct Address

The comma is also used to save time and words, to emphasize an important thought, and to set off names and terms in direct address.

Omissions

Sometimes writers can use the comma to avoid repeating words that have already been stated in the sentence. The comma makes the reader pause long enough to mentally supply the omitted words. An example is:

- Effective March 1, Mrs. Adams will be in charge of the Evans account; Ms. Dryfus, the Gleason & Norton account; Ms. Ollis, the Myers Shop account; and Mr. Wilson, the Kennedy Chemicals account. (Rather than repeat the words *will be in charge of* three times, the writer uses commas after *Dryfus, Ollis,* and *Wilson* to indicate the omission and cause the reader to pause long enough to supply these words.)

> **KEY POINT**
>
> Commas are usually substituted for repeated words when the clauses are separated by a semicolon.

Repeated Expressions

Repetition is one of the most effective ways to emphasize an important point. Repetitions must be planned if they are to be effective, and the repeated words must be separated by a comma. An example is:

- Company policy states, "Never, never smoke in the warehouse." (Note the comma that separates the repetition *Never, never.*)

Direct Address

In writing, when writers address people directly, called **direct address,** they set off their names (or similar terms) with commas. Some examples are:

- As you may know, Miss Trexler, this software program offers you direct online support.
- Without your encouragement and support, Dr. Rybnicek, I would not have recuperated so quickly.

7.2 Self-Assessment H

Check the following sentences for any errors in the use of commas. Write *OK* if the sentence is correct. If it contains errors, circle any error(s) and write the correction(s) on the line provided.

1. Mr. Vincent we enthusiastically support your fund-raising plan. _____

2. To pass the licensing exam, each trainee will have to study many many hours. _____

3. We are proud to announce that Wright, Inc., has donated $10,000 to United Way; Norstrom Industries $20,000; and Valley Communications $30,000. _____

4. Carol's testimony was the truth absolutely the truth. _____

5. The Baltimore plant is scheduled for a safety inspection on April 5; the Chicago plant April 15; and the Knoxville plant April 20. _____

6. Skydiving is a risky risky hobby! _____

In Numbers and Between Unrelated Numbers

Use a comma to separate thousands, ten thousands, hundred thousands, millions, and so on, in numbers of four or more digits. This function of the comma prevents misreading of numbers. Note that there is a trend toward omitting the comma in four-digit numbers like $4000. However, if the four-digit number is used in the same sentence as a number with five or more digits, use the comma for consistency.

Here are some examples of comma use to separate parts of numbers:

- Our sales exceeded $10,000,000 last year and are estimated to be $12,000,000 this year.
- Our bulk mailing list was 9,500 last year; this year it is 12,500.

When unrelated numbers are written together, use a comma to separate them. The comma slows down the reader and makes each number distinct. An example is:

- By September 5, 250 employees had completed the additional training.

More Comma Pitfalls

Now that you know all the important uses of the comma with numbers, be sure to master these principles for when *not* to use a comma with numbers.

In Numbers

Never use commas in the following numbers, regardless of the number of digits:

- Years   in 2007
- Page numbers   page 1418
- House numbers   3271 Oak Street
- Telephone numbers   201-555-8234
- ZIP Codes   Detroit, MI 48266-1274
- Serial numbers   No 3317265
- Decimals   11.37580

In Weights, Capacities, and Measurements

Never use a comma to separate the parts of *one* weight, *one* capacity, or *one* measurement. Some examples are:

- The videotape runs for exactly 1 hour 18 minutes 20 seconds.
- Jonah and Sandra's new baby weighs 10 lbs. 3 oz.
- Eliza stands 5 feet 7 inches tall.

All the above examples are considered one measurement with multiple elements. These elements should not be separated by a comma.

When to Use Commas with Numbers

When two unrelated numbers end up adjacent to each other in a sentence and both are numerals or spelled-out words, separate them with a comma. An example is:

- On May 15, 25 clients will be taking a tour of our plant.

However, when one of the numbers is a numeral and the other is a spelled-out word, no comma is needed.

- On May 15 twenty-five clients will be taking a tour of our plant.

Employability Skills

Making Decisions

Decisions are made daily in business, and the ability to make wise decisions is a key employability skill. In your daily life, practice making good decisions by evaluating all the alternatives and risks before making a decision.

Going Global

Commas Here and There

Writing numbers can be tricky in some countries if you are unfamiliar with the differences. For example, in Germany, decimal points indicate thousands, while commas indicate tenths. So the number 18.532,90 in Germany is the same as 18,532.90 in the United States.

7.2 Self-Assessment I

Check the following sentences for any errors in the use of commas. Write *OK* if the sentence is correct. If it contains errors, circle any error(s) and write the correction(s) on the line provided.

1. In 2005 the Beckworth Printing Company relocated to 2,967 Anderson Street. _____

2. Pages 3,996 through 4,017 of the book cover the details of the construction that cost $89000. _____

3. The panel allowed 1 hour, 10 minutes for questions from the audience. _____

4. By 2010 125 new stores will have been opened in 50 states. _____

5. Jacob received a bonus check for $1250; Andrew's was $2,000. _____

6. The ceilings in that room will be 8 feet, 9 inches high. _____

7. My copy of my car insurance policy, Policy 23,880, is in my file at home. _____

8. As you will see on Invoice 26683, 2 of the 7 items were back ordered. _____

Assessment   Section 7.2

Review of Key Terms

1. How is a *simple sentence* different from a *compound sentence*? _____
_____
_____
_____

2. When are commas used with *appositives*? _____
_____

Editing Practice

Call an Editor!   You have been asked to correct the following letter. Make the necessary corrections in the letter.

3. The new edition of *Consumer Facts* has named our software the No. 1 communications software in the nation. Obviously I am extremely proud of this accomplishment, I would like to congratulate our research and development staff, our marketing team and our office staff for all their hard work.

How were we able to achieve this goal. We had competent, energetic dedicated people whom worked many hours as a team. Im honored to work with you guys. _____

_____
_____
_____
_____
_____
_____
_____
_____

Practical Application

Correcting Sentences

4. Correct the following sentences.

    a. If I were in Miami, Florida or in Phoenix, Arizona I wouldn't be shoveling snow now.

    b. The announcement, that the city will be initiating a tax cut, excited the community.

    c. Amber will send you our internal audit report, and add any comments to the document that you would like to make.

    d. Denise Swartz one of the attorneys we met last year in Detroit is moving to Boston.

    _____
    _____
    _____
    _____

5. As a team, write the directions on how to operate an office machine, such as a personal computer, a copying machine, or a VCR. In your directions, include sentences that use the following: a series, introductory words or phrases, an explanatory element, and an introductory clause. _____

Discussion Point

Commas

6. How are commas like road signs? _____
    _____
    _____

7. If you are unsure about using a comma with interrupting, parenthetical, or explanatory elements, what could you do? _____
    _____
    _____
    _____

SECTION OBJECTIVES

When you have finished Section 7.3, you will be able to:

- Use semicolons correctly to join independent clauses.
- Use semicolons and colons correctly before enumerations and explanations.
- Use colons correctly to introduce independent clauses and for emphasis.
- Use dashes correctly in sentences.
- Correct errors in the use of semicolons, colons, and dashes.

WHY IT'S IMPORTANT

Using semicolons, colons, and dashes helps add variety to your writing.

KEY TERMS

- semicolons
- colons
- dashes

Semicolons, Colons, and Dashes

Essential Principles

This section discusses three marks of punctuation that are used *within* sentences—semicolons, colons, and dashes. These punctuation marks enable the writer to guide the reader through the message. At the same time, they enable the writer to add variety and interest to the message. Each mark has its own specific function.

Semicolons

Semicolons are intended to make the reader pause; by providing timing cues, they guide the reader in understanding the message clearly. **Semicolons** are used (1) in place of a coordinating conjunction to join independent clauses, (2) before an introductory word that begins the second clause in a sentence, and (3) before explanatory or enumerating words.

In Place of a Conjunction to Join Independent Clauses

As we have seen, in a compound sentence two or more independent clauses are usually connected by a comma or commas and one or more coordinating conjunctions. An example is:

- Thea completed her degree in physical therapy in June, and she started working at Cleveland Regional Medical Center in July. (This sentence is a compound sentence; it has two independent clauses connected by a comma and the conjunction *and*.)

The conjunction and comma in a compound sentence such as the one above may be omitted, and a semicolon may be used to replace them. An example is:

- Thea completed her degree in physical therapy in June; she started working at Cleveland Regional Medical Center in July. (Here, a semicolon joins the two independent clauses, replacing the comma and the conjunction.)

Before a Second Clause Starting with an Introductory Word

In some compound sentences, the second independent clause starts with an introductory word as shown in **Exhibit 7.3.**

Introductory Linking Words	
accordingly	however
again	indeed
also	moreover
besides	nevertheless
consequently	otherwise
furthermore	therefore

Exhibit 7.3
Linking Words
Thinking Critically. What is the function of the introductory words shown here?

KEY POINT

Semicolons are used:

1. Before the second clause in a compound sentence when the conjunction is omitted
2. Before an introductory word that begins the second clause in a sentence
3. Before explanatory or enumerating words

In such sentences, use a semicolon before the introductory word that introduces the second independent clause. The semicolon provides the necessary pause between the independent clauses, and the introductory word provides a connection between the two clauses. Some examples are:

- Many of our guests made reservations before the special offer was introduced; nevertheless, we will give them the discount. (The semicolon separates the two independent clauses, and the introductory word *nevertheless* signals the reader to contrast the two clauses.)

- This corporate bond offers a 7 percent after-tax return; consequently, we are increasing our total investment. (Again, the semicolon separates the two independent clauses and tells the reader to pause. The introductory word *consequently* establishes a specific relationship between the two clauses; it shows that the second statement is a result of the first statement.)

Note that the introductory word is not always the *first* word in the second clause. Some examples are:

- Many of our guests made reservations before the special offer was introduced; we are pleased, nevertheless, to give them the discount.

- This corporate bond offers a 7 percent after-tax return; we are, consequently, increasing our total investment.

Before Explanatory or Enumerating Words

Use a semicolon before terms such as *for example, for instance,* and *that is* when they introduce an independent clause, an enumeration, or an explanation that is incidental to the meaning of the rest of the sentence. Some examples are:

- Martha is seeking to advance her career; for example, she has completed two advanced accounting courses at the university. (*For example* introduces an independent clause.)

- Amy suggested several ways to advertise our company; for instance, (1) develop a home page on the Internet, (2) send promotional flyers to potential customers, and (3) sponsor a trade show. (*For instance* introduces an enumeration.)

- List units of measurement as abbreviations; that is, 8 in, 12 ft, and 5 yd. (*That is* introduces an explanation.)

7.3 Self-Assessment A

Check the following sentences for any errors in the use of semicolons. Write *OK* if the sentence is correct. If it contains errors, circle any error(s) and write the correction(s) on the line provided.

1. Dr. Madison's lecture on phobias was intriguing, indeed, 25 people registered for counseling to treat various phobias. _____

2. The airplane's arrival was about one hour late; the delay was caused by poor weather conditions. _____

3. Amanda will be transferred to San Francisco in February, we plan, therefore, to fill her position in early March. _____

4. We canceled our order for more fax machines, besides, most of our computers now have fax capabilities. _____

5. Elena is a full-time student, however, she does work at least 12 hours per week. _____

6. Riding in a hot air balloon provides a beautiful view, as the sun rises, the sky has many different hues. _____

7. Policy mandates two signatures for checks over $1000, consequently, both Phil and Amy must sign the reimbursement checks. _____
   _____

8. Invoices should be paid within the discount period, paying within the allotted time saved us $27,300 last year. _____

9. Most of the stockholders approved the merger; but the management did not. _____

10. She is highly qualified for this job; for example, she brought in 12 new clients in her last position. _____

Colons

Colons make readers pause and take note of what follows. A **colon** is a punctuation mark used chiefly to direct attention to information that follows.

Before Listed Items

When an expression such as *the following, as follows, this, these,* or *thus* is used to introduce a list of items, it is often followed by a colon. The list may appear on the same line as the colon, or it may start on a new line. Some examples are:

- Our next staff meeting will cover these topics: (1) research tools for paralegals, (2) new billing procedures, and (3) expansion of our client base.
- At our next staff meeting, we will discuss these topics:
  1. Research tools for paralegals
  2. New billing procedures
  3. Expansion of our client base

Employability Skills

Solving Problems

The ability to solve problems is a key employability skill. Whether it is equipment failure or conflict between people, learn to resolve problems appropriately.

Sometimes the words *the following, as follows,* and so on do not lead directly into the list; for example, an interrupting sentence appears between the lead-in sentence and the list. In such cases, use a period, not a colon. An example is:

- We have amended the course requirements. The new requirements are as follows. They may be completed in any order.

  1. Submit Form 470A.
  2. Meet with your supervisor.
  3. Request an examination date.

(A period, not a colon, is used after *as follows* because the actual list does not follow directly. A sentence separates the lead-in *as follows* and the actual list.)

If a list of items is preceded by an introductory clause that does not express a complete thought, do not use a colon to separate the clause from the list. An example is:

- Most of our computers contain internal modems, CD-ROM drives, and built-in Internet access. (No colon is needed before the list of items since the clause *Most of our computers contain* is not a complete thought.)

Instead of Semicolons

You already have learned that semicolons are used before expressions such as *for example* and *that is* when these expressions introduce independent clauses, enumerations, and explanations that are incidental to the rest of the sentence. However, when the explanation or enumeration is anticipated, a colon is used instead of a semicolon. An example is:

- We have changed our procedure for accepting new patients: namely, the patient must submit a complete medical history, and the patient must present proof of insurance.

To Emphasize

Writers use colons most often to emphasize important thoughts or words. Some examples are:

- Paul identified the most important feature: convenience. (The colon places special emphasis on *convenience.*)
- Remember: Beginning Monday, all employees must use their photo identification badges to enter the building. (More emphatic than, "Please try to remember that beginning Monday. . . .")

Capitalizing After Colons

Capitalize the first word following a colon if (1) it begins a complete sentence requiring special emphasis or (2) it begins a sentence stating a formal rule.

- The personnel changes will affect two departments: accounting and marketing. (Not a sentence; the first word is not capitalized.)
- Stephen stated an important reason for accepting the bid: It will cut costs. (Complete sentence; the first word is capitalized because the sentence requires special emphasis.)
- The first step is the most important: Create an outline for your report. (Complete sentence; the first word is capitalized because the sentence states a formal rule.)

7.3 Self-Assessment B

Check the following sentences for any errors in the use of colons. Write *OK* if the sentence is correct. If it contains errors, circle any error(s) and write the correction(s) on the line provided.

1. To be selected for a baseball expansion team, a city must have adequate support in these areas; demographics, economics, and facilities. _____

2. The concierge related this change in convention registration procedures, Registration is in the convention hall lobby instead of the main lobby. _____

3. We finally discovered why the mail had not arrived; The address was printed incorrectly. _____

4. Janet gave three reasons for hiring Alice. Each reason was justified. ____

5. Only two employees were recognized for distinguished service: My partner and Brianna Branson. _____

6. As soon as you hear the tornado alarm, follow this action. Go to the basement. _____

7. The committee consists of: Ms. Harrison, Mr. O'Reilly, and me. _____

8. Here's a list of what we need from the store: milk, a loaf of bread, and tomatoes. _____

Dashes

KEY POINT

Use dashes to indicate forceful summarizing, forceful repetition, and afterthoughts.

A **dash** is a punctuation mark that is used especially to indicate a break in the thought or structure of a sentence. Dashes share some of the features of semicolons and of colons: All three make the reader pause—but dashes do so more forcefully. Compare, for example, the differences in impact of the punctuation in each of the following examples. Notice how the dash provides greater impact than either the semicolon or the colon.

- Your Internet advertising will bring you the greatest return if you post ads on UniversalNet; this Internet service is the one most used by consumers worldwide. (A good sentence, but not a forceful one.)

- For the best return on your advertising dollar, do this: Buy ads on UniversalNet, the most widely used Internet provider in the world. (This is a better sentence, a more forceful one.)

- Your Internet advertising will bring you the greatest return if you post ads on UniversalNet—the Internet service most used by consumers worldwide. (The dash snaps off the main thought and thereby adds power to the rest of the message. This is the most forceful of the three sentences.)

The semicolon provides the needed pause between clauses. The colon provides more than a pause: It promises that something important will follow. The dash goes even further by drawing special attention to what follows the dash. Therefore, the dash makes the third example the strongest of the three.

For Forceful Summarizing and Forceful Repetition

In your writing you may wish to summarize the main points of your message to make sure that your readers remember these key points. Repeating a key point is another technique that you can use to make a stronger impression on your readers. (The same is true when you are speaking.) When you are summarizing or repeating main points, use a dash to separate the summary or the repetition from the rest of the sentence. Some examples are:

- Challenging games, helpful business programs, educational software—all are available at the CompuCenter nearest you. (The dash provides forceful summarizing.)
- Remember to get all your computer supplies from CompuCenter—CompuCenter, where we keep you and your computer needs in mind. (Forceful repetition. Here, the writer deliberately repeats the most important part of the message—the store's name.)

With Afterthoughts

To add variety to their writing, to arouse the reader's curiosity, to soften a statement that might otherwise offend, to provide special emphasis—for all these reasons, good writers *plan* their afterthoughts.

- Our Labor Day sale will surely save you money—and offer you some exciting unadvertised specials! (To provide variety in writing style and to arouse the reader's curiosity.)
- Of course, we wish that we could send you a free copy of our latest software as you requested—but company policy limits the free copies to educational institutions. (To soften a refusal.)
- This discount coupon is sent only to our credit customers—no one else receives one! (To emphasize a statement.)

7.3 Self-Assessment C

Check the following sentences for any errors in the use of dashes. Write *OK* if the sentence is correct. If it contains errors, circle any error(s) and write the correction(s) on the line provided.

1. Our team will be unable to travel to New Orleans—at least until spring semester ends. _____

2. Our marketing plans are almost complete but more about this at the meeting. _____

3. Only three reservations remain for the New York City trip fax your reservation request to us by Friday. _____

4. Get your music supplies from The Music Shoppe, The Music Shoppe, where we keep your music needs in mind. _____

5. Daisies, tulips, and petunias, these are just a few of the flowers we have in stock. _____

Punctuating Words Set Off by Dashes

Use dashes to set off words at the end of a sentence or within a sentence.

At the End of a Sentence.   When you want to set off words at the end of a sentence, use one dash before the words to be set off; a period, question mark, or exclamation point then ends the sentence. No spaces are used between a dash and the word or words it is setting off. An example is:

- This computer package has several features not usually found at this low price—12 gigabytes of memory, USB drive, a CD-ROM, a 17-inch color monitor. (The dash precedes the words to be set off; a period ends this declarative sentence.)

Note that no punctuation is used before the dash unless an abbreviation or quotation precedes the dash. No punctuation ever follows the dash. Some examples are:

- We became partners with MegaSoft Inc.—Ms. Swarez approved the merger. (The period before the dash belongs with the abbreviation.)
- The title of the article will be "The New World Climate"—the editor approved it this morning.

Within a Sentence.   To set off words within a sentence, two dashes are needed. Again, no punctuation is used before the first dash unless an abbreviation or quotation precedes the dash. The second dash may have a question mark or an exclamation point *before* it, but only if the words set off by the dashes require a question mark or an exclamation point. Some examples are:

- Our new vice president—have you met her?—will join us for lunch. (The dashes set off a question; thus a question mark precedes only the second dash.)
- Terry Ervin won—for the third consecutive year!—the company golf trophy. (The words set off by dashes require an exclamation point.)
- Company recruiters—Lillian Gray, Scott Miller, and Gary Parsons are among them—have requested a merit-based compensation package (no period before the second dash).

Note also that the first word after an opening dash is not capitalized even if the words between the dashes constitute a sentence.

7.3 Self-Assessment D

Check the following sentences for errors in the use of dashes. Write *OK* if the sentence is correct. If it contains errors, circle any error(s) and write the correction(s) on the line provided.

1. It will be Glen and Danny—do you know either of them—? who will remove the virus from your computer. _____

2. Competence, personality, and hard work,—these traits form the foundation for promotions. _____

3. Your flight leaves Newark at 11:35 a.m.—but you should arrive at the airport no later than 10:35 p.m. _____

4. Please send the completed forms—is overnight delivery available—? by the quickest way. _____

5. Tina ordered the snacks—bagels, pastries, and fruit—. _____

6. After she won the car—she won a brand new convertible!—she drove from coast to coast. _____

7. She gave me her answer—an emphatic yes—this morning. _____

8. All employees—except part-time clerks—need to attend this meeting.
    _____

Assessment   Section 7.3

Review of Key Terms

1. Why might a *semicolon* be preferred over other punctuation in a compound sentence? _____
    _____

2. When is it appropriate to use a *dash*? _____
    _____
    _____

Editing Practice

Vocabulary Alert!   Select the word from the list below that best completes each sentence.

exports	laptop	modem	virus

3. When opening documents on your e-mail, it is important to know the sender to avoid downloading a _____.

4. Computers are usually connected to the information highway through a _____.

5. Sherry is on the road three days a week, so she bought a _____ to use when she travels.

6. Imports, goods brought into the United States, decreased this year; however, _____ to foreign countries were on the rise.

Practical Application

Correcting Sentences

7. Correct any errors in the following sentences.

    a. Our proposal for flextime was accepted, however minor changes were made and approved by all.

    b. Investing has three possibilities making money, losing money, and breaking even.

    c. Clocks from Germany, chocolate from Switzerland, coffee from Colombia,—these are products we usually import.

    _____

    _____

    _____

    _____

    _____

    _____

8. Find an article in a professional journal of your team's choice. Look for use of the semicolon, colon, and dash. For each mark, discuss which rule is being implemented. Do you find an overuse of these punctuation marks? Do they aid in reading difficult material? Explain how. _____

    _____

    _____

Discussion Point

Colons

9. Colons are used in other situations than those listed in the text. What are they? _____

    _____

    _____

Quotation Marks, Parentheses, and Apostrophes

Essential Principles

Quotation marks serve primarily to tell the reader the exact words written or spoken by someone, but they also have other important uses. **Parentheses** share some (but not all) of the uses of commas and dashes. **Apostrophes** have one common use besides indicating ownership.

Quotation Marks

The common uses of quotation marks are described and illustrated in the following discussion.

For Direct Quotations

To indicate the exact words—a **direct quotation**—that someone has written or spoken, use quotation marks. In the following examples, note how commas, colons, and periods are used together with quotation marks.

- Mr. Olsen said, "Katrina and I are taking a class in money management." (A comma precedes the direct quotation.)
- "Katrina and I are taking a class in money management," Mr. Olsen said. (A comma ends the quotation, is placed inside the quotation mark, and separates what is being quoted from the explanatory words that follow.)
- "Katrina and I," Mr. Olsen said, "are taking a class in money management." (Note how two commas are used to separate the interruption, *Mr. Olsen said.* The quotation marks still enclose the speaker's exact words.)
- Mr. Olsen said: "Katrina and I are taking a class in money management. We feel that we are not saving and investing enough of our salaries. Looking ahead, we see that we will need to send two children to college and to finish paying for our home." (Use a colon before a long quotation, including a quotation of more than one sentence.)
- "Katrina and I are taking a class in money management," Mr. Olsen said. "We feel that we are . . ." (Again, note that the interrupting expression is separated from the exact words of the speaker by a comma and a period.)

SECTION OBJECTIVES

When you have finished Section 7.4, you will be able to:

- Use quotation marks correctly for direct quotations, definitions, special expressions, unfamiliar terms, titles of articles, and so on.
- Use parentheses correctly to enclose words that give additional information and for references.
- Combine other punctuation marks correctly with quotation marks and with parentheses in sentences.
- Use apostrophes correctly to form contractions and possessives.
- Correct errors in the use of quotation marks, parentheses, and apostrophes.

WHY IT'S IMPORTANT

Plagiarism is easily avoided if you know how to properly use quotation marks and parentheses.

KEY TERMS

- quotation marks
- parentheses
- apostrophes
- direct quotations
- indirect quotations

Remember that **indirect quotations** (restatements of a person's exact words, often introduced by the word *that*) are not enclosed in quotation marks. An example is:

- She said that they were taking a course in money management. (An indirect quotation.)

For Quotations within Quotations

Use single quotation marks for words quoted within other quoted material. Some examples are:

- Mrs. Cortez asked, "Did she say '15 percent' or '50 percent'?" (Note the position of the question mark: It is inside the double quotation mark because the question mark belongs to the entire sentence but outside the single quotation mark.)
- "In my opinion, this desktop publishing program is certainly not 'user-friendly,'" said Matt. (A final comma is placed inside both the single and the double quotation marks.)
- Matt said, "In my opinion, this desktop publishing program is certainly not user-friendly." (A period that ends a quotation is also placed inside both the single and the double quotation marks.)

For Definitions, Special Expressions, Unfamiliar Terms, Translations, and Slang

Use quotation marks to enclose definitions and special expressions following phrases such as *known as, marked,* and *signed.*

- In computer terminology, GUI means "graphical user interface" (for definitions).
- Computer equipment known as "peripherals" includes printers, scanners, and modems. (For expressions following *called, known as,* and so on.)

Note: Words introduced by *so-called* do not require quotation marks since *so-called* itself provides them with sufficient emphasis.

Also use quotation marks for unfamiliar terms and for translations:

- The illustration below shows a "light pen," which is used to read bar codes. (For unfamiliar terms.)
- *Par avion* is simply the French term for "by airplane." (For translations.)

Slang may be deliberately used to add punch to a message, to attract attention, or to make a point. (Such uses should be limited.) Use quotation marks to enclose a slang expression, a funny comment, or a grammatical error. Note that instead of quotation marks, italics or underlining is now more commonly used with definitions and special expressions. Some examples are:

- There is only one week left in the month, but Frank Stanley says the sales contest "ain't over yet!" (Quotation marks for intentional use of a grammatical error.)
- The city editor said to "kill" that investigative report on contract fixing. (Quotation marks for a slang expression.)

7.4 Self-Assessment A

Check the following sentences for any errors in the use of quotation marks. Write *OK* if the sentence is correct. If it contains errors, circle any error(s) and write the correction(s) on the line provided.

1. Colin said, "Mark all the cartons Handle with Care." _____

2. The check was signed Sonya Ellis, but the bank official said that the signature did not match the signature on file. _____

3. "Della will attend only the morning session announced Mr. Sanchez because she must catch an early afternoon flight to New York." _____

_____

4. Mr. Sanchez announced "Della will attend only the morning session because she must catch an early afternoon flight to New York. _____

_____

5. "Write Mr. Arnold a letter tomorrow and enclose our investment proposal" said Chris. _____

6. "The new catalog said Paula will be distributed to customers by the first of the month." _____

7. We decided that the so-called "photo opportunity" wasn't worth our time. _____

8. The cartons containing the framed pictures were marked Fragile, of course. _____

For Certain Titles

Use quotation marks for the titles of articles, poems, lectures, chapters of books, essays, and sermons and for mottoes and slogans:

- Jack Brantly wrote "E-Mail Etiquette," which appeared in the May issue of *Technical Trends.* (Quotation marks for article title.)

In the preceding example, note that, while the article title is in quotation marks, the title of the magazine is in italics. In addition, book titles are in italics, as are the titles of newspapers, booklets, epic poems, plays, operas, and movies:

- Hannah's new book, *Making Your First Million,* was favorably reviewed in *The Wall Street Journal.* (Italics for book title and for newspaper name.)
- This book, *Securing Your Financial Future,* contains a chapter entitled "Municipal Bonds Are Safe Investments."(Quotation marks for chapter title; italics for book title.)

Italics in printed copy are the equivalent to underscoring in typewritten or handwritten copy. Most word processing software and printers can print italics. Note, too, that while chapter titles are enclosed in quotation marks, other book parts are not. Words such as *preface, index, introduction,* and *appendix* are not enclosed in quotation marks.

- Dr. Negbenebor, our economics professor, wrote the preface to the enclosed volume as well as Chapter 7, "Analyzing Trends."
- Refer to the Glossary for these definitions. (This sentence appears in the same book as the Glossary.)

Punctuation at the End of Quotations

Review how to use periods, commas, colons, semicolons, question marks, and exclamation points with quotation marks:

1. Periods and commas are always placed inside the closing quotation mark.
   - "Prior to every scheduled meeting," said Ms. Botts, "the team leader will distribute an agenda to each of you."

2. Colons and semicolons are always placed *outside* the closing quotation mark.
   - Barbara buys only stocks that are considered "blue chips": Kemper Metals, Inc.; Martin Industries; Webb Hot Air Balloon Company; and World Plastics.
   - Wallace thinks that all the estimates are "not in the ballpark"; for this reason, he has asked the companies to revise their estimates.

3. Question marks and exclamation points may be placed either inside or outside the closing quotation mark, depending on whether or not the question mark or exclamation point is part of the quotation. Follow these rules to decide:

   a. If the quoted words are a question, then the question mark belongs *inside* the closing quotation mark.
      - Sandra Lance asked, "Do you think the sales forecast is realistic?" (Only the quoted words make up the question; thus the question mark belongs with the quoted words—*inside* the closing quotation mark.)

      Treat exclamations the same way as questions.
      - Robert Vance said, "I can't believe that the computer network is down again!" (Only the words in quotations make up the exclamation; thus the exclamation point belongs with those words—inside the closing quotation mark.)

   b. If the quoted words do *not* make up a question, the question mark belongs to the entire sentence. Place the question mark *outside* the closing quotation mark.
      - Do you agree with David Randall that their reaction to the budget cuts was "mean-spirited"? (The entire sentence is a question; the quotation is only part of the question. The question mark belongs *outside* the closing quotation mark.)

      Treat exclamations the same way.
      - Imagine calling these stocks "blue chips"! (The entire sentence is an exclamation; the quoted words are only part of the exclamation. The exclamation point belongs *outside* the closing quotation mark.)

Memory Hook

To help remember how to use end punctuation with quotation marks, use this tip:

- periods and commas   always inside
- colons and semicolons   always outside
- exclamation points and
  question marks   where they belong

7.4 Self-Assessment B

Check the following sentences for any errors in the use of quotation marks. Write *OK* if the sentence is correct. If it contains errors, circle any error(s) and write the correction(s) on the line provided.

1. Impatiently waiting for the sales figures for the meeting, Demetri exclaimed, "Where are those sales figures"! _____

2. The sales manager included these people as his "star performers:" Dave Brosi, Ted Gallagher, Martha Kay, Donna Martin, Nancy McCoy, and Barb Stover. _____

3. Her new book, The Secret to Public Speaking, has some excellent information that is not found in similar books. _____
   _____

4. A Penny Saved Is a Penny Earned is a fitting slogan for our cost reduction program. _____

5. During the inauguration, Maya Angelou read her poem "On The Pulse of the Morning". _____

6. Did Ted Cox specifically say "50 percent discount on all discontinued furniture?" _____

7. Bruce said that the budget requests were "ridiculously overstated;" moreover, he said that he wants each department head to revise and resubmit all requests. _____

8. Did you hear that one of the antique store owners said he was "selling his business immediately"? _____

Parentheses

Although commas, dashes, and parentheses share certain common uses, they should not be used interchangeably. Just as words that have similar meanings still have subtle distinctions, so, too, do commas, dashes, and parentheses. The careful business writer is aware of these distinctions.

> ### KEY POINT
>
> Parentheses are correctly used to enclose words that give additional information and to enclose references.

For Words That Give Additional Information

Commas, dashes, and parentheses may be used to set off words that give additional information:

1. The words set off by *commas* may be omitted, but they generally add something to the main thought.

2. The words set off by *dashes* are often given additional emphasis by the dashes.

3. The words set off by *parentheses,* however, are clearly deemphasized; they may be omitted.

Some examples are:

- Tom Kirby, after over 50 years of service, has finally retired. (The words set off by commas may be omitted, but they do add something to the main thought.)
- Ms. Teale selected four managers—including Joe Kennedy in Human Resources—for the task force. (The words set off by dashes may be omitted; however, the writer deliberately uses dashes to draw attention to these words.)
- In the past year, we lost only one account (Piedmont Productions, which had small billings for the past five years). (The words in parentheses are extraneous; they contribute little to the main thought.)

For References

Parentheses are very useful for enclosing references and directions. Some examples are:

- Refer to Appendix C for instructions on how to customize your keyboard.
- Include your credit card information (account number and expiration date) on the payment form.

Punctuation with Words in Parentheses

Parentheses may be used to enclose some of the words within a sentence, or they may be used to enclose an entire sentence.

Parentheses within a Sentence. No punctuation mark goes before the opening parenthesis within a sentence. Whatever punctuation would normally be used at this point is placed *after* the closing parenthesis. Some examples are:

- When we meet next Friday (at the weekly budget session), we will discuss the new billing system. (The comma that is needed after the clause *When we meet next Friday* is placed *after* the closing parenthesis.)
- Ms. Allen suggested that we limit the number of overtime hours each week (to 5 hours for every employee), and a long discussion followed. (The comma needed to separate the two independent clauses is placed *after* the closing parenthesis, not *before* the opening parenthesis.)
- Travis Tool Company estimated a unit cost of $3.63 (see the itemized statement enclosed); however, this cost applies only to manufacturing 100,000 units or more. (The semicolon is placed *after* the closing parenthesis.)

What's in a Name

Is her name Bev Saunders? (or is it Sanders).

Is her name Bev Saunders? (*or* is it Sanders?)

Note that these rules do not affect any punctuation needed *within* the parentheses. Study the following examples:

- She will be based in one of the West Coast offices (either San Francisco, California, or Seattle, Washington), once she accepts the position.
- I would like to revise the spreadsheet for the budget report (is it on this floppy disk?) and ask Sherry to comment on it.

If an independent clause in parentheses within a sentence is a question or exclamation, the question mark or exclamation mark is included within the parentheses. If the independent clause is a declaration, however, no period is used within the parentheses. Note, too, that when parentheses are included within a sentence, the first word in parentheses is not capitalized (unless, of course, the first word is a proper noun) even if the words in parentheses are an independent clause. An example is:

- Rob Bridges (he's the accounts receivable manager) is the person whom you should consult.

Parentheses for Complete Sentences.   When the words enclosed in parentheses are entirely independent (that is, they are not part of another sentence), the first word in parentheses is capitalized and normal end punctuation is used before the closing parenthesis. Some examples are:

- As you can see, we have depreciated the equipment over a 5-year period. (Please see Appendix A.)
- Please be advised that payments received after the due date will not be credited to your account. (A late fee of $20 will be added to your next bill.)

Employability Skills

Individual Responsibility

When working with business documents, it's important to edit and proofread them before sending them out to clients. To keep a level of professionalism, it is the individual responsibility of each person to review business documents for punctuation errors and other mistakes.

7.4 Self-Assessment C

Check the following sentences for errors in the use of parentheses. Write *OK* if the sentence is correct. If it contains errors, circle any error(s) and write the correction(s) on the line provided.

1. According to the revised company handbook (see the attached photocopy of page 34,) our vacation has been increased from two to three weeks. _____

2. Hoke International Travel, (formerly known as "Hoke Travel Services,") is the best travel service in town. _____

3. Take advantage of this exciting offer to trade in your printer for a color printer for only $239.95. (This special offer ends August 15). Call us today! _____

4. Do you think Bill will accept the transfer to the Atlanta office (after all, it is a lateral move?) _____

5. Shannon insists that all these checks (every one of them!) be processed and deposited before 2 p.m. _____

6. If Dave and Jillian buy a new car (We think they will do so.), we want them to get their loan from our bank. _____

Apostrophes

As you learned in Section 5.2, the primary use of the apostrophe is to form possessives of nouns, *Pete's office, several technicians' recommendations,* and so on. A second common use of the apostrophe is to form contractions—shortened forms of one or more words. Note the difference between a contraction, such as *cont'd,* and an abbreviation, such as *cont.* A contraction uses an apostrophe, and an abbreviation ends with a period. Some examples are shown in **Exhibit 7.4.**

Another use of the apostrophe is to show that the first two figures have been omitted from a year date; for example, *'09* is a shortened form of *2009.*

Contractions	
Contraction	**Full Form**
I'm	I am
you're, we're, they're	you are, we are, they are
she's, he's, it's	she is, she has; he is, he has; it is, it has
I've, you've, we've, they've	I have, you have, we have, they have
I'd, you'd, he'd, she'd	I had, I would; you had, you would; he had, he would; she had, she would
we'd, they'd	we had, we would; they had, they would
I'll, you'll, he'll, she'll, we'll, they'll	I will, you will, he will, she will, we will, they will
there's, where's	there is, there has; where is, where has
don't, doesn't	do not, does not,
didn't, can't, couldn't, won't, wouldn't	did not, cannot, could not, will not, would not

Exhibit 7.4
Contractions
Thinking Critically. *What is the difference between a contraction and an abbreviation?* Name a possessive and a contraction that can be homonyms.

Review of Key Terms

1. Why are words set off by *parentheses*? _____

_____

_____

2. What does an *apostrophe* indicate to the reader? _____

_____

_____

Editing Practice

Call an Editor!   Correct any errors in the following paragraph.

3. Once a month the children's Hospital allows volunteers to come, and join the children for lunch. These lunchons usually have a theme, such as Valentines Day or May day. However, they all have one thing in common they make the children forget about their illnesses', even if it is only for a short while. Wont you become a volunteer? _____

_____

_____

_____

_____

_____

Practical Application

Correcting Sentences

4. Correct any error in the use of quotation marks, parentheses, or apostrophes in the following sentences.

   a. When Martín completed his two-year degree, (he graduated in "99) he began working for Ms. Werner.
   b. "Without a doubt, we have produced the healthiest breakfast cereal on the market" said Lane Allen, "consequently, we must let the people around the world know the health benefits of our product".
   c. Nicole asked, "What is a non sequitur?" Sharon replied, "A non sequitur is a 'statement that does not follow."

_____

_____

_____

5. Write a dialogue between an employee and an interviewee. Then, rewrite the dialogue in paragraph form, deleting all quotation marks. Exchange dialogues with another team and insert the proper punctuation. _____

_____

Discussion Point

Quotations

6.   What is the difference between a direct quotation and an indirect quotation? How are they punctuated? _____
_____
_____

7.   What are the rules regarding the use of end punctuation (periods, commas, colons, semicolons, exclamation points, and question marks) with quotation marks? _____
_____
_____

Capitalization

Essential Principles

The rules of **capitalization** help writers make words distinctive, emphasize words, and show that certain words are especially important. Some of the rules for capitalization are easy to remember because they are well known and long established. These rules are reviewed briefly in this section. Other capitalization rules may cause writers problems; however, and these pitfalls are also fully discussed here.

First Words

Always capitalize the first word of the following:

1. A sentence or a group of words used as a sentence.
   - The most recent information must be downloaded by tomorrow morning (complete sentence).
   - Yes, tomorrow morning (a group of words used as a sentence).

2. Each line of poetry (unless the original shows other capitalization).
   - Pretty women wonder where my secret lies.
     I'm not cute or built to suit a fashion model's size
     But when I start to tell them,
     They think I'm telling lies.
     —Maya Angelou, from "Phenomenal Women"

3. Each item in an outline, numbered list, or bulleted list.
   - The results of the survey showed the following:
     1. Consumers dislike loud TV commercials.
     2. Viewers favor fewer commercial interruptions.
     3. Audiences respond to humorous commercials.

4. A sentence in a direct quotation.
   - The 911 dispatcher emphasized the urgency of the situation: "Please rush to the fire at the oil refinery; there are still workers in the main building."

5. A complete sentence after a colon when that sentence is a formal rule or needs special emphasis.
   - The store's rule is: Refund the customer's money if there is a receipt. (Rule.)
   - Computer experts issue this reminder: Always check your disks for viruses. (For emphasis.)

6. The first word after a colon when the material that follows consists of two or more sentences.

- She described in detail the two main reasons for changing delivery services: First, lower rates will substantially decrease shipping costs. Second, expanded access to global markets will make it easier to reach overseas customers.

7. A salutation.

- Dear Mr. Harmon:

8. A complimentary closing.

- Sincerely yours,

Main Words in Titles

Always capitalize the main words of headings and titles of publications. Do not capitalize articles, conjunctions, and short prepositions (prepositions of three or fewer letters), unless they are the first word or the last word in the heading or title. Some examples are:

- In this morning's edition of *USA Today,* under the headline "The Science of Staying Young and Enjoying Life," Alonzo Webb commended the American Medical Association for its research on aging. (*The* is capitalized in the title of the article because it is the first word. The preposition *of* and the conjunction *and* are not capitalized in the article title.)
- You should read "What Olympic Athletes Strive For," a well-written, perceptive article by Alicia McKinney that appears in the current issue of *Sports Today* magazine. (Here, *for* is capitalized because it is the last word in the title.)

Hyphenated titles follow the same rules:

- In "Out-of-Work Blues," Rachel Rosinni tells job seekers how to retain their self-esteem and their sense of humor.

Capitalize the first word that follows a colon or dash in a title.

- Dante Irvin wrote the book *The Emergence of the Computer: A Look Back.*
- Cheri Olsen is the author of a new book titled *Help!—A Virus Has Invaded My Computer.*

7.5 Self-Assessment A

Check the following sentences for any errors in the use of capitalization. Write *OK* if the sentence is correct. If it contains errors, circle any error(s) and write the correction(s) on the line provided.

1. At the close of the crash course to pass the constitution exam, the teacher said, "continue studying one hour a day until you take the exam." _____

2. She is writing "Tips For Purchasing a Computer And Printer" for the *Business Education Forum* magazine. _____
_____

3. Has the scanner been repaired? no, it hasn't. _____

4. We are now reviewing our office equipment needs:
   a. one computer desk _____
   b. one ergonomic office chair _____
   c. two bookcases _____

5. We are pleased to report the good news: Enrollment and revenue are up. _____

6. Did you read the article "How To Remember Names"? _____

7. Remember: when using your personal car for volunteer work, write down your mileage so you can deduct it from your taxes. _____
   _____

8. This audit report is easier to understand than the one from Clifton & Gunderson. significantly easier. _____

9. Lillian Greathouse uses the closing "professionally yours" in all her business correspondence. _____

10. Monday's seminar includes the following: An introduction to marketing grain, the fundamentals of selling grain, and testimonials by people involved in selling grain. _____

Names of Persons

The problems surrounding the capitalization of names concern the use of prefixes such as the following:

- D', Da, De, Di: D'Amato, d'Amato; Da Puzzo, daPuzzo; DeLorenzo, DeLorenzo, deLorenzo; DiFabio, Di Fabio, diFabio. Spell each name precisely as the person spells it.
- L', La, Las, Le: L'Engle, LaRosa, Las Varca, LeMaster. Follow the capitalization, spelling, and spacing used by the person.
- Mc, Mac: McMillan, Macmillan, MacMillan. The prefix *Mc* is followed by a capital letter and no spacing. The prefix *Mac* may or may not be followed by a capital.
- O': O'Brien, O'Toole, O'Malley. The prefix O' is followed by a capital letter and no spacing.
- Van, Von: Van Fossen, van Fossen; van Hoffman; Von Huffman; von der Lieth, Von der Lieth, Von Der Lieth. Follow the capitalization, spelling, and spacing used by each person.

In all cases, be sure to write each person's name precisely the way he or she writes it—this rule refers not only to capitalization but also to the spelling of and the spacing in names. Note, however, that even prefixes that begin with lowercase letters are capitalized when the surname is used without the first name:

- Larry received a fax from Elizabeth la Salle today. (She writes her name *la*.)
- He thinks La Salle's comments about the proposal are valid. (When her first name is not used, capitalize *La* to avoid misreading.)

Names of Places

Capitalize names of geographical localities, streets, parks, rivers, buildings, and so on, such as Europe, Park Circle Drive, Ebinport Road, Mississippi River, Metropolitan Medical Building.

Capitalize the word *city* only when it is a part of the corporate name of a city: Kansas City, but the city of Paris.

Capitalize the word *state* only when it follows the name of a state: Georgia State, but the state of Georgia.

Capitalize the word *the* in names of places only when it is part of the official name: The Hague, but the Maritime Provinces.

Capitalize the words *north, south, east,* and *west* whenever they refer to specific sections of the country and when they are part of proper names. They are not capitalized when they refer merely to direction. Some examples are:

- We established a shipping center in the East to expedite delivery in that region. (A specific part of the country).
- Shannon's sales territory includes North Dakota. (*North* is part of a proper name.)
- Significant tornado destruction occurred 10 miles west of town. (Here, *west* simply indicates direction.)

Names of Things

Capital letters identify official names of companies, departments, divisions, associations, committees, bureaus, buildings, schools, course titles, clubs, government bodies, historical events and documents, and so on. Some examples are:

- Millie and Kathy are taking Microcomputer Applications at Central Piedmont Community College. (*Microcomputer Applications* is the official course title; *Central Piedmont Community College* is the official name of the school.)
- Millie and Kathy are taking a microcomputer applications course at a nearby college. (No capitals.)
- Maria Dimitrios is a computer analyst for the Murphy Manufacturing Company, which has offices here in the Metrolina Building. (Capitalize the official name of the company and the building.)
- She is a computer analyst for a manufacturing company that has its headquarters in this building. (No capitals.)
- The Direct Mail Department has leased an entire floor in the Candler Building. (Official department name; official building name.)

Capitalize the following:

Names of the days of the week	Tuesday, Wednesday
Months of the year	March, June
Religious days and holidays	Easter, Passover
Names of eras and periods	the Middle Ages, the Roaring Twenties

Do not capitalize the following:

Seasons of the year	summer, fall, winter, spring

Proper Adjectives

Capitalize **proper adjectives,** which are adjectives formed from proper nouns; for example, *American, Canadian, Puerto Rican,* and so on. Note that certain adjectives—*venetian blind, india ink, turkish towel,* and *roman numerals*—are no longer capitalized, because through many years of use they have lost their identification as proper adjectives. Consult a dictionary when in doubt.

oops!

Status Day

Our department has a status meeting on the first tuesday of every month.

(*Tuesday* is correct, not *tuesday.*)

7.5 Self-Assessment B

Check the following sentences for errors in the use of capitalization. Write *OK* if the sentence is correct. If it contains errors, circle any error(s) and write the correction(s) on the line provided.

1. You should read the article on mexican exports in today's newspaper.

    _____

2. On the first friday in september, we will meet to plan our excursion to view the Autumn foliage. _____

3. Stephen LaRosa supervises our mexican trade office. _____

4. The Brendan Furniture Company has a showroom in Kansas city, Kansas.

    _____

5. My associate von Aspern owns and manages the Blue Ridge Bed and Breakfast inn on lake Lure. _____

6. Tori's speech, "Cash Flow In Business: a Guide For Today's Executives," offered many new accounting techniques. _____

    _____

7. The computers in schools association is exploring the possibility of moving its headquarters into the Murdock building. _____

    _____

8. The fireworks display sponsored by the city of Boiling Springs on the fourth of july was spectacular, Hans von hoffman tells me. Also, von hoffman reports that the display was safe. _____

    _____

Capitalization Pitfalls

The following discussion presents some useful solutions to some of the typical problems writers face in using capitals correctly.

Short Forms

Writers often substitute one word for the complete name of a person, place, or thing. Such substitutions are usually capitalized to give special distinction or emphasis.

Some short forms are capitalized if they are personal titles of high rank, organizational names, or governmental bodies. Some examples are:

- The most recent biography of the General is entitled *Powell in the Pentagon.* (Here, *General* is a personal title of a specific person.)
- She has written a book about a general who was famous in the Gulf War. (Because *general* does not refer to a particular person, it is not capitalized.)

The words *company, department, association, school, college,* and so on, are not usually capitalized when they stand alone, even though they may substitute for the official name of a specific organization. The word *company* may be capitalized when it carries special emphasis, as in legal documents and minutes of meetings.

- Her company developed the component with Glenn & Company.
- Alan visited the museum during a recent trip to Washington, D.C.
- Two sales associates in our department were promoted.

The terms *government* and *federal government* are not capitalized. Federal is capitalized, however, when it is part of an official name, such as *Federal Communications Commission.*

Personal and Official Titles

Always capitalize a title written before a name:

- Among the directors are Dr. Frieda Brown, former Senator Baker, and Professor Barbara Stansberry.

A title written after a name or without a name is capitalized when (1) it is the title of a high-ranking national or international official or (2) it is part of an address. Some examples are:

- In yesterday's editorial, she discussed the President's economic policies. (*President*—referring to the President of the United States—is always capitalized.)
- José Rodriques, president of Technology Enterprises, Inc., plans to retire in June. (Do not capitalize *president* in such situations.)
- Ms. Heide Stanton, President
  Williams Electronics, Inc.
  Post Office Box 975
  Naperville, Illinois 60566
  (Capitalize a title that is part of an address.)

When joined to titles, the prefix *ex-* and the suffix *-elect* are not capitalized. Also, *former* and *late* are not capitalized. Some examples are:

- The late Senator Joe Joliet will be remembered for his strong stands on business ethics.
- Next semester, ex-Senator Wheatley will teach a course in political science.

Commercial Products

Distinguish carefully between a proper noun that is part of the official name of a product and a common noun that names the general class of the product. For example, you would write *Arch Saver shoes,* not *Arch Saver Shoes,* because the official brand name is *Arch Saver.* Note the following:

- Coke (Coca-Cola)
- Kleenex tissues
- Ping-Pong balls
- Scotch tape
- Xerox machine
- Yellow Pages directory

Check the following sentences for errors in the use of capitalization. Write *OK* if the sentence is correct. If it contains errors, circle any error(s) and write the correction(s) on the line provided.

1. Creative Plastics is building an office and warehouse 15 miles West of Kansas City, Kansas. _____

2. Revirez Electronics will announce the appointment of a new President at a Monday morning press conference. _____

3. Throughout the country our company will lease over 12,000 General Motors Vans. _____

4. The federal Deposit Insurance Corporation is investigating the situation after receiving several complaints. _____

5. When your Manager speaks to the Rotary club monday in our Private Dining Room, his remarks should address the business aspects of managing a Charitable organization. _____

    _____

6. Of course, you should send the quality control reports to the Quality Assurance Division in Roanoke, Virginia. _____

7. Haley Archer, President of nashville Country Recordings, has announced that her company will construct its new facilities on Allen Road. _____

    _____

8. These Tastebud Cookies, made by a family-owned company, are low in sodium and high in fiber. _____

Assessment   Section 7.5

Review of Key Terms

1. What is a *proper adjective*? How can one be sure if a proper adjective should be capitalized? _____

    _____

    _____

2. What types of words are not capitalized in titles? _____

    _____

    _____

Editing Practice

Call an Editor!   Edit the following sentences to correct any errors in capitalization.

3. Mary said, "he did not accept our offer to be a Vice President." _____
_____

4. please read *How To Become A Millionaire,* which is published by our Company. _____
_____

5. The Late Mayor Palmer always talked to larry Hinkle in the college library in Danville. _____
_____

6. While in Washington, D.C., last Fall, we toured the white house. _____
_____

Practical Application

Correcting Sentences

7. Correct any capitalization errors in the following sentences.

    a. Our corporate offices are in Dallas, but our restaurants are located throughout the southwest, with most of them in the State of Arizona.

    b. Kent Mendoza, Vice President of our Company, has an option to purchase property.

    c. "Sailing In The Caribbean: a Vacationer's Paradise" was the title of the article that inspired me to take the trip.

    d. Danielle Miller, a former High School teacher, now gives classes in italian cooking.

_____
_____
_____
_____
_____
_____
_____

8. Choose a movie that you have seen that was originally a book. Write a brief review of each medium and state which format you preferred. Proofread your teams' reviews for errors in capitalizations. Share your results with your team.

_____

Discussion Point

Capitalization

9. When should words such as *north, south*, and *east* be capitalized? When should they remain lowercase? _____

_____

_____

10. Review the rules of capitalization in this book. Which rule do you find most confusing? Why? _____

_____

Abbreviations

Essential Principles

An **abbreviation** is the shortened form of a written word or phrase used in place of the whole. Abbreviations provide writers with shortcuts, and shortcuts are certainly appropriate *at times*. As a business writer, you must know when abbreviations are acceptable—and when they are *not*. In addition, you must know the correct forms of those abbreviations.

Personal Names

Study the following rules for using abbreviations before and after personal names.

Before Personal Names

Many of the titles used before personal names, such as *Mr., Mrs.,* and *Dr.,* are abbreviations. Some examples are:

Singular	Plural
Mr.	Messrs. (from the French *messieurs*)
Mrs.	Mmes. or Mesdames
Ms.	Mses. or Mss.
Miss	Misses
Dr.	Drs.

Other titles used before personal names are spelled out whether the full name or only the last name is given: *Governor* Fielding, *Superintendent* Presson, *Representative* Horn, the *Honorable* Elisabeth B. Thomas, the *Reverend* Jack Partain, *General* Streeter, and so on.

After Personal Names

A person's degree or other information may follow a name in formal writing. Be sure you understand how to punctuate and capitalize abbreviations following a name.

Academic Degrees and Similar Abbreviations. Abbreviations of academic degrees and religious orders and similar abbreviations generally have internal periods: M.D., D.D.S., Ph.D., D.V.M., Ed.D., S.J., D.D. Check your dictionary whenever you are not sure of the abbreviation.

Do not use *Mr., Ms., Mrs., Miss,* or *Dr.* before a person's name that is followed by an abbreviation of an academic degree or religious order. Some examples are:

- Jane D. Kirkpatrick, M.D., or Dr. Jane D. Kirkpatrick (not Dr. Jane D. Kirkpatrick, M.D.)
- Joyce Wang, Ph.D., or Dr. Joyce Wang (not Dr. Joyce Wang, Ph.D.)

Other titles before the person's name may sometimes be appropriate:

- Reverend Mark Seany, S.J.
- Professor Catheryn Holcomb, Litt.D.

Note that in a sentence, any such abbreviation following a name must be set off with two commas, unless the abbreviation ends the sentence.

- Lucy S. Miller, M.D., is the subject of today's "Pediatric Medicine" column.

Jr. and Sr. Omit the comma before *Jr.* or *Sr.* when either follows a person's name unless the person specifically uses a comma, as some people still do. Some examples are:

- Mr. Carlos Lopez Jr.
- Dr. B. Harrison Philpott, Sr. (Dr. Philpott does use a comma before *Sr.*)

Do not use *Jr.* and *Sr.* with a person's last name only.

- Ms. Owens faxed the summary to Charles J. Smith Sr., and Mr. Smith responded immediately.

Initials

Initials are abbreviations of names; in some cases, the initials *are* names because they do not really stand for anything. Write an initial with a period and a space after it (always following, however, a person's individual preference). Some examples are:

- Will J. B. speak at the conference next year?
- If possible, talk with J. B. Russell before noon.

Note: Reference initials written at the end of memos and letters are usually written in lowercase letters with no periods and no spaces (see Section 9.2).

7.6 Self-Assessment A

Check the following sentences for any errors in the use of abbreviations. Write *OK* if the sentence is correct. If it contains errors, circle any error(s) and write the correction(s) on the line provided.

1. Mr. Solon sent an e-mail to Henry J. Hunt Jr., and Mr. Hunt Jr. responded within 20 minutes. _____

2. Our coin collection was inherited by the four Messrs. Jacobs. _____

3. While Mister Lyttle is at the conference, one of his many assistants will handle any urgent matters. _____

4. Ms. Eleanor Jenkins, Ph.D., has resigned her university position to devote full time to her research projects. _____

   _____

5. Dr. Nancy Branyas, M.D., will be associated with the cardiologists who are already practicing at The Heart Institute. _____

   _____

6. Sen. Merritt announced his retirement, which would be effective at the end of the calendar year. _____

OOPS!

Abbreviated Title

Mister Parker is the guest speaker for our conference.

(Mr.)

Companies and Organizations

Always write the name of a company or an organization precisely as its *official* name on its letterhead stationery is written:

- Scott & Scott Inc.
- Kane and Cohen, Inc.
- Bits 'n' Bytes Software
- Bug Busters Pest Control Company
- Chandler Bros. Moving & Storage
- J. B. Wray & Sons

Inc. and Ltd.

As with *Jr.* and *Sr.,* omit the comma before *Inc.* and *Ltd.* in company names. Again, however, always follow the *official* name.

- Computer Dynamics Inc. specialized in software development.
- Fayla works for Bedow & Stern, Ltd., in Denver.

Note in the last example that two commas were used to set off *Ltd.* within the sentence.

All-Capital Abbreviations

Many names of organizations, associations, government agencies, and so on are abbreviated in all-capital letters with no periods or spaces between the letters. Some examples are:

- AAA   American Automobile Association
- AFL-CIO   American Federation of Labor and Congress of Industrial Organizations
- AT&T   American Telephone and Telegraph
- FBI   Federal Bureau of Investigation
- IRS   Internal Revenue Service
- NYSE   New York Stock Exchange
- UPS   United Parcel Service

An **acronym** is a shortened form of a name. The acronym is formed from the initial letters of the words in the complete name. Pronounce an acronym as you would a word. Some examples are:

- NASA   National Aeronautics and Space Administration
- OPEC   Organization of Petroleum Exporting Countries

The call letters of broadcasting stations are always written in all-capital letters without periods. Some examples are:

- WBTV-FM
- KCBT
- NPR

United States should not be abbreviated as a noun. When *United States* is abbreviated as an adjective, before the name of a government agency, periods are used. Some examples are:

- the U.S. Department of Commerce
- U.S. Air Force

Going Global

Proper Address

In some countries, addresses are written differently than in the United States. For example, the street name may be before the house or building number—Koperstraat 45.

Business Abbreviations

In addition to their use with personal names and in the names of companies and organizations, there are **business abbreviations** that are used in many other instances in business correspondence.

Address Abbreviations

Learn the standard method of writing addresses to speed business correspondence to its destination.

Street Names. On envelopes, space restrictions sometimes make the use of *St.* and *Ave.* necessary. In letters, however (and on envelopes whenever possible), avoid abbreviating the words *Street, Avenue,* and so on. When abbreviations such as *NW, SW,* and *NE* appear after street names, use a comma to separate the street name from the abbreviation. (Note that the abbreviations such as *NW, SW,* and so on, should be spelled out in other cases.)

- 221 East Third Street
- 1828 West Dixon Boulevard
- 186 Graham Avenue, NW

Post Office Box Numbers. The words *Post Office* may or may not be abbreviated with box numbers: *Post Office Box 249* or *P.O. Box 249.*

Rural Route Addresses. The U.S. Postal Service now requires addresses that update the old rural-style addresses to city-style addresses.

- Correct: 16750 E. 1000 North Road
- Incorrect: Rural Route 4—Box 24

City Names. Except for the abbreviation *St.* in city names such as *St. Louis* and *St. Paul,* do not abbreviate city names.

State Names. With inside addresses or correspondence, use either (1) the two-letter abbreviations of state names or (2) the spelled-out name. The U.S. Postal Service prefers the two-letter state abbreviations on envelopes. In both cases, always use a ZIP Code. An example is:

Mr. J. D. Faison
35 Harris Boulevard
New Orleans, LA 70124–1299
or New Orleans, Louisiana 70124–1299

When state names are used elsewhere, that is, not on envelopes or with inside addresses, spell them out or, if abbreviations are appropriate, use the traditional state abbreviations, such as *Conn.* or *Calif.*

Do not be surprised to see mail with computer-printed labels in all-capital letters with no punctuation and nearly every word abbreviated. Many companies that send large mailings use this style.

MR J D FAISON
ST LOUIS HOSP
2885 WOODLAWN ST
ST LOUIS MO 63121–1234

> **KEY POINT**
>
> In addresses, you may spell out or use abbreviations for the words:
>
> 1. Street (St.)
> 2. Avenue (Ave.)
> 3. Boulevard (Blvd.)
> 4. Post Office (P.O. or PO)

Units of Measure

Yard, inch, yd, in—when do you spell out **units of measure,** and when do you abbreviate? Your purpose for including units of measure in business documents will determine which forms you use.

General Use.   In routine correspondence, units of measure are spelled out: *yards, pounds, kilograms, degrees, meters, gallons,* and so on. Use numerals with units of measure. Some examples are:

- Photographs submitted for the contest must be 4 inches by 6 inches.
- Soft drinks are packaged in economical 2-liter bottles.
- The sample that we tested contained about 3 grams of zinc.

Technical Use.   In technical work and on invoices, units of length, weight, capacity, area, volume, temperature, and time are usually abbreviated. Among the commonly used terms are the ones listed in **Exhibit 7.5.**

Abbreviations for Units of Measure			
cm	centimeter, centimeters	L	liter, liters
ft	foot, feet	lb	pound, pounds
g	gram, grams	m	meter, meters
gal	gallon, gallons	mm	millimeter, millimeters
in	inch, inches	oz	ounce, ounces
kg	kilogram, kilograms	pt	pint, pints
km	kilometer, kilometers	yd	yard, yards

Exhibit 7.5
Abbreviations for Units of Measure
Thinking Critically. *Why are units of measure abbreviated in charts and diagrams?*

Expressions of Time

Write *a.m.* and *p.m.* in lowercase letters with periods but with no spacing. However, when using a computer, the accepted form is A.M. and P.M. using small capital letters with periods. Always use figures with these abbreviations, and do not use *o'clock* with *a.m.* or *p.m.* Remember: *a.m.* means "before noon" and *p.m.* means "after noon." An example is:

- The shipment will leave our offices at 8:30 a.m. on Tuesday. (Not 8:30 o'clock a.m.)

No. for Number

The abbreviations *No.* (for *number*) and *Nos.* (for *numbers*) are used only before a numeral: License No. 83465–75J; Patent No. 293,667; and so on. Note that *number* is spelled out when it is the first word in a sentence and that it may be omitted after words such as *Room, Invoice,* and *Check.*

- Have you found copies of the following purchase orders: Nos. 232–76, 232–78, and 232–81? When you do, bring them to Room 2127.
- Number 6232 is the only outstanding check, Ms. Radully.

Note: The symbol # may be used on forms or in technical copy.

Extend the Day and Date

The mayor has scheduled a news conference on Thurs., Nov. 25, at 4 PM.

(Thursday, November 25, at 4 p.m.)

Days and Months

The days of the week and the months of the year should be abbreviated only when space forces the writer to do so, as in tables and lists. In such cases, use the abbreviations shown in **Exhibit 7.6.** Note that *May, June,* and *July* are not usually abbreviated.

Abbreviations for Days and Months	
Days of the Week	**Months of the Year**
Sun., Mon., Tues. (or Tue.), Wed., Thurs. (or Thu.), Fri., Sat.	Jan., Feb., Mar., Apr., May, June (or Jun.), July (or Jul.), Aug., Sept., Oct., Nov., Dec.

Exhibit 7.6
Abbreviations for Days and Months
Thinking Critically. In general business communications, would you abbreviate or spell out these words?

Miscellaneous Abbreviations

In addition to the abbreviations discussed so far, there are many more that are used in business, including those shown in **Exhibit 7.7.** Check a dictionary or another reference book for a complete list of terms and their acceptable abbreviations.

Other Abbreviations	
ASAP	as soon as possible
CAD	computer-assisted design
ETA	estimated time of arrival
PE	price-earnings (ratio)
reg.	registered
atty.	attorney
CEO	chief executive officer
OTC	over the counter
RAM	random-access memory
ROM	read-only memory

Exhibit 7.7
Other Abbreviations
Thinking Critically. What is one explanation for why companies create abbreviations such as those in Exhibit 7.7?

7.6 Self-Assessment B

Check the following sentences for errors in the use of abbreviations. Write *OK* if the sentence is correct. If it contains errors, circle any error(s) and write the correction(s) on the line provided.

1. The technician asked how much R.A.M. and R.O.M. we have on each of our computers. _____

2. The parcel delivery service guaranteed that the package would arrive before 10:30 AM. _____

3. Governor Simpson has scheduled a news conference on Tues., Dec. 9, at 3:30 p.m. _____

4. The lab sample is about 4 inches long, which is equal to slightly more than 10 CM. _____

5. Valerie Zelesky moved to Ft. Wayne, IND., after she retired from IBM.

    _____

6. After she speaks in Tex., Emily will travel to New Mex. and to Nev.

    _____

7. Alexander now lives in Forest City, N.C., where he works for WBBO radio. _____

8. Since the box weighs more than 50 lb, we cannot ship it by City Parcel Service. _____

Assessment   Section 7.6

Review of Key Terms

1. When should *abbreviations* be used in business communications?

    _____

2. What are rules concerning the use of abbreviations in *units of measure*?

    _____

    _____

Editing Practice

Spelling Alert!   Rewrite the following sentences, correcting any spelling errors.

3. When Albert completed his tax forms in the personel office, he listed for dependents. _____

4. The consultent showed us how to write effective memorandoms and letters. _____

5. Most of the employees are sincerly interested in having a yard sale to raise money for the teen shelter. _____

6. The newspaper reports were clearly eroneous; there is no truth to the allegations. _____

Practical Application

Correcting Sentences

7. Correct any errors in abbreviation use in the following sentences.

   a. Has Mister Parker filed a complaint with the US Department of Commerce?
   b. The U.S.D.A. offers a variety of services to American citizens.
   c. One of our music professors, Dr. Stephen Plate, Ph.D., holds Copyright No 899,987,789.
   d. Halley worked for T.W.A. in LA, didn't she?
   e. Do you plan to run for gov. in the Nov. election?

   _____
   _____
   _____
   _____
   _____
   _____

8. As a team, browse through magazines, newspapers, and manuals. Look for use of abbreviations. With other teams in your class, discuss how often abbreviations are used and which format uses them the most. _____
   _____
   _____

Discussion Point

Interpreting Details

9. What is the difference between an *abbreviation* and an *acronym*?
   _____
   _____
   _____

10. Should all abbreviations be capitalized? Support your answer with examples. _____
    _____

SECTION OBJECTIVES

When you have finished Section 7.7, you will be able to:

- Determine when to express numbers as words and when to express them as numerals in sentences.

- Use ordinal numbers correctly in business communications.

- Use correct punctuation and symbols with numbers.

WHY IT'S IMPORTANT

The correct use of numbers is critical to communicating clear, accurate information.

KEY TERMS

- numbers
- ordinal numbers
- decimal numbers
- adjacent numbers

KEY POINT

Spell out numbers that begin sentences.

Numbers

Essential Principles

Numbers are commonly used in business to express sums of money, quantities for orders, discounts, time, measurements, percentages, addresses, dates, sales statistics, versions of computer programs, and so on. Business writers know that the correct use of numbers is often critical to clear, accurate communication. Errors in number use can cause more than simple confusion; they can be expensive, time-consuming, and exceptionally disruptive.

Be sure to follow the following principles of number usage, and make it a habit to proofread numbers carefully whenever you write business messages.

Using Words to Express Numbers

Why is it important to know when to express numbers in figures and when to express them in words? One reason is that long-established use dictates certain rules. Another reason is that figures and words have different effects on different readers. The use of numerals, for example, tends to emphasize a number, while the use of words tends to deemphasize a number: *$100* is more emphatic than *a hundred dollars*. Thus, we use numerals when the number is a significant statistic or deserves special emphasis, while we use words for numbers in a formal message and for numbers that are not significant and need no special attention.

The business writer must know the general rules for expressing numbers in words and for expressing them in numerals, and must be able to manipulate the rules when it is necessary to achieve a greater degree of formality or to provide greater emphasis. First, we will discuss when the writer should use words to express numbers. Then, we will discuss when the writer should use numerals to express numbers.

At the Beginning of a Sentence

At the beginning of a sentence, use a spelled-out word, not a numeral, to express a number. If writing the word seems awkward, then reword the sentence so that the number does not occur first.

- Seventy-seven percent of the customers we surveyed said that they were satisfied with our sales and delivery procedures (not *77 percent*).

- Of the customers we surveyed, 77 percent said that they were satisfied with our sales and delivery procedures (better than *Seventy-seven percent*).

Numbers From *One* Through *Ten*

In business correspondence, the numbers from one through ten are generally spelled out. Some examples are:

- We hired eight new accountants in May.

- Antonio's restaurant is located on Sixth Avenue.
- Susan ordered seven new computers for the accounting department.

Ordinal numbers indicate the order or succession: for example *first, second, third* or *1st, 2nd, 3rd*.

Note that the ordinal numbers *first* through *tenth* are also spelled out.

Fractions

Fractions are expressed in words in general business correspondence. A hyphen is used to join the number and the part:

- About one-third of the people surveyed said that they were dissatisfied with our banking services.

However, a mixed number (a whole number plus a fraction) is expressed in figures by using a decimal or a fraction:

- Our riding stable is located on 6.5 acres of land near the Blue Ridge Mountains. (The figure *6½ acres* is also acceptable.)

Indefinite Numbers

Spell out indefinite numbers and amounts, as shown in these phrases:

- a few million dollars
- hundreds of telephone calls
- several thousand people
- tens of children's charities

Ages and Anniversaries

Ages are spelled out—unless they are significant statistics:

- Mr. Anderson, our chemist, is forty-two years old today.
- Helen Brentworth is in her late sixties.
- Allison Buie, 27, has been appointed director of accounting (a significant statistic).

When ordinal numbers are used for ages and anniversaries, they are generally spelled out.

- her twenty-first birthday
- our thirty-first wedding anniversary

But when more than two words are needed to spell the number or when special emphasis is desired, express the numbers in numerals:

- our city's *125th* anniversary (not *one hundred and twenty-fifth*)
- a *10th* Anniversary Sale! (for emphasis)

Centuries and Decades

Centuries are generally expressed in words.

- the nineteen hundreds (but for emphasis, *the 1900s*)
- the twentieth century
- nineteenth-century factories

Decades, however, may be expressed in several ways. *Note:* Do not use an apostrophe to make the plural.

- the nineteen-nineties *or* the 1990s *or* the nineties *or* the '90s

oops!

Cardinal Error

We celebrated our wedding anniversary on the 21 of July.

(*21st of July* is correct)

7.7 Self-Assessment A

Check the following sentences for errors in the use of numbers. Write *OK* if the sentence is correct. If it contains errors, circle any error(s) and write the correction(s) on the line provided.

1. The auditor's report, which should be about 7 pages long, will be mailed to us next week. _____

2. Saxton & Company bought this building in the early 1980's, when it cost less than $400,000. _____

3. We have allocated about 1/10 of next year's budget to developing new products. _____

4. 32 percent of our telephone customers were satisfied with their long-distance service. _____

5. Customers between the ages of 55 and 60 will get a 10 percent discount on their purchases; customers over 60 will get 15 percent. _____

6. One sales representative has ten and a half times more expenses than any other producer. _____

7. 15 families have already called about renting the mountain cabin. _____
   _____

8. The local newspaper estimated the crowd at a few 1,000. _____
   _____

9. We received hundreds of résumés in response to our classified advertisement. _____

10. The museum curator thought the painting might be the work of an 18th-century French artist. _____

Using Numerals to Express Numbers

Polished communicators insist on expressing numbers correctly. The following simple rules will guide you in choosing between numerals or words to express a number.

For Numbers Higher Than Ten

As you know, the numbers from one through ten are spelled out. Numbers higher than ten are expressed in numerals:

- At last week's auction, 86 cars, vans, and trucks were sold.
- This 22-page manual lists and explains our rules and regulations.

However, express related numbers in the same way. If any of the numbers are above ten, express all the numbers in numerals:

- At Friday's meeting, we will need 6 tables, 36 chairs, and 2 laptop computers. (Because one of the related numbers—the numbers in the series—is above ten, all are expressed in numerals.)

Note: Numerals are more emphatic than words because numerals stand out clearly, especially when they are surrounded by words. Therefore, when greater emphasis is required for a number from one to ten, use a figure to express that number. For example:

- for 10 minutes (more emphatic than *for ten minutes*)
- a 3-year loan (more emphatic than *a three-year loan*)

For Sums of Money

Sums of money are written in numerals.

- Tony's travel expenses totaled $892.63.
- We gave her an advance of $800 (not *$800.00*—the extra zeros are unnecessary).
- We budgeted between $5,000 and $6,000.
- The unit cost is estimated to be 45 cents (not *$.45*—use the symbol ¢ in tables and in technical copy only.)

Note, however, the following usage for related numbers in the same sentence.

- The unit cost will be $.65 for the small vase and $1.12 for the large vase.

Words *and* numerals are often used to express amounts of a million or more.

- $7 million or 7 million dollars
- $15.5 million or 15.5 million dollars

To avoid misreading, be sure to repeat the word *million* in expressions such as this:

- between $3 million and $4 million (not *between $3 and $4 million*)

Also be sure to treat related numbers in the same way:

- between $500,000 and $1,000,000 (not *between $500,000 and $1 million*)

Remember that indefinite amounts are spelled out:

- Nathan's tax refund amounted to a few hundred dollars.
- Glenn and Nancy bought about a hundred dollars' worth of software at the exposition.

In Addresses

Use numerals for house numbers except for *One*. For street numbers, spell out the ordinal numbers *first* through *tenth*. Use figures for all other street numbers.

- The post office is located at One Dameron Street. (Spell out *One* when it is a house number.)
- The video store that was at 246 East 14th Street is now located at 486 East 12th Street.

(When the house and street number are not separated by *East, West,* use the ordinals *st, d,* and *th.*)

- 3214 85th Street (The ordinal *85th* helps to prevent possible confusion.)

ZIP Code numbers are always given in figures.

- New York, New York 10020 (Note that no comma precedes the ZIP Code number.)
- New York, NY 10020-1221. (ZIP plus four numbers.)

Number It

Our open house will start this Tuesday at eight p.m. (8 p.m.)

Mathematics

The ability to perform basic computation skills is important in the workplace. Understanding how to work with numbers and effectively using math techniques are valuable employability skills.

7.7 Self-Assessment B

Check the following sentences for any errors in the use of numbers. Write *OK* if the sentence is correct. If it contains errors, circle any error(s) and write the correction(s) on the line provided.

1. The interest rate is guaranteed for one hundred eighty two days. _____
   _____

2. Depending on the revenue, the budget will take from 6 months to 1 year to complete. _____

3. According to preliminary estimates, the potential sales for this camera is between $1 and $2 million. _____

4. Recent hurricane damage was estimated at 4 billion dollars. _____

5. FedEx guaranteed delivery by 10 a.m. today to Dr. Thomas Elliott, 404 13 Avenue. _____

6. This minibus has twelve seats but very little luggage capacity. _____
   _____

7. Our fleet of vehicles includes four vans, five trucks, and 12 cars. _____
   _____

8. The market located at One Curtis Lane has a special on bottled water for $.60. _____

9. If you pay 55¢ per day for your coffee, your coffee costs you $2.75 per week. _____

10. The new color printers cost $510.00, but you can get a 10 percent discount if you pay cash. _____

With Units of Measure and Percentages

Use numerals, even for numbers less than ten, with *units of measure* and with percentages, as shown in the following examples:

- Each bedroom measures 8 feet by 14 feet.
- This computer screen measures 17 inches diagonally.
- Each vial contains exactly 5 cubic centimeters of the serum.
- You will receive a 20 percent discount if you pay cash.

Note: Use the symbol % only in tables and forms. In other cases, spell out *percent*. Also note that *percent* is one word.

With Decimals

Decimal numbers (numbers with a dot or decimal point) are always expressed in figures:

- Mix this compound with water in a ratio of 4.5 parts compound to 1 part water. (A ratio may also be expressed as follows: *4.5:1 ratio of compound to water.*)

When no number appears before the decimal, add a zero to help the reader understand the number quickly.

- A very slight decrease—0.5 percent—was reported for the month of April. (Without the zero, the reader might read *.5 percent* as *5 percent* instead of *five-tenths of a percent*.)

With a.m. and p.m.

As you already learned, always use numerals with *a.m.* and *p.m.*

- at 11 a.m.
- between 10:15 a.m. and 11:15 p.m.

With O'Clock

With the word *o'clock,* either numerals or words may be used. For greater emphasis and less formality, use numerals. For more formality but less emphasis, use words. Some examples are:

- You are cordially invited to join us at eight o'clock on Friday, the first of July, to celebrate the one hundredth anniversary of the founding of Cullinan Enterprises. (*Eight o'clock* is more formal than *8 o'clock*.)
- All authors are invited to a brunch and book-signing party to be held at the Oak Terrace Inn on Friday, August 25, at 11 o'clock.

In Dates

Use figures to express the day of the month and the year in dates:

- April 19, 2009 (not April 19th, 2009)

When the day is written *before* the month, use ordinal numerals or spell out the ordinal number.

- the 4th of June or the fourth of June
- the 21st of April or the twenty-first of April

Note: The ordinal numerals are *1st, 2nd, 3rd, 4th,* and so on.

With Adjacent Numbers

Adjacent numbers (numbers next to each other) should be separated by a comma when both numbers are in numerals or when both are in words.

- In 2005, 250 employees were hired for the Forest City plant.
- Of the original seven, two employees still remain in the Asheville office.

But if one word is in numerals and the other is in words, no comma is needed.

- On June 12 two executives retired from Bost Bakeries Inc.

When one of the numbers is part of a compound adjective, write the first number in words and the second number in figures (unless the second number, when spelled out, would be a significantly shorter word). Do not separate the numbers with a comma.

- two 9-page booklets (but *200 nine-page booklets*)
- fifty $10 bills (but *100 ten-dollar bills*)

7.7 Self-Assessment C

Check the following sentences for any errors in the use of numbers. Write _OK_ if the sentence is correct. If it contains errors, circle any error(s) and write the correction(s) on the line provided.

1. Lorenzo rented a storage room that is twelve feet by twenty feet. _____
   _____

2. Our contract was signed and notarized June 2nd, 1998. _____

3. The press conference is scheduled for three o'clock Tuesday afternoon.
   _____

4. By January 15 97 employees had registered for our stop-smoking
   program. _____

5. To clean your tires, mix three and a half parts of Tirex to two parts
   water. _____

6. Your interest on your savings account is 2.8 percent. _____

7. A fireworks exhibition has been scheduled for the third of July at the
   mall. _____

8. According to the memo, the mandatory staff meeting will begin at
   4:30 p.m. and will end by 5:30 p.m. _____

9. The new company division will be staffed by one manager, 12 buyers,
   and two assistants. _____

10. She is the happy mother of five-year-old twin boys. _____

Assessment   Section 7.7

Review of Key Terms

1. Why is it important for business writers to accurately express _numbers_?
   _____

2. What are _ordinal numbers_, and when should they be spelled out?
   _____
   _____
   _____

Editing Practice
Mail Call!

3. Proofread the following excerpt from a letter and correct any errors.

September 10 20—
Ms. Renee Wallace
Fifteen Willow Drive
Altamonte Springs, FL 32714
dear Ms. Wallace,

Welcome to the Sunset Family! As a proud owner of a new Sunset sedan, you has our best wishes.

Our records show that you choose the 2-year or 20000-mile warranty. If you would like to extend your coverage, keep our 3-year and five-year warranty in mind. If you call now, you can save over $200.00 dollars! _____

_____

Practical Application
Correcting Sentences

4. Correct any errors in number use in the following sentences.
   a. Rachel said that our Web site has been accessed three thousand five hundred times since the first of the year.
   b. Ms. Teague said, "We are proud to announce that all 5 divisions showed a profit for the 3rd consecutive year."
   c. Our goal is to increase our profits by 10.5% before the end of the year.

   _____

   _____

   _____

   _____

   _____

5. Look at an appliance manual or a bank brochure. As a team, find examples of the rules covered in this section. Are there any rules that were not followed? Are there rules that were followed in an inconsistent manner? _____

   _____

Discussion Point
Thinking Critically

6. When are numbers spelled out in business correspondence? _____

   _____

   _____

   _____

7. Why are units of measurement, percentages, and decimals expressed in numerals? _____

   _____

Chapter 8

Sharpening Writing Skills

Workplace Connection

Good writing skills enable you to put words into appropriate thought units so that your message is clear. The ability to revise, edit, and proofread ensures that your documents will be correct and clear.

CHAPTER OBJECTIVES

When you have completed this chapter, you should be able to:

- Use a dictionary and a thesaurus to select the correct word.
- Use spelling rules to improve your spelling.
- Recognize and correct errors in thought units.
- Write effective sentences and paragraphs.
- Revise, edit, and proofread documents.

Using Words Effectively

Essential Principles

Words are the elements we use to communicate messages in writing. When we write, we create pictures with words, just as artists create pictures with paints. To write effectively, you must learn to use words precisely and clearly. Fortunately, help is available in two valuable reference books: the dictionary and the thesaurus. As you study this section, note how you could use a dictionary and a thesaurus to improve your writing skills.

The Dictionary

The dictionary is the most useful reference book for business writers. You should always keep a dictionary nearby and know how to use it. There is no good substitute for a comprehensive dictionary. However, you can use an online dictionary in many instances.

Word Information

As a writer, you have probably used the dictionary to find information on the spelling, definition, capitalization, and hyphenation of words, as well as synonyms and other information that help you use words effectively. As an example of the detailed information provided by a dictionary entry, review the entries for the words *complement* and *compliment* in **Exhibit 8.1** (see page 273).

Spelling. The dictionary entries in **Exhibit 8.1** show in bold type how the words *complement* and *compliment* are spelled. Keep in mind that many words have more than one spelling. Spellings that are equally correct are joined by "or," as in "adviser or advisor." When one spelling is less commonly used, the dictionary joins the spellings by *also,* as in "lovable *also* loveable."

Definition. A good dictionary lists all of a word's definitions, usually in the order in which they developed historically. Often the dictionary gives examples of the word's use in more than one sense. For example, see **Exhibit 8.1** (page 273), where the entry for *complimentary* shows several examples of the word's use.

Capitalization. The dictionary may show whether a word is to be capitalized when it is not the first word of a sentence. For example, the word *south* used as a direction is usually not capitalized, but when it refers to a specific region, as in *the South,* it *is* capitalized.

Hyphenation. Dictionary entries use centered periods to indicate the correct places for breaking or dividing words. Some examples are:

- com•mu•ni•cate
- ap•pre•ci•ate *but* ap•pre•cia•tive

SECTION OBJECTIVES
When you have finished Section 8.1, you will be able to:

- Use a dictionary to obtain information about the spelling, definition, capitalization, and hyphenation of words.

- Use a thesaurus to find words that will make your writing more precise.

- Avoid using words that are incorrect, overused, out of date, or inappropriate for the audience.

WHY IT'S IMPORTANT

Words are the building blocks of sentences, and sentences form our communication. To be accurate and effective in your written communication, you must use words effectively.

KEY TERMS
- phonetic spelling
- inflectional forms
- synonyms
- thesaurus
- homonyms
- pseudo-homonyms
- denotation
- connotation
- clichés
- antonyms
- derivative

271

Memory Hook

To use the dictionary to best advantage, follow these guidelines for verifying the spelling of a word:

- Place the letters in their correct order; for example, *neither*, not *niether*.
- Avoid inserting extra letters in a word, as in the incorrect *athaletic* (instead of *athletic*).
- Include all the letters that are in the word; for example, *mortgage*, not *morgage*, and *business*, not *busness*.
- Verify that the word is not some other word with a similar spelling. Read the definition. For example, would you give someone *complementary tickets* or *complimentary tickets*?
- Pay close attention to compound words to determine whether they are written as one word, *checkpoint*; two words, *check mark*; or a hyphenated word, *drip-dry*.
- Include any accent marks that are part of a word. For example, *exposé* is a noun that means "the revelation of something discreditable"; but *expose* is a verb that means "to cause to be visible."

KEY POINT

A good dictionary is the cornerstone of every writer's reference library.

Sometimes a word must be divided at the end of a line of writing. Unless the word is divided correctly, the reader may be confused. Here is an example of incorrect dividing:

- Please sign and return the enclosed statement promptly if you want a refund.

Pronunciation and Division into Syllables. Immediately after the regular spelling of a word, the dictionary shows the word's **phonetic spelling.** This feature indicates how the word should be broken into syllables, how each syllable should be pronounced, and which syllable or syllables should be accented. If phonetic symbols are new to you, refer to the section of the dictionary that explains them.

Look again at the sample dictionary entries for *complement* and *compliment* in **Exhibit 8.1.** The entries show that the pronunciation of both words is 'käm-ple-ment. The hyphens indicate syllable breaks. The accent mark indicates the syllable that should be stressed when pronouncing the word.

Inflectional Forms and Derivatives. **Inflectional forms** are forms of a word that show tense, number, and other meanings. For example, *goes* is an inflectional form of *go*. A **derivative** is a word formed from another word. For example, *affirmation* is a derivative of *affirm*.

The dictionary shows the irregular plurals of nouns, the past tense and participial forms of irregular verbs, and the comparative and superlative forms of irregular adjectives and adverbs. After the definition of the noun *contract*, for example, are its derivative noun *contractibility* and its derivative adjective *contractible*. The entry for the irregular verb *fall* gives its past tense, *fell*; its past participle, *fallen*; and its present participle, *falling*.

Synonyms. For many entries the dictionary lists **synonyms**—words that have almost the same meaning as the entry. The entry for *complement* in **Exhibit 8.1** lists the synonym *counterpart*; the entry for *compliment* lists the synonyms *honor* and *regards*. Note that although synonyms have what the dictionary calls a "shared meaning

com·ple·ment \'käm-plə-mənt\ *n* [ME, fr. L *complementum*, fr. *complēre* to fill up, complete, fr. *com-* + *plēre* to fill — more at FULL] (14c) **1 a** : something that fills up, completes, or makes perfect **b** : the quantity or number required to make a thing complete ⟨the usual ~ of eyes and ears —Francis Parkman⟩; *esp* : the whole force or personnel of a ship **c** : one of two mutually completing parts : COUNTERPART **2 a** : the angle or arc that when added to a given angle or arc equals a right angle in measure **b** : the set of all elements that do not belong to a given set and are contained in a particular mathematical set containing the given set **c** : a number that when added to another number of the same sign yields zero if the significant digit farthest to the left is discarded — used esp. in assembly language programming **3** : the musical interval required with a given interval to complete the octave **4** : an added word or expression by which a predication is made complete (as *president* in "they elected him president" and *beautiful* in "he thought her beautiful") **5** : the thermolabile group of proteins in normal blood serum and plasma that in combination with antibodies causes the destruction esp. of particulate antigens (as bacteria and foreign blood corpuscles)

complement 2a: *ACB* right angle, *ACD* complement of *DCB* (and vice versa), *AD* complement of *DB* (and vice versa)

com·pli·ment \'käm-plə-mənt\ n [F, fr. It *complimento*, fr. Sp *cumplimiento*, fr. *cumplir* to be courteous — more at COMPLY] (1654) **1 a** : an expression of esteem, respect, affection, or admiration; *esp* : an admiring remark **b** : formal and respectful recognition : HONOR **2** *pl* : best wishes : REGARDS ⟨accept my ~s⟩ ⟨~s of the season⟩

Exhibit 8.1
Dictionary Entry
Dictionary entries show the spelling, pronunciation, synonyms, and meanings of a word. ***Thinking Critically.*** *When you tell a person that you admire his or her work ethic, are you giving the person a* complement *or a* compliment?

element," each has its own distinct shades of meaning, as shown in the following examples of synonyms for *invent*.

- Edward Mellanby did not *invent* vitamin D, but he did *discover* it.
- The Wrights did not *discover* the airplane, but they did *invent* it.

Other Information

In addition to word information, a good abridged dictionary contains the following special sections that a writer may find helpful.

Signs and Symbols. This section consists of signs and symbols frequently used in such fields as astronomy, biology, business, chemistry, data processing, mathematics, medicine, physics, and weather. This section could be helpful in verifying the correct use of symbols in technical documents.

Biographical Names. The names of famous people, each with the proper spelling and pronunciation, are listed. Biographical data such as dates of birth and death, nationality, and occupation are also given. Use this material for checking the pronunciation of names or for identifying unfamiliar names encountered in reading or conversation.

Geographical Names. This section provides information about places—name, pronunciation, location, population, and so on. Therefore, it can be helpful when you are checking the spelling of place names in correspondence.

Going Global

Foreign Accent

It can be a challenge to proofread personal names or names of locations from other languages due to accent marks or different rules of spelling. Consult a dictionary for the language or a style guide for guidance.

Handbook of Style. Included in this very useful section are rules on punctuation, italicization, capitalization, and plurals; citation of sources; and forms of address.

The Thesaurus

If you know a word, the dictionary will give you its meaning. The **thesaurus** works the other way around: If you have a general idea of the meaning you want to convey, the thesaurus will give you a choice of specific words to express it. Look up the general idea, then choose the word or expression that best fits your meaning.

Roget's International Thesaurus and *Merriam-Webster's Collegiate Thesaurus,* two popular references, are arranged differently. *Roget's* has two parts: the main section, which lists synonyms and associated words, and the index to the main section. To find a synonym for a word, for example, the adjective *careful,* look up the word *careful* in the alphabetic index. There you will find entries followed by a key number, as in the following example:

careful
adj.   attentive 530.15

            cautious 895.8

            conscientious 974.15

            economical 851.6

            heedful 533.10

            judicious 467.19

interj.   caution 895.14

The key numbers refer to numbered paragraphs in the main section. Thus, if *cautious* is closest to the idea you wish to convey, turn to entry 895 in the main section, organized numerically, and find paragraph 8 for a listing of synonyms.

Merriam-Webster's Collegiate Thesaurus is organized like a dictionary, with one list of entries arranged in alphabetic order. To find synonyms for *careful,* just turn to the entry *careful.* Within this entry capital letters are used for the word *cautious,* an indication that more information can be found at that entry, which is also given in alphabetic order. *Bartlett's Roget's Thesaurus* has 350,000 references and includes contemporary words, phrases, foreign expressions, idioms, and many quotations.

To Find the Most Suitable Word

Imagine that you write advertising copy, and you're working on an advertisement about new fall fashions. One aspect you wish to emphasize is the smartness of the clothes. Using your thesaurus, you find that smart can be expressed by the words *chic, fashionable, dapper, well-groomed, dressed up,* and *dressy,* among a number of other words and expressions.

To Avoid Overusing a Word

Suppose you have written a letter in which you use the word *great* several times. Consulting the index of your thesaurus, you find a list of other adjectives, such as *grand, chief, important, large,* and *famous.* When you check these references, you discover additional words and expressions that are synonyms of *great.* You now have at your disposal a wide choice of words that you can use in place of *great.*

To Find the Most Specific Word

Sometimes you have a general word for an object or an idea in mind, but you want to use a more specific word. For example, you may be discussing the possibility of taking a *trial* vote, but that is not the specific word you are seeking. You look up the word *vote* in the thesaurus. Among the many choices shown is the expression *straw vote,* which is precisely the expression you are seeking.

To Replace an Abstract Term

Imagine that you are writing a memo and that you wish to replace the word *precipitous* in the phrase *a precipitous decision*. Among the substitutes that you would find in your thesaurus are *hasty*, *abrupt*, *hurried*, and *sudden*. You should choose the word that fits best.

Electronic Dictionary and Thesaurus

Word processing programs have an electronic dictionary and a thesaurus you can use to verify the spelling of a word or to find suitable synonyms. An electronic dictionary will indicate misspelled words, such as *apreciate* for *appreciate*. Most word-processing programs have an automatic correction feature. This feature will change *teh* to *the* automatically. See page 326 for more information on the automatic correction feature.

An electronic thesaurus will suggest possible synonyms for a word. If, for example, you have used the word *extravagant* three times in a report, you could check your thesaurus to find appropriate synonyms to substitute for one or two of them. Synonyms listed would include *abundant*, *excessive*, and *lavish*.

Improving Word Choice

The words that you use can either earn the respect and admiration of those with whom you communicate or mark you as unimaginative and even uneducated. To be an effective communicator, you must use the right word at the right time. You must also use words correctly, avoid excessive use of words, and predict how readers will interpret the words you use.

The Correct Word

Careful writers know the difference between correct and nonstandard usage. Usages that are unacceptable in standard English must be avoided in business writing.

Some nonstandard usages result from errors; for example, a speaker might use *irregardless*, which is not a word, for *regardless*. Some are correct words used incorrectly; for example, a writer might type *accept* for *except*. Some are glaring grammatical errors.

When you make errors such as these, readers may know what you mean, but they most likely will not have a positive view of your competency and expertise.

Homonyms

Homonyms are words that look or sound alike but have different meanings. Choosing an incorrect word, although it may sound or even look correct, is one of the most frequently committed errors in word usage.

For example, the tenants of a large apartment building receive a letter urging "all the *residence* to protest the proposed rent increase." This important message might cause confusion because the writer cannot distinguish people, *residents*, from place, *residence*.

Exhibit 8.2 (see page 276) lists homonyms that every business writer should know and use correctly.

Pseudo-Homonyms

Pseudo-homonyms are words that sound somewhat alike but have different meanings. When pronounced correctly, these words do not sound *exactly* alike. For example, the statement "David, Harry, and Susan placed orders for $800, $1,000, and $1,300, *respectfully*," is incorrect. The writer has confused the word *respectfully*, meaning "courteously," with *respectively*, meaning "in the order given." The pseudo-homonyms that give the most trouble are listed in **Exhibit 8.2** (see page 276).

Deadly Mistake

A teacher received the following note from a student's father. "John was sick yesterday. Please execute him."

(*Excuse* is the correct word, not *execute*.)

KEY POINT

Homonyms are words that look or sound alike but have different meanings.

KEY POINT

Pseudo-homonyms are words that sound somewhat alike but have different meanings, such as advice and advise. When pronounced correctly, these words do not sound alike.

Exhibit 8.2
Homonyms and
Pseudo-Homonyms
Easily confused
words. *Thinking*
Critically. What is the
difference between
a homonym and a
pseudo-homonym?

Homonyms and Pseudo-Homonyms

Homonyms

ad, add	dew, do, due	pedal, peddle
aisle, isle	discreet, discrete	plain, plane
allowed, aloud	dual, duel	presence, presents
altar, alter	foreword, forward	principal, principle
ascent, assent	forth, fourth	raise, raze
assistance, assistants	foul, fowl	rap, wrap
attendance,	gorilla, guerrilla	residence, residents
attendants	grate, great	right, write
aural, oral	hear, here	roe, row
bail, bale	hire, higher	so, sow, sew
base, bass	hole, whole	sole, soul
berth, birth	idle, idol	some, sum
born, borne	instance, instants	stake, steak
brake, break	intense, intents	stationary, stationery
canvas, canvass	lean, lien	straight, strait
capital, capitol	leased, least	taught, taut
cereal, serial	lessen, lesson	their, there, they're
cite, sight, site	lesser, lessor	threw, through
coarse, course	loan, lone	to, too, two
complement,	mail, male	vain, vane, vein
compliment	medal, meddle	waist, waste
core, corps	miner, minor	wait, weight
correspondence,	overdo, overdue	waive, wave
correspondents	pain, pane	weak, week
council, counsel	passed, past	weather, whether
dependence,	patience, patients	
dependents	peace, piece	

Pseudo-Homonyms

accede, exceed	dairy, diary	liable, libel
accept, except	deceased, diseased	loose, lose, loss
adapt, adopt	decent, descent,	moral, morale
addition, edition	dissent	our, are
adverse, averse	deference, difference	persecute, prosecute
advice, advise	desert, dessert	personal, personnel
affect, effect	detract, distract	precede, proceed
allusion, illusion	device, devise	quiet, quit, quite
anecdote, antidote	disburse, disperse	reality, realty
appraise, apprise	disprove, disapprove	recent, resent
carton, cartoon	elicit, illicit	respectfully,
casual, causal	eligible, illegible	respectively
clothes, cloths	emigrate, immigrate	statue, statute,
choose, chose	eminent, imminent	stature
conscience,	expand, expend	suit, suite
conscious	facilitate, felicitate	than, then
cooperation,	fiscal, physical	
corporation	formally, formerly	
correspondence,	ingenious, ingenuous	
correspondent	later, latter	

Spelling

If you were a business executive, would you hire an engineer whose résumé listed a degree in *compewter* science? Would you hire someone who had taken courses in *acounting*? Poor spelling would make you doubt that these people could do the jobs they were seeking. Good spelling shows readers the results of careful, hard work. Avoid being a poor speller by using a dictionary either in printed or electronic form.

You can improve your spelling by paying careful attention to the similarities and differences between homonyms, or pseudo-homonyms, and the suggestions in Section 8.2. The most important step to improved spelling, however, is developing the dictionary habit.

Words Suited to the Audience

In a letter to a customer, a computer specialist would lose the attention of the audience if, in discussing how a computer could be useful to everyone, he or she used such technical terms as *backups, checkdisk,* and *batch file.* By using nontechnical terms, the writer could better hold the attention of the audience. Using a specialized vocabulary that is unfamiliar to an audience is as serious a mistake as speaking in a language an audience doesn't know. Communication takes place only when a writer chooses words geared to the interests and knowledge of that audience.

Sounds Alike

The biologist identified the mushrooms that were audible.
(*Edible* is the correct word, not *audible*.)

 Memory Hook

Look up and remember the difference between prefixes that have similar meanings. Such words can be confusing.

biweekly—occurring every two weeks
semiweekly—occurring twice a week
disinterested—impartial
uninterested—bored; unconcerned
interstate—between states
intrastate—within one state

Words with Varying Connotations

The dictionary meaning of a word, the **denotation,** is often different from its **connotation,** which is the meaning readers associate with the word based on their experiences and emotions. For example, a solitary person might be called a *wallflower,* a *recluse,* or a *rugged individualist.* The wrong choice of terms can distort the writer's meaning and perhaps even offend someone.

Look at the shades of meaning in the two words *cheap* and *inexpensive.* Only an unskilled writer or speaker would use the word *cheap* to mean *inexpensive.* Certainly, no salesperson would make that mistake. *Cheap* means "worthless or shoddy"; *inexpensive* refers merely to cost, not to quality. Sometimes an *inexpensive* suit is a bargain; a *cheap* suit never is.

Whenever you are in doubt about a word's meaning, check the dictionary before using the word. If there is no time to look up the unknown word, then phrase your idea in a way that avoids it.

KEY POINT

Denotation is the meaning of a word that is listed in a dictionary. *Connotation* is the meaning readers associate with the word.

Words to Avoid

Building a successful business or career requires building goodwill. Because words play a vital part in establishing goodwill, a skilled communicator chooses words or phrases that the reader and listener can both understand and appreciate. In general, this means choosing positive rather than negative terms, presenting information directly and without repetition, and using fresh and current expressions rather than outdated and overused ones.

Avoid Negative Words

Which of the following statements is more likely to build or retain customer goodwill?

- You neglected to specify the sizes and colors of the dress shirts you ordered. We cannot ship the order with such incomplete information.
- The four dozen dress shirts you ordered will be shipped as soon as you tell us what sizes and colors you prefer.

The second statement is the better selection, although both statements try to convey the same idea. The second statement is positively worded and avoids such unpleasant expressions as *you neglected* and *cannot ship the order with such incomplete information*. Negative words are almost sure to evoke a negative response. The customer reading these negative words may cancel the order or may choose a different supplier for future orders.

Words result in negative responses when the reader feels blamed or accused. Most expert business writers consider *failed, careless, delay,* and *inexcusable* to be negative words, regardless of how the words are used, and they recommend avoiding these words. Actually, such words are unpleasant primarily when they are accompanied by *you* (*you failed*) or *your* (*your delay*). *Your oversight, your error,* and *your claim* signal the reader to react negatively; but *our oversight* and *our error*—though not necessarily wise choices of words—carry an entirely different impression.

The following words sound negative when used with *you* or *your*. To maintain goodwill, avoid using these words.

blunder	damage	inability	regret
careless	defective	inadequate	trouble
claim	delay	inferior	unfavorable
complaint	error	mistake	unfortunate
criticism	failure	neglected	unsatisfactory

Eliminate Unnecessary Words

Words that are repetitious are a waste of the reader's time. Such words clutter the message and can distract, delay understanding, and reduce emotional impact. The italicized words in the expressions in **Exhibit 8.3** on page 279 are unnecessary and should, therefore, be omitted.

Avoid Out-of-Date Words

Words that are out of date suggest that the writer is behind the times. Imagine the reaction to a sign that says "Eschew Smoking!" In certain uses, the words in **Exhibit 8.4** on page 279 have a similar effect.

Avoid Overused Words

Replacing overused words with more exact and colorful terms can make your writing lively and interesting. The adjective *good* is overused and weak: a *good* maneuver, a *good* negotiator, a *good* speech, a *good* worker. Instead, for greater interest, say a *clever, smart,* or *skillful* maneuver; a *patient, forceful,* or *crafty* negotiator; an *eloquent, informative,* or *engrossing* speech; a *qualified, intelligent,* or *competent* applicant.

Redundant Phrases

adequate *enough*	connect *up*
as yet	continue *on*
at above	*and* etc.
up above	*as* to whether
both alike	*past* experience
new beginner	*free* gratis or *for* free
cooperate *together*	inside *of*
same identical	my *personal* opinion
lose *out*	rarely (seldom) *ever*
meet *up* with	repeat *back* or *again*
modern methods *of today*	refer *back*
over *with*	*exact* same
customary practice	*true* facts

Exhibit 8.3
Redundant Phrases
Groups of unnecessary words. ***Thinking Critically.*** *Why is the pair* cooperate together *redundant?*

Outdated Language

advise *or* state (for *say, tell*)

beg (as in *beg to advise*)

duly (as in *comments are duly noted*)

esteemed (as in my *esteemed colleague*)

herewith (except in legal work)

kindly (for *please*)

party (for *person*, except in legal work)

same (as in *we will send you same*)

trust (for *hope, know, believe*)

via (for *by*)

Exhibit 8.4
Outdated Language
Imagine using some of these out-of-date words in a sales pitch for a new digital camera. ***Thinking Critically.*** *How would the words you chose affect your sales pitch?*

   Adjectives such as *awful, bad, fine, great,* and *interesting* are also overused. The following sentences show how meaningless these words can be.

Avoid: The new guidelines on hiring workers will result in a *bad* situation.

Use: The new guidelines on hiring workers will result in a (*difficult, painful,* or *troublesome*) situation.

Avoid: Kari Michaels gave an *interesting* sales presentation.

Use: Kari Michaels gave an (*informative, enlightening,* or *educational*) sales presentation.

Avoid: We have an *awful* backlog of orders.

Use: We have (*an enormous, an overwhelming,* or *a gigantic*) backlog of orders.

Avoid Clichés

Clichés are overworked expressions such as *crystal clear, needs no introduction,* and *at a loss for words* that lost their strength long ago. Outdated expressions such as *attached hereto, attached herewith please find,* and *under separate cover* still find their way into business documents, creating the perception of a stale, backward organization.

The use of clichés exposes a lack of imagination—the tendency to repeat the familiar, even when the familiar is not worth repeating. Clichés waste time, obscure ideas, and bore readers and listeners. Dare to use your imagination, which is sure to generate better expressions once you resolve to avoid clichés.

Some commonly overused words and expressions, together with suggested substitutions for them, are listed in **Exhibit 8.5.**

Exhibit 8.5
Clichés
Marketing pitches sometimes use clichés to describe a product's benefits to the consumer. *Thinking Critically. How might using clichés weaken your sales pitch?*

Clichés	
Cliché	**Substitute**
along the lines of	like
asset	advantage, gain, possession, resource
at all times	always
by the name of	named
deal	agreement, arrangement, transaction
each and every	each *or* every
face up to	face
factor	event, occurrence, part
field	branch, department, domain, point, question, range, realm, region, scene, scope, sphere, subject, theme
fix	adjust, arrange, attach, bind, confirm, define, establish, limit, mend, place, prepare, repair
inasmuch as	since, as
input	comment, information, recommendation
in the near future	soon (or state the exact time)
line	business, goods, merchandise, stock
matter	point, question, situation, subject (or mention what is specifically referred to)
our Mr. Smith	our representative, Mr. Smith
proposition	affair, idea, offer, plan, proposal, recommendation, undertaking
reaction	attitude, impression, opinion
recent communication	letter of (give exact date)
say	articulate, assert, declare, exclaim, express, mention, relate, remark

Use Creativity to Achieve Variety

Although you can use many reference books to help you achieve variety of expression, you won't find ready-made phrases to express every idea. Achieving variety in word usage requires creativity.

Select Suitable Synonyms

Choosing suitable synonyms is the most direct means of achieving variety in your vocabulary. Although synonyms have the same basic meaning, each synonym has a different shade of meaning. To select the best synonym, you must go beyond the basic idea and learn the distinctions.

A dictionary can help you create a phrase to achieve variety. Under the word *explore,* for example, the *Merriam-Webster's Collegiate Dictionary* lists no synonyms, but look at its definition: "to investigate, study, or analyze . . . make or conduct a systematic search." Instead of using *explore,* you can make a phrase to fit: "*study* the options" or "*systematically search* the files."

Use Appropriate Antonyms

An **antonym** is a word that means *exactly* the opposite of another word. For example, *light* is an antonym of *dark*. Antonyms are also formed by adding the prefixes "il," "in," "ir," "non," and "un" before a word.

Skill in the use of antonyms opens up broad possibilities to the writer. To *upset* someone seems harsh, to *unnerve* someone seems less critical. It is sad when the dead are *forgotten,* but sadder still when they go *unmourned.*

Choose Descriptive Words

Descriptive words make readers or listeners "see" what is being described. Notice how the first sentence uses vague words and the second sentence uses specific words to call an image to mind.

- **Vague:** Our building is well-located and the apartments are comfortable.

- **Descriptive:** Our new high-rise building is located on a quiet, tree-lined street near the center of town. The apartments are spacious and equipped with all the latest modern conveniences.

Using descriptive words will improve your written messages. To develop this skill, visualize a complete picture of what you want to describe, then consult the thesaurus until you find the most specific descriptive terms that apply. Use this technique to compose messages that hold the attention of your readers.

> **KEY POINT**
>
> Use a thesaurus to search for specific terms to make your writing more descriptive.

Assessment   Section 8.1

Review of Key Terms

1. How is a *thesaurus* different from a *dictionary*? _____
   _____
   _____

2. What is the difference between a word's *denotation* and a word's *connotation*? _____
   _____

Editing Practice

Using Language! Using a thesaurus, write an exact descriptive word for the italicized word.

3. The administrator made a *bad* decision. _____

4. Both the engineers and the technicians are *happy* with the design.

   _____

5. Our equipment operators receive *good* on-the-job training. _____

6. This new procedure is *hard* to understand. _____

7. Josh has a *good* work record. _____

Practical Application

8. Which words in the following sentences are used incorrectly? Write the incorrectly used word, and then write the word you should use in its place next to it.

   a. The storm damage was not quiet as severe as anticipated.
   b. Mr. Walters is adverse to changing his scheduled vacation.
   c. Reprimands will be issued to drivers who accede the posted speed limit in company cars.
   d. The assistant manager complemented her associates on their quick action.

   _____

   _____

   _____

   _____

9. Collect several travel brochures from a local travel agency. Then, identify words or phrases in the brochure that are used to attract potential guests. Are there any overused or trite expressions? Next, as a team, create a new brochure using your own descriptive words. You may want to consult a thesaurus.

   _____

   _____

Discussion Point

Thinking Critically

10. How can a misspelled word or a misused pseudo-homonym affect the credibility of a business writer? _____

    _____

    _____

11. How do negative words and overused words interfere with establishing goodwill? _____

    _____

Mastering Spelling Techniques

Essential Principles

Many employers screen applicants by giving them grammar and spelling tests. Such an assessment of an applicant's writing skill is important because misspelling a word in a document makes both the writer and the organization look unprofessional. To increase your chances for employment and advancement, make every effort to improve your spelling.

Guides to Correct Spelling

Although there are many variations in the spelling of English words, some spelling principles always hold true. Every writer must know and be able to apply these principles—the basic guides to correct spelling.

Final "y"

Many common nouns end in *y: company, industry, entry, territory, warranty, supply, day, attorney, survey.* The spelling of plurals of these common nouns depends on whether the *y* is preceded by a consonant or a vowel. The **vowels** are *a, e, i, o, u,* and sometimes *y*; the **consonants** are the rest of the letters in the alphabet.

- If *y* is preceded by a consonant, change *y* to *i* and add "es": *company, companies; entry, entries; industry, industries; supply, supplies; territory, territories; warranty, warranties.*

- If *y* is preceded by a vowel, leave the *y* and just add "s": *attorney, attorneys; day, days; survey, surveys.*

Ei and *ie* Words

Among the most frequently misspelled words are these: *believe, belief, conceive, conceit, deceive, deceit, perceive, receive, receipt, relieve,* and *relief.* Use the following Memory Hook to help you remember when to use *ie* and *ei.*

Memory Hook

Use the combination *li* and *ce* in *Alice* to remember that the correct spelling after *l* is *ie* (believe); after *c*, *ei* (receive).

Endings "ful," "ous," "ally," "ily"

To spell the endings *ful, ous, ally,* and *ily* correctly, remember the following:

- The suffix *ful* has only one *l*: *beautiful, careful, masterful, meaningful, skillful.*

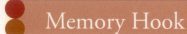

Memory Hook

To spell *ei* and *ie* words correctly, remember this saying:

Use *i* before *e*
Except after c
Or when sounded like *ay*
As in *neighbor* or *weigh.*

Exceptions:

- Words in which *ei* makes a long e sound (*either*, *caffeine*, and *seize*)
- for*ei*gn
- h*ei*ght
- forf*ei*t

- An adjective ending with the sound "us" is spelled *ous: humorous, miscellaneous, obvious, previous, various.*
- The ending *ally* has two *l*'s: *basically, finally, financially, incidentally, originally.*
- The ending *ily* has one *l: busily, gloomily, hastily, necessarily.*

Doubling a Final Consonant

Knowing when to double a final consonant before adding an ending to a word is a matter of distinguishing between vowel sounds.

Words of One Syllable. If you can hear the difference between long and short vowel sounds, you can tell whether or not to double the final consonant of a one-syllable word. If the vowel sound is long, do *not* double; if the vowel sound is short, double the final consonant. *Exception:* Do not double the final consonant of words ending in "w" (*saw*) or "x" (*fix*). See **Exhibit 8.6.**

Words of More Than One Syllable. The only rule needed is this one: Double the final consonant if the last syllable of the base word is accented, if the vowel sound in the last syllable is *short,* and if the suffix to be added begins with a vowel. Some examples are listed in **Exhibit 8.7.**

In each of the following base words, the accent is on the *first* syllable; therefore, in the preferred spelling, the final consonant is *not* doubled.

benefit	benefited	benefiting
cancel	canceled	canceling
differ	differed	differing
edit	edited	editing
equal	equaled	equaling
offer	offered	offering
travel	traveled	traveler

However, there are exceptions such as formatting, handicapped, and programmed. Check a dictionary if you are unsure of the correct spelling.

When to Double Consonants	
hope	hoping (*long vowel*)
mope	moping (*long*)
plane	planing (*long*)
scare	scaring (*long*)
stripe	striping (*long*)
tape	taping (*long*)
weed	weeding (*long*)
mix	mixing (*ends in x*)
hop	hopping (*short vowel*)
mop	mopping (*short*)
plan	planning (*short*)
scar	scarring (*short*)
strip	stripping (*short*)
tap	tapping (*short*)
wed	wedding (*short*)

Exhibit 8.6
When to Double Consonants
Words of one syllable that do and do not double the final consonant. ***Thinking Critically.*** *How does reading your writing out loud assist you in making doubling decisions?*

KEY POINT

For one-syllable words, do not double the final consonant before adding an ending if the vowel sound is long. Double the final consonant if the vowel sound is short.

Multisyllabic Words		
commit	committed	committing
equip	equipped	equipping
occur	occurred	occurring
omit	omitted	omitting
prefer	preferred	preferring
regret	regretted	regretting
transmit	transmitted	transmitting

Exhibit 8.7
Multisyllabic Words
Words of more than one syllable. ***Thinking Critically.*** *What resources can you use to assist you in doubling letters in words of more than one syllable?*

8.2 Self-Assessment A

Check the following sentences for any spelling errors. Write *OK* if the sentence is correct. Underline misspelled words. Write the correction in the spaces provided.

1. Katherine offered to work overtime during peak seasons. _____

2. The sales manager assigned the two new sales territorys to Steve Garner and Jane Johnson. _____

3. Dr. Sanders, the surgeon, said that scaring would be minimal. _____

4. I beleive that we can sell both buildings. _____

5. The sale will feature miscellanious tools and kitchen items. _____
   _____

6. Randall used his new equipment for tapping the wedding. _____

7. The lawyer transmited the document by fax. _____

8. Thank-you notes should be sent promptly after the weding gifts are received. _____

KEY POINT

Identify your personal spelling pitfalls and use a dictionary to verify the spelling of these words.

Dictionary Alerts

Even the best spellers need to use a dictionary. However, no one has time to look up every word. Therefore, you should learn how to recognize your own spelling pitfalls—words that you are most likely to misspell. These pitfalls alert careful spellers to consult the dictionary.

The most common spelling pitfalls are presented here. In addition, you may have your own list of problematic words. *Remember:* Use the dictionary whenever in doubt, but especially if the word in question contains one of these prefixes or suffixes.

Word Beginnings

These pairs of prefixes—*per, pur,* and *ser, sur*—present a spelling difficulty because the words in each pair sound like they could be spelled with the same prefix. Study the following words:

permanent	purchase
personal	purpose
persuade	pursuit
serpent	surplus
serenity	surprise
service	surtax

Word Endings

The following groups of word endings are tricky because they have similar sounds or because they may be mispronounced. The spellings of these endings differ, however. Do not try to guess at spellings of words with the following ending sounds.

Sounds "unt" and "uns."   The endings *ant, ance, ent,* and *ence* are all usually sounded "unt" and "uns." Because so many words have these endings, they are spelling danger spots. They must be spelled by eye, not by ear. Some common words with these endings are in the following list.

accountant	compliance	dependent	existence
defendant	maintenance	incompetent	independence
descendant	perseverance	permanent	interference
tenant	remittance	silent	occurrence

Sounds "uhble" and "uhbility."   The sound "uhble," which might be spelled *able* or *ible*, is another trap. The alert writer consults a dictionary in order to avoid misspelling words that end in *able, ible, ability,* or *ibility.* Some common "uhble" and "uhbility" words are found in the following list.

changeable	collectible	availability	credibility
movable	deductible	capability	flexibility
payable	illegible	predictability	possibility
receivable	reversible	probability	visibility

Sounds "shun" and "shus."   Words ending with the sound "shun" might be spelled *tion, sion, cian, tian, sian, cion,* or *xion.* The ending sound "shus" might be spelled *cious, tious,* or *xious.* Learn the spelling of the words listed here.

ambition	ignition	anxious	malicious
collision	profession	conscientious	pretentious
complexion	suspicion	conscious	superstitious
dietitian	technician	fictitious	suspicious

Navel vs. Naval

Several years ago, graduates were amused to find that they had graduated from the U.S. Navel Academy instead of the U.S. Naval Academy. The company that printed the diplomas apologized for the error and agreed to replace them.

8.2 Self-Assessment B

Check the following sentences for any spelling errors. Write *OK* if the sentence is correct. In the spaces provided, correctly write misspelled words.

1.   Our company requires a written receipt for all tax deductable expenses.

   _____

2.   Illegable handwriting is the direct cause of many medical errors. _____

   _____

3.   The defendent was charged with a DUI. _____

4.   Bill sent his remittence three weeks later. _____

5.   The sweater vest is reversable. _____

6.   The stockbroker was quite perplexed when he learned the training had been canceled. _____

Going Global

British Rule

Consider the differences in spelling when corresponding with businesses abroad. For example, the British spell the word "labor" with *ou* instead of *o* (labour), and the word "recognize" with an *s* instead of a *z* (recognise).

Sounds "shul" and "shent." The ending that sounds like "shul" is sometimes spelled *cial* and sometimes *tial*. A "shent" ending might be spelled *cient* or *tient*. Study the following words and learn how they are spelled.

artificial	deficient
beneficial	efficient
essential	impatient
judicial	omniscient
partial	proficient
substantial	quotient

8.2 Self-Assessment C

Check the following sentences for any spelling errors. Write *OK* if the sentence is correct. In the space provided, correctly write misspelled words.

1. Our new vice president, Max Stephens, is both aggressive and ambicious. _____

2. High school seniors found the Success in College workshop very benefitial. _____

3. People with blue eyes and a fair complection are more likely to get skin cancer. _____

4. The patient needs a capable and consciencious counselor. _____

5. Michal was ankcious about the medical procedure, even though her physician explained that the test was painless and routine. _____

Sounds "ize" and "kul." The ending "ize" might be spelled *ize, ise,* or even *yze* (*analyze*). A "kul" ending could be spelled *cal* or *cle*. A careful writer, therefore, consults a dictionary for words with these endings. Study the following "ize" and "kul" words.

apologize	advertise	identical	obstacle
criticize	enterprise	mechanical	particle
realize	improvise	statistical	spectacle
temporize	merchandise	technical	vehicle

Words That End in *ar, ary, er, ery, or,* and *ory*. Words that end in *ar, ary, er, ery, or,* and *ory* should be recognized as spelling hazards; you should always verify each spelling. For example, *stationary* (motionless) and *stationery* (paper) end with the same sound, but they are spelled differently. Memorize the spellings of the following words:

calendar	temporary	stationery	laboratory
grammar	advertiser	debtor	category
customary	adviser	advisory	depository
stationary	customer	inventory	crematory

Memory Hook

Do you get *stationery* and *stationary* confused? Simply put, think of *paper*, which ends in *er*, and you'll never confuse it with *stationary*—to *stay* in one place.

The sound "seed."   Even though merely a handful of words end with the sound "seed," they are often written incorrectly because the ending has three different spellings. As shown below, only one word ends in *sede* and only three words end in *ceed*—all other "seed" words are spelled *cede*. Some examples are:

sede	ceed	cede
supersede	exceed	accede
	proceed	concede
	(*but* procedure)	intercede
	succeed	precede
		recede
		secede

8.2 Self-Assessment D

Check the following sentences for any spelling errors. Write *OK* if the sentence is correct. In the spaces provided, correctly write misspelled words.

1.   Particals of dust can cause an allergic reaction in some people. _____
_____

2.   All of the contractor's bids exceeded the budget by more than $5,000. ___
_____

3.   We need a person with a technicle background to help us with the statisticle data. _____

4.   Since our inventory is getting low, this would be a logical time to design new letterhead stationary. _____

5.   Mr. Carson's calender is completely full for the next two weeks.
_____

Your Spelling Vocabulary

Business writers cannot take the time to verify the spelling of every word. Therefore, they must take the time to learn the correct spellings of the words used most often in their written communications. Knowing how to spell troublesome words requires more than memorization. You must analyze each word and fix in your mind its peculiarities. Use strategies like the ones shown in the following Memory Hook.

> **KEY POINT**
>
> Only one word ends in *sede* (*supersede*) and only three words end in *ceed* (*exceed, proceed,* and *succeed*). All other "seed" words end in *cede*.

> *oops!*
>
> **What Do You Mean?**
>
> We used two battery-operated ratios during the power outage.
>
> (*Radios* is the correct word, not *ratios.*)

Memory Hook

Remember the spellings of troublesome words by using tips such as these:

accommodate
(two *c*'s, two *m*'s)
aggressive (two *g*'s, two *s*'s)
convenient (*ven, ient*)
definite (*ni*)
develop (no final *e*)
embarrass (two *r*'s, two *s*'s)
forty, fortieth (the only *four* words without a *u*)

ninth (the only *nine* word without an *e*)
occasion (two *c*'s, one *s*)
privilege (*vile*)
recommend (one *c*, two *m*'s)
repetition (*pet*)
separate (*a rat*)
until (only one *l*)

Assessment   Section 8.2

Review of Key Terms

1. When should you double a final *consonant* before adding an ending to a word? Provide an example. _____

   _____

   _____

   _____

2. What spelling rule should you follow when writing words with the vowels *ei* and *ie*? _____

Editing Practice

Vocabulary Alert!   Select a word from the list below that best completes each sentence.

| delinquent | principal | principle | secede | supersede |

3. Although we stand to gain little from the lawsuit, we believe winning is a matter of _____

4. What is the dollar amount on all _____ accounts that are at least 60 days past due?

5. In planning for college, my _____ concern is getting a sound education at a reasonable cost.

6. Several nations are planning to _____ from the international trade alliance because they feel it is too restrictive.

Practical Application

7. Review some of the spelling errors that you have made—errors made while typing on the computer or perhaps on a term paper. Make a list of these words on a sheet of paper, writing the word correctly, circling problem parts, and listing a spelling rule for the word, if one applies. _____

_____

8. Write the correct forms of the words in parentheses.

   a. The charitable organization has established an (advise) board?
   b. The merger proved (advantage) to both companies.
   c. Due to excessive costs, the idea was (scrap) by top management.
   d. Jon has the (flexible) to play both sports.
   e. Mr. Davis is (commit) to providing insurance for all associates.

_____

_____

_____

_____

_____

Discussion Point

Evaluating Concepts

9. What are some ways in which you can improve your spelling? _____

_____

_____

10. If you do not know how to spell a word, how would you go about finding the correct spelling? _____

_____

_____

SECTION OBJECTIVES

When you have finished Section 8.3, you will be able to:

- Recognize and correct errors in thought units composed of words, phrases, and clauses.

- Recognize and correct errors in pronoun references.

WHY IT'S IMPORTANT

Appropriately placed phrases and clauses help make communication clear.

KEY TERMS

- thought unit
- which
- pronoun
- antecedent

Structuring Phrases and Clauses

Thought Units

A combination of words that properly belongs together is called a **thought unit.** One example of a thought unit is a noun or pronoun and its modifiers; another example is a verb and its complement. When the words of a thought unit are placed correctly, the reader can understand the meaning quickly and easily. When the writer incorrectly places the words of a thought unit, however, the reader may get a mistaken idea of the writer's meaning. Sometimes the mistaken idea is laughable, but in business communications, such mistakes are more likely to cause problems or confusion, as in the following example.

- Incorrect: Calling the meeting to order, the new Palm Pilot drew the praise of the vice president of sales.

Introductory phrases and clauses logically lead the reader to the words that directly follow. In the preceding example, however, a Palm Pilot cannot really call a meeting to order. In order to avoid a confusing statement such as this one, the writer should group together words whose meanings belong together.

- Correct: When the meeting was called to order, the new Palm Pilot drew the praise of the vice president of sales.

Words in Thought Units

Sometimes a confusing, laughable, or simply false meaning is conveyed because a single word is not connected with its proper thought unit.

The following advertisement is an example of a misplaced adjective.

- Incorrect: Gigantic men's clothing sale begins today!

The modifier *gigantic* has been misplaced—it seems to indicate that *gigantic men's* is a thought unit. However, few men want to be described as *gigantic*. The correct thought unit is *gigantic sale*.

- Correct: Gigantic sale of men's clothing begins today!

Misplaced adverbs can also cause confusion.

- Incorrect: The idea for changing our sales emphasis came to me after I had opened the meeting suddenly.

What happened suddenly—the opening of the meeting or the idea for the sales emphasis?

- Correct: The idea for changing our sales emphasis suddenly came to me after I had opened the meeting.

Phrases in Thought Units

Incorrectly placed phrases, as well as incorrectly placed words, can completely change the meaning of a message. Careful writers edit their work meticulously to see that they have placed phrases correctly.

- Incorrect: A hard drive can be installed by anyone who has studied the computer manual in 20 minutes.

No computer manual could be studied in 20 minutes, but someone who had studied the computer manual for a reasonable length of time could probably install a hard drive in 20 minutes.

- Correct: A hard drive can be installed in 20 minutes by anyone who has studied the computer manual.

Now, read the following classified advertisement and see the confusion that results from an incorrectly placed thought unit.

- Incorrect: Two-story townhouse apartment for rent. Ideal for working couple with balcony.

How many working couples can there be who have a balcony but don't have an apartment?

- Correct: Two-story townhouse apartment with balcony for rent. Ideal for working couple.

Two misplaced phrases can be even worse than one. Imagine receiving a direct-mail advertisement that contains the following sentence.

- Incorrect: Our interactive, multimedia games are guaranteed to give you hours of entertainment without qualification for your home computer.

The correct thought units are *games for your home computer* and *guaranteed without qualification*. The following revision would be more likely to encourage you to order a game or two.

- Correct: Our interactive, multimedia games for your home computer are guaranteed without qualification to give you hours of entertainment.

Clauses in Thought Units

We shouldn't be surprised to learn that a misplaced clause can have even more devastating consequences than a misplaced word or phrase. How would the public react if the president of your company made the following announcement?

- Incorrect: Our goal in marketing is to encourage the public to try our products until our health foods become better known.

oops!

Big Difference

Gigantic baby's furniture sale begins today!

(Gigantic sale of baby's furniture begins today!)

KEY POINT

Phrases may begin with:

1. **A preposition**
2. **An infinitive**
3. **A verb**

Employability Skills

Writing

Good writing skills are not only necessary but also required in specific careers. Using the correct phrases in your writing can make a strong impact on how your business associates receive the communications you write.

KEY POINT

Clauses contain a subject and a predicate.

The sentence sounds as if once the products are better known, no one will want to buy them. Moving the *until* clause clears up the matter.

- Correct: Until our health foods become better known, our goal in marketing is to encourage the public to try our products.

Because clauses pose a special hazard since they often are used to explain people's motives. Consider the following statement.

- Incorrect: The clerk hardly listened to the customer's complaint because she was concentrating so intensely on completing the form.

Was the clerk or the customer completing the form? While the original sentence is not wrong, the following sentence better describes the situation.

- Correct: Because she was concentrating so intensely on completing the form, the clerk hardly listened to the customer's complaint.

Ambiguous *Which* Clauses

The word **which** is a relative pronoun that refers to another word in the sentence. If the *which* clause is misplaced, the word being referred to is unclear and confusion will result.

- Incorrect: Our gallery has a book on important nineteenth-century American paintings, which you can purchase for a special price of $19.95 plus postage.

Placing *which* immediately after *paintings* is confusing. Can the *paintings* be purchased for $19.95? The writer of the sentence actually intended to say that the book could be purchased for $19.95.

- Correct: Our gallery has a book, which you can purchase for a special price of $19.95 plus postage, on important nineteenth-century American paintings.

While clear and a definite improvement, the rewritten sentence would gain force and polish if the *which* clause were removed, as in this revision:

- For a special price of $19.95 plus postage, you can purchase our gallery's book on important nineteenth-century American paintings.

Although it is acceptable for *which* to refer to a general idea rather than to a single noun, the writer must take extra care to see that the reference is clear. In the following sentence, the pronoun reference is ambiguous.

- Incorrect: Further resistance to the board of directors will only jeopardize your job, which neither of us wants.

The problem is that the *which* clause may refer either to the general idea *will only jeopardize your job* or to the single noun *job*. *Which* seems at first to belong to the thought unit *your job*. If neither of the persons referred to wants the job, why should either one care whether the job is jeopardized? A revision would clear up the confusion.

- Correct: Further resistance to the board of directors will only jeopardize your job, and we do not want that.

Here is an example of a *which* clause making clear reference to a general idea.

- Ms. Robinson predicted that an out-of-court settlement would be reached, which is precisely what happened.

Who Did What?

In written business communications, the writer must make it absolutely clear about *who* has done or will do a specific action. Sometimes, however, the writer confuses the thought by connecting the wrong person, place, or thing with an action. As a result, the intended meaning is not conveyed to the reader. Such a violation of the thought-unit principle can cause doubt or uncertainty as to *who* did *what*.

- Incorrect: If not satisfied, we will refund your money.

The thought unit is *If not satisfied, we.* The meaning here is that we (the manufacturer) are the ones who might not be satisfied. If a customer returned the goods and asked for a full refund, could the manufacturer refuse on the grounds that the manufacturer was well satisfied with the customer's money? The correct meaning is immediately apparent to the reader when the sentence is revised.

- Correct: If you are not satisfied, we will refund your money.

Occasionally, if the who-did-what principle is violated, the sentence becomes ridiculous, because an object, not a person, seems to be performing an action.

- Incorrect: Receiving the customer's urgent request, the order was immediately processed by Deanne.

The thought unit *Receiving the customer's urgent request, the order* suggests that the order was receiving the request. This kind of phrasing shows a serious lack of communication know-how. In a revision, Deanne performs the action.

- Correct: Receiving the customer's urgent request, Deanne immediately processed the order.

Here is another illustration of this type of error.

- Incorrect: After climbing to the top of the tower, the whole city lay spread before us.

What does the thought unit *After climbing to the top of the tower, the whole city* mean? How could a city climb to the top of the tower? In a revision, the people would perform the action.

- Correct: After climbing to the top of the tower, we saw the whole city spread before us.

A who-did-what violation, sometimes called a *dangling modifier,* does not necessarily occur at the beginning of a sentence. For example, note the error in the following sentence.

- Incorrect: Mr. Edwards saw the prospective customer leaving the stockroom.

As written, the thought unit is *customer leaving the stockroom.* Where was Mr. Edwards when he saw the customer, and why was the customer in the stockroom? Most likely it was Mr. Edwards who was leaving the stockroom. In order to eliminate the confusion, the writer should revise the sentence.

- Correct: Leaving the stockroom, Mr. Edwards saw the prospective customer.

Now, read the following sentence, which is another example of unclear word reference.

- Incorrect: Dana White was promoted to branch manager, thus confirming everyone's opinion that she is the most qualified person for the position.

oops!

What's What?

When stopped, the feet are needed by the cyclist to balance the motorcycle.

(When the motorcycle is stopped, the cyclist needs to use the feet for balance.)

Thus, as used here, is ambiguous. The thought could have been expressed more clearly and more directly by eliminating *thus*.

- Correct: Dana White's promotion to branch manager confirms everyone's opinion that she is the most qualified person.

Confusing Pronoun References

A **pronoun** is a word used in place of a noun. Each pronoun borrows its meaning from a noun. When the writer fails to make clear which noun a pronoun refers to, the pronoun loses its meaning or assumes an incorrect and unintended meaning. One vague or mistaken pronoun reference can garble an entire message.

Confusing *He* or *She*

When you use the pronoun *he* or *she,* you must make certain that the **antecedent**—the noun to which the pronoun refers—is clear. If more than one man or more than one woman is mentioned in the sentence, place the pronoun as near as possible to the person to whom you refer. The following sentence leaves the reader wondering "Who returned from the meeting?"

- Incorrect: Ms. Reynolds asked Adena to write a report immediately after she returned from the regional sales meeting.

Does *she* in this sentence refer to Adena or to Ms. Reynolds? If the reference is to Ms. Reynolds, the sentence should be revised.

- Correct: Immediately after she returned from the regional sales meeting, Ms. Reynolds asked Adena to write a report.

If, on the other hand, Adena is the one who attended the meeting, then the correct way to write the sentence is:

- Immediately after Adena returned from the regional sales meeting, Ms. Reynolds asked her to write a report.

Confusing *It*

Using the pronoun *it* to refer to something that is not immediately clear is a common mistake.

- Incorrect: I will place the football in the kicking tee, and when I nod my head, kick it.

Kick what? This *it* could result in a painful injury. The word *it* must be replaced by the noun to which it should refer.

- Correct: I will place the football in the kicking tee, and when I nod my head, kick the ball.

Other Confusing Pronoun References

Speakers who are uncertain of their sources frequently use the vague "they say" as a reference. In written communication, references must be definite and exact:

- Incorrect: They say that the joint venture between FedEx and the U.S. Postal Service will be launched early next year.

Who is meant by *they* in the preceding sentence? To be more precise, a writer should replace the vague *They say* with a more exact reference.

- Correct: *International Market News* reports that the joint venture between FedEx and the U.S. Postal Service will be launched early next year.

KEY POINT

Replace confusing pronouns with specific names of persons or things.

Call Who?

Patrick said to call them if you have problems using your new laptop.

(Patrick said to call someone in Customer Service.)

Another type of reference that is puzzling and annoying to a reader is an unclear pronoun reference.

- Incorrect: Although I dictated all morning on Tuesday, the administrative assistant typed only two of them.

The thought unit *two of them* is vague. Two of what? A clear thought could be communicated by:

- Correct: Although I dictated all morning on Tuesday, the administrative assistant typed only two of the letters.

Correcting *This* Faults

A common writing fault is the use of *this* to refer to an entire preceding thought. Lack of precision sometimes forces a reader to read a sentence several times to understand the writer's meaning. Inexact use of *this* can detract from the point the writer is trying to make.

- Incorrect: Employees can't find parking spaces. This has existed since we hired 50 new employees.

To what does *this* refer? Stating the point specifically makes the meaning clear:

- Correct: Employees can't find parking spaces. This shortage of parking spaces has existed since we hired 50 new employees.

KEY POINT

To correct *this* and *that* faults, ask yourself "*This* what?" or "*That* what?" Use your answers to these questions to complete the thought.

 Assessment   Section 8.3

Review of Key Terms

1. How can one avoid writing a confusing *thought unit*? _____
   _____
   _____
   _____

2. When using a pronoun, why must a writer use a clearly stated *antecedent*? _____
   _____

Editing Practice

Grammar Alert!   Correct the pronoun errors in the following sentences.

3. What one of the sales managers will be transferred? _____

4. Whom is going to the safety meeting in Atlanta next week? _____

5. The profit will be divided equally between you and I. _____

6. It was me who forgot to mail the check. _____

Practical Application

Analyzing Information

7. Rewrite the following sentences, making sure all thought units are clear.

   a. Matt put the video into the VCR, which everyone had been waiting to see.

   b. The veterinarian was unable to complete the exam for the cat's owner because she was nervous.

   c. Audrey ate the donuts at the bakery with coffee.

   d. The new equipment, with little or no training, can be operated by skilled technicians.

   _____

   _____

   _____

   _____

   _____

8. As a team, look in newspapers to find examples of inexact pronoun references and *this* faults. Sports articles or articles involving several participants are good starting points. Then, on a separate sheet of paper, rewrite the sentences to clarify any unclear references. _____

Discussion Point

Making Interpretations

9. It is often difficult for writers to find confusing thought units in their own writing. Suggest ways in which writers could revise their own work. _____

   _____

10. How do misplaced words, phrases, or clauses interfere with a writer's message? _____

    _____

Writing Effective Sentences

Essential Principles

A well-written letter, memo, e-mail, or report flows smoothly. The reader is more aware of the flow of ideas than of individual sentences, clauses, and phrases. Nothing should interrupt the reader's concentration—no awkward phrases, vague references, or unbalanced constructions.

Because a well-written document flows so easily, the reader may feel that the words flowed as easily from the writer's mind. In reality, however, the first draft was probably full of awkward phrases, vague references, choppy sentences, and unbalanced constructions. After completing that draft, the writer took the time to look for problems and to apply good writing techniques to eliminate them.

Word Usage

Writers combine words to make sentences and sentences to make paragraphs. You cannot write effective sentences without using the correct words. Here are some suggestions for writing effective sentences.

- Use the you-attitude and positive words.
- Use planned repetition of words to emphasize important points.
- Use pleasant-sounding words instead of harsh or awkward-sounding words.

Use the You-Attitude

Sentences that use the **you-attitude** emphasize the reader instead of the writer. By focusing on the reader, you are more likely to gain his or her acceptance or cooperation. Compare the following sentences:

- I-Attitude: I would like to thank you for your interest in Fibertec, Inc.
- You-Attitude: Thank you for your interest in Fibertec, Inc.
- I-Attitude: We need to receive your reply to this offer by Tuesday, May 16.
- You-Attitude: Please send us your reply to this offer by Tuesday, May 16.

One way to achieve the you-attitude in business writing is to use *you* with positive words. Such words create a receptive, pleasant impression in the mind of a reader. Compare the positive words and the negative words in **Exhibit 8.8** on page 300.

SECTION OBJECTIVES

When you have finished Section 8.4, you will be able to:

- Compose sentences that use the you-attitude and positive words.
- Use planned repetition for emphasis and avoid writing sentences with excessive repetition of sounds.
- Use subordination and coordination properly, and correct *so* and *and so* faults.
- Use the active and passive voices appropriately.

WHY IT'S IMPORTANT

Developing effective sentences will help ensure that your communication is consistent

KEY TERMS

- you-attitude
- voice

KEY POINT

The you-attitude focuses on the reader. The I-attitude focuses on the writer.

Positive or Negative?			
Positive Words		**Negative Words**	
advancement	happy	anxious	failure
agreeable	integrity	apologize	incapable
capable	pleasure	blame	loss
cheerful	profit	cannot	not
courage	success	complaint	problem
eager	warmth	damage	sad
easy	welcome	difficult	sorry
fun		dishonest	wrong

Exhibit 8.8

Positive or Negative?

Positive and negative words. *Thinking Critically. How can the following sentence become more positive?* It is not difficult to fill your order by April 19.

Note how using a negative word with *you* can result in a negative sentence. Such sentences should be reworded to make them more positive.

- Negative: You were not late in making deliveries last month.
- Positive: You made all of your deliveries on schedule last month.

Use Planned Repetition of Words

Although careless repetition of words shows a lack of imagination, *planned repetition* can sometimes strikingly emphasize an important idea. Repeating the words *too* and *flexible* in the following examples helps to emphasize each point.

- Sally arrived *too* late *too* often to keep her job.
- Take advantage of our *flexible* hours to keep your schedule *flexible.*

Repetition is most often used in advertisements where the major goal is to make readers remember the name and purpose of the product. Sometimes the goal is accomplished by simple repetition of the name. Clever writers manage to vary the order of the repeated words to prevent monotony, as in the following sentence.

- Flexicise Workouts will add muscles to your body, and Flexicise Workouts will add body to your muscles.

Use Pleasant-Sounding Words. Excessive repetition of certain vowel or consonant sounds can create tongue twisters that detract from the message. Even when reading silently, the reader cannot ignore a sentence like the following.

- Selina sold seven synthetic slipcovers on Saturday.

Such repetitious sounds can cause problems other than becoming tongue twisters. Although easy to say, the following sentence is hardly pleasant to hear.

- Steer your weary, dreary body to O'Leary's Health Club.

Avoid using words with unpleasant sounds, and do not attempt to write business letters that sound musical or poetic. A business document should be courteous and concise. For the greatest effect, concentrate on that function.

KEY POINT

Positive words make a pleasant impression on the reader.

8.4 Self-Assessment A

Check the following sentences for errors in either the you-attitude or pleasant sounding language. Write *OK* if the sentence is correct. Rewrite the sentence correctly if it contains errors.

1. Give me a response by Friday. _____

2. Include your payment with the completed order form. _____
    _____

3. The Werner account takes up four thick files. _____
    _____

4. To avoid being a failure, you should try harder. _____
    _____

5. I have enclosed the videos requested in your May 5 letter. _____
    _____

Proper Subordination of Ideas

Proper subordination of ideas depends on the ability to distinguish an important idea from a lesser idea. The important thought is expressed as a main clause, and the lesser idea is properly written as a subordinate clause. This principle can be remembered as follows: Main idea = main clause; subordinate idea = subordinate clause. Subordinate clauses begin with subordinate conjunctions such as *because, since, when,* and *although.*

- Incorrect: Your proposal is interesting, although it does not meet our specifications.

Which statement is more important—*your proposal is interesting* or *it does not meet our specifications*? That the proposal does not meet the specifications is the more important idea; therefore, it should be expressed as the main clause, as in the following example.

- Correct: Your proposal does not meet our specifications, although we did find it interesting.

Coordinate and Subordinate Ideas

When a sentence contains two ideas of equal importance, divide the sentence into two main clauses. Use a coordinating conjunction (*and, but, or, nor*) to join the ideas, as in the following sentences.

- Jess will review the cost estimates, and Maria will write the report.
- The work is difficult, but the rewards are great.

On the other hand, the writer can fail to see that the thoughts belong not in two main clauses but in a main clause and a subordinate clause.

- Incorrect: Other candidates were equally qualified, but the marketing director selected Lynn for the Webmaster position.

> **KEY POINT**
>
> When a sentence contains two ideas of equal importance, divide the sentence into two main clauses.

This sentence places equal stress on what the writer considers to be two main ideas. The emphasis should properly be placed on the director's choosing Lynn even though others were qualified. For force, as well as for clarity, the sentence should be rewritten.

- Correct: Although other candidates were equally qualified, the marketing director selected Lynn for the Webmaster position.

Eliminate Interrupting Expressions

Some writers destroy proper subordination by writing the lesser idea as an interrupting expression. For instance, read the following sentence:

- Incorrect: You are, considering the risks involved in such an investment, very fortunate.

The main thought, *you are very fortunate,* is interrupted by the lesser idea, *considering the risks involved.* This interruption breaks the flow of the main thought and detracts from the force of the statement. Properly written, the sentence should read as follows.

- Correct: You are very fortunate, considering the risks involved in such an investment.
- Correct: Considering the risks involved in such an investment, you are very fortunate.

Correct *So* and *And So* Faults

Whenever you read a sentence that uses *so* and *and so* to introduce a clause, you can improve the sentence by substituting a more meaningful conjunction. Notice how weak the connection is between the two clauses in the following sentence.

- Incorrect: Andrea has been a dedicated literacy volunteer for ten years, so we gave her a special tribute at last night's fund-raising dinner.

The first clause gives the reason for the second clause. *Because* is a better choice for joining clauses that give causes and results. The following sentence is stronger, clearer, and more polished.

- Correct: We gave Andrea a special tribute at last night's fund-raising dinner because she has been a dedicated literacy volunteer for ten years.

And so is not a two-word conjunction. It is two separate conjunctions used to form a vague connection between two clauses.

- Incorrect: Mr. Turner is a talented electronic publications specialist, and so we recommend that you hire him.

The first clause is the reason for the second. The relationship is easier to detect in the following revision.

- Correct: We recommend that you hire Mr. Turner because he is a talented electronic publications specialist.

8.4 Self-Assessment B

In the following sentences, make the corrections indicated in parentheses. Write the entire sentence.

1. Save the files in a new directory on the computer. Print a copy of each file. (Coordinate ideas.) _____

    _____

2. We are, despite the costs involved, committed to investing in current technology. (Eliminate an interrupting expression.) _____

    _____

3. The report is due March 4, and Betty has been working long hours on the calculations. (Subordinate an idea.) _____

    _____

4. Our editorial department is understaffed, and so we propose hiring three additional editors. (Correct the *and so* fault.) _____

    _____

5. Some additional options were presented, but the manager decided to go with Jessica's proposal. (Subordinate an idea.) _____

    _____

oops!

Active or Passive Voice?

A sample book was sent to us by Borders Bookstore.

(Borders Bookstore sent us a sample book. *Use the active voice.*)

Active Versus Passive Voice

Voice is that property of a transitive verb that shows whether the subject acts or is acted upon. In the active voice, the subject is the doer of an action; in the passive voice, the subject is acted upon. Any verb phrase composed of a past participle with a "being" verb helper is in the passive voice: *will be shipped, has been sent, was done, is frozen.*

> Passive: A program upgrade *was sent* to us by the company.
>
> Active: The company *sent* us a program upgrade.

The active voice expresses thoughts in a stronger, livelier way than does the passive voice. Compare these two sentences:

> Passive: Your computer *will be shipped* on Wednesday, June 1.
>
> Active: We *will ship* your computer on Wednesday, June 1.

Both sentences state the same information, but the active voice sentence is more direct.

In the following pair of sentences, note that the sentence using the active voice makes a stronger point than the weak, passive voice does.

- Passive: Last year our telecommunications systems *were sold* to three out of every four new businesses in the city.
- Active: Last year, we *sold* our telecommunications systems to three out of every four new businesses in the city.

> **KEY POINT**
>
> Use the active voice to express thoughts in a strong, direct way.

The passive voice is used in business writing to soften the impact of negative news. In the following sentences, note how the sentence using the passive voice is the more diplomatic of the two.

- Active: Because the college *did not send* us a copy of your transcript, we *cannot consider* your application to our program at this time.

- Passive: Your application to our program *will be considered* when a copy of your transcript *is sent* to us by the college.

Parallel Structure

Parallel structure is a must for similar parts of a sentence. A noun should be parallel with a noun, an adjective with an adjective, and a phrase with a phrase. For example, look at this sentence.

- Unparallel: The new assistant coordinator is eager, diligent, and has much knowledge.

Lack of parallel structure causes the sentence to lose momentum. The writer erroneously coordinated two adjectives and a clause. In the following revision, the writer has coordinated the three adjectives, making the sentence grammatically parallel and effective.

- Parallel: The new assistant coordinator is eager, diligent, and knowledgeable.

Balance Comparisons

Comparisons are balanced only if they are complete. They can be complete only if they include all the necessary words. The omission of one necessary word can throw a comparison out of balance, as in the following sentence.

- Unbalanced: Recent studies show that women spend more money on eating in restaurants than men.

As written, the sentence could mean that women spend more money on eating in restaurants than they spend on men. The comparison lacks balance, as well as sense, because an essential word is omitted. One word, properly placed, can make the meaning of the sentence clear.

- Balanced: Recent studies show that women spend more money on eating in restaurants than men *spend.*

- Balanced: Recent studies show that women spend more money than men *do* on eating in restaurants.

Here is another unbalanced comparison.

- Unbalanced: Ms. Taylor's role in the agency is more than a financial analyst.

This sentence lacks sense because essential words have been omitted. The following revision improves the clarity.

- Balanced: Ms. Taylor's role in the agency is more than *that of* a financial analyst.

An unbalanced comparison like the one that follows provides a chance for skillful revision.

- Unbalanced: Roby can program just as well, if not better, than Tommy.

Disregarding the words set off by commas, the sentence reads as follows: *Roby can program just as well than Tommy.* However, no one would say *as well than.* The first revision below is acceptable, but the second one is a much better sentence.

- Balanced: Roby can program just as well *as,* if not better than, Tommy.
- Balanced: Roby can program just as well *as Tommy,* if not better.

Balance Modifiers

Omission of single-word modifiers can destroy the balance of a sentence in several ways. Such an omission can produce, for example, an illogical message.

- Incorrect: The company is hiring a receptionist and software engineer.

Failure to write *a* before *software engineer* makes *a receptionist and software engineer* refer to one person. It is unlikely that one person could serve in this dual capacity.

- Correct: The company is hiring a receptionist and a software engineer.

Balance Verbs

Structural balance demands that whenever the parts of verbs in compound constructions are not exactly alike in form, no verb part should be omitted. The following sentence breaks this rule.

- Incorrect: Jaya always has, and always will, do a good job.

The word *do* cannot act as the main verb for the auxiliary verb *has. Has* requires the past participle *done.* Without the word *done,* the sentence seems to read "Jaya always has *do* and always will do a good job." The verbs required in this compound construction are not exactly alike in form; therefore, all verb parts should be included.

- Correct: Jaya always *has done* and always *will do* a good job.

The following sentence shows the same kind of error.

- Incorrect: Your revised report was received today and *copies* sent to the members of the advisory committee for their comments.

The omission of the auxiliary verb after *copies* makes the sentence read "Your revised report was received today, and copies *was* sent to the members of the advisory committee for their comments." The plural noun *copies* requires a plural verb; therefore, the sentence should be revised.

- Correct: Your revised report was received today, and copies *were* sent to the members of the advisory committee for their comments.

Balance Prepositions

The omission of a preposition can also throw a sentence off balance. Usage requires that some words be followed by specific prepositions.

When two prepositional constructions have the same object, use the preposition that is correct for each construction.

- Incorrect: Senior documentation writers must demonstrate expertise and knowledge of software programming.

In this sentence *expertise* and *knowledge* both are modified by the prepositional phrase *of software programming*. However, it is incorrect to say "expertise of software programming." The correct preposition to use with *expertise* is *in*. The sentence should read as follows.

- Correct: Senior documentation writers must demonstrate expertise *in* and knowledge of software programming.

Balance Conjunctions

In speech, subordinating conjunctions, particularly *that* and *when,* can often be omitted without causing any confusion. In writing, however, such omissions may destroy the balance of the thought units of a sentence and confuse the reader. Read the following example aloud.

- Incorrect: Neil often talks about the time he had neither money nor position.

If this were an oral communication, the speaker could make the meaning clear by pausing slightly after the word *time.* The reader, however, might see the thought unit as *Neil often talks about the time he had,* with the result that the words following *had* would not make sense. The reader would have to reread the sentence to understand the meaning. The sentence should read as follows.

- Correct: Neil often talks about the time when he had neither money nor position.

The following sentence may also be misread.

- Incorrect: I searched and discovered the contract folder was missing.

The reader may see *I searched and discovered the contract folder* as one thought unit. The subordinating conjunction *that* adds clarity.

- Correct: I searched and discovered *that* the contract folder was missing.

Balance Clauses

Another mark of writing distinction is to avoid incomplete, or elliptical, clauses. In the sentence *You are a faster typist than I,* the meaning "than I am" is clear. But note the following sentence.

- Incorrect: Did Mr. Chrisman pay the bill or his accountant?

This sentence could be interpreted as follows: "Did Mr. Chrisman pay the bill, or did he pay his accountant?" It could also be interpreted this way: "Did Mr. Chrisman pay his bill, or did his accountant pay the bill?" The following sentence clarifies the intended meaning.

- **Correct:** Did Mr. Chrisman pay the bill, or did his accountant pay it?

Balance Lists

The elements of a list should be parallel to each other. For example:

- **Incorrect:** You are responsible for:
    1. Researching the data.
    2. Analysis of the problem.
    3. The format of the report.

- **Correct:** You are responsible for:
    1. Researching the data.
    2. Analyzing of the problem.
    3. Formatting the report.

Assessment   Section 8.4

Review of Key Terms

1. How does using the *you-attitude* improve business writing? _____
   _____

2. When is it appropriate to use the *passive voice* in business writing? _____
   _____
   _____

Editing Practice

Using Language!   Rewrite each sentence to use positive language.

3. Accountants should not be dishonest. _____

4. I failed to complete the cost report by today, but I will try to finish it by
   tomorrow. _____

5. Your qualifications do not match our hiring needs, and you lack
   experience. _____

6. Discuss any complaints you have about your order with our 24-hour
   customer representative. _____
   _____

Practical Application

Revising Sentences

7. Rewrite each of the following sentences by correcting any faults. _____

    a. A pair of paralegals perused the evidence.
    b. You have successfully completed our sales training program, and you will get a promotion.
    c. The shipment was damaged in transit, and so I refused to accept it.
    d. We need temporary personnel to type documents, to proofread, and answering the phone.

    _____

    _____

    _____

    _____

8. Choose a famous speech, such as Abraham Lincoln's "Second Inaugural Address," Martin Luther King, Jr.'s "I Have a Dream," or John F. Kennedy's "Inaugural Address." As a team, discuss the use of parallel structure and how it affects the message.

    _____

Discussion Point

Thinking Critically

9. Why is it important to use correct grammar, spelling, and punctuation?

    _____

    _____

10. Why are subordination and coordination of ideas essential in writing effective communication? _____

    _____

Building Effective Paragraphs

Essential Principles

Writing effective paragraphs requires writing good sentences. Each sentence should support the main idea of the paragraph. If sentence structure is faulty, or if paragraph organization is poor, the entire communication will not convey the message effectively.

One Purpose, One Idea, One Thought

To be effective, a written message should have one purpose. Each paragraph in the message should have one main idea. Each sentence in a paragraph should have one main thought that supports the main idea of the paragraph.

Message	→	One purpose
Paragraph	→	One main idea
Sentence	→	One main thought

Message Control

A written communication, such as a letter or a memo, should be limited to one main purpose. Two or more main purposes within a message can cause confusion or can make one idea seem more or less important than another. In the following examples, note how the first message covers more than one purpose, while the second message focuses on one purpose.

- More Than One Purpose: Thank you for inquiring about our automobile loans. Enclosed is a loan application form for your review. You may also be interested in our certificates of deposit. We offer variable interest rates for three-month, six-month, and nine-month certificates.

- One Purpose: Thank you for inquiring about our automobile loans. Enclosed is a loan application form for your review. We offer flexible payment schedules for all automobile loans so that you can select a monthly payment that fits your budget.

Paragraph Control

To achieve paragraph control, the writer should relate all sentences to the main idea of the paragraph and keep paragraphs a reasonable length. In addition, the writer should use transitions and make sound decisions about where to begin a new paragraph.

SECTION OBJECTIVES

When you have finished Section 8.5, you will be able to:

- Write paragraphs that have one main idea, sentences that relate to the main idea of the paragraph, and messages that have a definite purpose.

- Use transitional words and phrases to connect sentences and paragraphs.

- Use variety in sentence length and sentence structure to make written communication more interesting.

WHY IT'S IMPORTANT

Writing effective paragraphs builds on the use of words, phrases, and sentences. Each part develops the main idea of the paragraph.

KEY TERMS

- paragraph unity
- readability
- transitional words and phrases

KEY POINT

Achieving paragraph unity requires the writer to focus on one main idea.

Paragraph Unity. The main idea of a paragraph is usually stated in a topic sentence. This topic sentence is often the first sentence in the paragraph. All other sentences in the paragraph should support the main idea, creating **paragraph unity.** For example, in the following paragraph, note how all the sentences relate to the main idea about techniques for improving your memory.

> There are several techniques for improving your memory. One technique is to use certain images to remember the names of people and things. For example, to remember the name of an important client, Ms. Flowers, you could remember her picking flowers. Another technique is to use a word or an acronym to remember a concept. For example, use the word *homes* to remember the names of the Great Lakes: *Huron, Ontario, Michigan, Erie,* and *Superior.* Still another memory technique is to associate a list of items with traveling a particular route. Each item becomes a part of your walk along this route. For instance, to remember the items on a grocery list, you might picture yourself putting a gallon of milk in the mailbox as you walk to your neighbor's house.

Before writing the first sentence of a paragraph, the writer should have the main idea of the paragraph clearly in mind. The writer must know where the paragraph is going before attempting to guide the reader there. The writer who does not know what conclusion the paragraph is to have should stop writing and start thinking.

Paragraph Length. In general, a paragraph should have no more than six to eight lines. If the development of the main idea requires more than six to eight lines, the writer should carry that thought over to another paragraph. Readers seem to need visual breaks (paragraphs) but not continuity breaks (interruptions in the message content). Visual breaks allow the reader to pause and think about the material presented.

Transitional Words and Phrases

To provide connections between sentences and between paragraphs, writers use **transitional words** and **phrases.** Skillful use of transitional words and phrases can move the reader through the communication—from one idea to another—without a break in continuity that could detract from the message.

Exhibit 8.10 on page 312 lists some common transitions you could use to show how items, ideas, or events are related to one another.

Note the transitions used in the following examples:

- Sequence: *After* he receives the spreadsheets, Dan will make a recommendation to management.
- Location: *Below* is a list of building specifications.
- Emphasis: *More important,* this new insurance policy will be cost-effective for all employees.
- Conclusion: *Therefore,* in recognition of Doris Gebel's outstanding sales record, we are naming her Employee of the Year.

As you read the following message, note the length of the paragraph and the lack of transitions.

> We were surprised to hear that you did not enjoy your tour of Denali National Park in Alaska last month. We feel that our literature gave you an accurate impression of what to expect. Our literature states that "Explorer Nature Tours are not for the faint of heart. Our naturalist guides take you to some of the most remote and pristine areas on Earth where you will see scenic landscapes and encounter native wildlife." Our tour literature does not explicitly say that you will wake up to find a grizzly bear in your tent, as you did. We do indicate that such encounters

are a remote possibility. Our experienced guides handled the situation quickly so that no harm resulted. We regret that you did not enjoy your tour. We must remind you that our policy, as stated in the tour literature, does not permit us to give you a complete refund. In your situation, we are willing to make an exception to our no-refund policy.

Let's look at how the preceding paragraph could be improved by making several shorter paragraphs and adding the transitions shown in italics.

> We were surprised to hear that you did not enjoy your Explorer Nature Tour of Denali National Park in Alaska last month. We feel that our literature gave you an accurate impression of what to expect. *For instance,* our literature states that "Explorer Nature Tours are not for the faint of heart. Our naturalist guides take you to some of the most remote and pristine areas on Earth where you will see scenic landscapes and encounter native wildlife."
>
> *Although* our tour literature does not explicitly say that you will wake up as you did, to find a grizzly bear in your tent, we do indicate that such encounters are a remote possibility.
>
> *Fortunately,* our experienced guides handled the situation quickly so that no harm resulted. *Nevertheless,* we regret that you did not enjoy your tour.
>
> We must remind you that our policy, as stated in the tour literature, does not permit us to give you a complete refund. *However,* in your situation, we are willing to make an exception to our no-refund policy.

Paragraphing Decisions

Paragraphing decisions can create an attractive, uncluttered format that makes business documents easier to read and understand. Ideally, content determines paragraph length. However, when it is practical, adjust paragraphs to fit the guidelines in the checklist in the next section. *Remember*: These are guidelines, *not* hard-and-fast rules.

- Keep the first and last paragraphs short, usually two to five lines each.
- Keep middle paragraphs an average of four to eight lines in length, and make them longer than the first and last paragraphs.
- Combine several short paragraphs to avoid a choppy appearance.
- Avoid writing several long paragraphs.
- Avoid a top-heavy appearance (beginning paragraphs too long); avoid a bottom-heavy appearance (ending paragraphs too long).
- Use an odd number of paragraphs. Three paragraphs look better than two, and five paragraphs look better than four.

Sentence Control

Maintaining sentence control is one way to improve the readability of a document. **Readability** refers to the ease with which something can be read. Sentence length and average number of syllables per word affect readability.

Variety in Sentence Length

Long sentences tend to be harder to understand than short ones. Yet, short sentences can seem choppy and boring. What is the solution to the sentence-length problem? Variety. Most sentences should range in length from 10 to 20 words. To provide variety, some sentences will have fewer than 10 words; others will have more than 20 words.

Digital Data

Word processing software programs have readability indexes that check spelling and grammar, and can display information about the reading level of a document, including readability scores. Each readability score bases its ranking on the average number of syllables per word and words per sentence.

KEY POINT

Transitional words and phrases signal relationships between sentences and between paragraphs.

Employability Skills

Improving or Designing Systems

A key employability skill is the ability to improve existing systems and develop new or alternative ways to improve operations. To communicate new ideas, it's important to effectively communicate both in writing and in presentations.

Common Transitions

Indicate Sequence

after	during	later
as soon as	finally	meanwhile
at present	first (second, third,	next
at the same time	fourth)	soon
before	immediately	then

Show Location

above	behind	inside
ahead	below	outside
	higher	

Compare or Contrast

also	however	on the other hand
although	instead	rather
both	likewise	similarly
but	neither	still
by contrast	nevertheless	yet
even though	on the contrary	

Add Information

also	besides	furthermore
and	despite	in addition
another	equally important	moreover
as well	further	next

Provide an Example

for example	namely	that is
for instance	specifically	
in particular	such as	

Add Emphasis

after all	even more	in fact
again	for this purpose	more important
especially	indeed	

Indicate a Result or Conclusion

as a result	consequently	therefore
because of	finally	thus

Exhibit 8.10

Common Transitions

Thinking Critically. *When explaining a new project to colleagues, how might transitions assist in determining objectives and responsibilities for each member of the group?*

Extremely long sentences seem to bury the main thought. Beyond a certain length, sentences seem to grow weaker with each added word. Overly long sentences may be grammatically correct, but often they are wordy. Compare the following examples.

- Wordy: Thank you for informing us in your letter of May 30 that you still have not received the illustrated *Complete Guide to Organic Gardening* that we shipped to you by parcel post on or about last May 1, but there's no need for you to worry because we are going to send you another copy of this excellent handbook on the techniques of successful gardening without chemicals.

The reader has to digest far too many words to learn that another copy of the book will be sent.

- Better: Thank you for letting us know that your copy of the *Complete Guide to Organic Gardening* has not reached you. We are mailing you a new copy at once.

On the other hand, a succession of short sentences weakens writing, because the reader is jerked along from thought to thought.

- Choppy: I received your proposal yesterday morning. Your approach to tracking inventory in our distribution center is interesting. We have a manufacturing committee meeting next Monday. I will present your proposal at that time.

The writer should smooth out the bumps, as in this revision.

- Better: Your proposal arrived yesterday morning. In my opinion, your approach to tracking inventory in our distribution center is promising. I intend to present your proposal to the other members of the manufacturing committee when we meet next Monday.

Short sentences are useful to bring out a series of important facts, to emphasize a point, and to break up a series of longer sentences. The following example uses a series of short sentences.

- The Fast-Action camera is made especially for quick-moving action photography. Its auto focus feature prepares you for your next shot a fraction of a second after you press the shutter. You just point and shoot—there's no need to focus! Its easy-open back permits you to insert a new roll of film faster than you can in any other camera. You can reload in 15 seconds! See your dealer for complete details.

Variety in Sentence Structure

A communication that lacks variety lacks interest. One sure way to produce a dull communication is to use only simple sentences, all compound sentences, or one with all complex sentences. Your goal should be to vary the sentence structure of a message. In the following example, note how too many compound sentences and too many *ands* make the paragraph dull.

What's the Real Reason?

I missed all my classes yesterday because I had a stomach.

(stomachache)

- Too many compound sentences: Your new Metro Spirit coupe costs more, *and* it offers a variety of convenient standard features. The fuel-injected engine is durable, *and* you will enjoy its trouble-free operation. The engine uses less fuel while idling, *and* it uses less fuel on the road. Our coupes stand up to years of wear *and* have a high resale value. You chose the right car, *and* you will find this out in the coming years.

In the following revision, note how variety in sentence structure improves the paragraph.

- Better: Your new Metro Spirit coupe costs more, *but* it offers convenient standard features. *Because* the fuel-injected engine is durable, you will enjoy years of trouble-free operation. You will use less fuel *both* when idling and when moving. *Finally,* because Spirit coupes stand up to years of wear, they have high resale value. The years will prove that you chose the right car.

You can also add variety to your message by including an occasional question or exclamation; inserting an interruption; or reversing normal word order. Some examples are:

- Why buy a Metro Spirit coupe? It offers . . .
- The fuel-injected engine is durable—voted Best Engine by *Auto* magazine—so you will enjoy years of trouble-free operation.
- *Never again* will you consider owning another make of car.

Assessment   Section 8.5

Review of Key Terms

1. How can a writer achieve *paragraph unity*? _____
   _____
   _____

2. How do *transitional words* and *phrases* provide connections between ideas? Provide an example. _____
   _____
   _____

Editing Practice

Grammar Alert!   Underline the grammar error in each sentence. Write the correction in the space provided.

3. Trina and myself will work on finishing the project after work. _____

4. The committee that organizes off-campus clubs meet tomorrow morning. _____

5. Mr. Owens and me were invited to tour the new county courthouse. _____

6. When was the chain saws shipped? _____

Practical Application

Creating Unity

7. Rewrite the following paragraph, varying the sentence structure. Some sentences should be combined. Omit the sentence that does not support the main idea.

There will be a reception on Friday, December 28. It will honor LaShon Oduba. He has been the purchasing director for 25 years. He just purchased a new house. He is retiring on December 30. The reception time is 5:30 p.m. to 7:30 p.m. It will be held in the corporate dining room. Everyone is invited.

_____

_____

_____

_____

8. Write a three-paragraph document that is informative. You may want 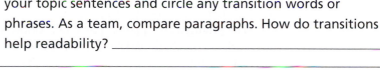 to tell your readers about a current news event. Underline your topic sentences and circle any transition words or phrases. As a team, compare paragraphs. How do transitions help readability? _____

_____

_____

Discussion Point

Thinking Critically

9. How does variety in sentence length and sentence structure improve the readability of a document? _____

_____

_____

10. In what ways does the appearance of a document affect readability?

_____

_____

SECTION OBJECTIVES

When you have finished Section 8.6, you will be able to:

- Describe *revising, editing,* and *proofreading.*

- Explain the importance of revising your written communications.

- Use a revision checklist to improve the organization, wording, and tone of your written communication.

- Apply the six Cs of editing to your written communication.

- Explain why proofreading written work is essential.

- Follow the five steps in proofreading.

- Use proofreaders' marks and technology when revising, editing, and proofreading.

WHY IT'S IMPORTANT

Even the most experienced business communicator has a need to edit and revise work.

KEY TERMS

- revising
- editing
- proofreading
- tone
- grammar-checker

KEY POINT

Revising improves the content and the organization of writing.

Revising, Editing, and Proofreading

Essential Principles

After writing the initial draft of a document, writers go through these three steps—revising, editing, and proofreading. Some do all three tasks simultaneously, while other writers focus on one step at a time. **Revising** improves the content and organization of writing; **editing** refines the revised draft and adds polish; **proofreading** spots content, grammatical, and typographical errors.

Using Proofreaders' Marks

When revising, editing, and proofreading documents, use proofreaders' marks as a quick, simple way to indicate changes or corrections in handwritten or printed copy.

The proofreaders' marks shown in **Exhibit 8.11** on pages 317 and 318 are standard marks used to indicate corrections in handwritten or printed copy. Study the marks and become familiar with their use.

Some of the proofreaders' marks are particularly useful in reorganizing the content of a memo, letter, or report. You can easily see from **Exhibit 8.11** how to use these marks to indicate the relocation of small and large segments of text. Simply identify the material to be moved by marking the beginning and the end of the segment with a vertical line and labeling the block with a letter of the alphabet. You can also use this block identification to mark material that should be checked for accuracy (a query) before the final document is printed. Place a question mark in the margin next to the block. Include marginal notes as needed for clarification.

Once you have marked changes and corrections on the hard copy, it is a simple process to make the changes on the computer. Remember to proofread the document after it has been printed to make sure all the indicated changes have been made correctly and no new errors have been introduced.

What Is Revising?

Revising is the process of "seeing again." In other words, when you revise, you have to stand back from your work and read it with fresh eyes in order to improve the writing. To do that, you need to allow some time to put your writing aside for a few hours or even for a day. Then, you should be able to read what you have written more objectively—as your potential audience will read it.

Checking Purpose, Audience, and Tone

Revising is not a hit-or-miss procedure. You need to ask yourself specific questions when revising any piece of writing. To begin the revision process, you should always ask questions about the purpose, audience, and tone of your message.

Exhibit 8.11
Proofreaders' Marks

Proofreaders' Marks

Capitalization

Capitalize a letter	texas	Texas
Lowercase a letter	This	this
Capitalize all letters	Cobol	COBOL
Lowercase a word	PROGRAM	program
Use initial capital	PROGRAM	Program

Changes and Transpositions

Change a word or amount	price is only 10.98 $12.99	price is only $12.99
Change a letter	deductable	deductible
Stet (do not make the change)	price is only $10.98 are	price is only $10.98
Spell out	2 cars on Rye Rd.	two cars on Rye Road
Move as shown	on May 1 write him	write him on May 1
Transpose letters, numbers, or words	hte time the of flight is 12:05	the time of the flight is 12:50

Deletions

Delete and close up	strooke or strooke	stroke or stroke
Delete a word	Wrote the the check	Wrote the check
Delete a punctuation	report is up-to-date	report is up to date
Delete one space	good day	good day
Close up	see ing	seeing

Insertions

Insert a word or letter	in office buildng the	in the office building
Insert a comma	may leave early . . .	may leave early, . . .
Insert a period	Dr Maria Rodriguez	Dr. Maria Rodriguez
Insert an apostrophe	all the boys hats	all the boys' hats
Insert quotation marks	Move up, she said	"Move up," she said
Insert hyphens	up to date report	up-to-date report
Insert a dash	They were surprised -- even shocked!	They were surprised —even shocked!
Insert parentheses	pay ten dollars $10	pay ten dollars ($10)
Insert one space	may leave	may leave
Insert two spaces	1. The new car	1. The new car

Proofreaders' Marks (*continued*)

Format Symbols: Boldface and Underscore

Print boldface	Bulletin
Remove boldface	**Bulletin**
Underscore	Title
Remove underscore	Title

Format Symbols: Centering

Center line horizontally	] TITLE [

Format Symbols: Page and Paragraph

Begin a new page	*pg* . . . order was delivered today by common carrier. We have all the . . .
Begin a new paragraph	. . . order was delivered today by common carrier. We have all the . . .
Do not begin a new paragraph (run-in)	. . . order was delivered today by common carrier. No ¶ We have all the . . .
Indent five spaces	5 We have raw materials in our warehouse. Production will . . .

Format Symbols: Spacing

Single-space	ss [XXXXXXXXXXXXXXXX XXXXXXXXXXXXXXXX
Double-space	ds [XXXXXXXXXXXXXXX XXXXXXXXXXXXXXX
Triple-space	ts [XXXXXXXXXXXXXXX XXXXXXXXXXXXXXX

Exhibit 8.11
Proofreaders' Marks, cont.
Proofreaders' marks provide a standard set of symbols for marking corrections. ***Thinking Critically.*** *Whom are proofreaders' marks written for?*

Is the Purpose of the Document Clear? If your purpose, for example, is to persuade your reader to take a certain action, does that message come across clearly, without the possibility of being misunderstood? If your purpose is to inform, have you included all pertinent information? If your purpose is to promote goodwill, have you used appropriate wording?

Is the Writing Tailored to the Audience? To tailor the writing to the audience, consider your audience's familiarity with the subject. Suppose you must write an e-mail to new employees about company copying and mailing procedures. Did you consider that your audience—the new employees—know very little about the company, its policies, or other procedures? Did you use any terms, abbreviations, or references that might not be understood by the new employees?

Is the Tone Appropriate for the Audience? **Tone** usually refers to the general effect a piece of writing creates. For example, the tone of your writing could be formal or informal, serious or humorous, positive or negative.

Although seldom stated directly, the reader infers tone through the author's choice of words and other elements of style. For example, if you were writing a memo to a supervisor, you would avoid a negative, critical tone—even if you were reporting on some aspects of company procedures that needed improvement. To keep the attention of your audience, you should establish a positive, upbeat tone that offers constructive suggestions for dealing with problems and challenges.

Digital Data

Training Resources

The most efficient way of improving your writing skills is to use various training resources available. Training courses specializing in improving writing skills are common, not to mention various self-help publications. Other means can include using the latest text editor which offers a spell-checker, a thesaurus, and a syntax editor.

Editing

Revision	Edited Draft
Identify block	and the catalog will be mailed.
Insert identified block	Your order will be mailed.
Delete identified block	Your order and the catalog will be mailed.
Move identified block	Your order and the catalog will be move shipped. The invoice will be mailed.
Query identified block	Ed will retire at the age of 96. ? B (Are the numbers transposed? Verify age.)
Query identified block	Make my reservation for June 31. ? C (June has only 30 days. Verify date.)
Query conflicting blocks	Call me Monday morning at 8 D ? E p.m. (Morning or p.m.? Verify time.)

Exhibit 8.12
Proofreaders' Marks for Editing.
Using proofreaders' marks to indicate copy to be moved or verified is convenient when you are writing a document as part of a team. *Thinking Critically. Can more than one person work from the marked copy at the same time?*

KEY POINT

When you begin revising a document, check for:

1. **Clarity of purpose**
2. **Suitability to the audience**
3. **Appropriateness of tone**

KEY POINT

Use transitions to help the reader move smoothly from one idea, sentence, or paragraph to another.

Reviewing the Organization

After answering the basic questions about purpose, audience, and tone, you should examine the organization of your message.

Is the Organization Logical?   Begin the message with a strong opening paragraph or introduction that states the main idea or purpose of the message. The middle paragraphs should sufficiently support or explain your stated purpose, and the conclusion should summarize your ideas or arguments.

One way to make sure that your writing is organized logically is to prepare an outline before you begin to write. Then follow that outline carefully as you write.

Do All Sentences Stick to the Point?   As you review the organization of your message, pay particular attention to any sentences that seem to stray from the main idea of each paragraph. Such sentences usually contain unnecessary details or information that should be deleted because it detracts from the message and creates confusion. For example, if you were making the point in a report that good math skills are necessary for all entry-level jobs in your company, you would be wandering off the subject if you described your own math training.

Are Transitions Used to Connect Ideas?   If your paragraphs are complete and if you have presented them in a clear, logical order, you should then make sure that you have included effective bridges (transitions) between ideas, sentences, and paragraphs. Refer to **Exhibit 8.10** on page 312 for some common transitional words and phrases.

Use Revision Checklist 1 in **Exhibit 8.13,** below, to improve the content, organization, and wording of your messages.

Reviewing the Language

KEY POINT

Use vivid, specific words to create concrete images in your reader's mind.

Once you are confident that you have included all the necessary information, take a close look at the words that compose the sentences and paragraphs.

Are Words Used Correctly?   First, make sure that you have used each word correctly. If you are unsure of the meaning of a word, either look it up in a dictionary to make sure the word is appropriate or find an alternative word that expresses your exact meaning.

Exhibit 8.13
Revision Checklist 1
A revision checklist to be used in checking for purpose, audience, tone, and organization.
Thinking Critically.
What effect does an inappropriate tone have upon readers?

Revision Checklist 1
Purpose, Audience, and Tone
○ Is the purpose clear?
○ Is the wording suited to the audience?
○ Is the tone appropriate?
Organization
○ Is the content complete?
○ Is the organization of the message logical?
○ Does the message have a strong introduction, middle, and conclusion?
○ Do all sentences relate to the main idea of each paragraph?
○ Are appropriate transitions used to connect sentences and paragraphs?

Are the Words Vivid and Specific?   Now, determine whether the words you have chosen will have the effect you intend. The purpose of all writing is to transfer your thoughts and ideas—as completely and as forcefully as possible—to someone else. Colorful, vivid, and specific words accomplish that purpose more easily than others. See page 281 for additional discussion of descriptive words.

When you revise, always examine your writing to make certain that the nouns, adjectives, and verbs are precise and sufficiently descriptive to convey your message. Use a thesaurus or a dictionary to find replacements for dull or overused words.

Are Any Words Overused or Unnecessary?   Check to see whether you have used the same words or expressions over and over. Reading something out loud is a particularly useful way to discover whether or not you have overused certain words. Readers sometimes become annoyed at such unnecessary repetition. For example, if you find that you have repeatedly used the word *told* throughout a report, consult a thesaurus for alternative words, such as *related, announced, declared, asserted, directed,* and *replied.* You will avoid repetition and at the same time describe more clearly the various ways people speak or make statements.

Is the Sentence Structure Varied?   Most people write exactly as they speak, and most people begin sentences with the subject. The monotony of this sentence structure is much more noticeable in a letter or report than it is in conversation. You can reduce reader boredom by adding some variety. For example, occasionally begin a sentence with an adverb or an adverbial phrase, a participial phrase, or a prepositional phrase.

- Subject: *Employees* often have to wait in line for 15 minutes in the cafeteria.
- Adverb: *Often* employees have to wait in line for 15 minutes in the cafeteria.
- Prepositional phrase: *In the cafeteria,* employees often have to wait in line for 15 minutes.

Is the Message Written in the Active Voice?   Another important step is to see if verbs are in the active voice wherever possible. In the active voice, the subject is the doer of the action; in the passive voice, the subject is the receiver of the action. Your writing will be much livelier if you use the active voice. Compare the following sentences.

- Passive: The long-awaited announcement was read by the president of the company.
- Active: The president of the company read the long-awaited announcement.

Use Revision Checklist 2 in **Exhibit 8.14,** on page 322 to improve the language use in your messages.

Revising with Grammar-Checkers

A **grammar-checker** is software that evaluates grammar and suggests ways to improve the grammar and wording of a document. Grammar-checkers identify certain weaknesses such as errors in subject-verb agreement, overuse of the passive voice, lack of variety in sentence structure, and wordiness.

Some grammar-checkers estimate the reading level of a text segment. You can revise your document if the reading level is too high or too low. For example, if your company is inviting employees' children to attend a summer day camp, you could use a grammar-checker to make sure the invitation was written on a level that children would understand.

Going Global

Works Both Ways

In some Arabic writing, the characters are read from right to left, not left to right. It's important to understand these differences when reading and writing documents.

KEY POINT

Using varied sentence structure holds a reader's interest.

Digital Data

Word processing software programs contain features in their readability indexes that detect the percentage of passive voice used in a document. Use these percentages as a guide for turning passive voice into active voice.

Revision Checklist 2

Language Use

- ○ Do the meanings of the words fit the content of the message?
- ○ Are there any dull or overused nouns, adjectives, or verbs that could be replaced with more colorful, specific words?
- ○ Are there any repeated words or expressions that could be deleted?
- ○ Should synonyms be used to make the message clearer and more forceful?
- ○ Are the sentence beginnings varied?
- ○ Are sentences written in the active voice whenever possible?

Exhibit 8.14
Revision Checklist 2
A revision checklist to be used in checking for language use. ***Thinking Critically.*** *How does overusing words hinder your communications with others?*

Most grammar-checkers highlight "potential" errors. You, as the writer, must decide if the highlighted text contains an actual error. You must also determine how to correct the error. You must ask yourself these questions: Is what I typed correct? Should I make a change? What is the correct change? Although grammar-checkers can be very helpful, they should not replace detailed revising and editing.

What Is Editing?

Editing is the process of checking a revised draft to make sure it meets the criteria of the six Cs of communication. That is, you make sure the document is clear, complete, concise, consistent, correct, and courteous. Editing not only helps improve the quality of your document but also helps improve your skill as a writer.

Developing editing skill is important for anyone involved with written communication. The purpose of editing is to make the document as effective as possible. Answer the questions posed in the Editing Checklist in **Exhibit 8.15** to improve your document.

Editing Checklist

Language Use

- ○ Is the message clear?
- ○ Is the message complete?
- ○ Is the wording concise?
- ○ Is the wording consistent?
- ○ Is the wording correct?
- ○ Is the message courteous?

Exhibit 8.15
Editing Checklist
Thinking Critically. *What else can you add to this editing checklist?*

The Six Cs of Editing

Editing a document to follow the six Cs of communication ensures that your message is straightforward and uses the you-attitude.

Is It Clear?

Business communications are written to get action—not to entertain or increase the vocabulary of the reader. Good business writers use simple words and proper English. They also make every effort to avoid clichés. Documents should be coherent; that is, they should flow appropriately. Using transitional words and phrases contributes to clarity.

Is It Complete?

A complete message includes all necessary information. Because the writer is so familiar with the message, omitted details are not always obvious to the writer. These missing details, however, may be obvious to the reader. Imagine receiving a brochure for a business seminar that gave only the hour, place, and topic of the seminar. The message would be incomplete without the date. Further communication would be needed to clarify the information.

Is It Concise?

Unnecessary words, phrases, clauses, sentences, and paragraphs are barriers to effective communication. Needless repetition of words decreases the effectiveness of your message because the reader must wade through a lot of words to get just a little information. To make your writing concise, include only necessary words and avoid repeating the same words several times in a message.

Is It Consistent?

Business messages should be consistent in fact, treatment, and sequence. A message is consistent in fact if it does not contradict itself, an established fact, or a source document.

Treating similar items the same way results in consistency in treatment. Follow these guidelines:

- When listing both men's and women's names, use courtesy titles for all or none of the names: *Mr. Lawrence, Ms. Ruiz, Mrs. Thomas.*
- Use a consistent style in writing numbers and amounts. For example, *$1,000* and *$10,000, 36 customers* and *67 customers.*
- Use the same formatting, such as indented paragraphs, throughout a document.
- Use special formatting techniques such as underlining and italics consistently for names of books and titles of articles.
- Use a consistent sequence (alphabetical, chronological, or numerical) to improve the flow of a message. For example, list names in alphabetical order to avoid conveying unintentional bias by listing one person's name before another's.

Note: Many companies use an established style guide. Be sure to refer to the preferred style guide used in your business.

Is It Correct?

Accuracy in content, typing, and mechanics (capitalization, grammar, spelling, punctuation, and so on) makes the message more effective. Proofread the document to eliminate these kinds of errors.

Is It Courteous?

Courtesy means that the document is pleasing to the eye, reader-centered, and positive. In addition to using the you-attitude and positive words, follow these suggestions for achieving courtesy:

- Select fonts that are easy to read. Cursive type fonts (*Cursive*) and solid-capital fonts (ALL CAPITALS) are more difficult to read than the more traditional fonts, such as Times or Times New Roman, in both upper and lowercase letters. Also, use a standard font size, such as 12 point. Very small point sizes are difficult to read.

- Create an eye-pleasing communication by using several short paragraphs instead of one long paragraph.

- Position your document attractively on the page, including enough white space (blank space) to make the page appear uncluttered.

- Use a table format or a bulleted or numbered list for appropriate information to add visual variety and to make reading easier.

What Is Proofreading?

KEY POINT

Ideally, proofreading should be a team effort by all those involved with the document preparation process.

Proofreading is the process of examining a document to find errors that should be corrected. Sometimes proofreading is a verification process, such as checking a letter typed from a handwritten rough draft. When you are proofreading your own work, however, you may not have a document to compare with the final draft. In either case, you should look carefully for errors in capitalization, content, format, grammar, word usage, number usage, punctuation, spelling, typing, and word division.

To be a good proofreader—to be able to identify errors—you must be familiar with all these types of errors. If you are unsure of a correct spelling, grammar points, and so on, rely on reference sources. You may, for example, see the word *reccomendation* and wonder if it is spelled correctly. After checking a dictionary, you change the word to *recommendation*.

The proofreading process should begin in the early stages of document preparation and continue throughout each stage, including the final copy. In other words, check the document for errors before typing from notes, a handwritten draft, or a typed draft. Today, with the use of electronic communication such as e-mail, some documents are not printed before transmission. However, for important documents, when errors could be extremely devastating, print a copy of the e-mail and proofread it before transmission.

Digital Data

Word processing software programs contain features that proofread for spelling and grammar errors auto-matically. Use this feature to eliminate errors in your document.

Responsibility for Quality

Business writers are responsible for the quality of their communications no matter who prepares the final document.

Office personnel often overlook the proofreading process because each person expects someone else to do it. The typist may think that the writer will proofread each communication. The writer may think that the typist will find and correct all errors before submitting the document for final approval or signature. Ideally, proofreading is a team effort. Both the typist and the writer should carefully proofread each document. The final responsibility, however, definitely rests with the writer.

Proofreading for Yourself and for Others

Proofreading is an essential step in the writing process, whether you are proofreading your own work or someone else's. As a student or as an office professional, you must get into the proofreading habit. Grades will suffer if errors are found in a research

Exhibit 8.16
On-Screen Proofreading
Proofreading on the computer offers the advantage of making corrections directly to the document. ***Thinking Critically.*** *What are some other advantages to proofreading on the computer?*

paper, and a potential salary increase or promotion may be lost if errors are found in a sales report you prepared. Habitual proofreading problems may even result in a loss of one's position.

In a business situation, you may be responsible for writing memos or reports. Consequently, you would need to proofread your own work. Often, a co-worker, realizing the importance of an error-free document, will ask you to check his or her work for errors. Occasionally, you might ask others to proofread your work, but you do not want to convey to them that you lack proofreading skills. If you type business letters, reports, or other correspondence, you must proofread as an important step in document preparation.

Proofreading your own writing is usually considered more difficult than proofreading the work of others, for two reasons. First, you, as the writer, may tend to be overconfident, believing that you corrected all errors. Second, you may be overly familiar with the document, which may cause you to "read" what you *intended* to type instead of reading what you *actually* typed.

Proofreading and Technology

Technology offers some assistance in proofreading for spelling and keyboarding errors. Most word processing programs have spell-checkers that will locate words not recognized by their built-in dictionaries. However, spell-checkers will not locate a missing word or a misused word if it is correctly spelled. For example, the errors in the following sentences would be undetected if you relied on a spell-checker alone:

- Incorrect: We submitted the completed *from bye* March 2.
- Incorrect: *Hour* company *if* the number *won* manufacturer of plastic containers in *their* country.
- Correct: *We* submitted the completed *form by* March 2.
- Correct: *Our* company *is* the number *one* manufacturer of plastic containers in *the* country.

Some spell-checkers will find repetition errors like this one:

- He gave me *the the* calendar.

Technology streamlines the process of making identical changes, called *global changes,* throughout a document. Suppose, for example, you mentioned the name *Steven Smathers* five times in a document. After typing, you learn that the correct spelling is *Stephen Smathers*. Using the global function, you would have to make the correction only once; the other four changes would be made automatically.

Proofreading has been made somewhat easier through the automatic correction features of word processing software. For example, the first sentence below was typed without the autocorrect feature. The second sentence was typed with the autocorrect feature.

> *Automatic correction feature off:*
> he boought theb ooks form sheila on thursday.

> *Automatic correction feature on:*
> He bought the books form Sheila on Thursday.

In the sentence *without* the automatic correction feature, note that the green wavy line indicates a possible grammar error and that the red wavy lines indicate either misspelled words or capitalization errors. The error of *form* for *from* was not detected.

In the sentence *with* the automatic correction feature turned on, note that the first word of the sentence was automatically capitalized, the word *bought* was correctly spelled, *the* and *book* were appropriately separated, and *Sheila* and *Thursday* were capitalized. The error of *form* for *from* was not detected.

Proofreading on the computer screen is similar in many ways to proofreading a printed page. However, you must adapt your eyes and mind to this different medium.

You should do your first proofreading on the screen, make the necessary changes and corrections, and then print a copy. You should also proofread the printed copy to make sure that your changes were entered correctly.

Even with all these automatic correction features, nothing yet replaces the human brain's ability to identify and correct errors.

Importance of Proofreading

Uncorrected errors create a bad impression. They also can cost your company money and cause other problems. Consider these two examples:

Suppose, in a handwritten draft, you quote a price of $32,453 for a new minivan. When the final copy is typed, the price is incorrectly listed as $23,453. If not detected, this simple transposition of numbers could cost your company $9,000. Correcting the error after the customer receives the incorrect quotation may cause ill will, the loss of a sale, and possibly legal action.

Suppose, on a travel itinerary, the airplane departure time is erroneously listed as 10:50 instead of the correct time of 10:05. This simple transposition could cause the recipient to miss the flight.

In both examples, efficient proofreading would result in the error being caught. For this reason, executives encourage the detection and correction of errors to prevent problems. Therefore, it is essential that you approach proofreading in a systematic way.

Steps in Proofreading

After using the electronic tools available to you, such as grammar-checkers and spell-checkers, use the Proofreading Checklist in **Exhibit 8.17** (page 327) both to proofread on-screen and later when you proofread printed documents. You need not use *all* these techniques for every document. Find the techniques that work best for you.

Proofreading Checklist

- ❍ Use a bright-colored pen to make changes easy to spot.
- ❍ Quickly scan for problems such as format errors. Are the date and other standard parts included in letters and memos? Do all headings in a report follow the same format?
- ❍ Check typeface styles and sizes. Is the same font style and size used for similar headings?
- ❍ Turn the document upside down to check for spacing and placement errors.
- ❍ Superimpose subsequent drafts over previous drafts and hold the drafts up to a light to detect possible errors.
- ❍ Read carefully for correct content, making sure that there are no factual errors and that no words, sentences, paragraphs, and other portions of text were omitted.
- ❍ Make sure that text that has been moved electronically does not appear in both the original position and the new location.
- ❍ Read for correct capitalization, grammar, word usage, number usage, punctuation, spelling, typing, and word division. Spell-check and grammar-check the entire document.
- ❍ Read the document backward to help detect spelling and punctuation errors by concentrating on each word separately.
- ❍ Give special attention to locations where errors frequently occur: (a) at the end and the top of a page, (b) in line endings and line beginnings, (c) in numerical and alphabetized lists, and (d) in cross-references.
- ❍ Check all numbers and technical terms for accuracy. Use a calculator to add columns of figures to verify that the total is correct.
- ❍ Ask a co-worker to proofread the document.
- ❍ Read the document aloud. Reading aloud increases concentration and thus helps you identify awkward sentences and omitted words.
- ❍ Use the print preview feature of your software to proofread your document.
- ❍ Temporarily enlarge the font to ensure that you are seeing everything clearly, including punctuation.

Exhibit 8.17
Proofreading Checklist
Thinking Critically.
What else can you add to this proofreading checklist?

Assessment   Section 8.6

Review of Key Terms

1. How does the audience of a document affect its *tone*? _____

_____

_____

_____

2. What are some advantages and disadvantages of using a *grammar-checker*? _____

_____

_____

Editing Practice

Proofreading Alert!   Proofread the following memo that was written quickly, using the proofreaders' marks on pages 317 and 318.

3. On Tuesday, January 30, Dr Sam Martinez will be at Phils Book Shop for a book signing from 10:30 A.M. to noon. His newest Book, *Healthy Eating for Busy Execturives,* will be availabel at a 20% discount while supplies last. _____

_____

_____

_____

Practical Application

Proofreading and Editing

4. Rewrite the following paragraph, making any necessary changes and corrections. Assume that Monday is July 1.

Nancy Seifken will assume the position of Director of Employee Activities on Monday, July 1. In this position, she will be in charge of and responsible for athletic teams, organizations, trips, and all other social events sponsored by our company. On Wednesday, July 3, she will attend a conference to learn about activities offered by other companies. She will have a meeting Tuesday, July 2, at 2:30 P.M., in the Recreation Hall, to get your suggestions for September and August activities.

_____

_____

_____

_____

_____

_____

5. Interview someone you know who writes daily. Consider interviewing a campus or local newspaper reporter or editor. Then, write a brief summary of how that person manages the writing process. What is the most difficult part of the process? The easiest? Share your findings with your team. _____

_____

_____

_____

_____

Discussion Point

Thinking Critically

6. Compare the role of revising with the role of editing. _____

_____

_____

_____

7. Why is it important to proofread documents throughout the entire writing process? _____

_____

Unit 4

Applying Communication Skills

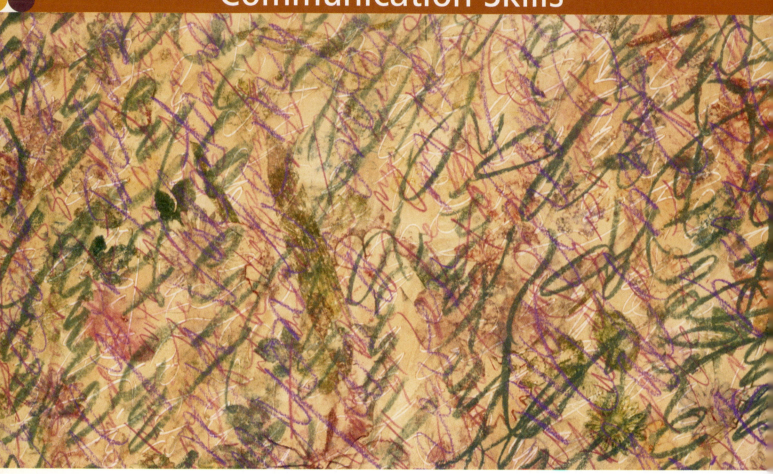

Unit Overview

In this unit, you will learn to apply communication skills to the workplace.

Chapter 9

Writing E-mail, Memos, and Letters

Chapter 10

Writing Specific Communications

Chapter 11

Preparing and Writing Reports

Stories From the Real World

Chris Ross had worked at Metropolis Medical Center for four years as a medical office assistant. In the *Medical Notes* weekly newsletter, the president of the medical center asked for volunteers to serve on a team to plan some special events and activities to recognize the medical center's 100 years of service to the community. Chris volunteered and was chosen as a member of the Centennial Celebration Team.

The team decided on several events and activities. One was to be a formal gala for approximately 500 people who were contributors to the Medical Center Foundation. The arrangements were made, the guest list was compiled, and the 500 formal invitations were printed and prepared for mailing.

Three weeks before the gala, the invitations were mailed. The next morning the phones did not stop ringing. The first caller said, "I received an invitation to the gala. When is it?" Other callers had the same question. It seems the invitations did not include a date for the gala.

The members of the team were certainly embarrassed. Chris said, "I thought the printer would check that information. I just signed the order form when it came; I assumed the invitation would be correct."

The team members decided to have the invitations reprinted and mailed again. The second invitation would have to be marked as a corrected or revised invitation so people wouldn't think it was a duplicate copy and discard the second one. Unfortunately, marking the second invitation "Corrected" or "Revised" would also draw attention to the error.

The cost of reprinting the invitations and the postage to mail them was an extra expense the team had not planned in their budget. The president of the medical center was not happy about the extra expense.

Thinking Critically

What strategies could Chris have used to ensure that the invitation was complete?

Who is responsible for catching proofreading errors?

Chapter 9

Writing E-mails, Memos, and Letters

Section 9.1
Planning Good News, Bad News, and Persuasive Messages

Section 9.2
Formatting Business Documents

Section 9.3
Writing E-mails and Memos

Section 9.4
Informing and Requesting

Section 9.5
Responding to Requests

Workplace Connection

E-mails and memos are primary methods of communication in the workplace. Most messages you write will be to inform, to make requests, and to respond to requests.

CHAPTER OBJECTIVES

When you have completed this chapter, you should be able to:

- Plan a good-news, bad-news, or persuasive message.
- Write and correctly format e-mails, memos, and letters.
- Write instructions, directions, and requests.
- Grant and reject requests while keeping recipient's goodwill.

Planning Good News, Bad News, and Persuasive Messages

Essential Principles

In business writing, careful planning and proper formatting are key to producing e-mails, memos, and letters that reflect positively on you and your company or organization.

Determine Your Reader's Reaction

The first step in planning a business message is to determine what your reader's reaction will be to your message. Recipients generally react in one of these four ways: pleased, neutral, displeased, or little or no interest. Depending on what you expect your reader's reaction will be, you will use one of three approaches for planning a message: direct, indirect, or persuasive.

Pleased or Neutral Reaction

If your reader will be pleased to get your message, or at least have a neutral reaction, you can get right to the point: the good news or the information. Use the **direct approach,** in which you state the main point of the message in the opening sentence. Follow the opening statement with supporting information. Close with an upbeat ending.

In a memo, you might close by stating what action to take or by requesting information. In a letter, you should close by reselling your service and/or product and building goodwill.

Displeased Reaction

When you expect the reader to be displeased, unwilling, or even hostile to your message, use the **indirect approach,** in which you begin the message with a buffer that presents background information.

Never start a message with bad news. This puts the reader in a negative frame of mind. Instead, sandwich the bad news in the middle of the message between neutral "buffers" and after an explanation for the bad news.

Little-or-No-Interest Reaction

If your recipient will have little interest in your message, you must sell the recipient on the message you are sending. This type of message calls for the **persuasive approach,** in which you begin by getting the reader's attention in the opening sentence. This "hook" is crucial in encouraging the reader to continue reading. Follow the hook by presenting benefits that generate the reader's interest. Then provide additional information that creates a desire on the reader's part for the plan, product, or service.

Exhibit 9.1

Message Approaches
Here are direct, indirect, and persuasive approaches to writing messages. ***Thinking Critically.*** *When is each approach most useful?*

Message Approaches		
Direct Approach	**Indirect Approach**	**Persuasive Approach**
Good news ⬇	Buffer ⬇	Attention getter ⬇
Supporting info ⬇	Reasons/explanations ⬇	Interest ⬇
Upbeat ending	Bad news ⬇	Desire ⬇
	Buffer	Action

Memory Hook

To remember the components of the persuasive approach for messages, think of the name "Aida."

A —attention

I —interest

D —desire

A —action

Close the message by asking for the desired action on the part of the reader. **Exhibit 9.1** illustrates all three approaches.

Improving the Message Content and Presentation

Once you determine your reader's reaction and the approach to use in organizing the message, plan to make a lasting impression on the reader. Two ways to make such an impression are to use the six Cs of communication and to use special formatting techniques.

Use the Six Cs of Communication

By using the six Cs of communication, you can write messages tailored to the reader's needs. Your writing should be:

- *Clear.* Use specific information, direct wording, and transitions. Replace specialized terms and jargon with words familiar to readers.
- *Complete.* Include all pertinent details so the reader has all the information needed to make a decision.
- *Concise.* Get to the point quickly without being abrupt, curt, or rude. Cut irrelevant words, sentences, or paragraphs. You will save your reader time and improve your letter or memo.
- *Consistent.* Use the same treatment for similar items, such as using courtesy titles and abbreviations of states. Also, use formatting techniques such as indenting, numbering, and single- or double-spacing consistently throughout a document.

- *Correct.* Verify that the information is accurate, and check the document for correct grammar, usage, spelling, and punctuation.
- *Courteous.* Write your message with the reader's viewpoint in mind.

Use Special Formatting and Mechanical Techniques

Formatting and mechanical techniques can simplify the overall organization of a memo or letter to encourage further reading. Some suggestions for using special formatting techniques follow.

1. Enumerate lists of important items.

   Please complete the following tasks before tomorrow morning:
   1. Make 20 copies of the inventory report and the sales report.
   2. Collate and staple the reports and put a copy in each manager's folder.
   3. Call the managers to remind them of the meeting.

2. Use bullets to emphasize several points when the sequence of the items is not important.

   Here are some topics we will discuss at next week's staff meeting:
   - Orientation program for new employees
   - Stock purchases by employees
   - Employee training programs
   - Education benefit program
   - Severance plan

3. Use **bold,** <u>underline</u>, *italics,* CAPITALS, or centering to emphasize important details.

   Tomorrow at 9:30 a.m. Bill Gates will be here to discuss
   EMERGING TECHNOLOGIES FOR MICROSOFT

<aside>
KEY POINT

Use a numbered list when the sequence of items is important, as is the case for steps in a set of instructions. Use a bulleted list when a series of items follows no particular sequence.
</aside>

4. Use columns with headings to make reading and understanding easier.

   Below are the inventory figures for March:

Number	Product	Cases
Y-3346	Wallpaper	1300
Z-4384	Cushions	2856
M-8729	Curtains	1438
L-4778	Comforters	1143

5. Use underlining or bold and side headings to show natural breaks in a message.

   Our new vacation policy rewards continued employment.

   Service—6 Months or Less

   Employees who have been with the company 6 months or less will receive a half-day of paid vacation for each month of full-time employment.

   Service—7 to 11 Months

   Employees who have been with the company 7 to 11 months will receive three-fourths of a day of paid vacation for each month of employment.

   Service—1 to 2 Years

   Employees who have been with the company 1 to 2 years will receive 14 days of paid vacation.

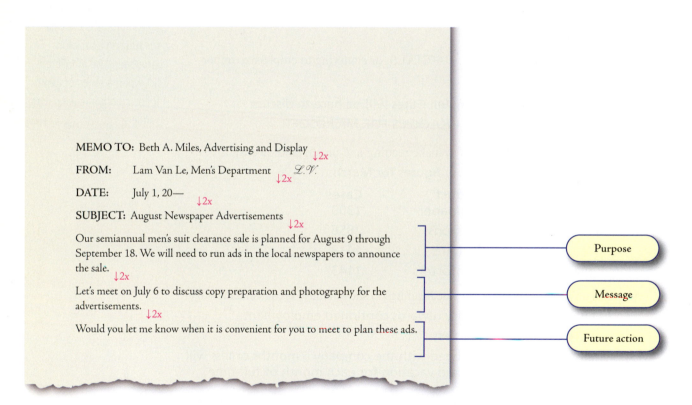

6. Use color coding to attract attention. For example, use yellow paper for all messages from the accounting department. Or use a colored highlighting pen to attract attention. The color used can have a special meaning. For example, blue could be used for general announcements (Our profits are up); red could signify needed information (All expense reports must be turned in by June 6).

Exercise caution in using these special techniques—overuse reduces their effectiveness.

Organization of the Memo

A memo tries to "sell" its reader a particular point of view. This is true whether the writer wishes to convince a superior of the need for new office equipment or to convince a subordinate employee of the need to maintain high work standards. A memo is more likely to achieve the writer's goal if it is brief and to the point without seeming abrupt or incomplete.

As shown in **Exhibit 9.2,** the organization of the body of a memo should be based on these three elements: (1) a statement of purpose, (2) a message, and (3) a statement of future action.

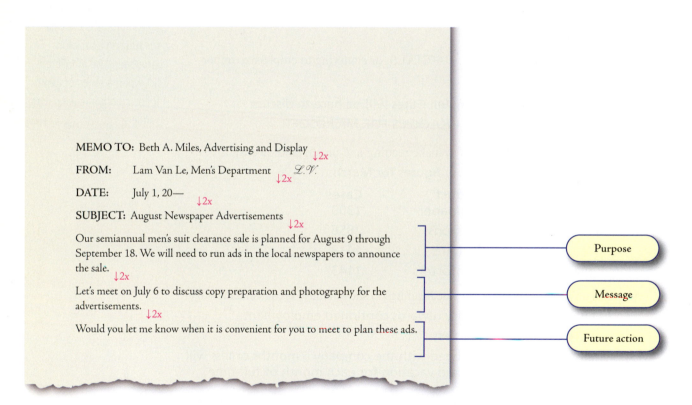

MEMO TO: Beth A. Miles, Advertising and Display ↓2x

FROM: Lam Van Le, Men's Department ↓2x *L.V.*

DATE: July 1, 20— ↓2x

SUBJECT: August Newspaper Advertisements ↓2x

Our semiannual men's suit clearance sale is planned for August 9 through September 18. We will need to run ads in the local newspapers to announce the sale. ↓2x — **Purpose**

Let's meet on July 6 to discuss copy preparation and photography for the advertisements. ↓2x — **Message**

Would you let me know when it is convenient for you to meet to plan these ads. — **Future action**

Exhibit 9.2
Organizational Elements
This memo is printed on plain paper using a standard memo format.
Thinking Critically. *What are the three organizational elements in the body of this memo?*

Misdirected

A confidential memo giving specifics about a new product was accidentally faxed to a competitor.

Statement of Purpose

The subject line tells the reader what the memo is about without stating the writer's reasons for writing. The writer usually can make the purpose clear by referring to an earlier memo or to a previous meeting or telephone conversation. Here are two examples of how a writer can state the purpose of a memo in the first paragraph:

- At the advertising meeting on October 15, you asked me to investigate and report on the comparative costs of print and broadcast advertisements in the Northeast. Here is a summary of my findings.

- Attached is the independent review of our admissions procedures from Dr. O'Choa. We will meet on May 2 from 9 to 11 a.m. in the Laura Lee Conference Room to discuss his recommendations:

Message

After making the statement of purpose, the writer should go directly to the main points of the message. The object is to help the reader grasp the main points as easily as possible, as in these two examples:

- We could admit patients more quickly and efficiently if we gave them a checklist to complete. The checklist would take the place of the long-answer forms now being used.

- A new form has been designed to simplify taking telephone orders. A copy of that form is attached.

Statement of Future Action

The body of the memo usually should end with a statement of action to be taken or with a request for further instructions, as illustrated in the following two examples:

- If you would like additional information on the benefits of this proposed checklist, call me at extension 6254. If you wish, I can investigate the amount of time such a checklist would save.

- Please notify me of your decision by February 16 so I can either put this procedure into effect or develop a new plan.

Special Techniques for Memo Effectiveness

Memos, like letters, can be effective or ineffective, depending on how they are written. Here are some suggestions for writing effective memos:

1. Cover only one main topic in a memo. When memos cover too many topics, a main thought may go unnoticed or may not receive the attention it deserves.

2. Consistently use a simple, familiar heading that includes the guide words *MEMO TO, FROM, DATE,* and *SUBJECT.* Using the words *MEMO TO* eliminates the need to type the word *MEMORANDUM* at the top of the page. People who receive messages from you regularly will know exactly where to look for specific information. Some companies use printed memo forms or a standardized template, which is provided with most software programs, for ease in composing memos. (Detailed information on memo types and parts appears in Section 9.2.)

3. Compose a brief but appropriate subject line. Subject lines should identify the topic, not give all the details. For example:
   - SUBJECT: Updated Personal Leave Policy
   - SUBJECT: Revised Salgada Contract

KEY POINT

The body of a memo should contain:

1. A statement of purpose
2. A message
3. A statement of future action

One Word

I like to read the company news letter online.

(*newsletter*)

Employability Skills

Solving Problems

Good problem-solving skills are valuable to employers. First you need to recognize a problem, create a plan of action, and implement your ideas. Learning to relay both good and bad news in a sensitive and professional manner helps alleviate additional problems.

4. Present the key idea in the first paragraph. The idea presented at the beginning will usually receive the most attention from the reader.

5. In most instances, use a personal, pleasant, and somewhat informal tone. You will know most of your receivers because they are members of your organization. Special situations such as writing to your superiors or reprimanding an employee, however, may require a more formal tone.

6. Strive to make memos clear, complete, concise, consistent, correct, and courteous.

Even though you will send most memos to people you know, you should not take shortcuts in your memos. Overusing shortcuts can decrease effectiveness.

Assessment   Section 9.1

Review of Key Terms

1. How is the *direct approach* in a memo different from the *indirect approach*? _____

2. Under what circumstances would a writer use the *persuasive approach*? What components are required for the persuasive approach? _____

Editing Practice

Using Language!   Revise the following underlined expressions to use clearer, more up-to-date wording.

3. <u>In regard to</u> your letter of the <u>17th of March</u> . . . _____

4. <u>At the present writing,</u> we still have not received . . . _____

5. <u>Please be advised that</u> your dividend will be $6,000, not $600. _____

6. <u>Due to the fact that</u> property sales are down this quarter . . . _____

Practical Application

Writing Memos

7. Using some of the special formatting techniques, write the body of a memo using the following information:

    Your supervisor, Rosa Hernandez, wrote you a memo on April 15. She asked that you give her a list of the sales by region for January, February, and March. The sales figures are, respectively, Region 1—$23,494, $22,577, $19,482; Region 2—$33,458, $32,722, $25,863; Region 3—$21,589, $21,887, $20,485. _____

    _____

    _____

    _____

    _____

    _____

    _____

8. Your team has been put in charge of arranging a continuing education class, and you need to know how many co-workers will attend. Write a memo to co-workers in which you provide all the necessary information about the class. _____

    _____

    _____

    _____

    _____

Discussion Point

Interpreting Information

9. What kinds of formatting techniques can improve the organization of a memo or letter? Why should writers be careful when using these techniques? _____

    _____

    _____

10. Name and describe the three elements of the body of a memo. _____

    _____

    _____

    _____

SECTION OBJECTIVES

When you have finished Section 9.2, you will be able to:

- Describe three types of printed memo forms and the circumstances in which each should be used.

- Identify both the standard parts and the optional parts of business letters.

- List the order in which letter parts appear.

WHY IT'S IMPORTANT

Selecting the appropriate type of memo for a particular purpose helps you communicate successfully with other members of your organization.

KEY TERMS

- guide words
- message memos
- routing slips
- style
- letterhead
- inside address
- salutation
- standard punctuation
- open punctuation
- reference initials
- copy notation
- block letter format
- modified-block format
- personal-business letter
- ream
- 20-pound paper
- watermark
- executive-sized stationery
- mailing notations

Formatting Business Documents

Memo Parts

Even though memos are internal documents, they are a vital link in achieving an organization's objectives. In addition, successful internal communication is important in achieving your career objectives. A memo has two parts: the heading and the body.

The Heading

The heading of a memo contains the guide words *MEMO TO*, *FROM*, *DATE*, and *SUBJECT*. Guide words may be typed in all-capital letters or with initial-capital letters. Never mix the all-capital letter format and the initial-capital format within the same memo. **Guide words** call attention to specific information.

The *MEMO TO* or *TO* Line

The *MEMO TO* or *TO* line contains the first and last name of the person or persons who are to receive the original copy of the memo. Courtesy titles are usually omitted on memos.

MEMO TO: Rodolpho Gonzalez
Stephanie Grimaldi
Carl Martin

The writer should include an addressee's job title in the following situations:

1. When the writer wishes to show respect:

   MEMO TO: Rodolpho Gonzalez, Chief Executive Officer

2. When the addressee has more than one job title, but the writer's message concerns the duties that pertain to only one of the titles.

   TO: Stephanie Grimaldi, Chair, Committee on Community Relations (Ms. Grimaldi is also the human resources director.)

3. When the addressee has the same name as another employee, or a very similar name, so that the writer must clarify which person should receive the memo.

   TO: Mike Boose, Assistant Chief Engineer (Another employee, also named Mike Boose, is the production manager.)

In large companies, it helps to include address information in the *MEMO TO* or *TO* line of an interoffice memo. For example:

- MEMO TO: Antonio Pappas, Room 3301, Benefits Office

- TO: Michelle Gold, Laboratory 3, Research Department

If the memo is being sent to more than a few people, type *See Distribution* or *Distribution Below* on the *TO* line and place the list of recipients at the end of the memo under the heading *Distribution*. Type *Distribution* on the third line below the reference initials, file notation, or enclosure notation, whichever appears last. Begin typing the list of names on the second line below *Distribution*.

Placing the distribution list at the end gives the memo a more balanced appearance and allows readers to focus on the message and not the list of recipients. List the names of recipients in alphabetical order; this is an objective way to determine the order of names. The memo in **Exhibit 9.3** shows a distribution list for individuals who are all branch managers.

TO: Branch Managers—Distribution Below ↓2x

FROM: Michael Ireland, General Manager ↓2x *m. l.*

DATE: August 18, 20— ↓2x

SUBJECT: Meeting for Branch Managers ↓2x

The Human Resource Department has announced improvements in the employee benefits plan. ↓2x

A meeting to explain our new benefits package will be held on Tuesday, August 28, at 9 a.m., in Conference Room A adjoining my office. ↓2x

Please read the enclosed booklet about the package before the meeting and let me know if you have any questions about it. ↓2x

dk emp-benf
Enclosure ↓3x

Distribution:

Carlos Alvarado
Joe Danford
Sally Dillon
Carroll Henderson
Tyler Jones
Paulette Meyers √
Harry Potter
Camille Weise

Exhibit 9.3
Distribution List
This memo is a template from a word processing program and shows how a distribution list is typed. ***Thinking Critically.*** *How are the names on the distribution list ordered?*

The FROM Line. The writer may include a job title, department affiliation, room number, and telephone extension in the *FROM* line.

- FROM: Edith L. Fitzpatrick, Researcher, Investment Department, Room 2403, Ext. 988

The DATE Line. Write the date in full rather than using abbreviations or all numerals.

- Business Style   December 19, 20—
- European Style   19 December 20—

The SUBJECT Line. The writer should state the subject of a memo clearly and briefly. To give a memo a more professional appearance, do not abbreviate the word *SUBJECT*. Only in exceptional cases should the subject require more than a single line. The following examples say all that is necessary; the rest should be left to the body of the memo.

- SUBJECT: Request for Additional Personnel
- SUBJECT: Submitting Time Sheets

The Body

A memo, unlike a business letter, includes no salutation. Instead, it begins with the first paragraph of the message. Leave one blank line, double-spaced, between the last line of the heading and the body of the memo. Single-space the body of the memo with a double-spaced blank line between paragraphs and use blocked paragraphs with no indenting. The block paragraph style is most often used because it is easy to type; paragraphs may be indented, but they usually are not. Many organizations determine these matters according to a style of their own; thus, new employees should find out whether there is a "house" style for memos.

Two lines below the body of the memo at the left margin, the typist should key his or her reference initials and any notations—for example, enclosure notations and copy notations—that may be needed. If the writer is the person who typed the memo, no reference initials are needed.

The trend today is to add the document name and location on the same line as or on the line below the reference initials. The notation may include the name of the document file or the location where the document is stored, such as:

- mls\winword\04\proposal
- Enclosure
- c: John W. Palmer

The Signature

The writer should sign each memo with a blue or black pen by writing his or her initials after the name on the *FROM* line. Typing or signing your full name at the end of a memo is unnecessary because the full name appears after the guide word *FROM*.

For information about other memo formats, consult a comprehensive reference manual.

Types of Memos

Memos may be printed on plain paper using a standard format (see **Exhibit 9.2**) or a template (see **Exhibit 9.3**) available with your word processing software. Memos may also be written on preprinted forms.

Using printed forms for specific purposes is a time-saver when one type of information is frequently communicated. Three examples of printed forms are the standard memo, the message memo, and the routing slip.

Standard Memos

Printed interoffice memo forms, which are usually 8½ by 11 inches, make it easy to both write and read memos. These printed forms often list the writer's name and telephone number. The writer simply writes in the appropriate information and forwards the memo.

The heading of a printed memo form usually contains (1) the name of the company, (2) the title *Interoffice Memorandum* or *Interoffice Memo,* and (3) the guide words *TO, FROM, DATE,* and *SUBJECT.* In some organizations, the preferred sequence is *DATE, TO, FROM,* and *SUBJECT.* In a large organization, the heading may also contain *Department, Location, Telephone Extension, Fax Number,* and *E-mail Address.*

Message Memos

Message memos are used to record phone messages and messages from visitors. These forms consist of lines for the caller's name and telephone number and for a brief message.

Routing Slips

Routing slips are used to channel messages to specific people. If a routing slip is not used often, the spaces following the guide words for names and office telephone numbers can be left blank. If a routing slip is used often, the names and office telephone numbers should be printed on the form.

Letter Parts and Formats

Think about the people you have seen within the past 24 hours. Were any two people dressed exactly alike? Did any two people say precisely the same thing?

Chances are, except for uniformed workers such as police officers, firefighters, and restaurant employees, no two people whom you have seen recently were dressed alike. The *appearance* of each person was different. Moreover, the *content* of the conversations you had with various people was probably different.

These two style factors—appearance and content—can also be used to describe a business letter. How does the letter *look,* and what does the letter *say?* The appearance and content of a business letter make up the **style** of a letter, just as a person's manner of dress and the content of his or her conversation contributes to that person's style.

The style of a business letter contributes as much to the success of that letter as a person's style contributes to his or her success. If your business letters are to achieve your goals, you must first learn how to control the appearance of a letter, which will be discussed in this section.

A writer conveys a professional appearance by using standard letter parts and arranging these parts according to accepted letter formats, thus, ensuring that the letter is arranged attractively on the page.

Business Letter Parts

Business letters often contain many parts. All the standard letter parts, plus some optional ones, are illustrated in **Exhibit 9.4.**

Letterhead. The word **letterhead** refers to either (1) the printed information at the top of business stationery or (2) the actual sheet of paper.

The printed information in a letterhead always includes the company's name, address, telephone number, and/or fax number. The company's slogan, a listing of its divisions, names of key personnel, and/or the company's logo may be included. Companies may also include their Web site and e-mail addresses. See the letter in **Exhibit 9.4** for sample letterhead. A company's letterhead may appear at the top, bottom, or along the side margin of business stationery.

> **KEY POINT**
>
> Letters that do not make a good first impression are not taken seriously by busy professionals.

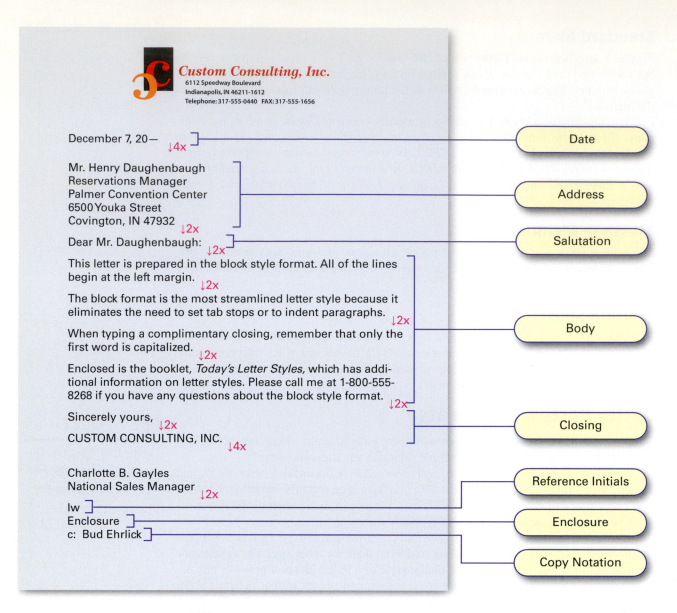

Custom Consulting, Inc.
6112 Speedway Boulevard
Indianapolis, IN 46211-1612
Telephone: 317-555-0440 FAX: 317-555-1656

December 7, 20— ↓4x **Date**

Mr. Henry Daughenbaugh
Reservations Manager
Palmer Convention Center
6500 Youka Street
Covington, IN 47932 ↓2x **Address**

Dear Mr. Daughenbaugh: ↓2x **Salutation**

This letter is prepared in the block style format. All of the lines begin at the left margin. ↓2x

The block format is the most streamlined letter style because it eliminates the need to set tab stops or to indent paragraphs. ↓2x

When typing a complimentary closing, remember that only the first word is capitalized. ↓2x **Body**

Enclosed is the booklet, *Today's Letter Styles,* which has additional information on letter styles. Please call me at 1-800-555-8268 if you have any questions about the block style format. ↓2x

Sincerely yours, ↓2x

CUSTOM CONSULTING, INC. ↓4x **Closing**

Charlotte B. Gayles
National Sales Manager ↓2x

lw **Reference Initials**
Enclosure **Enclosure**
c: Bud Ehrlick **Copy Notation**

Exhibit 9.4
Block Letter Format
The block format is very streamlined. This letter shows all the standard parts, as well as some optional ones. ***Thinking Critically.*** *Where should each part begin in a block format?*

When a letterhead is typed rather than printed, the information should be attractively arranged, starting 1 inch from the top of the page (on line 7). Word processing software simplifies typing a letterhead such as the following:

Electronic Designs Unlimited
575 Harborview Drive
Chelsea, MA 02150
800-555-0123

Date Line.   Most companies use a business-style date line with the month spelled in full, the day of the month written in numerals and followed by a comma, and all four digits of the year. The European or military style date line starts with the day of the month followed by the month, no comma, and all four digits of the year. Here are examples of each:

- Business style: July 10, 20—
- European style: 10 July 20—

Inside Address.   The inside address should match the name and address shown on the envelope. For example:

Ms. Camille R. Barry	Mr. Orris Patterson
Director	President
Habitat for Humanity	Patterson Consulting
85 East Perth Road	P.O. Box 1473
Conway, AR 72032	Golden, CO 80403-1473

The **inside address** includes the name of the addressee, the person's title, his or her company's name, street or post office box number, city, state, and ZIP Code. If the address has a post office box number, type it on the line immediately preceding the city, state, and ZIP Code. The U.S. Postal Service will deliver the mail to the location on the line preceding the city, state, and ZIP Code.

If you are sending a letter by a carrier other than the U.S. Postal Service, such as Federal Express or United Parcel Service, you must use a street address; these carriers cannot deliver to a post office box.

For an *international* address, type the name of the country in all-capital letters on a separate line at the end of the address. Do not abbreviate the name of the country.

Mr. Ferdinand Villa	Ms. Akiko Kagami
San Fernando, 2	The Togin Building
41004 Sevilla	4-1-20 Toranomon, Chuo-Ku
SPAIN	Tokyo 105
	JAPAN

Attention Line (Optional).   The attention line is an optional part of a letter. When used, it appears as the first or second line of the inside address or on the second line below the inside address. Type the attention line in all-capital letters or capital and lowercase letters. Use a colon after the word *Attention*.

- ATTENTION: TRAINING DIRECTOR
- Attention: Office Manager

Use an attention line when you want to stress that the letter is technically intended for the *company,* not the *person.* Also use an attention line when you do not know and cannot find out the name of the person to whom your letter should be directed. In this situation, the attention line should indicate the person's job title, such as *Sales Manager* or *Customer Service Representative.*

Salutation.   The **salutation,** or greeting, immediately precedes the body of the letter. Type the salutation on the second line below the inside address. Include a courtesy title, such as *Mr.* or *Ms.,* if it is known. If you do not know the courtesy title, use the recipient's first and last name, for example, *Dear Tracy Connor.* If you do not know the person's name, use the job title.

- Dear Ms. Metzen:
- Dear Marion Smith:
- Dear Mr. Tweedy:
- Dear Reservations Manager:

If the letter is intended to be less formal and more friendly, use just the addressee's first name.

- Dear Bob:
- Dear Annette:

A general salutation, such as *Ladies and Gentlemen,* is used to show that the company is being addressed. When you are writing to an individual whose name and gender you do not know, use a generic salutation, such as *Dear Customer, Dear Sales Manager,* and so forth.

Traditionally, the salutation ends with a colon; this is known as **standard punctuation** and is the style most often used by business writers. In **open punctuation,** no punctuation is used after the salutation and complimentary closing. Open punctuation is used by only a small percentage of business writers.

Subject Line (Optional).   Another optional part of a letter is the subject line, which is used to quickly identify the topic of the letter. Type the subject line in capital and lowercase letters below the salutation, leaving one blank line above and below. See the subject line in **Exhibit 9.5.**

Exhibit 9.5
Modified Block Letter Format
The modified-block format with indented paragraphs. ***Thinking Critically.*** *Where should the subject line be placed and should it be capital or lowercase letters?*

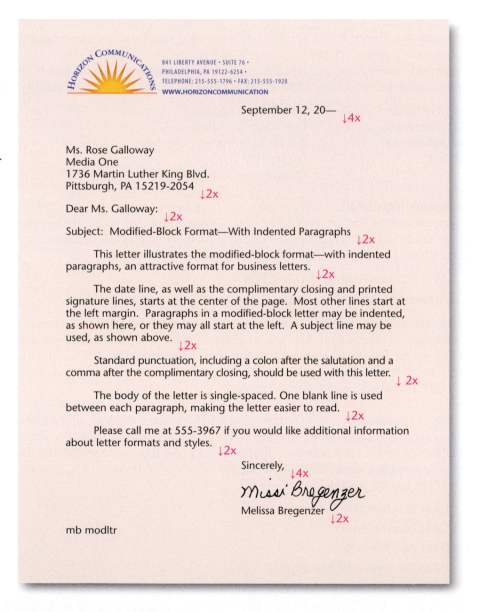

Chapter Nine   *Writing E-mails, Memos, and Letters*

Body. The body, or the main part of the letter, is typed single-spaced, with one double-spaced blank line between paragraphs. A good rule of thumb is to make the first and last paragraphs of the letter a maximum of four or five lines in length. Other paragraphs should be a maximum of eight lines in length, depending on the complexity of the message.

Complimentary Closing. The "good-bye" of the letter, or the complimentary closing, appears on the second line below the last line in the body of the letter. Some sample complimentary closings are:

- Cordially,
- Sincerely,
- Cordially yours,
- Sincerely yours,

Capitalize only the first word in a complimentary closing, and place a comma after the last word if you are using standard punctuation. If you are using open punctuation, do not use a comma.

Company Name (Optional). Some writers and companies use a company name; others do not. When used, the company name is typed in all-capital letters below the complimentary closing, with a blank line above and three blank lines below. See **Exhibit 9.4** for an example of a company name.

Writer's Identification. The writer's identification consists of the writer's typed name and job title. Key the writer's name on the fourth line below the complimentary closing or the company name, whichever is last. If the name and title are on the same line, separate them with a comma; if they are keyed on two separate lines, no comma is needed.

Reference Initials. **Reference initials** are the typist's initials—the initials of the person who keyed the letter. Key the reference initials in lowercase letters on the second line below the writer's identification. If the writer's initials are also used, they should appear preceding the typist's initials. If the writer is also the person who typed the letter, no reference initials are needed.

- JHK/prm
- RSZ/bar

Memory Hook

Remember the difference between standard and open punctuation:

Standard punctuation	Open punctuation
Colon after salutation	No punctuation after salutation
Comma after complimentary closing	No punctuation after complimentary closing

File Name Notation (Optional). A growing trend with business letters is to include the file name of a document that is created with word processing software, as in the following examples:

- proposal.131
- csmith.let
- cjibudget08

Type the file name notation on the same line as or on the line below the reference initials.

Enclosure Notation (Optional). When an item or items are sent with the letter, the word *Enclosure* or *Enclosures* is typed on the line below the reference initials or the file name notation, whichever is last.

Transmittal Notation (Optional). A transmittal notation is used to indicate that a letter and an enclosure or enclosures are to be sent by some means other than first-class mail. Type the transmittal notation on the line below the enclosure notation, reference initials, or file name notation, whichever is last. (See **Exhibit 9.6** on page 349 for a sample transmittal notation.)

- By Certified Mail
- By Federal Express
- By Fax

Copy Notation (Optional). When a copy of a letter is to be sent to a person or persons other than the addressee, the writer includes a **copy notation;** for example, *c: David Fischer,* on the line below the reference initials, the enclosure notation, or transmittal notation, whichever is last. The abbreviation *c:* or *c* means "copy to."

- c: Jerry Habanero
- c Melissa Temple

Postscript (Optional). The postscript is positioned at the *end* of a letter— deliberately or as an afterthought. Because it is part of the body of the letter, it is typed in the same way as the paragraphs in the body of the letter. Type the postscript on the second line below the last notation in the letter. Postscripts may be indicated by typing *PS:* or *PS.* before the message.

- PS: Be sure to bring a copy of your report with you.

Business Letter Formats

There are various acceptable formats for letters. Note that the sequence of the letter parts, including the optional parts, does not vary from one letter format to another. The differences in formats are primarily concerned with whether a particular part is aligned left, indented, or centered.

Block Format. In the **block letter format,** all letter parts begin at the left margin except tables and other setoff material. Because there are no indentions, the block style is easy to set up and, therefore, very popular. (See **Exhibit 9.4** for an example of a letter in block format.)

Modified-Block Format. Long popular, the **modified-block format** differs somewhat from the basic block style—namely, the date line, the complimentary closing, and the writer's identification, that is, name and job title, begin at the center of the page (see **Exhibit 9.5**).

Modified-Block Format—With Indented Paragraphs. One variation of the standard modified-block format involves indenting the first line of each paragraph a half inch rather than starting it at the left margin. (See **Exhibit 9.5** for an example.)

Other Letter Formats

In addition to the formats just discussed, you will find the personal-business and the social-business letter formats useful.

Personal-Business Letter Format. **Personal-business letters** generally are not typed on letterhead stationery; instead, plain paper is used. The writer's return address is typed directly beneath the writer's typed signature at the end of the letter. As shown in **Exhibit 9.6,** begin the writer's name and address on the fourth line below the complimentary closing.

Social-Business Letter Format. A special format, the social-business format (see Section 10.4), is sometimes preferred for letters written to business associates when the subject matter is more social than business.

Exhibit 9.6
Personal-Business Letter
Thinking Critically.
What format should a
personal business
letter use?

August 3, 20— ↓4x

DCS Electronics Company
Buena Vista Way
Suite 38
Orlando, FL 32800 ↓2x

Dear Sales Manager: ↓2x

On July 15 I purchased your new book, *Business Letter Formats for the Twenty-First Century.* I've enclosed a copy of your Invoice 254 for $21.99, which I paid in full. ↓2x

When I received the book this morning, I discovered that the cover was badly damaged and the corners bent. ↓2x

Please send me a new book to replace the damaged one.
If you would like me to return the damaged book, call me at
278-555-9748. ↓2x

Sincerely, ↓4x

Tyler Swider

Tyler Swider
378 Westwood Avenue
Dalton, MO 65246 ↓2x

Enclosure
By Certified Mail

Formatting Guidelines

Whichever letter style is used, the letter must be typed and formatted properly. The top, bottom, and side margins must be adequate, and the spacing between parts should adhere to certain standards.

Generally, 1-inch top and bottom margins and 1-inch side margins allow you to maximize the amount of copy on a page. Word processing software applications, such as Microsoft Word, have default margins that make formatting easier. For example, Microsoft Word has 1¼-inch default side margins and 1-inch default top and bottom margins.

The letters illustrated in Exhibits 9.4 to 9.6 have notations that show the number of lines of space generally left between letter parts. Use these notations to guide you in the vertical spacing of letter parts. Once you have used the proper spacing for all letter parts, use the center page command in word processing software to vertically center the letter on the page. An important point to remember is that the letter should look balanced on the page.

Stationery

The first impression of a letter will be determined by its physical appearance. The stationery used, the way the letter is folded, and the envelope used all influence that impression.

Paper

The paper used for letterhead contributes to the first impression of the letter. Paper is available in many different weights and finishes. For letterhead, 16-pound, 20-pound, or 24-pound paper is usually selected. The higher the number, the heavier the paper. The pound designations correspond to the weight of four reams of $8\frac{1}{2} \times 11$-inch paper. A **ream** is 500 sheets of paper. Therefore, if 2,000 sheets of paper weigh 20 pounds, the paper is called **20-pound paper.**

Paper quality is determined by the cotton fiber content, as well as by weight. Letterhead should have at least 25 percent cotton fiber content. The higher the percent of cotton fiber content, the better the quality of the paper. Any document that needs to last ten years or longer should be prepared on paper that is 100 percent cotton fiber content.

Better-quality paper also contains a **watermark,** which is the signature of the paper manufacturer. You can see the watermark by holding the stationery up to the light. If you can read the watermark from left to right, you are looking at the front side of the paper.

Color

Today, many colors of paper are used for letterhead. White is the most popular and is always correct. Studies have shown that colors send a message of their own. Most people react to certain colors in a predictable way.

Here are some examples of colors and what they suggest to people.

Colors	What they suggest to the reader
blue	sincere, harmonious
green	cool, restful
buff	dignified, conservative
gray	wise, confident
yellow	cheerful, vigorous
brown	strong, useful

Remember, people read more than the words in your message.

Size

In the United States, $8\frac{1}{2} \times 11$-inch paper is the standard size most commonly used for correspondence. Occasionally, a high-ranking employee will send a message of a personal nature—congratulations, thank-you, condolence—on **executive-sized stationery.** A sheet of executive stationery measures $7\frac{1}{4} \times 10\frac{1}{2}$ inches.

Correspondence in many foreign countries is often formatted on metric-sized paper. The most popular of these is called A4 paper, and it measures 210×297 millimeters— approximately $8\frac{1}{4} \times 11\frac{3}{4}$ inches.

Letterhead

Most organizations have a letterhead designed to create the image and impression they wish to convey. All letterheads should include the name of the company, the mailing address, telephone and fax numbers, and possibly Internet and e-mail addresses. Most letterheads also include a company logo.

The first page of a letter is prepared on letterhead. Continuation pages are prepared on plain paper of the same color, weight, and finish of the letterhead. The continuation page should have a heading that includes the following information: name of recipient, page number, and the same date that appears on the first page of the letter, as shown in the following examples:

- Ms. Molly Sullivan
  Page 2
  June 1, 20—

- Ms. Molly Sullivan   2   June 1, 20—

Envelopes

Envelopes should be the same color and quality as the letterhead stationery. The envelope should be large enough to hold the letter and enclosures without excessive folding.

In the United States, business envelopes come in a variety of sizes, but the two most common are the No. 10 envelope, which measures $9\frac{1}{2} \times 4\frac{1}{8}$ inches, and the No. 6¾ envelope, which measures $3\frac{5}{8} \times 6\frac{1}{2}$ inches. In foreign countries a business envelope for metric-sized paper is called DL, and it measures 110×220 millimeters—approximately $4\frac{1}{3} \times 8\frac{2}{3}$ inches. The metric envelope is not as deep as a No. 10 envelope, but it is slightly wider. An envelope has three printed or typed parts, as follows.

The Return Address

The return address goes in the upper-left corner of the envelope. Special instructions to be followed after the letter is delivered are indented three or four spaces from the left edge of the envelope and placed two to three lines below the return address.

Examples of special instructions are *Reply Requested* and *Personal and Confidential.*

Mailing Notations

Mailing notations are instructions for the post office, such as *Certified, Air Mail,* and *Registered.* They go on the upper-right side of the envelope, three lines below the stamp or postage meter insignia.

The Mailing Address

The mailing address should be typed on the envelope so there is a minimum of a ½-inch margin on the left and right and a minimum ⅝-inch margin on the bottom. These margins are needed by the U.S. Postal Service so that its scanning equipment will operate properly. See **Exhibit 9.7.**

To prepare standard business envelopes (No. 10 envelopes), follow these guidelines.

1. Begin typing the mailing address about 2¼ inches from the top of the envelope (on line 14), and about 4 inches from the left edge of the envelope.

2. Avoid italics and script fonts.

3. Use a block style, starting all lines of the mailing address at the same point.

4. Use single-spacing for the address.

5. Type the name and address in capital and lowercase letters or in all-capital letters with no punctuation. The U.S. Postal Service's optical character readers are programmed to read both styles of address. (See **Exhibit 9.7.**)

6. When using two-letter state abbreviations, capitalize both letters. Do not use a period after a two-letter state abbreviation.

7. Always include the ZIP Code, leaving one space between the state and the ZIP Code.

Exhibit 9.7

**Addressing Envelopes
Correctly**
The name and ad-
dress on an envelope
should match the
inside address of the
letter. The U.S. Postal
Service's (USPS's)
scanning equipment
can read addresses
keyed in either
all-capital letters with
no punctuation or
capital and lowercase
letters. *Thinking
Critically.* Why might
the scanners misread
punctuation?

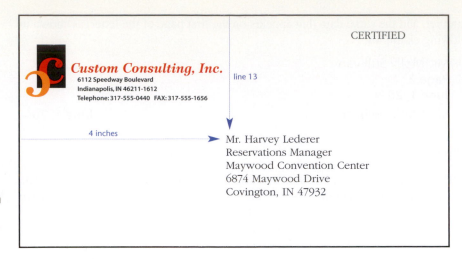

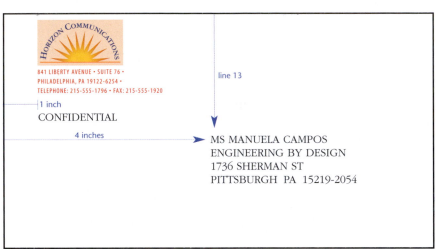

8. The last line of a U.S. address should contain the city, state, and ZIP Code. Do not type anything below the city, state, and ZIP Code. The area below the city, state, and ZIP Code is for a bar code that can be scanned by the post office. Many word processing programs can be set to automatically print the bar code below the address. For international addresses, type the name of the country in all-capital letters on the last line of the address. (See **Exhibit 9.7.**)

With today's global economy, international addresses require modifications to the address lines, including the addition of special codes, abbreviations, and capitalization. Here are four examples.

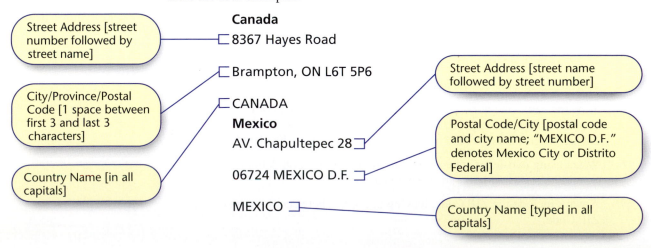

Germany
An der Hasenquelle 18 ——————————————————— Street Address [street name followed by street number]

55120 Mainz ——————————————————— Postal Code/City [Postal code and City name]

GERMANY ——————————————————— Country Name [typed in all capitals]

Japan
10-1, TORANOMON 2-CHOME ——————————— Division of the City

MINATO-KU TOKYO 105-8436 ——————————— Additional Division of the City, plus the City Name and Postal Code

JAPAN ——————————— Country Name [typed in all capitals]

If you need specific formatting instructions for envelopes, refer to a reference manual or business writing handbook.

Folding Letters for Envelopes

Letters should be folded so that the thickness of the paper is evenly distributed in the envelope. **Exhibit 9.8** shows the proper way to fold a business letter for No. 6¾ and No. 10 envelopes.

1. 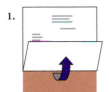 2. 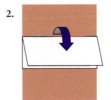 3.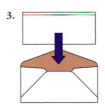

To fold a letter for a large envelope:
1. *Place the letter face up and fold up the bottom third.*
2. *Fold the top third down to 0.5 inch from the bottom edge.*
3. *Insert the last crease into the envelope first, with the flap facing up.*

1. 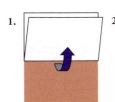 2. 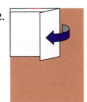 3. 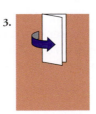 4.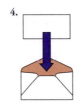

To fold a letter for a small envelope:
1. *Place the letter face up and fold up the bottom half to 0.5 inch from the top.*
2. *Fold the right third over to the left.*
3. *Fold the left third over to 0.5 inch from the right edge.*
4. *Insert the last crease into the envelope first, with the flap facing up.*

Exhibit 9.8
Sample Envelopes
How to fold and insert a letter into No. 6¾ and No. 10 envelopes.
Thinking Critically. *Why are there two methods of letter folding according to paper and envelope size?*

Employability Skills

Improving or Designing Systems

Many businesses that use charts and graphs in their reports follow a standard format. Depending on projects, visual formats can be improved or re-designed to communicate ideas better. Taking the initiative to improve them and present them is a valuable and an important skill.

Review of Key Terms

1. What is the purpose of *routing slips*? _____
   _____

2. What is the difference between the *block format* and the *modified-block format*? _____
   _____
   _____

Editing Practice

Call an Editor!   Rewrite the following paragraph, omitting the repeated words and adding missing words.

3. Aaron Singer of Caralia Draperies will be here tomorrow morning at
   10:30 a.m. to show us his line window treatments. His best-selling
   draperies are bow and ribbon swags and eyelet tiebacks. Our our competitors are doing quite with these two styles of, and we have lost business because do not carry these items. _____
   _____
   _____
   _____
   _____

Practical Application

Writing Letters and Envelopes

4. Type the following information on an envelope.

   The sender is Margaret English. She lives at 3568 Walnut Street in
   Rossville, Illinois, 60963. The recipient is Gary Blackmon, the president
   of Vintage Aircraft Owners on 396 Airline Boulevard in El Paso, Texas,
   79925. This letter will be sent registered mail. _____
   _____
   _____
   _____
   _____
   _____
   _____
   _____
   _____

5. Write a letter to your local Chamber of Commerce and request information about special events sponsored by the community. You
may want someone on your team to type the letter. Then,
identify the letter parts listed in **Exhibit 9.4** on page 344.

_____

_____

Discussion Point

Thinking Critically

6. Explain the function of each of the guide words in the heading of a
memo. _____

_____

_____

_____

_____

7. How does the appearance and content of a business letter affect the
reader? What are some of the standard parts used in a business letter
that improve its appearance? _____

_____

_____

_____

_____

When you have finished Section 9.3, you will be able to:

- Explain the differences among an e-mail, a memo, and a letter.
- List guidelines for writing professional e-mail messages.
- Name four advantages of using memos.
- List six purposes of memos and e-mails.
- Describe how to tailor the tone of a memo or e-mail to the recipient.

WHY IT'S IMPORTANT

E-mails and memos represent more than half of written communications in businesses today.

KEY TERMS

- electronic mail
- 24/7
- letters
- memos

Writing E-mails and Memos

Essential Principles

Electronic mail, more commonly referred to as e-mail, is written communication just like memos and letters. The primary difference is the method of transmitting the message. E-mail messages are sent instantly through the Internet via the modem in your computer and the modem in the recipient's computer. E-mail can be sent **24/7,** that is, "24 hours a day, 7 days a week," and, unlike a phone call or a fax, is received at the recipient's discretion.

Letters are printed on letterhead and sent to people outside your organization by mail or courier services. **Memos** are printed and sent to people within your organization through an interoffice mail delivery system. Memos may be sent within a department, among departments, and among company branches at different geographic locations. E-mail messages are sent to people both outside and inside your organization. E-mail can be stored on your computer, or a hard, or paper, copy can be printed for later reference. The hard copy automatically includes the date and time the message was sent.

E-mails, memos, and letters are essential to business communication because it is helpful to put important or complicated matters in writing.

E-mail

The use of e-mail today is so quick, easy, and inexpensive that its use is increasing at a phenomenal rate. Today's middle- and high-school students learn to use e-mail at school and through friends, so it will be second nature to them when they are employed.

Because e-mail messages are so easy to send, people tend to be careless about their spelling, grammar, and tone. Follow these guidelines to ensure that your e-mail messages will convey a professional image of you and your company.

Use the Correct Address

One typographical error in the address means your e-mail message will not be delivered. E-mail addresses have a username followed by the @ symbol and the host's domain name. For example, the e-mail addresses *yourname@eiu.edu* and *mcmillan@glencoe. com* follow this pattern. Always check the accuracy of an e-mail address.

Use a Greeting

When you meet someone or call someone on the phone, you greet that person with "Hi," "Hello," or something similar. Use a greeting to personalize the e-mail message. *Dear Sandy* usually is too formal for e-mail. Instead, just use the person's first name, *Sandy*, or *Hi Sandy*, as the greeting.

Use a Subject Line

E-mail messages with nothing in the subject line or something vague, such as "message" or "information," are read last, if at all. Subject lines should be concise phrases that clearly identify the content of the message. If your message is urgent, use the word *URGENT* in all caps as the first word in your subject line, followed by the topic. If your message is a request, use the word *REQUEST* in all caps as the first word in the subject line. If your message is an announcement or information that requires no response, use the abbreviation *FYI* (*for your information*) in all caps as the first word in the subject line.

- Subject: URGENT: Need Safety Mask
- Subject: REQUEST: Return First Aid Kit by Noon
- Subject: FYI: Free Ticket to Tonight's Hockey Game

Don't mark a message urgent unless it really is. You wouldn't call 911 if a colleague had a paper cut on his or her finger. Businesspeople today do not like to be tricked into reading an e-mail message.

Also, don't assume the recipient read your message just because you marked it *urgent*. The recipient may be away and unable to read e-mail for several hours or days. If you do not get a reply quickly to an urgent e-mail, follow up with a phone call.

Limit the Length, Topics, and Recipients

Limit your e-mail message to one topic, which makes writing a subject line much easier. E-mail messages are supposed to be brief and should be a maximum of about 25 lines of text. Use the default single-spacing with word wrap and keep the paragraphs short for easier reading. Leave a blank line between the paragraphs.

Send the e-mail only to those who need the information. Information overload and e-mail overload have a negative effect on productivity.

Watch the Tone of Your E-mail

When you talk with someone in person, you have additional means of communicating besides the words. The tone of your voice also conveys the intended meaning of the words. Your e-mail recipient may have trouble telling if you are joking or serious. Sarcasm is dangerous in any form of written communication because it is often misinterpreted.

Don't use all-capital letters in your e-mail because this format is hard to read, and is considered the same as shouting to your reader. Also, do not use all lowercase letters or very small type. This is interpreted as speaking so softly that people have trouble hearing you. The rules for proper language and capitalization rules apply to e-mail as well as other forms of communication.

Emoticons, or smileys, are a way of visually expressing your emotions in e-mail. Some common examples are:

:-)   to send a smile

:-(to send a frown

;-)   a wink and a smile

Remember that not all e-mail software, especially in other countries, can display special characters, so your recipient may not see the emoticon as you sent it. What you see on your screen may be different from what your recipient sees on his or her screen.

Digital Data

Convenience of E-mail

E-mail can be a convenient way of sending memos to groups of people without making separate copies for each recipient. The recipient can print a hard copy of the e-mail for reference or keep it in her or his message inbox.

KEY POINT

Some people use emoticons—a group of characters arranged to look like a face—to personalize e-mail messages.

:-(	I'm sad.
:-D	I'm happy.
:-+	I'm tired.
:-O	I'm surprised.

Use a Closing

Type your name at the end of your message. Some e-mail addresses do not use the name of the sender, so the signature may be the only clue to who the sender is. A complimentary closing is not necessary—just your first, or first and last, name. Many e-mail programs have an auto signature feature which can include your name, e-mail address, phone number, and mailing address in case the recipient needs to get in touch with you some way other than e-mail.

Check Spelling and Grammar

Always read and proofread your e-mail before you send it. If your message contains errors, people may assume you are uneducated. Some e-mail programs will automatically check your spelling or grammar before sending the e-mail. This feature does *not* take the place of proofreading. Automatic spelling and grammar checks will not detect a variety of errors, including allowing you to use a word in the wrong context. Misspelled words are a turnoff and do not convey a professional image of you or your company.

Do Not Send Confidential Information

E-mail is not private or confidential. A good rule to follow is: Do not send anything by e-mail that you wouldn't be willing to have published in the *USA Today* newspaper. Think of your e-mail as a postcard. Many people have the opportunity to read a postcard after it is sent and before it gets into the hands of the recipient. Remember, e-mail can also easily be forwarded to others.

Know Your Company Policy

Find out what your company's policy on e-mail is and follow it. If you violate the policy, you could be terminated. Some companies are very strict about not allowing employees to use the Internet or e-mail for personal use—either during or after working hours. Your company owns the e-mail system, and courts have subpoenaed e-mail messages as evidence. Even though you deleted the e-mail, it is probably still on the server's backup system and can be retrieved.

Whose Instructions

They're instructions were so general that I couldn't complete the request.

(*Their,* the pronoun, is correct, not the contraction *they're.*)

Spamming

Spamming is sending unsolicited e-mail, particularly advertisements, to others. It is the electronic version of junk mail. Spammers get your e-mail address the same way companies get your mailing address for junk mail—they buy lists. Send unsolicited e-mail only when you believe the recipient will want to receive it.

Reply to E-mails

Check your e-mail at least twice a day. Respond to urgent e-mails as soon as you read them, and respond to nonurgent e-mails that require an answer by the end of the day. It is common courtesy to respond to, and unprofessional to ignore, an e-mail that asks for a response.

When you reply to an e-mail, key your answer on top of the original message. This saves the recipient from having to scroll through the original message to see your reply. You may wish to delete parts of the original message and leave only the question(s) you are answering. If you choose to compose a new message for your reply, be sure to include enough information that your recipient will know which e-mail message you are answering and what you are talking about.

- AVOID: "I sure am."
- INSTEAD: "I am planning to attend the seminar this Friday in the Copper Penny Room."

Attachments

A document prepared in a word processing, spreadsheet, or graphics software program can be attached to an e-mail so it can be saved and printed by the recipient in its original form. Because of the increase in computer viruses, it is best to let your recipient know in your e-mail message that you are attaching a file to an e-mail and what the attachment is. It is also common courtesy to ask permission before sending a large attachment.

Viruses

A *virus* is a self-replicating code planted illegally in a computer program for the purpose of damaging or shutting down a system or network. Unfortunately, it is through attachments to e-mail that many computer viruses are spread to other computers. If you do not know the sender or you are not expecting an attachment, be cautious opening it.

Memos

Memos and e-mails are similar. They both include the same heading information of *TO, FROM, DATE,* and *SUBJECT.* Memos are perceived as more formal than e-mails, however. Confidential information should be sent as a memo rather than an e-mail because privacy cannot be ensured with an e-mail.

Advantages of Memos

Memos fill the needs for both effective internal communication and written documentation of messages. Organizations are often large and diversified, with branches or divisions of a company located in different states or even countries. Memos are a logical way to coordinate the efforts of many people within an organization—especially those who do not have access to e-mail.

Memos Are Quick. Using technology can reduce the time needed to write and send memos. Many software programs include memo templates that make it easy to compose a memo. By using e-mail and fax machines, a writer can quickly transmit memos to recipients.

Memos Are Inexpensive. Compared with telephone calls and meetings, memos are a cost-effective way to transmit messages within an organization because all recipients receive the same information. Using plain paper instead of letterhead or preprinted memo forms also reduces the cost of memos.

Memos Are Convenient. Memos offer access to people who are not seen on a regular basis. Memos also minimize interruptions for the receiver. In addition, reading a memo requires less time than a phone call or a personal visit.

Memos Are a Written Record. Memos serve as a written record for both the reader and the writer. Memos can, for example, clarify instructions or information given orally. In many situations, a well-written memo can help prevent misunderstandings.

Purposes of E-mails and Memos

Memos and e-mails are used for a variety of purposes. The main purposes are *to request, to inform, to report, to remind, to transmit,* and *to promote goodwill.*

To Request

Use memos or e-mails to ask for information, action, or reactions. Messages written for this purpose take the direct approach, as in the following examples from three different e-mails:

- We need revised sales figures from you before the cost estimates for the Bryant project can be completed.
- Please make arrangements for a one-day seminar for all trainees.
- Please review this proposal and give me your opinion of it.

To Inform

Use memos or e-mails to communicate procedures, company policies, and instructions. If the message contains good news, use the direct approach; if the message contains bad news, use the indirect approach. Here are three examples:

- Our safety procedures require a 15-minute break for every 4 hours of work.
- Company policy permits escorted visitors 16 years old and older to tour our plant.
- Use your key card to enter the Third Avenue gate.

To Report

Use memos or e-mails to convey organized data such as schedules, sales figures, and names of clients or patients, as in these two examples:

- Below is our schedule for the completion of Lincoln Hall.
- Here is a list of the donors who will attend the fundraiser.

To Remind

Use memos or e-mails as reminders about deadlines, important meetings, and so on. Such reminders should be brief and should use the direct approach. Here are two examples:

- Please send me your travel itinerary by May 6.
- Our appointment with the Southern Telcom representatives should be on your calendar for Monday, April 3, at 2 p.m. in the main conference room.

To Transmit

Use memos or e-mails to tell readers about an accompanying message. The message could describe, explain, or simply identify the attachment or enclosure. The direct approach works best for such memos. Here are two examples:

- Attached are the time sheets to be distributed to all hourly employees.
- Enclosed is a printout listing the names and home addresses of all regional managers.

To Promote Goodwill

Use memos or e-mails to establish, improve, and maintain goodwill. These messages can congratulate, welcome, or convey appreciation, such as in these examples:

- Congratulations on your promotion!
- Welcome to Howard Industries.
- Renee, your advertising designs got us the Wright Corporation account. Thanks for a great job!

Tone of the Memo and E-mail

The tone of a memo or e-mail depends largely on the position of, and the writer's relation to, the recipient. In general, use a more formal tone when addressing top management than when writing to a peer or a subordinate, unless you know that the addressee prefers an informal tone.

If you are not certain which tone to use in a memo or e-mail, choose a balanced one—neither too formal nor too casual. Avoid using contractions like *you'll* and *here's,* but do not use stilted language either. Stick to business. Note the balanced tone in the following example:

- Attached (or enclosed) is the report on last month's video camera sales with the changes you requested yesterday. The figures on Model A26 are now broken down to show the number of these video cameras sold in each sales region. In addition, the appropriate tables now have an added line showing Model A26 sales by region for the same period last year.

Subject matter also determines the choice of tone for a memo or e-mail. A message announcing the schedule of the company's bowling team would obviously have a lighter tone than a message justifying costs that ran over budget. The more serious the topic, the more serious the tone should be. Here are some words that convey a positive tone.

able	great	outstanding
absolutely	guarantee	particular
advantage	happy	patronage
appreciation	helpful	perfect
approval	honest	permanent
assist	important	pleasure
assure	initiative	productive
bargain	invaluable	progress
benefit	kind	promise
complimentary	lasting	recommended
comprehensive	long-lasting	revolutionary
congratulations	major	reward
delighted	markedly	satisfactory
determine	marvelous	save
easy	modern	security
effective	monumental	superior
efficient	motivation	terrific
enhanced	multifaceted	thank you
enriched	necessary	timely
expanded	notable	total
favorable	offer	unique
free	often	unlimited
genuine	opportunity	valued
grateful	original	wonderful

Review of Key Terms

1. What advantages does *e-mail* have over a *letter*? _____

_____

_____

2. What are the six purposes of *memos* and *e-mails* discussed in this section? _____

_____

Editing Practice

Mail Call!   Correct the following excerpt from a business letter.

3. September 12 20—
Kimberly Johnston
2443 Southpark Dr
Tampa, Flo.
33678

Dear Ms Johnston
    Last week I received a shipment of 60 wine glasses from your company. To my dismay, half of the glasses were broken. I have returned the damaged goods. Please send me 30 more wine glasses and credit my account for the return postage. _____

_____

_____

Practical Application

Writing Memos and E-mail

4. Write an interoffice memo notifying staff that new insurance coverage will take effect at the beginning of next month. Representatives from Prudential, the new company, will be in Conference Room A to provide information and to answer any questions regarding the new policy. Remember to include the time and date. _____

_____

_____

5. You are the manager of your department. You have just hired a summer intern. As a team, write an e-mail to your staff introducing the intern. Create any necessary background that you think your staff would find helpful. _____

_____

_____

_____

Discussion Point

Evaluating Concepts

6. Describe three specific situations in which you would use e-mail on the job. Is it appropriate to use e-mail for personal use on the job? Why or why not? _____

   _____

   _____

   _____

7. When writing a business e-mail to someone you have never met, explain what adjustments you must make in style and tone. _____

   _____

   _____

   _____

SECTION OBJECTIVES

When you have finished Section 9.4, you will be able to:

- Identify several types of informative messages.

- Apply the completeness test to all informative messages.

- Write request letters that are complete, precise, reasonable, and courteous.

WHY IT'S IMPORTANT

As a business communicator, you will be called upon to write messages to give information to others. Informative messages include giving instructions; giving directions; and making announcements about events, people, meetings, procedures, and so on.

KEY TERMS

- informative messages
- procedures book

Specify Addressee

Sending a fax addressed "To Whom It May Concern" will certainly reduce the likelihood of a positive response—or of any response.

Informing and Requesting

Essential Principles

Some of the most routine business tasks involve making requests; for example, asking for appointments, reserving conference rooms, obtaining price lists and catalogs, asking for copies of reports and studies, seeking technical information about goods and services, and asking favors.

Giving Instructions

As a business writer, you will have opportunities to provide written instructions, or **informative messages,** on how to complete a task or how to carry out a procedure. Follow these guidelines when writing step-by-step instructions:

1. Number the steps to make them easy to follow, and use phrases rather than complete sentences.

2. Include only necessary information. Avoid giving all the "what-ifs" so your instructions won't seem too complex.

3. List the steps in the order they are to be completed.

4. Write the instructions with the user in mind—define unfamiliar terms and explain complicated items.

5. Avoid unnecessary cross-references to information in another document. Instead, provide all the necessary information in the set of instructions.

6. Use white space, headings, and indentions to make the instructions visually clear. Start each new instruction on a separate line.

7. Test your instructions by having someone read them to see if they are clear and complete. The best test is to have someone who does not know the procedure try your instructions.

Giving Directions

As you give directions for getting from one location to another—whether to a different location in the building or to a different state—remember that some people learn visually and others learn verbally. Keep the following guidelines in mind as you prepare your directions.

- For visual learners, draw a map from the point of departure to the point of destination or, if possible, photocopy a map and use a light-colored highlighter to mark the route.

- For verbal learners, write the directions so that each part of the directions appears on a separate line.
- Differentiate between stop signs and stoplights, indicate turns as right or left, and give specific compass directions as in "Drive north for 2 miles" or indicate landmarks.

Writing Requests

Although written requests are common, you should not treat them routinely. Moreover, extraordinary requests require extraordinary planning and writing skills. Whether you are asking for a company catalog or asking a busy executive to speak at your conference, your requests should be:

- Complete
- Precise
- Reasonable
- Courteous

Be Complete

When writing a request, ask yourself, "What can I provide the reader to make sure that he or she has *all* the information needed to grant the request?" Also, "Would any more information be helpful?" Consider the following two situations:

- You are requesting information from Gateway, Inc., about CD-RW systems for a report that you are preparing. Tell the reader at Gateway, Inc., the purpose of your request. He or she might have additional materials to share with you or might grant the request solely to get publicity for his or her organization.

- You send a letter to a company asking them to send you the office supplies that you discussed yesterday during your telephone conversation. You are assuming the reader will remember facts from your conversation. Don't assume! Repeat the model or type, the catalog number, the price, the preferred shipping method, and any other facts that will help your reader.

Put yourself in the reader's place so that you can better understand how the reader might feel and what information he or she might need to know. Note how the requests in **Exhibit 9.9** and **Exhibit 9.10** successfully answer the questions Who? What? Where? When? Why? and How? or How much?

In your effort to be complete, however, do not give the reader an excessively detailed description or needless information. For example, decide whether it will help the reader to know that you are planning to write a detailed report about the subject. If it will help, include this fact in your request; if this information is not relevant to the reader, omit it. Likewise, decide whether you must include the model or type, the catalog number, and so on. If all this information is already included in the enclosed purchase order, then there may be no need to repeat it in the letter.

Be Precise

To ensure that your written requests are precise, you should present material in a format that makes it easy to comprehend. Using a table is a precise way to present facts and figures. Proofreading carefully is another way to make your written requests

Exhibit 9.9
Memo with a Request
Thinking Critically.
Whether a request is
routine or compli-
cated, what are the
four things the mes-
sage should aim to
achieve?

Employability Skills

Reasoning

Reasoning skills are necessary and important in business. When dealing with different types of business correspondence, the ability to use the appropriate forms of communication can make a difference in the outcome.

MEMO TO:	Maria Espinosa, Office Manager
FROM:	Jamie Martin, Copy Center Supervisor *J. M.*
DATE:	December 9, 20—
SUBJECT:	Request for Another Photocopy Machine

The use of our large photocopy machines in the Copy Center has more than doubled in the past year. The number of copies per day has risen from 12,000 on June 7 to about 26,000 in December. As a result, the length of our turnaround time to duplicate materials has increased from one day to three days. To meet this increase in demand, I propose purchasing a small photocopy machine to use for simple, quick jobs.

This new photocopier would be used for jobs that take less than ten minutes to complete, thus freeing the Copy Center to handle larger duplication efforts. The new photocopy machine would handle duplexing, collating, and stapling—the most used features. Jobs requiring special features such as special-size paper, enlargement, reduction, and color can be submitted to Copy Center personnel for copying.

Attached is a comparison of price quotes from two vendors for comparable photocopy machines. I would appreciate your feedback on this request by December 14 so that we can take advantage of the vendors' discount offer that is in effect until December 15.

st
Attachment

precise, and it also helps you eliminate errors that may be embarrassing, costly, and time consuming. See the example that follows:

Swider Computer Connections
2357 Vermilion Street
Cumberland, MD 21502
Attention: Order Department

Please send by Federal Express the following computer supplies to us. I have enclosed our company check for $369.40.

Item (Catalog No.)	Quantity (Units)	Unit Price	Total Price
Mouse Pad (42063)	6	$5.00	$ 30.00
Wrist Pad (42068)	6	$11.90	$ 71.40
Copy Stand (42035)	6	$8.50	$ 51.00
Computer Lamp (42092)	6	$39.50	$237.00
TOTAL			$369.40

We would appreciate receiving the entire order by May 15.

SHESKEY INSURANCE AGENCY
617 Crossroad Square Suite 21 Duluth, MN 55346
Telephone: 218-555-9692 FAX: 218-555-9760
www.sheskeyinsurance

September 23, 20—

Ms. Jerry Gasche
Training Director
MetLife Financial Services
38 Alexandria Drive
Painesville, OH 44077

Dear Ms. Gasche:

One of your insurance representatives, Ivan Chansuvan, told me that MetLife has produced a research report about the frequency and types of claims filed by policyholders. I would like to obtain this report.

Our company is interested in receiving information for claims relating to both homes and automobiles. We would like to incorporate this information into update sessions for our agents and to disseminate it to agents we may hire in the future.

Ivan did not know the answers to these questions:
• Is the report free, or would there be a charge?
• What would the charge be?
• Would I need to buy multiple copies, or could I duplicate portions for our employees?

We want to make applicable portions of the research report immediately available to our personnel. Please give me a call at 501-555-6245 so I can clarify the order, costs, and duplication issues. We are certainly willing to pay duplication costs and costs for mailing the materials by Federal Express two-day delivery service.

Sincerely yours,

Lance Sheskey

Lance Sheskey
President

tr

Respond with Respect

Responding to a request: "You are the only person who found our shampoo product unsatisfactory."

(Use pleasant-sounding language when responding to requests.)

Be Reasonable

Everyone makes unreasonable requests when they are faced with job pressures or do not understand how difficult, time consuming, or complicated the request is.

Consider your request *from the reader's perspective.* Are you requesting too much of someone's time? Are you asking for a character reference from someone who hardly knows you? Can you reasonably expect this person to spend much effort on your request? Consider these factors before making a request.

Be Courteous

Courtesy is a must in business communications. Whether you are requesting something that is legally or morally owed to you, something that you have paid or will pay for, something that is yours and should be returned, or something that the reader should be delighted to send to you—you should always be courteous in writing your request. Just as you deserve common courtesy, you must show common courtesy.

Although few people intentionally write discourteous requests, people *do* sometimes write impolite requests. Read this request for a free videotape describing vacation time-shares.

> Send me the free videotape about vacation time-shares at Morning Glory Resorts. I saw it in your ad in Leisure Days.

KEY POINT

Show courtesy in making requests of others.

The company *did* advertise free videotapes, obviously in the hope of selling vacation time-shares. Does this mean, however, that the recipient of the request letter does not deserve common courtesy? Of course not! The writer should have shown more thoughtfulness and more respect for the reader by writing the request along these lines:

> Please send me the free videotape advertised in *Leisure Days* magazine that describes vacation time-shares at Morning Glory Resorts. My husband and I enjoy golf and tennis, and your resort sounds like an ideal place to spend our two-week summer vacation each year.
>
> We are also interested in buying a two-week time-share at a ski resort during the month of January. We would appreciate receiving information about time-shares at winter resorts.
>
> Please mail the video and the other information to us at the address in the letterhead. We look forward to hearing from you.

The writer might have reaped additional benefits from this revised, more courteous request. The recipient will gladly send not only the free videotape advertised in the magazine but also any information about vacation time-shares at winter resorts since the writer took the time to state specific needs and did so *courteously*.

KEY POINT

Test every announcement for completeness by asking:

1. Who?
2. What?
3. Where?
4. When?
5. Why?
6. How or how much?

Making Announcements

A great deal of information is communicated through various forms of announcements. Announcements can be made through news releases, flyers, and formal cards, as well as by e-mails, memos, and letters. Every announcement should be tested against the completeness test. Does the announcement include answers to the questions Who? What? Where? When? Why? and How? or How much? Anticipate the questions your receiver may have, and answer them in the announcement.

Events

Events such as open houses, anniversary celebrations, special programs, commemorative events, holiday celebrations, ribbon-cutting ceremonies for new buildings or additions to existing buildings, and so on are frequently communicated through announcements.

People

Occasions for announcements about people include when a new employee is hired, when someone is promoted, when a person retires, when someone is elected or appointed to a position, when a person receives an award or another recognition, and so on. An announcement about someone's accomplishments is an excellent way to recognize the person and to let others know about the person's achievements.

Meetings

When meetings are needed, a meeting notice is the most efficient way to get the information to everyone, whether it is sent as a memo, an e-mail, or a flyer. When meetings are scheduled weeks in advance, a reminder notice close to the date of the actual meeting will ensure better attendance.

Going Global

Making a Meeting Significant

In some countries, such as Nigeria, business conducted by phone or mail is considered trivial. For a business transaction to be considered important or significant, personal meetings are required. Personal meetings help develop understanding and respect in relationships.

Procedures

Many organizations have a **procedures book,** a written, step-by-step guide that contains copies of all the procedures they follow. It is important to date each procedure, especially when a new procedure is implemented or an existing procedure is revised, so employees can easily identify the most recent version. These procedures may also be posted on an organization's Web site for easy access by users who have been given passwords.

Other Occasions

Other examples of occasions for informing others include announcing new office hours, a new toll-free telephone number, a new delivery service, a new product, a new address, the opening of a branch office, and so on.

Assessment   Section 9.4

Review of Key Terms

1. What types of *informative messages* do business writers make?

   _____

   _____

2. What are some examples of when you would need to use a *procedures book*? _____

   _____

   _____

Editing Practice

Using Language!   Rewrite these excerpts from letters, replacing any dated expressions.

3. The information on your application has been duly noted. _____

   _____

4. We wish to extend our thanks to you for taking the time to complete the questionnaire. _____

5. I have before me your letter of October 10. _____

   _____

6. In the event you will be unable to meet the deadline, please advise.

   _____

Practical Application

Writing Letters

7. Write a letter to Alvarez Office Furniture, 1199 Memorial Boulevard, Des Plaines, Illinois 46043, to order a desk. Before writing the letter, answer each of the questions below.

   - *Whom* should the desk be shipped to?
   - *What* kind of desk are you ordering?

- *Where* do you want the desk to be shipped?
- *When* do you want the desk?
- *Why* are you writing?
- *How* do you want to pay for and receive the desk?

_____

_____

_____

8. Write a news release that announces a new company. Your team will decide the name of the company and the nature of its business. Remember to answer the questions Who? What? Where? When? Why? How? or How much? You may want to preview news releases in *The Wall Street Journal* or similar news reports. _____

_____

_____

_____

Discussion Point

Analyzing Information

9. Discuss ways in which a writer can present clear written instructions or directions. _____

_____

_____

10. Why is it essential that business requests be precise, reasonable, and courteous? _____

_____

Responding to Requests

Essential Principles

Writing and answering requests are common business tasks. In this section you will learn how to effectively answer requests and how to use techniques for both granting and denying requests.

Answering Requests

Common courtesy dictates that a prompt reply be sent to request letters. Also, the writer should try to *help* the reader as much as possible, even if the request must be refused.

Writing a response—whether the reply is positive or negative—presents an opportunity to promote goodwill and to make a sale. Thus, the response should be *sales-minded*. In addition, the response, like the request, should be *specific* and *complete*.

Be Prompt

Many companies have policies requiring their employees to respond to letters within 48 hours—some, within 24 hours. Why? These companies realize that being prompt in replying is simply good business.

Even when an inquiry cannot be answered in detail, common business courtesy demands that a reply—at a minimum, an acknowledgment of the request—be sent *promptly*.

> Dear Mr. Miller:
>
> Your recent request for a price quotation for two cases of glossy photo paper (HP C6039A) is being handled by Michelle Cornell. Our supplier, Shick Office Supplies, now has this paper on back order. Ms. Cornell is checking with Shick Office Supplies to determine how soon this paper will be available and what the price change, if any, will be.
>
> Ms. Cornell expects to have this information for you by May 4. In any case, she will write to you before then to give you an update on your request.
>
> Sincerely,

This prompt response (1) acknowledges the request, (2) tells the potential customer who is taking care of the request, and (3) tells when the customer can expect an answer. The writer in this situation would send a copy to Michelle Cornell and place another copy in a **tickler file**—"a reminder file"—for May 4.

Dear Subscriber:

MANY THANKS . . .

for renewing your subscription to *U.S. News and World Report.* Your check for $23—half our usual subscription price—indicates that this publication meets your high standards and expectations because you chose to invest your money in this product.

We believe *U.S. News and World Report* presents a variety of issues and perspectives in a different way from any other media. Our magazine attempts to bring the facts to you with many points of view and in an objective, rational way. Our short, easily readable stories allow you to have current information.

By renewing *U.S. News and World Report,* you have indicated that we are doing our job in providing the information you need about national and international politics. However, we know it is always possible to improve a product. Therefore, please take a few moments to jot us a note and tell us how we can improve any aspect of your magazine. Simply return your comments in the enclosed, postage-paid envelope.

Sincerely,

Exhibit 9.11
Printed Form Letter
Thinking Critically. *What does this printed form letter aim to achieve?*

Because promptness is both a courtesy and a sign of good business, your reader will be impressed by your quick response. Note how one writer capitalized on a quick response:

> When I received your request by fax this morning, I checked immediately to make sure that we could make 58,000 tassels for the programs for the presidential inauguration you requested by January 10. I am pleased to tell you that we can make and deliver the tassels by. . . .

Another way for writers to achieve promptness when faced with a large volume of responses is to use a **preprinted reply card.** The card may have blanks that the writer can quickly fill in, or it may simply give a printed message with no blanks. Despite their lack of personalization, preprinted responses allow a company to respond to hundreds or thousands of requests *promptly.* See **Exhibit 9.11.**

Be Helpful

A customer, or a potential customer, who asks for information expects to receive assistance, whether he or she is asking in person, on the telephone, or in writing.

When responding to a request, try to understand *why* the person is asking for help, and remember why your company wants you to help. Remember, too, that you are the expert. Whether or not you can grant the request, consider if there is something additional you can do to help the person. Do you know of a store where the person can find the product he or she needs? Do you know of a company that makes the product he or she is looking for? Do you know of a book that covers the very topic the person wants to research? Do you know of a service organization that can assist the person?

Note how the writer of the following letter did more than fill the request—the writer anticipated Mrs. Golseth's interest in a closely related product. Good sales expertise? Good business? Both!

Dear Mrs. Golseth:

It's good to know that you are considering the ImageMaker, our telephone facsimile transmitting system. One of our most popular items, the ImageMaker, will enable you to send any graphic design 24 × 24 inches or smaller to any office in the world equipped with an ImageMaker and a telephone. The ImageMaker should be particularly valuable to you and your architects in other cities. Now you won't have to wait days to react to one another's latest sketches.

A wonderful complement to ImageMaker is our reducing, high-resolution photocopier, the ImageReducer. With no discernible loss in precision, the ImageReducer will reduce graphic designs as large as 48 × 48 inches to 24 × 24 inches—small enough to be transmitted by the ImageMaker. The combination of the ImageMaker and ImageReducer will save not only the transit time of regular mail or of shipping by an express mail service but also the cost.

We very much appreciate your interest in our products and would be happy to demonstrate them for you soon.

Sincerely,

Although it is rather easy to be helpful when you are granting a request, you can also be helpful many times when you cannot grant the request, as the writer of the following letter proves.

Dear Mr. Meechem:

Thank you for your recent order for the 15-millimeter, f/2.8 Canon underwater lens. Although we generally carry this superb lens, we are currently out of stock, and Canon will not be shipping more until September or October.

Because you mentioned that you wanted the lens for your upcoming scuba-diving trip, I called another supplier to find this lens. Good news: The Shutter Shop, a photography specialty store, has the lens that you want. You may call the Shutter Shop toll-free at 800-555-6763.

Good luck! And please be sure to try us again next time.

Sincerely,

This letter writer has certainly won a friend for his or her company—just by being helpful.

Be Sales-Minded

Whenever you respond to a request letter, you should look for possible ways to make a sale. After all, whether you work in the sales department or not, your company depends on sales to make a profit and to pay your salary.

The hard-sell approach is rarely effective; you will not make much progress by bluntly saying "Buy this product!" Yet you can help sell your company's products or services by responding promptly to requests and by being helpful. Both responses will make your readers appreciate the quality customer service that your company provides and will convince them to deal with your firm.

In addition to these indirect sales techniques, there are several direct ways to help sell your company's goods and services when you are responding to requests. For example, if you are sending a potential customer a catalog, include *both* an order blank *and* an addressed envelope to make it easy for the customer to place an order. If a customer complains about having had to wait a long time to receive a previous order, take a few minutes to write an apology and an explanation. Better yet, tell the customer to write directly to you next time so that you can personally track the order. Such extras are selling techniques.

Can you uncover the indirect selling methods the writer of this letter used?

Dear Mr. Neumann:

Thank you for asking about the service contract for Gorden's Model-X camcorder. We are pleased to share some information with you.

The enclosed booklet includes a list of all the specific items that are covered by our service contract. In fact, Mr. Neumann, it also lists, in equally large print, the few items that are not covered in the contract, so that there will be no surprises if something should happen to the product; you will know exactly what is covered. By doing so, we avoid the unfortunate experience that you described in your letter.

Because service is such an important factor in your buying decision, I recommend that you ask your local Gorden dealers how they rate the service of two or three of the brand names that they sell. (A list of dealers in your area is enclosed.) Further, I invite you to visit Peter Cleary of Cleary & Sons in Woodmere, which I believe is near you. Mr. Cleary has operated an authorized Gorden service center for more than 20 years. Not only will visiting Peter be informative, it will also give you a chance to meet the person who would service any Gorden product that you own.

Please review the enclosed booklet; then let me know of any way that we can help. You may call me toll-free at 800-555-9250 whenever you have any questions for us. We would be delighted to be of service.

Sincerely,

Throughout the letter the writer stresses what is most important to the reader—*service*.

Be Specific

The need to be *specific* is a general rule; it applies to any letter or memo, whether the message is a request, a response to someone's request, or any other type of communication.

When acknowledging receipt of money, cite the exact amount, form of payment, and purpose of the payment:

Thank you for your Check 3689 for $1,250 in payment of Invoice 17290.

When discussing dates, times, airline flight numbers, or other specific statistics, cite them clearly.

I am delighted to accept your invitation to discuss my career in graphic design with your students. It has been a long time since I visited the Art and Design Institute, and I look forward to our discussion on April 28 at 3 p.m. As you suggested, I will bring samples of my newest designs to share with your students.

My Northwest Airlines flight 741 arrives at John Wayne International Airport at 2:30 p.m. on Monday, July 8. . . .

When you receive something of value, acknowledge its receipt, including any specific information that is appropriate. Remember that your letter will become part of the sender's files—proof that you received the important mailing.

> Your portfolio of industrial photographs arrived this morning. When Kim Luttrell, our art director, returns from vacation next week, she will call you to discuss the prints she has selected for the April issue of *Modern Manufacturing.*

When acknowledging receipt of an order, include the date of the order and the purchase order number. Although the reader already knows this information, it is repeated because the letter will be filed for future reference. In addition, mention how the materials will be shipped, when the reader can expect to receive the merchandise, and so on.

> We are delighted that you are taking advantage of our annual stock-reduction sale. Your order No. 3598, dated July 14, will be shipped by UPS this afternoon. As you requested, the merchandise will be delivered to your Warrington Avenue store.

Be Complete

Although many writers try to be complete, important information is often omitted due to carelessness.

One way to make sure that your responses are complete is to *underline the specific points* in the request letter. Another way is to *note in the margin* each answer to a specific point in the request letter. The underlined points or marginal notes serve as an outline in writing the reply. For example, when Judy Anderson received the letter of inquiry illustrated in **Exhibit 9.12** she made marginal notes to make sure that her response, illustrated in **Exhibit 9.13,** would be *complete.*

One technique that fosters completeness is listing, either with numbers or bullets, major points in your response. The great advantage of bullets is that readers can see that important points are coming long before they get to them. Use bullets only when the order of the items is not important. Use numbers when priority or sequence matters. Note how the writer of the follow-up letter in **Exhibit 9.13** lists the major points the customer mentioned in his letter, as illustrated in **Exhibit 9.12.** In the follow-up letter, the writer enumerates each point and discusses them in the same order as in the customer's letter.

Be Positive

The need to be positive is especially important when handling **problem requests.** Saying no to people who have applied for credit, who do not qualify for discounts, whose warranties have expired, who have asked for confidential information, who have requested contributions that must be turned down—these situations require tact and diplomacy from the writer. *Never* start your message with bad news; use the indirect approach. *Remember:* Whatever the cause of the problem, the writer's goal is to retain the reader's goodwill.

To begin, consider the contrast between the statements listed below. Note how the positive statements say "no" without greatly hurting the reader's ego.

Negative	Positive
• Your product does not meet our specifications.	• Our engineers believe that the brand we selected is closest to our specifications.
• You do not meet our standards for this particular job.	• Although your qualifications are excellent, we feel that we must continue to search for someone who meets all the unique qualifications for this job.

KEY POINT

To give a complete response to a request, outline the specific points mentioned by the person making the request.

Singular Mistake

Your order will be not guaranted to arrive on time for the holiday.

(*Guaranteed* is the correct word, not *guaranted.*)

Exhibit 9.12
Annotated Request
Letter
Thinking Critically.
How do the annota-
tions help the reader
respond to the letter?

October 27, 20—

Judy Anderson
Sales Manager
Majestic Fireplaces
4929 Lincoln Avenue
Galveston, TX 77513

Dear Judy Anderson:

I am interested in installing a gas log in my fireplace. I have studied your brochure but have some additional questions before deciding whether to invest in this product.

1. How would the unit be mounted in the fireplace? *Middle of fireplace on floor*
2. What special electrical hookup would be required? *None*
3. How much installation time would be required by your technicians? *2 hours*
4. How would a gas log affect my gas consumption? *Minimally*
5. What would be the total cost of the unit, including installation? *$259*
6. What type of warranty exists for this product? *full 10-year*

I am thinking about having the gas log installed before December 25. Please answer these questions in time for me to make my decision.

Very truly yours,

Daniel Lutje

Daniel Lutje
245 South Hill Street
Houston, TX 77034

Employability Skills

Reading

When responding to requests that were submitted in writing, it's important to read carefully, interpret information correctly, and respond accordingly. Reading and writing skills are essential employability skills.

- In view of your poor payment record, we are unable to grant you credit.

- We must say no.

- Your prices are too high.

- We shall be glad to evaluate your credit record after you have settled some of your obligations.

- Unfortunately, we cannot say yes at this time.

- While your quality is indeed top-notch, we cannot afford to make a purchase at this time.

Note how the negative comments stress *you,* while the positive comments stress *we.* Always avoid saying "Because of your mistake" or "You failed to." Placing blame on the reader will accomplish nothing. Remember, preserving goodwill toward your company should be your goal in all business writing.

Exhibit 9.13
Response to a Request
Thinking Critically.
How should the
writer answer the
reader's questions to
reply effectively?

Majestic Fireplaces

4929 LINCOLN AVENUE
GALVESTON, TX 77513
TELEPHONE: 409-555-6218
FAX: 409-555-6359   WWW.MAJESTICFIREPLACES.COM

November 1, 20—

Daniel Lutje
245 South Hill Street
Houston, TX 77034

Dear Mr. Lutje:

Thank you for inquiring about our fireplace gas logs. I'll be glad to answer the questions you asked in your October 27 letter.

1. The gas log would be mounted in the middle of the fireplace on the floor.
2. The catalytic igniter does not require electricity so no special electrical hookup would be required.
3. Assuming no complicating factors, our technicians can install the gas log in about two hours.
4. Your gas log has three settings of flame; the lowest setting would use as much gas as a gas stove burner.
5. The total cost of the gas log and the installation would be $259.
6. Our gas log units carry a full, 10-year warranty.

Enclosed is a brochure that describes the gas log in which you are interested. I am sure you will find that this unit is an outstanding product for the money.

Please call me at 1-800-555-4793 if you have further questions and to set up an installation date.

Sincerely,

Judy Anderson

Ms. Judy Anderson
Sales Manager

lam
Enclosure

**Embarrassing and
Inappropriate**

Darla was attending the
funeral of a business colleague, and she forgot to
turn off her beeper. She
was embarrassed when
the beeper went off
during the service.

Although it is important to phrase comments positively and to avoid placing blame, you should not make false statements in refusing a request. If possible, share with the reader some of the genuine reasons *why* the request is being rejected.

- As much as we would like to help you with your research project, gathering the information you requested is beyond our present resources. As you can imagine, Ms. Granger, we simply cannot take that much time away from our usual duties.

- Perhaps the most positive aspect of such refusals is to offer the possibility of future cooperation.

- Perhaps next year we will be able to . . .

When you consider your reply from your reader's perspective, remember to put yourself in your reader's place.

Review of Key Terms

1. What is a *tickler file* and why should it be used? _____

   _____

2. What are the advantages and disadvantages of using a *preprinted reply card?* _____

   _____

   _____

Editing Practice

Public Relations Alert!   Rewrite each of the following sentences so that it promotes goodwill.

3. You must be too lazy to open your mail because we have already written to you about this matter. _____

   _____

4. Your April 3 letter fails to explain satisfactorily your delay in paying.

   _____

5. We will repair the microwave that you claim was damaged in transit.

   _____

6. You made a mistake of $27 on our March 15 invoice. _____

   _____

Practical Application

Writing Letters

7. You work at Allword Publishing Inc. Stefan Crowell at 23 Saltway Drive, Saltway, Florida 33596, requested a copy of your new magazine, *Video Visions.* Demand has exceeded expectations, and the first issue has sold out. Write an appropriate letter in response to Mr. Crowell's October 1 letter. _____

   _____

   _____

8. You are the manager of Los Comales, a Mexican restaurant located at 655 Lamar Street, Austin, Texas 78654. You received a new, heavy-duty commercial food processor, but your chef shows you that it does not slice food as advertised. As a team, write the manufacturer, Whirling Wonder Kitchen Co., One Bluegrass Way, Lexington, Kentucky 40506, requesting replacement of the food processor. _____

Discussion Point

Thinking Critically

9. If you have just received a request letter, what steps would you take to answer the request? _____
_____
_____
_____

10. How does the company, the claimant, the transaction, and the law determine the outcome of a claim? Provide current examples. _____
_____
_____
_____
_____
_____

Chapter 10

Writing Specific Communications

Section 10.1
Persuasive Communications

Section 10.2
Writing Claim and Adjustment Messages

Section 10.3
Public Relations Letters

Section 10.4
Social-Business Communications

Section 10.5
Form Paragraphs, Form Letters, and Templates

Workplace Connection

It's important to be able to write effective letters to sell your products, ideas, and services and to persuade your reader to pay for these items. When you purchase a product that is defective, you need to be able to write a claim letter to get an adjustment. Writing public relations and goodwill messages improves your working relations with others.

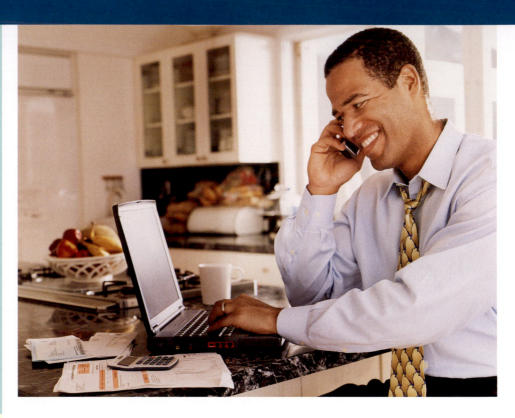

CHAPTER OBJECTIVES

When you have completed this chapter, you should be able to:

- Explain the objectives of sales letters.
- Write claim letters and adjustment letters.
- Identify special public relations writing opportunities.
- Use the social-business format when writing goodwill letters.
- Describe the advantages and disadvantages of using form letters.

Persuasive Communications

Writing Sales Letters

Businesses spend millions of dollars on sales letters every year because letters have two major advantages over radio and television advertisements. First, letters give recipients something they can touch and see or read more than once. Second, letters sent to a carefully selected audience can be more direct and personal than commercials, which are produced for a mass audience.

Targeting Audiences

Think about the sales letters you receive. They range from magazines to insurance offers to invitations to join a CD or DVD club. Do you think that everyone on your street or in your town gets the same sales letters that you do? You might be surprised to learn that marketing specialists make a living by choosing very select target audiences for different products and services. A **target audience** is a group of potential customers chosen on the basis of certain characteristics, such as age, geographic location, income, or lifestyle.

If the new product is exercise equipment, for example, the target audience will be fitness trainers or athletes who might be able to use such equipment. If the product is a new line of children's clothing, the target audience will be families with young children. Of course, finding the target audience is not always as easy as in the two preceding examples. Companies that want to sell a new digital camera or color laser printer to prospective business customers may have to do extensive research to determine the best target audience.

When the target audience for a product is the general public, the challenge facing writers of sales letters is to determine which of the following buying motives are most likely to appeal to the readers.

Understanding Buying Motives

Identifying buyers' needs and wants, and then satisfying those needs and wants, is the key to understanding buying motives.

Identifying Needs and Wants. In general, people buy products and services to satisfy specific needs and wants. **People's needs** are vital, of course, but relatively few: food, shelter, clothing, and perhaps transportation. **People's wants,** by contrast, are endless. People want not just any food, but delicious food; not just any shelter, but a comfortable apartment or house; not just any clothes, but the latest fashions. As you learned in Chapter 1, most people also want security, status, the approval of others, health, personal attractiveness, conveniences—microwave ovens, remote controls, home security systems, for example—and various forms of recreation and entertainment.

While people are usually aware of their wants in a general way, they may not know how a new product or service would fulfill any of those wants. The job of a sales letter writer, therefore, is to convince people that a specific product or service will satisfy one or more of their wants.

Satisfying Needs and Wants.   To make readers interested in a product or service, a sales letter writer must show how purchasing the item will provide the reader with prestige, good health, fun, beauty, savings, romance, freedom from drudgery, and so on. For example, the following list indicates the kinds of personal wants and needs that can be satisfied by the products and services shown.

Product or Service	Want or Need
Pillow-top mattress	Comfort
Ready-to-serve salad in a bag	Convenience
Toothpaste	Health and attractiveness
Home swimming pool	Recreation, status, or prestige
Outdoor lighting	Security
Charitable contribution	Self-esteem

Objectives of Sales Letters

After identifying the target audience's motives for buying a particular product or service, the writer proceeds to write the sales letter. Keep in mind, however, that there is no standard formula for all sales letters. They can vary in length, organization, and content. Nevertheless, an effective sales letter generally accomplishes the following five objectives:

1. Attract the reader's attention.

2. Establish a close relationship with the reader.

3. Appeal to one or more specific buying motives.

4. Persuade the reader to act.

5. Provide the reader with an opportunity to act.

KEY POINT

The goal of a sales letter is to persuade the reader to buy a specific product or service.

Attracting Attention

A sales letter must immediately attract favorable attention. The appearance of a sales letter often determines whether the letter is read or tossed into the wastebasket. Because appearance starts with the envelope, sales letters often come in envelopes that promise big prizes, valuable certificates, and great savings inside. Creative advertisement writers take advantage of computers to add personalized attention-getting questions to envelopes.

• Would you like your next vacation to be FREE, Mrs. Anderson?

Many readers would react by opening the envelope to see what they will have to do to get a free vacation.

Once a reader opens the envelope, other factors come into play. For example, heavy-stock stationery and an engraved letterhead give an appearance of importance, or the facsimile of a telegram gives the appearance of urgency. An enclosed free sample is another good way to get a reader's attention.

Establishing Familiarity

To keep the sales prospect reading, the writer needs to establish a **familiar tone** with the reader. One way to achieve this goal is to refer to the reader as *you* as often as possible. Another good device for establishing a mood of familiarity is to start the letter with a question that will result in a *yes* answer. If you combine these two techniques, you might develop an opening sentence such as the following:

- Isn't it time you took a really good photograph?
- Would you like to lose 5 pounds this week?

You can also establish a familiar tone with the reader in the first paragraph by (1) using imperative sentences; (2) using informal punctuation such as dashes, exclamation points, underscores, ellipses, and parentheses; (3) using contractions; (4) using short, informal sentences; (5) repeating the reader's name once or twice in the letter; and (6) complimenting the reader. The sentences that follow are additional opening lines that illustrate these techniques.

Opening	Product or Service
• Protect your family with Intruder Alert.	Security system
• Do it now! Don't wait a minute longer. Health—happiness—fitness: they're all yours at Exercise World!	Fitness club
• Mr. and Mrs. Shemesh, don't you want your child to get better-than-average grades?	Encyclopedias
• You can't let this opportunity pass—lowest prices of the year. Come test drive a car of your choice today!	Automobile

Appealing to Buying Motives

The writer uses market research and other knowledge about the target audience of the sales letter to make a connection between the features of the product or service and the presumed buying motives of the reader. The goal is to induce the reader to buy. "Incentives to buy" are called **sales appeals,** and they are the main act of the sales letter. Keep in mind, therefore, that the envelope, the stationery, and the opening line only set the stage. Notice how the following excerpts use sales appeals to stimulate the reader's buying motives.

Sales Appeal	Buying Motive
• Your family will ask for more each time you serve Barilla Pasta.	Family approval
• You can get twice the work done in half the time if your employees use Dell computers.	Convenience and economy
• You can relive all your happy moments time and time again if you record them with a Sony camcorder.	Enjoyment; nostalgia
• Don't drive just any car. Drive a car that people will notice. Drive an elegant Mercedes!	Personal status

The sales appeal brings the reader to the point of wanting to buy a product. The writer must then nudge the reader just a little further by persuading that person to act on his or her desire to buy.

---

oops!

Public Image

When you represent your company at a public meeting, your communication skills can affect the company's public imagery.

(*Image* is the correct word, not *imagery.*)

KEY POINT

The rhetorical question is the most effective technique to develop a close relationship between the writer and the reader.

Persuading Someone to Act

To increase the pressure on the reader to say, "Yes, I want to buy this!" the writer often uses techniques that help develop a close relationship between writer and reader. The most effective of these techniques is the rhetorical question. A **rhetorical question** is a question that is posed solely for effect, with no expectation of a reply or a clear yes or no. Rhetorical questions are asked to stimulate thought about a specific topic. Although a sales letter may contain several rhetorical questions at various points, a question can be used most effectively after the sales appeal. For example, after the virtues of the product have been described and the sales appeal has been made, imagine how effective questions such as the following could be:

- Do pressures, deadlines, and difficult people leave you feeling frazzled?
- Are your fuel bills too high?
- Would you like to be free from back pain?

After answering yes to rhetorical questions like these, readers are as ready to act as they will ever be. However, the writer's job is still not over.

Providing the Opportunity to Act

What happens if the reader has no opportunity to act on an urge to buy? Writers of sales letters include at least one of the following opportunities for immediate reaction:

- A postage-paid reply card.
- An order form.
- Coupons.
- A toll-free, 24-hour telephone number.
- A Web site address.
- Store locations.
- Product samples.
- Fax number.

The sample sales letter (see **Exhibit 10.1**) gives the reader simple instructions.

Writing Credit and Collection Letters

Another type of persuasive letter is the **collection letter**, a letter in which a company reminds certain customers that they have not paid their bill. Collecting an overdue account is not an easy task because no one likes to ask for money. Yet businesses must ask—or they lose money. Consequently, the goal is to get customers to pay without losing their goodwill.

Making Sure Customers Understand Credit Terms

The terms of credit should always be explained to the customer at the time credit is granted. Laws will vary from state to state. In fact, in certain states the law requires such an explanation. In commercial credit, that is, between a wholesaler and a retailer, it is also advisable to review credit terms pleasantly, but firmly, when acknowledging a customer's first order. If the terms are 30 days net, expect your money in 30 days and do not hedge with weak statements like, "We hope you will send your check within 30 days." Instead, say, "Our terms are 2 percent discount if you pay within 10 days; the net amount is due in 30 days."

KEY POINT

The goal of credit and collection letters is to get customers to pay their bills without damaging the goodwill relationship between the customer and the company.

August 11, 20—

Mr. Bill Brandenberger
531 Chester Avenue
Danville, VA 24540

Dear Mr. Brandenberger:

Studies show that . . .

> . . . the successful people in business control time and do not let time control them.
> . . . remembering important events strengthens friendships and relationships.
> . . . being organized and getting things done result in advancement opportunities.

We know these statements describe you, Mr. Brandenberger, because you purchased one of our convenient Day Planners last year for just $102. You and the many other individuals who use our day planning products are better organized and get more accomplished than those who do not use them.

Now we offer you a special, three-year subscription to calendar refills for 2003, 2004, and 2005 for an incredible $72.86. The price includes shipping and handling for all three years. Your 2003 calendar will ship immediately.

To reserve your Day Planner fillers and have them shipped at the appropriate times, just check the "Yes" option on our enclosed postage-paid return card, and mail it to us. We will bill you later.

Your time is valuable, Mr. Brandenberger. Let our Day Planner continue to help you make the most of it by acting now on this special offer.

Sincerely,

Mason Hicks

Mason Hicks
President

Enclosure

Exhibit 10.1
Sales Letter With a Return Card
Thinking Critically. *How does the return card make it easier for the reader to respond?*

Assuming Customers Will Pay

When a customer first fails to pay a bill on time, it is wise to assume that this failure is an oversight. Therefore, if the usual monthly statement does not produce results, companies often send the customer a second statement a week or ten days later. Sometimes this second statement is stamped "First Reminder" or "Please Remit." Some credit departments use printed reminder forms such as the one shown in **Exhibit 10.2.**

Most customers will respond to gentle hints that their accounts are overdue. Remember, the first reminder should never be an attack. Rather, it should be a highly impersonal nudge.

Exhibit 10.2

Overdue Reminder Form
An impersonal printed form provides a gentle reminder that an account is overdue. *Thinking Critically.* Why is it important to have an impersonal approach to overdue collections?

Moser's Fine Footware

Market Place Shopping Center
2000 North Neil Street
Champaign, Illinois 61820
217-555-8873

January 15, 20—

Have you forgotten . . . ?

Because of the holidays, you may have overlooked mailing your December payment for your charge account at Moser's Fine Footware.

Sending your payment for the amount due will be appreciated. In case you have already mailed the payment, please disregard this reminder.

Credit Account:	FF376-829-50
Amount Due for December 20—	
Charges:	$240.57
Minimum Payment Due:	$24.57

Thank you for shopping at Moser's Fine Footware, and Happy New Year!

Employability Skills

Thinking Creatively

Persuasive communication involves the ability to think creatively. Creative thinking entails quick thinking as well as generating new and credible ideas.

Sending Additional Reminders and Follow-Up Letters

If there is still no payment after a second statement has been sent, most companies will send a series of three to five follow-up letters before turning the account over to a lawyer or a collection agency.

In a typical five-letter **follow-up series,** all letters should include the amount owed and the date due.

1. *First* follow-up letter—though clear and firm, should still give the customer the benefit of the doubt.

2. *Second* letter—which should be mailed no later than 15 days after the first letter, should remain friendly and courteous but should be firmer and more insistent than the first.

3. *Third* letter—should be even more insistent and forceful than second letter.

4. *Fourth* letter—should demand payment.

5. *Fifth* letter—should state what legal action will be taken if the delinquent customer fails to take advantage of this last opportunity to pay.

The goal of this last letter is to urge the reader to pay the bill in order to avoid legal action.

Using the five-letter follow-up series provides a business with an effective and efficient plan for collecting payment before taking legal action. It provides customers with plenty of time to remit their payment. The follow-up letters also allow a business to document its efforts in collecting the truant customer's payment if legal action becomes necessary.

Assessment   Section 10.1

Review of Key Terms

1. What advantages do *sales letters* have over radio or television commercials? _____

   _____

2. What procedure do businesses follow when writing *collection letters*?

   _____

   _____

   _____

Editing Practice

Proofreading Alert! Rewrite the following excerpts so that they are more diplomatic.

3. You claim that your VCR was not tested after it was repaired. _____

   _____

4. You have never bought anything from us before, so why would we deliver the furniture free? _____

   _____

5. You didn't include your warranty number; therefore, we won't repair your CD player. _____

   _____

6. If you don't have the coupon, you can't get the discount. _____

   _____

Practical Application

Thinking Critically

7. Look through magazines, catalogs, and sales letters you have received. List at least ten different types of sales appeals you find. Prepare the list under the following headings: (1) Type of Product, (2) Trade Name, and (3) Sales Appeal. _____

   _____

   _____

8. As a team, write a sales letter—including an attention-getting envelope—that asks young married couples to buy a new home in a new housing development. Be sure to attract the readers' attention, set up a close relationship, appeal to a specific buying motive, persuade the readers to act, and give them an opportunity to act. _____

_____

_____

Discussion Point

Analyzing Details

9. How do businesses find their target audience? _____

_____

_____

10. What is the goal of a sales letter? Discuss examples of sales letters you have received in the mail. Were they effective? Why or why not?_____

_____

_____

_____

_____

_____

Writing Claim and Adjustment Messages

Writing Claim Letters

A **claim letter** is a type of request letter written when there is a problem with a product or service.

The person who writes a claim letter believes, of course, that he or she has been wronged. Indeed, the claim is justified if, for example, the writer:

- Ordered Model R-75 but received Model R-57.
- Requested 150 booklets but received only 100.
- Requested size 10 but received size 14.
- Enclosed full payment but was billed anyway.
- Specified brand Q but received brand T.

Sometimes, however, the writer *intended* to order brand Q but forgot to specify this particular brand. Or the writer neglected to proofread the order letter or purchase order and did not correct the "100" booklets to "150." Or the writer wrote the check for the full amount but did not enclose it. The first step in making a claim, therefore, is to get the facts—before you write your claim.

Get the Facts

Before you make a claim, try to find out what happened and why.

- If part of the order is missing, is there a packing slip that clearly says the rest of the order will be shipped separately? Check your original order to be sure that the "missing" merchandise was ordered.
- If merchandise was damaged, should you write your claim to the supplier, or should you write it to the shipping company? You will be embarrassed if you write a strong letter to the supplier and later discover that the shipping company was at fault.
- If the wrong merchandise was delivered, check the original order first. Before you write your claim letter, try to find out if anyone phoned in a change in the order.

When you write a claim letter, you should rely on facts as the basis of your claim. Until you have sufficient facts, do not write the letter. When you do have all the facts, use them to describe the claim completely and accurately.

SECTION OBJECTIVES

When you have finished Section 10.2, you will be able to:

- Gather the appropriate facts needed to write a claim letter that is complete and accurate.
- Evaluate claim letters received and make an appropriate adjustment.
- Write effective adjustment letters.

WHY IT'S IMPORTANT

One way customers let businesses know they are unhappy is through a *claim letter*. Businesses allowing claims respond with *adjustment letters*. Knowing how to write both effectively helps make you a more competent communicator.

KEY TERMS

- claim letter
- adjustment
- equitable adjustment
- claimant

KEY POINT

When writing a claim letter, be complete and accurate in presenting your claim.

Describe the Claim Completely and Accurately

It is especially important to be complete and accurate when you are writing a claim letter because you are, in effect, making an accusation. Both to make a convincing argument and to be fair to the reader, you should present all the facts, and you should do so accurately.

Read the following letter. As you do so, note how the writer cites all the necessary details—weights, quantities, times, descriptions, and so on.

Dear Mr. Barnett:

We have received your invoice for 25 100-pound bags of polypropylene resin for injection-molding. When we placed this order 17 days ago, we stressed the need for speedy delivery of the resin and were promised delivery within 10 days. Your invoice for 25 bags arrived on the tenth day, but none of the resin was delivered until the fifteenth day, when we received only 5 bags.

We would appreciate that you check your records to make sure that all the resin has been shipped. If it has, please notify our shipping company at once. Our customer desperately needs the items to be made from this resin and is understandably upset that we have not delivered them as promised. We are counting on you to help us make up for lost time.

Please telephone me at 614-555-8214 by June 5 to let us know the status of this vital shipment of resin. We will hold your invoice until we receive all 25 bags of resin. Then, of course, we will be happy to send payment.

Sincerely yours,

The writer not only tells the reader *everything* that happened concerning the materials that were ordered but also does so in chronological order. By giving complete information and delivering it accurately, the writer makes an honest, believable claim.

Let's look at another example of a claim letter that is both complete and accurate.

Dear Ms. Draper:

I was distressed to receive your notice of March 1 indicating that you have canceled my homeowner's insurance policy No. AZ1843687 for failure to pay the premium of $350 due on January 15.

On January 4, I mailed Check 186 for $350. On January 17, the check, endorsed by your company and stamped "Paid," was returned to me. I reported this information to you on the back of a notice of cancellation mailed to me January 30. Since I received no further word from you, I assumed that the matter had been resolved.

Enclosed is a photocopy of the front and back of my canceled check. Would you please send me a notice of the reinstatement of my insurance?

Very truly yours,

The letter gives *all* the details—completely and accurately—so that the insurance company can quickly correct its error. Note, however, that, even though the preceding letter presents facts, the writer does not accuse, threaten, or demand.

KEY POINT

The goal of a claim letter is to get results, not to accuse, threaten, or demand.

Avoid Accusations, Threats, and Demands

The goal of the claim letter is to get the missing merchandise, to correct the billing error, to return the damaged goods—in other words, to get results, not to accuse, to lay blame, to threaten, or to demand. For example, assume that the preceding letter to the insurance company was not answered in a reasonable time. What would you do? Write a threatening letter? Demand that the company send you a formal apology? These are reactions, not solutions. Writing a letter that begins, "You know very well that I paid my premium," or "You failed to reply," or "I will sue you," would be a waste of time.

Instead, write a reasonable letter, this time addressed to someone with more authority. For example, a letter to the president of the agency that handles your insurance would probably get results:

Dear Mr. Kovacs:

I am enclosing a photocopy of a letter I wrote to Marie Draper at your main office on March 5. My letter has not yet been acknowledged, and I am concerned about whether my homeowner's insurance is in force.

I would very much appreciate your looking into this matter for me and providing written notification regarding the status of my homeowner's insurance policy.

Very sincerely yours,

Without accusing, threatening, or demanding, the letter will get results. After all, if you were the president of the agency, would you overlook this letter? The president would understand that the next step is legal action.

Suggest Reasonable Solutions

The opposite of accusing, threatening, or demanding is suggesting reasonable solutions. *Remember:* Except in rare circumstances, you are dealing with honest business people who have made a mistake *and realize it*. By suggesting reasonable solutions, you strengthen your chance of getting a just settlement quickly. For example, if you placed an order and received only part of it, one solution might be to indicate that you will accept the missing portion if it arrives by a specific date, as shown by the following statement:

- We will gladly accept the 25 camping tents if they reach us by May 15, the first day of our Great Outdoors Savings Spectacular.

Or suppose that you were overbilled $100 on an order. In this case, you might say:

- We were billed $650 for the merchandise on our Purchase Order 3290, dated July 7. The figure should have been $550. Therefore, please credit our account for $100 and send us a credit memorandum for this amount.

It is usually best to suggest the kind of solution that you consider acceptable. If you received defective merchandise, for example, you might request replacement of the merchandise, cancellation of the order, a credit of the amount to your account, or substitution of a similar item. Suggesting a solution tells the company what kind of action you want taken. When your suggestion is reasonable, there is a good chance that the company will follow it.

Fairly Evaluating Claims and Making Adjustments

Whether a business is a multinational corporation or a small family store, it will have customers who claim that they received fewer items than they ordered; damaged goods; the incorrect size, color, or model; unsatisfactory merchandise; and so on. Each customer's claim must be answered, and each situation must be studied. The business must (1) determine whether the claim has any merit and (2) examine *how* the merchandise was damaged or *why* the wrong item was shipped so that the same mistake will not happen again.

In many cases, an **adjustment** will be made—the customer will receive a full or a partial credit, will be allowed to exchange the merchandise, or will be granted a refund.

> **KEY POINT**
>
> Suggesting a reasonable solution improves your chances of getting a just settlement quickly.

Several qualities are required to evaluate a claim, determine a fair adjustment, and approve the adjustment: (1) business experience; (2) company authority; (3) familiarity with company policy, industry standards, and consumer laws; and (4) common sense. You are essentially playing the role of judge; but since you have a vested interest in the case, being impartial is difficult. Yet an **equitable adjustment** requires you to be reasonable, fair, honest, and impartial in making your decision.

Making the right decision is, therefore, a difficult task. The sources of evidence that you must weigh are the company; the **claimant,** that is, the person making the claim; the transaction; and, in some cases, the law. Let's look at each source to see how it influences or affects the final decision.

The Company

As an ethical business, your company will want to examine its responsibility in light of a claim. Ask yourself the following questions to determine the extent of your company's responsibility in causing the situation.

- Do you know, without a doubt, that the company is not at fault?
- Could anyone in the company have made a misleading statement?
- Could the advertising be misinterpreted?
- Could your records be at fault?
- Is it possible that someone in the company made a mistake?

If such questioning reveals an element of blame on the part of the company, you, the adjuster, will probably decide to honor the claim, at least in part.

The Claimant

To help you evaluate the claimant's share in causing the claim, ask questions like these:

- Could the claimant be mistaken?
- Is the claim, if true, a reasonable one to make?
- Has the claimant provided all the information you need to check the claim and place responsibility for it?
- Does the claimant have a record of fair dealings with your company?

Even if you find that the claimant is wrong beyond any doubt, good business sense tells you that perhaps the claim should be honored anyway.

The Transaction

The answers to the following questions will help you arrive at an equitable decision about the transaction.

- Did your company carry out all its obligations—both stated and implied—to the customer?
- Has your company made any claims with reference to this product, such as, "Double your money back if you are not absolutely satisfied"?
- Were any misleading statements made to the customer by your sales personnel?
- Is there evidence of faulty materials or workmanship in the product?
- Were the instructions for use of the product clear and complete?

If you find a defect, either in the product or in the handling of the transaction, you should decide in favor of the claimant. This correction is just one more application of the commonly practiced business rule of trying to please the customer.

Sometimes you will have to seek further information before you can answer the previous questions. You may need to question some of your co-workers or to write the claimant before you have all the facts. The following letter is an example of an inquiry addressed to a claimant:

Dear Mrs. Lane:

Thank you for your October 17 letter about your StairTrainer treadmill. We are sorry that you are having problems with the treadmill, a product that is usually quite reliable.

We cannot locate a copy of your warranty agreement, which should be on file here. The period of the warranty is normally one year. If you could send us the transaction number from the top right corner of your receipt, we could confirm the purchase. If you do not have the receipt, then please give us the name of the dealer from whom you made the purchase and the approximate date of purchase.

As soon as we receive the information, we will be happy to make an adjustment.

Sincerely yours,

When you receive the necessary information, you will be able to make an equitable decision on the claim.

The Law

In some cases, laws will determine what you must decide regarding a claim. Laws intended to protect consumers, for example, allow a consumer to cancel certain contracts within three days "without penalty or obligation." State or local laws may apply in special situations in your industry.

In any case, you should realize that there are potential legal problems in some situations. Although you have learned that you should not threaten when making a claim, many writers will threaten you with legal action in their first claim letters just because they believe that making such threats will get results. Does your company have a policy that requires all employees to notify the legal department any time there is the possibility of a lawsuit? Whether or not it has such a policy, you *should* notify someone in authority, perhaps your supervisor *and* the legal department, whenever legal action is even remotely possible.

Writing Adjustment Letters

After probing all the sources of evidence and reviewing all the facts in a claim, you may determine that (1) the claim is indeed allowable, (2) the claim is only partially allowable, or (3) the claim is not allowable. Now comes the task of using your writing skills to respond to a claim letter with an adjustment letter.

An Allowable Claim

Mistakes occur in every business. What separates a well-run business from a poorly run business is not *whether* the company makes mistakes but *how it handles* its mistakes.

Question: What do you do when the error is yours? *Answer:* Use the direct approach and *grant* the adjustment in the opening sentence. Admit that it was your fault, without arguing or trying to avoid responsibility. Note how effectively this is done in **Exhibit 10.3.**

The writer also strives to keep the customer's goodwill throughout the letter. In an effort to maintain goodwill, some companies will even grant doubtful claims if the costs are not excessive. In this way, they develop an excellent reputation among their customers and gain new business.

KEY POINT

Be sure you have all the information you need before handling a claim.

Misstating the Case

You may also want to make souvenirs for your guests to take home as memorandums.

(*Mementos* is the correct word, not *memorandums*.)

Turbak Instruments

9376 West Century Boulevard
Los Angeles, California 90045
213-555-4678 • FAX: 213-555-4699
www.turbakinstruments.com

November 5, 20—

Dr. Carlos A. Gotardo
Anderson Manufacturing Corporation
3976 State Street
Prestonburg, Kentucky 41653

Dear Dr. Gotardo:

A new barometer has been shipped to you by airfreight.

From your description in your November 2 letter, we believe that your aneroid barometer was mistakenly calibrated for use as an altimeter. We manufacture altimeters and aneroid barometers using the same mechanism—only the calibrations are different.

Somehow the wrong model number and nameplate were placed on the barometer you received. Please accept our sincere apology. We are reviewing our procedures in an effort to prevent this kind of mix-up from happening again.

When we can be of further assistance to you, Dr. Gotardo, please write or call.

Sincerely yours,

Art Dale

Art Dale, Supervisor
Customer Service Department

yr

Exhibit 10.3
Letter Granting an Adjustment
Thinking Critically. *Why should a letter granting an adjustment start with the good news?*

A Partially Allowable Claim

Allowing a claim is rather easy. Slightly more difficult is reaching a compromise with a claimant. For instance, if the transaction involves a heavy piece of equipment worth $10,000, the manufacturer will probably be reluctant to exchange the equipment and pay for double shipping charges besides. Yet, that may be what the claimant asks for.

Suppose, for example, that a recent purchaser of a commercial automatic film processor wants to exchange the processor. The customer states that the processor is unsatisfactory because the developed film comes out wet instead of dry. You feel certain that the problem is caused by failure of the small fan under the drying hood. Replacement of the fan will take one of your technicians ten minutes and cost you only $25. Exchanging the entire processor, which weighs 200 pounds and is valued at $9,000, will be expensive because of shipping costs. Moreover, the customer will have to wait at least three weeks for a new processor. You decide to seek a compromise adjustment.

How much of an adjustment a company makes in a case like this depends on company policy. You believe that the customer will be satisfied with the processor after the fan is replaced. You are also willing to offer the customer a $100 discount toward the purchase price as compensation for the inconvenience caused by the failure of the fan. Your letter describing this proposed adjustment might read as follows:

Dear Ms. Mihm:

>Thank you for your letter about the problem you are having with your new Kodiak Mammography Film Processor. Replacing the fan under the drying hood is the solution. Although we thoroughly test each processor before it leaves our plant, the machines are sometimes damaged by rough handling in transit.

>Exchanging your processor for a new one would require subjecting another unit to the hazards of shipping. In addition, you would be without a processor for at least three weeks. We seriously question the wisdom of exchanging the entire unit when only one small component is the cause of all the trouble.

>Ms. Mihm, we want you to be satisfied with our products and service. We realize that the fan's failure has inconvenienced you. We can send a service technician to your mammography center with a new drying fan. Replacement of the defective fan should take only ten minutes, and you can test the processor immediately to make sure that everything is working properly. Please call our service center at 555-2243 to make an appointment for our service technician to visit your center.

>In addition, we have enclosed a $100 discount certificate.

>We are confident that your Kodiak Mammography Film Processor will provide good service for years to come.

Sincerely yours,

The writer is trying to reach a fair settlement with the customer. Nonetheless, Ms. Mihm may reply by asking to be compensated for all the film wasted as a result of the fan's failure.

A Nonallowable Claim

Although a business may strive to satisfy its customers and may have the most lenient claim policy in its industry, it will encounter situations in which claims simply cannot be allowed. For example, one customer may try to return a perfectly good lamp that he ordered simply because he no longer wants that style. Another customer may wrongly insist that she ordered merchandise before a price increase. If the business granted such claims once, it would set a questionable precedent. Besides, granting such a claim would be poor business. Whatever the reason, the company is faced with the uncomfortable but necessary task of saying no to a customer.

Assume, for example, that you are employed by Essex Distribution Company, a computer products wholesaler. Last month, you featured a special offer on the complete Epic Model KL computer system. In your mailer to dealers, you specifically stated that you are discounting your current inventory of the KL model by 30 percent "to make room for new inventory." Many dealers took advantage of the superb discount offer. You specifically stated in the mailer that this sale was a "clearance sale" and that no returns would be permitted.

Toni Gleisner, manager of the Inacom Computer Center, purchased 50 of the discounted Epic KL systems, sold 20, and then asked permission to return the remaining 30 systems. Because Inacom is a good customer, you have "bent the rules" in the past to allow Ms. Gleisner special return privileges for unsold merchandise. This time, however, you simply cannot accept the 30 Model KL systems. You must write to

KEY POINT

Strive to keep a customer's goodwill when writing an adjustment letter.

Ms. Gleisner to tell her this, but you must also try to retain her goodwill—and her future business. To do so, perhaps you would send the following letter:

Dear Ms. Gleisner:

Thank you for complimenting us on our special offers of the top brand names in computers. We at Essex pride ourselves on being the number one computer distributor in the state, and we sincerely appreciate having the opportunity to do business with the number one computer store in the state, Inacom Computer Center.

As you know, Ms. Gleisner, no other distributor has offered such a drastic discount on Epic computers as our recent 30 percent discount. We did so, frankly, because we were forced to make room for new inventory. We simply had to clear our stock at the time of the special sale. That's why we specifically stated that the sale was on a no-return basis. I'm sure that you, too, have been faced with similar situations.

As much as we would like to help you, we really cannot accept a return of 30 Epic KL systems. For one reason, we now have on order more than 500 of the new Epic XP systems. As you can imagine, these 500 systems will take up a lot of warehouse space and eat up many inventory dollars. We are also increasing our inventory of other major brands so that we can continue to deliver to dealers like Inacom all computer merchandise in the minimum amount of time. By serving you better, of course, we help you serve your customers better.

May I make a suggestion? A few days ago Bill Kline of Computer World, located in the Warren Mall, was eager to get more Epic Model KL systems. Perhaps you can arrange to sell your stock to Mr. Kline. Of course, if I should hear of any other dealers who are looking for Epic KLs, I will be sure to call you.

By the way, let me give you some "advance notice" of a special sale we are planning for next month. We will be offering the popular Speedex ZIP disk drive for only $75 and the Lark DSL modem for only $95!

Sincerely yours,

Although the reply is clearly no, the letter has a positive tone and maintains the customer's goodwill. The writer used the indirect approach; start with a buffer, which gives the reasons *before* the refusal, and then end with another buffer.

Assessment   Section 10.2

Review of Key Terms

1. What guidelines should a writer follow when writing a *claim letter*?

   _____

   _____

   _____

2. What kind of *claim adjustments* do customers receive from businesses? How does a business determine how to make an *equitable adjustment*?

   _____

   _____

   _____

   _____

Editing Practice

Call an Editor! Underline the errors. Then edit and rewrite the following paragraph.

3. Send me the compleat two-volume set of *Marketing and Distribution.* I understand I will also recieve a one-year subscription to *American Business Today*, along with a calender for business executives. Please - refrane from placing my name on any mailing lists. Enclosed is my check for $53.99. _____

_____

Practical Application

Writing Letters

4. Review the adjustment letter addressed to Ms. Mihm (page 395). Assume that in addition to the replacement fan, she also wants full compensation for all the film wasted as a result of the defective fan. Write a letter to Ms. Mihm, offering to send a claims adjuster who will examine the film and determine its value. You are not committing yourself at this point to reimburse her for all the wasted film. _____

_____

5. You ordered a CD player from Orion Inc. on December 5 as a gift. Orion promised shipment by December 20. The CD player didn't arrive until December 27, however, and without the necessary hardware to connect it to an amplifier! The catalog stated that all necessary hardware would be included. As a team, write the body of the claim letter that explains what happened and suggest a solution. _____

_____

Discussion Point

Thinking Critically

6. Why are claim letters that use a negative, threatening tone a waste of time? What approach would ensure the claimant a quick and reasonable settlement? _____

_____

_____

7. How do the company, the claimant, the transaction, and the law determine the outcome of a claim? Provide current examples. _____

_____

_____

_____

_____

_____

SECTION OBJECTIVES

When you have finished Section 10.3, you will be able to:

- Write a letter effectively promoting a new business.
- Write a letter encouraging credit account use.
- Apply general public relations techniques to the writing of routine business letters.

WHY IT'S IMPORTANT

Favorable public relations with a business means that the public has a positive opinion of the company or organization; unfavorable public relations means a negative opinion.

KEY TERMS

- public relations
- public relations specialist
- public relations campaign

KEY POINT

Public relations is the business of positively influencing the public's feeling or attitude toward a company or an organization.

Public Relations Letters

Essential Principles

Major corporations have public relations departments that specialize in creating favorable images of their firms and minimizing the negative impact when their firms get unfavorable news coverage in the media. Although you may not work in the public relations department, as an employee you will certainly affect your company's public image. **Public relations** is the business of influencing the public to have understanding for and goodwill toward a person, firm, or institution.

Whenever you communicate with the public as a representative of your company—when you talk with or write to anyone outside the company—you have an opportunity to influence the public's attitude toward your firm. Your communication skills can definitely contribute to your firm's favorable public image.

Special Public Relations Opportunities

You have seen advertisements that say, for example, "Working Hard to Keep You and Your Family Safe . . . FIRST-ALERT SMOKE DETECTORS." This ad is not designed specifically to sell First-Alert's Model 911-E smoke detector or to sell First-Alert's line of products but instead to promote the First-Alert Company in general. The ad is designed to convince you that the First-Alert Company has your safety in mind. Why? So that, when you do shop for smoke detectors, you will—either unconsciously or otherwise—select First-Alert—a name you can trust.

The **public relations specialist** looks for opportunities to show the company in the best possible light. When an employee receives a commendation from his or her community for civic work, the company might send a news release to various newspapers to share this good news with the public. The good civic work of one of its employees helps to enhance the firm's image. On the other hand, the public relations specialist tries to minimize anything the public could interpret in a negative way.

Unfavorable public opinion can ruin a firm. For example, if a newspaper report states or implies that the All-Natural Breads Company uses chemical preservatives and artificial coloring despite claims that its breads contain only natural ingredients, public opinion of that company will certainly drop—even if the report is later proved false. Consumers who remember the negative report may start buying another brand if they doubt the integrity of the company.

Knowing the benefits of good public relations, all businesses strive to create—and to maintain—a favorable image of their organizations in the eyes of the public. An oil company may televise a short film showing the public that the company works to protect the environment wherever it drills for oil. A well-known, reputable person may narrate the film to lend it additional credibility. At no time does the narrator say, "Buy your oil and gas from

Enviro-Go." Instead, the narrator points out all the benefits the company offers the public.

The public relations specialist tries to win friends and customers when faced with the opportunity to:

- Promote a new business.
- Announce a special privilege or service to preferred customers.
- Offer special incentives to encourage charge customers to use their credit cards.
- Welcome new residents—who are potential customers—to the community.
- Congratulate someone for a special achievement.
- Invite someone to a lecture, art show, demonstration, or film.
- Thank someone for his or her business.

Promoting a New Business

To promote a new business, the first step toward establishing good public opinion is to announce the grand opening—for example, in a letter such as this one:

> May we introduce you to—Piérre Maigrete, chef and managing partner of Chicago's premier and most exciting restaurant:
>
> ### Entre Nous
>
> Chef Maigrete, a graduate of the American Culinary Arts Institute and the author of two best-selling cookbooks, has practiced his culinary magic in several fine restaurants in New York and Boston. *Good Food* magazine has hailed Piérre Maigrete as "one of America's most creative young chefs."
>
> Come to Entre Nous for the ultimate dining experience. Surrounded by understated elegance, you and your guests will be attended by a well-trained staff who will describe in detail the tempting appetizers, entrées, and desserts that Chef Maigrete and his staff will prepare for you.
>
> Reservations are necessary, and all major credit cards are accepted. As a courtesy to all guests and for your personal dining pleasure, separate dining rooms are reserved and designated as smoking and nonsmoking.
>
> Join us at Entre Nous for a relaxed evening of fine dining.
>
> Cordially,

This letter alone is simply one step in a public relations campaign, though. To effectively promote this grand reopening requires newspaper ads, spot announcements on local radio stations, circulars, and news releases, all focused on the general theme and tone of this letter. Together, these messages make up a **public relations campaign** that will surely reach the potential diners who live or work in the Chicago area.

Through these public relations communications, Entre Nous seizes every opportunity to put its name before potential customers in a favorable light.

Handling Special Opportunities

The sharp businessperson has an eye for opportunities to improve public relations—and takes every advantage of those opportunities. For examples of how to *create* letters for special occasions, see the letters illustrated in **Exhibits 10.4** and **10.5**.

Everyday Public Relations Opportunities

Unless your job is in the public relations department, you may not have all the special opportunities that have been discussed so far. But the techniques will be useful because you will have everyday opportunities to improve public relations for your company.

KEY POINT

Astute business people look for opportunities to improve public relations.

Unappealing Error

Sales letters or promotional letters are written to appeel to a specific audience.

(*Appeal* is the correct spelling, not *appeel*.)

Important Facts

Please check all names and dates when preparing the press release. The factuals are very important.

(*Facts* is the correct word, not *factuals*.)

TRAVEL DESIGN AGENCY
449 North Leisure Boulevard, Louisville, KY 40205
Phone: 520-555-8728, Fax: 520-555-8728
E-mail: traveldesign@cactusnet.com
www.traveldesign.com

April 21, 20—

Ms. Inge Colby
23849 Lucas Street
Louisville, KY 40205

Dear Ms. Colby:

Do you need a vacation? Like many people, you probably enjoyed your last few days away from the office during the holidays. That seems so long ago as you wade through the endless piles of paper on your desk, as you sort through endless requests, and as you hurry from one meeting to another.

We invite you to visit our summer getaway representative at the Travel Center. We can offer you many alternatives for the weekend, week, or month vacation you deserve. We can offer suggestions that fit your preferences. We have the networking capability to make all arrangements so you don't have to worry about any details. All you have to do is think about a glorious vacation that lies ahead for you beyond that stack of papers on your desk!

Right now, you can take advantage of many airline and tour discounts. Give yourself something to look forward to. Come in and talk to one of our representatives today.

Sincerely yours,

Angela Williams

Angela Williams
Travel Manager

Exhibit 10.4
Sales Letter with a Special Offer
Thinking Critically. *How do companies use sales letters to attract interest in a product or service?*

In **Exhibit 10.4,** note how the writer of the letter uses a rhetorical question to catch the reader's interest. The writer continues the letter by stating how the company can assist the reader.

Note in the following letter that the writer sells the company. In other words, the writer employs good public relations techniques in replying to a routine request for information.

Dear Mr. Foster:

All of us here appreciate your thinking of the Raccoon Lake Inn as the place to hold your annual sales conventions. Thank you for the compliment!

For several years now, you have used our facilities to host your special dinners, to demonstrate products to customers, to train your new representatives, and to lodge your employees and guests whenever they are in our area. We do, indeed, make a special effort to make all your meetings successful because your appreciation of our efforts always shows.

Mr. Foster, we sincerely enjoy serving you, your employees, and your customers. Thank you for doing business with us.

Cordially yours,

In **Exhibit 10.5,** the writer contacts a former customer to pave the way for future business.

As you see, public relations is part of every letter you write for your company. When you write your letters, even routine letters, look for ways to incorporate good public relations techniques.

38767 Walnut Street ❖ Alhambra, CA
Telephone: 818-555-8835 ❖ www.agf.net

October 8, 20—

Mrs. Lynn Dubea
9376 Valley View Parkway
Pasadena, CA 91116

Dear Mrs. Dubea:

Congratulations! You now own the big screen television you purchased one year ago. Our enclosed canceled note is your record that all payments have been made on this product.

We are sorry to lose you as a customer because you have always made all your payments on time. We hope you will consider us again to finance your purchase of additional major household items.

Please file our enclosed certificate that will entitle you to our lowest possible finance rates when you seek loans from us for indoor and outdoor household items as well as new vehicles. Present the certificate to a representative at any one of our conveniently located offices for service on your loan requests. We will be most pleased to work with you again.

Cordially yours,

Sofia Martinez

Sofia Martinez
Vice President

ms/note3689
Enclosure

Exhibit 10.5
Public Relations Letter
The writer makes an opportunity to contact a former customer. ***Thinking Critically.*** *What are the objectives of this public relations letter?*

Review of Key Terms

1. Why are *public relations* important to business? _____
   _____
   _____

2. How can a *public relations campaign* promote a business? _____
   _____
   _____
   _____
   _____

Editing Practice

Call an Editor!   Rewrite the following sentences to improve any poor writing techniques.

3. Arriving to pick up the package, I asked the messenger to wait while the cover letter was signed by Ms. Drake. _____
   _____

4. Employees must now submit their health insurance claim to Robert Bergman in the personnel office. _____
   _____

5. Ellen borrowed the dictionary which was on my desk. _____
   _____

6. You can use either of these four spreadsheets as a model for your training course. _____
   _____

Practical Application

Public Relations Letters

7. You are the manager at Morrison's Hardware Store located near the city limits. Traditionally, most of your customers have come from the city, but with new neighborhoods springing up beyond the city limits, you are looking for a way to develop business with these new residents. Write a letter, enclosing a $5 coupon, which invites each resident of the new area to visit your store. _____
   _____
   _____
   _____

8. You work for Newlook Decorators. You want to encourage prior customers with good credit to make another purchase of your new line of furniture. As a team, write a letter that invites your charge customers to a special preview showing of the new line. Admission will be by ticket only, and you are enclosing a ticket with each invitation. The general public will not see the new line until after the special showing. _____

_____

_____

Discussion Point

Making Generalizations

9. What effect can one negative incident have on public opinion? Discuss some examples of unfavorable public opinion and their effects. _____

_____

_____

_____

10. How do companies promote public relations through their business letters? _____

_____

_____

_____

_____

SECTION OBJECTIVES

When you have finished Section 10.4, you will be able to:

- Use the correct social-business letter format both on plain stationery and on printed stationery.

- Write effective congratulatory letters, thank-you letters, and condolence letters.

- Correctly write—and reply to—formal invitations.

WHY IT'S IMPORTANT

Common courtesy and tradition require people to communicate their congratulations or sorrow.

KEY TERMS

- social-business communications
- format
- executive letterhead

Social-Business Communications

Essential Principles

Common courtesy and tradition demand that co-workers send **social-business communications** to congratulate someone on a special occasion, to express condolences when a business associate suffers the loss of a loved one, to reply properly to a formal invitation, to thank someone for a special favor or a gift, and so on. Just as you would appreciate hearing from your co-workers and business associates in these situations, you should let them hear from you whenever appropriate.

Social-Business Letter Format

As you learned in Section 9.2, the **format** of a letter refers to the arrangement of letter parts on the page.

On Company Letterhead

For a social-business letter typed on company letterhead, use the social-business letter format illustrated in **Exhibit 10.6.** As you see, in this social-business letter format, the letter parts are in the usual position *except* that the inside address is placed last, positioned at the bottom left of the page. In addition, there is a change in the usual punctuation pattern for business letters: The salutation ends with a comma rather than with a colon. Reference initials, copy notations, and so on, are not included.

Some companies provide **executive letterhead** for social-business and other letters. Executive stationery measures $7\frac{1}{4} \times 10\frac{1}{2}$ inches (monarch) or $5\frac{1}{2} \times 8\frac{1}{2}$ inches (baronial). Standard stationery, on the other hand, measures $8\frac{1}{2} \times 11$ inches. Many people consider these sizes especially fitting for executive correspondence.

Whether you are using monarch or baronial letterhead or standard-sized stationery, follow the same format described in this section.

On Plain Stationery

When a social-business letter is typed on stationery with no printed letterhead, include the return address as you would for personal business letters. See the letter illustrated in **Exhibit 10.7.**

Lakeside Community College
DEPARTMENT OF COMPUTER SCIENCE

ONE TOWNE CENTRE
LEE'S SUMITT, MO 64063
TELEPHONE: 573-555-3576
FAX: 573-555-7413
E-MAIL: LUNGREN@LCC.EDU

October 14, 20—

Dear Ms. Childs,

Congratulations on your recent promotion to Executive Editor. As an author who has worked with you for two years, I know the promotion is well deserved.

You have played an important part in developing the concept for my computer applications text. You have also secured approved funding, completed and implemented input from reviewers, and kept me on track in terms of meeting manuscript and production deadlines.

As a result of your efforts, my text is now being used in community colleges around the country. Not only do you have superb editorial skills but also you have the people skills to pull everyone together as a team to complete this project.

I hope your promotion will not affect our working relationship when the text revision begins. I look forward to working with you again. I do wish you continued success in your new position and with all projects for which you have increased responsibility.

Sincerely,

Merle Buss

Merle Buss
Associate Professor

Ms. Lynn Childs
Beacon Publishers
321 National Boulevard
Brechenridge, MO 64625

Exhibit 10.6
Congratulatory Letter on Standard Letterhead
Thinking Critically. *What are the two unique features of social-business letters?*

Congratulations Letters

Special honors and special events provide ideal public-relations opportunities. They present you with an appropriate occasion to say "Congratulations!" Your reader will appreciate your thoughtfulness, and you will certainly win favor both for yourself and for your company. *Remember:* Everyone wants to be respected and admired, and a congratulatory message shows your respect and admiration for someone's accomplishment or recognition.

The 24-Hour Clock

In many countries, times are expressed according to the 24-hour clock. For example, a 3 p.m. meeting would be the same as 15:00 hours.

1003 Bridge Street
West Lafayette, IN 47906
April 7, 20–

Dear Ms. Liu,

My best wishes to you upon your election as national president of the National Reading Literary Council. You have shown your dedication to the goals of this organization at both the local and state levels.

With your experience, you will continue to work hard and be influential in helping everyone learn to read. By doing so, you will improve the quality of life of many people nationwide.

I know you will have a productive and successful term in this very important leadership position.

Cordially yours,

Michael Finkle

H. Michael Finkle

Ms. Luci Liu
334 Emerson Street
Chicago, IL 60606

Exhibit 10.7
Congratulatory Letter on Plain Stationery
What style does this congratulatory letter follow?

For Promotions

The degree of friendliness or informality of your congratulatory note will depend on the specific relationship you have with the reader. For two examples of similar congratulatory notes, one more formal and the other more casual, see the letters in **Exhibits 10.6** and **10.7,** respectively.

Congratulatory letters often are written to employees of the same company. In fact, it is virtually *mandatory* for executives to acknowledge promotions of employees in their company. The following letter is written to a valued employee.

Dear Arthur,

Congratulations to you on your promotion to Regional Sales Manager! You certainly are "the right person for the right job."

Maria Velazquez has been talking about promoting you to this position since she became Marketing Manager six months ago. All of us in management are equally convinced that you will be able to continue to turn in the high sales volume for which the Southern Region is well known.

In any case, Arthur, I certainly am happy to welcome you to the sales management team for our Consumer Division, and I wish you success in your new position.

Sincerely,

For Anniversaries

A co-worker's anniversary also calls for written congratulations. Note the friendliness and informality—and the sincerity—of this letter.

Dear Monte,

Congratulations on your tenth year with Apelern Inc.! I remember your first day with the company, when Jim Gieseke introduced you to me and my staff. When Jim retired one year later, I knew that you were the right person to replace him—and you've continued to prove that for the past nine years.

Monte, I think you know just how pleased I've been to have the opportunity to work with you during your time here. Thanks to your manufacturing expertise and management leadership, our production department is the best in the industry. My staff and I appreciate your fine work. You certainly help make things easier for the rest of us!

Cordially yours,

For Retirements

The retirement of a co-worker or of a business associate also deserves recognition. Retirement letters deserve extra care; if you are not sure that the person welcomes retiring, be especially sensitive to the retiree's feelings in writing the note.

Dear Alice Marie,

What will Pilár Publishing be like without you? Our clients, our suppliers, and all our co-workers have come to depend on your smiling face, your cheerful voice, and your friendly attitude whenever we bring work for you and other graphic arts department staff to do. It seemed as if you were always there to help a lost visitor, to reroute a messenger, and to answer the phone when no one else was around. I know that you were always there to help me.

Thank you, Alice Marie, for all you have done to help me since the first day I joined the company. All my best wishes to you in your retirement. I hope that you will enjoy many years of health and happiness with your family and your good friends. I hope, too, that you will visit us from time to time.

Sincerely,

For Individual Honors

When a business friend or associate has been named, appointed, or elected to a special position, show your congratulations with a message such as the one illustrated in **Exhibit 10.6.**

Thank-You Letters

A special occasion requires a *written* thank-you—for example, when we receive a special courtesy from a business associate.

Employability Skills

Individual Responsibility

Individual responsibility is necessary in the workplace. When communicating in social or business settings, it's important to be respectable and act with integrity.

KEY POINT

In many cases, a written thank you is expected. A timely thank-you letter demonstrates to employers that you are a thoughtful person who knows business etiquette.

For Gifts

Business executives may receive gifts from suppliers and vendors. When they do, courtesy demands that they write a thank-you note to the giver.

> Dear Reese,
>
> Thank you for your thoughtfulness in sending me such a beautifully bound edition of *Modern Art in America.* You certainly selected a book of special interest to me, as you very well know. Since I received your package late Friday afternoon, I have done little else but read, read, read. Admittedly, I spent lots of time on the photographs too!
>
> Reese, please accept my sincere appreciation for your kindness. You may be sure that I will enjoy this book again and again.
>
> Cordially yours,

Some companies have policies prohibiting employees from accepting such gifts under any circumstances. If your firm has such a policy, you will obviously adhere to it. Your thank-you letter, then, will require a different approach.

> Dear Reese,
>
> Thank you for your thoughtfulness in sending me *Modern Art in America.* You certainly selected a book of special interest to me.
>
> I wish that the company permitted me to keep this thoughtful gift, but we have a specific policy that prohibits my doing so. Therefore, when I have completed reading the book, I will give it to the company library, with this inscription: "Donated to the Monsanto-St. Louis Library by Interstate Publishers Inc."
>
> Reese, please accept my sincere appreciation for your kindness.
>
> Cordially yours,

For Hospitality

A business associate's hospitality is not to be taken for granted. Even if the person is also an employee of your company, he or she still deserves a thank-you letter for special hospitality.

> Dear Mrs. Fridy,
>
> Thank you for the many courtesies extended to me on my recent visit to Evanston. My stay was certainly most pleasant because of your thoughtfulness in arranging for my comfort.
>
> The high spot of the entire visit was the evening spent in your beautiful home. You and Mr. Fridy are gracious hosts. The food was excellent; the conversation stimulating; the people delightful.
>
> Enclosed is a small token of my appreciation for the many kindnesses shown me. I shall not soon forget my visit to Evanston.
>
> Sincerely yours,

For Recommendations

Many businesses flourish almost solely on the basis of the recommendations of clients, friends, suppliers, and other business associates. When someone recommends you or your firm, he or she is doing you a special favor—a favor that deserves a thank-you letter.

oops!

Dental Dilemma

All our employees participate in the dentist insurance program.

(*Dental* is the correct word, not *dentist.*)

KEY POINT

Thank-you letters build business relationships with co-workers and colleagues at other companies.

Dear Ms. Marrs:

This morning we visited John Lodge of Lodge's Discount Store. Mr. Lodge mentioned your recommendation when he placed an order for display and storage equipment for the chain of new stores that he will open this fall.

We thank you, Ms. Marrs, for recommending us to Mr. Lodge. We appreciate the order immensely, but not one bit more than we appreciate your confidence in us. Please accept our thanks for this favor. I hope we will be able to repay your kindness at the earliest opportunity.

Cordially yours,

Condolence Letters

When business associates and friends suffer tragedies or misfortunes, common courtesy requires you to communicate your sympathy with a condolence letter; or depending on your specific relationship, you may send a printed sympathy card.

Condolence letters present difficulties simply because it is not easy to console and comfort someone who has recently suffered a tragic loss. For the same reason, however, condolence letters are always very much appreciated. The important element is to let your business associate or friend know that you are thinking of him or her. You may type a condolence letter, but if you really wish to give your letter a personal touch, write a legible handwritten note.

Dear Sarah,

The news of your brother's untimely death yesterday has stunned and saddened me. I know that you have suffered a great loss. Please accept my sincere sympathy.

When my mother died last year, a friend sent me a copy of Dylan Thomas's poem "And Death Shall Have No Dominion." I found the poem, a copy of which is enclosed, a source of consolation again and again. I hope the poem will serve you as well as it did me. My heart goes out to you and your family in your time of grief.

Sincerely yours,

Formal Invitations and Replies

From time to time, businesspeople receive formal invitations to events such as an open house, a special reception to honor a distinguished person, a special anniversary, or a formal social gathering. Such invitations are usually engraved or printed and are written in the third person.

The illustration in **Exhibit 10.8** shows a formal printed invitation. Handwritten invitations and replies are written on personal stationery, special note-sized stationery, or plain white notepaper. Historically, an acceptance or a refusal was handwritten; today, if a phone number is provided on the invitation, a telephone response is acceptable.

Exhibit 10.8
Printed Formal Invitation
Thinking Critically. *Which voice is a formal invitation written in: first, second, or third?*

The Vermilion Fitness Center

requests the pleasure of your company
at its presentation of expanded health facilities
Friday, the sixth of February
at six o'clock in the evening
3170 South Hamilton Road in Muncie.

Our health bar will be serving refreshments.

R.S.V.P.

317-555-6786

 # Assessment　　　Section 10.4

Review of Key Terms

1. How does *social-business communication* improve a company's public relations? _____
_____

2. How is *executive letterhead* different from standard stationery, and when should it be used? _____
_____
_____

Editing Practice

Mail Call!　Rewrite the following wordy e-mail message.

3. One of the nation's outstanding experts on stress is Dr. Alice Burns of New York. We are fortunate to have Dr. Burns as a speaker for two presentations that she will give here in our company auditorium next month.

   The title of her talk is "Stress on the Job." The first presentation will be at 10 a.m. on April 18, the second presentation will be at the same time on the next day, April 19. If you are interested in hearing this noted author and lecturer, you are welcome to attend either one of the scheduled sessions. _____
_____
_____

Practical Application

Writing Social-Business Letters

4. You read in the newspaper that Annette Rossi, a fellow classmate in college, has been chosen Outstanding Financial Analyst at Harvard Investment (HI). After just three years at HI, she has been promoted to Assistant Director of Financial Analysis. Write a letter of congratulation to Annette on her achievements. _____

_____

_____

_____

5. Your team just returned from a business trip in New Orleans. During your three-day stay, employees from your sister company, Brandon Inc., personally drove you to business appointments, took you to restaurants, and planned a night on Bourbon Street. Write a note of thanks to the team at Brandon. (You have also ordered a gift to be sent to them as a small token of your appreciation.) _____

_____

_____

Discussion Point

Interpreting Information

6. Discuss the appropriate business situations that call for congratulation letters, thank-you letters, and condolence letters. _____

_____

_____

_____

_____

7. How should you reply to a formal business invitation? _____

_____

_____

SECTION OBJECTIVES

When you have finished Section 10.5, you will be able to:

- Explain the advantages and disadvantages of using form letters.
- Name and describe the three categories of form letters.
- Create and use a form letter with variables.
- Create form paragraphs and use them to develop form letters.
- Create a form letter.

WHY IT'S IMPORTANT

Form letters can help save time, money, and, in some cases, are more accurate than letters developed for individually created communications.

KEY TERMS

- form letters
- variables
- boilerplate
- data file
- form file
- template

Cartridge Catastrophe

The printer cartriage is out of ink so we cannot print the letter.

(*Cartridge* is the correct spelling, not *cartriage*.)

Form Paragraphs, Form Letters, and Templates

Essential Principles

You have learned that writing quality business communications takes much time and effort. Because time and effort cost money, many companies look for acceptable ways to reduce the amount spent. One very good way to reduce writing costs is to use form letters. **Form letters** are letters in which the same message is sent to many addressees. Sometimes, details of the message, called **variables,** change from letter to letter. Sometimes, form letters are composed by combining various prewritten paragraphs, called **boilerplate,** into a particular communication.

Advantages of Using Form Letters

Here are the major advantages of using form letters:

- Using form letters saves time in planning, dictating, and transcribing.
- Company representatives can respond more quickly to routine writing situations, and thus the receiver gets an answer sooner.
- The content quality will be better. Much time and thought can go into writing form letters.
- Fewer errors will result because the spelling, punctuation, and grammar have to be approved only once.
- Form letters and paragraphs do not have to be retyped. They are simply selected and printed.

Disadvantages of Using Form Letters

As with most good ideas, there are some disadvantages of using form letters. Here are three:

- Some of the "personal touch" can be lost in mass-producing letters. Attempts should be made to make letters more personal. You could, for example, include the person's name within a sentence. "I look forward to seeing you, Ms. Tate, on Friday at 2 p.m."
- If readers find out that they have received a form letter, they may feel somewhat disappointed. For example, a manager wrote you a congratulatory message when your son finished college. You felt good about the letter until your co-worker showed you one exactly like it that he had received when his daughter graduated from college. The purpose of the letter was goodwill, and the goodwill was lost. For this reason, form letters should be revised and updated at least once a year. Do not knowingly send

personal form letters to people who would have the opportunity to compare content.

- Form letters and boilerplate can be abused. Some business writers use them when they do not quite fit the situation and are thus inappropriate.

Types of Form Letters

Executives often find that they are repeatedly writing the same content in response to frequently occurring—almost identical—writing situations. When this happens, they should invest some time and effort in developing general responses that can be used and reused. These general responses fall into the following three main categories:

- Form letters
- Form letters with variables
- Letters with form paragraphs

Form Letters

Form letters are used when you must respond to identical situations. The letter shown in **Exhibit 10.9** would be used to respond to any general inquiries about cruises in

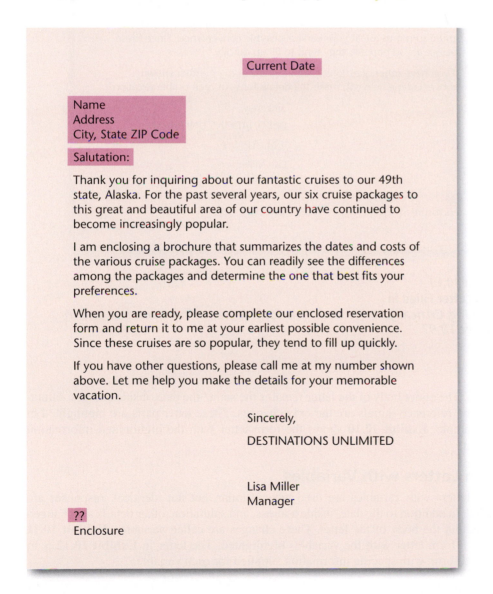

Current Date

Name
Address
City, State ZIP Code

Salutation:

Thank you for inquiring about our fantastic cruises to our 49th state, Alaska. For the past several years, our six cruise packages to this great and beautiful area of our country have continued to become increasingly popular.

I am enclosing a brochure that summarizes the dates and costs of the various cruise packages. You can readily see the differences among the packages and determine the one that best fits your preferences.

When you are ready, please complete our enclosed reservation form and return it to me at your earliest possible convenience. Since these cruises are so popular, they tend to fill up quickly.

If you have other questions, please call me at my number shown above. Let me help you make the details for your memorable vacation.

Sincerely,

DESTINATIONS UNLIMITED

Lisa Miller
Manager

??
Enclosure

Exhibit 10.9
Sample Form Letter
Thinking Critically.
How is the reader guided by this form letter?

Destinations Unlimited
344 East Canyon Place, Tucson, AZ 85704
Telephone: 520-555-8728, Fax: 520-555-8728
E-mail: destunl@cactusnet.com   www.destinationsunlimited.com

February 10, 20—

Tina Monfredini
5 Fenster Way
Fargo, ND 58103

Dear Ms. Monfredini:

Thank you for inquiring about our fantastic cruises to our 49th state, Alaska. For the past several years, our six cruise packages to this great and beautiful area of our country have continued to become increasingly popular.

I am enclosing a brochure that summarizes the dates and costs of the various cruise packages. You can readily see the differences among the packages and determine the one that best fits your preferences.

When you are ready, please complete our enclosed reservation form and return it to me at your earliest possible convenience. Since these cruises are so popular, they tend to fill up quickly.

If you have other questions, please call me at my number shown above. Let me help you make the details for your memorable vacation.

Sincerely,

DESTINATIONS UNLIMITED

Lisa Miller

Lisa Miller
Manager

dp
Enclosure

Exhibit 10.10
Form Letter Filled In
Thinking Critically. *How does this form letter differ from the one in Exhibit 10.9?*

Alaska. The entire body of the letter remains the same; the date, inside address, salutation, and reference initials are the only changes. These letter parts are highlighted in the example. **Exhibit 10.10** shows the form letter with the highlighted information filled in.

Form Letters with Variables

Form letters with variables are used when similar, but not identical, responses are needed. In addition to the date, inside address, and salutation, other details are changed throughout the body of the letter. These changes are called variables. **Exhibit 10.11** shows a form letter with the variables highlighted. The letter in **Exhibit 10.12** is in finished form, with specific information supplied for each variable.

Current Date

Name
Address
City, State ZIP Code

Salutation:

Your reservations for eight tickets to see "The Sound of Music" have been made, and your tickets are enclosed. You should be pleased with the seats you have been assigned. Four individuals will sit in Row 2, center; four individuals will sit in Row 3, center.

A total amount of $640, including taxes and service fees, has been charged to your Visa credit card. These tickets cannot be exchanged, and no refunds can be given.

We thank you for ordering tickets from us, and we know you will enjoy this fabulous Broadway musical. Seeing this show will certainly enhance your trip to New York City.

Sincerely,

Nanette Mellon
Reservation Agent

Exhibit 10.11
Form Letter with Variables
Thinking Critically. *How is the reader's attention directed to the variables in this form letter?*

Letters with Form Paragraphs

For similar writing situations that occur frequently but vary in content, experienced business communicators use form, or boilerplate, paragraphs. Paragraphs dealing with most common situations are written. Each paragraph has a number. Instead of dictating or keying each letter, the originator gives the office assistant the date, inside address, salutation, and a list of paragraphs by number. A letter that uses form paragraphs and sample boilerplate for those paragraphs is shown in **Exhibit 10.13.**

Using the word processing program on a computer makes writing letters with form paragraphs even easier. Boilerplate paragraphs and complete letters can be stored on disk and retrieved and altered as necessary. Only the variables need to be typed. As a result, routine letters can be prepared quickly and efficiently.

Travel Design Agency
449 North Leisure Boulevard, Louisville, KY 40205
Phone: 520-555-8728, Fax: 520-555-8728
E-mail: traveldesign@cactusnet.com
www.traveldesign.com

August 15, 20—

Mr. Rick Rotramel
247 Magnolia Drive
Huntington, WV 25701

Dear Mr. Rotramel:

Your reservations for two tickets to see "The Sound of Music" have been made, and your tickets are enclosed. You should be pleased with the seats you have been assigned. Two individuals will sit in Row 4, center.

A total amount of $160, including taxes and service fees, has been charged to your MasterCard credit card. These tickets cannot be exchanged, and no refunds can be given.

We thank you for ordering tickets from us, and we know you will enjoy this fabulous Broadway musical. Seeing this show will certainly enhance your trip to New York City.

Sincerely,

Nanette Mellon

Nanette Mellon
Reservation Agent

Exhibit 10.12
Form Letter with Variables Filled In
Thinking Critically. How does this form letter differ from the one in Exhibit 10.11?

Merged Letters

Merged letters save time when you need to send the same letter to a group of people. Merging requires a **data file,** which contains the names and addresses of people on your mailing list, and a **form file,** which contains the form letter and the codes to merge the information with the data file. Merging the two files allows you to print letters that appear to be individually typed and addressed. Then, the next time you wish to send a letter to this group of people, you need only change the body of the letter.

DOYLE LEGAL SERVICES

1237 OCEAN WAY SEAHORSE PLACE   TELEPHONE: 813-555-4159
VENICE, FL 34293   FAX: 813-555-4367

April 5, 20—

Ms. Mellisa Ronto
401 Veterans Parkway
St. Petersburg, FL 33712

Dear Ms. Ronto:

Thank you for expressing an interest in employment with our firm. We feel complimented that you want to discuss your career plans with us.

Before we consider you for any position, your application file must be complete. Please send us the name, company name (if appropriate), address, and phone number of three references.

As soon as we receive the information requested, we will call you to arrange an interview with our human resources manager.

Thank you for your interest in Doyle Legal Services. We look forward to hearing from you.

Sincerely,

Wes Rush

Wesley Rush
Senior Partner

eb

Exhibit 10.13
Form Letter with Form Paragraphs
Thinking Critically. *What changes would you make if you were sending the above form letter to a business instead of an individual?*

Templates

Many word processing programs today come with templates of letters. A **template** contains the format for a letter and can include the letterhead in addition to the skeleton of a letter. To use a template, you either insert it into your blank document or you open a copy of it, add the text in the places indicated, and print. This saves time and helps the user who is unsure of the correct letter format. Unfortunately, not all templates in all software applications are set up according to the correct formats you learned about in Chapter 9.

Review of Key Terms

1. Why do businesses use *form letters*? _____

_____

2. What are *boilerplate* paragraphs? Why are they used in business letters? _____

_____

_____

Editing Practice

Proofreading Alert! A word has been left out of each of the following sentences. Select a word that will correctly complete each sentence.

3. A helpful highway gave us directions to your plant. _____

_____

4. Most of the employees have decided participate in the dental insurance program. _____

5. Newspaper articles magazine articles aroused our interest. _____

6. Our sales in your area is Carla White. _____

Practical Application

Using Form Letters

7. Use the form letter in **Exhibit 10.11,** page 415, to model a letter to Denis Prior, P.O. Box 2849, Birmingham, AZ 85643. You made reservations for Mr. Prior for four tickets in row 8, center, to see *Bells Are Ringing*. The total came to $400, which has been charged to Mr. Prior's Visa credit card. _____

_____

_____

_____

_____

_____

_____

8. You work for a restaurant supply company. As a team, create three boilerplate paragraphs: one to list and describe some of the products you sell; a second to reply to restaurants that request a catalog; and a third to thank potential customers for their interest in your company. _____

_____

_____

Discussion Point

Thinking Critically

9. What are some of the advantages and disadvantages of using form letters? _____

_____

_____

_____

_____

10. Explain how variables in form letters provide a personal touch. _____

_____

_____

_____

_____

Chapter 11

Preparing and Writing Reports

Workplace Connection

Many careers rely on various kinds of reports to assist in decision making. Competent office personnel should understand the basics of report writing. They should also be able to use the Internet and the World Wide Web to access information.

CHAPTER OBJECTIVES

When you have completed this chapter, you should be able to:

- Use technology to research a report topic.
- Write an informal or a formal report.
- Keep meeting records.
- Prepare a news release.

Technology and Reports

Types and Purposes of Reports

Before writing a report, you need to determine its purpose and analyze your audience. This will determine the type of report you prepare. The two basic kinds of reports are informative reports and analytical reports.

Informative Report

An **informative report** gives facts and other information on some aspect of an organization's operations. Examples of informative reports include reports on company policies and procedures; sales reports of company's products or services; and reports on patient admissions, clients served, cases processed, bids submitted, customer service requests, and so on. An informative report usually identifies a problem or gives background information but does not make recommendations or persuade. Informative reports are divided into three report types: periodic, progress, and unsolicited.

Periodic Report. A **periodic report** is prepared at regular intervals, for example, weekly, monthly, or quarterly. Any report prepared at specified intervals is considered a periodic report. A quarterly sales report is an example. It is prepared four times per year at the end of each calendar quarter. A calendar quarter is three months, making the end of the first quarter March 31 if a business uses the beginning of the calendar year as its fiscal start.

Progress Report. A **progress report** gives the current status of a project, tells what has been completed since the last progress report, and states when the project will be completed. Progress reports usually are done for projects that require an extended period of time, such as three months or more. They are often done informally in memorandum format but can include details of the progress in separate documents created in project-management software (such as Microsoft Project). Progress reports may also include supporting documents to show the progress of the entire project or specific parts of the project. For example, a progress report describing the progress of a new product release that your company is developing with another company may include e-mail messages from the other company describing its progress on the project.

Unsolicited Report. An **unsolicited report** is, quite simply, one that you make on your own initiative rather than one you are asked to prepare or a periodic report that you are expected to prepare at regular intervals. In business, any idea for increasing efficiency, saving money, increasing productivity, or increasing profits will usually be welcome. It's advisable to put your idea in writing so that you can present it in the most complete, logical, and generally effective manner. Unsolicited reports can be done

KEY POINT

The purpose of your report determines the type of report you prepare.

formally or informally and include specific intended results, proposed new products, or proposed new procedures to accomplish an existing task. If an unsolicited report includes a great deal of detail about a new idea, the report can turn into an analytical report, which is covered below. Unsolicited reports usually also include a request to meet with the intended recipient to discuss any new ideas or products presented in the report.

Analytical Report

An **analytical report** examines a situation or problem, draws conclusions, and makes recommendations, in addition to providing information and data. This type of report may explore the feasibility of taking possible actions by looking at several alternatives, systematically analyzing each alternative, and then making recommendations.

Examples of analytical reports are justification reports, feasibility studies, and proposals. These three types of reports are somewhat similar.

Justification Report. A **justification report** is usually prepared for someone at a higher level of management; it gives the rationale for a recommendation or a decision. Sample subjects would include making a major expenditure for new equipment, expanding facilities, and hiring additional personnel.

If you wanted to update the computer infrastructure company-wide, for example, you would probably be asked for the reason. You would then write a justification report, justifying the cost involved by reporting reasons such as "The system is outdated and causing problems." You would give positive reasons for the update, such as reduced maintenance on the new system and increased speed in performing operations.

Feasibility Study. A **feasibility study** describes the pros and cons of proceeding with a project in addition to giving the costs and a time frame for the project. This type of report would include recommendations on whether to go ahead with the project.

Proposal. A **proposal** is a report that may be prepared for someone inside or outside your company. It is designed to persuade the reader to purchase your products or services, to adopt your idea or plan, or to provide or donate money or services for a worthwhile project. The proposal may offer a solution to a problem and usually gives the cost of the plan. Proposals usually include a plan of action, in which the author proposes the initial step or set of steps to be taken to get the proposed result.

Gathering Information

The value of any report depends on the quality of the material going into it. A term used by computer specialists—*GIGO* (pronounced "guy-go"), standing for "garbage-in, garbage-out"—expresses this idea vividly. With reliable facts behind it, a reliable report can be written; with questionable data, only a questionable report can result.

Information for reports can be obtained through two types of sources—*primary sources* of data and *secondary sources* of data. Your first step should be to see what secondary data already exist to save yourself the time and trouble of gathering data that may already be available. Also, you want to include in your report information that is common knowledge. Primary and secondary sources of information are explained in the pages that follow.

Secondary Sources of Information

A **secondary source** is a document or other material that contains information gathered by someone else. This information is usually published in books and periodicals, or it may be found in company records and reports. **Periodicals** are journals, magazines, pamphlets, newsletters, and so on that are published on a regular basis. Indexes of these periodicals include the *Readers' Guide to Periodical Literature,* the *Business Periodicals Index,* and *The New York Times Index.*

KEY POINT

Obtain information for reports by consulting primary and secondary sources of data.

Today, secondary information is also widely available through electronic databases and World Wide Web sites. In gathering secondary information, you should be familiar with the authoritative references in your field. There are, in addition, many general references that are invaluable to help every writer, some of which are listed here.

Databases.   In library usage, a database is usually an electronic version of a print index. Most of these allow for a computerized search for your topic. A database may include citations or references to (1) where the article appeared originally or (2) the citations as well as the full text of the article in an electronic form. A popular database that libraries use is ABI/Inform.

Almanacs and Yearbooks.   These sources contain concise information on important events that occurred during a given year. Examples include *The World Almanac* and *Book of Facts, Information Please Almanac,* and *Facts on File*. These sources are also available online through databases or in some cases for free on the Web.

Periodicals.   Periodicals that are of general interest to report writers include magazines such as *Time, U.S. News & World Report,* and *BusinessWeek*. Newspapers such as *The Wall Street Journal, The Washington Post,* and *The New York Times* are reliable secondary sources of information. Many professional journals are published in every field, and the applicable ones should also be reviewed frequently by report writers. Popular publications will also have online editions, but readers should realize that online content is often different from and less permanent than the print version. Also, many publications' Web sites will charge for access to articles that can readily be obtained for free from the library.

Naturally, anyone doing research must first learn how to find and use books, periodicals, and databases, as well as the many sources available through the Internet. After you know the topic of your report, make a list of keywords and key phrases that might give you information on your topic. Also make a list of the sources (books, periodicals, magazines, and so on) that you plan to search for additional information on your topic.

A word of caution about secondary data—always check the *date* of publication and the *source*. You don't want to use outdated information, and you want it to be from a credible (reputable and unbiased) source. For example, an article on the benefits of a certain medication for allergies published by a drug company that manufacturers and sells the medicine may present a slanted view. Remember, just because information appears in print or on the Internet doesn't necessarily make it true.

Use the following checklist to help you determine the reliability of a secondary source of information

- Does the source provide current information on the topic?
- Is the source reliable?
- Is the information pertinent to your topic?
- Is the author an authority on the subject?
- Does the author identify his or her opinions?

When the information you need is not available from secondary sources, you have to gather the information and collect the data for your report from primary sources.

Primary Sources of Information

A **primary source** is a source from which information or data are obtained firsthand for your particular need. Primary source data may be obtained through surveys (such as questionnaires), personal interviews, or telephone interviews as well as through observation or experimentation. Eyewitness accounts, given by someone who experienced the event firsthand, are also considered primary sources.

One problem with many primary sources is the accuracy of the information you receive. For example, many people will not bother to complete and return a questionnaire, so you may not get a representative sampling. Other people may not answer the questions truthfully, so your results are not accurate. Eyewitness accounts also can lead to unpredictable or even inaccurate data. Be sure, when possible, to interview multiple eyewitnesses to corroborate the data provided by each of them.

Surveys are done to identify customer likes and dislikes, to identify customer wants and needs, to poll patients on the care they received, to learn the level of customer or client satisfaction, to determine public opinion on a controversial topic or project, and so on. Well-constructed surveys require much time and effort. Even after you think that your survey is as good as it can be, you should conduct a pilot test of the survey. When you conduct a **pilot test** for a survey, you survey a small group to check the quality of your survey. Analyzing the results from this small test group will help you find survey questions that could be misunderstood, incomplete, or confusing. It can also point out problems if you are performing some statistical analyses on the responses.

Surveys can be conducted by several methods. These may include telephone surveys, questionnaires, interviews, and observations.

Telephone Surveys.   Telephone surveys seek responses to your prepared survey by direct vocal contact. To conduct an effective telephone survey, you should have a printed copy of the survey before you; this ensures that you ask the same question of each person you call. Identify yourself and your organization, and state the purpose of the survey at the beginning of each telephone interview. Ask questions that provide data that can be compared or measured. For example, if you are conducting a survey about how good the service was during a recent visit to the hospital, ask each person to rank the service using a scale from 1 to 10, with 1 being the worst ever, and 10 being the best ever. (See **Exhibit 11.1.**)

Exhibit 11.1
Telephone Survey
Thinking Critically. What is the most efficient way for a customer service representative to complete a telephone survey?

Finally, keep the number of questions manageable so as not to bore or anger the person surveyed. Record the responses accurately and thank the person at the end of the survey.

Questionnaires. Questionnaires are printed surveys, which can be delivered personally, by mail, or by e-mail. As with any type of survey, you should determine the types of questions that will yield the most helpful answers and get the data needed. The most effective types of questions to yield measurable data include yes-or-no questions, multiple choice questions, ranking according to preference, and rating in order of importance. For example, a questionnaire on a new product line to be sent to current and potential customers might ask the respondent to rank the new products in the order in which they might be purchased.

Interviews. Interviews are surveys that use the face-to-face method to get the needed responses. To gather information by interviewing, you should first familiarize yourself with the topic and terminology of your subject, then create your survey using this information. After constructing the printed survey, you should identify the people whom you will survey. Schedule an appointment for each interview and give an estimate of how much time you need. Begin the interview by explaining its purpose and, if you plan to use them, asking if you can record the interview using a tape recorder or videotape. Continue the interview by asking your questions in an objective manner, and thank the person for his or her time at the conclusion of the interview. (See **Exhibit 11.2**.)

Always ask at the end of the interview if the interviewee has anything he or she would like to add; there may be relevant information that you did not ask about in your interview. Be sure to take copious notes and ask if the interviewee can be quoted and identified in your report. For example, to gather information about starting a child-care facility at your company, you might interview human resources managers at companies that have child-care facilities and companies that do not have child-care facilities. Your questions could cover topics such as how in-house child-care facilities affect hiring policies, employee absenteeism, turnover rates, and employee morale.

Observations. Observations provide data by having someone physically watch a practice or procedure. The survey in this case would give details on which practice or

Exhibit 11.2
Interview
Thinking Critically. *How is interviewing similar to surveying?*

procedure would be observed and which specific information should be recorded from each observation. This method can help you determine if the procedure and policy could be improved. Use facts and statistics, not opinions, to present your observations. For example, you might record the number of telephone calls received in a doctor's office during the lunch hour. If you observe a significant number of calls during the lunch hour, your observations may help you conclude that the office telephone should be answered during lunch. Your recommendation may be to have a receptionist work at this time to better serve the patients.

Technology

Technology has opened a whole new world of electronic resources to help the researcher and report writer. These sources are available in public and university libraries and can also be accessed from many commercial enterprises. In addition, some large organizations, as well as some medical facilities, have libraries of their own. Individuals can access these sources from their offices or homes through the Internet.

Computerized Library Listings

Today, most libraries have online library catalogs that tell you not only what books are in a library but also what books are in other library systems. These online library catalogs enable researchers in remote locations, as well as those physically located in the library, to have access to the library's list of holdings. Many colleges, universities, and municipal libraries often offer interlibrary loan opportunities, giving researchers access to books and periodicals housed in different locales. Remember, if you require a book or periodical that is not located in your library, it may take days or weeks for the item to arrive so that you can use it. This will add time to your research and delay the completion of your report.

Searching Library Listings.   Online library catalogs can be searched by author, by title, and by subject. You can also search for keywords and get a listing of all the books that may have information about the keywords. When you are learning to use the computerized catalog, ask the librarian for help, or use the help menu on the screen. Reference librarians are specially trained to help you locate information on just about any topic.

The Internet

The **Internet** is an electronic communications network that connects computer networks and organizational computer facilities around the world. The Internet is the fastest-growing electronic source of information. People from all over the world and in all professions, including governments and educational institutions, can exchange and retrieve information through the Internet. Internet tools that can be used to find information include the World Wide Web, online services, Usenet newsgroups, chat services, and listservs. The way to access this information is through the use of Internet software, including Web browsers, e-mail software, and chat tools.

World Wide Web.   The **World Wide Web** (WWW) is a segment of the Internet that contains electronic documents. Information on the Web is in the form of Web pages that contain text, graphics, video, audio, and hypertext to link pages. Almost all companies, government organizations, and educational institutions have their own Web pages.

Internet Service Providers (ISP).   ISPs offer access only to the Internet and the World Wide Web—not any other services.

Online Service Providers (OSP—also Online Services).   **Online services** are self-contained services (sometimes fee-based; sometimes free) that provide their own independent content (extensive resources) to their members. Typical resources are discussion groups, e-mail, online banking, news, and software. Many online services also provide a gateway to the Internet. Two popular online services are American Online (AOL) and Microsoft Network (MSN).

Connecting to the Internet through an OSP is an alternative to connecting through one of the national Internet service providers, such as AT&T or NetZero, or a regional or local Internet service provider (ISP).

Online services make extensive use of content providers. Information services or content providers include Lexis-Nexis and Hoovers Online. These services are highly reliable; businesses and libraries pay fees to access them.

Usenet Newsgroups. Usenet is a worldwide system of thousands of discussion groups. Each Usenet group has a unique name and specializes in a specific type of news. Members send messages for other people to read. Many times these newsgroups are the best source for certain kinds of information—fixing computer bugs, getting a sense of the reliability of products from users, certain kinds of problem solving such as car troubles or locating obscure sources, because of the self-selective nature of the users.

Internet Software. To access resources on the Internet, you must use special Internet software. Software you need includes the following:

- **Web browsers.** A Web **browser** enables you to navigate on the World Wide Web and displays Web pages. Popular browsers include Microsoft Internet Explorer, Mozilla Firefox, and Netscape Navigator.

- **E-mail software.** E-mail software allows you to create, send, receive, and read electronic mail and listserv messages. **Listservs** are automated services that send out electronic messages on a given topic to a list of recipients. An e-mail software program is often bundled with a Web browser.

- **Chat tools.** Chat tools are used to allow real-time communication between two or more users on the Internet. Most chat tools enable you to type text to another person or group of people, send that message to others immediately, and receive responses back from them immediately. Chat tools are bundled with browser software. Instant messaging (IM) software typically is too. They are distinct though. Technically chat establishes a "room" for conversation, whereas IM simply coexists between users. Thus users in a chat room can also directly IM one another.

Searching the Internet for Information for a Report

When you are ready to start your search on the Internet, you must visit special Web sites that provide searching capabilities. These sites are called **search engines.** Some of the popular search engines are Google, Yahoo!, and Ask Jeeves.

You must give some thought to how you will approach your search on the Internet. Develop a plan to make the best use of the search engines. Such a plan might include the steps in the following tips:

1. Identify the topic you want to research.

2. Determine keywords to use for your search. For example, if you are searching for job listings, you might use keywords such as *job listings, employment opportunities,* and *job postings.*

3. Choose a search engine or set of search engines to assist in your search. If necessary, do some research on the search engine and how it works to identify the appropriate Web pages for your search.

4. Be certain that the information is the quality that you need. Not every article on the Internet is research based; it may just be someone's opinion. The contributor controls the quality of the information on the Internet. Thus,

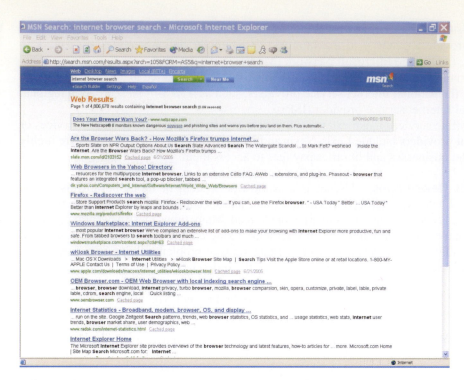

Exhibit 11.3
Internet Browser Search
Thinking Critically. Explain how a browser allows you to search for information. *What browser do you use in your business communications?*

there is some excellent research, and there is some research that is questionable, if not inaccurate.

5. Develop a plan for using the keywords and the search engines to search for the information you need.

6. Begin searching using your first keyword and first choice for a search engine.

7. Examine the information you receive initially and adjust your plan, perhaps using a different search engine as necessary to obtain the information you seek.

8. Repeat the procedure in step 7 for each keyword that you have identified.

The sample screens shown in **Exhibits 11.3** and **11.4** illustrate some steps in a keyword search on the Internet.

Documenting Sources

Once you have identified the sources of information for your report, you need to read and review the articles and take notes.

Working Bibliography. As you consult the various reference works pertinent to the topic of your report, you should make a list of the books, periodicals, reports, and other sources to be used as references in the report. This preliminary list of sources is called the **working bibliography.** If you make each entry of the working bibliography on a separate card (3 × 5 or 4 × 6 inches), the final bibliography of sources actually used will be easy to assemble because you can simply arrange the cards in the appropriate order. You will also find the bibliography cards useful when footnoting material in the report.

KEY POINT

A working bibliography is a preliminary list of sources.

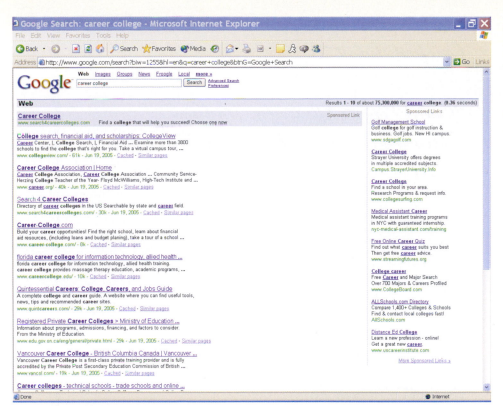

Exhibit 11.4
Internet Browser
Keyword Search
Thinking Critically.
Where are the results
of a keyword search
displayed within the
browser?

Some researchers prefer taking a laptop computer with them to the library and entering the bibliographic information directly, bypassing the 3 × 5-card step. The laptop method is efficient because the researcher can use the word processing program to automatically sequence the bibliography entries each time a new one is entered. If you decide to use a laptop computer, set up your working bibliography the same way as you would on index cards.

Create a document in a word processor, such as Microsoft Word, and list each resource on a separate page or in a table so that you can quickly locate the resource when you get to the point of putting together your report.

A bibliography or source card for a book or reference should contain all the information shown in **Exhibit 11.5.** In addition, it is helpful to include for your own use the library's call number for the reference.

When consulting a magazine, newspaper, or other periodical, prepare a bibliography card like the one illustrated in **Exhibit 11.6.**

Highlighting.   Many times you will have a photocopy of the article or a printout from the computer. (Be sure you have the bibliographic information for the article listed on the article or on your working bibliography matched to the article name and author.) Start by reading the article. As you read, underline or highlight the information you might need. This practice will make note taking easier.

Note Taking.   Taking notes from your sources helps you pick out the information you can use, organize the information, and retain the information. You should use note cards for taking notes because they are sturdy and can be sorted and re-sorted easily. Notes also can be taken on a computer by creating separate documents for each source or for each topic. Then, you can print out the notes and sort them easily.

Exhibit 11.5
Book Bibliography Card
Thinking Critically.
What are the elements listed on this bibliography card?

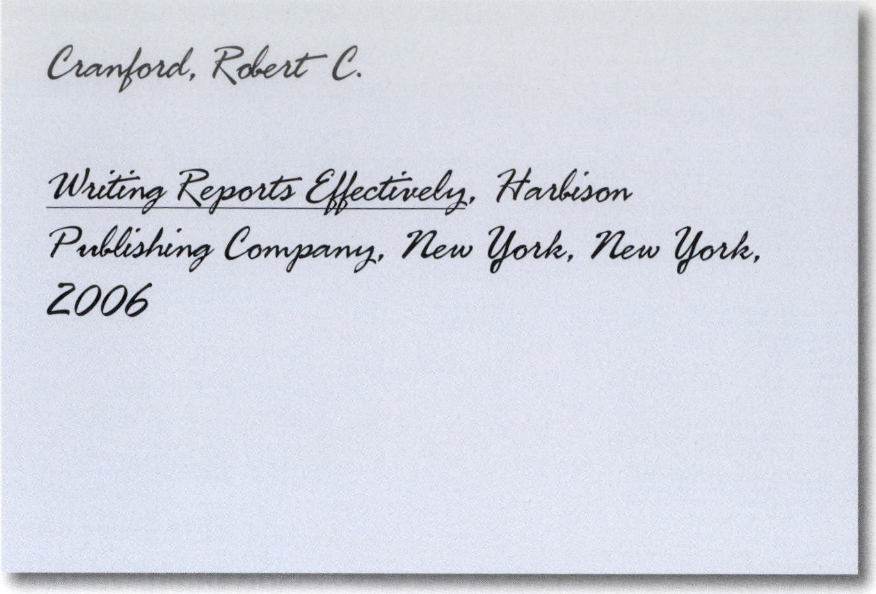

Cranford, Robert C.

Writing Reports Effectively, Harbison
Publishing Company, New York, New York,
2006

Exhibit 11.6
Article Bibliography Card
Thinking Critically.
How do the elements differ on a bibliography card for an article versus a book?

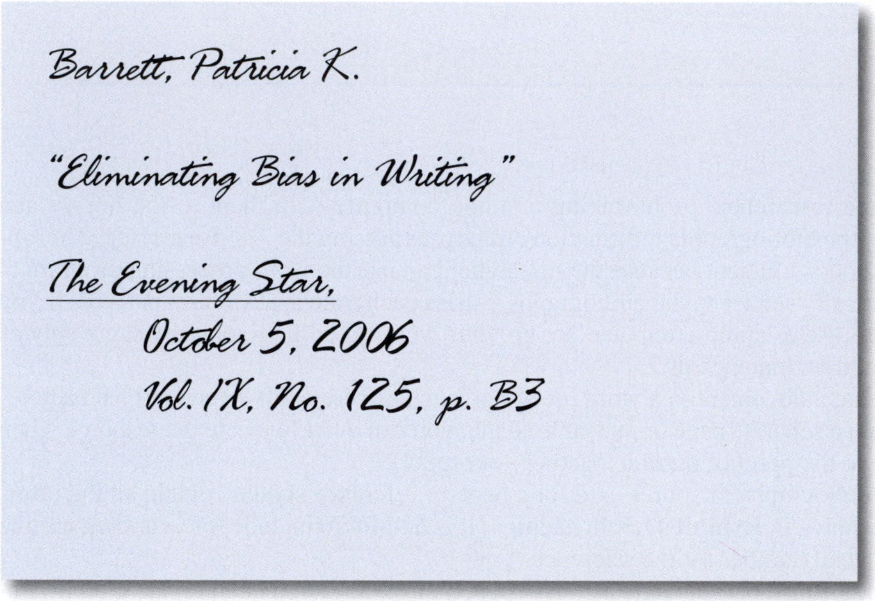

Barrett, Patricia K.

"Eliminating Bias in Writing"

The Evening Star,
        October 5, 2006
        Vol. IX, No. 125, p. B3

Taking detailed notes as you read makes it easier for you to organize and write a report. This practice gives you a great deal of information, which you can use as the basis for your report.

When you take notes from your reading, follow these tips:

- Identify each source, including the name of the writer, the title of the work, resource name (such as the periodical name), the name of the publisher, and the date published.

- Use a new card for each new source or topic. Normally, summary statements or phrases with page references are sufficient for note cards.

- Copy quotations word for word, exactly as they appear in the source. Enclose each quotation in quotation marks, and list the page number from which the quotation was taken.

As you organize your research, include a brief subject reference at the top of each note card; for example, if you are tracing the development of a product, you might identify each card by subject references like "year," "developer," or "site of development."

Plagiarism and Paraphrasing

Careful note taking will help you to keep from plagiarizing material. **Plagiarism** is using someone else's words—exact or paraphrased—or ideas as your own; that is, without giving credit to the original author. **Paraphrasing** is taking someone else's idea and stating it in your own words. When you paraphrase, you should give credit to the original author.

Credit for exact written words (quotes) and paraphrases can be given to the originator by doing the following:

- Mentioning the source in your text.
- Using quotation marks for direct quotes.
- Documenting the source in a footnote or endnote.

Avoid plagiarism by following a simple rule: When taking notes from published sources, use quotation marks around any material that you copy word for word. When writing your report, either quote and acknowledge the source or summarize the material in your own words and acknowledge the source.

Plagiarism is a serious offense and can result in criminal prosecution. It is usually grounds for expulsion at many educational institutions. Consult your school's code of conduct for information on how plagiarism is handled at your institution.

Protecting Your Report

Technology has made keyboarding reports much easier and faster. However, some caution should be exercised to prevent loss of text, especially when working with long documents. Most students know someone who has worked hours on a report only to lose it because of technical difficulties or sudden power outages. Losing an entire document, however, is preventable. Tips that will help you protect your document are on page 432 .

Documentation Formats

Several methods of documenting sources are used in the business world today. Some organizations have even adopted their own format for documentation. Some of the more widely used formats appear in *The Chicago Manual of Style, The Publication Manual of the American Psychological Association,* and *The MLA Style Manual.*

CMS Style. The documentation format preferred in the humanities, *The Chicago Manual of Style,* is well established and has been used for years. This style uses consecutive raised (superscript) numbers to identify quoted or paraphrased ideas throughout the report. Complete information on the source for each number is given either as a footnote at the bottom of the page or on an endnote page, usually titled "Notes," at the end of the report. Note the example:

. . . most recent information.[1]

In addition to your "Notes" page, you will also need, after the body of the report, a **bibliography**—that is, an alphabetical listing by author's last name of all the sources used in your report. If a source has no author, it is alphabetized by the first important word in the title of the work. A hanging indention style (first line of each entry located at the left margin with the second and succeeding lines indented one-half inch) with a blank line between each entry makes it easier to quickly locate a particular reference.

KEY POINT

Paraphrasing is taking someone else's idea and stating it in your own words.

KEY POINT

Ideas taken from someone else or from another source should be cited even if you are not quoting the material word for word. Taking credit for an idea presented by someone else is a form of plagiarism, in the same way that using the words of someone else without enclosing those words in quotation marks is plagiarism.

KEY POINT

Several methods of documenting sources are used in the business world today.

Protecting Your Document

- Save your document frequently—every 5 to 10 minutes.
- Save your document in at least three places—in case a disk, CD, or USB drive becomes defective.
- If you have your own computer, save your document on your hard drive and on two additional external storage media such as disk, CD, or USB drive.
- If you use a classroom computer, save your document on your own storage media. Documents left on a classroom computer are usually not secure.
- Print your document at various intervals. It is much easier to reenter the document from a printout than to have to compose it again and verify all your information and sources.
- Keep your backup storage media in separate locations. The reason is logical. If all your backups are in your backpack and it is lost, your storage media containing your document will probably not be found in time to submit your document by the deadline.
- Keep your storage media in a location that is dry and is not extremely hot or cold.
- Always complete your document and print it at least one day before the deadline to allow for delays caused by technical difficulties, such as printer problems.

APA Style.   The American Psychological Association (APA) style gives reference information immediately following the quote or paraphrased material in the body of your report. APA style is heavily used in the social science and education fields. APA style emphasizes the date of publication because it is important that information be current in these fields. The author's name, the year of publication, and the page numbers are separated by commas and given in parentheses in the text. If the author's name is given as part of the quote or paraphrased material, it does not need to be included again in the parentheses.

> . . . most recent information (Masters, 2005, p. 148).

A **references** section is the same as the bibliography in *The Chicago Manual of Style*. The entries are arranged in alphabetical order by author's last name, and a hanging indention style is used for ease of locating information quickly.

For additional information on APA style, see the most recent edition of the *Publication Manual of the American Psychological Association*.

MLA Style.   The MLA style was developed by the Modern Language Association and is heavily used in the humanities area. MLA style emphasizes the page number to facilitate locating the exact information. It is similar to APA style in many ways. The author's last name and the page number appear in parentheses immediately following the quoted or paraphrased material. One difference is that no comma is used to separate the author's name and the page number.

> . . . most recent information (Masters 148).

The complete list of sources used in an MLA paper is given at the end of the paper. This list is titled "Works Cited" and is similar to the bibliography used in *The Chicago Manual of Style*. The entries are double-spaced and arranged in alphabetical order by the author's last name. A hanging indention style makes it easy to locate a specific source quickly.

For detailed information on MLA style, see the most recent edition of the *MLA Handbook for Writers of Research Papers*.

Documenting Electronic Sources. When you cite material taken from an electronic source, such as an online database or a Web page on the Internet, you need to provide enough information so that someone reading your report can access the source. With electronic sources, this means identifying information such as that described in the following chart:

Citing Electronic Sources	
Source	**Citation Information**
E-mail	Author's name, e-mail address, subject line, date the message was posted
Mailing list	Author's name, e-mail address, subject line, date the message was posted, mailing list address, date the material was accessed
Web site	Author's name, title of the document, last date updated or revised, the address of the Web site, date you accessed the site

For detailed information on citing electronic sources, consult *The Chicago Manual of Style*; the *Publication Manual of the American Psychological Association*; or the *MLA Handbook for Writers of Research Papers*.

Review of Key Terms

1. How is an *informative report* different from an *analytical report*? Provide examples of each type of report. _____
   _____
   _____
   _____

2. Why is a *working bibliography* an important part of a report? What information should be included in a bibliographic entry? _____
   _____
   _____
   _____
   _____

Editing Practice

Proofreading Alert!   Check the following paragraph for errors.

3. The 1st 20 seconds in a job interview our the most important. The first impression at a job intervew is a mayor factor in weather or not your will be hired. You should make eye contact, smile, and give a firm hanshake as soon as you met the interviewer's. _____
   _____

Practical Application

Preparing for a Report

4. Choose a topic of interest, and find three different types of sources of information. Photocopy the pertinent pages; make source cards for each one. Then, take notes on what you read, paraphrasing the information you might use in a report. _____
   _____
   _____

5. Your team will conduct an Internet search on purchasing new computers. Make a list of keywords you might use. Print out several reports, including some whose reliability may be questionable. Highlight important information. Once your team has read the articles and discussed the merits of each computer, write a brief memo to your instructor, proposing which computer would better serve the needs of the company. Consider the computer's capability, performance record, and cost. Turn in all notes, keywords used, and highlighted articles along with your memo. _____
   _____
   _____

Discussion Point

Identifying the Main Idea

6. What is the difference between primary and secondary sources? What are some methods to use for gathering primary data? How can you be sure a secondary source is reliable? _____

_____

_____

_____

_____

_____

7. If you incorporated someone else's ideas into your report, are you required to provide the source of that information? What are the consequences of plagiarizing information in business? How can you avoid plagiarism? _____

_____

_____

Writing Informal Reports

Essential Principles

In the business world, the report is probably the primary method for providing information. Report information is vital in improving the effectiveness of decision making. This information is intended to help executives, supervisors, managers, department heads, and others understand their roles and perform their duties more effectively. Therefore, anyone who wishes to succeed in today's business world must be able to gather information and prepare reports.

A report may be given orally, in writing, or both. Important information in an oral report may be quickly forgotten; whereas, a written report can be referred to again and again. A written report that is also delivered orally will have increased impact.

One way to classify reports is according to the length of the report—informal reports are usually shorter, and formal reports are usually longer. Because formal reports usually require extensive research, documentation, investigation, and analysis, the style of the presentation is usually different from the style used for a short report.

Style of Informal Reports

In Chapter 9, you learned how to use a memo as a means of corresponding with other employees within an organization. The same memo form is used for writing informal reports, hence the name **memo report.**

The memo report begins with the same information contained in the memo format that you learned to use for interoffice correspondence.

MEMO TO:
FROM:
DATE:
SUBJECT:

Whether you use this format exactly as it is or adapt it will depend upon the report style preferred by the company where you work.

File Copies

Whenever you write an informal report, even if you think it is not important, be sure to make a copy for your own files. Anything important enough to be put in *writing* is important enough to be *retained.* You may never need to refer to your file copy, but someone else in the company may need some of the information contained in the report sometime in the future.

Planning and Writing Informal Reports

Many people think that writing involves merely sitting down and dashing off a few words, a simple task anyone can do with little or no effort. Partly as a result of this widespread but false notion, good business writers are scarce and, therefore, very much in demand.

Indeed, first-class writing of any kind involves hard work and results from much thought, careful planning, many drafts with revisions, and excellent training. Before you can write informal reports of the highest quality, you need to study, think about, and apply the following principles.

Be Clear, Complete, Correct, and Concise

As you know, concise writing should also be complete writing. To be concise, you must say everything that needs to be said, but you must say it in the fewest possible words.

You are also well aware that your writing must be clear and complete. You would not write a fuzzy sentence like this:

- Zach Mendoza told Mr. Ruiz about the construction delays at the industrial park, and he said he would have the report to Mr. Ruiz by Monday.

Instead, you would write a clear, complete message, such as this one:

- Zach Mendoza told Mr. Ruiz that he would have the report on the construction delays at the industrial park on Mr. Ruiz's desk on Monday, April 25, 20—.

All reports must be correct in every detail. Perhaps we should use the stronger term *accurate*, because any information important enough to be reported must be more than substantially correct; it must be completely accurate. For example, if you are asked to report the number of free-sample requests that come in on a given day, you had better be sure that you give an exact, not an approximate, count.

Wording

The wording of reports differs from that of letters. A letter is designed to do more than convey a message, for its accompanying purpose is to win new customers or clients for the company and to retain old ones. Therefore, the tone of a letter is warm and friendly. A report, on the other hand, is a straightforward, factual presentation—and it should be worded as such.

As an illustration, read the following opening paragraph of a letter answering a request for information about your company's free tuition program for employees.

> In response to your May 30 request, we are pleased to tell you that we do provide free tuition for employees taking work-related courses in local schools under the following circumstances: [At this point, you would itemize and explain the circumstances under which your company pays the tuition for its employees.]

Now, note how the wording changes when the same information is given in a report.

> Employees taking work-related courses in local schools will be reimbursed for tuition when the following requirements have been met:
>
> 1. The course has been approved in advance by the employee's supervisor.
> 2. The employee earns a grade of B or better.
> 3. The employee has been with the company for one year or more.

KEY POINT

Preparing reports requires high-quality writing. Reports should be clear, complete, correct, and concise.

Formats of Written Reports

How brief or how detailed should your informal report be? Should you give the requested information in a single paragraph? Should you present the information in outline form? Should you tabulate the information? Should you show the information in a graph?

Because you are preparing the report, you are the one who must answer these questions. Only you are close enough to the situation to know why the report was requested, to project the probable uses of the information, and so on. To make a wise decision about the form your report should take, though, you must be familiar with the different types of presentations and their uses.

Paragraph Form

The **paragraph form** is often used for the presentation of simple facts. For example, if your supervisor has requested that you report how many hours of overtime were paid the previous month—and you are certain that the only statistic of interest is the total number of hours—you might write the following in a memo-style report:

> In the month of February 20—, the total number of hours of overtime in the Printing Department was 25 hours.

Or, if you want to give a little extra information, you might add the following to the above statement:

> There are 50 employees in the department, and 10 employees (20 percent) accounted for the 25 hours of overtime.

Outline Form

If, however, you know that your supervisor has a personal interest in the staff, you might correctly believe that you should list the names of the people who worked overtime. You could present all the information necessary in outline form. The **outline form** uses the format of an outline to list information.

> Information regarding overtime in the Accounting Department during March 20— is as follows:
>
> 1. Total employees in department: 50
> 2. Total hours of overtime: 25
> 3. Employees working overtime: 10 (20 percent)
>
> > William Carter, 3 hours
> > Reba Evans, 2 hours
> > Estévan Gomez, 3 hours
> > Elyse Levy, 3 hours
> > Nancy Murphy, 3 hours
> > Habib Odish, 4 hours
> > Sabeeha Sedik, 3 hours
> > Chen Sui-Ling, 2 hours
> > Ping Yu, 1 hour

Table Form

In some cases, a table is the most effective way to present information. The **table form** uses a systematic arrangement of data, usually in rows and columns for ready reference. The advantage of a tabulated presentation is that the reader can easily see the total situation at a glance without wading through a great many words. The decision to tabulate should be influenced by the amount and the kind of information to be included as well as by the uses to which the information is likely to be put. In table form, the example overtime report would look like this:

ACCOUNTING DEPARTMENT OVERTIME
Month of March 20—

Employee	Hours	Reason
Carter, William	3	To complete January billing
Evans, Reba	2	To prepare expense statement
Gomez, Estévan	3	To prepare cost analysis
Levy, Elyse	3	To work on computer program
Murphy, Nancy	3	To update all client information
Odish, Habib	4	To analyze travel expenses
Sedik, Sabeeha	3	To design a company brochure
Sui-Ling, Chen	2	To prepare for business trip
Yu, Ping	1	To complete checking cost estimates

Total employees: 50
Overtime hours: 25
Total employees working overtime: 10
Percentage of employees working overtime: 20

Most office suites providing word processing software also have a table feature that makes tables easier to set up. This table feature will make the information neat and more readable.

Assessment   Section 11.2

Review of Key Terms

1. How is a *memo report* similar to a standard memo? How is it different?

   _____

   _____

   _____

2. What are the different formats of a written report? _____

   _____

Editing Practice

Spelling Alert!   Find any spelling or homonym errors in the following sentences.

3. Our magazine sales acceded 1.5 million copies in the month of December. _____

   _____

4. We expect sales of our February addition to reach 1.6 million copies.

   _____

5. The managing editor was formally a schoolteacher. _____

6. Several sports editors took a coarse in interviewing. _____

   _____

Practical Application

Writing Informal Reports

7. Select two or three stocks or bonds that are listed in your local newspaper's stock market report. From the information that is provided in the newspaper, write an informal report about the status of these two securities during the past five days. Address the report to your instructor. _____

8. As a team prepare a table form report, similar to the one on page 439. The table will be a report of students in your class. Use the following information in your table: Student, Number of College Hours Completed, Number of College Hours This Semester, Proposed Major. Provide figures for total students and working students. _____

Discussion Point

Thinking Critically

9. What are the steps to writing a quality report? _____

   _____

   _____

   _____

10. When would a writer use the paragraph form in an informal report? When would a writer use an outline or a table in an informal report?

    _____

    _____

    _____

    _____

Writing Formal Reports

Essential Principles

How do formal reports differ from the memorandum reports that you learned to write in the previous section? **Formal business reports,** in addition to being longer than informal memorandum reports, are usually concerned with more complex problems or questions necessitating more investigation, analysis, research, and documentation. Some typical formal report subjects might be an analysis of the methods of marketing a company's products, a study to determine which type of computer accounting and billing system to install, or an experiment to determine how to improve the quality control of a product.

Writing a formal business report may require weeks or even months of extensive research and reading related to the report topic. The completed report could contain anywhere from several pages to more than a hundred pages. Regardless of its length, however, a formal report must be accurately documented and well written, because often a company decides whether to spend many thousands of dollars based on the report.

Not everyone can write an effective formal report. Even though an executive, an engineer, or a technician may conduct the research that is the basis for the report, often an administrative assistant will be closely involved in the report preparation.

Preparing to Write Formal Reports

Not all reports look alike. There are some variations in the style and form used in formal reports. These variations are usually determined by the nature of the subject being investigated. For example, a technical report that specifies the requirements for manufacturing computer components may be organized in outline form with very little text. Similarly, the reports of chemists, engineers, and other scientists are likely to include many tables, charts, and graphs, with a relatively small amount of narrative interpretation. On the other hand, many business reports are mainly narrative, possibly with some tabular material. Despite this variation in the style and form, most formal reports include these main sections:

> Introduction
>
> Summary (often called an Executive Summary in business reports)
>
> Body of the report
>
> Conclusions and recommendations
>
> Supplementary material

Before beginning to write a formal report, the writer-investigator must first determine the purpose and the scope of the report. To make this determination, the investigator must gather reliable facts; assemble and analyze those facts; draw conclusions

SECTION OBJECTIVES

When you have finished Section 11.3, you will be able to:

- List and describe the main sections of a formal report.
- Explain how to plan and write a formal report.
- Explain how to write progress reports.
- Describe the mechanics of report writing.

WHY IT'S IMPORTANT

Writing effective formal reports takes preparation. Some reports take weeks or months of research. Learning to prepare a variety of reports will put you ahead of the game in your career.

KEY TERMS

- formal business reports
- purpose
- scope
- procedures
- summary
- body of the report
- conclusions
- recommendations
- supplementary material
- appendix
- bibliography
- letter or memo of transmittal

KEY POINT

Formal reports often cover more complex problems and questions that frequently require extensive study or investigation.

from the factual analysis; and, finally, make recommendations that are reasonable in view of company needs.

Defining Purpose and Scope

The **purpose** of the report is the reason it is being written. Why is the report being written? The answer to this question should appear in the introduction of the report. For example, in a study to determine whether a company should buy laptop computers for each sales representative to use in submitting orders from the field, communicating with the home office, and maintaining current inventory figures and prices, the purpose of the report might be stated as follows:

1. To determine the benefits of providing laptop computers to sales representatives
2. To determine the cost of providing laptop computers to sales representatives
3. To determine if the benefits will justify the costs

The **scope** of a report determines the extensiveness of the research; that is, the scope specifies boundaries that keep the research within reason. A report writer must avoid selecting a topic that is too large in scope to be handled effectively. The experienced report writer, therefore, clearly defines the scope of the problem and sets reasonable boundaries. For example, think how difficult it would be to do research for a report entitled "Computer Uses by Office Personnel." This topic is much too broad in scope to be treated in one report, if it could be treated at all. The topic needs to be limited to a more specific group. A revised title that would be more practical might read "Computer Uses by Accountants at Cassidy Sales and Service, Inc."

Organizing the Report

After all the material related to the topic has been collected and studied, the writer can begin to organize the report. At this time, the note cards should be revised, sorted by topic, and tentatively organized into a logical sequence for the report.

Outline

Using organized note cards as a guide, the writer creates an outline to serve as the structure, or framework, of the report. The outline should be kept as simple as possible. While determining the outline, the writer should keep in mind the kinds of topic headings the report requires. If outline entries are carefully thought out, many of them can be used as topic headings in the final report.

KEY POINT

Using a consistent style for headings helps the reader better understand the organization and content of a report.

Headings

Most books, articles, and business reports use headings to indicate the organization of the material. Headings of equivalent weight should be formatted alike. For example, the main divisions of an article, a report, or a chapter in a book may be centered, and the subdivisions of each main heading may be typed as paragraph headings. When there are more than two divisions, however, the following arrangement of headings (excluding the report title) should be used:

CENTERED FIRST-ORDER HEADING

Side Second-Order Heading [on a line by itself]

Run-In Third-Order Heading. Text follows on the same line . . .

If the report writer is consistent in the use of headings, the reader will better understand the content because the organization will be easy to follow. Consistency should be observed in the wording as well as in the style of the headings. In general, topic form is preferred to sentence form. For example, "How to Write Reports" is preferable to "This Is How to Write Reports."

Writing the Report

There are considerable differences between the informal writing style of business letters and memorandums and the writing style commonly found in formal reports.

Writing Style

Long business reports are important documents upon which management bases many of its high-level decisions. Consequently, such reports tend to be written in a *serious, formal style,* usually in the *third person.* The *impersonal style* helps the writer avoid interjecting a personal tone that might weaken a report by making it seem merely a statement of one person's opinions and beliefs. The more the writer can deemphasize the *I* and cite facts to back the evaluation, the more objective and more persuasive the report will be.

In the following example, the writer carefully avoids any expressions that may imply that the evaluations are based on personal opinions instead of sound reasons and facts.

> The evidence revealed by this survey indicates that the modified-block letter style takes 10 percent more typing time than the block style.
>
> Use of the block letter style would be appropriate for Action Team News, Inc., because the style has the modern look of simplicity and is also faster and easier to type.
>
> Three of the five departments studied use standard punctuation; however, adoption of open punctuation would have the following advantages: (Explanation of these advantages would follow.)

The same impersonal writing style illustrated above should characterize every section of the report. Remember: Making it possible for the reader to reason from the facts presented is an important factor in the success of any business report.

Title Page

The title page usually includes the complete title of the report, the name and title of the author, the name and title of the person for whom the report is prepared, and the date the report is submitted. These items should be attractively arranged on the page. A typical title page is shown in **Exhibit 11.7.**

Table of Contents

This section is prepared after the report has been completed. It should start at the top of a new page and list in sequence each separate part of the report. The main part of the report (the body) should list the side headings used and possible paragraph headings. The paragraph headings would be indented to indicate that they are a lower level. Use dot leaders to align the elements of the report with the page number they start on, as illustrated in **Exhibit 11.8.**

Introduction

The introduction section tells the reader why the report was written, what the scope of the report is, and how the data were gathered.

Suppose that Lynn Vernon, president of Southern Regional University, has assigned Douglas Ling, the director of administrative services, to investigate the feasibility of establishing an international business center as a way to improve the university's service to the corporate business world. In the introduction to such a report, Mr. Ling would include the purpose and scope of the report, as well as a description of the procedures followed to collect and analyze the data presented in the report.

Statement of Purpose.   First, the writer should state the problem that the report addresses—the need to improve the university's service to the corporate business

Edition/Addition

The fourth addition of the book will be published this year.

(*Edition* is the correct word, not *addition.*)

Not Acceptable

She wood not accept our sincere apology.

(*Would* is the correct word, not *wood.*)

Exhibit 11.7
Title Page of a Report
Thinking Critically.
What are the elements listed on this title page of a report?

THE FEASIBILITY OF ESTABLISHING
AN INTERNATIONAL BUSINESS CENTER
AT
SOUTHERN REGIONAL UNIVERSITY

Prepared by

Douglas Ling
Director of Administrative Services

Submitted to

Lynn Vernon
President

August 25, 20—

world. Next, the writer should list the objectives of the report as in the following example:

> This report was prepared at the request of Lynn Vernon, president of Southern Regional University. The report addresses the need to improve the service to the corporate business world. The purposes of the report are:
>
> 1. To determine the need for an international business center
> 2. To determine the functions of an international business center
> 3. To determine the resources involved in the initial start-up of the center
> 4. To determine the proposed budget of the center
> 5. To determine a potential list of corporations that would benefit from the services provided

Scope or Limitations. A brief statement of the investigation's scope may be included in the introduction, including limitations.

> This investigation is limited to the corporate community within a 50-mile radius of the Southern Regional University campus in Atlanta, Georgia.

Exhibit 11.8
Table of Contents Page of a Report
Thinking Critically.
Name the elements on this table of contents. *What are the dot leaders used for?*

CONTENTS

Procedures.   The introductory section of the report should describe the research procedures. **Procedures** are the methods that were used to collect and analyze the data. Here is an example:

> Information for this report was collected through telephone interviews with corporate CEOs of companies within a 50-mile radius of Atlanta, Georgia. The interview questions are in Appendix B of this report.
> A survey was mailed to each Chamber of Commerce located within the 50-mile radius of Atlanta, Georgia. The survey instrument appears in the report as Appendix C.
> The consulting firm of Friedman, Stedham, and Kline prepared a budget that includes start-up costs.

Summary

The **summary,** often called an *executive summary* in business reports, is a brief review of the report. It is placed early in the report, usually following the introduction. The summary may range from one paragraph to several pages, depending on the amount of material covered. The following example is the opening paragraph of the summary of the study to determine the feasibility of establishing an international business center as a way to improve the university's service to the corporate business world.

KEY POINT

A summary contains the most significant information in capsule form, which helps the reader who cannot take time to read the entire report.

This study recommends that an international business center be established at the Atlanta, Georgia, campus of Southern Regional University and demonstrates that such a center would serve the corporate community within a 50-mile radius of the campus. The specific data gathered during this investigation resulted in the following conclusions that led to the above recommendation:

1. A distinctive need for an international business center exists in the geographic area studied.

2. Three major functions of an international business center were determined.

3. The major resources involved in the initial start-up of the center were identified.

4. A proposed budget for the center has been projected for a five-year time period.

5. A potential list of corporations that would benefit from the services provided has been identified.

Body of the Report

The **body of the report** is the actual text of the report. In this section, the writer tells what research was done, how it was done, and what the writer found. For example, in the report on the international business center at Southern Regional University, the body of the report would include the following:

- An analysis of responses to the telephone interviews with corporate officers

- The results of the surveys mailed to each Chamber of Commerce

- A list of the major resources involved in the start-up of the center

- A justification for the five-year proposed budget

- A discussion of the categories of businesses that would benefit from the services provided

Writing the body of the report should present few difficulties if the writer follows a carefully prepared outline and has detailed notes. The writer should stick to accurate, verifiable facts and present them in a clear, concise manner. The suggestions given in Chapter 8 for forceful, clear writing apply also to writing reports.

Conclusions and Recommendations

This section can easily be the most important one in any report, for it is here that the real results of the report appear. The writer's **conclusions** tell the busy executive, on the basis of the most reliable data available, "Here is what the report tells us."

Personal observations should be kept to a minimum—conclusions should be drawn only from the facts. In light of the conclusions and from experience with the company, the writer can make **recommendations.** As a guide to making worthwhile recommendations, the writer should refer to the listed purposes of the report. As a rule, there should be at least one recommendation for each stated purpose.

By referring to the purposes stated in the introduction of the report on the feasibility of a telecommunications center at Southern Regional University, the writer might include the following conclusions and recommendations:

From an analysis of the data gathered in this study, the following conclusions are drawn:

1. An international business center would be an asset to the specified business community.

2. The major function would be to facilitate business transactions between the specified business community and international markets.

Going Global

International Time Differences

Be knowledgeable about the differences between time zones when making an international phone call. Make sure that both parties are comfortable with the time when scheduling a phone conference. For example, if it is 7 a.m. in New York City, in Tokyo it is 9 p.m. the same day.

3. The resources involved in the initial start-up include office space with utilities, computer equipment with Internet access, typical office expenses, and a three-person staff.

4. The proposed budget is accurate and comprehensive.

5. Corporate personnel in the identified geographic area are eager to use the international business center.

With these conclusions in mind, the following actions are recommended:

1. Southern Regional University to establish an international business center to be operational by January 1, which will require approval of the university's Board of Trustees.

2. Staff members to be employed as soon as feasible to begin establishing contacts with the corporations and contacts in the international markets.

3. Expenditure approvals to be initiated to acquire and equip an office for the international business center.

4. Adopt the proposed budget and establish financial liaisons and the necessary bank accounts.

5. Establish a board of directors for the international business center with representatives from the corporate community.

Supplementary Material

Supplementary material, which is given *after* the conclusions and recommendations, provides substantiating data for the report. One or all of the features discussed below may be included.

Illustrations. A formal report can often be enhanced by the use of *graphics* or *illustrations.* Consider using graphics when any or all of the following situations occur:

1. The information—ideas, facts, or figures—being presented is complex and illustrations will help simplify it.

2. Visuals can reinforce the logic of your conclusions and recommendations.

3. You are comparing or contrasting two sets of data, or you are analyzing trends.

4. Statements need to be documented, and tables and other displays will provide the necessary information.

Tables can be prepared in spreadsheet software programs (such as Excel) that can convert the data to a visual representation such as a line, bar, or pie chart.

What kinds of graphic or visual displays should be included? It depends on the information you are presenting and your purpose in presenting this information. The possibilities include:

- **Tables** to provide a visible comparison of two or more sets of data and ready access to information.

- **Bar graphs** to depict relationships between fixed groups of data or to compare or contrast two sets of data.

- **Line graphs** to illustrate trends or show how sets of data have changed over a period of time.

- **Pie charts** to show the relationships between parts and a whole.

- **Diagrams, flowcharts, organizational charts** to simplify complex relationships or operations.

- **Photographs** to document information or statements.

Employability Skills

Allocating Human Resources

Creating a lengthy and formal report entails many hours. Before finalizing any document, it's important to ask for valuable input from colleagues and teammates. Whether researching, writing, editing, and proofreading, allocating the jobs to the appropriate people is a good idea.

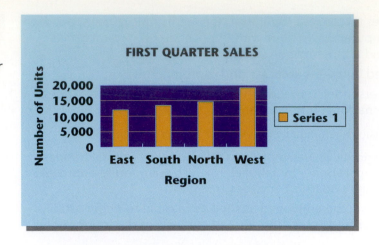

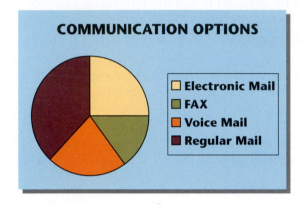

Refer to **Exhibits 11.9** and **11.10** for some examples of illustrations used to present data in a report.

How graphic displays are prepared varies from company to company. Using color in the graphic displays is usually acceptable in reports prepared for industry. Unless you are a business writer with artistic ability, you may wish to have visuals prepared by your corporate art department or by an independent artist or agency. Another alternative is to use a graphics software program to prepare visuals. Several excellent programs that produce sophisticated, professional-looking graphic displays are available, and they are easy to learn. These graphic displays may be used as visual aids if the report is presented orally to the management team.

Appendix. The **appendix** is a report section that consists mainly of supporting information to back up the material in the body of the report. Long tables, charts, photographs, questionnaires, letters, and drawings are usually placed in this section. By including such material at the end of the report, you keep the body of the report free of the kind of detail that makes reading difficult.

Bibliography. The **bibliography** section is an *alphabetical* listing of all the references used in the report. Bibliographic entries are listed in alphabetic order by author. Forms for book and periodical entries are shown in the following examples:

Books
Brown, Frieda F., *International Markets,* Bently Publishing Company, New York, 20—.
Lane, S. C., *Exporting for Profit,* Harrison Book Company, New York, 20—.

Editing Practice

Call an Editor! Edit or rewrite the following sentences to improve clarity and conciseness.

3. Ms. Andrews is the new administrative assistant, and she is very proficient in computer operations. _____

4. Spend an afternoon at the job fair, and there you can learn about job opportunities for recent college graduates. _____

5. Not having been able to obtain any information about loans, and not knowing the procedures for making such loans, the new manager decided we must deal on a cash basis. _____

6. I liked the graphics in your report. They were readable. They contained accurate and complete information. _____

Practical Application

Analyzing Information

7. The appearance of a formal report must be impeccable. Write a summary for your instructor in which you address issues in appearance, mechanics, and the use of graphics. _____

8. Have each member in your team interview someone who is in business or works for a state or government agency. Ask what kinds of reports they read or write. Ask for a copy, if possible, and bring it to class. Compare the formats of the samples your team has obtained with the format presented in this section. Prepare a short oral report to give to the class.

_____

_____

_____

Discussion Point

Thinking Critically

9. What kind of writing tone and style is appropriate for a formal report?

_____

_____

10. Discuss the content and function of each of the following parts of a report: Introduction, Summary, Body of the Report, and Conclusions and Recommendations. _____

SECTION OBJECTIVE

When you have finished Section 11.4, you will be able to:

- Record and prepare for distribution a set of minutes from a meeting.

WHY IT'S IMPORTANT

Meetings are an important part of life as a business communicator. Recording notes or minutes from business meetings is also important.

KEY TERMS

- minutes
- agenda
- quorum
- verbatim

KEY POINT

Minutes are the written record of a meeting.

Keeping Meeting Records

Essential Principles

Every organization, business or social, has meetings and must keep a record of what happens at these meetings. These records of the proceedings of meetings, called **minutes,** are another type of report used in business. The minutes serve as a permanent record of the decisions reached and the actions that are to be taken. The minutes can also be used to inform those who were not at the meeting of what took place. At one time or another, most business employees serve as recorder in a group or committee and are responsible for keeping an accurate set of minutes.

Recording the Minutes

The minutes of a meeting are the record of the proceedings of that specific meeting. Accurately recording the business conducted at a meeting is important, because the minutes usually serve as the only historical record of a meeting. Minutes are taken, prepared in an acceptable format, and distributed to meeting participants and others who have reason to see them.

There is probably no one best way to record what happens at a meeting. If an agenda of the meeting has been prepared beforehand, the *recorder* (the person taking the minutes) should receive a copy. As you will learn in Chapter 14, an **agenda** is a brief chronological list of the business to be transacted at the meeting and acts as a guide to the person presiding at the meeting. The agenda also helps the recorder check that all scheduled items are accounted for in the minutes. Any recorder preparing to record the proceedings of a meeting should find the following general guidelines helpful:

1. List the name of the group, committee, or team and whether the meeting is a regular or special one.

2. Record the day, date, time, and place of the meeting.

3. With a small group, list the persons attending and those absent. One way to do this is to list all the group members and place an asterisk beside group members in attendance. (Be sure to explain the asterisk as follows: *Denotes members present.) In a large group, however, either state the number of people present, as in "Forty-five members were present," or list the names of the absentees only. Some minutes simply note that a quorum was present. A **quorum** is the number of group members required by the group's bylaws (or other document) to conduct business.

4. In the opening section of the minutes, mention that the minutes for the previous meeting were read and approved, amended, approved as printed, or not approved.

Exhibit 11.11
Thinking Critically. *What purpose does the recording of minutes serve in a meeting?*

5. Record the important points in the discussion of each item on the agenda. Presenting supporting facts helps those who were present recall the discussion and informs those who were not present. Reports or papers read during the meeting are often attached to the final minutes.

6. Record **verbatim** (exact quotation) all resolutions and motions, as well as the names of the people who introduced and seconded the motions. If the assistant was unable to record the information, request that the motion be repeated or even put in writing so that the exact motion is recorded.

7. Keyboard, edit, and prepare the minutes in final form. Sometimes the assistant may want to get another person's approval before issuing the minutes in final form.

8. File one copy of the minutes in the folder, notebook, or binder used for this purpose. Usually minutes are duplicated and sent to each member of the group and to designated officers who would be interested in the business of the meeting.

Format of Minutes

Various formats are used for meeting minutes. Regardless of the format used, all essential information should appear in a neat, well-arranged form. Some organizations prefer to emphasize the main points on the agenda by using a standardized format with headings.

The minutes shown in **Exhibit 11.12** illustrate an acceptable format. Notice the standard pattern and the topical headings that are used for all meetings of this group and the way in which the motions and the discussion are summarized.

Digital Data

Make a Note of It

When keeping records of meetings or researching information, it's important to take good notes. Many software programs have note-taking or outline features that allow you to arrange and rearrange notes on the page. Some programs even allow you to expand notes into narrative copy without retyping the information from the notes.

Employability Skills

Self-Management

A part of self-management is the ability to be organized and keep your goals and priorities intact. Be responsible in keeping records of your work to help monitor progress and growth in your career.

**KINGSTON HOMEOWNERS ASSOCIATION
MINUTES OF MEETING OF APRIL 1, 20—**

Time, Place, Attendance	The quarterly meeting of the Kingston Homeowners Association was held in the Recreation Room at 7:30 p.m. The president, Betty Talbert, presided and noted that a quorum was present.
Minutes	The minutes of the last meeting on January 3, 20—, were read and approved.
Treasurer's Report	The treasurer distributed a printed report reporting receipts of $10,500 and disbursements of $5,200, leaving a cumulative balance of $24,300 as of March 15. Anthony Moreno moved the acceptance of the report. Morgan Meadows seconded the motion. The motion carried.
Nominating Committee Report	Chairperson William Ferris presented the report of the nominating committee. The nominees for the year beginning July 1 are:

        President: Mitchell Perry
        Vice President: Hannah Cortez
        Secretary: Lisa Anthony
        Treasurer: Luis Prado

Rosa Sanchez moved that nominations be closed and that a unanimous ballot be cast for the slate of officers presented by the committee. Yamen Abdulah seconded the motion. The motion carried.

Unfinished Business	Plans for the Annual Neighborhood Street Party to be held July 4 were finalized. Entertainment contracts were extended to Tony's Fireworks, Inc., The Beach Bums Band, and Party Rides, Inc. The president will report to the group by e-mail when these contracts are signed and returned.
New Business	The president reported that the Board of Directors is considering a policy change concerning pool and tennis court hours. A survey was distributed and collected at the meeting to determine the preferred hours. The results of the survey will be e-mailed to the association members. The Board will recommend the hours of operation based on the survey results.
Adjournment	The meeting adjourned at 8:45 p.m.

Respectfully submitted,

Ron Paige

Ron Paige, Secretary

Exhibit 11.12
Minutes of a Meeting
Thinking Critically. *What kind of information is contained within the column headings?*

Assessment   Section 11.4

Review of Key Terms

1. Why are *minutes* an important part of business communication? _____
    _____
    _____
    _____

2. What is the purpose of an *agenda*? _____

_____

_____

_____

Editing Practice

Spelling Alert!   Correct any spelling errors in the following paragraph.

3. Harrison, who dislikes meetings, thought the comittee meeting was a waist of time. Everyone else, of corse, disagreed. Alice Croft chairred the meeting and encouraged the members to particpat fully. Clark recorded the minuets—a task that he enjoys and takes seriusly. Accept for Harrison, we all left the meeting convinced that a productive meeting had been adjorned. _____

_____

_____

_____

_____

_____

Practical Application

Evaluating Concepts

4. Attend a meeting, such as a homeowners association meeting, a club meeting, or a public university meeting. Take minutes of the first half-hour of the meeting. Remember to include the name of the organization, the date, and place held. You may want to follow the model on page 454. _____

5. With your team, research how meetings are conducted in your local government. Find out what rules and guidelines apply to a meeting. Is there a quorum requirement? How are the minutes taken? Is the meeting recorded? Did you receive an agenda beforehand? Write a brief summary for your instructor about your experience. _____

Discussion Point

Thinking Critically

6. Discuss how listening skills and note-taking skills are important for the person recording minutes at a meeting. _____

_____

_____

_____

7. If you were asked to record minutes at a meeting, what steps would you take to prepare yourself? _____

_____

What a Waste!

Do not waist time in doing silly things when you have a deadline.

(*Waste* is the correct word, not *waist*.)

Preparing News Releases

The Function of the News Release

An important means of getting the planned publicity of business into the hands of the public is the **news release.** Whenever a business plans an announcement or an event that it considers newsworthy or capable of enhancing its public image, its public relations personnel prepare and submit a news release to various news outlets for publication or broadcasting. Such a news announcement may publicize the introduction of a new line or new product, or it may concern the awarding of some honor to a member of the organization. Any item that will interest the public and create goodwill for the organization is an appropriate subject for a news release.

Any news story sent by a company must be approved for release. In large companies, the director of public relations would have this responsibility. In small companies, individual department heads might handle their own news and distribute it in keeping with company policy, or releases might be issued from the office of the president or of one particular executive.

To be printed or broadcast and thereby serve its purpose, the release must be *newsworthy*; that is, the contents of the release must be of interest to the public. Naturally, the writing style of the news release, as well as the form in which it appears, will have a strong effect on the news editor, who decides whether the story is worth printing or broadcasting.

The Format of the News Release

With hundreds of releases coming to their desks each week, news editors will select for publication or broadcast the items that require the least amount of rewriting, everything else being equal. Therefore, the news release must give complete, accurate information in a news style of writing that presents the facts in a clear and interesting way.

Many organizations use a special form for issuing news releases. These forms are arranged so that editors can get to the heart of the story without wasting time. Like a letterhead, a news release form usually contains the name and address of the company or organization and the name, address, and telephone number of the person responsible for issuing the release to the public as shown in **Exhibit 11.13.**

1367 Baxter Avenue
Knoxville, Tennessee 37916
865-555-3405

NEWS RELEASE
Gloria Linquist
Director of Public Relations

Loren Williams, Manager
Knoxville Daily Star
865-555-7500

For Immediate Release
June 1, 20—

**JOHN J. MAXWELL NAMED MANAGER
OF RIVER DEVELOPMENT CORPORATION**

Knoxville, June 1, 20—. John J. Maxwell has been named manager
of River Development Corporation by its president, Sybil Cannon.

Mr. Maxwell succeeds David Gomez, who retired from River
Development on May 15 after serving for 30 years.

The new manager joined River Development Corporation over two
years ago as assistant manager in the Chattanooga office. Before that, he
was in the management training program at Foxworthy Construction
Company, also in Chattanooga.

Mr. Maxwell is a graduate of the University of Tennessee and a
member of the Rotary Club. He enjoys mountain hiking and volunteer-
ing at the hospital and children's homes.

###

Exhibit 11.13
News Release
Thinking Critically. *What kind of information is contained within a news
release?*

The following information lists some standards for preparing news releases:

1. Double-space the news release and leave room in the margins for editing by
the news editor.

2. Include a tentative headline in all-capital letters to identify the story. An editor may change this title to fit the space requirements and style of the publication or broadcast.

3. Indicate the time when a story may be published. In the example in
Exhibit 11.13, note the prominence of the phrase *For Immediate Release.*
A release may be sent to the media before an event occurs so that news will
reach the public at almost the same time the event takes place. For example,

KEY POINT

A news release does not
have a single prescribed
format. However, follow-
ing certain rules in preparing a news release will
provide greater assurance
that the story will be
published.

oops!

Discussion Leader

My husband charred the
meeting and encouraged
everyone to participate
in the discussion.

(*Chaired* is the correct
word, not *charred.*)

**Employability
Skills**

Integrity

When preparing company
news releases, it's crucial
to double-check the facts
and events with your
communications depart-
ment before releasing it
to the public. Errors or
mistakes diminish the
integrity of your work as
well as harm the image of
the company.

if a company plans to announce a million-dollar gift to a local hospital at a banquet on Saturday, April 20, the release might read *For release after 6 p.m., Saturday, April 20.*

4. In a long release, insert subheads between parts of the release to guide the editor who wants to scan the story.

5. If there is more than one page to the release, type the word *MORE* in parentheses at the end of each page but the last one. At the end of the last page, type one of these symbols -XXX-, ###, o0o, or type *END* to indicate the end of the release.

Writing the News Release

However good the form of a written communication, the subject and the words determine whether the release will be read and used. In writing a news release—just as in writing letters, memorandums, and reports—certain guides will help the writer develop an effective writing style and will improve the chances of getting the release printed. Especially important is the arrangement of paragraphs in the news release.

The opening paragraph of a news release should summarize the entire story and present the most newsworthy information first. In this opening section, the writer should give the *who, what, where, when, why,* and *how* of the news story in such a form that this paragraph can stand by itself, as in the following example.

> Ms. Linda Starr has been named international marketing director of Miller Aviation, Inc., by its president, Natalie Patrilla.

Each succeeding paragraph should supply background facts in the order of decreasing importance. In this way, editors who need to shorten the release because of space or time limitations can easily cut the story from the bottom up. For example, notice that the first two paragraphs in the news release in **Exhibit 11.13** make a complete news story by themselves. The remainder of the copy provides additional details. A common practice is to include quotations from an official or another important person commenting on the news in the release.

Assessment   Section 11.5

Review of Key Terms

1. What is the purpose of a *news release?* _____
   _____

Editing Practice

Vocabulary Alert! Replace any words with negative connotation with a more positive word.

2. If this booklet does not give you the information you demand, please write us again. _____
   _____

3. Replacing the merchandise is not a hassle. _____
   _____

4. Your problem can be dealt with in customer relations. _____

_____

5. Noir's Restaurant serves cheap lunches. _____

_____

Practical Application

Analyzing Information

6. As vice president of Northwest Paper Company, you have been asked to write a news release announcing the retirement of the company president, Philip Suarez. Mr. Suarez has worked with the company for 25 years, serving as president for the last ten years. He started his career with Northwest Paper as a shop supervisor and became manager within two years. Following his retirement, Mr. Suarez will serve as chairperson of the board of directors. Supply any additional information that should be included, using the news release on page 457 as a model.

_____

_____

_____

_____

_____

_____

_____

_____

_____

_____

_____

_____

7. Each member of the team should find examples of news releases in business magazines or newspapers. (If possible, cut them out to submit with your report.) Prepare a short analysis of each news release, citing common themes and stories. Decide which news release presented its company in the best light. _____

Discussion Point

Making Generalizations

8. What effect does a business-related news release have on the public?

_____

_____

9. Can a news release ever provide information that may interfere with a company's business? Explain. _____

_____

_____

Unit 5

Communicating in a Business Environment

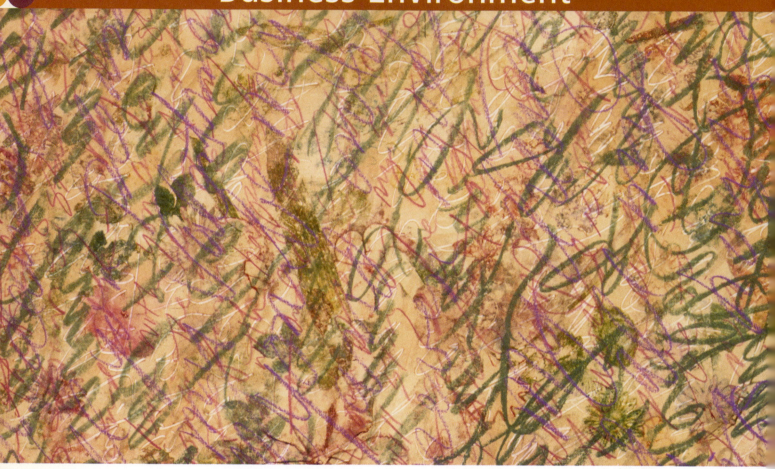

Unit Overview

In this unit, you will learn the various ways that people communicate in business.

Chapter 12

Working with Technology

Chapter 13

Communicating with Customers

Chapter 14

Developing Presentation Skills

John and Sarah rushed to the emergency room of a large metropolitan medical center after being awakened at 11:30 p.m. by a telephone call delivering the alarming news that Sarah's father apparently had had a heart attack. John and Sarah entered a bustling reception room and hurried to the receptionist's desk.

John and Sarah heard one side of the receptionist's phone conversation. "I'll be late getting off from work tonight. We have several critical patients who have just arrived. Can you pick up something for dinner?

John waited patiently and then interrupted the receptionist, "Please, can you help me?"

"Sir," the receptionist responded, her expression showing her annoyance at being interrupted, "I'll be with you just as soon as I finish this call."

Sarah interjected, "Please, we just received a telephone call that my father was brought here and . . ."

"Ma'am," the receptionist impatiently interrupted, "I said that I will be with you just as soon as I finish this call. What's his name?" Then the receptionist continued with her telephone conversation.

"Now, what is it you want?" the receptionist scowled.

Sarah, who was very upset, asked the receptionist about her father. After getting Sarah's father's name, the receptionist gave Sarah a clipboard with a questionnaire. "Fill this out. We need his insurance information."

Sarah completed the insurance questionnaire and returned it to the receptionist, who was talking on the telephone again. The receptionist took the clipboard from Sarah and motioned for her to take a seat. The receptionist continued to chat on the phone.

Fifteen minutes later, John and Sarah again approached the receptionist's desk. The night shift receptionist was now on duty. Sarah emphatically said, "I want to know how my father is."

The night shift receptionist asked for the patient's name and immediately telephoned to find out his status. A moment later the receptionist reported that the emergency room physician was transferring Sarah's father to a room for overnight observation. "If you and your husband will go to Room 385, Dr. Feldman will talk with you. He has been waiting for you for a half hour. He has some good news. Your father did not have a heart attack."

John and Sarah thanked the receptionist and hurried to see Sarah's father. Several days later, they began to think about the treatment they had received from the first receptionist.

Thinking Critically

Make a list of *good* communication strategies used in the above story.

Make a list of *poor* communication strategies.

Chapter 12

Working with Technology

Workplace Connection

Because we live in an advanced society, each of us must understand the technology all around us. To be successful in the workplace of the future, we must be proficient in using technology.

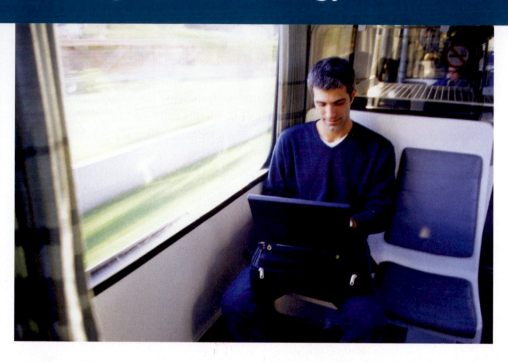

CHAPTER OBJECTIVES

When you have completed this chapter, you should be able to:

- List four technological factors that affect productivity and give examples of these technologies.
- List and describe technological devices that aid in communications.
- Describe ways in which technology networks allow worldwide communication.
- Show ways in which teleworking has influenced and will influence the marketplace.

Ways Technology Affects Communication

Essential Principles

Technological advances are causing constant changes in the way we work. Some recent changes include:

- Software that allows us to be more productive.
- Increasingly accurate voice and handwriting recognition software to cut down on keyboarding time.
- Handheld computers that allow us to stay organized and connected to our offices from almost anywhere.
- Cellular telephones that connect us to the Internet and some that are small enough to fit in our ears.

Most technological advances take years to come to market. Of those, very few become widely used. Once devices become common, you should be prepared to use them in today's business world. You should also be open to trying new devices as they become available.

An important aspect of any job is communicating with others. New and constantly changing technology makes communicating with co-workers, customers, and suppliers easier and more efficient. You will use technology to communicate with people regardless of your location. Your customers, co-workers, or employer may be thousands of miles away but only a few seconds or minutes from you electronically. Whatever job you hold—accountant or computer programmer, paralegal or sales representative, teacher or technician—you need to know how to use technology to be an effective global communicator.

Impact of Technology on Your Job and Your Future

Technology has revolutionized business communication. Just 30 years ago, standard office equipment comprised the typewriter, telephone, copying machine, and calculator.

Today, companies and organizations are equipped with computerized information processing systems including:

- Personal computers (PCs).
- Computer networks.
- Fax machines.
- Electronic mail (e-mail).
- Phone systems integrated with personal computers and networks.

SECTION OBJECTIVES

When you have finished Section 12.1, you will be able to:

- Describe how technology will affect you in your working life.
- Describe four main areas where productivity is enhanced when using technology.

WHY IT'S IMPORTANT

Communication technology is constantly changing. In order to be your professional best, you must be up to date with current and emerging technologies.

KEY TERMS

- remote technology
- wizards
- peripherals
- styles
- routing
- intranet

When you're working away from the office, **remote technology** allows you to communicate with others—employees, colleagues, customers, and so on. Some types of technology you may use remotely are:

- Notebook computers.
- Digital pagers.
- Personal digital assistants (PDAs).
- Cellular telephones.

All these devices will help you receive, process, and transmit information faster and more efficiently.

Productivity Enhancements With Technology

Businesses rely on technology to enhance productivity of both products and services and to compete globally. There are four main areas where technology enhances productivity:

- Time
- Convenience
- Quality
- Environment

Technology Reduces Time to Complete Tasks and Projects

One of the primary reasons companies invest in technology is that workers are able to be quicker and more efficient. This results in lower costs and higher profits. For example, e-mail is used to transfer information, both text and images, across the Internet. A worker in Chicago can e-mail information about a wastewater treatment project to an engineer in Atlanta. This transfer of information is quick and reduces the amount of time these workers wait to hear from each other. Compare this to years ago when the primary means of transferring documents was by postal delivery.

Technology can also reduce the time required to complete a project by enabling you to reuse or recycle information, which eliminates the need to re-create and rekey data. Rekeying data means that you must retype information. An example of recycling information would be when a worker creates an electronic address book of contacts. This address book, which is usually stored in a personal information management (PIM) program, could then be shared with other workers, thereby eliminating the need to type in addresses for letters, envelopes, business correspondence, mass mailings, presentations, and other documents.

Technology Makes the Way We Work More Convenient

With technology, correspondence can be distributed via methods such as:

- E-mail.
- Fax machines.
- Pagers.
- Voice messaging.
- Text and instant messages.
- Telephones.

Technology offers workers convenience. For example, correcting errors in electronic documents can be done instantly by deleting a character, a word, a phrase, or the entire document, then typing in new information. Moreover, most word processing programs automatically correct or highlight spelling and grammatical errors. For example, in Microsoft Word, if you type *teh* instead of *the,* MS Word automatically corrects the transposition after you press the spacebar to continue with the next word in the sequence.

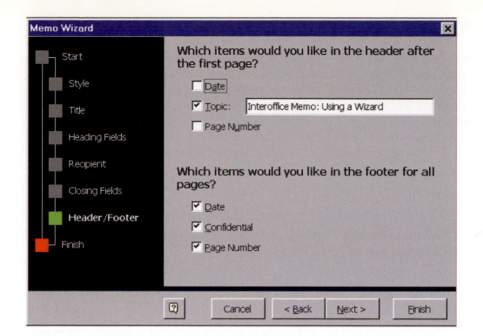

Exhibit 12.1
Working with a Wizard
Thinking Critically.
*How does a Wizard
help create common
documents between
co-workers?*

One recent advancement in user convenience is the invention of software wizards. **Wizards** are features in software applications that walk users through tasks to achieve the desired results. For example, Microsoft Publisher, a desktop publishing program, includes wizards to help users design and create a company newsletter. The wizards include separate screens that prompt the user to fill in blanks or that ask pertinent questions related to the type and style of the newsletter the user wants to create. Each screen includes buttons that allow the user to return to any previous screen in order to change settings or text. At the final wizard screen, the user can press a "Finish" button to create the document, which can then be edited. See **Exhibit 12.1.**

Technology Enhances Quality of Communications

In many ways, technology has improved the quality of communications. In a classic example, telephone voice mail enables a caller to leave detailed and accurate messages about projects, meetings, contact information, and so forth.

Another example of how technology affects the quality of your communication is in the documents you create. Because of the ease of correcting errors using electronic tools, high-quality documents can be produced in the electronic office.

Some of these electronic tools include the following:

- Spelling checkers
- Grammar checkers
- Electronic thesauruses

With technology, you can also make your documents look good using basic personal computer software and **peripherals**—hardware devices you connect to your computer to input and output information. Desktop publishing software, scanners, digital cameras, laser printers, and color printers enable you to produce professional-looking documents with your personal computer. You can choose from hundreds of fonts that today's software provides. In addition, you can emphasize text through **styles,** such as *italics,* **bold,** ~~strikeout~~, text coloring, and shading. Finally, documents can be enhanced by downloading noncopyrighted clip art images and photos to use in your publications.

Technology Makes Our Work Environment More Pleasant

Another way that technology affects productivity is through improving our office environment. Technology has improved our environment by streamlining tasks. For

KEY POINT

Messages sent to several people at the same location are easily handled by voice mail or E-mail if the messages are relatively short.

example, voice mail has all but eliminated the need to take written telephone messages. A voice mail message should always include your name, your phone number, and a concise but complete message. When you are on the phone and you receive another phone call, voice mail can automatically inform the second caller that you are already on the phone and that the caller can leave a message.

Technology has also helped reduce a lot of the waste found in offices. For example, sending an electronic version of a standard form via e-mail or posting the form on a Web site reduces the need for large numbers of paper copies.

These e-forms can include the following types of information:

- Subject
- Instructions
- Fill-in-the-blank areas in which recipients can type information
- Check boxes, radio buttons, and drop-down menus that allow recipients to select predefined options
- List of other recipients
- Controls that let the recipient send the form to another listed recipient, known as **routing**

In any business, the need to conduct daily, weekly, or monthly meetings is important. Meetings enable groups to discuss projects, to disseminate information, and to gather and discuss new ideas. One downside is that a meeting must be scheduled at a time and place where all participants can meet. If an important member of the meeting is unavailable, the meeting can be a waste of time for all other participants.

With technology, even a person who cannot physically attend a meeting can participate. For example, teleconferencing allows employees to call a conference room or office and participate remotely in a meeting.

As you will learn later in this chapter, teleworking allows employees to work at home, reducing expensive and redundant overhead in many office complexes. Finally, technology can enhance workplace morale through wider dissemination of information and better customer support. IBM is an example of a company that has enhanced communications through technology. They have an **intranet,** which is similar to the Internet but located on a network within a company. The intranet provides a place for IBM's employees to post want ads and other personal messages that only other employees can read.

Intranets are popular for several reasons:

- Because they use standard TCP/IP protocols rather than the proprietary protocols used by network operating systems, they are simpler and less expensive to install and configure.
- Because they enable users to work in standard (and usually free) Web browsers, they provide a consistent, friendly interface.
- Because they function readily with firewalls and other standard Internet security technologies, they provide excellent security against infiltration, viruses, theft, and other problems.

KEY POINT

The sender's level of familiarity with the receiver determines the amount of personalization needed in sending a message.

Digital Data

Benefits of the Intranet

Intranets are beneficial because information can be widely distributed within a company without using the traditional method of paper and mailings.

Assessment   Section 12.1

Review of Key Terms

1. How does *remote technology* improve business transactions? _____
_____
_____

2. How do *wizards* make work more convenient? _____

_____

Editing Practice

Proofreading Alert! Revise the following telecommunications so that neither exceeds 15 words. Aim for brevity, clarity, and completeness.

3. Phillip Goetz expects to arrive in Boston on Skylark Flight 15 on Friday morning at 8:00 a.m. Please arrange to pick him up at the airport and brief him on the Tracy-Phelps contract en route to the board meeting. (39 words) _____

_____

4. The computer printout of the March sales forecast was lost and never reached us. Please fax two copies of the March forecast immediately. (23 words) _____

Practical Application

Evaluating Concepts

5. Compose a greeting that will be recorded on your voice mail indicating that you will be away for several days. Let callers know that they can either leave a message or contact Simone Rubin at 555-3939 if they need immediate help. Make sure your message is brief but that it contains all the necessary information. _____

_____

_____

_____

6. Your company is considering installing a voice mail system, and your team has been appointed as the committee to gather information about voice mail. The team will be making its case to the Chief Financial Officer (CFO), who will approve the request to purchase the system. As a team, you will need to research the information and talk to current users of voice mail systems. In your research, ask these questions:

- What benefits/costs has your company derived/incurred from using voice mail? What are your ongoing costs?
- Have you experienced any problems? If so, what were they and how were the problems solved?

_____

Discussion Point

Determining Cause and Effect

7. How has the communication revolution changed business? _____

_____

_____

_____

SECTION OBJECTIVES

When you have finished Section 12.2, you will be able to:

- Discuss the different advanced technologies available today.
- Discuss the different input and output devices used by computerized information systems.

WHY IT'S IMPORTANT

As a business communicator, making technology work for you is important. Developing competencies in technologies that help you communicate can make you more efficient.

KEY TERMS

- voice mail system
- fax machine
- pager
- cellular telephone
- analog data
- digital data
- smart phone
- PCS
- GSM
- GPS
- VoIP
- computer workstation
- notebook computer
- tablet PC
- embedded computer device
- printer
- ppm
- modem
- bandwidth
- DSL
- cable modem

Using Technology to Communicate

Essential Principles

Someday, all computers and handheld devices are expected to be able to connect in a global communication network that will allow access to information from a multitude of worldwide sources.

The Internet is only the start of this communication revolution. Other forms of electronic communication, including PDAs, pagers, cellular telephones, and e-mail, offer expanded possibilities for communicating with others around the globe. Soon, wireless technology will make traditional landline systems obsolete. In many developing nations, cellular telephones are the primary means of telecommunications because conventional telephone lines do not have to be installed.

In the following sections, we will look at how specific technologies allow us to communicate. These technologies are divided into two main areas of discussion—basic and advanced. Basic technologies include devices that are common in many homes and offices today, such as the telephone and fax machine. Advanced technologies include devices that have become readily available in the past decade but are still not present in all homes or businesses.

Using Basic Technology to Communicate

We've seen how most companies rely on some technology to help their employees communicate with co-workers, vendors, and customers. Now, let's look at how some specific telephone and computer technologies are used.

Voice Mail Systems

Voice mail systems provide a fast, convenient way of managing telephone messages. Unlike traditional answering machines, which can record messages only when the telephone is not in use, voice mail can take messages while you're on the phone with someone else. That way, you do not miss a phone call, and the caller knows that her call is just as important as the one you're currently engaged in.

Voice mail allows workers to record greetings for incoming calls and to listen to and forward messages. A caller can leave a detailed message that includes the reason for the call and information about how and when the caller can be reached. Instead of responding to a written telephone message, which may be illegible or incoherent, the recipient listens to a caller's message at a convenient time and responds accordingly. More importantly, by dialing the voice mail number directly, you can use voice mail 24/7/365: that is, 24 hours a day, 7 days a week, 365 days a year.

When communicating with your telephone and voice mail systems, follow these guidelines:

- Eliminate busy signals for incoming calls. Companies lose business when potential callers cannot reach them. Use a high-quality voice mail system from your local telephone carrier that can handle multiple incoming calls at once.
- Use voice mail and an answering machine. Voice mail systems can store messages for a finite amount of time, sometimes for merely ten days, and can hold only a specific number of messages, usually no more than 25. If your voice mailbox is full, new callers cannot leave their messages. Use an answering machine to pick up all calls after the first two or three rings, then have voice mail pick up after that—after the fourth ring, for instance—to make sure you never miss an important call.

Facsimile (Fax) Machines

A **facsimile (fax) machine** can transmit exact copies of handwritten, typed, or printed documents, as well as graphs, illustrations, and photographs over regular telephone lines. In the past, both the sender and the receiver needed a fax machine. The sender's fax machine scanned the document and transmitted it via telephone lines to the receiver's fax machine, which printed out the document for the recipient to read.

Today, many word processing programs can fax documents on computers that have a fax/modem. A computer with a fax/modem can send a fax to or receive a fax from another computer with a fax/modem. A computer can also send a fax to or receive a fax from a fax machine. Likewise, a fax machine can send a fax to or receive a fax from a computer. All the following combinations that are possible for sending and receiving faxes are:

- Fax machine to fax machine.
- Fax machine to computer.
- Computer to computer.
- Computer to fax machine.
- Fax machine to cellular telephone.
- Cellular telephone to fax machine.

Broadcast Fax. A broadcast fax service allows you to fax the same document to hundreds or thousands of fax machines simultaneously using programmed telephone lists. You can think of this as a form of electronic direct mail. Direct mail includes advertisements and other marketing information sent to a list of targeted customers who are considered to be the most likely purchasers of a product or service. When using broadcast fax, be careful not to violate the state and federal Do-Not-Call laws enacted in 2003.

Fax by Request. Fax by request is a process by which you call or dial an organization to request copies of documents or forms. For example, to request tax forms, you can call an IRS phone number from your fax machine and follow the instructions on the recorded message—select the option for getting forms, then enter the catalog number for each item that you want, hang up the phone, and the fax will begin.

Internet Faxing. Internet faxing enables users to send and receive faxes via the Internet. This is commonly done by using a faxing service provider that lets a person fax a document to the provider, who, in turn, sends it to a recipient on the Internet who then retrieves and reads it using a World Wide Web browser or software provided by the service provider. Conversely, a person can send a fax, using the browser, to the

KEY POINT

To decide which medium to use for a message, ask:

1. "Is the recipient familiar with the technology?"
2. "Which medium is best suited for sending the type of message?"

KEY POINT

Internet faxing allows you to send and receive faxes anywhere you access the Internet.

service provider, who, in turn, sends the message to a recipient's fax machine. Faxing service providers generally charge a nominal fee for their service.

Pagers

Pagers, sometimes known as *beepers,* notify you by a tone, vibration, or visual display that someone is trying to reach you. Pagers have a small digital display that shows the number of the person calling you and, depending on the type of pager you have, can also display a short message from the caller. After receiving a page, you can then use a standard telephone or cellular telephone to call the person who paged you.

Pagers are lightweight and small enough to carry in a pocket or a purse. If you are carrying a pager, people can contact you regardless of your location. When critical decisions or emergencies arise in business, it is advantageous to be able to reach a co-worker who is away from his or her desk or away from the office; a pager allows you to have that contact.

Some newer pagers also include short text displays to allow senders to send a brief message to the recipient. A small keypad on the pager doubles as a number keypad and character keypad, allowing users to enter numbers, letters, and other keyboard characters. Recipients can then reply with a brief message or use a telephone to call the sender.

Using Advanced Technology to Communicate

Along with understanding how to use the preceding basic devices, we also need to understand and know how to use many advanced devices, such as cellular telephones, personal computers, and the like. Let's look at some of these now.

Cellular Telephones

Cellular telephones, or *cell phones,* are small, wireless, lightweight, portable phones that allow you to communicate from almost any location where your phone can pick up a signal. Cell phones can also have such traditional features of a regular phone service as call waiting, caller ID, speed dialing, and voice mail. You can use cell phones to talk to someone, to send and receive e-mail, to surf the Internet, and even to download music.

Advanced cell phone technology even allows users to snap digital pictures while traveling in another country, riding in a vehicle, walking through the mall, or shopping at the grocery store.

Note: A word of caution—a cell phone call is not secure. Equipment as simple as a police scanner may allow someone to listen to your cell phone calls.

Here are some tips on how to choose the right cell phone for you:

- Choose a cell phone service company for your area. Each phone service has its own area of coverage, so make sure the company you enter into an agreement with covers the area you are most likely to work in.

- Buy a phone that works with your service provider. You can get great deals on cell phones in some retail stores, but certain phones may not work with your service.

- Choose digital over analog. Digital technology allows more features and functions on your phone and usually has a much clearer sound than analog. The first cell phones were analog; today most are digital. **Analog data** is continuous data—there are no individual elements, such as light, voice, and video, that can be distinguished from any other element. Any analog data must be digitized in order to store it on a computer. **Digital data** is composed of items, such as text, numbers, and Morse code, that are distinct from one another. Digital data is stored as a combination of numbers: specifically, a series of 0s and 1s. If your area has digital phone service, you should consider using it.

- Buy a phone with a long battery life and/or short recharging time. Because you want your cell phone with you wherever you go, you don't want to worry about its battery running out.

- Look for ease of use and size. Get a cell phone that fits nicely in your hand and is easy to store without the potential of damaging its keys. Also, look for one that has a large liquid crystal display (LCD) screen that is easy to read.

Smart Phone Technologies. **Smart phones** are wireless cell phones with a computer—an enabled feature not usually associated with telephones. A smart phone is a cell phone, PDA, and handheld computer with an Internet connection combined into one device. Smart phone capabilities include the following:

- Sending and receiving e-mail and faxes.
- Accessing Web sites.
- Scrolling through menus.
- Accessing stock quotes, sports, and news.
- Viewing and modifying calendar and address book items.

A smart phone also allows online banking and remote control of computers and other devices at work and at home.

The Massachusetts Institute of Technology has released a device that a heart patient can wear that transmits heart data wirelessly to a doctor through a cell phone. If the monitor detects a problem, the doctor can call the patient on a cell phone before the patient suffers a heart attack.

PCS, GSM, and GPS Phone Technologies. **Personal Communication Service (PCS)** is a system of digital, wireless communications used especially for mobile/cellular phones that often includes additional features, such as caller ID or paging.

The **Global System for Mobile Communication (GSM)** is a digital, wireless mobile telephone system that is already widely used in Europe and in 120 countries throughout the rest of the world. The United States is just beginning to use GSM.

The **Global Positioning System (GPS)** is available in some automobiles and will soon be a standard feature in many cell phone products. GPS is a system of 24 satellites that orbit the earth and make it possible for people with ground receivers to pinpoint their geographic location. The receivers are small enough to fit in a cell phone. GPS also allows an emergency response service to locate you. Accuracy within 1 meter—a little over 3 feet—is possible. Today many new cars come with a GPS system installed.

Another recent technological advance is the convergence of smart phones and GPS. This convergence will soon be able to give your exact location or transmit your whereabouts to a 911 operator in an emergency.

VoIP Technology. Voice over Internet Protocol (**VoIP**) is technology that permits you to make telephone calls using a broadband Internet connection instead of a conventional telephone. Some VoIP services allow calls only between persons with the same service, while others allow you to call anyone who has a telephone number—local, long distance, mobile, or international. Some VoIP services work only over a computer or special phone, while others permit you to use a regular phone with a special adaptor. (*Source:* Federal Communications Commission, www.fcc.gov/cgb.)

Computerized Information Systems

Computerized information systems enable business personnel to handle a variety of tasks. One innovation that saves time and increases accessibility is the computer workstation. The **computer workstation** can be a microcomputer or personal computer

KEY POINT

The smart phone further extends the value of a mobile phone by providing a mix of online and offline applications to keep people connected to their important, time-critical information

operating independently, or a computer terminal linked, or networked, to the company's main computer. Using the computer simplifies tasks, such as creating spreadsheets, databases, and documents, and allows you to communicate with others in your office or virtually any place in the world.

Two types of personal use computers are the Apple Macintosh and the IBM-clone or compatible. The Macintosh is referred to as a "Mac" and the IBM-clone or compatible is simply called a personal computer, or PC. To make things more confusing, Macintosh computers are classified as personal computers because they are designed to be used and managed by individuals.

Let's look at each of the two main personal computers.

The Macintosh. The Mac was the first widely sold computer for personal use that included a graphical user interface (GUI). GUI systems display text and graphics on a page just the way the document would look printed out. Today, Mac users represent about 5 percent of the total number of personal computer users. Macs are preferred by graphic designers and online visual artists.

The IBM-Clone or Compatible Personal Computer. The IBM-clone or compatible personal computer is the most popular type of personal computer in the world. It accounts for nearly 90 percent of the market for homes, businesses, and schools. Originally created by IBM, the PC is now manufactured by a number of companies. These computers are called *clones* or *compatibles* because their design is similar to the original IBM machine and they use the same software.

Notebook Computers

A **notebook computer** is a lightweight, portable battery-powered computer. You can use a notebook computer to work on documents and to send information to and receive information from an office computer in almost any location. With a notebook computer, businesspeople can be productive during periods that would otherwise be downtimes, such as time spent waiting in airports and during flights.

Notebooks provide flexibility for workers who have to be mobile. For example, a sales representative can leave the office and take along a computer. With a modem and phone line connection, or with a wireless modem, the worker can stay "connected" to the office using the Internet or other dial-up networking options. The worker can send, read, and receive e-mail; access shared files; or run applications installed on a desktop computer from a remote site. Finally, full-size keyboards and monitors can be plugged into the back panel of the notebook to allow the employee to work more comfortably.

Tablet PC

A **tablet PC** is similar to a notebook computer but is smaller and thinner and allows the user to take notes on the screen by writing with a stylus or digital pen instead of a keyboard. The concept of a tablet PC originated in a Xerox laboratory in 1971. The first commercial version was Apple Computer's Newton, which was not commercially successful. The latest version is Microsoft's Tablet PC, which is about the size and thickness of a lined notepad.

Handheld Devices

Handheld devices, such as PDAs, are portable computers that fit into one hand and are sometimes the size of a wallet or checkbook. Handhelds usually offer a limited number of applications, including contact management software, spreadsheet programs, word processors, and e-mail programs.

Some handhelds include a small keyboard on which users can type messages. Others may include an electronic pen with which users can write messages or click on-screen buttons. Most use standard battery sizes, usually AA or AAA. Handhelds include communication devices like fax/modem cards, cellular cards, and input/output ports to connect the device to a desktop computer.

Handheld devices are popular with workers who travel a lot and need to stay connected to the office but do not want the extra cargo of a notebook. For example, some real estate agents carry handhelds to get their e-mail messages and have access to their electronic Rolodex, rather than carrying a bulkier notebook when showing houses to their clients.

Some new PDAs include cell phone and digital camera capabilities.

Exhibit 12.2
PDA
Thinking Critically.
How do handheld devices, such as PDAs, enable workers to communicate?

Embedded Computer Devices

An **embedded computer device** is a tiny computer built into a larger product to control functions of that product. Many functions of today's automobiles, such as antilock brakes and electronic door locks, are controlled by microprocessors connected to a central computer. The remote controls for your TV and VCR are other examples of embedded computer devices.

Soon, household appliances such as microwave ovens will have embedded computer devices that can scan bar codes on food packages, enabling the microwave to cook the food correctly, provide nutritional information, and give serving suggestions.

Advanced Input and Output Devices

Some advanced technologies used by workers include input and output devices for PCs. These devices enable users to send information into a computer (inputting) or retrieve information from a computer (outputting). These devices are discussed below.

Scanners

Scanners are input devices that copy a printed page into the computer's memory, then transform the image into a digital format. The most common item scanned is a photograph or magazine illustration. Scannable items include book pages, written documents, contracts, receipts, and other hard copy.

> **KEY POINT**
>
> Embedded computer devices are used to control, to monitor, or to assist the operation of equipment and machinery.

Scanners work with software that interprets the digital data sent from the scanner to the computer. After loading the data into the computer, the user can use it just like any other computer data. For instance, scanned images can be inserted into desktop publishing documents for newsletters, yearbooks, or Web sites. Scanned text can be converted to digital text using software called optical character resolution (OCR) software. This software converts the hard-copied text to digital text so it can be inserted into your spreadsheets, word processing documents, databases, and e-mail.

Printers

Printers accept text and graphics from a computer and transfer the information to paper or another medium, such as a transparency. Many printers also have scanning, copying, and faxing capabilities. The two most common types of printers today are laser printers and ink-jet printers.

Laser Printers. A laser printer is a high-resolution printer that uses a laser beam reflected from a mirror to attract ink, called *toner,* to appropriate areas of the paper as the sheet rolls over a drum. Laser printers are the more expensive of the two types of printers, but the professional look of the printed materials they produce enhances the image and credibility of a company. Businesses also use laser printers to produce camera-ready copy.

Ink-Jet Printers. An ink-jet printer forms an image by spraying ink from several tiny jets, or ink cartridges, at close range as the paper rolls by. The ink used by some ink-jet printers is watersoluble and may smear easily. Because of their relatively low cost compared to laser printers, many ink-jet printers in use today are color. In fact, in many businesses and educational institutions, a color ink-jet printer is the standard output device.

When buying a printer, consider:

- Color resolution, or the sharpness of text and images on paper.
- Speed, rated as "pages per minute" (**ppm**).
- Memory, or the amount of information that a printer can store and print per print job.
- The cost of color cartridges.

Digital Cameras

Digital cameras store images digitally on special reusable film cards like flash-memory cards, instead of on film. Some digital cameras use a memory stick or a smart media or xD-picture card. Others use 3¼ inch CD-R or CD-RW disks. Digital images stored on the camera can be uploaded to your computer using a direct link from the camera or a special film card reader attached to your computer. The images then can be viewed, edited, printed, or embedded in documents. The quality of pictures taken by digital cameras depends on the megapixel rating. A 2- or 3-megapixel camera is inexpensive and adequate for casual photographers.

Digital Video Cameras

Another type of input device is the digital video camera, or PC video camera. These devices are like standard video camcorders, but they store images and video in digital format instead of on videotape. You can then copy the images or video to your computer to edit, view, or embed the data in documents. Some PC video cameras are used to capture live images or full-motion video for videoconferencing; that is, when multiple users see and talk to each other in real time over a network or the Internet.

Modems and Online Connections

A **modem** is a device connected to, or included inside of, a computer. It is used to exchange programs and data with other computers and to get on the Internet. Traditionally, this occurred via *telephone lines and cable or fiber optics;* today, this exchange can be *wireless or transmitted through airwaves*. A modem makes it possible to have instant access to all types of information.

Bandwidth.   When discussing modems and online connections, you need to understand **bandwidth,** which is used to measure how fast and how much data flows on a given transmission path. Any analog or digital signal has a bandwidth. For example, when you connect to the Internet using a 56K modem, the bandwidth is 56,000 bits per second. That is, 56,000 bits transfer to or from your modem every second.

Digital Subscriber Line.   A **digital subscriber line (DSL)** is a technology for bringing high bandwidth information to homes and small businesses over ordinary copper telephone lines. Sending data over a DSL is ten times faster than sending it over standard telephone lines.

Cable Modem.   Sending data over a **cable modem** is 100 times faster than sending it over telephone lines. Not only does the cable modem provide a much faster rate of data exchange, users also do not have to wait for the modem to dial up to make a connection. Instead, users log on to the Internet and can stay connected until they log off, unless any technical difficulties arise. One disadvantage of cable modems is that they require a specific Internet address, or IP address, which can make them vulnerable to security threats from outside hackers.

Assessment   Section 12.2

Review of Key Terms

1.   How do *voice mail systems* and *faxes* improve business transactions?

   _____

   _____

   _____

   _____

2.   How can a *pager* be beneficial to a worker who does not hold predictable office hours? _____

   _____

   _____

Editing Practice

Spelling Alert!   Circle any errors and rewrite the following paragraph, correcting problems with numbers and spelling errors.

3.   Too administrative assistants wanted two share the use of a computer workstation equiped with a fax machine an a modem. Both assistants felt this arrangment would work because each assistant types only for

hours per ate-hour day. Each assistants works with three executives. The six executives agree two the trade. _____

_____

Practical Application

Evaluating Concepts

4. You work with a consulting company that has been hired by a local real estate company to investigate and make recommendations on how technology can be used to communicate with potential customers. What types of information would be communicated between the business and its customers? Is there a certain type of technology that would work well for each of the types of communication you identified as being used in this organization? _____

    _____

    _____

    _____

5. As a team, interview someone in business and evaluate the importance you think technology has in that business. Begin by using the following suggested list of questions:

    - What percentage of your job is spent using technology?
    - What kinds of communication problems do you encounter on the job due to a lack of technology?
    - What could your company do to improve technology?

    _____

    _____

Discussion Point

Making Inferences

6. How has technology enabled people with disabilities to join the workforce? Provide specific examples. _____

    _____

7. What effect has advanced technology had on business communication?

    _____

    _____

    _____

    _____

Communicating with the World

Essential Principles

The issue of communicating using technology is one you should be very familiar with by now. But one area of communication that is not yet common to all of us is that of communicating with people from around the world. With the Internet boom of the 1990s, it became possible to communicate almost instantaneously with anyone connected to the Internet. We'll look now at some of the technologies that make this communication possible.

The Internet and the World Wide Web

The **Internet,** often called the Net, is a system of computer networks that links computers from around the world in one large network. Internet users can send e-mail messages, chat with one another, post and read messages on electronic bulletin boards, and gain access to databases and Web sites almost any place in the world.

Electronic Mail

Electronic mail, or **e-mail,** is a keyboarded message transmitted instantly from your computer to the computer of your recipient via the Internet, other computer networks, or online services. You can attach a file—a word processing document, image, or spreadsheet that you've prepared in a software program, for example—and send it to a recipient along with your message. When the recipient receives the message, the attached file can be opened as long as a program that supports the attached file is installed on the recipient's computer. E-mail can be sent to one person or a group of people.

E-mail can be sent to almost any place in the world—even into outer space—provided the sender and the recipient have access to a computer network. This technology benefits businesses because messages can be sent immediately. Vint Cerf is known as "the father of the Internet" because he coauthored the TCP/IP protocols that created cyberspace as we know it. Cerf's latest project is to create protocols to extend the Net into outer space. "It sounds a bit crazy, sending e-mail to other planets," he admits. "But we never expected the Net to grow as fast as it did. This is just the next logical step."

Finally, with advances in smart phone technology, you can even read and send e-mail using a cell phone. Cell phones with embedded video cameras now allow you to snap pictures or video, create e-mail, and send your video e-mail to another person using your cell phone.

Instant Messaging

Instant messaging, or "chat," is real-time communication via the Internet. Presently, there are more than 60 million worldwide users of instant messaging, and that number is growing daily.

SECTION OBJECTIVES

When you have finished Section 12.3, you will be able to:

- List and describe different features of the Internet.
- Discuss how the World Wide Web is used in business communication.
- Discuss how the Internet has changed the way we shop and connect with the outside world.
- Describe asynchronous and synchronous communications.

WHY IT'S IMPORTANT

Being familiar with the Internet and World Wide Web is mandatory in today's working world.

KEY TERMS

- Internet
- e-mail
- instant messaging
- e-commerce
- World Wide Web
- URL address
- hypertext links
- firewall
- extranet
- smart card
- groupware
- asynchronous
- synchronous
- teleconference

Instant messaging can be used for chat rooms, but it can also allow two people to communicate with one another over the Internet or an online service. Because the cost of chatting is free (you pay only your online service fee), this is one way workers, students, homemakers, and others eliminate costly long distance telephone calls to colleagues, friends, and relatives.

Electronic Commerce

One way that technology is transforming the way we communicate with each other around the world is with the advent of electronic commerce. Electronic commerce (**e-commerce**) is buying and selling merchandise and services over the Internet.

The volume of e-commerce worldwide is growing astronomically. Today, you can buy almost anything over the Internet, from ink pens to automobiles. Many retail establishments have set up Web sites to advertise their goods and services and to allow consumers to order these items from the comfort of their own homes. For example, Wal-Mart, the largest U.S. retailer, has Walmart.com, a Web-based retail outlet where you can buy most products that are in Wal-Mart stores. After you place an order, you can track it to find out when it will be delivered.

Problems with E-Commerce.   Although e-commerce promises convenience and lower prices, you should be aware of some problems with it. First, be careful when giving your credit card or other payment information over the Internet, even to major Internet sites that indicate they have encrypted data protection. Some of these databases have been subject to recent attacks by hackers who like to steal credit card numbers and personal and financial data.

Second, you don't always get what you expect, or when you expect it. For example, some online auction sites have been hit by lawsuits charging fraud. Also, if you order an item from a company you have never dealt with, you may never see the product you ordered—or the money you paid for it. Scam artists operate on the Web just as they do in brick-and-mortar businesses.

New Market Arena.   E-commerce opens up a new market arena that allows everyone to take advantage of worldwide commerce via the Web. Everyone has an opportunity to purchase goods from or to sell goods to a global audience.

With the world Internet population at 1.1 billion in 2005 and projected to be 1.4 billion in 2007, worldwide e-commerce growth will be phenomenal. (*Source:* Computer Industry Almanac.)

Managed Travel

The Internet is a valuable tool for travelers who need to schedule trips and to book reservations. Instead of relying on travel agents, you can get on the Web 24/7/365; use online travel booking agents like Orbitz.com, Travelocity.com, and Expedia.com to book a flight, set up hotel reservations, and reserve a rental car. Most online travel booking agents have "booking engines" to automatically search and find the best deals for travel arrangements.

You can also make restaurant reservations in larger cities. Similarly, the Internet enables you to order tickets to music concerts, amusement parks, and sporting events. Before you leave for your trip, you can use the Internet to research your destination and even create a map of each of the cities you will be visiting.

Corporate policy is expected to dictate that more and more business travel be booked online.

World Wide Web

The **World Wide Web,** also called the Web and often abbreviated as WWW, is the most widely used part of the Internet. The Web gives you access to millions of pages of information, often in other languages, that are presented in multimedia form, including text, animation, virtual reality, sound, and music files.

Uniform Resource Locator

The outstanding feature of the Web is the ease of getting information. Information is stored on one or more Web pages with a Uniform Resource Locator (URL) address. A **URL address** is the Internet address of a given site: *http://www.dacc.edu,* for example. The URL address needs to be entered exactly as it is written; however, you can usually omit the *http://* portion depending on the World Wide Web browser—the software used to access Web pages—you use.

Hypertext Links

Information on the Web is linked by connections that are made between data at different Web sites. These connections are called **hypertext links,** words or graphics that are highlighted in some way. When you click on the link, you go immediately to that related site, display a related image, or download software. What is hyperlinked to a specific link is determined by the author of the Web page. Much of the information on the Internet can be accessed free of charge other than your monthly Internet provider access fee. Some Web sites, however, charge for premium content. For example, magazine and newspaper Web sites often charge for archived articles, and some software companies require you to pay before you can download their software. As the Internet becomes more popular and the technology for payment transactions becomes more secure, you probably will see a rise in fee-based sites and the types of goods and services you can acquire over the Internet.

A word of caution: Just because information is posted on an Internet site doesn't mean that it is true or correct. Currently, anyone can post anything on the Internet—it is not regulated. So, you should always verify information you obtain from the Internet.

Intra and Extra Nets

As noted in Section 12.1, an intranet is similar to the Internet except it is a private network within an organization, but not necessarily within the same building. A company's intranet could connect operations at several locations. These locations include hyperlinks to other resources within the intranet and often have links to content posted on the Internet. An intranet is protected by firewalls to prevent outsiders from getting into the private network. A **firewall** is an integrated collection of security measures designed to prevent unauthorized access to a networked computer system.

An **extranet** is a private intranet that gives limited access to select outsiders, such as customers or vendors. These outside users can access certain company databases with a password. For example, if you are a consultant working with a company and need access to certain documents or data, you may be given a username and password to use in connecting to and accessing an organization's extranet to obtain the limited information you may need.

Smart Card Technology

Basic smart cards have been around for more than a decade, though mostly in Europe. A **smart card** looks like a standard credit card but it contains a battery-powered, wafer-thin computer. Up until now, smart cards have been used primarily as prepaid, disposable phone cards. As a person uses the phone card, the amount of time left on the card decreases. Information transfers between the card and the reader are protected through security encryption. Smart cards of the near future, however, will be able to combine all of a person's cards—such as credit, phone, driver's license, medical information, among others—into one card. This smart card could then allow payments to be made at your doorstep to the plumber or the delivery person or purchase something from a vending machine.

Neither/Nor

Dana neither participates in office parties or socializes with her co-workers.

(*Nor* is the correct word, not *or.*)

Technology and Group Communication

Group communication is a key component of any organization. Often, it is done by conducting on-site meetings with project teams, staff members, and other groups. But technology has changed the way group communication occurs. Now, we have software that enables multiple users to access the same document at the same time and mark it for edits or other changes. You also can use group-based project-management software to send project assignments to team members, then track the assignments through completion. The following paragraphs discuss these types of technological advancements in group communication.

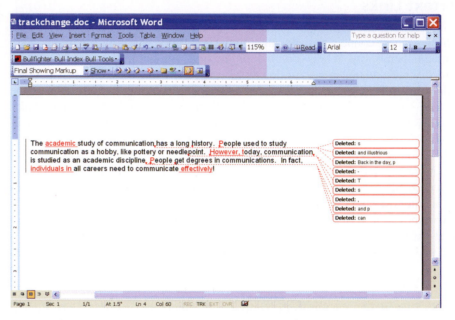

Exhibit 12.3
Tracking Changes
Thinking Critically. How does Microsoft Word's "Track Changes" feature enable workers to work on the same document?

Group, or Collaborative, Writing Tools

Group, or collaborative, writing tools are used in business to:

- Maximize the expertise of different people
- Improve the quality of the document by combining the talent of several people
- Produce the document faster by dividing the work

Groupware is software that allows people to work together. All users have access to the document, and the software will maintain a current version for all of the users. Microsoft Word has a feature called "Track Changes" (See **Exhibit 12.3**) that allows a group to work on a document and keep track of changes. Each member of the group may use a different color for the changes and comments. The software tracks who made the changes, the date of the changes, and any comments about the changes. It also allows you to "lock" the document with a password so only those authorized to view and edit it can do so. This provides a layer of security for those files that may need it, such as budget memos, payroll documents, and so on.

Asynchronous Communication

The computer tools used to facilitate learning and communication can be divided into two categories: asynchronous and synchronous.

Asynchronous means sending the communication at one time and the receivers retrieve or access it at their convenience. E-mail is a type of asynchronous communication.

Advantages of Asynchronous Communication. Schools use asynchronous teaching and learning with Internet courses. Businesses also use asynchronous training for employees. The teacher or trainer puts the documents, tests, video clips, etc., online, and the learners can access the information 24 hours a day and use it when it is convenient. This is much like an old-fashioned correspondence course except that an Internet course is done on the Web and usually incorporates multimedia. Multimedia is a combination of two or more of the following: text, graphics, animation, sound, and motion video.

Synchronous Communication

Synchronous means at the same time, or real time. In synchronous distance education, teachers and learners are connected at the same time and communicate in real time. This is much like going to class where the teacher and the students are physically present.

Teleconferencing. A **teleconference** is where the participants are at two or more locations and can participate in a conference without traveling; it is a form of synchronous communication. A teleconference can be an audioconference or a videoconference. In addition to businesses, medical facilities are using teleconferencing nowadays. For example, a surgeon can conduct a consultation with a patient before surgery. The surgeon is in the main hospital, and the patient and a nurse may be at a remote site. This procedure saves the patient, who may be in fragile health, from traveling a great distance to consult with the surgeon.

Digital Data

Teleconferencing

Teleconferencing enables workers located in different areas to communicate using text, audio, and video. Teleconferencing can minimize travel expenses and can be an effective way to conduct meetings.

Assessment   Section 12.3

Review of Key Terms

1. How can the *World Wide Web* improve office productivity? Provide an example. _____

_____

_____

2. What is a *firewall,* and how do firewalls help businesses? _____

_____

_____

_____

Editing Practice

Grammar Alert!   Circle any usage errors and rewrite the following e-mail, correcting the errors.

3. All employee in maintenance will be required to attend a safety workshop. Workshops is scheduled for the following day and times: Monday 9:00–10:00 a.m., Wednesday 1:30–2:30 p.m., and

Thursday 3:00–4:00 p.m. If there are topics you will like to have covered, please submit your requests to Human Resources before noon this Friday. A sign-up sheet for the workshops are posted in the break room. Personnel who does not sign up by Friday will be assigned. _____

Practical Application

Evaluating Concepts

4. Assume you need to make travel arrangements for your supervisor. She will be traveling to Dallas for a sales convention. Using the Internet, find at least three options for air travel, hotel reservations, and car rental. Remember, you want to be frugal but not cheap. Prepare the information in a chart. _____

5. As a team, research the topic of smart cards in businesses on the Internet. Document your sources, either by writing down the URL, the date, and other pertinent information, or by printing out a copy of the information. Prepare a one-page memo for your classmates that presents your team's findings. _____

Discussion Point

Analyzing Information

6. Discuss how the Internet can be used in the workplace. In your discussion, consider how hypertext links are used. How might a company use such links? Why do some Web sites charge a fee? How can you be sure the information you obtain on the Internet is reliable? _____
   _____
   _____
   _____
   _____
   _____

7. What effect has e-commerce had on businesses? What are some advantages and disadvantages to e-commerce? _____
   _____
   _____
   _____
   _____

Teleworking as a Way to Communicate

Essential Principles

We are beginning to witness another transformation of the workplace. In the pre-industrial era, workers lived mostly in isolation on farms and had limited contact with one another. The industrial era brought people together into cities and factories to work in a structured environment. The Information Age is returning workers to their homes where they are physically isolated, yet connected via modern technology to the virtual office.

Within this decade, it is predicted that many changes will occur regarding who is using technology to get jobs done. Technology will permeate almost every business practice and drive enormous strategic and practical progress. Gone will be most secretarial and administrative jobs. Also, managers will have to focus on measuring efficiency and productivity rather than on tracking a group of employees and tasks.

Telecommuting versus Telework

The terms *telecommuting* and *telework* are frequently used interchangeably, although telework is the preferred term today. Both save time, space, and travel costs.

According to the International Telework Association & Council, or ITAC, **telecommuting** refers to salaried employees who work at home for part or all of the work week instead of going to the office.

ITAC broadly defines **telework** to mean using telecommunications to work wherever you need to in order to satisfy client needs. This could mean from a home office, a telework center, a satellite office, a client's office, an airport lounge, a hotel room, the local Starbucks, or from your office to a colleague ten floors below in the same building—wherever!

Telework can also be defined as an employment arrangement in which employees work from a location away from the employer's main office, using electronic connections, such as phone lines, cellular/wireless circuits, and Internet access. Some people telework full time, but more people telework one to three days per week.

Hot Desking and Hoteling

If teleworkers come to the office occasionally, they must have a place to work. It would not be cost-effective to have a specific desk sitting empty on the days teleworkers are out of the office. Therefore, desks and office space are shared. This sharing has given rise to terms such as *hot desking* and *hoteling*.

SECTION OBJECTIVES
When you have finished Section 12.4, you will be able to:

- Describe the types of jobs suitable for telework.
- Explain the advantages and disadvantages of telework for the employee.
- Explain the advantages and disadvantages of telework for the employer.

WHY IT'S IMPORTANT

As technology develops, more workers will have the opportunity to work, at least part of the time, from home.

KEY TERMS

- telecommuting
- telework
- hot desking
- hoteling
- ergonomics

KEY POINT

Telework is a flexible way of organizing work without the physical presence of workers at their work places during important working hours.

Hot Desking. **Hot desking** means that workers do not have their own desks but simply use an available desk when they are in the office. They keep their personal belongings in a locker or file cabinet when they are out of the office. "Hot" refers to the desk and chair still being "warm" from the previous worker.

Hoteling. **Hoteling** is a way for workers to share workspace—without stepping on each other's toes—by either calling a staff concierge or logging onto a Web-based scheduling system. You can reserve your favorite office spot, if available. Today, hoteling is an effective tool for managing the physical needs of diverse staffs that include the following:

- On-site workers.
- Teleworkers who work from a remote site.
- Mobile workers.
- Flex-timers who work a nonstandard schedule.

Hoteling uses the analogy of a hotel—you reserve a room (office) for the nights (days) you need to stay (work) with the features (that is, equipment and supplies) you need.

Ideal Teleworkers

The ideal teleworker must be suited to the new work environment and must share the work ethic and values of her or his employer. Teleworkers should possess time management skills, be self-motivated and trustworthy, and have the ability to work independently. In addition, they must have the trust and support of their employers, so that they will conduct their work from a remote site and be as productive off site as they would be working in the company's offices.

The International Telework Association and Council (ITAC) estimates 23.5 million employed Americans worked from home during business hours at least one day per month in 2003. JALA International, in association with ITAC, forecasts over 40 million teleworkers in the US by 2010. (*Source:* www.ivc.ca/studies/us.html, printed 7/19/2005.)

Types of Telework

Telework is best suited to information-based, portable, and predictable jobs, or ones that demand a high degree of privacy and concentration. Typically, teleworkers are information workers in mid-level or senior positions, but the trend is toward teleworking at all levels. Some typical telework jobs include:

- Information processing.
- Sales.
- Customer service.
- Research consultant.
- E-commerce manager.
- Design engineer.
- Graphics designer.
- Medical transcript accountants.
- Writers.
- Teaching (online classes).
- Telehealth/telemedicine.

Jobs that require face-to-face contact with co-workers or customers, however, are difficult to perform as telework. This would include some managers, retail sales staff, construction workers, and the like.

Benefits of Telework

Gains in computing and communication technologies have fueled the growth in teleworking. In many cases, the four walls of an office are not required to get the work done as was the case just a few years ago. Affordable technology lets workers outfit a home office for just a small percentage of what it costs a business to build an office infrastructure. The following sections list the advantages of teleworking for both the employee and employer.

Benefits for the Teleworker

A teleworker saves money and time by not commuting. In addition, he or she may be more productive because of the flexibility of working during off hours, such as late nights, early mornings, holidays, or weekends.

Teleworkers also are free from interruptions that occur in a normal office environment. Dedicated and self-disciplined teleworkers usually can finish projects quicker because they are not disrupted by office gossip and frequent meetings.

Another plus for the teleworker is being able to spend more time at home, a special advantage for those with young children, those who care for elderly relatives, and for those with disabilities.

Finally, the teleworker may be able to take a tax deduction for a home office. Business supplies, equipment, utility costs, use of dedicated office space and storage, etc., may apply for a teleworker.

Benefits for the Employer

Unless it affected the bottom line, most companies would not even consider integrating teleworking into their overall business model. However, many companies have realized great gains in productivity, employee morale, and efficiency since instituting teleworking. In addition, some companies save money over the long term by using teleworkers.

Size Reduction. Companies that have teleworkers can reduce the size of their office spaces and overhead or avoid moving to larger premises. Reducing office space saves money on furniture, rent, heat, air conditioning, and utility expenses.

Best Talent. Another benefit of using teleworkers is that the company is able to utilize the best employees, regardless of their location. For example, many publishing houses use teleworkers to write, edit, proofread, and design manuscripts. This allows them to search for and acquire teleworkers from around the world. All the teleworker needs is e-mail, a phone, and sometimes a fax to send and receive documents, memos, and other information from the publisher.

Productivity. Companies may also see an increase in teleworkers' productivity. One reason is because people who telework use less sick leave than traditional office workers. Teleworkers' schedules, as noted above, can also be flexible rather than limited to 8 a.m. to 5 p.m., thereby freeing them to work longer hours on special projects that may demand extra time.

Disadvantages of Teleworking

Teleworking is not for everyone or every company, though. Before an employee decides to telework, he or she should be aware of some of the disadvantages of working from home. Likewise, not all companies are suited to provide teleworking environments, so they too should look carefully at teleworking before deciding to implement it. The following sections discuss some of these disadvantages.

Employability Skills

Allocating Time

The ability to manage time well is a crucial employability skill. Whether you're telecommuting or working at the office, it's important to prioritize tasks, set goals, and use time wisely to complete projects on schedule.

Going Global

Scheduling to Avoid Conflicts

When you are conducting business in another country, make sure that you do not schedule business on a cultural or religious holiday. Find out the dates of the various holidays observed in that country before scheduling a meeting.

oops!

Determining Your Own Schedule

When working at home, you determines your own work schedule.

(*Determine* is the correct word, not *determines*.)

Disadvantages for the Teleworker

Teleworkers may experience isolation from other workers, and they may be the victims of resentment expressed by nontelecommuting co-workers. Some teleworkers tend to overwork, never turning off their PCs and never taking necessary breaks to avoid burnout. Home distractions might make it difficult for some people to stay on task. For others, there may be extra utility costs at home, although these may be offset by the reduced commuting expenses or may be paid for by the teleworkers' companies. As a teleworker, you become your own technical support department. As a result, teleworkers must become more technically savvy about their computers, printer, fax machines, scanners, and, in some cases, phone lines.

Disadvantages for the Employer

Only some kinds of work are appropriate for teleworking. Some managers have difficulty managing by results only; they need to see that tasks are being done. Here are other potential problems for employers:

- Meetings are hard to schedule.
- Technology infrastructure may be too expensive.
- Data security is harder to ensure.
- Customers may object to dealing with home-based workers.
- There is increased liability in having workers off-site.
- There is the additional expense of software licensing for off-site computers.

Setting Up the Home Office

Considerations for setting up a home office include ample workspace in a separate hazard-free room or other self-contained area. The area should be temperature controlled and well lit, with no glare on the computer monitor. The home office should be isolated from distracting noises, and the furnishings, particularly the computer chair, should be ergonomically designed to prevent strains and injuries. **Ergonomics,** sometimes called human engineering, is the design of devices, systems, and physical working conditions that meet the physical needs of the worker.

Ergonomics and Health Issues

Any office worker will tell you that sitting at a desk all day can become extremely uncomfortable. Using a computer all day long can be even worse. Many hand and wrist injuries result from keyboarding or using a mouse for long periods of time. Eye strain is common after staring at a monitor for hours on end. Such injuries can be extreme, threatening the sufferer's general health.

Much is being done to make computers easier, safer, and more comfortable to use. Thanks to the publicity that computer-related injuries have received over the past decade, most people now recognize the importance of ergonomically correct computer furniture and proper techniques for using the computer. The term *ergonomically correct* means that a product is designed to work properly with the human body, reducing the risk of strain, stress, or other types of injuries.

Repetitive Stress Injuries

The field of ergonomics did not receive much attention until repetitive stress injuries (RSIs)—a group of ailments caused by continuously using the body in ways it was not designed to work—began appearing among clerical workers who spend most of their time entering data on computer keyboards. One injury that is especially well documented among these workers is carpal tunnel syndrome, a wrist or hand injury caused by extended periods of keyboarding.

The carpal tunnel is a passageway in the wrist through which a bundle of nerves passes. In carpal tunnel syndrome, the tunnel becomes misshapen because the victim has held the wrists stiffly for long periods, as people do while keyboarding. When the tunnel becomes distorted, it can pinch the nerves that run through it, causing tingling, numbness, pain, and even an inability to use the hands. Carpal tunnel syndome is the best-known RSI. Is can become so debilitating that employees suffering from it have to take time off work. In some extreme cases, surgery is required.

If you routinely use a computer, you can avoid fatigue and strain by choosing the proper furniture for your workspace. The most important piece of furniture is a comfortable, ergonomically designed chair. See **Exhibit 12.4.** Look for these three characteristics in any office chair:

- Adjustable height.
- Lower-back support.
- Armrests (preferably adjustable).

Your desk should also be well suited to computer use, permitting you to place your keyboard and mouse at the proper height. Ideally, your hands should be at the same height as your elbows, or slightly lower, when they hover above the keyboard.

Another important factor in avoiding keyboard-related RSIs is the keyboard itself. A few years ago keyboard designers realized that a flat keyboard is not well suited to the shape of our hands. If you relax your arms, your thumbs tend to point up. Logically, then, keyboards should be designed with two sides, one for each hand. Ergonomic keyboards allow the user's hands to rest in a more natural position than traditional flat keyboards.

A padded wrist support can also help prevent an RSI. The support can be built onto the keyboard or placed in front of it. A wrist support allows you to rest your hands comfortably when you are not actually typing. Remember, however, that you should never rest your wrists on anything, even a comfortable wrist support, while you type. Use the support only when your fingers are not touching the keys.

Eyestrain

Eyestrain is the most frequently reported health problem associated with computers.
Here are some ways to protect your vision and reduce eyestrain:

- Avoid staring at the screen for long stretches of time.
- Remember to blink; lack of blinking causes dryness of the eye and eyestrain.

oops!

Helpful Hyphen

We all gasped when we saw that the meeting had a four hour agenda.

(*Four*-hour—a hyphen is needed.)

Going Global

An International Audience

Be careful about making jokes while speaking to an international audience. A cultural joke may be unfamiliar to the audience and might even be offensive.

KEY POINT

Position your monitor so that no light reflects off the screen.

- Position your monitor between 2 and 2½ feet away from your eyes.
- Position your monitor so that no light reflects off the screen. If you cannot avoid reflections, purchase an antiglare screen.
- Keep your screen clean.
- Look for a monitor that holds a steady image without appearing to pulsate or flicker.

Electromagnetic Fields

Electromagnetic fields (EMFs) are created during the generation, transmission, and use of low-frequency electrical power. These fields exist near power lines, electrical appliances, and any piece of equipment that has an electric motor. A debate has continued for years whether EMFs can be linked to cancer. Though not conclusive, there is enough data to raise suspicion.

EMFs are composed of an electrical and magnetic component. Of the two, the magnetic field is the one that raises the health concern. Electrical fields lose strength when they come in contact with barriers, such as clothing and skin. A magnetic field will penetrate most materials, however, even concrete or lead. Magnetic fields lose strength rapidly with distance. Options to reduce your risk from EMFs include the following:

- Take frequent breaks away from the computer.
- Sit an arm's length away from the system unit and monitor.
- Use a flat-panel display, which does not radiate EMFs.

Assessment   Section 12.4

Review of Key Terms

1. How has technology allowed workers to *telecommute* or *telework*? ____
   _____
   _____

2. What is the difference between *hot desking* and *hoteling*? _____
   _____
   _____
   _____

Editing Practice

Using Tact!   Each of the following items lacks sensitivity to the reader. Rewrite each one to correct the problem.

3. You forgot to tell us what color towels you want (catalog No. 0R114). If you want to get your towels, send us the color ASAP! _____
   _____
   _____
   _____

4. We recently sold 6,000 CD players in our fantastic sale. You are the only one complaining. Although we have 5,999 satisfied customers, you should get your new CD player tomorrow. _____

_____

_____

5. The terms of our contract were crystal clear. We offered a discount if we received payment within 10 days. You took a total of 30 days to pay. Now you owe us the $50 balance. _____

_____

Practical Application

Drawing Conclusions

6. There are two main issues to consider about telecommuting—working alone and being self-disciplined. Is telecommuting for you? Write a short report in which you evaluate your characteristics and work style to determine if you would make a productive telecommuter. _____

_____

7. Each person on the team should interview several people who telecommute. Take notes on what their professions are, and find out what they like and don't like about telecommuting. Once you have gathered your data, share your notes with the team to find common issues. Then, write a report for your instructor that summarizes your team's findings. _____

_____

Discussion Point

Making Comparisons

8. What are the advantages and disadvantages of teleworking? What jobs are more suitable for this? _____

_____

_____

_____

_____

_____

_____

9. How does teleworking benefit the employer? _____

_____

_____

_____

_____

_____

_____

Chapter 13

Communicating with Customers

Workplace Connection

In the last two decades, we have seen "mom-and-pop" grocery stores, corner drugstores, and traditional downtown shopping districts approach extinction. However, keeping customers satisfied, no matter where or how the goods and services are purchased, is key to business profits and longevity.

CHAPTER OBJECTIVES
When you have completed this chapter, you should be able to:

- Explain the importance of good customer service.
- List some strategies for maintaining good customer service.
- Discuss ways to improve contacts with customers.
- Suggest ways to respond to customer-service needs.

The Importance of Good Customer Service

Essential Principles

Customer service is the consistent performance of activities or services for the purpose of ensuring customer satisfaction. Customer satisfaction occurs when the customer's wants and needs are met and when the customer feels valued by the company. Goods and services must be provided to the customer when and where they are wanted and needed and at a competitive price. Making customers feel valued instills the feeling that their business is appreciated, that they will be treated with respect, and that their business will receive conscientious attention.

Customer service is a proactive function that should exist and be practiced throughout every business organization. The requirement that customer-service procedures be implemented throughout an organization must come from top management. Without top management's support and specific directives to key employees, customer service will not receive the attention it deserves.

You should establish a customer-service culture that instills a courteous, helpful, professional attitude at all levels of your organization. Employees should convey this attitude to customers, letting them know that they are eager to help them. Communication is vital to any effective customer-service program. If customer-service policies appear only in the company handbook and are not effectively conveyed throughout the organization and to customers, the customer-service culture mentioned above does not exist.

An excellent customer-service reputation can become the feature that gives your company a competitive edge in the marketplace. Always remember that if you do not take care of your customers, your competitors will.

Need for Customer Service

Why should your company implement customer-service procedures? In a highly competitive world, outstanding customer service helps you retain your current customers and attract new ones. Outstanding customer service also helps develop a reputation that encourages people to do business with you. Satisfied customers become loyal customers who continue to use your product or service, resulting in repeat business. Chief executive officers (CEOs) say it is easier to keep a customer than to attract a new one. In addition, businesses derive much of their new business through referrals. **Referrals** are recommendations from satisfied customers.

SECTION OBJECTIVES

When you have finished Section 13.1, you will be able to:

- Explain the concept of customer service.

- Understand the importance of customer service.

- Explain the difference between external and internal customers.

WHY IT'S IMPORTANT

No matter what job you choose in the future, you will have to deal with customers. Learning the basics of effective customer service will help you interact with internal and external clients.

KEY TERMS

- customer service
- referrals
- external customers
- internal customers

KEY POINT

External customers are people outside your organization who purchase your goods or services.

We often think of customers as being from outside the business. However, there are two categories of customers: external and internal. **External customers** are people outside the business who purchase its goods or services. External customers include individual consumers and businesses. A company may work with external customers in person, through its Web site, or by telephone, fax, or e-mail.

An **internal customer** is a co-worker or supervisor—someone within the company who depends on products, supplies, or services from a different department. Suppose, for example, you work in the marketing department. Before the marketing department can determine the selling price for an item, the company's budget office must supply the cost figures. The marketing department is the internal customer of the budget office. If the marketing department asks the accounting department for the credit rating of a prospective customer, the marketing department is an internal customer of the accounting department.

KEY POINT

Internal customers are people within your own company who depend on co-workers for products, supplies, or services.

Today, much emphasis is placed on maintaining good relationships with internal customers. Internal customers must work as a team and communicate with a courteous, positive attitude. Good communication skills and a positive attitude allows the internal team to produce the best product and service possible.

Assessment   Section 13.1

Review of Key Terms

1. What is *customer service*? _____
    _____

2. Why are *referrals* an important business tool? _____
    _____
    _____

Editing Practice

Spelling Alert!   Rewrite the paragraph below, correcting any spelling errors.

3. Chris, a disatisfied customer, wanted to speak with the store manager. He said if the manager did not speak with him immediatly, he would make a scine. The manager spoke with Chris, who critecized the quality of work he recently had done on his car. Their were oil stains on the upholstery and cigarette butts left in the ashtray. The condition of the car was not acceptable. Chris announced he would go elsewhere if the car was not restored satisfactorily. _____
    _____
    _____
    _____
    _____
    _____

Practical Application

Analyzing Information

4. Interview a customer-service representative at a local business, such as a retail store or government agency. Are staff members trained to handle customer inquiries? Write a brief essay describing the customer-service policy and practices of the organization. _____

_____

5. Role-play a customer-service situation involving a face-to-face conversation, a telephone call, or an e-mail. Team members will write scenarios to show both the "wrong" way and the "right" way to handle a particular situation. Volunteers will role-play the scenes for the class or display the e-mails on a screen. _____

_____

Discussion Point

Making Comparisons

6. How can good customer service enhance a business? How does bad customer service hurt a business? Give examples of both good and bad customer service that you have received. How did these encounters affect your opinion of the company? _____

_____

_____

7. Define *external customers* and *internal customers*. _____

_____

_____

_____

SECTION OBJECTIVES

When you have finished Section 13.2, you will be able to:

- Define a customer-focused organization.
- Understand the importance of positive customer contact.
- Discuss customer-service guidelines.
- Discuss the usefulness of PDAs and laptop computers.
- Explain how companies can be accessible to their customers.
- Understand the importance of knowledgeable responses to customers.
- Explain the role of continual contact with customers.

WHY IT'S IMPORTANT

Developing a customer-focused attitude not only helps the "bottom line" of a company, but it can also help you as an individual. Your colleagues and clients will be more likely to deal with you in a fair manner if you adopt a customer-focused attitude.

KEY TERMS

- customer-focused organization
- personal digital assistants (PDAs)
- laptop computers

KEY POINT

Any employee who comes in contact with a customer directly or indirectly can influence that customer's perception of the company and its products and services.

Maintaining Good Customer Service

Customer Service as an Ongoing Function

Customer service is a complex function that has many facets. Some people view customer service as a problem-solving function that comes into play only when there has been a complaint. In fact, customer service should be an ongoing function that allows employees to anticipate and prevent problems.

Employees at all levels should be trained to communicate with customers. They should be committed to being a **customer-focused organization.** A customer-focused organization makes customer service an ongoing function. Its approach is proactive in anticipating problems. If a business satisfies its customers and is managed efficiently, profits should naturally follow. Employees should be taught the following good customer-service practices:

- Good customer service is a part of internal as well as external communication and service.
- Good customer service is an attitude that should be demonstrated by all employees.
- Customers are important to business and should never be considered a nuisance.
- Treat customers with respect and courtesy.
- Customers do not depend on us nearly as much as we depend on them.
- In addition to helping solve customer problems, good customer service includes creating a positive business atmosphere in which customers can do business.
- Satisfied customers continue doing business with us and recommend us to their friends.

Customer Contact

Any employee who comes in contact with a customer, directly or indirectly, can influence that customer's perception of the company. Advertisements, phone calls, faxes, e-mail, letters, and face-to-face conversations can increase or diminish the likelihood that a customer or potential customer will do business with your firm.

Limited Customer Contact

First impressions are important in establishing a good rapport between customers and employees. Employees should exhibit positive attitudes and perform their jobs in such a way that they build trust.

There are many opportunities to cultivate a positive customer-service image. Use the following guidelines when working in a business environment in which only limited contact with external customers takes place.

- Maintain a clear, uncluttered business environment.
- Greet the customer with a smile and an appropriate greeting.
- Address the customer by name.
- Be attentive to the customer and treat him or her with respect.
- Assist the customer in conducting his or her business.
- Thank the customer, and say good-bye with a smile.

Listen when customers speak. Get to know them and what is important to them without being intrusive. Make notes each time you visit a customer or talk with him or her. Include pertinent information about the contact and the customer's personal interests. You might write: "Susan's daughter will graduate from college next week. Send her a card." Another entry might be: "Ivan and his wife are expecting a baby in July." Or, "Alice will be competing in the local marathon in March." Keep the information current, and read your file on each customer before making a call or visit. Your customers will be impressed by your seemingly impeccable memory, but you are really just being organized and doing your homework. This tactic communicates that you respect and value the customer and that you value the business the customer conducts with you. Taking notes can be as simple as writing on an index card. However, technology has provided us with two extremely helpful tools for note taking and other functions: the personal digital assistant (PDA) and the laptop computer.

Personal Digital Assistants (PDAs) are computers that fit in the palm of your hand. Computer companies offer many different functions on these small devices. Most offer an address book, a calendar, a calculator, and a note function. Others offer Internet capabilities, including e-mail. Data are entered into the PDA by tapping the tiny, on-screen keyboard or by handwriting data on the screen using a special stylus. These devices provide convenience for employees who are frequently away from their desks or anyone else who has complex responsibilities. One benefit of a PDA is that you can synchronize its data with the data on your desktop or laptop computer. In other words, when you are away from your desk, you can enter new appointments, notes, and other information into the PDA. When you return to your office, you can then use software that comes with the PDA to update both the PDA and the desktop computer simultaneously. (See **Exhibit 13.1.**)

Laptop computers also are convenient tools for executives. A **laptop computer** functions like a desktop computer but is small enough to be portable and may be battery-operated. Laptop computers have become standard equipment for sales representatives and others who often work away from the office. (See **Exhibit 13.1.**) Laptops can be connected by telephone or wireless modem through the Internet to the home office. Laptop users can immediately enter and transmit information to the main office, thus improving work efficiency. Sales representatives use laptops to retrieve updated price lists, inventory figures, delivery information, graphics of specific products, and a multitude of other data. With this kind of readily available information, the employee can serve the customer more efficiently. For example, both laptops and PDAs can be operated on major airlines at times specified by the flight crew.

Accessibility

A company is "accessible" if business can be conducted easily and at a convenient time. Here are a few examples of those services:

- Web sites allow customers to conduct business at any time from a computer.
- Banks provide automated teller machines, or ATMs, and 24-hour banking via computers.

Going Global

Friendly Greetings

Greeting a customer in his or her native language demonstrates an effort to be friendly. Here are some frequently used English words and their Spanish equivalents.

English	Spanish
Hello	Hola
Good-bye	Adiós
Thank you	Gracias

Digital Data

Convenient Shopping and Flying

Many airlines and retail clothing stores have online services to help customers. Using your home computer, you can reserve and book airline tickets that meet your requirements, and you can conveniently shop for clothing without having to leave your home.

Exhibit 13.1
The Laptop
Laptop computers are standard equipment for business professionals who are frequently away from their offices. *Thinking Critically.* How have laptop computers changed the way we work?

KEY POINT

Your company is accessible to customers if you make it easy for them to conduct business at convenient times.

Know Your Representative

As a sales representation, you should get to know your customers.

(*Representative* is the correct word, not *representation*.)

- Some companies have toll-free telephone numbers that are answered 24 hours per day, 7 days per week.
- A catalog-sales company installed a TDD to communicate with deaf customers by telephone.
- A school district encourages parents to pay for school lunches online.
- Hotels that cater to business travelers have rooms wired for Internet and fax connections. (See **Exhibit 13.2** on page 497.)
- Some companies offer e-mail addresses to answer customer questions.
- Mail-order pharmacies offer 24-hour, automated prescription refills by telephone or online.
- Pacemakers can now be checked by telephone to ensure proper operation.
- Major airlines provide telephones for passengers to use in flight. (See **Exhibit 13.3** on page 498.)
- Some dentists and doctors schedule evening and Saturday appointments.
- Las Vegas has drive-through wedding chapels.

Toll-free phone numbers are often established to assist customers. Many of these toll-free numbers operate around the clock—not just from 9 a.m. to 5. p.m., Monday through Friday. When a problem occurs, the customer wants an immediate answer.

Exhibit 13.2
Guest Room with Dataport
Many hotels offer guests a variety of business services. *Thinking Critically.*
How might hotel personnel assist business travelers during their stay?

Consumers place calls to furniture manufacturers when they have trouble assembling an item, to beauty product companies when their hair dye is wrong, and to poultry companies when their Thanksgiving turkey is not cooked right. Customers want what they want when they want it. The astute executive makes his or her company's products and services available when customers need them.

Knowledgeable Responses

Employees who come into contact with customers should be knowledgeable about their company's products and services, as well as its policies. When customers ask questions, give them a timely answer. If you don't know the answer, tell the customer that you will find out and call back with the answer. Don't let that promise be "lip service." If you say that you will get information for a customer, do it as soon as it is feasible to do so.

Here are some ways you can give knowledgeable responses to customers and clients:

- Familiarize yourself with the products and services your company offers.
- Know the functions of key departments and personnel to whom you can refer a customer or client.
- Have copies of pertinent company information, such as brochures, fliers, and catalogs, available for your reference.
- Provide specific information such as dates and costs.

Employability Skills

Maintaining and Troubleshooting Equipment

Equipment, such as cash registers or computers, can fail during working hours. When you are dealing with customers, the ability to troubleshoot is important in maintaining good service. One way to improve customer service is to inspect equipment from time to time to prevent mishaps.

Exhibit 13.3
In-Flight Telephone
Making an in-flight telephone call may be a little expensive, but it's worth the cost when important messages must get through to their destinations. ***Thinking Critically.*** *When might you use an in-flight telephone?*

Continual Contact

After you have sold a product or provided a service, keep the customer informed. Let the customer know if merchandise will be delayed or if there is a shipping problem. If there are changes in the service that your company has provided, such as a change in a policy or a warranty, notify the customer in writing or with a telephone call. Let the customer know what to expect.

Even after the sale has been made and the customer has paid for the merchandise, you should follow through and reinforce the relationship between the company and the customer. For example, an Internet provider e-mailed a customer to make sure that the connection was working correctly. A dermatologist called a surgery patient several days after the procedure to find out if she was experiencing any difficulties. A computer sales representative called clients who had recently bought computers and software to ask if he could provide additional technical assistance.

In any situation in which employees are in direct contact with the public, that contact becomes the basis for the customer's judgment about the services or products provided by the company. If the contact situation is pleasant and rewarding, the customer will likely view the company positively; any unpleasantness will create negative impressions and discourage the customer from doing business with the company.

Review of Key Terms

1. What is a *customer-focused organization*? _____

_____

_____

2. How can *laptop computers* increase business productivity? _____

_____

_____

Editing Practice

Proofreading Alert!   Proofread the following sentences, eliminating all unnecessary repetitions.

3. We are planning to revert back to personal contacts as our main sales strategy. _____

4. These forms confuse me because they are both alike. _____

5. Please repeat the instructions again so that everyone understands them. _____

6. What files are stored inside of this cabinet? _____

7. Past experience shows that Michael is reliable. _____

8. In addition, other evidence indicates that the volcano erupted within the past 200 years _____

_____

Practical Application

Drawing Conclusions

9. Explain the importance of making knowledgeable responses and maintaining continual contact in customer-service situations. _____

_____

_____

_____

10. Divide the team into two or three groups. Each group will visit and observe the customer-service techniques at three local businesses, such as restaurants, supermarkets, or video stores. Meet as a team and compare the positive and negative actions that you observed. Write a summary of your findings. _____

_____

_____

_____

Discussion Point

Evaluating Concepts

11. What are guidelines to use when you have limited contact with a customer? _____

_____

_____

12. Give examples of technologies that customer-service companies use to be accessible to customers. How do policies affect these media? _____

_____

_____

_____

_____

13. Discuss ways to establish continual contact with a customer. Under which circumstances is continual contact important? _____

_____

_____

_____

_____

Improving Contact with Customers

Essential Principles

Both initial and continuing customer contacts are important in establishing and maintaining good customer relations. Every employee can influence a customer's image of your firm. The assistant who greets visitors and answers telephone calls can have a significant impact on a customer's perception of your firm. A sales representative who has product knowledge instills confidence in the company. A friendly and helpful assistant who directs a visitor or caller to the person who can best offer assistance creates customer goodwill. **Customer service** deals with customers' needs, complaints, and inquiries. Good customer service skills are critical, not just for the sales representative and the assistant but for everyone in the organization. Communication plays a vital role in customer service.

Receiving the Public

Some companies designate an employee, such as a receptionist, to greet visitors. However, almost all employees come in contact with customers. Chances are, no matter which field you choose, you will have interaction with customers. You should, therefore, be familiar with the basic procedures for meeting the public. **Exhibit 13.4** on page 502 illustrates a professional yet friendly approach to greeting a client.

Give Prompt Attention to Visitors

Recognize a visitor's presence immediately. Even if you are busy, interrupt your work for a moment to smile and say to the new arrival, "I'll be with you in a moment. Would you like to sit down?"

Be Courteous to All Visitors

Every visitor should receive friendly and courteous treatment, regardless of the purpose of the visit. Even if the visitor is upset about something and acts accordingly, you must overlook any discourtesy and show that you are concerned. It may be that your visitor is annoyed about what he or she believes is unfair treatment from your company. There may be some justification for this belief, but you have an opportunity to mend it. Even if you can do nothing about the situation, you can listen in an understanding way to the complaint. Treating an annoyed customer discourteously will only make the situation worse. Your courteous attitude is likely to help calm the visitor and give your company a chance to make amends.

Apologize for Delays

If someone cannot keep an appointment, you should explain the delay. For example, "I'm sorry, Ms. Welch, Mr. Farber has been

Employability Skills

Organizing Ideas

Organizing ideas is a key component of communicating with co-workers and customers. Business documents that present information in an organized manner help prevent miscommunication.

Exhibit 13.4
Welcoming a Visitor
The way you welcome a visitor to your company can make a good impression on the visitor and create a positive mind-set for the business that will be conducted. ***Thinking Critically.*** *How might this receptionist make a good impression on the visitor?*

delayed at a meeting." You should tell the visitor about how long the wait will be: "Mr. Farber should be back in about 20 minutes." Make the visitor comfortable. A selection of current magazines and today's newspaper should be available, and you should offer a cup of coffee if it is convenient to do so.

Find Out the Purpose of the Visit

Almost every visitor will have an appointment with a staff member of the company. For example, a visitor may say to you, "I'm Michael Werner. I have a 10 a.m. appointment with Susan Mangum." You will escort Mr. Werner to the appropriate office or telephone Ms. Mangum, letting her know that her visitor has arrived. If you do not know whether the visitor has an appointment, you must ask, "May I help you?" or "Whom do you wish to see?" If the visitor has no appointment, take his or her name, the name of the company he or she represents (if any), and the purpose of the call. Relay this information to the person who you think can be of most help to the visitor. After getting permission to show the visitor in, invite him or her to follow you to the appropriate office. Then, present the visitor like this: "Mr. Morgan [host], this is Mary O'Neill [visitor]."

Be Discreet and Tactful

Discretion is cautious reserve in speech. Protect the privacy of both your manager and your company by being discreet in your comments to visitors. For example, if your employer is late arriving at the office in the morning or returning from lunch, it is not appropriate to supply these details to the visitor. Also, avoid making conversation about company business or personnel.

Be discreet in giving any opinions solicited by the visitor. For example, the visitor may want to show you certain products and ask whether you think your company might be interested in buying them. Unless you are responsible for company purchases, however, you should not give an opinion about the company's possible interest in buying the products. Simply reply that you can't make decisions about purchases and that you will contact someone who can.

Communicating by Telephone

Many transactions are handled by telephone. All telephone relationships—regardless of the initial contact system your company uses—require special consideration. In almost all cases, the customer expects speed, knowledge, courtesy, and action.

Speed

Answer the telephone within three rings, sooner if possible. Since the customer has called rather than visited, he or she is interested in saving time. Although the customer's expectation of a speedy response is frequently unrealistic, your demeanor will affect the customer's attitude.

Knowledge

If you have answered the call, it is important to find out quickly what is being requested. Do not assume that the first statement or request is the customer's primary motive for calling; getting to that may take a while. Respond in those areas in which you are qualified, and quickly redirect the customer to other staff members if necessary. If possible, after making the transfer, check to find out whether the transfer occurred. There is nothing more frustrating to a customer who has called long distance than to be transferred to another extension and get a busy signal, or to be accidentally disconnected.

Courtesy

Always use a respectful tone when answering calls from customers. Maintaining a courteous tone can be difficult, especially when the day grows long or the customer becomes hostile. However impatient and frustrated you become, remember that each call is a new situation to the caller. No matter how far up or down the chain of command you are, a customer remembers discourtesy—and often the name of the person who was discourteous.

Action

When you make a commitment to a customer, make sure that you keep it. If you promised to replace a defective product, do so as soon as possible. Broken commitments foster distrust.

Employability Skills

Monitoring and Correcting Performance

Maintaining customer service is important, but improving it is more important. Predicting trends, correcting performance failures, and monitoring operations are essential to improving and maintaining a successful business.

Employability Skills

Listening

To establish credibility with your customers, carefully listen to their requests and take appropriate actions. Listening is an important employability skill when you are working with customers.

Assessment Section 13.3

Review of Key Terms

1. Which employees in an organization should have good *customer-service* skills? _____

_____

2. What is *discretion,* and in which business situations should it be used?

_____

_____

Editing Practice

Public Relations Alert!   Rewrite any sentences from the following telephone conversation that do not display tact and courtesy.

3.   Shawna: Hello. Whom do you want to speak with?

Customer: My name is Ruby Devane. I am trying to contact Megan Diaz.

Shawna: Do you know what department she's in?

Customer: No. Do I need that information?

Shawna: What do you want to talk to her about? _____

_____

_____

_____

_____

Practical Application

Analyzing Information

4.   With your team, develop and role-play the following situations and the appropriate responses:

- A customer walks into the reception area and looks confused.
- A customer standing in line with a small infant is becoming agitated about the long wait.
- An annoyed customer approaches you about a problem and begins yelling.
- You must put a caller on hold; when you do, you disconnect the person and that person calls back.
- You clearly know that the company is at fault for nonperformance of a product; a customer is calling about a matter indirectly related to your company's services or products. _____

_____

Discussion Point

Making Generalizations

5.   What is the appropriate way to let a customer know that his or her appointment will be delayed because your employer is late? Discuss other situations in which you must be tactful with customers. _____

_____

_____

_____

6.   How does telephone etiquette affect customer relations? Do you think that communicating with customers over the phone is easier or more difficult than talking face-to-face with a customer? _____

_____

_____

Responding to Customer-Service Needs

Essential Principles

The best way to curb customer complaints is to prevent them. A visitor to the Scottsdale Princess Hotel in Arizona was impressed with the exceptional service she received from all levels of the hotel staff. When the visitor commented on the exceptional service, a human resources spokesperson at the hotel told her that all employees receive customer-service training. The spokesperson said that employees are encouraged to help make memories for the guests and to cater to the "internal guest" (like an "internal customer") by becoming a "team player." The spokesperson showed the guest a card that is given to all associates to remind them of the level of service that guests should receive. The following quotes are from that card:

> "We provide our guests with a unique and luxurious resort experience through attentive and professional service."
>
> "By anticipating needs and exceeding expectations, we provide our guests with sincere, personalized service, ensuring a memorable stay."

Top management must set the standard for good customer service throughout the organization. No matter how hard a company tries, however, there will be some dissatisfied customers. The goal then is to minimize dissatisfaction and take corrective action when it does occur.

Technology and Customer Satisfaction

Some customers communicate by e-mail. E-mail, just like telephone calls and correspondence, should be answered promptly. E-mail transmissions happen so quickly that the sender expects a fast response. If companies use e-mail for correspondence, they should ensure that employees respond quickly.

Some employees use their e-mail's auto-responder function when they receive messages and are unavailable to answer them. The **auto responder** is a message-response system that automatically replies to e-mails in the employee's absence. A sample auto-responder message follows: "Gordon Lang is attending an engineering show and will be back in his office Monday, May 5. Please e-mail his assistant, Robert Baker at rbaker@city.com if you need immediate help with your computer system." Such a message conveys that Gordon Lang is not simply ignoring the message and that he will be available on May 5 to reply to the e-mail. The e-mail also tells the reader who could be of assistance in Mr. Lang's absence.

Companies also improve customer service by hosting Web sites. A Web site allows a customer to conduct business with the company 24 hours per day, 7 days per week. Web sites should make it easy for customers to do business. If the customer finds the Web site difficult to use, the customer finds another company's Web site just a quick click away. See **Exhibit 13.5.**

Here are some common Web site features:

- A **Frequently Asked Questions (FAQs)** section. Clicking on this section takes you to a list of common questions and the answers to them, often letting the customers solve their problems without further assistance.

- A **Contact Us** section. Clicking on this section takes you to a screen with a preaddressed e-mail. This makes e-mailing the company easier.

- An **order confirmation function.** When you place an order electronically, you will have an e-mail confirmation within about 15 minutes. This confirmation assures you that the products have been purchased. The confirmation also lists the tracking number, which enables you to follow your shipment as it makes its way to your office.

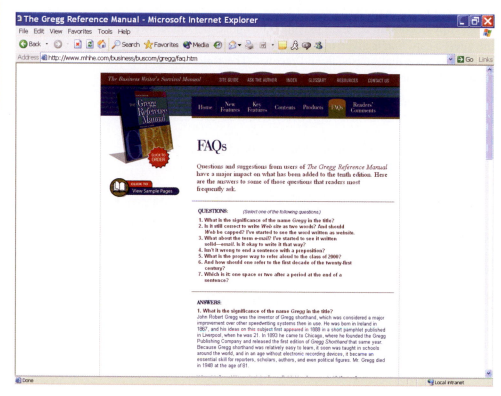

Exhibit 13.5
Frequently Asked Questions (FAQs)
This Web site has a Frequently Asked Questions (FAQs) section and a Contact Us section. ***Thinking Critically.*** *What does the FAQ section give customers? What does the Contact Us section give customers?*

Sometimes technology increases customer frustration. Imagine how you would feel if you called a company about a defective product and were connected to the following message:

"Hello! This is Low Country Communications. If you want to subscribe to our services, press 1 now. If you want information about your bill, press 2 now. If you want Customer Service, press. . . ."

If your company uses such technology, your "live" voice or presence becomes especially important. When your personal contact with a customer occurs, his or her stress level probably is already high. Your recognition of the customer's state of mind is crucial. Greet the customer by making a positive statement: "Hi. I'm Maxine in Customer Service. May I help you?"

When formal greetings are required, express genuine interest in helping the caller: "Hello. This is Shawn Vandenberg at City Electronics. Thanks for calling. How may I help you?" Control your speed of delivery and tone of voice to sound fresh. It helps to vary your responses to avoid the impression of a worn-out greeting. Communicating boredom or impatience in the delivery of a "warm" greeting is worse than bland impersonality. Here are some suggestions for responding to customer concerns:

- Answer the telephone call promptly in a courteous, enthusiastic tone.
- Listen carefully and take notes on important details.
- If a customer is irritated, let him or her vent about the problems.
- If a customer becomes hostile, maintain self-control. You must remember that you represent your company. Nothing is gained by becoming angry.
- Talk *with* the customer—not *at* the customer.
- Express interest in and an understanding of the caller's problem.
- Remember that all customers are different, and they will come to the situation with different levels of negotiating skills.
- Clarify any misunderstandings that may have occurred.
- Don't blame someone else for the problem.
- Take enough time to help the customer. If the customer senses that you are rushed, he or she will think that you consider the call unimportant.
- Tell the caller what action you will take. If the customer has experienced problems, make repairs and exchanges cheerfully. Provide whatever relief is available through warranties and company policy. Be honest and fair, yet firm.
- If you cannot make the adjustment yourself, refer the caller to someone who can. Don't make the caller repeat the entire story to someone else.
- Take the action that you promised the customer as soon as possible.
- Follow up within three to five days to make sure that the customer is now satisfied.

Maintaining your air of helpfulness decreases a customer's resistance and establishes a basis for success. Never respond to a customer's demand for speed with frustration. Simply tell the customer when you can do something. If the complexity of the request clearly requires a face-to-face exchange, suggest that a visit would be more productive and arrange for the customer to meet with you. Here are some suggestions for dealing with customers who have a complaint or need to exchange an item.

Always keep the customer's expectations in mind when you are trying to resolve the complaint. Be creative, but stay within the limits of your customer-service policies, when suggesting solutions to the customer's concerns. Customers who do not receive a satisfactory remedy often will communicate their dissatisfaction to others using the Internet. This phenomenon is called **e-whining.** Several Web sites exist that will list the customer's complaints. Other Web sites will send an anonymous e-mail, letting companies know that someone is dissatisfied with a product or a service. Aim to provide the best customer service available to avoid this kind of publicity.

Going Global

When Are Gifts Acceptable?

In business settings, gift giving is expected in some cultures like Japan. In other cultures, it is not an acceptable practice. Many U.S. companies enforce strict guidelines about the kind of gift an employee may accept or give.

Customer-Service Policies and Procedures

Most companies have customer-service policies and procedures. Policies and procedures set up by a company determine the boundaries of your behavior as an employee. Do not assume, however, that the company's recommended procedures anticipate every situation. Also, do not assume that company procedures are infallible. Of course, you cannot make policy by yourself or make arbitrary changes that do not conform to the spirit of the policy. Be especially careful of personal interpretation in situations with legal repercussions.

Every contact situation requires your alertness, sensitivity, and judgment in handling customers in the best interest of a positive relationship. Let managers know if you have suggestions for improving your company's customer-service policy.

Organizations often hang up fancy posters and banners touting such claims as, "The customer is always right," "The customer is No. 1," or "We're here to serve YOU!" But at the moment of truth, when customers come into contact with employees, they frequently hear, "Please take a number so we can better serve you," "I can't do that," or (on the phone), "ABC Company, please hold—[CLICK]." Clearly, when these things occur, the organization is not customer-focused and a service has broken down. The important question is, "How do we fix our system?" The answer: Make a commitment to the customer and establish an environment that will support that commitment. This is where you come in as a customer-service professional. Through conscientious and concerned assistance to customers, you and the organization can form a solid relationship with the consumer.

Assessment   Section 13.4

Review of Key Terms

1. Explain how an *auto responder* aids in customer service. _____
   _____
   _____
   _____

2. How can an *FAQs* section of a Web site help customers? _____
   _____
   _____

Editing Practice

Grammar Alert! Circle the agreement errors in the following sentences. Write the correction in the space provided.

3. The security officer who sits next to the elevators have been receiving multiple complaints. _____

4. One of the copying machines are not working properly. _____

5. Chris or the new interns is answering the phone today. _____

6. The faculty are meeting to create a procedure to handle parental complaints. _____

7. One of the visitors left their coat in the lobby. _____

Practical Application

Analyzing Information

8. Describe a situation in which an employee at a company or business frustrated you. Identify the factors that produced the frustration, and explain how, in the role of the employee, you would have handled the situation better. Do not mention the name of the company or real names of the people involved. _____

_____

9. Assume that your team works in a bank. Write a customer-service policy for the employees in your branch office. Present your policy to the class, and discuss the differences and similarities in each team's policies. _____

_____

Discussion Point

Evaluating Concepts

10. What are some appropriate ways to deal with irate customers or customers who need to exchange an item? _____

_____

_____

_____

_____

_____

11. If you are in a situation that you cannot handle and tempers are beginning to flare, what should you do? _____

_____

_____

_____

_____

Chapter 14

Developing Presentation Skills

Section 14.1
Basics of Oral Communication

Section 14.2
Communicating in Groups, Teams, and Meetings

Section 14.3
Formal and Informal Presentations

Section 14.4
Using Visual Aids and Technology

Workplace Connection

Good oral communication encourages a flow of information and ideas between management and employees. Spoken communication from every employee should contribute to effective public relations. Expertise in producing and using visual aids can improve an employee's promotability status.

CHAPTER OBJECTIVES

When you have completed this chapter, you should be able to:

- Discuss the basics of oral communication.
- Plan and conduct a meeting.
- Deliver both formal and informal presentations.
- List the qualities of good visual aids.
- Discuss how technology can facilitate the use of visual aids.

Basics of Oral Communication

Essential Principles

Some business positions require the extensive use of oral communication. The people who fill these jobs are hired on the strength of an ability to speak well. Sales associates, administrative assistants, customer-service representatives, paralegals, and medical assistants— all these people must be highly skilled in oral communication. These and other business professionals use oral communication extensively in carrying out their job responsibilities.

Your ability to speak clearly, correctly, and convincingly will play a vital role in helping you achieve success in the business world. The manner in which you use your oral communication skills at work can either help or hinder your daily performance on routine tasks as well as on special projects. In many work-related situations, you will do much of the talking. You will try to solve problems; you will be assigned to project teams; you will participate in and conduct meetings and small-group discussions; you will speak to supervisors and colleagues, to the public, and to business and professional groups. In your daily contacts with those inside and outside your organization, you will use oral communication to make requests, provide instructions, and give information.

The Role of Oral Communication in Business

Business professionals use oral communication in a variety of ways and settings. Professionals depend upon oral communication when engaged in activities such as those described below.

- Explaining or reporting to supervisors, subordinates, and associates on the same level. Examples: Report to a supervisor about the status of a project. Direct a subordinate to complete a task. Work with peers as part of a team.

- Giving information to customers and potential customers. Examples: Answer face-to-face or telephone inquiries about items or services offered by your company. Give presentations describing products and services provided.

- Acquiring information necessary to conduct the everyday affairs of business. Examples: Speak with vendors and suppliers to request information about products or to order supplies. Speak with outside consultants, such as accountants, attorneys, and computer specialists.

SECTION OBJECTIVES

When you have finished Section 14.1, you will be able to:

- Explain the importance of oral communication in business.

- Describe the various forms of oral communication.

- List guidelines for effective one-on-one communication.

- Discuss basic procedures for meeting the public.

- Describe proper techniques for originating and receiving telephone calls.

WHY IT'S IMPORTANT

Although written communication is important during business transactions, oral communication is used more often and by more people. The success of any business organization depends, to a very large degree, upon the success of its members in making themselves understood and in persuading others to accept their ideas.

KEY TERMS

- voice recognition software
- volume
- pitch
- intonation
- tone
- tempo
- enunciation
- pronunciation

- Participating in meetings. Examples: Meet with all personnel levels to discuss current and future projects. Meet with consultants or customers to discuss products and services. Meet with teams to complete an assigned project.
- Participating in informal discussion with fellow employees. Examples: Ask co-workers to contribute for flowers for a hospitalized colleague. Plan recreational functions for employees. Attend an informal social event for employees at someone's home.
- Giving instruction to an individual or a group. Examples: Train new employees. Instruct customers in the use of newly purchased products. Instruct patients in caring for themselves.
- Interviewing employees and prospective employees. Examples: Interview job applicants. Participate in performance appraisals.
- Participating in social-business conversations. Examples: Engage in conversations with representatives from civic and professional organizations. Congratulate associates and business acquaintances on their accomplishments.
- Giving formal speeches before groups. Examples: Give a speech before a civic group. Talk to students (elementary, high school, or college level) about your work experience.

These are just a few examples of oral communication activities that take place every day in professional settings—activities that rely heavily upon effective oral communication for their success.

Forms of Oral Communication

Oral communication occurs in many different forms; some are used more frequently than others. Among the most commonly used methods of oral communication are the following:

- Face-to-face conversations—interviews, sales, social-business situations, informal discussions with co-workers.
- Group discussions or meetings—employee group discussions, team meetings, meetings of business and professional organizations.
- Telephone conversations—with a colleague, a supervisor, a customer, or a supplier.
- Voice mail messages—recording a telephone message for someone to hear later.
- Formal speeches—debates; panels; addresses to employees, the public, customers, or professional groups.
- Instruction—conducting training for new employees, such as sales representatives and users of information processing systems.
- Dictation and recording—dictating letters and memos for transcription or recording meetings electronically.
- Using **voice recognition software** to enter text or data into the computer, thus bypassing the traditional keyboard method of entry.

Each of these forms of oral communication requires a slightly different technique. The difference may be (1) the amount and kind of preparation, (2) the manner in which the voice is projected, or (3) the style in which the speaker makes the presentation. For example, speaking over the telephone requires knowledge of how far to hold the telephone mouthpiece from the lips and how much the speaker's voice should be projected. Leading a meeting requires knowledge of parliamentary procedure. Speaking to a large group requires experience with a microphone. Teaching a class requires that the instructor know how to ask questions properly. Participating in a team meeting requires the ability to think quickly and to put thoughts into understandable language without hesitation.

The Role of Nonverbal Communication

In most business situations, oral communication is probably used more frequently than written communication. Furthermore, both obtaining a good position and succeeding in it depend heavily upon persuasive oral skills. For these reasons, it is important that you pay attention to two major factors that determine a person's effectiveness in communicating orally—physical appearance and speech qualities. At this point, it would be helpful to refresh your memory on nonverbal communication by reviewing Chapter 2, Section 1. Nonverbal communication contributes significantly to the effectiveness of oral communication, especially in meetings, job interviews, and presentations.

Appearance

Except for situations involving the telephone or voice mail, the speaker is visible to the listener and creates an impression that influences the acceptability of his or her words. This impression is based primarily on the speaker's posture, gestures, eye contact with the listener, body and head movements, and overall personal appearance—dress, grooming, and so on.

Video telephones, though available, are not in common usage. This next generation of the telephone combines the advantages of a computer, telephone, and videophone. It is projected that this device will be widely accepted and become the market standard.

In both casual and formal speaking situations, a speaker's physical appearance often sets the stage for the acceptance or nonacceptance of the speaker's words. A person who makes a good physical impression quickly gains the interest of listeners. Of course, a speaker must have something interesting and worthwhile to say—and must say it in an effective manner—to hold the attention of the listeners for any length of time. An experienced speaker has good posture, is dressed appropriately, is well-groomed, and uses eye contact to make each listener feel that he or she is being spoken to directly.

Posture. Many people underestimate the importance of good posture to overall physical appearance. Good posture will also make you appear more confident and give your listeners the impression that you know what you are talking about and that your message is important.

Of course, no speaker should appear stiff or pompous. Instead, develop a natural posture, constantly reminding yourself to stand erect, with your shoulders back and your stomach in.

Gestures. While you are talking, do not distract your listeners by pulling at your clothing; putting your hands to your face or hair; or toying with an object such as a paper clip, a rubber band, or your eyeglasses. Listeners will become distracted by your physical maneuvers and will lose track of what you are saying.

If you are standing, place your arms and hands in a relaxed position at your sides, rather than behind your back or folded in front of you. From time to time, make natural gestures. If you are delivering a speech and there is a lectern in front of you, you may wish to place your hands on either side of it. However, remember never to lean on the lectern!

When you are talking from a sitting position, you will be heard better if you sit slightly forward in your chair. Rest your arms and hands in your lap, on the arms of the chair in which you are sitting, or partially on the edge of the table or desk in front of

you. However, never rest your elbows on the desk or table. Lazy-looking speakers encourage apathy on the part of their listeners.

Facial Expressions. A speaker's facial expression influences the listeners' impressions. A relaxed, pleasant, interested expression will create a better atmosphere for communicating than a wrinkled brow and turned-down mouth. Evaluate a videotape of yourself rehearsing a presentation. Try to be objective as you look at the tape and answer the following questions:

- Are your facial muscles relaxed?
- Is your smile natural, pleasant, and genuine?
- Does your facial expression convey interest and enthusiasm?
- Do your facial expressions help convey your message or contradict it?

Practice developing animation and showing enthusiasm in your facial expression.

Eye Contact. One of the best ways to show interest is to look at your audience, whether that audience includes just one person or more than a hundred people. Everyone likes to feel directly addressed by the speaker. Therefore, your eyes should never leave your listeners for any extended period of time; it's hard for them to stay interested when you are looking constantly at your notes, at the ceiling, at your own visual aids, or out the window. When talking to one or two people, look them squarely in the face without staring at them. When speaking to a large group, move your eyes over the entire audience; look into the faces of your listeners and not over the tops of their heads.

Body Movement. Body movement also contributes a great deal to the physical effect a speaker creates. When walking to the podium to speak, you should choose a confident, purposeful gait. After you begin speaking, you should balance on both feet and not pace back and forth, because excessive movement will distract listeners. You may turn from side to side or move forward to add emphasis to a remark. Occasionally, you may even want to take a step toward your listeners to emphasize an important point or a step sideways to signal a transition in what you are discussing. If you are using a chart or other visual aid, move to it from time to time.

Nervousness. When you are talking to a group, pretend that you are carrying on a face-to-face conversation with just one person in the group. Remember that the audience is just as eager for you to perform well as you are to do so. Try to relax and convert your nervousness to energy and enthusiasm—even experienced speakers are apprehensive. Feeling nervous is a result of anxiety about doing a good job, and most authorities believe that a little stage fright provides needed tension that makes you mentally alert.

Grooming and Dress. Personal appearance—grooming, cleanliness, and attire—is also an important factor in effective oral communication. How you look and dress expresses your personality just as much as your speech and conduct do. Feeling good about your appearance gives you confidence. Appearing clean and neatly dressed; avoiding extremes in jewelry, hairstyles, and clothing styles; and selecting clothing and accessories that are tasteful are some of the factors that you should consider.

Speech Qualities

Although a speaker's physical appearance creates the first impression on listeners, the quality of speech may have an even greater influence on them. The quality of speech is determined by these voice attributes: volume, pitch, tone, tempo, enunciation, and pronunciation.

Volume

For oral communication to be effective, your voice must be heard clearly. Sufficient **volume,** achieved through good breath control, is important. If your voice is too soft and you have trouble being heard, practice breathing deeply and controlling your breath with your diaphragm and abdominal muscles, just as a singer does. The large abdominal cavity should be used to store a supply of air that can be released evenly to produce a clear, sustained tone. How much force you must use is determined by the acoustics in the room in which you are talking, the size of your audience, and whether or not you are using a microphone to amplify your voice.

Pitch (Voice Level)

A speaker's voice should have a pleasing pitch. **Pitch** refers to the level of a sound on a musical scale. Practice can help correct the shrillness of a voice that is pitched too high or the excessive resonance of a voice that is pitched too low. Another pitch-related problem is the constant pitch that results in a monotone speech. An effective speaker varies the pitch of his or her voice to help communicate the message. **Intonation,** the rising and falling of voice pitch, can indicate that a statement is being made, that a question is being asked, or that a speaker is pausing.

A drop in pitch usually signals finality or determination and is, therefore, used at the end of a declarative sentence. For example, in reading the following sentence you should close with a drop in pitch:

- I cannot *possibly* finish responding to all the e-mails by 5 p.m. (Emphasize the word *possibly.*)

A rise in pitch can signal a question or an expression of suspense, doubt, or hesitation. Read the following sentence, closing with a rise in pitch.

- What *more* do you expect? (Emphasize *more.*)

Gliding the pitch up and down or down and up usually expresses sarcasm or contempt, as in the slang expression "Oh, yeah?"

The most important aspect of pitch is variation. Variation of pitch not only helps hold listeners' attention but also helps listeners know the exact meaning intended by the speaker. A rise in pitch can stress important words. Using the same pitch for each element can stress comparisons; pitching the first element high and the second low, on the other hand, can denote contrasts.

Notice the different shades of meaning that emerge as you read the following sentences and emphasize the italicized words.

- *Lydia* gave him the special project. (Lydia did, not someone else.)
- Lydia *gave* him the special project. (He did not earn it.)
- Lydia gave *him* the special project. (Only he was given the special project.)
- Lydia gave him the *special* project. (The particular, or special, project.)
- Lydia gave him the special *project.* (She gave him the special project, not something else special.)

Tone

The **tone** of your voice often reveals your attitudes and feelings. A pleasant and cheerful tone is desirable because it will have a good effect on your listeners. On the telephone, the tone of your voice must substitute for your facial expression. In addition, you can use variation in tone, as well as in volume and pitch, to add interest to your speaking voice. The kind of tone you use should be appropriate for the words and ideas you are expressing.

Digital Data

Presentation Video Star

Some meetings and conferences allow visitors to use tape recorders or videos to record presentations. Reviewing and critiquing others' presentations are good ways to learn, evaluate, and improve your own presentation and speaking skills.

Tempo

Tempo, the rate at which you speak, should be varied to avoid extremes in either direction. Most people tend to speak too rapidly. Although you should not speak so rapidly that your words are not understood, neither should you speak so slowly that your listeners lose track of what you are saying. Regulate your rate of speaking so that you can say each word clearly. The listener should hear each word without difficulty.

A good speaking rate is 125 words a minute; oral reading rates tend to run slightly faster—about 150 words a minute. To determine what a rate of 125 words a minute sounds like, read aloud the paragraph below in a half minute. Reread the paragraph as many times as necessary until you achieve the desired rate. At the end of 15 seconds, you should be at the diagonal line. Use this line as a guide to increase or decrease your speaking rate.

A good speaker talks slowly enough to be understood by the listeners and speaks in a pleasant voice, articulating and pronouncing each word correctly and distinctly. To develop a good/speaking voice, you must spend sufficient time practicing the elements of good speech. An effective speaker is a definite asset to a business and will usually find more opportunities for advancing in the job. (64 words)

Changing the rate contributes to variety, as well as clarity. Important words and ideas should be spoken slowly, while unimportant words or phrases should be spoken more rapidly.

Try to speak in thought units so that you can assist the listener in interpreting your words. If the sentence is short, the thought unit can be the entire sentence, as in "My job is very exciting." When there are several thought units within a sentence, pause slightly after each thought group.

- My job is very exciting; / but I must admit, / some days are almost too exciting.

Use pauses to stress major points. By pausing between major points or after important statements, you add variety and emphasis to the points you want your listeners to remember.

Enunciation and Pronunciation

In business—and even in social situations—it is important for those who have face-to-face or telephone contact with customers and vendors to speak clearly and correctly. Speaking clearly and correctly conveys that you are an intelligent, well-educated person. Two terms relate to speech quality: enunciation and pronunciation. Even though they are closely related, they do have slightly different meanings. Understanding the difference between the two terms and practicing problem words or difficult words will help you improve your speech.

Enunciation

Enunciation refers to the distinctness or clarity with which you articulate or sound each part of a word. For instance, saying "gonna" for *going to* is an example of careless enunciation. Careless enunciation often occurs in *ing* words, such as "willin" for *willing* and "askin" for *asking*. Also, when we speak rapidly, most of us have a tendency to run our words together, dropping some of the sounds. Saying "dijago" for *did you go* and "meetcha" for *meet you* are examples. A person who slurs too many words is likely to be misunderstood, particularly over the telephone, on transcribing equipment, or when using voice recognition software. It is annoying for both the listener and the speaker if the listener must ask the speaker to repeat something several times. When using voice recognition software, an incorrect word or words will be entered. Such difficulties can often be avoided if we simply speak more slowly and distinctly.

Pronunciation

Pronunciation refers either to the sound that a speaker gives to the letters or letter combinations that make up a word or to the way in which the speaker accents the word. Note the following examples of mispronunciation and correct pronunciation.

Incorrect Pronunciation	Correct Pronunciation
pro•noun•ci•a•tion	pro•nun•ci•a•tion
li•ba•ry	li•bra•ry
com•par'•able	com'•par•able

Of course, there are regional differences in pronunciation; and, in addition, a number of words have more than one acceptable pronunciation. In the latter case, the dictionary lists the preferred pronunciation first.

Many difficulties in pronunciation arise because some letters or combinations of letters are pronounced one way in some words and another way in others. For example, the combination *ow* has an "oh" sound in *know* but an "ow" sound in *power,* and in *now.* Other difficulties in pronunciation arise because a letter may be sounded in some words but silent in other words.

For example, *k* is sounded in the word *kite,* but it is not sounded in words such as *know* and *knee.* Consult the dictionary whenever you are in doubt about the pronunciation of a word.

Pronunciation errors are most likely to occur with (1) unfamiliar words, (2) words of foreign origin, (3) names, and (4) multisyllable words. Such errors tend to distract the listener and may give the impression that the speaker is careless or uneducated. The business associate who is eager to succeed does not wish to be marked with either of these labels.

Communicating One-on-One

High on the list of communication activities for most business employees is communicating orally on a one-on-one basis. Business employees talk with colleagues in their own departments, with their supervisors, with top management, and with service personnel many times during the working day.

In addition, many employees talk either on the telephone or in person with individuals outside the company—customers, clients, patients, sales representatives, suppliers, visitors, and various people soliciting or giving information. Many business employees depend heavily on their oral communication skills to earn their living—sales representatives, personnel interviewers, and customer-service representatives are just a few examples.

Use the following suggestions as guidelines for communicating effectively on a one-on-one basis.

Establish the Best Atmosphere

One way to establish good relations with colleagues and customers is to create a relaxed, conversational atmosphere. You can accomplish this in one-on-one conversations by sitting or standing so that there are no physical barriers between you and the listener. Focus on the conversation instead of doing other tasks, such as working at the computer. Giving the other person your undivided attention shows courtesy and respect.

Listen Attentively

Listening attentively and showing interest in the other person are just two attributes of a good communicator. In a one-on-one conversation, you alternate between the roles of speaker and listener. As a speaker, part of your responsibility is to listen to what the other person says, to be courteous, and to get the necessary information. For example, a sales associate should listen to a customer's inquiry in order to know how to answer

---

oops!

Costly Enunciation

Because of her manager's poor enunciation, Mona transcribed a statement from his dictation as "forty wall units for $14,000" instead of "fourteen wall units for $14,000." If her supervisor hadn't spotted the discrepancy in the letter, the mistake could have been costly.

KEY POINT

Enunciation refers to the distinctness or clarity with which a speaker sounds each part of a word.

KEY POINT

Pronunciation refers either to the sound that a speaker gives to the letters or letter combinations that make up a word or to the way in which the speaker accents the word.

---

the customer. A medical assistant needs to ask questions, then listen to the patient's responses to find out about the patient's illness.

Use the Person's Name

Be certain that you hear and remember the name of a person whom you have met or talked with for the first time. Repeat the name right after it is given to you: "I'm happy to meet you, Ms. Blasczynski." If you aren't absolutely sure of the person's name, ask that it be repeated; you can say, "I didn't hear your name clearly" or "How do you pronounce, or spell, your name?" Then, after hearing the name, pronounce it aloud in order to fix it in your mind. Whenever it is appropriate, use the name once or twice during the conversation: "Yes, I understand, Ms. Blasczynski." Finally, always be sure that you say the person's name in your good-bye: "Goodbye, Ms. Blasczynski. I enjoyed talking with you."

Permit Others to Talk

Do not do all of the talking. Give the other person an opportunity to talk, while you listen attentively. Watch for signs that the other person wants to say something or is becoming bored and is not listening carefully. No matter how interesting you think the conversation is or how well informed or articulate you think you are, you must give your listener a chance to speak. Otherwise, you will lose your listener's attention and respect. For example, you might ask questions to let the listener know you are interested in receiving feedback.

Compliment When Appropriate

Compliments are always welcome, so compliment someone whenever the occasion is appropriate. Paying a compliment is especially effective during tense situations. If a valued employee or a customer has a complaint that you cannot justify or remedy, you can put that person in a better frame of mind for a "no" answer by paying a compliment. For example, compliment the employee for work well done and compliment the customer for paying promptly. However, never pay a compliment unless you can do so honestly and convincingly. Insincerity is easily detected.

Keep Conversations Concise

Since time is valuable, you should keep your conversations to the point. If you are asked for opinions, give them clearly and concisely. Being concise, however, does not mean you must be brusque. Try to sense the amount of information the situation warrants and act accordingly. Most people do not want to hear unnecessary details or to listen to prolonged excuses for your inability to do something they have requested. Give enough information to satisfy the listener. If you are in doubt, the best policy is to keep your conversation short.

Communicating by Telephone

Communicating by telephone requires techniques that are somewhat different from those used in one-on-one conversations. Since the speaker and the listener in a telephone conversation are unable to see each other, they must depend entirely upon their voices to communicate friendliness, interest, and a willingness to be helpful.

The manner in which a customer is treated on the telephone is just as important as effective written communication is in developing goodwill—sometimes even more important. All employees—technicians, salespersons, administrative assistants, accountants, paralegals, medical assistants, receptionists—create a public image of the company they represent by the manner in which they speak to current and potential customers. A curt or rude employee can cause a business to lose potential customers—and even to lose long-standing customers. In a telephone conversation, the associate must, through the words and tone used, make listeners feel that their interests are important and that the company wants them to be satisfied.

The telephone is one of the most important communication media in business. You must use it with great skill, whether you are speaking to callers from inside or outside the organization.

Although you are familiar with using the telephone, you may not be using it properly. Some of the following suggestions may seem obvious. Nevertheless, you should read them carefully and follow them whenever you use the telephone for either personal or business use.

- Talk directly into the mouthpiece.
- Talk slowly and naturally. Exaggerate your enunciation slightly. Do not shout.
- If you must transfer a caller to someone else in the company, say, "If you will please hold for a moment, I will transfer your call." Give the caller the name and phone number of the person to whom you are transferring the call, in case the transfer does not go through. Stay on the line to announce the transfer.
- If, while talking, you must put down the receiver, either put the caller on hold or place the receiver on a book or magazine rather than on a hard surface.
- Place the receiver gently in the cradle when you hang up.

Courtesy is the key to effective telephone communication. Greet all callers pleasantly. Pleasantness is achieved both by the words you use and by the tone of your voice. If you know who the caller is, use a greeting such as "Good morning, Mr. Ackley" or "Hello, Abigail." If you do not know who the caller is, identify yourself first: "Ms. Cheney speaking" or "Phyllis Cheney." When answering the telephone for a department, identify both the department and yourself: "Engineering Department, Ms. Cheney."

Smile as you speak on the telephone. The smile will relax your facial muscles and vocal cords, making your voice sound relaxed and pleasant. Your voice should be friendly and your manner courteous, regardless of who is calling. This manner is especially important when you are talking to outside callers. Remember that the impression created by your voice should be that of a friendly smile. Show the caller that you want to be helpful: Always listen attentively and don't interrupt. Make an occasional comment, such as "Yes" or "I understand," to let the caller know you are listening. Use the caller's name at least once before hanging up, and conclude the call with a remark like "Thank you for calling, Ms. Donohue" or "We will look into the matter for you right away, Mr. Hill."

Originating Calls

To make the best use of your telephone time, follow these suggestions for originating calls:

1. Plan the conversation before you call. A little preparation will save both time and money. If your conversation will be an involved one, jot down notes in advance.

2. Identify yourself promptly and state the purpose of your call. For example, say, "This is Richard Epstein of Gilmore Industries. I would like to speak to the person in charge of new accounts."

3. Be prepared to leave a voice mail message if the person you are calling does not answer.

4. Get to the point quickly.

5. Listen carefully.

6. Focus on the job at hand; do not surf the Web, etc., while making a call.

7. Set an approximate time limit for the call before you dial.

> **KEY POINT**
>
> Smile as you speak on the telephone. The smile will relax your facial muscles and vocal cords, making your voice sound relaxed and pleasant.

Receiving Calls

To ensure efficient use of the telephone when you receive a call, follow these suggestions:

1. Answer promptly and identify yourself immediately. You should answer at the first ring, if possible, and no later than the third ring.

2. Respond to inquiries graciously; verify important details, such as account numbers, model numbers, dates, and names.

3. Keep a phone log, listing the caller, the company name, and the decisions made during the call.

4. If the call involves controversial information, confirm in writing the decisions made.

5. At the close of the conversation, take the required action. Be certain that you keep all the promises you make to the caller.

6. Allow the caller to hang up first.

7. If you are going to be away from your telephone, leave a voice mail greeting that directs callers to leave a message or refers them to someone who could help them in your absence.

8. Inform the caller if you must place him or her on hold. Ask the caller if he or she would prefer to be placed on hold or would prefer for you to return the call later. For example, "Can you hold, please, or would you prefer that I call you later?"

9. Smile as you speak on the telephone.

10. Relax your facial muscles and vocal cords to make your voice sound relaxed and pleasant.

11. Do not say, "Hold on," or, "Hang on."

12. Give the caller on hold an option to continue waiting every 20 seconds. This lets the caller know that you have not forgotten that he or she is on hold.

13. Be prepared to take a message. Give appropriate information as requested.

Assessment   Section 14.1

Review of Key Terms

1. How do *pitch* and *intonation* affect the quality of speech? _____
   _____
   _____
   _____

2. What is the difference between *enunciation* and *pronunciation*? How do they affect oral communication? _____
   _____
   _____
   _____

Editing Practice

Call an Editor! Some of the following sentences contain spelling errors or misused words. Underline the incorrect words and write the correction in the space provided. Sentences may have more than one error.

3. How will the new policy effect office morale? _____

4. Which proceedures apply to this job? _____

5. The new superviser was formerly introduced to the team today. _____

_____

6. On which sight will the new factory be build? _____

_____

Practical Application

Applying Skills

7. Write the following headings on a separate sheet of paper: Home, School, Business. Then, list as many oral communication activities as you think would be typical. You may want to choose a specific position for your Business heading. _____

8. Without using any gestures or diagrams, each team member should give oral directions for the following situations:

   - How to get to your classroom from the campus library.
   - How to get to the administration building of your school from your classroom.
   - How to fold a letter for insertion in a standard-sized envelope.
   - How to reboot a computer.

   Then, write a brief critique of each member's directions. _____

_____

Discussion Point

Making Generalizations

9. How does the physical appearance of a speaker affect his or her oral communication? Provide examples in which you were affected by the physical appearance of a speaker, either positively or negatively. Do not include names or other identifying descriptions in your response to this question. _____

_____

10. What are some guidelines you should use when communicating one-on-one in a business situation? _____

_____

_____

SECTION OBJECTIVES

When you have finished Section 14.2, you will be able to:

- Discuss the steps to take to plan for effective meetings.
- Discuss the steps to take to lead effective meetings.
- Describe the interaction method of conducting meetings.
- List the six basic rules for effective participation in meetings.

WHY IT'S IMPORTANT

Meetings are among the most important ways to exchange ideas and report information within businesses.

KEY TERMS

- standing committee
- ad hoc committee
- minutes
- agenda
- *Robert's Rules of Order*
- directives

KEY POINT

Before the meeting takes place:

1. **Prepare thoroughly.**
2. **Arrive early.**
3. **Check the meeting site.**

Communicating in Groups, Teams, and Meetings

Essential Principles

Meetings are among the most important ways to exchange ideas and report information within businesses. A meeting may involve a supervisor and an employee, several employees at various levels, or employees and vendors or customers. With an increase in global competition, many businesses are adopting a team approach to conducting business. Using the team approach helps involve employees at all levels of planning and decision making. Rather than working independently, employees work in groups where they share ideas and responsibilities.

As a business communicator, you are likely to have frequent opportunities to participate in a variety of capacities in many types of meetings. You might be selected as a member of a **standing** (permanent) **committee** that meets regularly, such as a finance committee or a nominating committee. You may also serve on an **ad hoc** (temporary) **committee** formed for a particular purpose, such as a grievance committee. You may even be selected as chairperson of one of these committees, with the responsibility for planning and conducting the meetings. After attending meetings during working hours, many business professionals often go to meetings and serve on other committees outside the company—for example, in professional, cultural, social, religious, political, and civic groups.

Planning Meetings

You should determine the kind of meeting that would best suit your needs: a traditional meeting, an electronic meeting, a teleconference, etc. (See Chapter 12 for information on electronic meetings.) The success or failure of a group meeting is often determined by preparation. Skillful planning can turn an ordinary meeting into an extremely profitable experience for each participant. Without careful advance work, the most promising meeting can result in a waste of time for everyone. (See **Exhibit 14.1.**)

Determine the Reason for the Meeting

Unless a specific group is required to meet on a regular basis, it is up to the meeting chairperson to decide if a meeting should be called. If you are calling a meeting to distribute information, an e-mail or memo with attachments might best serve this purpose. Meetings should be held when the exchange of ideas from different people needs to be processed for decision making.

Exhibit 14.1
A Meeting
How can meetings be the most productive?
Thinking Critically.
What responsibility does the chairperson have in ensuring that the meeting is a success?

Determine the Meeting Participants

Having meetings is time consuming and expensive because it takes the participants away from their usual tasks and responsibilities. Consequently, you want to include only those people who have direct input to the causes, results, solutions, or impacts of the discussions that will take place at your meeting and the resulting decisions that will be made. And you want to invite those who have the knowledge of the issues, the creativity to solve them, and the authority to put the decisions made into action.

Prepare Thoroughly

A successful meeting or conference requires that the leader or leaders prepare adequately and make all the necessary arrangements. Preparations should include determining the starting time, the length, and the site of the meeting; the names of those who are to attend; the objectives to be accomplished at the meeting; and potential problems.

Notification of a meeting is usually done by e-mail or memo. The notification should include the time, date, and location of the meeting. You should attach a copy of the meeting agenda and a copy of the minutes from the previous meeting, if not already distributed. The **minutes** of a meeting are the official record of the meeting proceedings. An **agenda** is a list of the topics to be discussed and the names of the people who are to lead the specific discussions. It usually specifies the name of the group and the date, time, and place of the meeting. Sometimes the agenda also specifies the anticipated ending time of the meeting. Refer to **Exhibit 14.2** for a sample agenda. Some tips for agendas follow:

- Send the agenda prior to the meeting, allowing sufficient time for the group members to prepare for participation.
- Ask that the agenda be prepared in Braille for visually impaired participants.
- List topics in the order in which they will be discussed. You may want to include the names of the people responsible for each agenda item to alert them to be especially prepared for that particular topic.
- Under "New Business," list the most important items first in case there is not enough time to discuss them all.
- If meeting length is a concern, include a suggested time limit for the discussion to encourage completion of the agenda.

oops!

Don't Stay Out Too Late

Hillary won the employee of the month award for February. As she gave her acceptance speech, she stood slouching against the podium because she was tired from staying out late the night before.

BAXTER AND BRADSHAW, INC.

AGENDA

Quarterly Sales Meeting

Tuesday, April 18, 20—
9 A.M.–10 A.M.

Conference Room #2

Call to order	Tracy Dillard
Approval of minutes of January meeting	George Sanders
Announcements	
Old Business:	
a. Report on new incentive compensation plan	Melinda Regan
b. Review of customer service survey results	Steve Horowitz
New Business:	
a. Review of previous January, February, and March sales	Jared Adams
b. Recommendations for proposed new sales territories	Teresa Atkins
c. Report on college intern applications	Brooke Kinkaid
Adjournment	

Employability Skills

Participating as a Member of a Team

Contributing to the group effort is a key component to being successful in working with a team. Sharing creative ideas and suggestions can help the team efficiently progress toward positive outcomes.

Arrive Early

The leader of the meeting should arrive a few minutes early to check the facilities and to set an example for the participants. Arriving early also gives the leader a chance to greet the participants and offer them a copy of the agenda. Even though everyone should have an advance copy of the agenda, not everyone will remember to bring it to the meeting. Extra copies of reports or other papers to be discussed should be available, even though copies may have been distributed in advance.

Check the Meeting Site

Arrangements for the meeting site must be planned so that the room, the furniture, and the equipment to be used are set up in time for the meeting. A list of routine meeting tasks associated with meeting preparations can be found on page 525.

Routine Meeting Checklist

- Make sure that the meeting room is clean and ready for use.
- For small meetings, arrange seating so that participants have eye contact with one another, such as around a conference table.
- Make needed adjustments to the ventilation, room temperature, and lighting.
- Request any special equipment, such as a computer, an overhead projector, a slide projector, or multimedia projection equipment.
- Check all equipment to make sure that it is working properly.
- Check to see that electrical receptacles are accessible for your equipment. Bring extension cords if they are needed.
- Have handouts at the door ready for distribution when meeting participants arrive. Make sure you have enough handouts for everyone at the meeting.
- Request a meeting recorder to take the minutes.
- Request any special services needed for participants. For example, you may need an interpreter for a deaf participant or a note-taker for a visually impaired participant.
- Arrange for refreshments if appropriate.

To start the meeting promptly, check the room at least 45 minutes before the scheduled time to ensure that everything is ready. By checking in advance, you can take care of any problems before the meeting begins and, thereby, avoid delays. Problems are more easily solved if they are discovered in a timely fashion.

Managing Meetings

Being able to run a meeting smoothly is an important skill to acquire. You can follow the same guidelines for a small informal meeting as for a large conference.

Establish a Businesslike Atmosphere

The chairperson or facilitator sets the tone of the meeting. If the leader begins late or is slow to start the meeting, the participants are likely to lose whatever enthusiasm they may have had when they came to the meeting. Generally, it is best to start a meeting precisely at the scheduled time, even though there may be latecomers. Starting at the appointed time encourages participants to be punctual.

Determine the Procedural Methodology

Some groups meet very informally, with an open discussion. Other groups, however, conduct their meetings on a formal basis, following parliamentary rules. If you are elected to office in such a group, you should read ***Robert's Rules of Order,*** the standard guide to parliamentary procedure.

KEY POINT

During the meeting:

1. **Establish a businesslike atmosphere.**
2. **Determine the procedural methodology.**
3. **Guide the discussion.**
4. **Manage conflicting opinions.**
5. **Encourage participation.**
6. **Discourage excessive talkers.**
7. **Keep the discussion pertinent.**
8. **Summarize periodically.**
9. **Know when to conclude.**
10. **Complete after-meeting tasks.**

Guide the Discussion

A good leader talks as little as possible and draws out the opinions and ideas of the participants. The leader's function is not to show how much he or she knows but to steer the discussion in the proper direction. An experienced leader knows that the greater the participation—that is, the more minds constructively at work on issues—the better the chances of accomplishing the meeting objectives.

Manage Conflicting Opinions

Participants should feel free to disagree tactfully with one another. There would be little reason to meet if all participants held the same opinions on the topics to be discussed. Healthy, stimulating discussions can lead to new ideas and solutions. It is up to the chairperson to ensure that the disagreements are productive and tactful. The chairperson should monitor all discussions to make sure they do not get out of control.

Encourage Participation

Everyone invited to a meeting should be able to make some contribution to the discussion. Sometimes, ground rules are needed to encourage the members of the group to participate. The leader of the meeting should make it clear that individuals are not allowed to interrupt the person who is speaking. Speakers should know that they will be able to express their ideas without being criticized or attacked.

Some people are shy and will not say anything unless they are encouraged to speak. The leader should make a statement that offers encouragement. For example, "Andrea, you have had much experience in marketing. What do you think of Emily's design for the product label?"

A leader can encourage positive participation by complimenting a speaker who has made a worthwhile contribution; for example, "Thank you, Anna Grace, for that cost-cutting suggestion."

Comments of this type are effective when they are obviously sincere. Negative comments, on the other hand, discourage participation and should, therefore, be kept to a minimum and presented so tactfully that they do not discourage others from making suggestions. "If that idea could be implemented in a cost-effective way, our problem would be solved." The previous sentence tactfully says that the idea will not work because it costs too much.

Discourage Excessive Talkers

In any group, there will always be one or two people who want to do all the talking. Unless these individuals are listed on the agenda as principal contributors, they should not be permitted to monopolize the discussion. A leader should be firm in preventing a single person from taking over the meeting. "That's very interesting, Corey, but I think we ought to hear what Danielle has to say," or, "Let's get back to you a little later, Joyce. I think we would all be interested in hearing as many points as we can in our brief meeting."

Keep the Discussion Pertinent

Meetings sometimes tend to get off the track. All too often, a subject comes up that is of genuine personal interest to all those present at the meeting but has little or no bearing on the main topic. When side issues begin to waste valuable time, they must be cut off tactfully by the leader and the discussion must be brought back on track. "That certainly was an interesting experience, Will, but let's get back to our discussion on safety in the parking deck. Ellen, were the video cameras that we installed last month a deterrent to theft from employee vehicles?"

Usually you can keep the discussion on track without being rude to anyone, but bluntness is sometimes necessary as a last resort. "Alex, time is getting away from us, and we want to avoid having to call another meeting to settle this problem. Do you have any specific solutions?"

Summarize Periodically

The group leader should always listen attentively but does not need to comment except to stimulate further discussion. "Excellent—that's an interesting point. I gather that you think this plan will be more effective than the one we have been following. Is that a correct assumption?" Above all, the leader should not tear down ideas or argue with participants; doing so will only discourage others in the group from expressing themselves. The leader of the meeting is only one member of the group; thus, it is usually poor practice for the leader to judge every idea expressed instead of letting other members of the group participate.

From time to time, the chairperson should summarize the major points that have been presented. "We all seem to agree that we should not add more branch stores at the present time. Instead, you feel we should enlarge the existing branches and increase our advertising budget. Is that correct? Well, let's discuss which branches should be enlarged and how we should make use of an increased advertising budget. Norris, do you have any suggestions regarding which branch stores should be enlarged?"

Know When to Conclude

If the chairperson has prepared the agenda carefully and has conducted the meeting efficiently, the meeting should end close to the time scheduled for adjournment. If the discussion seems likely to extend beyond the closing time and it is important to continue, get the approval of the group; for example, "It is five minutes of twelve, and it looks as though we won't get out of here by noon. Shall we continue the discussion, or would you rather schedule another meeting for this afternoon?"

Complete After-Meeting Tasks

After the meeting, the recorder should prepare the minutes and distribute them as soon as is feasible. E-mails or memos should be written to those who were assigned special responsibilities at the meeting. **Directives** (formal authorizations for changes) should be composed, signed, and sent to those responsible for implementing the decisions that were made. The chairperson should make notes on his or her calendar as a reminder to verify that these special responsibilities have been completed and the decisions made have been implemented.

Participating in Meetings

Everyone invited to participate in a group discussion has an obligation to contribute his or her best thinking and suggestions. Here is an opportunity to exhibit your interest in, and knowledge of, the work you are doing. Too often, time and money are wasted because employees take meetings for granted and do not contribute their maximum effort to the discussion. They often come to a meeting unprepared, uninterested, and uninspired.

The six basic rules for participating effectively in a meeting are:

1. Prepare for the meeting.

2. Express opinions tactfully.

3. Make positive contributions.

4. Be courteous.

5. Keep remarks concise and pertinent.

6. Take notes.

KEY POINT

To prepare for a meeting, read about the topic and discuss the topic with knowledgeable people.

Prepare for the Meeting

The first rule for effective participation in a meeting is to come prepared. Learn all that you can about the topics to be discussed at the meeting. If there is an agenda, study each item carefully and learn more about topics that are unfamiliar to you. For example, if the subject of employee absenteeism is to be discussed, be sure that you know what the current company procedures are for dealing with absenteeism, as well as the advantages and disadvantages of these procedures. You may refer to books or articles dealing with this topic or examine company forms that are currently in use. In addition, you might get the opinions of knowledgeable people who will not be present at the meeting. If there is to be a discussion of a revision to the evaluation form, study the form thoughtfully, try it out yourself, and ask various people who use the form to tell you what they like and do not like about it.

Being prepared also means coming to a meeting with a set of well-founded ideas. Ideas that are worth listening to in a business meeting are the ones backed up by facts. People are often opposed to a new idea merely because they don't know enough about it. Make certain that you can supply facts that will support your ideas and that will help convince others of the validity of your position.

Express Opinions Tactfully

When someone asks you for your opinion or when you volunteer an opinion, be tactful in expressing yourself. Often, opposing points of view can cause strong disagreement. No matter how strongly you may feel, your chances of winning that person's support are better if you are tactful in presenting your views.

For example, don't say, "You're wrong, and here's why." Instead, you might say, "Your point of view certainly has merit, Henry, but I have doubts because. . ."

Never tell someone that he or she is wrong—*wrong* is a strong term, and your right to use it requires indisputable evidence. In selling your point of view, you will find the "Yes, but . . ." technique is more effective; in other words, acknowledge the other person's point of view and show your respect for it. Then, present your own ideas. For example, "Yes, I agree that the solution seems simple and that your idea represents one way to approach the problem, but. . ."

In expressing yourself, separate facts from opinions. Label as facts only those statements for which you have solid evidence. Opinions should be signaled by such phrases as, "It seems to me," "As I understand it," or, "In my opinion."

Make Positive Contributions

Most meetings are held for the purpose of solving problems, and problems cannot be solved in a negative atmosphere. Participants must be willing to approach a problem with the attitude that the only way to solve it is to present as many ideas as possible. No one should immediately veto an idea; instead, each person should try to see the idea's merits and try to enlarge upon the idea's possibilities, no matter how weak the idea may seem at first. To dismiss ideas before they are fully aired is not only rude but also extremely disheartening to those who are genuinely trying to reach intelligent decisions.

Be Courteous

The ideal meeting is one in which everyone participates freely. A speaker who monopolizes the discussion will discourage the participation of others. Even though you may be more knowledgeable about the topic than anyone else in the group, you should never display your knowledge in an offensive, overbearing manner.

More victories have been won in group discussion by modesty and tact than will ever be achieved by over-aggressiveness. Don't jump in while others are speaking; wait your turn patiently. Show interest in what others are saying. You will win more support by listening and taking notes on remarks by others than by interrupting their remarks—

regardless of how inane the remarks may seem to you. Acknowledge that others may have as much information or insight as you have or perhaps even more than you have.

Courteous group members do not (1) resort to sarcasm when they disagree with someone, (2) interrupt the person who is talking, (3) fidget, (4) gaze into space, or (5) carry on side conversations with other members of the group while someone else is speaking. If someone interrupts you while you are speaking, say something like "Please let me finish" and continue with the point you are making.

Keep Remarks Concise and Pertinent

Some participants in a meeting take a roundabout route to reach the point they want to make. They ramble endlessly. If you have something to say, get to your point quickly. Meetings become boring and unproductive mainly because participants insist on relating personal preferences, experiences, and opinions that have little or no bearing on the discussion at hand.

Take Notes

It is a good idea to develop the habit of taking notes at meetings, because the act of taking careful notes (1) keeps you alert, (2) tells speakers that you consider their remarks worth remembering, and (3) provides a valuable reference source both during and after the meeting. Take notes not only on what the speaker is saying but also on what you want to say when it is your turn to speak. Jot down your key remarks in advance so that your comments will be well organized and complete.

Assessment   Section 14.2

Review of Key Terms

1. What is the difference between a *standing committee* and an *ad hoc committee*? _____

   _____

2. Under what circumstances would you use *Robert's Rules of Order*? _____

   _____

   _____

Editing Practice

Service Please!   Revise the following letter excerpts to promote good customer service.

3. We fail to understand why you claim that the two lamp bases do not match. _____

4. We are unable to grant you credit because you are a poor payer. _____

   _____

5. You claim you sent your check last week, but we have not yet received it. _____

6. You have put us through a great deal of trouble getting the merchandise to you on the date you requested. _____

   _____

Practical Application

Thinking Critically

7. Evaluate your ability to conduct a meeting, using your previous experience, if any, and the qualities you consider necessary in an effective leader of group discussions. _____

8. Each team will select a subject for an ad hoc committee. First, choose a chairperson for your committee; then, develop a list of topics concerned with phases of this subject. Each team member should write notes about his or her phase. Create an agenda, using the sample agenda on page 524. Teams will role-play the meeting, with the chairperson bringing the meeting to order and leading the meeting. _____

_____

_____

Discussion Point

Identifying the Main Idea

9. Discuss the steps you would take to prepare a meeting room for an all-day discussion. How would you handle an emergency, such as a power outage or an unscheduled fire drill? _____

_____

_____

_____

_____

10. How can you establish a businesslike atmosphere at a meeting? _____

_____

_____

Formal and Informal Presentations

Essential Principles

Most professionals routinely make presentations as part of their job. In some cases, they are asked to introduce speakers to their associates or to their civic clubs. They may be addressing a student group that is touring their facility, making a formal sales presentation to a prospective client, or explaining a proposed policy to the regional medical center board. Being able to develop and make formal and informal presentations is a competence that you should achieve. Practice is the best way to improve your presentation skills.

The Importance of Developing Presentation Skills

For many business professionals, the ability to speak effectively to groups is an important requirement of their positions.

A business executive may be expected to represent the company before professional organizations or cultural, civic, religious, or educational groups. These external speaking duties are beyond those duties involved in speaking to members of one's own organization at employee meetings, at board meetings, or at stockholders' meetings.

However, even those who are not top executives often are called upon to participate in activities involving speeches before either large or small groups—instructing subordinates, reporting to an executive committee, introducing a speaker, explaining a new company policy to a group of employees, or greeting a group of visitors.

Presentations can influence an audience either positively or negatively. It is a reflection not only on the presenter but also on the company that the speaker represents. An effective speech should convey a message clearly and convincingly and, at the same time, it should build goodwill. Because nearly everyone is called upon at one time or another to "say a few words" to an audience, every business professional should be prepared to represent his or her company in a way that will reflect favorably. Whatever your responsibility—introducing the speaker or making the presentation—you should be prepared and do a superb job.

Introducing a Speaker

A brief, informative introduction sets the stage for the speaker and the presentation. If the introducer does an outstanding job, the main speaker's task is greatly simplified. When introducing a speaker, observe the following points.

1. Use an appropriate, brief introduction.
2. Set the stage for the speaker.

3. Keep your eyes on the audience.

4. End with the speaker's name.

5. Make closing remarks brief and appropriate.

Use an Appropriate, Brief Introduction. The audience has come to hear the speaker, not the person who is introducing the speaker. Therefore, keep the introduction short—not more than two or three minutes in length. Avoid giving specific information on the topic; the speaker will do that.

When you are introducing a speaker, avoid such trite expressions as, "The speaker for this evening needs no introduction," "I give you Professor Terricita Gomez," or "Without further ado, I present Dr. Andrew Pearson Devane."

Set the Stage for the Speaker. A human-interest story about the speaker's hobby, family, or generosity will warm the audience. Although you should have a complete résumé supplied to you itemizing the speaker's experience, education, and attainments, you do not need to use them all. An audience is quickly bored, and sometimes a speaker is embarrassed by a straight biographical introduction, no matter how impressive the speaker's background is. Give only the most significant dates, positions, and accomplishments. You need only to convince the audience that the speaker is qualified to speak on the topic assigned, is worth knowing, and has something important to say.

Keep Your Eyes on the Audience. Do not turn from the audience to face the speaker you are introducing—always keep your eyes on the audience. After you have made the introduction, wait until the speaker has reached the lectern before seating yourself.

End with the Speaker's Name. Some people recommend that you not mention the speaker's name until the very end of the introduction. During the introduction refer only to "our speaker." Then, at the end of the introduction, say something like, "It is my pleasure to present Dr. Mary Elizabeth Johnson."

Make Closing Remarks Brief and Appropriate. At the end of the speaker's remarks, someone on the platform or at the speaker's table should assume the responsibility for closing the meeting. If the speech was a particularly effective one, you may say with sincerity, "Thank you, Mr. Bandall, for your most informative and insightful message. We are most appreciative. Members of the audience, the meeting is adjourned."

On the other hand, if the speech has been average or even disappointing, as indicated by the audience reaction, you may close by merely saying, "Thank you, Dr. Danner, for giving us your ideas on how to manage a multinational sales force. Members of the audience, thank you for coming to our meeting and good night."

Under no circumstances should you prolong the closing remarks. If the speech was a good one, there is nothing more you can contribute to its effectiveness. If the speech was a poor one, the audience is probably tired and eager to leave.

Preparing for a Presentation

Preparation is the key to a good presentation. You have an obligation to prepare and to deliver a presentation that will be worthwhile for your audience.

Analyze Your Audience. One of the first steps in preparing for a presentation is to analyze your audience. You should learn everything you can about your audience, including its knowledge of, and interest in, the subject. Doing so helps you plan what to say. The following tips will help you analyze your audience:

- Determine the occasion for your presentation. Is it a staff meeting? Birthday dinner? Retirement banquet?

Employability Skills

Selecting Technology

Preparing for a presentation is as important as doing it. Choosing the appropriate tools, such as computers, visual aids, and video screens, is vital to making a successful presentation. Be prepared by selecting the right materials.

Refresh Your Memory

Tom is chairperson of the refreshing committee for the seminar.

(*Refreshment* is the correct word, not *refreshing*.)

- Tailor every presentation to the audience and to the occasion or theme of the meeting.

- Know the expectations that your audience has for your presentation.

- Respect your audience. This includes remaining within your allotted time. Using more time than allowed is discourteous. A good speaker knows the requirements of the program and adapts to them.

- Put yourself in the shoes of the people who will be listening to your presentation and ask, "Would this speech be interesting to me?"

- Determine information such as gender, job titles, education, interests, and general age range of the audience.

- Find out how many people will attend so that you can prepare enough handouts.

- Determine how much your audience knows about your topic. Your audience may know much about your topic or very little.

- Choose the appropriate level of communication. Talking over the heads of your audience or talking down to your audience is considered rude. A good rule of thumb is to talk just a little below the level of the audience so that they can understand you easily.

Memory Hook

Don't wait until the last minute to prepare your presentation. There will always be last-minute adjustments, but keep these to a minimum.

Develop Your Speech.   An important step in preparing a presentation is developing your speech. Sometimes you are asked to speak about a specific topic; other times, you may choose your own topic. Whatever your topic, you should always have a strong introduction and conclusion. A brief, but strong, introduction grasps your audience's attention and clearly identifies your topic. You may choose to use a rhetorical question, a startling fact, or a true story to introduce your topic. A **rhetorical question** is a question that is posed—with no expectation of a response—to stimulate thought about a specific topic.

The body, or "meat," of your presentation should have substance for your listeners. You should develop your points and support them. Be careful to avoid information overload. Most audiences will remember about five major points. You may want to use a handout to reinforce your major points.

Your conclusion should be well prepared, and you should end on a positive note. Remember that your audience, during these last critical minutes, is formulating a lasting impression of you and your presentation. A strong conclusion summarizes your major points and helps the audience remember what you said. Note the chart that follows. It suggests an amount of time for each major part of your presentation.

Part	Purpose	Percentage of Time
Introduction	Stimulate interest in the topic	15%
Body	Convey the content	70%
Conclusion	Summarize and give a positive ending	15%

Here are some tips to help you develop your speech:

Going Global

Accommodating Native Languages

Most international businesspeople speak some English. However, many visitors might be more comfortable speaking their native language. If possible, the host company should try to arrange for a translation or interpreting service.

Content

- Determine the purpose for your presentation, and make sure that it is clear in your mind.
- Brainstorm ideas about the subject and outline your presentation, keeping the organization simple.
- Write your ideas about the subject in words that your audience can understand.
- Create an outline which includes an introduction, the body, and a conclusion. Allot about 15 percent of your time to the introduction, 70 percent to the body, and 15 percent to the conclusion.
- Stick to your topic. Avoid rambling.
- Include brief examples to illustrate your main points.
- Do whatever research is necessary. A good guideline is to know ten times more about your subject than you are able to say during the allotted time. This extra knowledge will help you field questions and feel self-confident.

 ## Memory Hook

Here is a tough challenge:

Don't overestimate or underestimate your audience's knowledge on your presentation topic.

Clarity

- Be specific, avoid making too many broad generalizations, and stay on your subject.
- Don't try to ad-lib or add material on the spot.
- Use repetition as an effective way to emphasize main points.
- Summarize after each main point.
- Explain difficult points as you go along, and define unfamiliar terms the first time that you mention them.
- Do not use abbreviations, acronyms, or technical terms that are unfamiliar to the audience.
- Bring the presentation to a deliberate conclusion. Reemphasize the basic message, and summarize your main points.
- Even though the audience is not reading your presentation, it is a good idea to use the readability function in your word processing software to estimate the grade level of the content. Then, make any necessary adjustments to gear your presentation to the appropriate level for your audience.

Treatment

- Try to give an overall impression of the subject rather than just facts and figures. The audience will get bored if all you do is give statistics.
- Use illustrations and examples to help your audience relate to your content.
- Use human-interest stories and phrases that appeal to the senses and tend to create pictures in the mind of your audience.

Humor

- Use humor only if you are comfortable with it. Omit telling jokes if you know that you always forget the punch line or that no one ever laughs at your jokes.

- Remember that starting with a joke is risky. If the joke bombs, recovering is almost impossible.

- Use humor only if it pertains to your topic.

- Do not make fun of an individual or group of individuals. If you are questioning whether to use a specific joke, the rule of thumb is not to use it.

- Always prepare an extra joke, because the person who speaks before you may use the joke that you intended to use.

- If there are humorous aspects to your subject, make reference to them. Humor can be a true story that has a humorous side. A speaker telling how to give CPR might say, "When you first see a person lying down, check to see if he or she is breathing. I almost gave CPR to a person who was simply sleeping."

Memory Hook

When trying to decide whether or not a certain anecdote, joke, or story would be appropriate, use the following rule of thumb: When in doubt, leave it out!

Prepare Notes, Rehearse, and Anticipate Problems.   After you have analyzed your audience and developed your presentation, you should prepare your notes, rehearse, and anticipate problems. Speakers, just like musical performers and actors, should practice before the actual presentation. Here are some tips to help you get ready for the presentation:

- Develop speaking notes from the text of your presentation.

- Print your outline or keywords on your note cards. Writing out every word on note cards will confuse you during the presentation.

- Print your notes on index cards, not full sheets of paper. Sheets of paper look unprofessional, and even the slightest movement of papers will cause noise, which will be amplified if you are using a microphone.

- Use large print (14–16 point) on your note cards, which will allow you to see the text easily. The distance from the lectern to your eyes will probably be slightly greater than your normal reading distance.

- Use a bright-colored highlighter pen to mark important points.

- Don't put your notes on the podium ahead of time. The speaker before you may inadvertently remove them.

- Indicate on your note cards the visual aid that should be used at that particular point in the presentation.

- Practice until you feel confident and can coordinate your visual aids with your presentation.

- Rehearse for timing. Plan what you can cut if it becomes necessary and what you can add if you finish ahead of schedule.

- If possible, rehearse in the room in which you will be presenting with the equipment you will be using.

- Practice with a microphone if you will be using one.
- Videotape your presentation to detect and fine-tune details, such as speaking too fast, speaking without expression, and using distracting mannerisms.
- Evaluate all aspects of the videotape. Ask a friend to complete an evaluation and make suggestions for improvement.
- Remember that skipping meals before you speak can take the edge off your energy level. Overeating can cause you to become sluggish.
- Make sure the audience can hear you. Ask for a microphone if you know that you have difficulty projecting in a large room.
- Examine podium lighting to make sure you can read your notes.
- Adjust the room temperature if possible. Set the temperature a few degrees below the comfort level. The temperature will rise when people assemble in the room.
- Make sure that all equipment is working properly.
- Take an extension cord and a three-prong/two-prong receptacle adapter.
- Prepare a brief autobiographical sketch to send to the person introducing you. Take an extra copy with you to the presentation.

Conveying a Professional Image

Now that you have finished your preparation, you should be concerned with conveying a professional image during your presentation. You should realize that audience members start forming their opinions of you as soon as they see you. Use your best manners, be sure that you are dressed appropriately and that you demonstrate a confident, professional image as you enter the room and walk to the podium.

The following tips should help you convey a professional image:

- Be real, be sincere, be yourself. Being pompous or arrogant destroys audience rapport.
- Remember that much of your message is communicated nonverbally through your posture, tone of voice, expressions, gestures, attire, and so on.
- Dressing appropriately will boost your confidence and convey credibility to your audience. Appropriate attire demonstrates that you respect your audience.
- Be well groomed. Make sure that your hair is neat and your clothes are fastened.
- Decide what you will wear for your presentation in time to have your garments pressed or cleaned. Allow time to press clothes again if you packed them for travel.
- Select clothes and accessories that look professional. Wear comfortable shoes that are appropriate for the occasion. Always have an extra blouse or shirt in case your clothes become accidentally soiled.
- Use appropriate facial expressions.
- Avoid mannerisms that take your listeners' attention away from your content. Lean toward your audience, not away from it.
- Use relaxed, natural movements and appropriate gestures. Moving around while you are speaking conveys confidence; a stiff, statuelike posture conveys apprehension.
- Avoid rocking back and forth, standing on one foot, chewing gum, or jingling keys or coins.
- Convey confidence and purpose as you walk to the lectern, and stay poised throughout your presentation.

Delivering Your Presentation

Now, you are ready to actually deliver your presentation. You should greet your audience and convey your pleasure at being asked to speak to them by smiling and using a friendly tone. In greeting your audience, you should observe the courtesies that are dictated by the formality of your speaking situation. For example, at a committee meeting, you might say, "Madam Chair and Committee Members." A simple "Good morning" would be appropriate in casual circumstances.

Probably the most-mentioned audience expectation is that the speaker not read his or her presentation. A second expectation is that the speech be substantive. The third expectation is that the speaker should end on time. The smart speaker, when assigned 45 minutes, plans on 35 to 40 minutes. If there are 5 to 10 minutes left, the time may be used to answer questions.

Following are some suggestions for improving your delivery.

- A strong opening sets the pace and immediately captures your audience's attention.

- Deliver your presentation; don't read it. Reciting from memory or reading a presentation makes you seem insincere, apprehensive, and unprepared.

- Use notes, but use them sparingly.

- Radiate energy, be enthusiastic, and be sincere.

- Maintain eye contact. Focus on one person for several seconds, letting the person sense that you are talking to him or her. Then, focus on someone else in another segment of the room.

- Adjust your volume to make sure that everyone can hear you. Groups of 45 or over usually require a microphone.

- Speak at a slow, deliberate pace, and pause occasionally. Silence can be an effective way to get your audience's attention.

- Concentrate on your words so that you do not slur your speech.

- Properly pronounce words, use correct grammar, and choose appropriate vocabulary.

- Stay focused and keep ideas moving.

- If it is appropriate to your situation, interact with your audience. Ask questions and respond to the answers.

- Deliver your first words in a loud voice to gain your audience's attention.

- Repeat important points. Audience members are more likely to remember details that they hear more than once.

- Avoid fillers, such as *uhs, ums,* and clichés, such as "to make a long story short" or "That reminds me of a story. . . ."

- Monitor expressions and nonverbal cues to determine if your audience is confused, listening, disagreeing, or bored. Respond by adjusting your presentation accordingly.

- Use appropriate gestures to emphasize major points. Move naturally, avoiding a stiff, robotic appearance.

- Coordinate content and visual aids. Do not show a visual aid until you are ready for your audience to see it.

- Use a laser pointer or other pointing device to get your audience to focus on a certain aspect of a visual aid.

- Display a blank slide with a pleasant color between slides.

KEY POINT

Audiences expect the speaker to:

1. **Not read the presentation.**
2. **Make substantive comments.**
3. **End on time.**

- Speak to your audience, not to your visual aid.
- Anticipate potential noise such as sirens or people talking in the halls. When noise occurs, keep your composure and pause for the noise to end.
- Stay within your assigned time limit.
- Leave time for questions from your audience.
- Conclude with a strong ending that will make your audience remember you and the content delivered.

 ## Memory Hook

Put prompts or reminders to yourself on your note cards. For example, you could draw a smiley face to remind you to have a pleasant expression. You could write "Slow DOWN!" on several cards if you have a tendency to speak too fast. A clock drawing would remind you to check your time.

KEY POINT

Good questions can help clarify important concepts, identify misunderstandings from audience members, and recognize specific areas that should be pursued.

Fielding Questions

You should cultivate a positive attitude about questions from your audience. Good questions can help clarify important concepts, identify misunderstandings from audience members, and recognize specific areas that should be pursued. Most presentation situations offer a question-and-answer period. When someone asks you a question, acknowledge the person and listen closely to the question. Following are some guidelines for fielding questions:

- At the beginning of your presentation, tell your audience your preference for handling questions—at the end or as they occur throughout the presentation. An inexperienced speaker may prefer handling questions at the end.
- If you like handling questions throughout the presentation, you may want to stop at convenient points and ask for questions.
- Repeat the questions for the audience members who may not have heard them. Restating the question gives you time to formulate your response.
- Ask for clarification if a question is unclear to you.
- Give brief, direct answers to questions.
- Try to anticipate possible questions by the audience, and think of answers in advance.
- If you don't know the answer to a question, offer to find the answer and forward it to the person who asked the question if he or she will leave a business card with the question on the reverse side.
- Stay calm and polite if you receive antagonistic questions. Avoid displaying negative emotions.
- Never permit an antagonistic audience member to take control of your presentation or to speak from the microphone. Always maintain control of your temper and control of the presentation.
- If the audience member continues to be confrontational, offer to talk with the person after the session ends.

KEY POINT

Remember that speaker's anxiety is normal and that you are not alone in this emotion.

Managing Stage Fright

What are the symptoms of stage fright or speaker's anxiety? Some speakers report cold hands, sweaty palms, shaky knees, or a quivering voice. Others sense a pounding heart. Most experienced and inexperienced speakers have anxiety when addressing a group of people. Experienced speakers, however, value the benefits produced by speaker's anxiety and attempt to convert the anxiety into a positive energy that keeps them sharp and alert during their presentations.

If you experience stage fright, remember that nervousness is normal and that you are not alone in this emotion. Most people list the fear of public speaking as their number one fear, above snakes and dying. Experienced speakers do not eliminate stage fright, but they learn how to manage it. The following are some suggestions for managing anxiety:

- Remind yourself that almost all speakers have some level of apprehension and that audiences really want you to succeed.

- Prepare adequately. The key to conquering stage fright is preparation.

- Master your content and visual aids to boost your self-confidence.

- Because much of the anxiety comes as you begin your presentation, make sure that you are especially prepared with a very strong opening.

- Go to the meeting room early, and talk with members of your audience. Introduce yourself to those whom you do not know, and initiate an informal conversation with those you already know.

- While in a rest room or other private place, loosen up by bending from the waist and letting your hands and arms hang limp.

- Just before you go to the podium, take three deep breaths to help you relax.

- When you are speaking, focus on your topic and your audience.

- Don't apologize for being nervous. An apology attracts attention to your nervousness, and your audience may not have noticed.

- Develop a positive attitude toward speaking. Speak every time you have the opportunity, whether at school, work, club meetings, or church or synagogue functions.

Memory Hook

Good advice for managing stage fright used to appear on the lid of a popular brand of mayonnaise: "Keep cool, but don't freeze."

Evaluating Your Presentation

After each presentation, you should evaluate yourself. Also, ask a friend or co-worker if he or she will constructively criticize your presentation. Be receptive to any suggestions received. Try to complete the evaluation within two to three days after the presentation, while you still clearly remember the details. This self-evaluation process will help you become a better speaker. Here are some evaluation techniques:

- Seek constructive criticism of your presentation from people you respect.

- Maintain a good attitude about negative comments.

- Profit by your mistakes, and convert them into learning experiences.

- Note any segments that receive several questions. It is possible that your content was incomplete or unclear in this particular area.

- List any changes you would make if you were presenting the same topic soon.
- Compare yourself with others who spoke on the same program.
- List your strengths and weaknesses that are related to speaking.
- Accept as many opportunities to present as practical. Each speaking experience and subsequent evaluation will help you improve your presentation skills.
- Keep a presentation file. The file will be helpful should you be asked to speak to the same group again or another group on the same or similar topic. Include your evaluation in this file.

Memory Hook

Number your note cards and your visual aids. If you drop them, the numbers will make it easy to put them back into the correct order.

Assessment   Section 14.3

Review of Key Terms

1. When you are beginning a speech, how can a *rhetorical question* help set the stage? _____
_____

Editing Practice

Vocabulary Alert!   In each of the following sentences, underline the word that does not fit the context. Write the correct word in the space provided.

2. Please call the personal office to arrange an interview. _____
_____

3. We attended to complete the project by Saturday. _____
_____

4. To countenance serious problems, we must make drastic budget cuts.
_____

5. The threat of a tax audit compiled us to consult with our tax attorney.
_____

6. His actions did not ward our taking any steps at this time. _____
_____

Practical Application

Applying Skills

7. Prepare and present a three-minute informal presentation to your class on how to do something. You must use visual aids. _____
_____

8. Your team has been asked to make a presentation to all employees regarding company activities for the upcoming year. Among the activities are a blood drive in March, a food drive for the local food bank in April, a company picnic in July, and an adopt-a-family program for the December holidays.

   The team will develop an outline of the presentation it would give to encourage all employees to participate in these activities. Analyze the audience, choose appropriate visual aids, prepare a list of questions that might be asked, and include possible answers. Role-play the presentation to the class. Include introductions if appropriate. _____
_____
_____

Discussion Point

Analyzing Details

9. What are some techniques you could use to introduce a speaker? _____
_____
_____
_____

10. Discuss how audience and content play a role in how a presentation is developed. How does content dictate the treatment of a topic? Should humor be used in all speeches? _____
_____
_____
_____
_____

SECTION OBJECTIVES

When you have finished Section 14.4, you will be able to:

- Discuss the basic guidelines for visual aids.

- Discuss the use of handouts in a presentation.

- Discuss multimedia rooms and projectors.

- Discuss the use of presentation software.

- List the guidelines for using presentation software.

- List most of the checklist items for presentation software visual aids.

WHY IT'S IMPORTANT

Creating useful, appropriate visual aids is vital for presentation success. Visual aids should help convey your message, keep your audience focused, and improve retention of your subject matter.

KEY TERMS

- document camera
- design templates
- clip art gallery
- slide animation
- slide transitions

KEY POINT

Remember that visual aids are not the presentation and that good visuals are not a substitute for good content.

Using Visual Aids and Technology

Essential Principles

Creating useful, appropriate visual aids is vital for presentation success. Visual aids should help convey your message, keep your audience focused, and improve retention of your subject matter.

Visual aids can include electronic slide shows, 35-millimeter slides, handouts, overhead transparencies, videos, traditional photographs, scanned or digital photographs, demonstrations, objects, samples, flip charts, and skits. Some presentations might use a combination of the mentioned methods. For example, a presentation on CPR might include an actual demonstration of CPR techniques and an electronic slide show giving the statistics on the number of lives that can be saved using the procedure.

Basic Guidelines for Visual Aids

Visual aids should support and enhance your presentation and reduce the amount of effort that your listener needs to understand what you are saying. In other words, visual aids should help convey your message. Suppose, for example, you were doing a presentation on credit card abuse and your visual aids consisted of a stack of credit cards and your most recent statement. Would the credit cards and the statement help convey your message? No, everyone has seen credit cards and statements. Neither aid would help convey the message about the huge amount of credit debt accumulated by people who overextend their purchases based on their current salaries. Facts and figures in an electronic slide show would be a good choice to convey the details about credit card abuse.

Your content, your presentation location, and the equipment available will determine the best visual aids to help you get your points across. Remember, the quality of your visual aids strongly influences your audience's perception of you. When preparing your visuals, strive for professional-looking quality. If your presentation is extremely important or before a very impressive audience, you might consider having an office graphics professional prepare them for you. Most of the time, however, you or someone in your company can create impressive visual aids.

One of the basic rules of communication also applies to the preparation of visual aids. The KISS rule should be emphasized. KISS stands for *Keep It Short and Simple.* For example, when preparing handouts, slides, and other printed visuals, you should use key words instead of complete sentences. In addition to verbal simplicity, you should keep the visuals uncluttered. Suppose there is a book page that has an illustration that you would like to use. Instead of copying the entire page, extract the illustration from the rest of the page, then make your visual.

Use an appropriate number of visuals in relation to the length of your presentation. Oversaturating your presentation with visuals loses an audience. One or two visuals per minute is a good guide. Remember that visual aids are not the presentation and that good visuals are not a substitute for good content. Impressive visual aids will not disguise poor content that lacks substance. You want your audience to grasp your message. You do not want them to say, "Sam is a wizard with the visuals, but what was he trying to get across to us?"

Visual aids should be visible from any location in the room. For that reason, posters are usually ineffective for group sizes over ten. Passing around samples is also ineffective for large groups, because the distribution causes a distraction and, in most instances, the speaker is finished before the samples reach everyone in the room.

Make sure that you do not stand between your audience and the visual aid. Also, make sure that you do not talk to your visual aid but face your audience. You should, however, quickly glance at your visual as soon as it is displayed to make sure that it is indeed there and is positioned correctly. When you are projecting transparencies or other documents onto a screen, try not to project your fingers onto the screen as you are adjusting the documents.

Integrating the visual aids throughout the presentation—as opposed to clustering them at the beginning or end of the presentation—helps sustain your audience's attention. Use a variety of visual aids in long presentations. This tactic helps keep your presentation moving.

Always practice your presentation with your visuals. Sometimes it is advisable to use an assistant to handle your visual aids and to adjust the lights as needed throughout your presentation. Always number your visuals and indicate on your note cards when the visual should be shown.

Handouts

Experienced speakers recommend that you give your audience at least one handout. Having something to take away from the presentation helps the audience remember you and your topic. Always include contact information such as your name, postal address, e-mail address, and fax and telephone numbers on your handouts.

Handouts are a good choice for visual aids when the information is too complex or too small to be projected onto a screen. They are also useful when you want audience members to evaluate the material or react to the content at a later date. Always prepare extra handouts. Some audience participants will take more than one copy.

If you are going to use your handouts during your presentation, ask someone to distribute the handouts for you, preferably as audience members enter the room. This saves time and avoids the distraction of distributing them during your presentation. If your handout will not be used during your presentation, distribute them as your audience is leaving. You could also choose to have your audience download the handouts from your Web site.

Numbering or color-coding handout pages makes it easier for audience members to locate a specific page when you refer to it during your presentation: "Find page 7," or "Turn to the blue page in your handouts." It is helpful to leave generous margins on handouts for additional notes. Many presenters provide miniature slide printouts to make note taking easier for listeners.

Multimedia Rooms and Projectors

Corporations often have multimedia rooms for meetings and presentations. These multimedia rooms are equipped with the latest technology to make presenting easier and more effective. The rooms have attractive, comfortable, yet functional furniture. (See **Exhibit 14.3.**)

KEY POINT

Visual aids should support and enhance your presentation and should reduce the amount of effort that your listeners need to understand what you are saying.

Employability Skills

Applying Technology to Task

One effective way of communicating in a business meeting is to organize information and create visuals to help others understand better. Use graphs, pictures, and other visuals to enhance your presentation.

Exhibit 14.3
Multimedia Room
Thinking Critically. *How can multimedia rooms help the competent, well-prepared speaker effectively and efficiently convey his or her ideas?*

Multimedia rooms use a combination of equipment. The presenter stands at a console that houses a computer and the other needed equipment. Some rooms have rear projection capabilities; others have a projector mounted from the ceiling. The projector can be activated and the screen can be raised or lowered by remote control.

From the console, the presenter can show transparencies and project hard-copy documents using the document camera. The **document camera** projects a photograph, a drawing, or the printed page onto the screen. The presenter, from the console, can also play a videotape or access an Internet connection or a cable television show. Additionally, anything on the computer screen, such as an electronic slide show, can be projected.

The quality of multimedia equipment varies. Several companies make portable equipment that can be transported in a rolling case to different locations within the firm or to distant locations. Portable multimedia equipment, including a laptop computer, necessary to operate the multimedia equipment, can be purchased at various prices. Of course, the quality depends on how much money you are willing to spend.

Using Presentation Software

Presentation software, such as PowerPoint (see **Exhibit 14.4**), will let you generate electronic slides that can be used as visual aids during a presentation or as a presentation that will run automatically. Automatic slide show presentations have many uses because they run uninterrupted and can be left unattended. For example, a college admissions staff developed an automatic slide show to be used when the staff visits high schools to recruit students. Using a laptop computer, the slide show runs continuously on a television monitor at the admissions booth during college fairs.

Additionally, presentation software can be used to write, edit, and print the speaker's outline or notes. You can use the software to print miniature copies of your

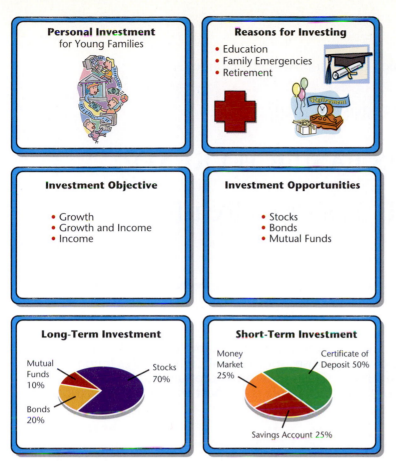

Exhibit 14.4
PowerPoint Slide Show
Thinking Critically. What are two benefits of an electronic slide show?

slides to be used as part of your notes or to distribute as handouts to your audience to facilitate note taking. One of the major advantages of using presentation software is that you can update your electronic slides within a few moments.

Presentation software provides design templates to make slide show creation easy for the novice. **Design templates** are preformatted layouts that let you add text, while keeping layout, color, fonts, etc., consistent. You can add clip art, animation, or slide transitions to make your visual aids more interesting. The **clip art gallery,** provided with your software, is a collection of simple drawings that can be used to illustrate your slides. In addition to the clip art that comes with the presentation software, there are Web sites that provide a variety of clip art that can be used in your electronic slides. Slides can be animated in several ways. **Slide animation** is a feature that lets parts of the slide—titles, bulleted items, and clip art—appear on the screen at different times. For example, the title would appear first, the clip art next, then each bulleted item would be added one at a time as the speaker talks about each one. Slide transitions are another presentation software feature. **Slide transitions** are special effects that introduce each slide as it appears on the screen. Examples would be sounds announcing the next slide or special visual effects like having the slide fade in or out.

Exhibits 14.5 and 14.6 and the Checklist for Presentation Software will help you prepare and use an electronic slide show. Most authorities recommend a maximum of three font sizes per slide.

Which of the following three lines...

is easier to read?

IS EASIER TO READ?

Is Easier to Read?

Exhibit 14.5
Fonts for Visual Aids
Read the text in Exhibit 14.5. In the first example, the first font is hard to read. The second example uses solid capitals, which takes longer to read than the third example, which uses initial capitals and lowercase letters. **Thinking Critically.** *Which example is the best choice for visual aids?*

36 Point
24 Point
18 Point

Exhibit 14.6
Font Size
Thinking Critically. *How many font sizes should be used per slide?*

Memory Hook

Your audience should remember your content—not merely that you had "spiffy" slides.

Checklist for Presentation Software

- Make sure all information on the graphics is correct and up to date.
- Use an appropriate number of visuals in relation to the length of your presentation.
- Create slides on the important points that you want your audience to remember. Use only one point per slide, with supporting bulleted items below.
- Use color effectively to make your visuals interesting and pleasing to the eye.
- Keep slides simple and uncluttered. Slides that require lengthy explanations are ineffective.
- Limit each slide or transparency to three to four lines of text; seven lines should be the maximum.
- Use block lettering, not fancy or script type. Limit type sizes to three per visual. Using more than three sizes complicates the visual.
- The three preferred font sizes are 36, 24, and 18. A size 18 font should be the smallest font that you use.
- Project each slide for about 30 seconds.
- Use uppercase and lowercase letters. Solid capitals are hard to read.
- Use bullets to emphasize important points.
- Vary the visuals. Use a combination of pictures, graphs, text, and cartoons.
- Test visual aids on the equipment that you will be using during the presentation.
- Place the projector screen in a prominent location. Make sure that it is large enough to be seen from all areas of the room.

Memory Hook

Your content drives the visual aids—not the other way around.

Anticipating Problems

No matter how much you prepare and how well you are organized, situations can develop over which you have no control. Anticipate as many of these situations as you can and plan how you will handle the situation.

One of the most common problems with technology is the incompatibility of software. A slide show that works perfectly on your office computer will not work in the hotel conference room because two different software applications are involved.

Prepare backup visuals; for example, transparencies for your slide show or slide miniatures as handouts. Also, be able to give your presentation without visual aids should it become necessary. You, your content, and the manner in which you deliver the content *are* the presentation. Prepare and rehearse—these are the keys to successful presenting.

Assessment   Section 14.4

Review of Key Terms

1. How can *design templates* aid in creating a slide show? _____
_____

2. When would you want to use *slide animation* in an electronic slide show? _____
_____

Editing Practice

Vocabulary Alert!   In each numbered list below, circle the pair of synonyms or pair of antonyms. Tell whether the words are synonyms or antonyms. Use a dictionary if necessary.

3. (a) busy   (b) boisterous (c) happy   (d) clever   (e) quiet
_____

4. (a) faultless   (b) modest   (c) serious (d) pretentious (e) extraneous
_____

5. (a) demise   (b) hope   (c) death   (d) vision   (e) contrive
_____

6. (a) excellence (b) disparity (c) slander (d) reference   (e) equality
_____

7. (a) affable   (b) garrulous (c) erratic (d) joyous   (e) talkative
_____

Practical Application

Analyzing Information

8. Interview someone in education, human resources, or staff development, and find out what kinds of visual aids are used. Find out if more advanced technological aids are being introduced and what the advantages and disadvantages are to using these tools. Write a brief essay about your findings for your instructor. _____
_____
_____

9. Your team will prepare a three-to-five-minute presentation about your campus. Include some form of visual aid—electronic slides, 35 mm slides, overhead transparencies, videos, handouts, etc. If available, schedule a multimedia room to make the presentation. Remember to rehearse the presentation using the visuals. _____

_____

_____

Discussion Point

Making Comparisons

10. When should a presenter use visual aids? How does the quality of visual aids affect the audience and the message? _____

_____

_____

11. When should a presenter use handouts? What are some guidelines for using handouts? _____

_____

_____

Unit 6

Searching for Jobs and Writing Résumés

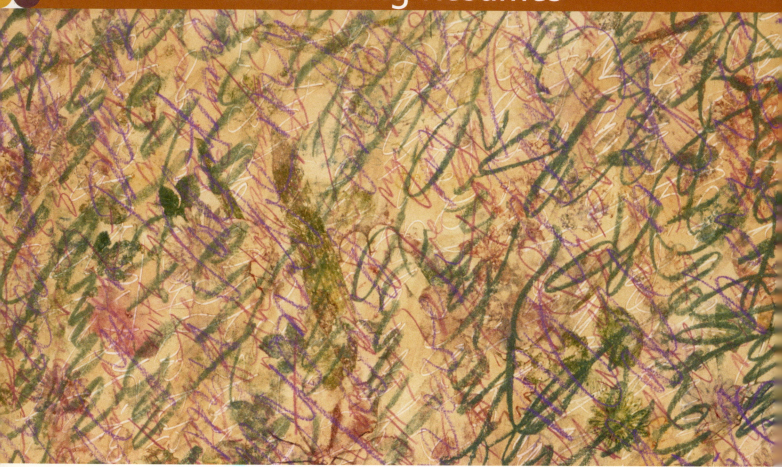

Unit Overview

In this unit, you will learn to use your communication skills to secure employment.

Chapter 15

Searching for Jobs

Chapter 16

Interviewing and Employment Issues

Harold is one of ten graduates at Centerville Community College to be interviewed for two positions that would begin June 1 at HiTech Solutions, Inc., a local computer company. Lonnell Russell, HiTech's interviewer, will meet with all ten as a group at the college to tell them about the company and the two available positions. All had similar academic programs, each had at least a 3.5 grade point average, and all had work experience.

Harold arrived late for the group meeting and took a seat near the door. Mr. Russell was telling the group about HiTech and the two available positions. Harold felt uncomfortable as he glanced around the room. Everyone else had worn business attire. He had on jeans, a school sweatshirt, and a baseball cap.

After Mr. Russell finished the information session, he asked those students who were interested to sign up for an appointment at his office the next day. Harold signed up for the 1:30 slot.

Harold was determined to dress appropriately and to arrive early for the interview—two tasks that he hadn't accomplished at the group meeting. On the day of the interview, Harold was running late. To save time, he ate on the way. Harold noticed that his gas gauge was on empty. He stopped at a self-service gas station and filled his gas tank. In his haste, Harold spilled some gas on his shoes. He used the napkins that came with his meal to wipe his shoes. Soon after, he arrived at the interview site.

In the reception area, Harold sat down beside his classmate, Max Wilson, and started a conversation. The receptionist asked, "Sir, may I help you?"

From his seat, Harold identified himself and told the receptionist he had an appointment with Mr. Russell.

Max asked Harold, "What's that spot on your shirt?"

"Must be catsup from the french fries. Got a Kleenex?"

"And, what's that smell?" Max queried.

"Must be the gas that sloshed on my shoes. Sorry," Harold said apologetically.

Mr. Russell's administrative assistant walked over to Max and Harold. Max stood up, while Harold sat and rubbed the stain on his shirt. Ms. Moreno took Max to Mr. Russell's office for his interview. Harold finally gave up on the stain.

Thinking Critically

If you were interviewing Harold, what would have been your first impression of him?

What did Harold do incorrectly?

Would you have hired Harold?

Chapter 15

Searching for Jobs

Workplace Connection

Every year, thousands of positions are available to graduating students, each of whom is in search of that first big job. The challenge is to get it. The job search procedure is exciting, but it can also be frustrating if you do not know what to expect. Chapters 15 and 16 will guide you through the job search process.

CHAPTER OBJECTIVES

When you have completed this chapter, you should be able to:

- Discuss job search methods and which ones best suit your needs.
- Compose a résumé that markets your qualifications to prospective employers.
- Identify the strategies for preparing a scannable résumé.
- Compose a persuasive application letter.
- Compose and present an employment portfolio.

Job Search Skills

Essential Principles

Finding the position you want is similar to taking a comprehensive final exam. You are taking the knowledge you acquired and are applying it to a specific situation.

The job search process is becoming extremely sophisticated and competitive. Technology makes online job applications possible. Résumés and application letters can be transmitted instantaneously. The information and related assignments in this chapter will prepare you for a modern-day job search. The process will be easier if you approach it systematically in separate steps. You need to:

1. Analyze yourself and your qualifications.

2. Assess the job market.

3. Develop personal packaging information, including résumés and application letters.

Analyzing Yourself and Your Qualifications

The first step in the job search process is to analyze yourself and your professional qualifications. You need to consider what kind of work interests you and what qualifications you have that would help you perform that particular work.

Career Goals

To determine your career goals, ask yourself these questions: What professional position, if any, do I have now? What position do I want when I complete my course of study? What position do I want two years from now? What position do I want five years from now? These are the basic questions many people use to create a five-year plan, a fundamental building block in career planning.

Education

Think about how education affects your career goals by asking yourself these questions: What courses, degrees, or training have prepared me for my career goals? Can I achieve my career goals with the education I now have? Do I need additional courses to qualify for the position I want? Will I need additional education and training for the position I want in the future?

Experience

Analyze your work experience by asking yourself these questions: What work experience do I have that is related to the position I want? How is this experience related to my career goals? If I do

When you have finished Section 15.1, you will be able to:

- Analyze yourself and your professional qualifications.
- List the methods for assessing the job market.
- Discuss placement agencies and employment contractors.

WHY IT'S IMPORTANT

Technology has significantly affected the job search process, much as it has affected the rest of our professional and personal lives. With a click of the mouse, you can log on to a company's Web site, learn about positions available, and apply for the position that you choose. Some companies prefer that you apply through their Web site; others prefer the traditional method of mailing your résumé and application letter.

KEY TERMS

- hidden job market
- placement agencies
- employment contractors

not have related experience, how can I acquire such experience? Do I have additional—though unrelated—experience that will demonstrate a successful work history?

Personal Characteristics

Define your personal characteristics by asking yourself these questions: What are my major strengths and weaknesses? Do I enjoy working with figures, computers, or people, or a combination of these? Do I like variety? Do I want responsibility? Do I like challenges and problem solving? Would I accept a position that offers advancement but frequently requires overtime? What do I like to do?

Your Ideal Job

The next step is to become very specific. Begin by describing your ideal potential employer and the position you would want with that firm. It is okay to dream a little when writing this description—your goal is to determine the type of position you want.

Here are some questions to consider when writing the description of your ideal job:

- Which products or services am I interested in providing?
- Which position do I want?
- Am I looking for a career opportunity that offers promotions, transfers, additional education, and training?
- Do I want to work in a small community or a large city? In the United States or abroad?
- Would I like to work for a small, medium, or large company?
- What salary range would be acceptable?
- How important are benefits, such as a flexible schedule, vacation policy, health insurance, and retirement options?
- Am I prepared to travel for my job?

Compare your description of your ideal company and position with your analyses of your goals, education, experience, and personal characteristics to see how the two sets of information fit. If almost every category is in harmony with the others, proceed to the next step. If your personal assessment and the description of your ideal position and company do not agree, however, work through both sets of information again to decide where you should make changes.

For example, you may learn that the type of job you want as a computer programmer exists, but the available positions are in southern California, and you were hoping to work in Texas. Should you stick to your original plan or rethink your choices? You must consider your choices and establish your priorities. This leads to the second step in the job search: assessing the job market.

Look for connections as you examine your career goals, education, experience, personal characteristics, and your ideal job. Similarities can indicate a potential career path.

Assessing the Job Market

After you have analyzed yourself and your qualifications and identified the type of employment you want, begin looking for positions that meet your specifications. Many convenient sources of information about job opportunities are at your disposal. Traditionally, listings on college bulletin boards, newspaper classifieds, chambers of commerce, and library reference books offer up-to-date information and reliable resources. Depending on the size and geographic region of your desired location, some sources of information may be more accessible than others.

Use the Internet to find potential employers. Many companies use their Web sites to post general information about their purpose and goals, the locations of their branches, and current employment opportunities. The Internet also has a number of job search engines that offer listings of professional openings in numerous fields. Also, using a standard search engine to search for job openings in many categories is helpful. More information on searching for jobs on the Internet is found later in this section.

Your Personal Contact Network

Your personal contact network of friends, relatives, and college instructors can be an effective source of employment opportunities, particularly in a small community. Employees of a company often know when positions will become available because of transfers, promotions, resignations, retirements, and the creation of new positions. Inform people in your personal contact network about the kind of job you are seeking and the date when you will be available to accept a position. Even if your personal contacts do not know of an available position, they may know others who do.

Your Professional Contact Network

You can establish your own professional contact network of friends and acquaintances in the business world using the following tips:

Join the College Affiliate of Civic and Professional Organizations.   The Rotary Club sponsors Rotoract—its collegiate organization—on many campuses, and International Management Accountants (IMA) encourages student participation in its organization.

Use Every Opportunity to Mingle with Professionals in Your Chosen Field. When you hear a guest speaker at a conference, be sure to talk with the speaker after the presentation. Introduce yourself, express your appreciation for the speaker's time and expertise, and comment on some specific point that was made during the presentation.

Arrange to Meet Professionals Who Are Affiliated in Some Way with Your College.   Find out if the department in your major has a board of advisers or a similar group. You might suggest holding a reception that gives students the opportunity to interact with members of this group.

Acquire Work Experience through Internships, Summer Jobs, and Part-Time Employment.   In addition to the work experience positions like these provide, you have an opportunity to develop relationships with professionals who can serve as mentors and employment references. You also develop links to other employers who might have positions available that match your qualifications. Internships and temporary employment situations give you a chance to see if a career in a particular field is right for you.

Build Cordial Relationships with the Business Professionals with Whom You Work.   Through your job performance, impress upon the employer your willingness to accept new assignments and to work as a team member. Many employers use internships and temporary employment situations to determine the potential temporary employees possess for permanent employment. Employers particularly look for traits that are complex to measure, such as the ability to work in teams, a positive attitude, and creativity in coming up with new ideas or suggestions for solving problems. They also look for a good attendance and punctuality record.

Hidden Job Market

The hidden job market is not really a new concept, but today it seems to be used more and more. The **hidden job market** refers to job opportunities that are not advertised in the traditional venues, such as newspapers or journals. This market, which represents a majority of available jobs in some fields, should not be overlooked. Most of these job openings are filled through word-of-mouth contacts or sometimes through online announcements that encourage submission of applications and résumés.

College Placement Centers

Most educational institutions have placement offices whose career counselors are eager to assist you in finding a position. Visit your school's placement center or Web site to see what services are available. Besides listing employment requests from area businesses, career counselors often coordinate job fairs that bring potential employers to the campus to interview students. Career counselors often arrange for students to attend regional job fairs. Regional job fairs attract a larger number of employers and are open to students from many schools.

A comprehensive placement center would offer workshops on résumé preparation and interviewing techniques. These placement centers can also serve as the disbursement center for employment-related credentials that each student selects to be sent to prospective employers. These credentials would include a résumé, a list of references, and an unofficial transcript. Many career placement centers offer software programs which help you make career decisions, as well as books, pamphlets, and magazines related to current employment trends. These centers can also assist in researching employers.

Often, career counselors can help you get a part-time job while you are in school. Many college placement centers offer to help students long after they graduate. If you want to change positions several years after you graduate, contact your college's career placement center and ask if you can still use its services.

Newspaper Advertisements

The classified advertisement section of newspapers carries announcements of job openings in many types of business positions. Generally, the Sunday edition of a newspaper has the most extensive listings. If you want to apply for a position in a distant city, you should start checking the classified advertisements several months in advance for job openings in that location. Your college library, local library, or bookstore may subscribe to a newspaper from the city you have chosen. If not, you may need to take out a short-term subscription to selected newspapers.

Specialized Journals

Another place to look for employment opportunities is in specialized journals, such as those for accountants, medical personnel, office personnel, teachers, and other professionals. Published annually, *The College Placement Annual* offers information on a variety of employment opportunities and is available through college placement centers. This publication lists employers alphabetically and geographically. It also gives general background information about companies and lists anticipated position openings.

Online Searching for Employment

The many employment-related sites on the Internet and the World Wide Web make it possible for you to conduct an online employment search. Many companies have home pages on the World Wide Web that provide information about the company and its employment opportunities. In addition, online services provide job postings and employer profiles for job seekers, and they collect résumés for employers seeking new employees. Many of these sites allow you to post your résumé electronically, either free of charge or for a fee. In the next section, you will learn how to write an electronic résumé.

Listed below are a number of online employment services and their Internet addresses.

CareerBuilder Inc.	careerbuilder.com
Internet Career Connection	iccweb.com
Monster.com	monster.com
NationJob Network	nationjob.com

KEY POINT

Online employment services offer a variety of job listings.

Placement Agencies and Employment Contractors

Private employment agencies can be found in most metropolitan areas. Their business is to fill jobs for companies. Some of these **placement agencies** fill job openings in a wide range of occupations, while others focus on one area of employment, such as management, construction, or office personnel. These agencies charge a fee, which is usually a percentage of the annual salary for the position. The fee is paid either by the company seeking to fill a vacancy or by the person who gets the job. Be sure to determine if the company will pay the fee, or if you will be responsible for it. Also, read carefully any contract that you might consider signing with a placement agency. You need to know all of the contract stipulations.

Employment contractors, also known as temporary agencies, supply personnel on a temporary basis for a given company's specific requests and needs. Temporary workers gain valuable workplace experience, establish a positive relationship with a company, and possibly attain permanent employment.

Assessment   Section 15.1

Review of Key Terms

1. How can you find out about employment in a *hidden job market*? _____
   _____
   _____

2. What are some disadvantages with using *private employment agencies*? _____
   _____

Editing Practice

Call an Editor!   Rewrite the following sentences for clarity and correctness.

3. Each of the 3 applicants are qualified. _____

4. Its company policy to conduct drug screening on all new employees'.
   _____

5. Our team was asked to develope a schedule for the Spring projects.
   _____

6. The report is up-to-date and will be distributed tommorow. _____
   _____

7. Jan wrote a reccomendation letter in march. _____

Practical Application

Analyzing Information

8. Describe your ideal position. List five jobs that would fit your description. _____

9. Visit your college placement center and local employment agencies. Find out how these organizations can help you in your job search. Inter-

view someone in one of these organizations, and research what the job market is like in your area. What kinds of openings are most available in your area? What markets are tight? Write a report of the team's findings for your instructor. _____

_____

Discussion Point

Identifying the Main Idea

10. What are some sources you might consult for information about job openings in your chosen career? _____

_____

_____

11. Discuss how internships and summer jobs are valuable employment contacts. _____

_____

_____

_____

_____

Chronological and Functional (Skills) Résumés

Résumés

The résumé is an outline, or summary, of your background and qualifications for the job you want. As you prepare your résumé, remember that the care in its preparation and the information it supplies often determine whether you will be invited for an interview. Résumés for your first job after college should be one full page in length. Proofread and edit your résumé carefully to make sure the spelling, grammar, and facts are correct and that the wording is clear. Ask several people to proofread your résumé as well. Creating an error-free résumé will help make your first impression a favorable one.

All messages, including your résumé and application letter, to a potential employer must communicate a professional image. Use a businesslike e-mail address. Addresses like funguy@ . . . or shoptilidrop@ . . . convey that you are immature and not serious about the job search process. Your outgoing voice mail message also should sound professional. If a potential employer hears a message like the following one, he or she will probably not leave you a message or call back. "You're here. I'm not. You know what to do at the tone." Job seekers must establish a professional image with prospective employers.

Always be honest when listing your qualifications on a résumé. Fabricating academic credentials or job titles and responsibilities is not worth the risk involved. Falsifying your credentials or application documents is grounds for immediate termination in many companies. It is also dishonest and unethical.

Most employers avoid asking the age, sex, marital status, religion, or race of applicants. Supplying such information is optional. Most people, however, prefer to omit such information.

Be prepared to submit your résumé and application letter electronically. If you cannot do this, a prospective employer will perceive that you do not have technical skills—a must in today's professional environment. Today, many résumés are sent as attachments to e-mails.

Résumé Sections

Résumés usually have standard sections. This makes it easy for prospective employers to review a job candidate's credentials. You can individualize the information in these standard sections to present your qualifications in the best light. When creating your first résumé, it is okay to get ideas from a résumé template (available in most word processing programs) to help you get started. However, when preparing a résumé for actual submission to a potential employer, you should develop a customized résumé that highlights your individual qualifications. Many applicants may use the same template, and you want your résumé to stand out from other résumés. The generic approach to résumé writing is a negative, because you don't want a potential employer to think that you have taken a shortcut to prepare this vital document in the job search process. Include the following major sections in your résumé.

Identification.   Begin with your name, address, telephone number, cell phone number, e-mail address, and fax number, if applicable. If you have a temporary address while you are in college, be sure to include both your temporary and your permanent address information. You may want to have the following heading above your temporary address: Address Until May 10, 2007.

Position Objective.   Your position objective should express your employment goal. If you prepare your résumé in response to an advertised position, you may want to reflect the specifics noted in the ad, such as "A position as a paralegal in the area of probate, trusts, and estates." If you are preparing a résumé to send to many companies, your objective should be more general, such as "A position as a nursing assistant in a clinic." You can easily change the position objective with each résumé that you send.

Education.   If you have attended several colleges, list your most recent education first. Include your degree, college, and major; also list your grade point average if it is 3.2 or higher on the 4.0 scale. If your overall grade point average is less than ideal, consider limiting your grade point average calculation to your major, but only if it is higher; for example, "Grade Point Average in Major 3.8." Be sure to add "in Major" to make it clear that 3.8 is not your overall grade point average. If you have not yet received a degree, list the date the degree will be awarded, for example: "Associate of Arts in Accounting to be awarded May 2007." As a prospective college graduate, you will find that your education can be your strongest selling point.

If your résumé is too brief, you can expand the education section by listing your major courses. List the topic of the course (Managerial Accounting) rather than the course number (Accounting 320).

Special Skills.   Use this optional category to list distinctive competencies, such as proficiency in another language, ability to interpret for the hearing impaired, experience with specific software programs, or certification in CPR. Some skills may be position specific; for example, a potential teacher may list that he or she is licensed to drive a school bus.

Experience.   You have several options in listing work experience. You may choose to list every job you have had, even though past jobs may be unrelated to the position for which you are applying. A steady work history demonstrates you are industrious, have initiative, and are dependable.

List your current or most recent work experience first and continue backward. Give the months and years of employment, such as May 2003 to June 2005, along with the company name, city, and state. Include brief, specific descriptions of your job responsibilities using active verbs. For example:

- Reduced mailing costs by 10 percent.
- Developed training program for new salespeople.
- Increased the sales of electronics equipment by 25 percent.
- Implemented voice mail system to handle customer inquiries.

If you have had many jobs, you may use the heading "Selected Experience" or "Related Experience" to focus on those most related to the position you seek. Use one of these headings to let potential employers know your résumé does not include your entire employment history.

Using action verbs in your résumé to describe your work responsibilities makes you seem more competent and qualified. Include the following action words as you compose your résumé:

achieved	expanded	presented
arranged	implemented	programmed
completed	improved	reduced
coordinated	increased	researched
created	initiated	simplified
designed	managed	solved
developed	minimized	supervised
evaluated	organized	trained

To let a potential employer know that you are honest and trustworthy, include experience, as appropriate, that communicates that you had responsibility for money or property in previous jobs. Here are some examples:

- Balanced the cash drawer at shift change.
- Opened and closed restaurant on weekends.
- Made deposits twice daily.
- Substituted for shift manager.

Activities. List your participation in school and community organizations, sports, and volunteer activities. Specify any offices you held, such as president, secretary, or treasurer. This section demonstrates your leadership abilities and community involvement, qualities that many employers look for in job candidates. You can expand the section on activities to include special recognitions such as dean's list, academic scholarships, honor societies, and so on. If you expand this list, use a heading such as "Honors and Activities."

References. As part of the résumé preparation process, you should create a reference list. The stationery for the reference list should match the stationery for the application letter and the résumé. Use the statement "References supplied upon request" to indicate you will provide references when a prospective employer requests them. Use the statement "References are attached" if you are sure that you want a particular job or if you are taking your résumé with you to an interview. See **Exhibit 15.1** on page 562 for an example of a reference list.

You should carefully select three individuals who know you well and who will communicate with prospective employers on your behalf. You could choose an instructor in your major field, a former employer or supervisor, and someone who knows you personally but is not a relative. Give the name, job title, if applicable, complete address, e-mail address, and telephone number of each reference.

As a courtesy, you should ask each person if you may give his or her name as a reference. Although you can request permission by telephone or in person, you may also make this request in writing, as in the following example.

> Would you be willing to serve as a reference for me in my job search? As you are aware, I will graduate in May 2006 from Anderson Piedmont Community College with an Associate Degree in Computer Science. Enclosed is a copy of my résumé for your reference.
>
> Please indicate your answer in the space provided and return this letter to me in the enclosed stamped envelope by March 15.

Digital Data

Résumé Templates

When creating your résumé for the first time, templates available in word processing programs will help you get started. However, you should develop a customized résumé for actual submission, because other applicants may use the same templates to create their résumés.

KEY POINT

Always ask for permission before listing someone as a reference.

Janet Hardiman	238 East Park Circle Shelby, North Carolina 28150	704-555-2367 (Cell) janet@community.net

Reference List

Employment Reference:	Mr. Steve Davis Davis Accounting Services Post Office Box 3389 Charlotte, NC 28202 704-555-8293 sdavis@davis.net
Academic Reference:	Dr. Phyllis Taylor Holly Hills Community College Post Office Drawer 3885 Casar, NC 28154 704-555-7864 ptaylor@hollyhills.edu
Character Reference:	Ms. Sarah Massey 5323 East 33rd Street Casar, NC 28154 704-555-2354 smassey@haven.net

Exhibit 15.1
Reference List
Thinking Critically. *What kinds of information did Janet provide in her reference list?*

You may also use an e-mail to request permission. Be sure to attach a copy of your résumé. When you accept a position, you should let your references know and thank them for their willingness to be used as a references. Be cordial with your references, because they took the time to help you and you may need them again.

Additional Headings. Additional headings such as *Certifications, Profile,* and *Qualifications* may be included on your résumé. You should use all the standard headings and then select others that showcase your attributes to their fullest potential.

After you have completed your résumé, be sure to store it on a separate disk (or other device) labled *Résumé*. Update the résumé to reflect each new accomplishment as it occurs; for example, "Volunteered at soup kitchen," "Selected for nursing honor society," "Dean's list for fall 2007 semester," "Secretary for business club." Maintaining an up-to-date résumé will prepare you for unexpected job interviews. You can proofread, print, and be ready to interview.

KEY POINT

Maintain a current résumé, updating it immediately when significant accomplishments occur.

William Kirkpatrick

418 Barton Street
Lansing, Michigan 48914

405-555-2841 (Cell)
405-555-2943 (FAX)

wkirkpatrick@lanmich.net

OBJECTIVE	To obtain a position as an accountant with opportunities for advancement based on performance.
EXPERIENCE January 2001 to Present	**Accountant** Great Brands Outlet Store, Lansing, Michigan • Implemented Inventory System that Saved Company $100,000 • Wrote Company Accounting Policy Manual • Developed and Maintained Web site • Supervised Data Entry • Completed Quarterly Reports
May 1998 to December 2000	**Customer-Service Representative** Atkins Jewelry Store, Lansing, Michigan • Handled Billing Inquiries from Customers • Obtained Customer Credit Reports • Established Security Procedures for Jewelry
June 1996 to April 1998	**Sales Associate and Management Trainee** Capers Department Store, Lansing, Michigan • Simplified Inventory Procedures for the Children's Department • Counted Cash Receipts and Made Deposits Twice Daily • Trained New Sales Associates
EDUCATION	Bachelor of Science in Accounting Awarded May 2001 Abernathy State College, Lansing, Michigan • Additional Hours in Management Information Systems • 3.8 GPA
SPECIAL SKILLS	Bilingual in English and Spanish Proficient in Microsoft WORD, PowerPoint, Access, and Excel Experience with Accounting Software
HONORS AND CIVIC ACTIVITIES	President, Rotary Club, 2004 Youth Camp Board of Directors 2003 Dean's List All Semesters, Abernathy State Golf Team, Abernathy State—Won Regional Tournament Capers Round Table, 1997 and 1998 (Awarded to Top Ten Sales Associates)
REFERENCES	Provided on Request

Exhibit 15.2
Chronological Résumé
Thinking Critically. Why did Will Kirkpatrick choose the chronological format?

Employability Skills

Individual Responsibility

In a chronological résumé, one of the key elements is to describe your increasing responsibilities in reverse chronological order. From one job to another, it's crucial to show how you've improved and grown in your position.

Misspelling

Be sure not to mispell words on a résumé.

(*Misspell* is the correct spelling, not *mispell*.)

Résumé Types

Résumé formats are usually chronological, functional, or a combination of these two types. Scannable résumés are discussed in Section 15.3.

Chronological Résumés

Chronological résumés list work experience in reverse chronological order, with the most recent experience listed first, as shown in **Exhibit 15.2.**

Chronological résumés are appropriate when you have a steady work history and work experience in your field of interest. You want to demonstrate that your responsibilities have increased as you have accepted new positions. Most new college graduates do not use the chronological format.

Permanent Address	Campus Address
Post Office Box 3849	Davis College Apartment 223
Charlotte, NC 28102	Cherryville, NC 28021
704-555-1688	704-555-3820

Objective: An Administrative Assistant position where my computer skills can be used.

Education: Davis College, Cherryville, North Carolina
Associate in Applied Science to be Awarded May 2006
Administrative Assistant Curriculum plus 15 Hours in Computer Courses

Qualifications:

Computer Skills
Competent in latest Versions of Popular Software

WORD	WordPerfect
Excel	Access
PowerPoint	PageMaker

Administrative Skills
Proficient in Office Procedures:

General Office Duties	Complex Switchboard Operations
Typing—75 WPM	Calendar/Appointment Management

Organizational Skills
Efficient in Accomplishing Assignments:

Prioritizing Tasks	Scheduling Part-Time Employees
Multitask Capabilities	Meeting Deadlines
Self-Starter	Working without Close Supervision

Experience: Davis College Data Services Department-September 2004 to May 2006
Established Log for Equipment Problems
Completed Work Orders on Equipment Problems
Assisted in Loading New Software on Campus Computers
Assisted in Installing Wireless Network

Barnett's Ice Cream Shop-June 2002 to August 2003
Served Customers
Opened and Closed Shop on Weekends

Activities at Davis College:

Treasurer, Phi Beta Lambda	Member, Basketball Team
Vice President, Interact Club	Member, Davis College Chorus

Volunteer Work: Prepared Meals on Saturdays for Homeless Shelter
Mentored for the Cherryville Youth Assistance Program
Taught Crafts at the Wendall Retirement Home

References: Available on Request

Exhibit 15.3
Functional Résumé
Thinking Critically. *Why did Brendan choose a functional format for his résumé?*

Employability Skills

Knowing How to Learn

The key element of a functional or skills résumé is to describe your expertise and talents in a specific field. However, an employer might look for an applicant who has the willingness to learn new skills on the job. Being flexible and willing to acquire new skills is a great employability skill.

Functional Résumés

Unlike chronological résumés, **functional résumés,** which are also called skills résumés, highlight professional skills and related accomplishments and deemphasize work history. A functional résumé, as shown in **Exhibit 15.3,** is appropriate for recent graduates who wish to emphasize their education and training over their work experience. This is especially true when most work experience is part-time and does not relate to the position that you seek. Note that the functional résumé includes a section titled "Qualifications." This section is specific to the functional résumé but may be included, as appropriate, in other résumé types.

Combination Résumés

Combination résumés employ the best features of chronological and functional résumés to present a prospective employee's strongest qualifications. As shown in **Exhibit 15.4,**

Janet Hardiman

238 East Park Circle
Shelby, NC 28150

704-555-2367 (Cell)
janet@community.net

Objective:	Position as office manager in a growing firm.
Profile:	Excellent oral and written communication skills.
	• Proficient in word processing desktop publishing.
	• Typing speed of 70 words per minute.
	• Adept at integrating spreadsheets and graphic elements into reports.
	• Familiar with photography programs.
	• Quick learner who enjoys working with people.
Education:	Associate of Arts in Secretarial Science, May 2005, GPA 3.6 in Major
	Holly Hills Community College, Casar, North Carolina
	Selected coursework in addition to required major courses:

Human Resource Management	First Aid and CPR
Management Principles	Golf and Tennis
Music Appreciation	Psychology

Certifications:	Notary Public, 2005 CPR, 2005
Experience:	Office Manager, Davis Accounting Services, Charlotte, North Carolina, June 2004 to present.
	• Conduct software training classes for management.
	• Arrange domestic and international travel for executives.
	• Write company newsletter.
	• Coordinate quarterly board meetings.
	• Supervise two administrative assistants.
	Secretary, Farnsworth, Brentworth, and Schmidt, Attorneys at Law, Charlotte, North Carolina, Summers of 2002 and 2003.
	• Scheduled appointments and court dates.
	• Assisted attorneys in preparing and filing briefs.
	• Handled correspondence for three attorneys.
Honors And Activities:	Outstanding Student Award, 2005.
	Software Applications Award, 2004.
	Dean's List, All Four Semesters
	Vice President, Phi Beta Lambda
	Secretary, Holly Hills Honor Society
	Member, Students Against Drunk Driving (SADD)
Volunteer Efforts:	Habitat for Humanity
	Community Homeless Shelter
References:	References will be furnished on request.

Exhibit 15.4
Combination Résumé
Thinking Critically. Why did Janet choose a combination format for her résumé?

KEY POINT

As a courtesy, you should supply your references with a copy of your résumé so that they will be prepared to answer questions about you. You should also notify your references when you accept a position.

a combination résumé emphasizes education and skills while also mentioning work experience. The "Profile" heading can include both skills and personal characteristics, or a combination of the two. A combination résumé is shown in **Exhibit 15.4.**

While writing a résumé is not a difficult task, you should devote sufficient time and effort to do it well. A sloppy, poorly written, or incomplete résumé is likely to be tossed aside by a potential employer—and with it your chance for a job.

If you are just beginning your academic career, you should start building your résumé by acquiring work experience, doing volunteer work, and participating in appropriate campus organizations. Establishing a solid work history can assist you in the job search by providing sources for excellent recommendations on your job performance. Having a sufficient work background in your field of interest and being involved in a variety of activities certainly makes writing your résumé much easier.

Résumé Formatting

Once you have identified the information to include in your résumé, you need to arrange and format the information for the most attractive, professional, and eye-catching appearance. Use the following checklist:

Checklist for Formatting a Résumé

- Limit your résumé to one full page, unless you have extensive work experience. While your résumé should contain all pertinent information, it should not be crowded.

- Place your résumé attractively on the page. Include an eye-appealing combination of printed information and white space to make the résumé easy to read.

- Use 1-inch side and bottom margins and a 1 1/2-inch top margin.

- Use headings with bold or capital letters to identify your sections of experience, education, activities, etc.

- Select a readable font in 11- or 12-point type for your text and a somewhat larger font, such as 14-point type, for headings. The smallest acceptable font is a 10-point size. It should be used sparingly; reserve it for less important details.

- Select a good-quality paper with matching envelopes. Ideally, your matching envelopes should be large enough to accommodate your résumé and application letter unfolded. Use the same type and color stationery for your résumé, application letter, and list of references. White stationery is used most often, but light colors—cream, buff, or gray—are acceptable.

- Avoid stapling the application letter and résumé because the receiver must often separate them for photocopying or scanning.

- List your personal information (name, address, telephone, cell phone, fax, e-mail) at the top.

- Choose sections that are appropriate for representing your background and qualifications.

- Include a career objective at the beginning.

- List your education in reverse chronological order, most recent first. Include specific information, such as college name, dates attended, location, and degree.

- The phrase, "References available on request," or, "References are attached," can be used to finish a résumé. Make sure that address information for all your references is up to date.

Review of Key Terms

1. Why is it better not to staple or fold your résumé? _____
_____

Editing Practice

Vocabulary Alert!   Choose the word that correctly completes each of the following sentences:

2. Adam used the new software program to (excess, access) the database.
_____

3. Tomás had to drive through the (dessert, desert) during the hottest part of the day. _____

4. Severe (weather, whether) delayed his arrival. _____

5. Ms. Epstein asked the members of her staff for (they're, their, there) views on the new procedure. _____

6. Will Kirkpatrick told the sales manager to (chose, choose) a site for the upcoming sales meeting. _____

Practical Application

Writing a Résumé

7. Based on your education, work experience, and skills, determine which résumé style is best for you. Explain your choice. Then, make a list of people you could use as references. _____
_____
_____
_____

8. Write your résumé using the style you selected above. Use one of the sample résumés as a guide. Once your résumé is completed, do peer editing in your team. Make a checklist, noting use of action words, clarity, organization, spelling, grammar, and mechanics. Make sure the formatting is professional. Then, write your final résumé on good-quality paper. Also, if requested to do so, submit the assignment to your instructor as an e-mail attachment.
_____
_____
_____
_____
_____

Discussion Point

Thinking Critically

9. Some people "pad" their skills and work experience on a résumé. Why is it important for you to be honest when you list your qualifications in a résumé? _____

_____

10. If you have little work experience, how can you build your résumé?

_____

_____

_____

Scannable Résumé

Essential Principles

A scannable résumé is one that has been written to enhance the writer's chances of being selected when computers, using a data tracking system, scan for specific keywords and nouns.

Computers are programmed to scan résumés posted on the Internet for specific keywords associated with a particular industry and specific positions within that industry. If a résumé contains enough keywords to match an advertised job opening, the résumé is selected for further consideration.

To prepare a scannable résumé, use keywords, such as the following, to describe your accomplishments and responsibilities.

ability to delegate	detail minded	problem solving
ability to implement	flexibility	public speaking
accurate	industrious	relocation
adaptable	leadership	self-starter
analytical ability	multitasking	team player
communication skills	oral communication	willing to travel
customer oriented		

A New Way to Prepare Résumés

Increasingly, companies review résumés using databases and computer scanners to reduce the cost and time involved in assessing job applicants. Besides the traditional method of submitting résumés by mail, job applicants now have the opportunity to post résumés on the Internet. These postings can be viewed 24 hours a day, 365 days a year, and they are available to users in the United States and more than 100 other countries. Many online services offer tips for writing a résumé that can be scanned or searched for keywords.

Below and on the following page are guidelines to help you correctly prepare your résumé in a format compatible with computers, fax machines, photocopiers, and scanners:

- The applicant's name should be the first line of text on the résumé.
- Put your career objective on the second line of the text.
- Print in black ink and only on one side of the paper.
- Place keywords within the text of your résumé, or group them in a separate paragraph at the end.
- Minimize the use of abbreviations.
- Align the text at the left margin.
- Avoid centering the text or using right justification.

SECTION OBJECTIVES

When you have finished Section 15.3, you will be able to:

- List the keywords that computers look for when scanning résumés.
- Prepare a scannable résumé.
- Explain in simple terms how résumé scanning works.

WHY IT'S IMPORTANT

To take advantage of all the employment opportunities available today, job applicants must consider the preparation of a résumé to be stored and viewed electronically. Résumés may be scanned by a computer, entered in a database, posted on the Internet, sent via e-mail, or faxed.

KEY TERM

- scannable résumé

- Avoid bullets, columns, tables, graphics, and shading.
- Do not use tabs or indenting.
- Single-space the text.
- Remove hard returns to allow the text to wrap.
- Do not condense the spacing between letters.
- Use asterisks instead of bullets.
- Do not use italics, script, or underlined text.
- Avoid using horizontal or vertical lines, which are difficult for computers to read.
- Do not use two-column text.
- Send an original of your résumé, not a copy.
- Print your résumé on a laser printer for the best quality.
- Do not staple or fold your résumé.
- Use the high-resolution or detailed mode when faxing your résumé to make it easier to read.

It is a good idea to follow up an electronically submitted résumé with a printed résumé, application letter, and list of references for any job you feel is a possible match for you. You should exercise caution in sending personal information and your list of references over the Internet to employers you do not know by reputation.

When sending a printed résumé to a prospective employer, remember it may be scanned electronically, hence the type font you choose and color of paper can either help or hinder you in your job quest. Dark or colored stationery and exotic type fonts may render your document electronically unreadable and hence unintentionally remove you from consideration.

How Does Scanning Work?

Today's business organizations are trying to be efficient as they strive to identify people who can do specific jobs. Computers—not human resource people—screen résumés to identify potential employees. Corporate tracking systems search databases for keywords like those previously mentioned. In traditional résumés, the emphasis is on action verbs. With the scannable résumés, the emphasis is on keywords and nouns. Scanned résumés, because they are stored in large databases, remain active longer than traditional résumés.

Do I Need Both Types of Résumés?

Even though you prepare and submit a scannable résumé, you still need a traditional résumé in the standard format. Most prospective employers expect you to bring a printed copy of a traditional résumé to a job interview. Also, you may need to attach a copy of a traditional résumé to an e-mail. This traditional résumé should be eye appealing and should follow the appropriate format as presented in this chapter.

oops!

Threat to Job Security

Lagging behind in technological skills poses a treat to job security.

(*Threat* is the correct word, not *treat*.)

Assessment   Section 15.3

Review of Key Terms

1. What is a *scannable résumé*? Why are these résumés used? _____
_____
_____
_____

Editing Practice

Spelling Alert!   Check the following sentences for any errors in spelling. Write *OK* if the sentence is correct. Write the word correctly in the space provided.

2.   The employment agency reccommended me for the job. _____

3.   We were asked to print the address lables for the company newsletter.

_____

4.   I was truely shocked to learn about the factory lay-off. _____

5.   Make sure the colors of your stationery and envelops match. _____

6.   We have a vacency for an adminstrative assistant. _____

Practical Application

Writing a Scannable Résumé

7.   As a team, write a fictitious résumé for John W. Doe. Create his address information, qualifications, etc. Complete a chronological résumé and a functional résumé. _____

_____

8.   Using the information created in item 7, complete a combination résumé and a scannable résumé. Use the cut-and-paste function of your word processing software to avoid retyping each résumé entirely. _____

_____

_____

Discussion Point

Making Generalizations

9.   What are some guidelines to follow in preparing a scannable résumé?

_____

_____

_____

10.   What effects have technology and the Internet had on job searching? How can lagging behind in technological skills affect your career? _____

_____

_____

_____

Application Letter and Application Form

Essential Principles

The **application letter** is a companion document to your résumé and list of references. It should show the connection between your qualifications and those specified for the available position. It is intended to highlight your most important qualifications and to persuade the employer to grant you a personal interview. Your résumé will help the employer determine whether you have the education and skills required for the job. A sample application letter appears in **Exhibit 15.5.**

When writing an application letter, always address the letter to a specific recipient. Use the person's name, if you know it. If you cannot find out the person's name, use a job title, such as Human Resources Manager or Personnel Director. The salutation, "To Whom It May Concern," should not be used.

Get to the Point Immediately

In the first paragraph of your application letter, you should:

- State your intent to apply for a position with the company.
- Describe the position for which you are applying.
- Indicate how you learned about the position.

If you are submitting a résumé to a company that has no advertised openings in your field of interest, identify the type of position you seek.

There is no one best opening for an application letter. The following opening sentences are suggestions that have been used successfully. Adapt them to suit your needs.

For newspaper ads:

- Please consider me an applicant for the position of management trainee, as advertised in the August 25 issue of the *Orlando Times.* (Note that newspapers are italicized.)
- The position of paralegal, which you advertised in the April 1 issue of the *Gazette,* matches my qualifications and experience. Please consider me an applicant for this position.

For referrals:

- A mutual friend, Anna Grace Bankhead, suggested I contact you concerning a position as administrative assistant with your company.

238 East Park Circle
Shelby, North Carolina 28150
May 2, 20—

Mr. Howard Benton
Asheville Technical Supplies
2388 South Washington Street
Asheville, NC 28801

Dear Mr. Benton:

Please consider me a candidate for the position of office manager with your company as advertised in the April 30 issue of *The Asheville Citizen Times*.

As you will see from the enclosed résumé, my experience in a variety of office settings has prepared me to handle multiple tasks—a must for the position you advertised. In addition, my familiarity with the latest versions of Microsoft Office Suite and Corel Suite would allow me to handle your office tasks and record-keeping needs in an organized, efficient manner.

Because of my interest in working with people, I opted to complete courses in human resources management, psychology, and management principles. The sensitivity to others I developed through this coursework and through my work experience enables me to deal effectively with individuals from a variety of backgrounds and organizational levels. My experience in conducting software training for all levels of management and in supervising five associates has prepared me to assume a managerial role. I thrive on hard work, and I am quick at learning new software and skills.

After you have had an opportunity to review my résumé, I would look forward to the opportunity to answer any questions you might have. I will call next week to see if scheduling an interview might be possible. Thank you for your time in reviewing my qualifications.

Sincerely,

Janet Hardiman

Janet Hardiman

Enclosure

Exhibit 15.5
Application Letter
Thinking Critically. *What four things does the job seeker do in this application letter?*

- Your company has been recommended to me by Mrs. Lisa Fullbright, the placement director of Midlands Community College, as one with exceptional opportunities for accountants. Do you have a position for a self-starter with two years of experience in accounts payable?

For applications made directly to a company, whether or not a position is open:

- I believe my qualifications for a position as insurance sales representative will interest you.
- I am interested in working for a progressive real estate firm such as yours. My enclosed résumé lists my qualifications for the position.
- Here are five reasons why you should consider me for a sales position with Chapman, Williams, and McNeilly.

Explain Why You Should Be Considered

In the second paragraph of your application letter, state how your skills and accomplishments make you a desirable candidate for the position referred to in the first paragraph. Your goal is to convince the employer you are the best person for the job. Don't be afraid to write about your accomplishments. For example:

> As you can see from my enclosed résumé, my coursework in accounting, human resource management, and economics has prepared me to assess a variety of financial and personnel needs. In all my courses, I consistently ranked in the top 5 percent of my class.

Of course, the nature of the second paragraph will depend on what you have to offer. If your work experience is limited and unlikely to impress the employer, you should emphasize your education and training. In such a case, you might follow the above paragraph with a statement such as this:

> Of particular interest to me in the accounting courses I completed were the applications of accounting theory to computerized procedures and equipment. Working for a large organization, such as Johnson Associates, would allow me to implement my training with spreadsheets and databases on a wide scale.

The writer of the following paragraph lacks business experience but compensates for this by demonstrating interest and enthusiasm.

> I am very interested in working as a paralegal for Brantley and Sharpe. As a result of conversations with Nancy Kellerman, a paralegal with your firm, I feel the varied duties and opportunities for advancement fit well with my legal research background. With my willingness to learn and my attention to detail, I can become an asset to your company within a short period of time.

If you have work experience related to the position for which you are applying, make the most of it, as in the following example:

> As an intern with Creedmore, Baxter & Company last summer, I participated on the total quality management team that drafted information-processing procedures. This opportunity gave me valuable experience in team problem solving that I could put to use for your company.

Show a Willingness to Work and Learn

The employer who hires you is taking a risk that you may not be suitable for the position. One of the best ways to convince the employer of your suitability is to demonstrate a willingness to learn and to express genuine interest in the job. The following are examples of ways you can convey your enthusiasm:

- As a self-starter who absorbs new information quickly, you will find me willing to learn and eager to improve.
- I am not afraid of hard work; in fact, I enjoy it.
- You will find I am a quick learner and am adept at problem solving.

Point Out How Your Qualifications Meet or Exceed the Employer's Needs

The reason a position is open is that the employer has a need. The employer does not want just any employee but an employee who can fulfill that need. When an ad specifies particular qualifications needed for a position, be sure you underscore your own qualifications in your cover letter and/or résumé that will fulfill that need.

> Your ad for a senior administrative assistant specified a two-year degree plus five years of related experience. With a four-year degree and six years of experience, I exceed both of these requirements.

Make It Easy for the Employer to Ask for an Interview

Write the last paragraph of your application letter with the goal of asking the prospective employer for an interview. Make it easy for the employer to contact you by including your telephone number and the best time to reach you.

> I look forward to meeting with you to discuss the paralegal position available with your firm. You may contact me at 314-555-7613 or at the address at the top of this letter. I am available to meet with you between 11 a.m. and 3 p.m., Monday through Thursday.

Some job seekers prefer to follow up on the letter rather than wait for the employer to contact them. For example:

> If it is convenient for you, I am available for an interview between 9 a.m. and 5 p.m. on Tuesdays and Thursdays until April 1. After you have had a chance to review my qualifications, I will contact you to request an appointment.

The Application Form

An **application form** is a form used by potential employers to request specific information from someone seeking employment. Most companies require prospective employees to complete an application form, as shown in **Exhibit 15.6** on page 576. Some companies require it to be completed before the interview; others want it after the interview. You may be asked to complete the form at the company office, or you may be asked to take the form home to complete. A few companies have their application form online. If you take the form home with you, you should photocopy it and do a rough draft on the photocopy, then transfer it to the original form. Completing a rough draft helps you think about your responses and do a better job.

Be Prepared.   When applying for a job, take with you the information you will need to complete an application form. Most application forms ask for details about your education, work experience, and references. You should have this detailed information with you, along with a copy of your résumé and a list of your references. These documents will help you complete the application form accurately and completely. These tips will help you be prepared:

- Read the application form before you start.
- Take two working pens, preferably black.
- Write legibly.
- Follow any directions given on the application form. If the instructions say "print," don't use cursive writing.
- Take your social security card with you.

The Hidden Questions.   A prospective employer can tell a great deal about you by the way you complete the application form. Your completed application shows:

- How neat or sloppy your work habits are.
- How well you can follow written directions.
- How detail oriented you are.
- How accurately you can complete a task.

Going Global

Bilingual Skills
One way to prepare for today's global marketplace is to study a foreign language. Being fluent in two languages gives you an advantage over others when seeking a position in an international business that requires using both languages.

The McGraw-Hill Companies
Employment Application

An Equal Opportunity Employer
McGraw-Hill Policy Forbids Discrimination Because of Age, Citizenship Status, Color, Disability, Marital Status, National Origin, Race, Religion, Sex, Sexual Orientation, or Veteran Status.

Personal Data _____ **Date** _____

Applying for position as _____ Salary required _____ Date Available _____

Name _____
(Last)   (First)   (Middle)

Address _____
(Street)   (City)   (State)   (Zip)

Telephone no. _____ Social Security no. _____
(Area code)

E-mail Address _____

Are you legally entitled to work in the United States?   Yes   No

If hired, can you show proof of age?   Yes   No

Relatives employed by McGraw-Hill:

Name _____ Department _____

Name _____ Department _____

Have you previously applied for employment with the McGraw-Hill Companies?   Yes   No

If "Yes," when? _____

How were you referred to the McGraw-Hill Companies?

Agency   School

Advertisement   Direct contact

McGraw-Hill employee

Other _____

Name of referral source above _____

I understand that the submission of any false information in connection with this employment application may be cause for immediate discharge at any time thereafter should I be employed by The McGraw-Hill Companies. _____   _____
(Signature)   (Date)

The Job-Related Questions.

The basic categories of information on an application form include:

- Your name, mailing address, e-mail address, and phone number (cell or landline), so the employer can contact you.
- Your educational background, including schools attended, dates attended, mailing addresses, and phone numbers.
- Your work experience, including names and addresses of employers, dates employed, job duties, reasons for leaving, and—sometimes—beginning and ending salaries.
- References, including names, mailing addresses, e-mail addresses, and phone numbers.

Some application forms include questions you are expected to answer in complete sentences. The purpose of these questions is to test your ability to communicate clearly in writing; your knowledge of spelling, punctuation, and grammar rules; and your proofreading skills.

Accuracy

Be honest about your qualifications and make sure that all information is accurait on your résumé.

(*Accurate* is the correct spelling, not *accurait*.)

Tips for Completing the Application Form

Keep these suggestions in mind the next time you fill out an application form:

- Read the entire application before completing it so you know what information is requested.
- Use black ink, because it photocopies better than blue ink.
- Type the form, if possible; otherwise, use your neatest printing.
- Double-check your answers to be sure all the dates match the dates on your résumé.
- If the form asks for "Salary Desired" or "Salary Requirement," never include a figure; answer "Open" or "Negotiable." The job interview is the appropriate time and place to discuss salary.
- Don't leave anything blank. If the category does not apply, write "N/A" or put a line in the blank to show that you read the question. The only exception to this would be if the answer is very negative and you believe it might eliminate you from consideration for the position. In that case, leave the answer blank and be prepared to discuss it in the job interview.
- Avoid stating a negative reason for leaving a job. Use reasons such as better job opportunity, career advancement, return to school, and summer/seasonal job. Obviously, negative reasons will reflect poorly on you.

The Signature

Application forms have a place at the end for your signature. A paragraph above the signature line often states that the information you have put on the application is true and accurate to the best of your knowledge. You are expected to sign that statement. If you lie or significantly misrepresent yourself on an application form and the employer finds out, the employer has a legal right to terminate you—even if you are doing a good job.

Remember that your application form becomes part of your permanent record at your company.

 ## Assessment   Section 15.4

Review of Key Terms

1. What is the purpose of an *application letter*? _____

   _____

   _____

   _____

2. What are some tips to follow when completing an *application form*?

   _____

   _____

   _____

Editing Practice

Grammar Alert! Check the following sentences for any errors in the use of pronouns. Write *OK* if the sentence is correct. Strike through the incorrect word and write the correct word in the space provided.

3. Are you going to give your expense report to Gordon or I? _____

    _____

4. With who did you have your appointment? _____

5. Mr. Willis stated that it was the operator and them who made the shipping error. _____

6. The article was written by she last summer. _____

7. Lori and him volunteered to work overtime during inventory. _____

    _____

Practical Application

Finding Employment

8. From the "Help Wanted" advertisements in your local newspaper, select a position that appeals to you and for which you are qualified, or will be upon graduation. Write an application letter answering the advertisement, and enclose a résumé targeted specifically for this job.

    _____

    _____

9. As a team, complete an Internet search for sites that advertise job openings. Select two or three companies that interest you. Then, make a list of current listings and qualifications needed for those openings, and find out if the companies accept online applications. Compose a short presentation for your class, and share URLs for these companies. _____

    _____

    _____

Discussion Point

Interpreting Information

10. Interviewers often read the application letter before looking at the résumé. What can you do to ensure that your application letter and résumé get you an interview? _____

    _____

    _____

    _____

11. In addition to specific requested information, what does an application form communicate about you to a prospective employer? _____

    _____

    _____

Employment Portfolio

Essential Principles

Portfolios are folders or notebooks that contain evidence and examples of your achievements, skills, and qualifications. A résumé and a list of references form the basis of the portfolio, but your creativity and your prospective employment position determine the contents of your portfolio. For example, teachers might include lesson plans and pictures of bulletin-board displays. Sales representatives might include pictures, scripts, or videos of mock sales presentations they have developed. Administrative assistants might include spreadsheets and examples of correspondence they have prepared. Medical personnel might include copies of their licenses and certificates.

Every item in your portfolio should be of high quality. Start with an attractive binder that has pockets for odd-shaped items, such as a videotape. Documents, such as your résumé, transcripts, and certificates, should be placed in plastic sheet protectors—never laminate them.

The following items could be included in a portfolio, if applicable:

- Title page.
- Divider pages with labeled tabs.
- Résumé.
- References.
- A copy of diplomas and certificates.
- Transcript of grades, if your grades were good.
- Perfect attendance awards.
- Software examples that you've created in class.
- Document examples from a job or internship.
- Anything else that will serve as "proof" of your ability.

Presenting Your Portfolio

Your interview time with a potential employer is limited, so manage your portfolio presentation well. You may have to narrate to provide flow to the presentation and a coherent picture of your credentials to the employer, but be prepared to have only one or two succinct comments about each page you show. Plan what you will say to complement your interview, not monopolize it.

It is important for you to tell the employer at the beginning of the interview that you have your portfolio with you and will speak about it later in the interview. This alerts the interviewer that you are well prepared. The initial stage of the interview is the time for general discussion about the company, your career interests, and the type of position available. Once these topics have been covered, the interviewer will get into more specific questions about

SECTION OBJECTIVES

When you have finished Section 15.5, you will be able to:

- Determine the appropriate contents for an employment portfolio.
- Introduce your portfolio during the job interview.

WHY IT'S IMPORTANT

Portfolios are gaining in popularity and acceptance in the job search arena. For many years, artists, models, and advertising associates have used portfolios to display examples of their work during job interviews. Prospective employees in other fields have noted the value of this method and are using it too.

KEY TERM

- portfolios

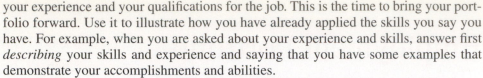

your experience and your qualifications for the job. This is the time to bring your portfolio forward. Use it to illustrate how you have already applied the skills you say you have. For example, when you are asked about your experience and skills, answer first *describing* your skills and experience and saying that you have some examples that demonstrate your accomplishments and abilities.

Find the right time to introduce your portfolio during a job interview. Few interviewers will ask to see your portfolio; they expect you to present it to them. Here are ways to introduce it:

When Discussing Your Educational or Work Background

You might reply: "I learned a great deal at Southern Community College about how to prepare professional-looking documents in a timely manner. I've brought my portfolio with some samples of what I learned. Would you like to look at it?"

When Answering Specific Questions about Your Computer Skills

You might say as you open your portfolio to the appropriate section: "Here's a Power-Point presentation I prepared for my supervisor. I enjoy working with presentation software."

When You Have an Opportunity to Ask Questions

If you have not found an opportunity during the interview to present your portfolio, you can do it as the interviewer asks if you have any questions. After your questions, you could say: "I'm very interested in this position, and I believe I have the qualifications you are looking for. Would you like to look at my portfolio and see the kinds of work I'm capable of doing?"

When You Are Asked to Take a Test or Complete Additional Paperwork

If the interviewer asks you to take tests or to complete additional paperwork, say: "Would you like to look at my portfolio while I'm taking the test?"

Application Letter

She sent out her applicator letter and résumé today.

(*Application* is the correct word, not *applicator.*)

Employability Skills

Writing

Often the first two things an employer judges an applicant by are the cover letter and the résumé. Proofread these carefully to make sure you have correct grammar and spelling. Mistakes in your cover letter or résumé can cost you the job.

Assessment   Section 15.5

Review of Key Terms

1.   What is a *portfolio*? How can portfolios help you in a job interview?

_____

_____

_____

_____

Editing Practice

Vocabulary Alert!   Choose the word that correctly completes each of the following sentences.

2.   Alicia attended a seminar for patients that helps them improve their (moral/morale). _____

3. After falling down the stairs, Charles required (minor/miner) surgery on his ankle. _____

4. I wanted to print my résumé on high-quality (stationary/stationery). _____

5. Alex complained that the conference was a (waste/waist) of time. _____

Practical Application

Starting a Portfolio

6. Make a list of some items you can include in your work portfolio. Then, begin to collect these items, making sure that everything looks professional. Write a summary about what you will include in your portfolio, and submit it to your instructor. _____

_____

7. Meet with your team and review your lists for items to include in your individual portfolios. Team members may have suggestions that have not occurred to you. Discuss ways in which you can make your portfolio more attractive. Visit an office supply store and see what is available to help you make a professional-looking portfolio. If you know someone who already has a portfolio, ask if he or she would visit your class to share ideas and provide suggestions. _____

_____

Discussion Point

Identifying the Main Idea

8. What are some items that can be placed in a portfolio? What specific items would you add that are not listed in the text? _____

_____

_____

9. When should you present your portfolio to the interviewer? Should you let your portfolio do the talking, or should you provide narration as the interviewer flips through the pages? _____

_____

_____

_____

Chapter 16

Interviewing and Employment Issues

Workplace Connection

It's important to know and practice good interview skills so that you get a job that matches your skills with the requirements of the job. Because you will spend many of your waking hours at work, finding the right job is a key component of your happiness and well-being.

CHAPTER OBJECTIVES

When you have completed this chapter, you should be able to:

- Prepare for several types of interviews.
- Use your communication skills effectively during a job interview.
- Write other employment-related letters.

Preparing for the Interview

Essential Principles

An **employment interview** is a formal conversation to evaluate the qualifications of a prospective employee. The job interview is a critical factor in determining whether or not a person is hired. For this reason, you should be well prepared for each interview in which you participate. No matter how impressive your background, your résumé, and your application letter, you may fail to be hired if you cannot "sell" yourself when you meet a prospective employer face to face. In Chapter 15, you learned that a résumé and an application letter are the first phase in marketing yourself to potential employers. The interview is the second phase of the marketing process.

During an interview, you have an opportunity to sell yourself. Your responses to questions, your descriptions of experiences and activities, your explanations of procedures and methods—all contribute to the interviewer's impression of you. Therefore, you must prepare thoroughly to interview well.

Mental Preparation for the Interview

Although you were not aware of it at the time, you began preparing for a job interview some time ago. You chose the type of work you wanted to do; then you acquired the education and training necessary for your chosen career. You then targeted prospective employers, compiled a résumé and a list of references, wrote an application letter, and obtained the interview. Now, you must prepare for the job interview itself.

Remember the Goal of the Interview

Remember that your goal is twofold: first, to sell yourself; and second, to find out if the job fits your qualifications and your career plans.

Research the Prospective Employer

Conduct some research on your prospective employer. Find out about the company's products, services, and history. Knowing something about the organization will help you decide if it is a place you would like to work.

Having this background knowledge will also help you effectively and convincingly answer the often-asked question, "Why are you interested in employment with our company?" Your answer will demonstrate that you know something about the company. "I have always been interested in investments, and I know that your company is one of the leading investment firms in this area. . . ." Or, "I'm interested in the telecommunications industry,

KEY POINT

To prepare mentally for an interview:

1. **Remember the goal of the interview.**
2. **Research the prospective employer.**
3. **Prepare questions to ask the interviewer.**
4. **Know your strengths and weaknesses.**
5. **Anticipate questions.**
6. **Become knowledgeable about industry trends and current events.**

Employability Skills

Acquiring and Evaluating Data

One way to prepare for an interview is by discovering how the company started, its goals, and the people involved. Evaluate the company's Web site and see if its goals align with yours. Then, be ready to share how you can be of benefit to the company with your skills and experience.

and I know that your company has recently developed a wireless next-generation cellular telephone that has the potential to revolutionize the way we use cellular telephones."

Most employers agree that thoroughly researching the employer's company is one of the most important things you can do to prepare for an interview. Follow these guidelines when researching a company:

- Speak with the person who referred you to the organization or to an employee of the organization to find out the information you need.
- Contact the career services center at your school for tips on researching a company.
- Explore the Internet for information about the company or organization. Many companies have home pages on the World Wide Web that provide background information about the company, including the type of business and a description of its products and services.
- Search print or computerized databases in the library for information about local, national, or international companies.
- Obtain a copy of the company's annual report.
- Contact the local Chamber of Commerce for information on companies in the area.

Remember that print media may not be current. Always check the date of the information to see if it is up to date.

When researching an organization, find answers to as many of the following questions as possible:

- How long has the company been in business?
- Is the company publicly or privately owned?
- Is the company a subsidiary or a division?
- What services and products does the company offer?
- How many people does the company employ?
- Who are the company's competitors in the industry?
- Does the company show a certain pattern of growth in the past 10 to 20 years?
- What are the company's annual sales?
- What are the company's assets and earnings for the previous year?
- Does the firm have divisions and subdivisions?
- Are there offices in more than one state?
- What vision does the company have for new products and services?
- Are there any international operations? Plans for expansion into other countries?

A survey conducted by the National Association of Colleges and Employers revealed that job applicants who have researched the company they are interviewing with (1) are better able to discuss how their experiences and qualifications match the company's needs, and (2) can also talk about how they can make an immediate contribution to the organization. The ability to do these two things makes a very positive impression in a job interview. The candidate who does the best usually gets offered the job.

Prepare Questions to Ask the Interviewer

During an interview, you will be asked many questions designed to help the employer find out about your specific skills and qualifications for the job. Remember: The interview is also your opportunity to find out more about the company. Prepare a list of questions you would like to ask and take the list with you to the interview.

Research-Related Questions. Researching a company will help you prepare intelligent questions to ask the interviewer. Here are some examples:

- I read that your company exports products to South America. What percentage of your product is shipped abroad?
- I know that your company has eight branch offices. Which office is experiencing the most growth?

Job-Related Questions. After you are comfortably into the interview, plan to ask some questions related to the prospective job. Questions you might ask the interviewer include:

- Describe the type of person who does best in your company.
- What would my primary duties be? How will these change in the future?
- Tell me how my work in this position fits into the whole operation of your company.
- What are the opportunities for advancement?
- Would travel be required for this position?
- What is your company's dress code?
- What is the most difficult part of the job?
- Whom would I be working with, and what does he or she do?
- How will my work be evaluated and how often?
- Why was this position created? *Or:* What happened to the last person who had this job?
- Are internal candidates being considered for this position?
- How soon will the decision for this position be made?

Questions about Salary and Benefits. After the company shows an interest in hiring you, it is permissible to ask questions that deal with salary, benefits, vacation, or job security. If you ask these questions too early in the interview, an employer may interpret them as self-centered questions that reveal that you're more concerned about yourself than you are about what you can offer the company. **Salary** is fixed compensation paid regularly for services. **Benefits** are payments or services provided for under an annuity, pension plan, or insurance policy. Holidays, sick leave, and vacation days are also considered benefits.

Examples of these types of questions are:

- Does the company provide training and additional education for employees who want to develop their skills?
- What health insurance benefits do you provide for employees?
- What is the salary for this position?

Digital Data

Increase Your Chances of Getting Hired

Thoroughly research the company you are interviewing with before the interview. Review the company's Web site, read articles that highlight the company in business publications, and be informed about all its business practices. The more prepared and informed you are about the company, the better you will perform during the interview and the more you will increase your chances of getting hired.

KEY POINT

Prepare questions about the company and the position based on information in the job posting and on your research of the company.

Sometimes, a job applicant knows the salary offered for a position before the interview. However, if you do not know the salary, you should ask about the salary near the end of the interview. The best time to negotiate for salary and benefits is after you've been offered the job.

Listen closely during the job interview and take notes. You don't want to ask a question that was answered earlier in the interview.

Know Your Strengths and Weaknesses

As a job applicant, you are a sales representative, and the product you are selling is you! Preparing a résumé gives you an excellent opportunity to put on paper what you have to sell—to emphasize your strengths and to present your education, experience, special interests, and skills in a way that makes you a strong candidate for the job. You should know your qualifications so well that you can communicate them orally without hesitation.

Anticipate Questions

Anticipate questions that the interviewer may ask about your education, work experience, and personal qualities. Interview questions are discussed in the next section. You should practice answering these questions out loud to prepare for the actual interview. Ways to practice include: (1) videotape your questions and answers, then evaluate the tape; and (2) watch your facial expressions and eye contact by answering the questions as you sit in front of a mirror. The best way to practice is to have a friend or family member ask you interview questions and videotape the mock interview. The videotape will help you detect any detracting mannerisms that you may have.

Become Knowledgeable about Industry Trends and Current Events

Acquire a working knowledge of trends and issues in the industry in which the company does business. Also, keep up to date about local and national current events. Read a local newspaper to learn about issues as well as cultural, religious, civic events, and other opportunities. Such knowledge demonstrates interest in the business and thoroughness in preparing for the interview.

Physical Preparation for the Interview

Make sure you have the information and materials you need to keep your appointment for an interview and to do well.

Confirm Your Appointment

If your interview is more than a week ahead, call a day or two before the interview, or send a short letter a few days beforehand, to confirm the appointment time, date, and place.

> Thank you for the opportunity to interview for the paralegal position with Grant and Jennings, Inc. I look forward to meeting with you on Tuesday, April 19, at 10:30 a.m., in your State Street offices.

Get Directions to the Interview Site

Ask for directions to the interview site. If you are taking public transportation, double-check the departure and arrival times. If your interview is in a city or town you are not familiar with, get a map of that city and study it. Sometimes you can find good driving instructions and street maps on the Internet. If possible, drive to the interview site the day before the interview to determine the travel time, route, and exact location of the building. Make sure you have enough gas and money for the trip.

Identify Items to Take

Take the following items to an interview:

- Two black ballpoint pens.
- A professional-looking folder with a letter-sized pad of paper.
- Three or four copies of your résumé and list of references, placed in the professional-looking folder. Often, you will interview with more than one person, and each interviewer may not have a copy of your résumé. You can also use a copy of your résumé as a reference in completing a job application form.
- A portfolio, if appropriate, that contains documents or projects you prepared that demonstrate your knowledge and qualifications.
- A list of questions to ask the interviewer. You should not read the list to the interviewer but have it available to refresh your memory. Review the list while waiting for your appointment.

Get a Good Night's Sleep

Get eight to ten hours of sleep the night before the interview. Being sharp for the interview will boost your energy level and help you answer questions clearly.

Assessment   Section 16.1

Review of Key Terms

1. What kind of opportunity do you have during an *employment interview*? _____

   _____

2. What may happen if you ask questions about *salary* too early in an interview? _____

   _____

   _____

Editing Practice

Call an Editor!   Correct any errors in the following sentences.

3. The messengers bicycles should not be parked in this area. _____

   _____

4. Please continue on until you finish. _____

   _____

5. Complete your questionaire and your assingment before you leave.

   _____

6. This months menu was given to Porter and I this week. _____

   _____

Practical Application

Thinking Critically

7. Prepare written answers to each of the following questions, which are likely to come up during an employment interview.
   - What are your job goals for the next five-year period?
   - What are your strengths?
   - What are your weaknesses?

   _____

   _____

   _____

8. Make an appointment to interview with someone who gives screening interviews at a business or government agency. As a team, prepare a list of questions to determine what makes some interviews effective while others fail. Find out what specific behaviors or answers made an ineffective interview. Determine which strategies made the interview positive. Write a summary of your findings for your instructor. _____

   _____

   _____

Discussion Point

Evaluating Concepts

9. Why is it important to have some background knowledge of the company you are interviewing with before the interview? How can you obtain information about a company? _____

   _____

   _____

   _____

   _____

10. How can you prepare for an interview? What are some errors that people make during an interview? _____

    _____

    _____

    _____

    _____

    _____

    _____

Interviews and Interview Questions

Essential Principles

The questions you are asked during a job interview will be determined by the type of interview that you are given. There are several types of interviews.

Screening Interview

A **screening interview** is conducted to determine if you have the skills and qualifications for the job. This type of interview may be conducted over the telephone and may also serve as a preliminary screening of your communication skills and interpersonal skills. Keep your responses concise; giving too much information in a screening interview can hurt you.

One-on-One Interview

As the label implies, in a **one-on-one interview,** you will be interviewed by one person only. The interviewer wants to see if you will fit in with the company and to determine how your skills will benefit the company.

Panel or Committee Interview

The **panel** or **committee interview** is fairly common today as companies look for ways to make better hiring decisions. The interview team members usually take turns asking interview questions. When answering questions, focus your attention on the person who asked the question rather than on the whole group. Some applicants feel that this kind of interview is more stressful than a one-on-one interview because there are more interviewers and the questions can be asked very quickly.

Group Interview

In a **group interview,** several applicants meet with one or two interviewers. (See **Exhibit 16.1** on page 590.) This type of interview is designed to uncover leadership potential among the applicants and to see how you interact with others. Walt Disney World uses this type of interview.

Stress Interview

A **stress interview** is a deliberate attempt to put you under stress to test how you react under pressure. Some techniques used in stress interviewing are rapidly firing questions at you, placing you on the defensive with irritating questions and sarcastic comments, or long periods of silence after you answer a question. Remain calm during this type of interview.

SECTION OBJECTIVES

When you have finished Section 16.2, you will be able to:

- Describe several types of interviews.
- Answer interview questions.

WHY IT'S IMPORTANT

Learning about the different types of interviews will help you to better prepare for your meeting. Remember that an interview is an opportunity for you to showcase your abilities.

KEY TERMS

- screening interview
- one-on-one interview
- panel or committee interview
- group interview
- stress interview
- unstructured interview
- behavioral interview
- situational interview

Preventative Preparation

"What do you make here?" Asking this question during a job interview can prevent you from being considered for the position because it makes you look unprepared.

Exhibit 16.1
Group Interview
Thinking Critically. When you are being interviewed by a team, whom should you focus your attention upon?

Unstructured Interview

An **unstructured interview** usually consists of one or two broad questions, such as, "Will you please tell me about yourself?" The purpose is to find out if the applicant is wise enough to focus on his or her qualifications for the job and to find out how good his or her communication skills are.

Behavioral Interview

In a **behavioral interview,** the idea is to see how a candidate handled a situation in the past. The theory is that past behavior is a good predictor of future behavior. The interviewer uses questions and statements to get applicants to relate specific examples of how they have successfully used the skills required in the job. An example of a behavioral interview question is, "Tell me about a conflict you had with a co-worker and how you handled it."

Situational Interview

A **situational interview** is similar to a behavioral interview. Instead of being asked to relate past experiences, the applicant is given a situation—for example, "One of your subordinates has been late three days this week"—then asked, "How would you handle this situation?"

Interview Questions

There are literally hundreds of questions you might be asked during the course of an interview. Here are examples of possible interview questions you should be prepared to answer.

Employability Skills

Interpreting and Communicating Information

During an interview, it's critical to interpret the questions carefully and communicate your answers thoughtfully. Remember to keep eye contact and speak clearly. Employers look for good interviewing skills from applicants.

Standard Interview Questions

- Why did you select this particular course of study?
- Which of these courses did you like best? Why? Which course did you like the least? Why?
- Tell me something about your course in communications (or other subject).
- I see by your application that you worked as an intern at Austin Accounting for one semester. Describe the work you did. What did you like most about your job? What did you like least?
- What hobbies or activities do you enjoy in your spare time?
- Were you active in school organizations? Which ones?
- Do you like to write? How would you rate your English skills?
- Tell me about yourself. (This request will give you a chance to emphasize your most salable features, such as what you do best. Never discuss your family, marital status, financial problems, or health problems.)
- Summarize your college courses and your work experience. (Emphasize the college courses or work experience that will best support your qualifications for this job.)
- What are your strongest points? Your weakest points?
- Tell me why you think you should be hired for this position.
- Why do you want to work for this company?
- Why did you leave your last position?
- What job would you like to have five years from now?
- Would you be willing to work overtime if necessary?
- Would you be willing to travel?
- Would you be willing to relocate?

Surprise Interview Questions

- If you could be an animal, which animal would you be, and why?
- Give me three words that would describe you.
- What is the worst mistake you ever made?
- What was the last book you read?
- Why do you think manhole covers are round?

Behavioral Interview Questions

- Describe a situation in which you recognized a potential problem as an opportunity. What did you do?
- What are the key ingredients in building and maintaining successful business relationships? Give me examples.
- Tell me about a time when you failed to meet a deadline. What happened? What did you learn?
- Describe a time when you got co-workers or classmates who dislike each other to work together. How did you do this?
- Give me an example of a time when you set a goal and were able to meet or achieve it.

- Tell me about a time when you had to go above and beyond the call of duty in order to get a job done.
- What is your typical way of dealing with conflict? Give me an example.
- Tell me about a recent situation in which you had to deal with a very upset customer or co-worker.

Your answers to interview questions will help the interviewer assess your qualifications for the position, determine how quickly you would adjust to the job, and gauge your potential for growth.

Interviewing Techniques for International Employment. At times, students may need to recognize cultural differences that exist between different countries so that they can communicate effectively when interviewing with a prospective employer. The information provided in **Exhibit 16.2** is only a general comparison of some of the differences that may exist between U.S. and international employers.

Always Take Careful Directions

Be sure to get directives to the interview site.

(*Directions* is the correct word, not *directives*.)

Cultural Differences in the Interview Process	
In the United States	**In Some Other Countries**
Self-Promotion • Assertiveness. • Confidence in openly discussing goals and accomplishments. • Appropriate dress.	• Unless presented as part of a group activity, citing accomplishments and skills is viewed as boastful, self-serving, and too individualistic. • Asking employer directly about status of application is rude.
Directness in Communication • Open and direct responses to questions. • Eye contact with interviewer and relaxed posture are appropriate.	• Appearance of criticism must be avoided to save face. • Eye contact, especially with persons of higher status, is considered disrespectful.
Self-Disclosure • Personal descriptions of experiences, hobbies, strengths, weaknesses. • Answers to questions related to personality (e.g., leadership style, problem-solving abilities).	• Personal questions about likes, dislikes, and so on are considered an invasion of privacy, and such matters are discussed only with close friends and family.

Exhibit 16.2
International Interviewing Techniques
Here are some techniques to use when interviewing for a job outside the United States. ***Thinking Critically.*** *Why might these techniques be useful?*

Review of Key Terms

1. What is the purpose of a *screening interview*? _____

   _____

2. Why does a *behavioral interview* help determine how a candidate
   handled a situation in the past? _____

   _____

Editing Practice

Proofreading Alert!   Some companies require a written test as part of the interviewing process. Proofread the following paragraph. Underline errors and write the corrections in the space provided.

3. At Laurel electronics, we make sure our customers come first. We
   redeem any costs the consumer may incur for shipping. Due to the fact
   that many of our customers shop online, we want them to feel free to
   order and return merchandize without worrying about shipping costs.
   If we do not accomodate our customers, they will shop elsewhere. A
   satisfied customer is a loyal customer. _____

   _____

   _____

   _____

   _____

   _____

Practical Application

Analyzing Information

4. Knowing how to answer a question during an interview will decrease
   your anxiety. Prepare written answers to each of the following
   questions or statements.
   - Tell me about yourself.
   - Summarize your college courses.
   - Summarize your work experience.
   - What is your typical way of dealing with a conflict? Give me
     an example.

   _____

   _____

   _____

   _____

   _____

5. Assume your team members are applying for positions at a major airline. Your team is scheduled for a group interview. Your instructor will be interviewing your team in front of the class. Dress appropriately on your day, and bring your résumé. Be prepared to show your leadership skills. Your classmates will decide on the two best applicants through a secret ballot.

_____

_____

_____

Discussion Point

Making Comparisons

6. Compare a *one-on-one interview* with a *committee interview*. _____

_____

_____

_____

_____

7. Would you be better prepared to answer standard interview questions or behavioral interview questions during an interview? Explain your answer. _____

_____

_____

Communication Skills During the Interview

Essential Principles

When you arrive at the interview site, state your name and the purpose of your visit. While you wait, review your résumé, check your completed application form, and skim any literature about the company that may be available in the reception area. Always convey a professional image.

Interviewing—From the Interviewer's Perspective

Most interviewers have three standard goals for an interview:

- To give the applicant general information about the company and specific information about the position. Sometimes the interviewer will give the applicant printed information about the company and a printed job description.
- To establish a positive **rapport** (relationship) that makes the interview comfortable for the applicant. A skilled interviewer will try to put the applicant at ease to facilitate the interview process.
- To get enough information from the candidate to make a decision about the person's suitability for employment with the company.

Making a Positive First Impression

Your punctuality and appearance contribute to the impression you make. Follow these suggestions to create a positive first impression:

Arrive Early

Plan to arrive for your appointment at least 15 minutes early. Traffic problems, weather, or simply getting lost could result in your being late. Last-minute traffic delays can cause you to feel frustrated, apprehensive, and stressed. Allow an extra 30 minutes to arrive at the interview site on time and relaxed.

Dress in a Businesslike Way

It is most important to look your best at an employment interview. (See **Exhibit 16.3** on page 596.) Therefore:

- Make sure your hair, nails, and shoes are neat and clean.
- Avoid wild colors. Stick to more neutral or conservative colors, such as blue, green, gray, and brown.
- Men should wear a suit and tie. A suit is preferred over slacks and a sport coat.

SECTION OBJECTIVES
When you have finished Section 16.3, you will be able to:

- Describe interviewing from the interviewer's perspective.
- Make a positive first impression.

WHY IT'S IMPORTANT
Making a positive first impression is always important when interviewing.

KEY TERM
- rapport

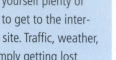

KEY POINT

Do Not Be Late

Give yourself plenty of time to get to the interview site. Traffic, weather, or simply getting lost might cause you to be late. Being late will only make you frustrated and increase your stress level before the interview.

Employability Skills

Organizing Information

If you have an organized portfolio, you can have an advantage over an applicant who does not. Be prepared for an interview by having all your materials in order and ready to show to the interviewer.

- Women should wear a skirted suit. You want the interviewer to perceive you as a professional, and a suit definitely contributes to that image.

- Women should avoid carrying a purse; put your car keys and any other essentials in a pocket or a briefcase that contains your résumé.

- Wear long sleeves. Women should wear a blouse or top that comes up to the neck, and men should wear a shirt buttoned up to the neck.

- Be conservative about accessories. Avoid dangling and gaudy jewelry. Men should not wear earrings, and women should limit their rings to one finger per hand. Visible body piercings and tattoos do not make a professional impression.

- Watch your personal grooming. Ensure that you are clean and that your breath is fresh. Be cautious about wearing too much perfume or after-shave lotion. Avoid smoking before going into an interview because the smoke smell will be on your clothes and your breath. Do not chew gum during an interview.

Check Your Appearance

Before going into the reception area for the interview, visit the restroom and make sure that your hair and clothes are neat. Women should check their makeup, and men should make sure their ties are straight.

Exhibit 16.3
Interview Attire
Your appearance creates the first impression your interviewer has.
Thinking Critically. *Which of these three applicants do you think will make the best first impression on an interviewer?*

Demonstrate Your Self-Confidence

The impression you make when you first walk into the room will very likely influence the interviewer's attitude toward you throughout the entire interview. Stand up straight, smile, and project self-confidence. Preparing yourself, as outlined in this chapter, is the key to building self-confidence.

Beginning the Interview

When you are being ushered into the interviewer's office, try to be relaxed—but not casual or arrogant—and to look pleasant. Greet your interviewer with a firm handshake, a smile, and good eye contact. Introduce yourself and express your interest in employment with the company. Seat yourself only when you are invited to do so.

Keep with you the materials you have brought. Don't place anything on the interviewer's desk unless you are invited to do so. When asked about your education and work experience, say something like: "Here is my résumé, which summarizes that information. I also have completed the application form." Then, hand both to the interviewer.

Follow the interviewer's lead. You will know at once whether the interviewer is going to ask most of the questions or whether he or she prefers that you take the initiative.

During the Interview

During the interview, conduct yourself in a professional manner. Follow these suggestions:

- Be attentive and speak clearly. Face the interviewer directly and speak to him or her. It is fine to shift your gaze occasionally, but don't stare at the floor or out the window while either of you is talking. It is okay to take a few notes on details. However, don't take so many notes that you are writing more than listening.

- Speak slowly and enunciate carefully. Give your answers and statements in a straightforward manner; show that you have thought them through and that you can speak with precision. For example, if the interviewer states, "I see you have had one course in accounting; did you like it?" it is not enough simply to say yes. You might add, "I enjoyed the course very much, and I plan to take more accounting in evening school."

- Be specific and honest about your qualifications. For example, "One of the most challenging tasks in my internship was handling customers' reservations. It wasn't always easy to meet their requests because we had so many clients, but I was successful and learned much from the experience."

- When asked about your achievements or experiences, show the interviewer appropriate items from your portfolio.

- Be objective when you must explain why you left a previous position. If you make negative comments about the people or the company policies of former employers, you may give the impression that you are a complainer. Say something like, "I had learned much from working at Donavan's Hardware Store. With this experience and recent additional course work, I wanted to seek more opportunity and responsibility."

- When you are asked about your strengths, respond by identifying your strongest point without bragging about it. "I am very task-oriented and work diligently until the project is completed."
- When asked about your biggest weakness, answer the question truthfully and positively. "I'm a perfectionist and always want my work to be the best that I can do. I realize that this sometimes results in project delays or missed deadlines, however, and I'm working on being more realistic. I am now able to complete a project on schedule, doing the best job I possibly can within the time and with the resources I've been given."

If you're asked about leisure activities, mention interests that involve either physical energy or mental capabilities. Good answers would include jogging, playing tennis, reading, and working on your computer. Avoid giving poor answers such as watching television, shopping, and sleeping. Develop constructive leisure activities, because many interviewers ask about leisure activities to find out if you have initiative.

Relax and smile occasionally. Remember: the interviewer needs someone to fill an open position and is just as eager to make a decision in your favor as you are to get the job. Avoid nervous habits such as brushing lint off clothing, fussing with hair, toying with an object such as a pen or a paper clip, or putting your hand to your face. Give your full attention to the interviewer.

Avoid the temptation to read materials on the interviewer's desk. He or she would likely view you as being nosy and unprofessional.

If your interview involves dining, follow the lead of your interviewer. Ask for suggestions on menu items, but don't order the most expensive meal. Avoid foods such as spaghetti that are messy to eat. Let your interviewer begin eating first. Enjoy your meal, but remember that you are still under scrutiny. Be sure to thank the interviewer for your meal.

Ending the Interview

The interviewer generally will let you know when the interview is over. The usual signal is when he or she stands up. As soon as the interviewer rises, you should do so also. The exchange that takes place might be something like the following:

Interviewer (rising):	I enjoyed meeting and talking with you.
Applicant (rising):	Thank you, Ms. Alyman. I enjoyed meeting you and appreciate the interview with your company.
Interviewer:	We have your telephone number, and we will call you just as soon as we have reached a decision.
Applicant:	Thank you. I'll look forward to hearing from you.
Interviewer:	Good-bye.
Applicant:	Good-bye.

Leave quickly and thank the receptionist as you depart.

After an interview, use the checklist on page 599 to evaluate your progress.

When you go home after an interview, write down all the questions you can remember and what your responses were. This will help you remember your conversation with the employer in case any questions arise about what was communicated during the interview.

Always send a thank-you letter immediately after an interview—in fact, on the same day. If you are interested in the job, the letter will jog the employer's mind about you as an applicant and will relate your interest in the job. If you are not interested in the job, still send a thank-you letter for the time the employer spent with you. A few years from now, you may want to work for that employer, and you would not want to have created a negative first impression of your professionalism.

Completing an Interview Checklist

Before the interview, I . . .

- arrived slightly early.
- was courteous to the receptionist.
- had my résumé and other necessary items.
- dressed appropriately and was well-groomed.

During the greeting, I . . .

- used the interviewer's name.
- shook hands firmly.
- waited to be invited to sit.

During the interview, I . . .

- sat up straight and appeared self-assured.
- maintained eye contact.
- listened carefully.
- used a pleasant tone of voice.
- answered questions completely and precisely in a straightforward manner.
- showed knowledge of, and interest in, the company.
- explained my work experience briefly and clearly.
- presented my portfolio at an appropriate time.
- asked pertinent questions about the company.
- asked for clarification about the job.
- demonstrated a confident, positive attitude.

Following the interview, I . . .

- left suitable paperwork (résumé, reference list, and/or application form).
- thanked the interviewer and shook hands firmly.
- was courteous to the receptionist.

KEY POINT

Be Attentive
Don't take so many notes in the interview that you are writing more than listening.

Employability Skills

Cross-Cultural Eye Contact

In the United States and Japan, good eye contact is considered to be a sign of respect. However, in some Latin American countries, establishing direct eye contact is considered to be rude.

Assessment   Section 16.3

Review of Key Terms

1. Why will an interviewer attempt to establish a positive *rapport* with an applicant? _____

_____

_____

Editing Practice

Spelling Alert!   Rewrite the following sentences, correcting all spelling errors. Write *OK* if the sentence is correct.

   2. Did you provide the human resource office with a list of referances?

   _____

   3. The committee made a unanimus decision to hire an additional security
       guard. _____

   4. Please check my résumé and application letter for any mispelled words.

   _____

   5. In your absense, we asked Jim to take the minutes. _____

   6. On your résumé, list memberships in any organizations or asociations.

   _____

Practical Application

Analyzing Information

   7. Discuss the reasons that men should wear a suit—not a sport coat and
       slacks—to an interview. Discuss the reasons that women should wear a
       skirted suit not sport slacks and blouse to an interview. _____

   _____

   _____

   8. Form pairs and take turns being the interviewer and the applicant. Each
       pair should prepare a list of questions to be asked by the in-
       terviewer. Videotape the interview. Then, write an analysis
       of your performance as an applicant—address areas of
       strengths and weaknesses. _____

   _____

Discussion Point

Evaluating Concepts

   9. Discuss the *dos* and *don'ts* in dressing for an interview. _____

   _____

   _____

   _____

   _____

   10. Many interviewers are looking at your body language for clues about
        your truthfulness to questions being asked. Discuss some nonverbal
        language that may alert the interviewer about your truthfulness.

   _____

   _____

   _____

   _____

After the Interview

Essential Principles

As soon as is feasible after the interview, jot down the names and titles of the people with whom you talked. Later the same day, write a summary based on your notes and your opinions about what you learned during the interview regarding the company and the position. If you are interviewing for jobs in several different companies, these written summaries will prove an excellent way to refresh your memory about an interview when you are trying later to make your final job choice.

Post-Interview Thank-You Letter

After you have been interviewed, it is a good strategy—not to mention common courtesy—to write the interviewer a thank-you letter. Getting the thank-you letter on the interviewer's desk a day or two after the interview will make an extremely good impression. If a potential employer receives a letter from you the day after your interview, you may be perceived as having initiative, manners, and promptness. This thank-you letter may be the thoughtful act that moves your résumé to the top of the stack.

The thank-you letter puts your name before the interviewer again, and it gives you a second opportunity to sell yourself by mentioning pertinent qualifications.

> Dear Ms. Tyson:
>
> Thank you for meeting with me on April 15 to discuss the medical assistant position at Rose Valley Clinic.
>
> Your description of the position gave me a clear picture of the responsibilities that a medical assistant has at your facility. The duties you discussed fit well with my training and my internship experience at Belmont Manor.
>
> After visiting your facility, I am convinced I could make a positive contribution to your patient-care team. I look forward to hearing from you soon.
>
> Sincerely,

If you do not hear from the company, call after about one week to find out whether a hiring decision has been made or a second round of interviews has begun. Whatever the response, be careful to answer graciously and without getting defensive or angry—there will be other interviews.

Follow-up Letters

Follow-up letters get your name before a prospective employer yet another time. If you have not heard from the company in one to two weeks after the interview, write a follow-up letter to each

SECTION OBJECTIVES

When you have finished Section 16.4, you will be able to:

- Write a thank-you letter after an interview.
- Accept or reject a job offer in writing.

WHY IT'S IMPORTANT

Since your interviewer will probably see many interviewees in a day, it is important to write a thank-you letter after the interview. A thank-you note will remind the interviewer about your skills.

KEY TERM

- follow-up letters

KEY POINT

Mail the interview thank-you letter the same day as your interview. This act may move your résumé to the top of the stack.

KEY POINT

A follow-up letter gets your name before a prospective employer yet another time.

person with whom you interviewed. Express your continued interest in the position and ask that your application remain on file.

> Dear Mr. Abernathy:
>
> On May 10, I interviewed with you for the position of administrative assistant. During the interview, you indicated that you would make a decision within two to three weeks.
>
> I am still very interested in the position and would like you to keep my application current. Please contact me at 216-555-4253 if you need additional information about my qualifications.
>
> Sincerely,

Employability Skills

Negotiating

When accepting a job offer, consider the art of negotiation. When discussing salaries and benefits, learn to work toward agreements that are comfortable and acceptable for both parties.

Accepting a Job Offer

Suppose that you receive a letter offering you a position for which you applied and interviewed. You decide to take the job. If you are to start work almost immediately, or if a reply has been requested by a certain date, you should probably telephone to inform the employer of your decision. Writing a letter is appropriate if your reporting date is two or more weeks away or if the representative is out of town.

> Dear Mrs. Williams:
>
> I am pleased to accept the position as editorial assistant with the catalog department of Dynamic Designs. I know that I will enjoy working with you in designing and producing your promotional and sales materials.
>
> As you requested, I shall report to work on Monday, May 28. Thank you for the confidence you have expressed in me by giving me this opportunity.
>
> Sincerely,

Declining a Job Offer

For various reasons, you may decide not to take a position. Declining a job offer should be done tactfully because you may be interested in working for that firm later in your career.

> Dear Dr. Tyndall:
>
> Thank you for offering me the position of office manager with your medical practice. Since we last talked, I have been offered and have accepted a position as office manager in a real estate office.
>
> Working in a real estate office will help me achieve my long-term goal of becoming a commercial real estate sales representative. My new employer is already encouraging me to begin studying for the licensing exam.
>
> Thank you, Dr. Tyndall, for your time and courtesy in interviewing me. I very much appreciate that you considered me worthy of the position in your office.
>
> Sincerely,

Declining a Position You've Accepted

Occasionally, it may be necessary to inform an employer that you will not be taking a job that you have already accepted. You should avoid this situation if at all possible. If, however, you find yourself in this awkward position, you need to give the firm that offered you the first job some solid reasons for your change of heart. Here is a sample:

> Dear Mr. Arnold:
>
> This morning, I received an offer from another firm that closely matches my qualifications and career plans. The person who will be my supervisor in this firm considered my experience and education sufficient to place me well above entry-level status. In addition, he has arranged for me to take several advanced training courses in my field of interest.
>
> I feel that I must accept this opportunity, which means declining the position you offered me. I apologize for any inconvenience my decision may cause you.
>
> Sincerely,

Thank-You Letters to Others

After you have accepted a job, you should personally thank each person who helped you get the job. You should write a brief note or letter to the people who provided job leads, introductions to potential employers, or personal references.

> Dear Mr. Nelson:
>
> You will be pleased to learn that I have accepted a position as medical technologist with Rush-Presbyterian St. Luke's Medical Center in Chicago. I start work next week, and I am eager to begin my new position. The job fits well with my qualifications.
>
> Thank you very much for letting me list you as a character reference. I am sure that your recommendation was instrumental in my being hired.
>
> Sincerely,

Handling Rejections

Be positive, but be realistic. You may get the job for which you interview, but you may not. Whether you are turned down once or many times, don't take the rejection personally. View each interview as a learning experience. Take note of the strategies that worked well and use them over and over again. Eliminate or improve the strategies that were ineffective.

oops!

Help Yourself to the Correct Tense

After you have accepted a new job, you should thank each person who help you get the job.

(*Helped* is the correct word, not *help.*)

KEY POINT

Deal with rejections in a positive way by considering each one as a learning experience. Then, adjust your strategies accordingly.

 Assessment   Section 16.4

Review of Key Terms

1. When is it appropriate to write a *follow-up letter*? _____

_____

Editing Practice

Service Please!   The following sentences lack writing polish. Edit and rewrite them.

2. The reason Will Kirkpatrick was late is because he had to make a deposit at another branch. _____

_____

---

3. I have difficulty in distinguishing one to the other. _____

    _____

4. Nothing should be done to change the procedure. You must see to it that
    that nothing is changed regarding the procedure. _____

    _____

5. The ruling which takes effect today is the one concerning tardiness.

    _____

Practical Application

Thinking Critically

6. Assume you just interviewed with Worldwide Telephones, 1400 Spring-
    field Avenue, Lansing, Michigan 48901. Write a thank-you letter to
    Patricia L. Carmichael, director of the company.

    Now, assume that you were offered the job at Worldwide Telephones
    and accepted the job. However, a week later you were offered a job
    with their main competitor. This position has greater potential for
    advancement, a higher starting salary, and better fringe benefits. You
    decide to accept the better offer. Write another letter to Patricia
    Carmichael at Worldwide, explaining why you have changed your mind
    and must decline the position. _____

    _____

7. Each team of three or four students is the owner of a company of its
    choosing. Discuss how the four communications skills—listening,
    speaking, writing, and reading—are essential to successful
    employment at your company. Then, write a memo to
    your instructor that summarizes your team's findings.

    _____

    _____

    _____

    _____

Discussion Point

Making Generalizations

8. What is the benefit of sending a post-interview thank-you letter? _____

    _____

    _____

    _____

    _____

9. If you decide not to accept a position, or if you change your mind about
    a position you have accepted, why is it important to send a letter and
    thank the organization? _____

    _____

    _____

Requesting a Promotion or a Compensation Increase

SECTION OBJECTIVES
When you have finished Section 16.5, you will be able to:

- Request a pay raise.
- Ask for a promotion.

Essential Principles

Ideally, you will receive a periodic performance review or assessment and an adequate pay increase on a regular and timely basis. Unfortunately, in many organizations, the routine work tasks totally occupy the supervisors, and they simply forget that it is time for a compensation increase. A **compensation increase** is an increase in salary or benefits. Here are some tips for bringing this to your supervisor's attention in a tactful way:

How to Ask for a Raise

You got the job. You are making great progress and devoting extra time to making sure things are done correctly. Now, you think you deserve a raise but don't know exactly how to go about asking. What do you do? With a little research, a well-thought out presentation, and good timing, you can make a case for a salary increase.

Find Out What the Competitive Salary Is

Do some research on salary trends for employees with your job responsibilities. Using job titles for comparison purposes will not get you the data you need because there is no standard for job titles. An administrative assistant in one organization may perform only receptionist duties; whereas, in another organization, this is a lower-management-level position. Try to find out the salary range at your company for your job classification and where your current salary falls within that range.

Use salary surveys that are published nationally, such as the *Occupational Outlook Handbook* (published by the U.S. Bureau of Labor Statistics), which is available on the Internet, at *bls.gov*, as well as in printed form. Remember to adjust these figures for the cost-of-living differences in your area. Local statistics may be available from your Chamber of Commerce, Economic Development Corporation, Career Services office at your school, and private employment firms.

Another place to gather data is relevant help-wanted ads that list salaries. Or, look for and save magazine and newspaper articles that contain references and facts about salaries.

Prepare a Written Proposal

Your supervisor will probably have to justify and "sell" the idea of a pay raise for you to his or her supervisor. Prepare a written rationale that your supervisor can use when requesting a pay increase for you. List specific examples of your major accomplishments, in addition to the work you completed that was "above

WHY IT'S IMPORTANT

Asking for a pay raise or promotion takes tact. Developing your strategies for periodic performance reviews increases your chances for promotion or compensation increase.

KEY TERMS

- compensation increase
- promotion

oops!

Now That's Quite an Accomplishment

Be prepared to show your manager all your acomplishments when requesting a raise.

(*Accomplishments* is correct, not *acomplishments*.)

and beyond" what your job description requires. Give measurable comparisons where possible, such as, "increased sales 8 percent over previous year" or "handled 5 percent more customer service calls since January 1."

List skills that are indispensable to your company, as well as any new technical skills you have learned—either by attending training sessions or on your own.

Also state what you are doing to help the company meet its corporate goals. Include future goals you plan to achieve on behalf of the company. Review recent performance evaluations and other progress and periodic reports you've prepared to help you list these goals.

Anticipate Objections

You should anticipate the objections and problems that your supervisor will have with your request for a raise. Address these objections and problems in your written proposal and tell how they can be overcome. Be cautious about listing problems for which you have no solutions. You may be giving your supervisor the reasons he or she needs to deny your request for a raise.

Watch Your Timing

The best time to ask for a raise is when your supervisor is in a good mood and right after you've either completed a major project successfully or taken on additional responsibility. You should also be aware of the financial status of your organization. It's not good timing to ask for a raise when business is down.

You may also want to hold off if your supervisor is new to your department or the organization. Your supervisor will need to establish his or her own credibility in the job before seeking raises for subordinates.

Set a Meeting

After you've done your research and prepared your written proposal, schedule a meeting with your supervisor—do not "drop in."

Plan this meeting to demonstrate that you are organized. Speak respectfully and assertively but avoid any hint of "or else" threats. Review your accomplishments and share any salary comparison information you've gathered. Caution: Do not ask for a raise because of your personal financial situation; raises are given based on your job performance and the value you bring to your company.

Asking for the Raise.   Don't ask for a raise in general; have a specific amount in mind and ask for it. Also have some alternatives in mind that you would find acceptable. For instance, if your supervisor can't approve an 8 percent raise, perhaps you can get a 4 percent raise now and another 4 percent in six months.

Be open-minded about taking such perks as more paid vacation days, flexible scheduling, telecommuting opportunities, company-paid parking, travel allowance, subsidized childcare, new technology training, formal education reimbursement, bonuses, and permission to attend company-paid seminars and workshops in lieu of a salary increase.

If your supervisor asks for time to think it over, ask for another meeting in two weeks. Don't leave the meeting with an open-ended time limit.

How to React When the Boss Says No.   If your supervisor turns down your request for a raise because "the timing is not right," ask, "Could we discuss my proposal again at a more appropriate time?" Then, try to find out what conditions would need to be present to qualify as a better time to revisit the request.

If your supervisor tells you "the request cannot be justified," ask, "What can I do to earn an increase in salary?" Make notes of what the boss suggests and then start immediately to accomplish those objectives.

End the Meeting with a Thank You.   If you get the raise, end the meeting with a verbal thank you, but be sure to follow up with a written thank-you note or card. If you do

Going Global

Weathering Other Countries

When visiting another country, find out the current weather of your destination. Selecting the proper clothes will make a difference in how comfortable you feel during a meeting. Search for Web sites that can provide international weather information.

Employability Skills

Reasoning

When requesting a promotion, you need to be ready to discuss with your supervisor the reasons for your request. Be prepared to show samples of your work and demonstrate how your skills have improved operations. Displaying great leadership skills is essential in reasoning with your employer.

not get the raise, you should still say thank you. Let your supervisor know you appreciate his or her honesty and that you appreciate his or her taking the time to meet with you.

How to Ask for a Promotion

A **promotion** is an increase in position or rank. Many of the same principles discussed in getting a pay raise apply when you are seeking a promotion. You should start thinking about a promotion the day you start work. Be sure you develop a reputation for being dependable by getting your job done on time and correctly—the first time.

Once you learn your job, start taking on additional responsibilities. Take advantage of any opportunities to cross-train in other related areas, including some of your supervisor's job responsibilities. Volunteer for more difficult and responsible assignments.

Demonstrate a strong work ethic by showing up for work punctually every day. Have a customer-service attitude toward everyone, both internal and external customers, and maintain a friendly, cheerful, and enthusiastic manner. Dress for the job you *want*, not the job you have. This makes it easier for your supervisor(s) to visualize you in a higher-level job.

Following the tips in this section will prepare you to apply for a higher-level position when one becomes available. Another option for a promotion is to make a case for having your job level and job title raised because of the additional responsibilities you've assumed. Prepare a written rationale for promotion using the same guidelines that were explained in the preceding section on justifying a salary increase.

Exhibit 16.4 presents a list of factors that may stand in the way of your getting a promotion. Can you add to the list?

Factors That May Stand in the Way of Promotion

- Lack of liveliness.
- Inability to accept criticism.
- Prejudice.
- Low professional standards.
- Lack of interest in company.
- Indecisiveness.
- Immaturity.
- Unwillingness to complete seemingly menial tasks.
- Lack of self-confidence.
- Being inarticulate.
- Tardiness and leaving early.
- Shabby appearance.
- Laziness.
- Bitter sarcasm.
- Discourtesy.
- Excessive absences.
- Internet surfing.
- Personal telephone conversations.
- Failure to meet deadlines.
- Personal cell phone interruptions to work.

Exhibit 16.4
Undesirable Qualities
Here are some factors that may stand in the way of a promotion. ***Thinking Critically.*** *Why would these factors stand in the way of a promotion?*

Review of Key Terms

1. What are some useful ways to ask your employer for a *compensation increase*? _____

   _____

2. What strategy should you use when seeking a *promotion*? _____

   _____

   _____

   _____

Editing Practice

Grammar Alert!   Check the following paragraph for errors in usage. Underline the errors and write the corrections in the space provided.

3. At tomorrow's meeting, we will be discussed the proposed manufacturing of several of our products. Many new issues will be risen that will be sensitive to some committee members. Please put your personal feelings aside, and look for the better outcome for the company. Incidentally, several members will be sitting in from management on our meeting to get suggestions and answering questions. _____

   _____

   _____

   _____

   _____

   _____

Practical Application

Asking for a Raise

4. Assume you are a manager with The Diamond Grill, a statewide restaurant. You have worked there two years and have not yet received a raise. Write a list of some of your accomplishments and skills that make you an exceptional employee. If you are not familiar with what a restaurant manager does, interview a manager at a local restaurant.

   _____

   _____

5. Writing a list of accomplishments is easy. Verbalizing your accomplishments is often more difficult. With your list that you created above, take turns asking for this raise. One team member can be the supervisor, while the others provide feedback about your communication skills. _____

   _____

   _____

Discussion Point

Identifying the Main Idea

6. Before asking for a raise or a promotion, what background work should you do? _____

_____

_____

_____

7. What are some guidelines you should follow in regard to asking for a raise? _____

_____

_____

SECTION OBJECTIVES

When you have finished Section 16.6, you will be able to:

- Write a letter of resignation.
- Know what to do if you are downsized.

WHY IT'S IMPORTANT

In today's economy it is likely you will have many different jobs. Knowing how to handle the end of a job will make the beginning of the next job easier.

KEY TERMS

- resignation
- downsize

KEY POINT

It is easier to get a job if you have a job.

Leaving a Position

Essential Principles

Most people change jobs several times in the course of their careers. You may leave a position to take another job or for personal reasons. You may be terminated. Your job may be eliminated because the company is restructuring, downsizing, or going out of business.

Unless there are extremely negative situations with your current employment, it is better not to resign from your current position until you have a new position. If you have a job, you avoid having to answer an awkward question from an interviewer: "Why did you leave your last position?" It's hard to believe, but it is easier to get a job if you have a job.

Resigning from a Position

Resignation is formal notification of giving up employment. Resigning from a job requires almost as much tact, diplomacy, and care as applying for a job. You should leave on good terms with your employer for two key reasons. First, you might want to work for this company again, and second, you may need references.

Your resignation letter should contain three elements: the date of your resignation, a positive explanation for your resignation, and a thank you for the experience. This letter will become part of your permanent employment file.

Follow these guidelines when you resign from a job:

- Make an appointment with your immediate supervisor, and hand your letter of resignation to him or her.

- In your letter and in the comments you make during the appointment, indicate that you enjoyed working for the organization. You might mention that the experience gained with the company has definitely moved you forward in your career.

- Give a two-week advance notice that you are leaving, unless your company handbook or employment agreement specifies that you must give longer notice.

- If you are leaving due to job dissatisfaction, express your reasons in a positive way. For example, "I feel that Casey & Casper Accounting will offer me some new challenges and a greater opportunity for advancement."

- Make certain that all your work is up to date and that your papers and files are clearly marked and well organized.

- Leave a list of instructions or suggestions that may be helpful for your successor.

Here is a sample letter of resignation:

Dear Matt:

Last week, I received a job offer from Upstate Computer Solutions in South Carolina. They have offered me a position as senior systems analyst, which represents a major career advancement for me. I have accepted the position.

Please accept my resignation effective November 8. I would be happy to help you find and train a replacement for my position.

Working with you has been a pleasure, Matt. You hired me directly after I graduated from college, and you helped me grow and develop professionally. I have learned a great deal about computer programming and troubleshooting through working with you and the other programmers in our department. I appreciate DataTrac's investment in my career development.

Sincerely,

Being Downsized

To **downsize** is to reduce in size. The economy has a great deal to do with whether companies need employees or downsizing to survive. Be aware of what's going on with the local and national economy. Always keep your résumé up to date. If you lose your job, follow these tips:

- Stay calm. Don't show your anger or frustration. Try to negotiate continued health insurance for a transition period, a severance payment, outplacement services, etc. Always remain professional.

- Seek the support of family and friends. Eat right and get adequate rest. Take advantage of job counseling offered by the company.

- Network. Let people know that you are looking for a job, and ask the people you know to suggest others to contact.

- Negotiate a good severance package. When presented with a severance package, get all the details and ask for time to consider it. Discuss it with a lawyer or a financial adviser, and when you are calm enough to talk about separation, point out your many achievements and contributions to negotiate a better deal.

- Assess your skills; upgrade them; examine your attitude; explore your vocational passions; and decide if you should make a career change.

As you have learned in these last two chapters, communication skills of all types play a critical role in the job application and interview processes. In other words, the written and oral communication skills you learn in school form the basis for the skills you will use throughout your career.

Time to Resign

When you redesign from a job, leave on good terms with your employer. You may want to work for this company again or you may need your supervisors as references.

(*Resign* is the correct word, not *redesign*.)

Employability Skills

Self-Management

Learning to manage your time, goals, and progress is part of self-management. When making changes in your life, such as leaving a job, it's important to evaluate all the alternatives and options before making a final decision.

Review of Key Terms

1. When giving your *resignation,* why is it important for you to leave on good terms with your employer? _____

_____

_____

2. What should you do if your company is *downsized*? _____

_____

_____

Editing Practice

Grammar Alert!   Rewrite each of the following sentences, making sure that each word or phrase is in the right place. You may have to add some words.

3. Looking back at my last job, the people were exceptionally nice. _____

_____

4. Dr. Freeman noticed a misplaced chart making his rounds. _____

_____

5. We noticed several firetrucks speeding from our office window. _____

_____

6. I was fortunate that I was only working part-time because my salary was not cut. _____

_____

7. Lynn Wells turned in her resignation with complete self-restraint when she was asked to take a pay cut. _____

_____

Practical Application

Writing a Letter

8. Assume you have worked for Treasured Vacations, a local travel agency, for five years. You have been offered a job at the specialized travel agency, Cruises Unlimited. Write a resignation letter to your supervisor, André Garcia, and notify him of the day you are leaving, why you are leaving, and any other pertinent information you think would be appropriate.

_____

9. Assume your team of classmates is being downsized. Make a list of proactive steps you should take. Ask friends and family if they know of anyone who is hiring, and document your findings. Investigate if your school or local employment agency offers any counseling to those who have lost their jobs. Write a summary of the support groups your team discovered. Submit the summary to your instructor. _____

_____

_____

_____

Discussion Point

Evaluating Concepts

10. Discuss why it is important to leave on good terms with your employer. Provide examples of this in your own life. _____

_____

11. Explain the following statement: It is easier to get a job if you have a job. _____

_____

_____

2.1 Self-Assessment
1. F
2. F
3. F
4. T
5. F
6. F
7. T
8. F
9. T
10. T
11. F
12. T

2.2 Self-Assessment
1. F   6. T
2. F   7. T
3. F   8. T
4. T   9. F
5. T   10. T

11. Answers may vary. Listening, however, is to hear something with thoughtful attention. Hearing, on the other hand, is the physical function of detecting sound.

2.3 Self-Assessment
1. F
2. T
3. T
4. F
5. F

2.4 Self-Assessment
1. F
2. T
3. T
4. T
5. T

4.1 Self-Assessment A
1. we (P) ticket (N) play (N) Broadway (N)
2. I (P) Julia Oscar Amar (N) our (P) tour (N) we (P) him (P)
3. They (P) Lamborghini (N) Chicago (N) week (N)
4. You (P) I (P) Saturday (N) wedding (N)
5. She (P) Orlando (N) and Miami (N) sights (N)
6. Mark (N) Anna (N) me (P) Northeast (N) their (P) part (N) country (N)

4.1 Self-Assessment B
1. seems
2. was planning
3. has been
4. hired, promoted

Answers may vary in 5–8.
5. plans (action)
6. received, completed, finished (action) started, began (action)

7. is (being)
8. passed (action)

4.1 Self-Assessment C
1. adjective, adverb, adjective
2. adverb, adjective
3. adjective, adverb
4. adjective, adverb, adjective
5. adjective, adverb
6. adjective

4.1 Self-Assessment D
1. P, C, P
2. P, P, C
3. P, P
4. P, C, P, P
5. C, P, P, P

4.2 Self-Assessment A
1. repairs (3)
2. I (1)
3. Caroline Madison (3)
4. You (2)
5. Donna Simpson (2)

4.2 Self-Assessment B
1. participant (simple)
2. employees (simple)
3. salons and bookstore (compound)
4. depositions (simple)
5. Susan or Jeff (compound)

4.2 Self-Assessment C
1. is scheduled for June 10.
2. have responded favorably to our new bank statements.
3. are our best home decorators.
4. has enrolled in a business communications course.
5. should have at least three years' experience.

4.2 Self-Assessment D
1. INT
2. IMP
3. D
4. E
5. D

4.2 Self-Assessment E
Suggested completions on 2, 4, and 5 will vary.)
1. dependent (, they review each patient's medical reports.)
2. dependent (, she will explain the problem.)
3. dependent (, the other administrative assistants will be asked to work overtime.)
4. sentence
5. sentence

4.2 Self-Assessment F
1. IP, PP, PP
2. IP, VP, IP, PP

3. VP, PP, PP
4. VP, PP
5. IP, PP, VP, PP

4.2 Self-Assessment G
(Suggested sentence completions will vary.)
1. fragment, we can complete the transaction today.
2. sentence
3. sentence
4. fragment, it has now expired and must be renewed.
5. fragment, you should ask Mr. Marcos and Ms. Fisher to sign them.

4.3 Self-Assessment A
1. has accepted
2. invited
3. seemed
4. was, was announced
5. want
6. are

4.3 Self-Assessment B
1. painted
2. carrying
3. typed
4. answered
5. baked
6. marked
7. marrying
8. trusted
9. used
10. walking

4.3 Self-Assessment C
1. have been waiting
2. should have attended
3. will be inspecting
4. can complete
5. want
6. have received
7. has been drafting
8. has been promoted
9. will enter
10. will introduce

4.3 Self-Assessment D
Student sentences will vary.
1. We have studied for months to take the CPA exam.
2. I wished that we could visit with you during the holidays.
3. Jim has stopped smoking. Congratulations!
4. She evaluates each scholarship applicant carefully.
5. Bill had remembered my birthday.
6. They are listening to all of the explanations.
7. The manager will have adjusted all of our schedules by tomorrow.
8. Hilton will be inspecting the elevators tomorrow.

4.3 Self-Assessment E
1. has spoken (or spoke)
2. had begun
3. has gone (or went)

4. has seen (or saw)
5. knew
6. OK
7. OK

4.3 Self-Assessment F
1. is (B)
2. has been deliberating (B)
3. was employed (B)
4. have been (B) (*Been* is the main verb; *have* is a helper.)
5. have been sympathizing (B)
6. is (B)

4.3 Self-Assessment G
1. were
2. OK
3. was
4. were
5. were

4.3 Self-Assessment H
1. has told (T)
2. have left (I)
3. has been (B)
4. had been appointed (T)
5. will be (B)
6. will be televised (T)
7. confirmation (DO); him (IO)
8. books, magazines (DO)
9. report (DO); pilot (IO)
10. awards (DO); Jillian, Justin (IO)

4.3 Self-Assessment I
1. laid
2. rise
3. raise
4. set
5. sits
6. raised
7. set
8. lay

4.4 Self-Assessment A
1. has; its; its
2. is; its
3. wants; his
4. is; her; she
5. does; its
6. are; their; them

4.4 Self-Assessment B
1. there are
2. is
3. there are
4. is
5. OK
6. there are

4.4 Self-Assessment C
Simple subjects are given in parentheses.
1. has submitted (Nobody)
2. he or she must; present his or her (student) (Using plurals could make this sentence more readable.)

---

3. OK (Anyone)
4. has (Neither)
5. his or her (manager)
6. wants; his or her (Each)

4.4 Self-Assessment D
1. has been criticized
2. is
3. are
4. is printed
5. is leaving
6. OK
7. were discussing
8. are used

4.4 Self-Assessment E
1. have already begun
2. has risen
3. were damaged
4. OK
5. are concerned
6. OK

4.4 Self-Assessment F
1. has
2. OK
3. are
4. are
5. is; his or her
6. is

4.4 Self-Assessment G
1. likes; her
2. is
3. are; their
4. have; their
5. have

4.4 Self-Assessment H
1. that have three
2. OK
3. purchase his or her uniforms
4. OK
5. OK
6. have
7. that are now
8. Zach is one of those accountants who always double-check their figures.
9. have
10. who wants to

5.1 Self-Assessment A
1. editors-in-chief
2. companies
3. countries
4. attorneys
5. counties, companies
6. lenses
7. Marcys
8. OK
9. editors in chief

5.1 Self-Assessment B
1. Misses Smith (or Miss Smiths)

2. OK
3. I's
4. OK
5. women, companies
6. IDs
7. shelves
8. women, Messrs., Mses.
9. geese
10. CEOs

5.1 Self-Assessment C
1. tomatoes
2. logos
3. thieves
4. loaves
5. concertos
6. gulfs
7. sheriffs
8. handkerchiefs
9. volcanoes
10. solos

5.1 Self-Assessment D
1. editors-in-chief
2. syllabi
3. analysis
4. discos
5. OK
6. OK
7. OK
8. women's
9. civics
10. stimuli

5.2 Self-Assessment A
1. Riley's
2. actress's
3. fathers'
4. Women's
5. applicants'
6. representatives'
7. accountant's, company's
8. Corporation's

5.2 Self-Assessment B
1. OK
2. else's, Adrian's
3. vice presidents'
4. Juan and Maria's
5. OK
6. OK
7. mother-in-law's
8. Anita's

5.2 Self-Assessment C
1. there's (or there is)
2. who's (or who is)
3. (OK)
4. (its)
5. you're (or you are)
6. it's (or it is)
7. there's (or there is)
8. who's (or who is)

5.3 Self-Assessment A

1. change *him* to *he*
2. OK
3. change *me* to *I*
4. OK
5. change *I* to *me* ("to be" has the pronoun "him" before it)

5.3 Self-Assessment B

1. whom
2. who
3. whoever
4. whom
5. whoever
6. who

5.3 Self-Assessment C

1. to us
2. Dr. Cordez or me
3. Tanya and him
4. asked us
5. than I.
6. OK
7. Radmilla or he
8. none of us
9. OK

5.3 Self-Assessment D

1. he said
2. OK
3. . . . she herself wants . . .
4. Suzzana and I
5. OK

6.1 Self-Assessment A

1. CR
2. CO
3. S
4. S
5. CR
6. S
7. CR
8. CO
9. S
10. S

6.1 Self-Assessment B

1. is *that* technology
2. *who* would be (or that)
3. OK
4. *as if* you are (or as though)
5. *unless* the mail
6. *as if* she has (or as though)
7. *unless* you check
8. *but* he is
9. *as if* most (or as though)
10. *unless* he approves

6.1 Self-Assessment C

1. by e-mail
2. traveling
3. raw
4. accurate

5. exercising
6. OK

6.1 Self-Assessment D

1. and "surfing"
2. either to form
3. mailed either to
4. and colorfully illustrated
5. by either Mr. Ormanni
6. went neither to

6.2 Self-Assessment A

1. <u>of</u> the customers; <u>with</u> the billing procedures
2. <u>into</u> the auditorium; <u>with</u> her guest
3. <u>on</u> the site; <u>of</u> the midtown helicopter landing pad; <u>by</u> the planning board
4. <u>in</u> a hurry; <u>to</u> the airport
5. <u>in</u> my file cabinet
6. <u>Between</u> you and me; <u>out of</u> college
7. <u>for</u> the delay; <u>on</u> the computer
8. <u>of</u> the invoices; <u>on</u> my desk; <u>to</u> the Accounts Payable Department

6.2 Self-Assessment B

1. OK
2. discrepancy between
3. retroactive to
4. identical with
5. OK
6. in regard to
7. OK
8. different from
9. angry with
10. plans to open

6.2 Self-Assessment C

1. help singing—omit *from*
2. have gone to—omit *to*
3. all these decorations—omit *of*
4. Both the—omit *of*
5. like her—omit *for*
6. OK
7. go into the new
8. *within*
9. is opposite—omit *to*
10. *off* your wrist
11. *behind*
12. among
13. into
14. beside
15. all his cars and trucks are—omit *of* omit *at*

6.3 Self-Assessment A

1. A <u>special</u>(D) seminar is being scheduled for <u>new</u>(D) paramedics to learn <u>these</u>(DM) <u>life-saving</u>(C/D) procedures.
2. The <u>Reno</u>(PR) attorney who represents <u>that</u>(DM) company asked <u>our</u>(P) associates for <u>their</u>(P) opinions on <u>Will's</u>(P/PR) character.
3. <u>Dr Cooper's</u>(P/PR); administrative(D) <u>three</u>(L) <u>well-known</u>(C/D) speakers will be featured at the <u>fall</u>(D) conference.

4. In six(L) months his(P) older(D) brother will visit this(DM) country and intern in our(D) Atlantic City(PR/C) plant.
5. In Andy's(P/PR) opinion, we should request a two-year(C/L) assignment in scenic(D) Alaska.
6. One of Lenny's(P/PR) crucial(D) accounts is a new(D) client who represents an East Coast(C/PR) retail(D) store.
7. These(DM) bonds are tax-free(D/C) investments, according to their(P) new(D) prospectus.
8. The first(L) T-shirt(C/D) outlet we opened has contributed a substantial(D) profit to our(P) struggling(D) company.

6.3 Self-Assessment B
1. is larger
2. is unique
3. more nearly full
4. are better; quieter; bigger
5. OK
6. was empty
7. uses more energy
8. is happier

6.3 Self-Assessment C
1. 15-minute; two-hour
2. word-of-mouth
3. court-appointed
4. OK
5. either one of them
6. with each other
7. five-time
8. any other

6.3 Self-Assessment D
1. PA
2. PN
3. PA; PA
4. PN
5. PN

6.4 Self-Assessment A
1. SC; SA; SA
2. SA; CA; SA
3. SC; SA
4. SC
5. CA
6. SC
7. SA; SA; CA
8. SA; SC

6.4 Self-Assessment B
1. bad
2. well
3. angry
4. OK
5. really
6. somewhat
7. really
8. OK
9. OK
10. surely

7.1 Self-Assessment A
1. Q
2. P
3. P
4. Q
5. P
6. P
7. Q
8. P

7.1 Self-Assessment B
1. OK
2. OK
3. Jr.
4. III,
5. OK
6. $570

7.1 Self-Assessment C
1. OK
2. hours, when
3. meeting, we
4. noon. We (or noon; we)
5. ago, Rafael
6. Monday; he (or Monday. He)
7. deposit. He (or deposit; he)
8. hour, she

7.1 Self-Assessment D
1. system.
2. tornado?
3. they?
4. truck.
5. she?
6. OK
7. pier.
8. OK

7.2 Self-Assessment A
1. Dallas, nor
2. June but
3. September, but
4. OK
5. a.m. but
6. OK
7. drove and
8. Phil; and

7.2 Self-Assessment B
1. alarm, etc.
2. Jonas & Smith
3. etc., will
4. reservations, and
5. airplane; or
6. John,
7. train,
8. OK

7.2 Self-Assessment C
1. rep requires
2. August 1, you
3. Capitol, each
4. today, we
5. therefore, she

6. windows, took
7. OK
8. Boston, we
9. Dean, she
10. approved, moreover, adding

7.2 Self-Assessment D
1. alternative, Jon . . . think, will
2. OK
3. technician who . . . lab is
4. Jonas, waiting . . . office, did
5. solution, as . . . yesterday, is
6. OK
7. attorney whom . . . consult is
8. received, but . . . owned, are
9. staff who . . . CPA is
10. cartridges if

7.2 Self-Assessment E
1. OK
2. Reynolds, will
3. Houston, Texas, for
4. King Jr. will
5. OK
6. Meyers, were
7. 2005, our
8. divisions, Ace Pharmaceuticals, has
9. Arkansas, to
10. Inc., this

7.2 Self-Assessment F
1. shift are
2. brochure, which . . . tickets, is
3. software that . . . catalog may
4. products that
5. outlet, which . . . U.S., is
6. OK

7.2 Self-Assessment G
1. brilliant, ambitious, resourceful
2. OK
3. OK
4. solid, high-yielding
5. OK
6. creative, talented

7.2 Self-Assessment H
1. Mr. Vincent, we
2. many, many
3. Nordstrom Industries, $20,000, and Valley Communications, $30,000.
4. truth, absolutely
5. Chicago plant, April 15, . . . Knoxville plant, April 20.
6. risky, risky

7.2 Self-Assessment I
1. to 2957 Anderson
2. Pages 3996 through 4017 . . . cost $89,000
3. 1 hour 10 minutes
4. By 2010, 125
5. for $1,250
6. 8 feet 9 inches

7. Policy 23880, is
8. OK

7.3 Self-Assessment A
1. intriguing; indeed
2. OK
3. February; we
4. machines; besides,
5. student; however,
6. view; as
7. $1000; consequently,
8. period; paying
9. merger, but
10. OK

7.3 Self-Assessment B
1. areas: demographics
2. procedures: Registration
3. arrive: The
4. OK
5. service: my
6. action: Go
7. of Ms.
8. OK

7.3 Self-Assessment C
1. OK
2. complete—but
3. trip—fax
4. shoppe—The
5. petunias—these

7.3 Self-Assessment D
1. them?—who
2. work—these
3. OK
4. available?—by
5. fruit.
6. OK
7. OK
8. OK

7.4 Self-Assessment A
1. 'Handle with Care!'"
2. "Sonya Ellis,"
3. session," announced Mr. Sanchez, "because
4. announced, "Della . . . New York."
5. proposal,"
6. catalog," said Paula, "will
7. so-called photo opportunity
8. "Fragile,"

7.4 Self-Assessment B
1. figures!"
2. performers"; Dave
3. , *The Secret to Public Speaking,* or , <u>The Secret to Public Speaking,</u>
4. "A Penny Saved Is a Penny Earned."
5. Morning.
6. furniture"?
7. overstated"; moreover
8. OK

7.4 Self-Assessment C

1. page 34),
2. Travel (formerly . . . Services"), is
3. August 15.)
4. move)?
5. OK
6. (we think . . . so),

7.5 Self-Assessment A

1. said, "Continue
2. "Tips for Purchasing . . . Computer and Printer"
3. No, it
4. One; One; Two
5. OK
6. How to Remember
7. Remember: When
8. Significantly
9. "Professionally yours"
10. following: an

7.5 Self-Assessment B

1. Mexican
2. Friday in September, autumn foliage
3. Mexican
4. Kansas City
5. Von Aspern; Inn: Lake Lure
6. ". . . in Business: A Guide for . . ."
7. Computers in School Association; Building
8. Fourth of July; von Hoffman; Von Hoffman

7.5 Self-Assessment C

1. west.
2. president
3. vans
4. Federal
5. manager; Rotary Club; Monday; private dining room; charitable
6. OK
7. president; Nashville
8. cookies,

7.6 Self-Assessment A

1. . . . and Mr. Hunt responded . . .
2. OK
3. While Mr. Lyttle
4. Dr. Eleanor Jenkins has . . .   or Eleanor Jenkins, Ph.D., has . . .
5. Dr. Nancy Branyas will . . .   or Nancy Branyas, M.D., will . . .
6. Senator Merritt . . .

7.6 Self-Assessment B

1. RAM; ROM
2. 10:30 a.m.
3. Tuesday, December 9,
4. 10 centimeters
5. Indiana,
6. Texas; New Mexico; Nevada
7. North Carolina,
8. 50 pounds,

7.7 Self-Assessment A

1. seven
2. 1980s
3. one-tenth
4. Thirty-two
5. OK
6. 10.5 or 10½
7. Fifteen
8. thousand.
9. OK
10. an eighteenth-century

7.7 Self-Assessment B

1. for 182 days.
2. . . . from six months to one year . . .
3. . . . between $1 million and $2 million.
4. OK
5. 404 13th Avenue.
6. . . . has 12 seats . . .
7. . . . 4 vans, 5 trucks
8. . . . for 60 cents . . .
9. . . . pay $.55 per . . .
10. . . . cost $510, but

7.7 Self-Assessment C

1. 12 feet; 20 feet
2. June 2, 1998
3. 3 o'clock
4. January 15, 97
5. 3 1/2 parts . . . 2 parts
6. OK
7. OK or 3rd of July
8. OK
9. 1, 2
10. OK

8.2 Self-Assessment A

1. OK
2. territories
3. scarring
4. believe
5. miscellaneous
6. taping
7. transmitted
8. wedding

8.2 Self-Assessment B

1. deductible
2. Illegible
3. defendant
4. remittance
5. reversible
6. OK

8.2 Self-Assessment C

1. ambitious
2. beneficial
3. complexion
4. conscientious
5. anxious

8.2 Self-Assessment D

1. Particles
2. exceeded
3. technical; statistical
4. inventory; stationery
5. calendar

8.4 Self-Assessment A

1. Please give me your response by Friday.
2. Please include your payment with the completed order form.
3. Material on the Werner account is in four large files.
4. To be successful, you should try harder.
5. The videos you requested in your May 5 letter are enclosed.

8.4 Self-Assessment B

1. Save the files in a new directory on the computer, and print a copy of each file.
2. Despite the costs involved, we are committed to investing in current technology.
3. Because the report is due March 4, Betty has been working long hours on the calculations.
4. Because our editorial department is understaffed, we propose hiring three additional editors.
5. Although some additional options were presented, the manager decided to go with Jessica's proposal.

A

ab•bre•vi•a•tion a shortened form of a word or phrase (3.1, 7.6)

ab•so•lute ad•jec•tives adjectives whose qualities cannot be compared (6.3)

ac•ro•nym a word formed usually using the first letter of each word in a phrase (3.1)

ac•tive lis•ten•ing using a high level of concentration to listen for information (2.2)

ad hoc com•mit•tee a temporary committee formed for a particular purpose (14.2)

ad•jec•tives words that describe nouns or pronouns by modifying them (4.1, 6.3)

ad•just•ment an answer to a customer claim of unsatisfactory service or defective product. The company decides if the claim is allowable, partially allowable, or not allowable (10.2)

ad•ver•bi•al clauses dependent clauses that serve as adverbs to modify an adjective, verb, or adverb in the main clause (6.4)

ad•verbs words that describe verbs, adjectives, or other adverbs by modifying them (4.1, 6.4)

agen•da a brief chronological list of the business to be transacted at a meeting (11.4, 14.2)

an•a•log da•ta in early cellular telephones, continuous data (12.2)

an•a•lyt•i•cal re•port examines a situation or problem, draws conclusions, and makes recommendations in addition to providing information and data (11.1)

an•te•ced•ent a noun or a noun phrase that is referred to by a pronoun (5.3, 8.3)

an•to•nyms words that mean exactly the opposite of another word (8.1)

apos•tro•phe a punctuation mark used to form possessives, contractions, and some plurals (5.1, 7.4)

ap•pen•dix report section that consists mainly of supporting information for the material contained in the body of the report (11.3)

ap•pli•ca•tion form a form used to make a request for employment (15.4)

ap•pli•ca•tion letter or *cover letter,* a companion document to a résumé and references that highlights important qualifications and persuades an employer to grant an interview (15.4)

ap•pos•i•tives words or groups of words that give more information about a preceding word (7.2)

ar•ti•cles the words *a, the,* and *an* (6.3)

asyn•chro•nous sending a communication that allows the receiver to retrieve or access it at his or her convenience (12.3)

au•to re•spond•er a message-response system that automatically replies to e-mails in the employee's absence (13.4)

B

band•width measures how fast and how much data flows on a given transmission path (12.2)

bar•ri•ers factors that block or interfere with communication (1.1)

be•hav•ior•al in•ter•view an interview where the applicant is asked questions that test how he or she would handle a situation (16.2)

be•ing verb a verb that does not describe an action or condition, but is a form of the infinitive *to be* (4.3)

ben•e•fits payments or services provided for employees under an annuity, pension plan, or insurance policy (16.1)

bib•li•og•ra•phy an alphabetical listing of all the references used in a report (11.1, 11.3)

block let•ter for•mat all letter parts begin at the left margin, except for tables and other offset material (9.2)

body lan•guage gestures, movements, and mannerisms used to communicate ideas to others (2.1)

body of the re•port the actual text of a report (11.3)

boil•er•plate a form letter that combines various prewritten paragraphs that fit certain or varied situations (10.5)

brib•ery giving or receiving payment as a method of influence (3.2)

brow•sers devices that enable the user to navigate the World Wide Web (11.1)

busi•ness ab•bre•vi•a•tions shortened forms of words or phrases used in business (7.6)

C

ca•ble mo•dem allows data to be transmitted 100 times faster over telephone lines (12.2)

cap•i•tal•iza•tion the rules for writing certain important words with capital letters (7.5)

case the form of the pronoun: possessive, nominative, and objective (5.3)

CD-ROM or *compact disk—read-only memory,* a computer storage medium that can hold up to 250,000 pages of text (11.1)

cel•lu•lar tele•phones or *cell phones,* small, wireless, lightweight portable telephones that allow communication from almost any location that can pick up a satellite signal (12.2)

chro•no•log•i•cal ré•su•mé emphasizes work history and education; lists work experience in reverse order with the most recent first (15.2)

claim•ant the person who makes a claim of unsatisfactory or damaged goods and services (10.2)

claim let•ters or *written requests,* that ask the receiver to provide something or some service for the sender (10.2)

clause a group of words containing a subject and a predicate (4.2)

cli•chés overworked expressions, such as *crystal clear, needs no introduction,* and *at a loss for words* (8.1)

clip art gal•lery software that contains a collection of simple drawings and art (14.4)

code of eth•ics the operating goals of a company toward its customers and competitors (3.2)

col•lec•tion let•ter a letter in which a company reminds a customer that he or she has not yet paid his or her bill (10.1)

col•lec•tive noun a noun that refers to a group or collection of persons or things (4.4)

co•lons punctuation used to direct attention to the matter that follows (7.2)

com•bi•na•tion ré•su•mé employs the best features of the chronological and functional résumés (15.2)

com•mas punctuation used to separate elements within a sentence (7.2)

com•ma splices commas used to join two independent clauses (7.1)

com•mis•sion the fee paid to a sales associate as a result of a sale (3.2)

com•par•a•tive de•gree words that compare the qualities of two or more people or things (6.3)

com•pen•sa•tion in•crease an increase in salary and/or benefits (16.5)

com•plete pred•i•cate the simple predicate plus all the words that modify it in a sentence (4.2)

com•pound ad•jec•tives two or more words used to modify one noun or pronoun (6.3)

com•pound noun a noun that consists of two or more words (5.1)

com•pound ob•jects nouns or pronouns joined by coordinating conjunctions (5.3)

com•pound sen•tences sentences that have two or more independent clauses, each containing a subject and a predicate (7.2)

com•pound sub•jects two or more subjects joined by a conjunction (4.2, 5.3)

com•pre•hen•sion understanding something read, heard, seen, or felt (2.4)

com•put•er work•sta•tions a microcomputer or personal computer operating independently or a computer terminal linked/networked to a company's main computer (12.2)

con•clu•sions place where the real results of a report appear (11.3)

con•fi•den•tial in•for•ma•tion spoken or written ideas that are private or secret (3.2)

con•junc•tions words that join other words, phrases, or clauses (4.1)

con•junc•tive ad•verbs adverbs that join elements within a sentence, also called "transitions" (6.4)

con•no•ta•tion the meaning readers associate with a word, based on their experiences and emotions (8.1)

con•sec•u•tive ad•jec•tives adjectives that come together but separately modify a noun (7.2)

con•so•nants the letters of the alphabet that are not vowels: *b, c, d, f, g, h, j, k, l, m, n, p, q, r, s, t, v, w, x, y, z* (8.2)

"Con•tact Us" a section on a Web site that takes the user to a screen with a preaddressed e-mail (13.4)

co•or•di•nat•ing con•junc•tions words that connect only like elements of grammar (6.1)

copy no•ta•tion on a letter, the last line under the reference initials to state to whom a copy of the letter should be sent (9.2)

cor•rel•a•tive con•junc•tions pairs of conjunctions used to connect like elements (6.1)

cross-cul•tur•al com•mu•ni•ca•tion communicating with people from cultures different from your own (3.1)

cul•ture the customs, beliefs, lifestyles, and practices of a group of people (3.1)

cus•tom•er-fo•cused or•gan•i•za•tion an organization that emphasizes customers and their interests and satisfaction (13.2)

cus•tom•er ser•vice consistent activities that ensure customer satisfaction (13.1, 13.3)

D

dash•es punctuation used to indicate a break in thought (7.3)

da•ta file   a file that contains the names and addresses of people used for mailing lists (10.5)

dates   times in which events occur or a statement of time (7.7)

dec•i•mals   numbers in units of ten (7.7)

de•clar•a•tive sen•tence   a sentence that makes a statement (4.2, 7.1)

de•mon•stra•tive ad•jec•tives   pronouns that are used to modify one noun or pronoun (6.3)

de•no•ta•tion   the dictionary meaning of a word (8.1)

de•riv•a•tive   a word formed from another word (8.1)

de•scrip•tive ad•jec•tives   words that tell "what kind of" or describe (6.3)

de•sign tem•plates   preformatted layouts in presentation software (14.4)

dig•i•tal da•ta   in more modern cellular telephones, data stored as a combination of numbers—0s and 1s (12.2)

di•rect ad•dress   speaking to the person directly (7.2)

di•rect ap•proach   the main point of the message is stated in the opening sentence (9.1)

di•rec•tives   formal authorizations for changes (14.2)

di•rect ques•tions   sentences that ask a question (7.1)

di•rect quo•ta•tions   the exact words spoken or written by someone else (7.4)

dis•cre•tion   cautious reserve in speech to protect the privacy of both your manager and your company (13.3)

dis•crim•i•na•tion   treating or judging someone on the basis of age, ethnic group, sex, etc. (3.3)

dis•crim•i•na•to•ry lan•guage   offensive terminology based on characteristics, beliefs, values, and attitudes (3.3)

dis•tance learn•ing   studying or watching a college or university lecture via the Internet at home or at work (2.4)

doc•u•ment cam•era   projects a photograph, a drawing, or a printed page onto the screen (14.4)

do•mes•tic   originating from your own country (3.1)

dou•ble neg•a•tive   two negative expressions used together (6.4)

down•size   to reduce in size the staff of a company or organization (16.6)

down•ward com•mu•ni•ca•tion   communicating with others of a rank lower than your rank (1.3)

DSL   or *Digital Subscriber Line*, technology for bringing high bandwidth information to homes and small businesses over ordinary copper telephone lines (12.2)

E

e-com•merce   buying and selling merchandise and services over the Internet (12.3)

ed•it•ing   the process that refines the revised draft and adds polish (8.6)

ed•u•ca•tion•al dis•trac•tion   lack of knowledge about a subject matter leading to confusion (1.2)

elec•tron•ic mail   or *e-mail*, messages transmitted instantly through the Internet via the modem in a computer (9.3, 12.3)

em•bed•ded com•pu•ter de•vice   a tiny computer built into a larger product to control the functions of that product (12.2)

emo•tion•al-phys•i•cal dis•trac•tion   mental and physical factors leading to confusion (1.2)

em•ploy•ment con•trac•tors   or *temporary agencies*, supply personnel on a temporary basis (15.1)

em•ploy•ment in•ter•view   a formal consultation to evaluate the qualifications of a prospective employee (16.1)

enun•ci•a•tion   the distinctness or clarity with which words or sounds are pronounced (14.1)

en•vi•ron•men•tal dis•trac•tion   factors such as noise or room temperature leading to inattentiveness (1.2)

eq•ui•ta•ble ad•just•ment   reasonable, fair, honest, and impartial decision making when deciding on customer adjustments (10.2)

er•go•nom•ics   or *human engineering*, the design of devices, systems, and physical working conditions that meet the physical needs of the worker (12.4)

eth•ics   the moral principles of right and wrong (3.2)

eth•no•cen•trism   believing that your own ethnic group or culture is superior to others (3.3)

e-whin•ing   unsatisfied customers communicate their dissatisfaction to others using the Internet (13.4)

ex•change rate   the ratio at which the principal unit of two currencies can be traded (3.1)

ex•cla•ma•tion points   punctuation used at the end of a sentence to indicate strong feeling or emotion (7.2)

ex•clam•a•to•ry sen•tence   a sentence that expresses strong feeling (4.2)

ex•ec•u•tive let•ter•head   company-provided stationery for social-business and other company communications, measuring 7¼ × 10½ inches; also called "monarch" (10.4)

ex•ec•u•tive-sized sta•tion•ery   stationery that measures 7¼ × 10½ inches (9.2)

ex•plan•a•to•ry el•e•ments   additional information that is not essential to the sentence (7.2)

ex•ter•nal com•mu•ni•ca•tion   the transferring of information to and from people outside the company (1.3)

ex•ter•nal cus•tom•ers   people outside a company who purchase its goods and services (13.1)

ex•ter•nal noise   sounds created externally or outside the body that distract the listener (2.2)

ex•tra•net   a company's private intranet that gives limited access to select outsiders, such as customers or vendors (12.3)

F

fa•mil•iar tone   a writing device for establishing a mood of familiarity with the reader (10.1)

FAQs   or *Frequently Asked Questions,* a section on a Web site that lists common questions and the answers to them (13.4)

fax ma•chine   or *facsimile,* transmits documents, illustrations, and photographs over regular telephone lines (12.2)

fea•si•bil•i•ty study   describes the pros and cons of proceeding with a project in addition to giving the costs and time frame for the project (11.1)

feed•back   receiving an oral, written, or nonverbal response from a receiver (1.1)

fire•wall   integrated security measures designed to prevent unauthorized access to networked computer systems (12.3)

fol•low-up let•ters   maintain contact with a previous interaction (16.4)

fol•low-up se•ries   a series of three to five follow-up letters that remind delinquent bill payers to settle their account before it is turned over to a lawyer or collection agency (10.1)

for•mal busi•ness re•ports   long reports that usually address more complex problems or questions (11.3)

for•mat   refers to the arrangement of letter parts on the page (10.4)

form file   a file that contains a form letter and codes to merge information with the data file (10.5)

form let•ters   letters in which the same message is sent to many addresses (10.5)

frag•ments   incomplete sentences (7.1)

func•tion•al ré•su•mé   or *skills résumé,* highlights professional skills and related accomplishments and de-emphasizes work history (15.2)

fu•ture per•fect tense   the form of a verb that tells that an action will be completed by a specified time in the future (4.3)

fu•ture pro•gres•sive tense   the form of a verb that tells that the action will be in progress at a certain time in the future (4.3)

fu•ture tense   the form of a verb that tells that the action will happen in the future (4.3)

G

gen•der-bi•as words   terms that show favoritism toward a particular gender (3.3)

gen•der-spe•cif•ic words   terms indicating whether a subject is male or female (3.3)

ger•und   a verb that ends in *-ing* and is used as a noun (5.2)

ger•und phrases   groups of words that contain a gerund (7.2)

GPS   or *Global Positioning System,* a system of 24 satellites that orbit the earth and make it possible for people with ground receivers to pinpoint their geographic location (12.2)

gram•mar-check•er   computer software that evaluates grammar and suggests ways to improve the grammar and wording of a document (8.6)

group in•ter•view   an interview where several applicants meet with one or two interviewers (16.2)

group•ware   software that allows several users to work together and have access to the same document (12.3)

GSM   or *Global System for Mobile Communication,* a digital, wireless mobile telephone system that is widely used in Europe and 120 other countries (12.2)

guide words   words that call attention to specific information (9.2)

H

hear•ing   the physical act of detecting sound (2.2)

hid•den job mar•ket   job opportunities not advertised in traditional venues (15.1)

hom•onyms   words that look or sound alike but have different meanings (8.1)

hot desk•ing   workers use whatever desk is available when they are in the office (12.4)

ho•tel•ing   workers share a workspace by calling a staff concierge or by logging onto a Web-based scheduling system to reserve a space (12.4)

hu•man re•la•tions skills   understanding and relating to people in a way to foster goodwill (1.1)

hy•per•text links   highlighted words or graphics that can make connections between data at different Web sites (12.3)

I

I-at•ti•tude   putting your own interests before those of your readers or listeners (1.1)

---

idi•o•mat•ic us•age expressions that are considered correct even though there isn't a rule or logical reason (6.2)

im•per•a•tive sen•tence a sentence that states a command or request (4.2, 7.1)

in•di•rect ap•proach using background information as a buffer to bad or unpleasant information in a message (9.1)

in•di•rect ques•tions questions restated as declarative sentences (7.1)

in•di•rect quo•ta•tions restatements of a person's exact words (7.4)

in•fin•i•tive phrase a group of words that contain an infinitive and any words that modify it (4.2, 7.2)

in•flec•tion•al forms the form of a word that shows tense, number, and other meanings (8.1)

in•for•ma•tive mes•sages written instructions on how to complete a task or carry out a procedure (9.4)

in•for•ma•tive re•port gives facts and information on some aspect of an organization's operations (11.1)

in•side ad•dress on a letter, includes the name, title, company name, street address, city, state, and ZIP Code of the addressee (9.2)

in•stant mes•sag•ing or *chat*, is real-time communication via the Internet (12.3)

in•ter•jec•tions words used to express extremely strong feelings or emotions (4.1)

in•ter•nal com•mu•ni•ca•tion transferring information within a company (1.3)

in•ter•nal cus•tom•er a co-worker or supervisor who depends on products or services from another department within a company (13.1)

in•ter•nal noise feelings or sensations inside the body that distract the listener (2.2)

in•ter•na•tion•al originating beyond a country's borders or viewpoints (3.1)

Inter•net or *Net*, a system of computer networks that links computers around the world into one large computer (11.1, 12.3)

in•ter•per•son•al com•mu•ni•ca•tion communicating with others (1.1)

in•ter•pret•ing analyzing the sounds you hear, then relating that information to past experiences (2.2)

in•ter•rog•a•tive sen•tence a sentence that asks a question (4.2)

in•ter•rupt•ing el•e•ments words that add extra meaning, but not essential information, to sentences (7.2)

in•to•na•tion the rising and falling of voice pitch (14.1)

intra•net similar to the Internet but located on a network within a company (12.1)

in•tran•si•tive verbs verbs that do not have objects (4.3)

in•tra•per•son•al com•mu•ni•ca•tion communicating with yourself based on interpretations of previous experiences.

ir•reg•u•lar verbs verbs that do not follow the regular pattern of verbs (4.3)

J

jus•ti•fi•ca•tion re•port gives the rationale for a recommendation or a decision, usually prepared by someone in upper management (11.1)

L

lap•top com•put•er functions like a desktop computer but is small enough to be portable and may be battery-operated (13.2)

lat•er•al com•mu•ni•ca•tion communicating with people who are the same rank as you (1.3)

let•ter•head refers to either 1) the printed information on the top of business stationery or 2) the actual sheet of paper (9.2)

let•ter or memo of trans•mit•tal a short letter that documents that a report has been completed and is being submitted to the person(s) in the memo (11.3)

let•ters messages printed on letterhead and sent to people outside an organization by mail or by courier service (9.3)

lim•it•ing ad•jec•tives adjectives that tell "how many," "how much," or "in what order" (6.3)

lis•ten•ing hearing something through thoughtful attention (2.2)

lis•ten•ing bar•ri•ers distractions that interfere with listening (2.2)

lis•ten•ing pri•or•i•ties determining the listening opportunity that is most important to you (2.2)

M

mail•ing no•ta•tions on an envelope, instructions for the post office, found in the upper-left corner (9.2)

mem•o•ran•dum re•port an informal, written report used for correspondence with other employees within an organization (11.2)

mem•os messages printed and sent to people within an organization through an interoffice mail delivery system (9.3)

mes•sage mem•os used to record telephone messages and messages from visitors (9.2)

min•utes a written record of the proceedings of a meeting (11.4, 14.2)

mo•dems a device connected to, or included inside, a computer that can exchange data with other computers (12.2)

mod•i•fied-block for•mat similar to block format, except that the dateline, complimentary closing, and writer's identification begin at the center of the page (9.2)

mul•ti•na•tion•al com•pa•ny a company that operates in more than one country (3.1)

N

news re•lease an announcement prepared for release to the public that enhances the image of an organization (11.5)

non•dis•clo•sure agree•ment a promise not to divulge company trade secrets or procedures (3.2)

non•ver•bal com•mu•ni•ca•tion communication without words; actions, expressions, or tone of voice used to convey information (1.1, 2.1)

note•book com•pu•ter a lightweight, portable battery-powered computer (12.2)

noun a name of a person, place, thing, concept, or quality (4.1)

num•bers sums of units in a mathematical system (7.7)

O

ob•ject the person or thing that receives the action of the verb (5.3)

ob•ject of the prep•o•si•tion the noun or pronoun that follows the preposition in a sentence (6.2)

one-on-one in•ter•view an interview conducted by one person (16.2)

on•line ser•vices self-contained, fee-based services that provide extensive resources to their members (11.1)

open punc•tu•a•tion in a business letter, no punctuation is used after the salutation and complimentary closing (9.2)

oral com•mu•ni•ca•tion spoken words used to exchange ideas and information (1.1, 1.2)

or•der con•fir•ma•tion func•tion an e-mail confirmation that assures the customer that his or her products have been purchased (13.4)

or•di•nal num•bers numbers designating a place in an ordered sequence; first, second, etc (7.7)

out•line form a form of formal, written report that uses an outline to list information (11.2)

P

pag•er a lightweight device that notifies the user that someone is trying to reach him or her (12.2)

pan•el in•ter•view an interview conducted by a team of people (16.2)

par•a•graph form a form of formal, written report used for the presentation of simple facts (11.2)

par•a•graph uni•ty created when all sentences in a paragraph support the main idea (8.5)

para•lan•guage nonverbal communication, such as tone, pitch, and sighing, used to reinforce verbal messages (2.1)

par•al•lel struc•ture expressing parallel ideas in the same way (6.1)

para•phras•ing restating the words or ideas of someone else in your own words; you should still give credit to the original author (11.1)

par•en•the•ses punctuation used to set off amplifying or explanatory words (7.4)

par•en•thet•i•cal el•e•ments words, phrases, and clauses added to sentences to emphasize a contrast, express an opinion, etc. (7.2)

par•ti•ci•pial phrases groups of words that contain a participle; a phrase containing a verb and any words that modify it (7.2)

pas•sive lis•ten•ing concentrating on the spoken words at a low level of effort (2.2)

past per•fect tense the form of a verb that tells which of two actions occurred first (4.3)

past pro•gres•sive tense the form of a verb that tells that an action was in progress some time in the past (4.3)

past tense the form of a verb that tells the action happened in the past (4.3)

PCS or *Personal Communication Service*, a system of digital, wireless communications used especially for mobile/cellular telephones (12.2)

PDAs or *Personal Digital Assistants*, computers that fit in the palm of the hand and offer many functions (13.2)

peo•ple's needs things that are vital to survival: food, shelter, clothing, and perhaps transportation (10.1)

peo•ple's wants things that are not vital to survival: security, status, approval from others, health, personal attractiveness, conveniences, and various forms of recreation and entertainment (10.1)

per•cent•ages parts of a whole expressed in hundredths (7.7)

pe•ri•od faults an incomplete thought or sentence fragment (7.1)

pe•ri•od•ic re•port prepared at a regular interval (11.1)

pe•ri•ods punctuation used to end a sentence (7.1)

pe•riph•er•als hardware devices that connect to computers to input and output information (12.1)

per•son•al-busi•ness let•ters letters not typed on letterhead stationery, with the writer's address typed beneath the signature at the end (9.2)

per•sua•sive ap•proach getting the reader's attention in the opening sentence, using a "hook" that encourages the reader to continue reading (9.1)

pho•net•ic spell•ing a dictionary feature that shows the word broken into syllables, how each syllable should be pronounced, and which syllable or syllables should be accented (8.1)

phrase a group of words with neither a subject nor a predicate (4.2)

pi•lot test uses a small test group to check the quality of a survey (11.1)

pitch the level of sound on the musical scale (14.1)

place•ment agen•cies fill permanent job openings for companies in a wide range of occupations (15.1)

pla•gia•rism using the ideas of or exact or paraphrased words of someone else as your own without giving credit to the original author (11.1)

port•fo•lio a notebook or folder that contains evidence and examples of a person's achievements and skills (15.5)

pos•i•tive de•gree words that express the quality of one person or thing (6.3)

pos•ses•sive ad•jec•tives possessive personal pronouns used as adjectives to modify nouns (6.3)

pos•ses•sive forms of nouns and pro•nouns adding an apostrophe and sometimes an "s" to nouns and pronouns (5.2)

ppm means "pages per minute" (12.2)

pred•i•cate part of a sentence that tells what the subject does or what is done to the subject (4.2)

pred•i•cate ad•jec•tives adjectives that follow a being verb and modify or describe the subject of the sentence (6.3)

pred•i•cate agree•ment the verb and its modifiers agree with the subject in number and in person (4.4)

pred•i•cate nom•i•na•tives words that follow a being verb and rename the subject (6.3)

prej•u•dice a negative attitude about an individual, race, or supposed characteristics (3.3)

prep•o•si•tion•al phrase a group of words containing a preposition, an object, and a modifier of the object (4.2, 6.2, 7.2)

prep•o•si•tions connecting words that show a relationship between nouns or pronouns and other words in a sentence (4.1, 6.2)

pre•print•ed re•ply card a form that allows a company to respond to many requests promptly (9.5)

pre•sent per•fect tense the form of a verb that tells that the action occurred in the past and may still be occurring now (4.3)

pre•sent pro•gres•sive tense the form of the verb that tells that an action that is currently in progress (4.3)

pre•sent tense the form of a verb that tells that the action is happening now (4.3)

prin•ci•pal parts of verbs the present, past, past participle, and present participle forms of verbs (4.3)

print•ers accept text and graphics from a computer and transfer the information to paper or another medium (12.2)

prob•lem re•quests a message that requires the writer to say "no" to someone (9.5)

pro•ced•ures the methods that are used to collect and analyze data (11.3)

pro•ced•ures book a step-by-step guide that contains written copies of all the procedures an organization follows (9.4)

pro•fes•sion•al cour•te•sy using good manners in professional dealings (3.2)

pro•gress re•port gives the current status of a project (11.1)

pro•mo•tion an increase in position or rank; sometimes meaning an increase in salary and/or benefits as well (16.5)

pro•nouns words that take the place of nouns (4.1, 8.3)

pro•nun•ci•a•tion the sound a speaker gives to the letters or letter combinations that make up a word; the way in which a speaker accents a word (14.1)

proof•read•ing the process that detects typographical and grammatical errors (8.6)

pro•per ad•jec•tives words derived from proper nouns (6.3, 7.5)

pro•po•sal designed to persuade the reader to purchase products, adopt an idea or plan, or provide or donate money or services to a worthwhile project (11.1)

pseudo-hom•onyms words that sound somewhat alike but have different meanings (8.1)

pub•lic re•la•tions the business of positively influencing the public's feeling or attitude toward a company or an organization (10.3)

pub•lic re•la•tions cam•paign the concentrated effort of a company to put its name before potential customers in a favorable light (10.3)

pub•lic re•la•tions spe•cial•ist a person who looks for opportunities to show a company in a favorable light (10.3)

pur•pose the reason a report is being written (11.3)

Q

ques•tion marks   punctuation used to indicate a question (7.1)

quo•rum   the number of group members required by the group's bylaw to conduct business (11.4)

quo•ta•tion marks   punctuation used to tell the reader the exact words written or spoken by someone else (7.4)

R

rap•port   to establish a positive relationship (16.3)

read•abil•i•ty   refers to the ease with which something can be read (8.5)

ream   500 sheets of paper (9.2)

re•call•ing   using retained and recalled sounds for comprehension (2.2)

rec•om•men•da•tions   suggested actions to be taken, drawn from the facts of a report (11.3)

ref•er•ence ini•tials   in a letter, the typist's initials (9.2)

ref•er•ences   source entries arranged alphabetically by the author's last name (11.1)

re•fer•rals   recommendations from satisfied customers (13.1)

re•flec•tive lis•ten•ing   attentively listening to the speaker's actual words and tone of voice, and observing body language or emotions (1.2)

reg•u•lar verb   verbs that follow the simple form (4.3)

rel•a•tive pro•nouns   pronouns that relate to other words called antecedents (4.4)

re•mote tech•nol•o•gy   allows a worker to communicate with co-workers while he or she is away from the office (12.1)

res•ig•na•tion   a formal notification of giving up employment (16.6)

re•tain•ing   recalling interpreted sounds for later use (2.2)

re•ten•tion   remembering something read, heard, seen, or felt (2.4)

re•vis•ing   the process that improves the content and organization of writing (8.6)

rhe•tor•i•cal ques•tion   a question that is posed solely for effect, with no expectation of a reply or a clear "yes" or "no" (10., 14.3)

Robert's Rules of Order   a standard guide to parliamentary procedure (14.2)

rout•ing   a feature on e-mail forms that lets the recipient send the form to another listed recipient (12.1)

rout•ing slips   used to channel messages to specific people (9.2)

RSVP   French for "please reply" (3.2)

S

sal•a•ry   fixed compensation paid regularly for services (16.1)

sales ap•peals   a writing device that is used to induce the reader to buy a product or service (10.1)

sal•u•ta•tion   or *greeting*, immediately preceding the body of a letter (9.2)

scan•nable ré•su•mé   written to enhance the résumé writer's chance of being selected by a data tracking system, which uses specific keywords and nouns (15.3)

scope   determines the extensiveness of research (11.3)

screen•ing in•ter•view   a preliminary screening, usually by telephone, to determine if the applicant has the skills and qualifications for the job (16.2)

semi•co•lons   punctuation used to indicate a stronger break between items in a series (7.2, 7.3)

sen•tence   a group of words that expresses a complete thought and contains a subject and a predicate (4.2)

sen•tence frag•ment   a group of words that does not express a complete thought and is missing either a subject or a predicate (4.2)

se•ries   three or more items in a sequence (7.2)

sim•ple pred•i•cate   the main verb plus any helping verbs in a sentence (4.2)

sim•ple sen•tences   groups of words that contain subjects and verbs (7.2)

sim•ple sub•ject   the main word or words in a complete subject, the core of the subject (4.2)

sit•u•a•tion•al in•ter•view   an interview where the applicant is asked to relate past experiences and how he or she handled them (16.2)

slide an•i•ma•tion   a feature that lets parts of a slide arrive on the screen at different times (14.4)

slide tran•si•tions   special effects that introduce each slide as it appears on screen (14.4)

smart card   looks like a credit card but contains a battery-powered, wafer-thin computer—prepaid, disposable telephone card (12.3)

smart phones   a wireless cellular telephone with a computer (12.2)

so•cial-busi•ness com•mu•ni•ca•tion   communication among co-workers to congratulate someone on a special occasion (10.4)

space   the physical distance maintained between yourself and others (2.1)

stan•dard punc•tu•a•tion   the style most used by business writers, where the salutation ends with a colon (9.2)

stand•ing com•mit•tee a permanent committee that meets regularly (14.2)

ster•e•o•typ•ing a simplified and negative image of a person or group (3.3)

stress in•ter•view an interview where the applicant is deliberately put under stress to test his or her reaction (16.2)

style used to emphasize important details—**bold,** *italics,* etc. (9.2, 12.1)

sub•ject a word in a sentence that names the person speaking, the person spoken to, or the person spoken about (4.2)

sub•or•di•nat•ing con•junc•tions words that join clauses of unequal rank (6.1)

sum•ma•ry often called an *executive summary* in business, this is a brief review of a report (11.3)

su•per•la•tive de•gree words that compare the qualities of three or more persons or things (6.3)

sup•ple•men•ta•ry ma•te•ri•al given after the conclusions and recommendations in a report and provides substantiating data for the report (11.3)

syn•chro•nous means "at the same time"; several people in different locations can communicate in real time (12.3)

syn•o•nyms words that have almost the same meaning (8.1)

T

20-pound pa•per the weight of 500 sheets, or a ream, of paper; for example, 500 sheets of 20-pound paper weigh 20 pounds, 500 sheets of 40-pound paper weigh 40 pounds, etc. (9.2)

24/7 an abbreviated term that means "24 hours a day, 7 days a week" (9.3)

ta•ble form a form of formal, written report that systematically arranges data in rows and columns (11.2)

tab•let PC smaller and thinner than a notebook PC, it allows the user to use a stylus or digital pen instead of a keyboard (12.2)

tar•get au•di•ence a group of potential customers chosen on the basis of certain characteristics, such as age, geographic location, income, or lifestyle (10.1)

team working with peers to complete a project (14.1)

tele•com•mut•ing salaried employees who work at home for part of or all of the work week (12.4)

tele•con•fer•ence a meeting via advanced telephone or computer technology that brings together people from several locations (2.3, 12.3)

tele•work using telecommunications to work whenever needed to satisfy client needs (12.4)

tem•plate contains the format for a letter and can include the letterhead in addition to the skeleton of the letter (10.5)

tem•po the rate of speed at which one speaks (14.1)

the•sau•rus a book that gives the synonyms and antonyms of words (8.1)

thought unit a combination of words that properly belong together (8.2)

tick•ler file a dated "reminder file," which reminds the user that something written earlier must be addressed or responded to by the date on the file (9.5)

time a measured or measurable period during which an action occurs (7.7)

tone usually refers to the general effect a piece of writing creates (8.6); attitudes and feelings revealed in the voice (14.1)

touch haptic communication used to communicate intention or emotion (2.1)

tran•si•tion•al words and phrases words or phrases that provide connections between sentences and paragraphs (8.5)

tran•si•tive verb a verb that has an object or a receiver of the action (4.3)

U

units of mea•sure terminology used to indicate weight, mass, length, distance, etc. (7.6)

un•so•lic•it•ed re•port one that is prepared on the writer's own initiative (11.1)

un•struc•tured in•ter•view an interview that usually consists of one or two broad questions (16.2)

up•ward com•mu•ni•ca•tion communicating with others of higher rank than you (1.3)

URL ad•dress the Internet address of a given site (12.3)

V

vari•ables form letter elements that change from letter to letter (10.5)

verbatim an exact quotation (11.4)

verb phrase two or more verbs working together as one verb (4.2, 4.3)

verbs words that express action, a state of being, or a condition (4.1, 4.3)

verb tense the form that tells when the action occurred (4.3)

voice the property of a transitive verb that shows whether the subject acts or is acted upon (8.4)

voice mail sys•tems a telephone answering system that can record messages even when the telephone is in use (12.2)

voice rec•og•ni•tion soft•ware software that allows the entry of text and data through voice instead of through traditional keyboard entry (14.1)

VoIP voice over Internet protocol. Technology that permits you to make telephone calls using a broad band Internet connection instead of a conventional telephone (12.2)

vol•ume the intensity of a sound (14.1)

vowels the letters *a, e, i, o, u,* and sometimes *y* (8.2)

W

wa•ter mark the "signature" of the paper manufacturer, found in better-quality paper (9.2)

which a relative pronoun that refers to another word in the sentence (8.3)

wiz•ards features in software programs that walk users through a task to meet a desired result (12.1)

work•ing bib•li•og•ra•phy a preliminary list of sources (11.1)

World Wide Web or *Web,* also *www,* gives the computer user access to millions of pages of information (11.1, 12.3)

writ•ten com•mu•ni•ca•tion communication using letters, words, sentences, and symbols to exchange ideas and information (1.1, 1.2)

you-at•ti•tude putting your reader or listener's interests first (1.1, 8.4)

Photo Credits

Antonio Mo/Getty Images 4; © Digital Vision 9; Keith Brofsky/Getty Images 12; Patrick Clark/Getty Images 18; Antonio Mo/Getty Images 25; Ryan McVay/Getty Images 28; Royalty-Free/CORBIS 31; © Getty Images 31; Ryan McVay/Getty Images 31; Royalty-Free/CORBIS 31; The McGraw-Hill Companies, Inc./Andrew Resek, photographer 48; PhotoLink/Getty Images 50; The McGraw-Hill Companies, Inc./John Flournoy, photographer 60; S. Wanke/PhotoLink/Getty Images 65; Royalty-Free/CORBIS 71; Steve Mason/Getty Images 79; Ryan McVay/Getty Images 84; S. Meltzer/PhotoLink/Getty Images 117; Jack Hollingsworth/Getty Images 134; Royalty-Free/Corbis 150; Keith Brofsky/Getty Images 162; Ryan McVay/Getty Images 198; Vicky Kasala/Getty Images 270; Jack Hollingsworth/Getty Images 304; Jason Reed/Ryan McVay/Getty Images 325; SW Productions/Getty Images 332; © Digital Vision 380; John A. Rizzo/Getty Images 420; Javier Pierini/Getty Images 424; Steve Mason/Getty Images 425; <http://search.msn.com> accessed June 21, 2005 428; <http://google.com> accessed June 21, 2005 429; PhotoLink/Getty Images 453; Patagonik Works/Getty Images 462; Comstock/PunchStock 473; PhotoDisc/Getty Images 487; Ryan McVay/Getty Images 487; Russell Illig/Getty Images 490; © Digital Vision 496; Janis Christie/Getty Images 497; Ryan McVay/Getty Images 502; Royalty-Free/CORBIS 498; http://www.mhhe.com/business/buscom/gregg/faq.htm accessed on August 22, 2005 506; C. Borland/PhotoLink/Getty Images 510; © Digital Vision 523; Ryan McVay/Getty Images 544; © Digital Vision 552; © Digital Vision 582; © Digital Vision 590; © Digital Vision 596